Healthy for Life

Brief Version

Healthy for Life

Brief Version

Brian K. Williams

Sharon M. Knight
East Carolina University

Brooks/Cole Publishing Company

I(T)P™ An International Thomson Publishing Company

Pacific Grove • Albany • Bonn • Boston • Cincinnati • Detroit • London • Madrid • Melbourne
Mexico City • New York • Paris • San Francisco • Singapore • Tokyo • Toronto • Washington

Sponsoring Editor: *Marianne Taflinger*
Marketing Manager: *Carolyn Crockett*
Production Coordinator: *Fiorella Ljunggren*
Production: *Stacey Sawyer, Sawyer & Williams*
Manuscript Editor: *Anita Wagner*
Interior Design: *MaryEllen Podgorski*
Cover Design: *Vernon T. Boes*
Cover Photo: *J. A. Kraulis/Masterfile*
Interior Illustrations: *GTS Graphics, Inc.*

Art Coordination: *Stacey Sawyer*
Permissions: *David Sweet*
Photo Research: *Linda Rill, LLR Research*
Index: *Lois Oster*
Typesetting: *GTS Graphics, Inc.*
Color Separation: *GTS Graphics, Inc.*
Cover Printing: *Phoenix Color Corporation, Inc.*
Printing and Binding: *Banta Company*

For more information, contact:

BROOKS/COLE PUBLISHING COMPANY
511 Forest Lodge Road
Pacific Grove, CA 93950
USA

International Thomson Publishing Europe
Berkshire House 168-173
High Holborn
London WC1V 7AA
England

Thomas Nelson Australia
102 Dodds Street
South Melbourne, 3205
Victoria, Australia

Nelson Canada
1120 Birchmount Road
Scarborough, Ontario

International Thomson Editores
Campos Eliseos 385, Piso 7
Col. Polanco
11560 México D. F. México

International Thomson Publishing GmbH
Königswinterer Strasse 418
53227 Bonn
Germany

International Thomson Publishing Asia
221 Henderson Road
#05-10 Henderson Building
Singapore 0315

International Thomson Publishing Japan
Hirakawacho Kyowa Building, 3F
2-2-1 Hirakawacho
Chiyoda-ku, Tokyo 102
Japan

Printed in the United States of America

10 9 8 7 6 5 4 3 2 1

Library of Congress Cataloging-in-Publication Data

Williams, Brian K., [date]
    Healthy for life / Brian K. Williams, Sharon M. Knight. — Brief
version.
        p.   cm.
    Includes bibliographical references and index.
    ISBN 0-534-24354-1
    1. Health.   I. Knight, Sharon M.   II. Title.
RA776.W684   1995   94-35242
613—dc20   CIP

Contents in Brief

Preface to the Instructor

There is a war on—the war of *information clutter.*

Too often, what we want to find in books, magazines, computer screens, and so on, is all but lost in a mishmash of distractions. Even college textbooks striving for supposed conciseness have too many "enrichments" and visual pyrotechnics that diminish rather than reinforce learning.

Frequently we hear students and instructors say, "There's too much information here! All I want is the basics!" In this book, we try to provide just that—the basics. We have attempted to present a book that provides information the same way other consumer-friendly products do—giving just what is needed.

The Audience for and Goals of This Book

Intended readers are college students in a one-term introductory health course. The principal goal of the book is to present a concise treatment of essential health matters. More specifically, the goals are to show students how to evaluate the accuracy and usefulness of health information, how to change health habits, and how to achieve high-level wellness and peak performance.

HEALTHY FOR LIFE: BRIEF VERSION is designed for use as a college textbook to accompany a one-semester or one-quarter introductory course in health science. It distills the essentials of our comprehensive text, *Healthy for Life: Wellness and the Art of Living.*

More specifically, the book is intended to help readers as follows:

- *Evaluate health information:* Hardly a day goes by that most people aren't exposed to some sort of health "information"—from family and friends, from the mass media, from various health authorities, reputable and otherwise. How do we know what is useful and what is not? Learning how to weigh health information is one of the major themes of this book.

- *Change health habits:* "Habits are simply things we create," says one observer. "If you've created something, you can uncreate it." This is an important point. However, students often think that a particular behavior "is just my nature" or that "I don't have the willpower she has." We take pains to show students how changing habits is a skill that can be developed—and is often needed in this era of lifestyle-related health problems.

- *Achieve high-level wellness and peak performance:* Health, of course, is not merely the avoidance of illness. We try to show readers how they can go beyond mere good health to achieve high-level wellness— that is, to realize themselves to the fullest, to become peak performers.

All three themes are constantly reinforced throughout the text in the sections headed "Strategy for Living."

Why This Book Is Different

This book presents essential concepts in concise form by leaving out boxes and other extraneous material, reinforces learning with built-in mastery devices and personalized ways to help students "own" the material, provides art that instructs as well as entertains, celebrates diversity with people who are "ordinary heroes," and offers a quick course in study skills.

This textbook is, we think, distinctive in a number of ways. It offers:

1. Concise yet complete treatment.
2. Reinforcement for learning with built-in repetition.

3. Reinforcement for learning with ways to help students "own" the material.

4. Art that instructs and informs as well as entertains.

5. Celebration of diversity through "Ordinary Heroes" boxes.

6. Quick course in study skills.

We elaborate on these features below.

1. Concise Yet Complete Treatment The material has been arranged into 12 self-contained chapters, which may be read independently of one another. *Chapters may be assigned in any order or eliminated entirely,* as the instructor chooses. To permit this smorgasbord of options, we have repeated the definition of key terms throughout the text.

We have been able to achieve conciseness in a very easy way by eliminating those "sidebar" devices that are intended to serve as student-enrichment materials but unfortunately all too often merely create "speed bumps" for the student's reading. *Except for text material appearing within some illustrations and the "Ordinary Heroes" boxes, all material in the book is to be considered testable.*

2. Reinforcement for Learning: Offering Built-In Repetition How do people learn? One major way, of course, is by repetition. Accordingly, *we have built repetition into the book* to reinforce the same information over and over, as follows:

- *Learning objectives:* Major sections within chapters begin with learning objectives setting forth the questions the student should try to answer in reading the material.

- *Subsection summaries:* Each subsection opens with a section summary or abstract—the material in blue boldface type immediately following the subsection heading—which offers a preview of the material to come.

- *Material in "bite-size" portions, with headings:* Major ideas are presented in bite-size form, with generous use of advance organizers, headings, bulleted lists, and new paragraphing when a new idea is introduced.

3. Reinforcement for Learning: Helping Readers "Own" the Material Another principle of learning is that students have to mentally "own" the material—personalize it, incorporate it into their own experience. We have tried to encourage this ownership through the following devices:

- *Interesting writing:* Studies have found that textbooks written in an imaginative style significantly improve students' ability to retain information. Thus, we have tried to employ a number of journalistic devices—such as the apt direct quote, the colorful fact, the short biographical sketch—to make the material as interesting as possible.

- *Clear writing:* We have taken great pains to express our ideas as clearly as possible. In particular, we have done two things: (1) We have expressed *key terms* in **boldface italic type** and their *definitions* in **boldface type.** (2) We have made sure that *most sentences do not exceed 22 words in length.* Both these measures will, we hope, benefit our readers.

- *Real anecdotes and examples:* We believe that examples take on much more significance when they are true rather than fictionalized. Accordingly, to introduce or support concepts, we have scouted the general press for real episodes involving real people of both traditional and nontraditional student age.

- *Self Discovery questionnaires:* Most people are curious about where they stand or how they are faring in matters of health. Our Self Discovery questionnaires help make material relevant to the reader and provide feedback on health practices. Some of our Self Discoveries cover somewhat unusual topics—for example, "How's Your Hearing?"

- ***800-HELP toll-free phone numbers:*** At the end of most chapters, we present toll-free 800 numbers of helpful sources dealing with the matters we have just discussed. Readers thus have the *immediate* opportunity to follow through on the material on their own.

4. Art That Informs as Well as Entertains Many college textbooks often use art, particularly photos, simply to break up a gray page of words (on the assumption that readers raised on television don't handle such pages well). We believe, however, that art should be *didactic*—it should inform and instruct as well as entertain.

With only a few exceptions, most of the illustrations in this book are designed to reinforce concepts discussed in the text. For example, we have tried to couple photos with additional information: an elaboration of the discussion in the text, some how-to advice, an interesting quotation from popular material, or a piece of line art.

In addition, we have tried to deal with the irritating matter of *page flipping* between text reference and illustration in two ways: (1) wherever possible, by positioning illustrations on the same page spread where the reference occurs and (2) by using colored dots (• • • •) to help readers easily find their way back from the illustration to the place in the text where they left off reading.

5. Tributes to Diversity Although in general the book avoids the distractions of boxes, we have made an exception in presenting a handful of boxes entitled "Ordinary Heroes: A Celebration of Diversity." These feature ordinary men and women of different ages, races, cultures, and physical abilities—people who have lifted themselves beyond the ordinary through exceptional deeds.

6. Quick Course in Study Skills For students whose study skills may be rusty, we have presented a crash course in study techniques and better organization and time management. This is the section entitled "To the Student: How to Win in a College Health Course—or Any Other Subject," which precedes Chapter 1.

Convenient, "Turn-Key" Teaching Package

The instructional package includes an instructor's resource manual with transparency masters, transparency acetates, test bank, computerized testing, study guide, and electronic study guide.

We offer a great deal of assistance in teaching materials in hopes that an instructor can simply "turn the key" to launch an instructional program. Knowing the value of instructors' time, we have stressed convenience and effectiveness, offering teaching materials that eliminate time-wasting preparations. This allows instructors to do what they do best: engage the students in this exciting subject, develop their enthusiasm and interest in health, and tailor topics as appropriate for their particular classes.

Instructor's Resource Manual The instructor's manual (prepared by Karen Vail-Smith of East Carolina University) includes lecture notes, class activities, and instructional resources.

The Instructor's Manual also includes:

- ***"How to teach health" tips:*** Teaching health science is not the same as teaching other disciplines. Thus, we have included in the Instructor's Manual suggestions for most effectively presenting health concepts.

- ***Informative, entertaining lectures:*** The startling statistic, the poignant story, the amusing anecdote—we include these as "asides" in the lecture notes for instructors to use to enliven their classroom presentations.

- **Large-type lecture notes:** The lecture notes in the instructor's manual are printed in large type to make them easily readable at a rostrum.

Transparency Visuals Health science is a particularly visual subject. Many times, however, the transparencies developed by publishers are created as an afterthought. As part of our "turn-key" instructional package, we have paid special attention to the preparation of transparencies. Particularly important, they have been *upsized,* so that they can be easily seen even from the back of a large lecture hall.

Test Bank The test-bank, also available in an electronic version, was created by the well-respected health educator Herb Jones of Ball State University, who has had over 30 years of teaching experience. He has prepared approximately 2000 meaningful questions linked to the learning objectives at the beginning of each chapter.

Study Guide for Students A separate study guide (and an electronic version) is available to provide students with further learning reinforcement. It consists of learning objectives, matching terms and definitions, short answers, multiple-choice questions, and a few personal-insight questions. The study guide provides reminders of key terms, questions that require more than word definitions to answer, and multiple-choice questions that test general knowledge of specific important points. The guide was prepared by Richard Reser and Anita Wagner.

Acknowledgments

Two names are on the front of this book, but a great many others are powerful contributors to its development.

We have been fortunate to have as our sponsoring editor Marianne Taflinger, who saw the need for a brief version of our big book. Marianne, thanks for your terrific support and assistance. We are also grateful to editorial assistants Virge Perelli-Minetti and Laura Donahue, who ably assisted us on many matters. In addition, we appreciate the support of Brooks/Cole management: Vicki Knight, managing editor; Craig Barth, vice president, editorial; Bill Roberts, president; and Wayne Oler, CEO of ITP Education Group.

The Brooks/Cole marketing staff has done everything authors could expect a publisher to do. It's been a pleasure to work once again with Adrian Perenon, director of marketing, and we've been delighted to have great allies in Carolyn Crockett, our very professional marketing manager; Adrienne Carter, our advertising coordinator; and Margaret Parks, the director of marketing communications.

Fiorella Ljunggren, production services manager, was our great liaison during the production process, and we appreciate her willingness to work with the somewhat unusual production arrangements, in which Stacey Sawyer and Brian Williams in effect "packaged" the book. We are also grateful to Vernon Boes for his imaginative cover design, the idea for which was initially suggested by Marianne. In addition, we wish to acknowledge Bill Bokermann and Vena Dyer for their manufacturing support.

Outside of Brooks/Cole, we were ably assisted by a community of first-rate publishing professionals. Directing the production of the entire enterprise was Stacey Sawyer— Brooks/Cole alumna and Brian's wife, who had also directed the production of our big book. Stacey, once again you showed just how good you are at putting together a production team of top-notch talent and at keeping your eye on the ball to keep the book on schedule. Thank you again for everything.

Photo researcher Linda Rill helped us obtain rights to reuse many of the photographs that we found worked so successfully in our big book, and we are grateful for her efforts. David Sweet once again ably helped us chase down permissions to reprint copyrighted material. Anita Wagner did a crackerjack job of copyediting the manuscript, especially in helping us reduce sentence lengths in order to improve the reading level. She was supported by proofreader Martha Ghent, whose keen eye helped us avoid several embarrassments. Lois Oster, an old friend of Brian's, provided an excellent index.

As usual, the work performed by GTS Graphics has been first class. We want to thank Elliott Derman, Bennett Derman, Gloria Fontana, and production coordinators Kathy Malloy and Gail Ward for delivering a superb job. Kathy and Gail were ably assisted by Mary Zelinski, Larry Weigert, Pat Anderson, and Danny Barillaro.

Both authors are grateful once again for the terrific assistance of Herb Jones for the great job on the test bank and of Rick Reser and Anita Wagner for their excellent work on the study guide. We also want to express our deep appreciation to Karen Vail-Smith, author of the instructor's manual, for her exceptional work.

Finally, there are always people who were not directly involved in the book but whose support must be acknowledged nevertheless. Brian wants to thank not only Stacey but also Gertrude, Sylvia, Kirk, Susan, Michael, and Dee for their continuing support. Sharon wishes to thank My Hoa and Alex for their understanding and support.

Acknowledgment of Reviewers

We are grateful to the following people for their reviews on early drafts of *Healthy for Life: Wellness and the Art of Living,* from which the present book was distilled: Nancy Baldwin, Edinboro State University; Danny Ballard, Texas A & M University; Rick Barnes, East Carolina University; Marsha Campos, Modesto City College; Rosemary Clark, City College of San Francisco; Bryan Cooke, University of North Colorado; Sandra Cross, California State University, San Bernardino; Paul Finnicum, Arkansas State University; Fred Fridinger, University of North Texas; Kathie Garbe, Youngstown University; Bernard Green, Valdosta State College, Leslie Hickcox, Linn Benton Community College; Norm Hoffman, Bakersfield College; William Hotchkiss, Slippery Rock University; Herb Jones, Ball State University; Henry Petraki, Palm Beach Community College; Frances Poe, Washoe Medical Center, Reno; Susan Radius, Towson State University; Kerry Redican, Virginia Polytechnic Institute and State University; Gayle Schmidt, Texas A & M University; Christine Hamilton Smith, California State University, Northridge; Sherm Sowby, California State University, Fresno; and Richard W. Wilson, Western Kentucky University.

We also wish to acknowledge the help of the following reviewers of *Healthy for Life: Brief Version*: Sharron Deny, East Los Angeles College; Neill Gunn, Contra Costa College; Norm Hoffman, Bakersfield College; Laurie K. Roeder, Point Loma Nazarene College; Allan A. Simmons, Jackson State University; and Carl Stockton, Radford University.

We welcome your response to this book, for we are truly trying to make it as useful as possible. Write to us in care of Marianne Taflinger, Editor, Brooks/Cole Publishing Company, 511 Forest Lodge Road, Pacific Grove, CA 93950-9968.

Brian K. Williams
Sharon M. Knight

Detailed Contents

CHAPTER 4   Physical Fitness: Activity and Rest   99

CHAPTER 5   Intimacy, Sexuality, and Safer Sex   129

CHAPTER 6   Birth Control, Pregnancy, and Childbirth   165

CHAPTER 7 Caffeine, Tobacco, and Alcohol 211

CHAPTER 8 Drug and Other Dependencies: Lifestyles and Gratifications 253

CHAPTER 9   Infectious and Noninfectious Illnesses   283

CHAPTER 10   Heart Disease, Cancer, and Personal Safety   333

To the Student

How to Win in a College Health Course—Or Any Other Subject

An essential part of the art of living is the art of learning. Both in college and thereafter, we are constantly involved in new situations that require us to take on new skills and habits.

How does one become a good learner? "Winning the game of higher education is like winning any other game," say learning experts Debbie Longman and Rhonda Atkinson. "It consists of the same basic process. First, you decide if you really want to play. If you do, then you gear your attitudes and habits to learning. Next you learn the rules. To do this, you need a playbook, a college catalog. Third, you learn about the other players—administration, faculty, and other students. Finally, you learn specific plans to improve your playing skills."[1]

Unfortunately, many students come to college with faulty study skills. They are not entirely to blame. In high school and earlier, much of the emphasis is on *what* is to be studied rather than *how* to study it.

"The secret to controlling time is to remember that there is always enough time to do what is really important," say Mervill Douglass and Donna Douglass. "The difficulty is knowing what is really important."[2]

What *is* important in college? Studying, going to classes, writing papers, and taking tests compete with social life, extracurricular activities, and perhaps part-time work. All must somehow fit into the same 24 hours available each day, yet—unlike high school or many paying jobs—time in college is often very unstructured. For students, the clash of college demands can lead to several health-related problems: sleep disturbances, alcohol and drug abuse, eating disorders, money difficulties, procrastination, and other maladaptations. Let us discuss how to improve academic performance, a top priority.

Developing Study Habits: Finding Your "Prime Study Time"

Here is a way you can use knowledge about your own body and mind to improve your academic performance: Devote the hours you *feel best* to *study best*. What is called "prime study time" is the time of day when you are at your best for learning and remembering.

Each of us has a different energy cycle. For example, two roommates may have different patterns. One (the "day person") may be an early riser who prefers to work on difficult tasks in the morning. The other (the "night person") may start slowly but be at the peak of his or her form during the evening hours.

The trick, then, is to effectively *use* your energy cycle, which tends to repeat itself from day to day, so that your hours of best performance coincide with your heaviest academic demands. If your energy level is high during the evenings, you should plan to do your studying then—especially for assignments requiring heavy concentration, such as writing papers or doing math problems. Yet you should recognize that evening hours are a time when others around you like to unwind or socialize or watch TV and that you will be tempted to join them. If, by contrast, your energy level is high during the mornings, you should hit the books then. But you may have to deal with the fact that others nearby are still sleeping or that many classes occur before noon. Probably most students will find that their energy levels are higher during the first part of the day and lower later on.

These different energy patterns and distractions suggest some important actions to take.

Make a Study Schedule First make a master schedule that shows all your regular obligations—classes and work, of course, but you may also wish to list meals and exercise times. This schedule should be indicated for the *entire school term*—semester, quarter, or whatever.

Now insert the times during which you plan to study. As mentioned, it's best if these study periods correspond to times when you are most alert and can best concentrate. However, don't forget to schedule in hourly breaks, since your concentration will flag periodically.

Next write in the major academic events—when term papers and other assignments are due, when quizzes and exams take place, any holidays and vacations.

At the beginning of every week, schedule your study sessions and write in the specific tasks you plan to accomplish during each session. It's best to try to study something connected with every class every day. If the subject is difficult for you (for example, language or math), try to spend an hour a day on it, which is more effective than 5 hours in one day.

In addition, rather than put off major projects, such as term papers, thinking you'll do them in one concentrated period of effort, it's more efficient to break the task into smaller steps that you can handle individually. This prevents you from delaying so long that you finally have to pull an all-nighter to complete the project.

Find Some Good Places to Study Studying means first of all avoiding distractions. No doubt you know people who study while listening to the radio or watching television—indeed, maybe you've done this yourself—but the fact is that most people *are* distracted by these activities.

Avoid studying in places that are associated with other activities, particularly comfortable ones. That is, don't do your academic reading lying in bed or sitting at a kitchen table. Studying should be an intense, concentrated activity.

You may wish to designate two or three areas as regular areas for studying. Assuming they are free of distractions, two good places are at a desk in your room or a table in the library. As these places become associated with studying, they will reinforce better studying behavior.[3]

Make sure the place you study is free of clutter, which can affect your concentration and make you feel disorganized. Your desktop should contain that which you are studying and nothing else.

Avoid Time Wasters, but Reward Your Studying Certainly it's much more fun to hang out with your friends, play sports, or to watch television than to study. Moreover, these pleasures are real and immediate, whereas getting an A in a course, let alone getting a degree, seems to be in the distant future.

Thus, at the same time you must learn to say no to distractions so that you can study, you must also give yourself frequent rewards so that you will indeed be *motivated* to study. Thus, you should study with the notion that after you finish you will "pleasure yourself" with a walk, a snack, a television show, a videogame, a conversation with a friend, or similar treat.

Improving Your Memory

Memorizing is, of course, one of the principal requirements of being in college. Distractions are one of the main impediments to remembering as they are to other forms of learning. *External* distractions are those you have no control over—noises in the hallway, an instructor's accent, people whispering in the library. If you can't get rid of the distraction by moving, you might try to increase your interest in the subject you are trying to memorize. *Internal* distractions are daydreams, personal worries, hunger, illness, and other physical discomforts. Small worries can be shunted aside by listing them on a page for future handling. Large worries may require talking with a friend or counselor.

Beyond getting rid of distractions, there are certain techniques you can adopt to enhance your memory.

Space Your Studying, Rather Than Cramming Cramming—making a frantic, last-minute attempt to memorize massive amounts of information—is probably the least effective means of absorbing information, especially if it tires you out and makes you even more anxious prior to the test. Research shows that, in general, it is better to space out your studying of a subject on successive days rather than try to do it all during the same number of hours on one day.[4] It is *repetition* that helps move information into your long-term memory bank.

Review Information Repeatedly—Even "Overlearn" It By repeatedly reviewing information—what is known as "rehearsal"—usually you can not only improve your retention of it but also your understanding of it.[5] Overlearning—continuing to repeatedly review material even after you appear to have absorbed it—can improve your recall substantially. Thus, although "cramming" is not an effective way to learn, reviewing material right before an examination can help counteract any forgetting that may have occurred since the last time you studied the material.

Use Memorizing Tricks There are several ways to organize information so that you can retain it better. Longman and Atkinson mention the following methods of establishing associations between items you want to remember:[6]

- *Mental and physical imagery:* Use your visual and other senses to construct a personal image of what you want to remember. Indeed, it helps to make the image humorous, action-filled, sexual, bizarre, or outrageous in order to establish a personal connection. For instance, to remember the name of the 21st president of the United States, Chester Arthur, you could visualize an author writing the number "21" on a wooden chest. This mental image helps you associate chest, author, and 21 to recall that Chester Arthur was the 21st president.

  You can also make your mental image a physical one by, for instance, drawing or diagramming. Thus, to learn the parts of the human gastrointestinal system, you could draw a picture and label the parts in order to assist your recall.

- *Acronyms and acrostics:* An acronym is a word created from the first letters of items on a list. For instance, *Roy G. Biv* helps you remember the colors of the rainbow in order: *r*ed, *o*range, *y*ellow, *g*reen, *b*lue, *i*ndigo, *v*iolet. An acrostic is a phrase or sentence created from the first letters of items on a list. For example, *Every Good Boy Does Fine* helps you remember the order of musical notes is E-G-B-D-F.

- *Location:* Location memory occurs when you associate a concept with a place or imaginary place. For example, you could learn the parts of the heart system by visualizing an imaginary walk across campus and associating each part with a building you pass.

- *Word games:* Jingles and rhymes are frequent devices used by advertisers to get people to remember their products. You may recall the spelling rule "I before E except after C or when sounded like A as in neighbor or weigh." To recall the difference between a stalactite (which hangs from the top of a cave) and a stalagmite (which forms on the floor of a cave), you might remember that the *t* in *stalactite* signifies "top." You can also use narrative methods, such as making up a story.

How to Benefit from Lectures

Are lectures really a good way of transmitting knowledge? Perhaps not always, but the fact remains that most colleges (and certainly most health courses) rely heavily on this method. Research has shown that students who are more often absent from class are more apt to have grades of C− or below compared to students attending class who have grades of B or above.[7]

Most lectures are reasonably well organized, but you will probably attend some that are not. Even so, they will indicate what the instructor thinks is important, which will be useful to you on the exams.

Regardless of the strengths of the lecturer, here are some tips for getting more out of lectures.

Take Effective Notes by Listening Actively Research shows that good test performance is related to good note taking.[8] Good note taking requires that you *listen actively*—that is, participate in the lecture process. Here are some ways to take good lecture notes:

- *Read ahead and anticipate the lecturer:* Try to anticipate what the instructor is going to say, based on your previous reading (text or study guide). Having background knowledge makes learning more efficient.

- *Listen for signal words:* Instructors use key phrases such as "The most important point is . . . ," "There are four reasons for . . . ," "The chief reason . . . ," "Of special importance . . . ," "Consequently . . . " When you hear such signal phrases, mark your notes with an asterisk (*) or write *Imp* (for "Important").

- *Take notes in your own words:* Instead of just being a stenographer, try to restate the lecturer's thoughts in your own words. This makes you pay attention to the lecture and organize it in a way that is meaningful to you. In addition, don't feel you have to write everything down, just get the key points.

- *Ask questions:* By asking questions during the lecture, you necessarily participate in it and increase your understanding. Although

many students are shy about asking questions, most professors welcome them.

Review Your Notes Regularly The good news is that most students, according to one study, do take good notes. The bad news is that they don't use them—that is, they wait until just before final exams to review their notes, when the notes have lost much of their meaning.[9] Make it a point to review your notes on a regular basis, such as on the day of the lecture or at least once a week. We cannot emphasize enough how important this kind of reviewing is.

How to Improve Your Reading Ability: The SQ3R Method

We cannot teach you how to speed-read here, but perhaps we can help you make the time you do spend reading more efficient. The method we will describe here is known as the *SQ3R method,* where "SQ3R" stands for *survey, question, read, recite,* and *review.*[10] The strategy for this method is to break down a reading assignment into small segments, each of which you master before moving on.

The five steps of the SQ3R method are as follows:

1. *Survey* **the Chapter Before You Read It** Get an overview of the chapter or other reading assignment before you begin reading it. If you have a sense of what the material is about before you begin reading it, you can predict where it is going, bring some of your own background experience to it, and otherwise become involved in it in a way that will help you retain it.

Many textbooks offer some "preview"-type material, such as a list of objectives or an outline of topic headings at the beginning of the chapter. Other books offer a summary at the end of the chapter. In the present book, for instance, at the beginning of each section, look at the objectives. You may also wish to flip through the chapter and read the summary at the beginning of each subsection.

2. *Question* the Segment in the Chapter Before You Read It   This step is easy to do, and the point, again, is to get yourself involved in the material. After surveying the entire chapter, go to the first segment—section, subsection, or even paragraph, depending on the level of difficulty and density of information—and look at the topic heading. In your mind, restate the heading as a question. After you have formulated the question, go to steps 3 and 4 (read and recite), then proceed to the next segment and restate the heading there as a question.

For instance, for the section heading in Chapter 1 that reads "The Five Dimensions of Health: Five Kinds of Well-being," ask yourself, "What *are* the five kinds of well-being?" For the heading of the subsection "High-Level Wellness," ask: "What does the term 'high-level wellness' mean?"

3. *Read* the Segment About Which You Asked the Question   Now read the segment you asked the question about. Read with purpose, to answer the question you formulated. Underline or color-mark sentences you think are important, if they help you answer the question. Read this portion of the text more than once, if necessary, until you can answer the question. In addition, determine whether the segment covers any other significant questions and formulate answers to these, too. After you have read the segment, proceed to step 4.

Perhaps you can see where this is all leading: If you approach your reading in terms of questions and answers, you will be better prepared when you see questions about the material on the examinations later.

4. *Recite* the Main Points for the Segment   Recite means "Say aloud." Thus, you should speak out loud (or under your breath) the an-

swer to the principal question about the segment and any other main points. Put these points in your own words, the better to enhance your understanding. If you wish, make notes of the principal ideas, so you can look them over later.

Now that you have actively studied the first segment, move on to the second segment and do steps 2–4 for it. Continue this procedure through the rest of the segments until you have finished the chapter.

5. *Review* the Entire Chapter by Repeating Questions   After you have read the chapter, go back through it and review the main points. Then, without looking at the book, test your memory by repeating the questions.

Although clearly the SQ3R method takes longer than simply reading with a rapidly moving color marker or underlining pencil, the technique is far more effective because it requires your *involvement and understanding.* This is the key to all effective learning.

How to Become an Effective Test Taker

The first requirement of test taking is, of course, knowledge of the subject matter, which is what the foregoing discussion has been intended to help you obtain. You should also make it a point to *ask* your instructor what kinds of questions will be asked on tests. Beyond this, however, there are certain skills one can acquire that will help during the test-taking process. Here are some suggestions offered by the authors of *Doing Well in College:*[11]

Reviewing: Study Information That Is Emphasized and Enumerated   Because you will not always know whether an exam will be an objective or essay test, you need to be prepared for both. Here are some general tips.

- **Review material that is emphasized:** In the lectures, this consists of any points your instructor pointed out as being significant or important, or spent a good deal of time discussing, or specifically advised you to study.

  In the textbook, pay attention to key terms (often emphasized in *italic* or **boldface** type), their definitions, and the examples that clarify them. Also, of course, material that has a good many pages given over to it should be considered more important.

- **Review material that is enumerated:** Pay attention to any numbered lists, both in your lectures and in your notes, whether it is the 13 vitamins, the major schools of psychology, or the warning signs for heart disease. Enumerations often provide the basis for essay and multiple-choice questions.

- **Review other tests:** Look over past quizzes as well as the discussion questions and review questions given at the end of chapters in many textbooks.

Prepare by Doing Final Reviews and Budgeting Your Test Time Learn how to make your energy and time work for you. Whether you have studied methodically or are only able to cram for an exam, here are some tips:

- **Review your notes:** Spend the night before reviewing your notes, then go to bed without interfering with the material you have absorbed (as by watching television). Get up early the next morning and review your notes again.

- **Find a good test-taking spot:** Make sure you go to the exam with any pencils and other materials you need. Get to the classroom early, or at least on time, and find a quiet spot. If you don't have a watch, sit where you can see a clock. Again, review your notes and avoid talking with others, so as not to interfere with the information you have learned and increase your anxiety.

- **Read the test directions:** Many students don't do this and end up losing points because they didn't understand precisely what was required of them. Also, listen to any verbal directions or hints your instructor gives you before the test.

- **Budget your time:** Here is an important point of test strategy: Before you start, read through the entire test and figure out how much time you can spend on each section. The reason for budgeting your time, of course, is so that you won't find yourself with only a few minutes left and a long essay still to be written or a great number of multiple-choice questions to answer.

  Write the number of minutes allowed for each section on the test booklet or on a scratch sheet and stick to the schedule. The way you budget your time should correspond to how confident you feel about answering the questions.

Objective Tests: Answer Easy Questions and Eliminate Options Some suggestions for taking objective tests, such as multiple-choice, true-false, or fill-in, are as follows:

- **Answer the easy questions first:** Don't waste time stewing over difficult questions. Do the easy ones first and come back to the hard ones later (put a check mark opposite those you're not sure about). Your unconscious mind may have solved them in the meantime, or later items may provide you with the extra information you need.

- **Answer all questions:** Unless the instructor says you will be penalized for wrong answers, try to answer all questions. If you have time, review all questions and make sure you have recorded them correctly.

- **Eliminate the options:** Cross out answers you know are incorrect. Be sure to read all the possible answers, especially when the first answer is correct (because other answers could also be correct, so that "All of the above" may be the right choice). Be alert that the test may provide information pertinent to one question in another question on the test. Pay particular attention to options that are long and detailed, since answers that are more detailed and specific are apt to be correct. If two answers have the opposite meaning, one of the two is probably correct.

Essay Tests: First Anticipate Answers and Prepare an Outline Because there is only a limited amount of time during the test, there are only a few essay questions that your instructor is apt to ask during the exam. The key to success is to try to anticipate beforehand what the questions might be and memorize an outline for an answer. Here are the specific suggestions:

- *Anticipate 10 probable essay questions:* Using the principles we discussed above of reviewing lecture and textbook material that is *emphasized* and *enumerated*, you are in a position to identify 10 essay questions your instructor may ask. Write out these questions.

- *Prepare and memorize informal essay answers:* Write out each of the questions and list the main points that need to be discussed. Put supporting information in parentheses. Circle the key words in each main point and below the question put the first letter of the key word. Make up catch phrases, using acronyms, acrostics, or word games, so that you can memorize these key words. Test yourself until you can recall the key words that the letters stand for and the main points the key words represent.

    For example, if the question you make up is "What is the difference between the traditional and the modern theory of adolescence?" you might put down the following answers:[12]

(1) Biologically generated. Universal phenomenon (Hall's theory: hormonal).

(2) *Sociologically generated.* Not universal phenomenon (not purely hormonal). BG SG   BIG GUY SMALL GUY

When you receive the questions for the essay examination, read the entire directions carefully, then start with the *least demanding question.* Putting down a good answer at the start will give you the confidence and make it easier to proceed with the rest. Make a brief outline, similar to the one you did for your anticipated question, before you begin writing.

The Peak-Performing Student

Good students are made, not born. They have decided, as we pointed out earlier, that they really want to play the college game, to learn the rules, the players, and the playing skills. We have listed some of the studying, reading, and test-taking skills that will help you be a peak-performing student. The practice of these skills is up to you.

Sources and Credits

F stands for Figure, **SD** for Self Discovery.

CHAP. 1. **F1** Adapted from Combs, B., Hales, D., & Williams, B. (1983). *An invitation to health* (2nd ed.). Menlo Park, CA: Benjamin/Cummings, 3. **F3** Brody, J. E. (1991, January 31). In pursuit of the best possible odds of preventing or minimizing the perils of major diseases. *The New York Times*, B6. Copyright © 1991 by The New York Times Company. Reprinted by permission.

CHAP. 2. **F1** Adapted from Menninger, K. (1963). *The vital balance.* New York: Viking; Combs, B., Hales, D., & Williams, B. (1980). *An invitation to health.* Menlo Park, CA: Benjamin/Cummings, 51; and Hales, D.(1992). *An invitation to health* (5th ed). Redwood City, CA: Benjamin/ Cummings, 70. **F5** Starr, C., & Taggart, R. (1992). *Biology* (6th ed.). Belmont, CA: Wadsworth, 643. **SD2** Mullen, K., & Costello, G. (1981). *Health awareness through self-discovery* (Edina, MN: Burgess International Group).

CHAP. 3. **F5** Adapted from Welsh, S. O., & Marston, R. M. (1982). Review of trends in food use in the United States, 1909 to 1980. *Journal of the American Dietetic Association, 81*, 120. **F10** U.S. Department of Agriculture.

CHAP. 4. **F1** Centers for Disease Control and Prevention. (1990). Coronary heart disease attributable to sedentary lifestyle— selected states, 1988. *Journal of the American Medical Association, 264*, 1392. **F4** From "Staying Loose" by James M. Rippe, M.D., *Modern maturity*, June–July 1990, 73–74. Used with permission of the author. **F5** Stretching before— and after. *American Health* © 1990 by Marc Bloom. **F7** Adapted from Borg, G. (1973). Perceived exertion: A note on history and methods. *Medicine & Science in Sports, 5*, 90. © by American College of Sports Medicine, 1973. **F8** (table). Adapted from DeWitt, J., & Roberts, T. (1991, September). Pumping up an adult fitness program. *Journal of Physical Education, Recreation, & Dance*, table 4, p. 70. **F9** Top: Data compiled from *The physiological basis of physical education and athletics* (3rd ed.) (p. 475) by E. L. Fox and D. K. Mathews, 1982, Philadelphia: Saunders College Publishing, and *Physiology of exercise: Responses and adaptations* (p. 281), 1978, D. R. Lamb, New York: Macmillan Publishing Co.. As shown in *Environment and human performance* by E. M. Haymes and C. L. Wells (p. 27), Champaign, IL: Human Kinetics Publishers. Copyright 1986 by Emily M. Haymes and Christine L. Wells. Adapted and reprinted by permission. Bottom: Adapted from Sharkey, B. J., 1975, *Physiology and physical activity*, New York: Harper & Row Publishers, 108–109.

As found in *Environment and human performance* by E. M. Haymes and C. L. Wells (p. 27), Champaign, IL: Human Kinetics Publishers. Copyright 1986 by Emily M. Haymes and Christine L. Wells. Adapted and reprinted by permission.

CHAP. 5. **SD1** Adapted from Reinisch, J., & Beasley, B. (1990). *The Kinsey Institute new report on sex.* New York: St. Martin's Press, 3–6. **F6** Adapted from Kinsey, A., Pomeroy, W., & Martin, C. (1948). *Sexual behavior in the human male.* Philadelphia: W. B. Saunders, 638. **F11** Based on data from Centers for Disease Control and Prevention. (1990). *Contraceptive options: Increasing your awareness.* Washington, DC: NAACOG. Hatcher, R. et al. (1990). *Contraceptive technology, 1990–1992.* New York: Irvington. Leads from the MMWR. (1988). Condoms for prevention of sexually transmitted diseases. *Journal of the American Medical Association, 259*, 1925–27. Harlap, S. et al. (1991). *Preventing pregnancy, protecting health: A new look at birth control choices in the United States.* New York: Alan Guttmacher. Anonymous. (1991, December). Deconstructing the condom. *Self*, 122–23. Consumers Union. (1989, March). Can you rely on condoms? *Consumer Reports*, 135–41.

CHAP. 6. **F1** Adapted from Starr, C., & Taggart, R. (1992). *Biology* (6th ed.). **F2** Adapted from Kost, K., Forrest, J. D., & Harlap, S. (1991). Comparing the health risks and benefits of contraceptive choices. *Family Planning Perspectives, 23*, 54–61, table 1. **F18** Adapted from Myers, D. G. (1989). *Psychology* (2nd ed.). New York: Worth Publishers, 59; and from Bevan, J. (1978). *The Simon & Schuster handbook of anatomy and physiology.* New York: Simon & Schuster, 17. **F19** Adapted from Bevan, J. (1978). *The Simon & Schuster handbook of anatomy and physiology.* New York: Simon & Schuster, 19. **F21** American College of Obstetrics and Gynecologists. Adapted from Anonymous. (1990, December). Older mothers: Chromosome defects. *American Health*, 11. **F24** Adapted from Starr, C., & Taggart, R. (1992). *Biology* (6th ed). Belmont, CA: Wadsworth, 768. **F26** Reproduced by permission from Jensen et al. (1979). *Biology.* Belmont, CA: Wadsworth, 237. **F29** Adapted from Starr, C., & Taggart, R. (1992). *Biology* (6th ed). Belmont, CA: Wadsworth, 775.

CHAP. 7. **F1** Data on coffee, tea, tea products, and chocolate products: Institute of Food Technologists. (1987, June). *Evaluation of caffeine safety.* Data on soft drinks: National Soft Drink Association. **F3** *Smoking and health.* (1990). Rockville, MD: Health and Human Services. **F4** Adapted from Zaret, B. L. et al. (1992). *Yale University School of Medicine heart book.* New York: Hearst,

76. **F9** Starr, C., & Taggart, R. (1992). *Biology* (6th ed.). Belmont, CA: Wadsworth, 643. **F11** Centers for Disease Control and Prevention. (1990). Alcohol-related mortality and years of potential life lost—United States, 1987. *MMWR, 39*(11), 175. **F13** American Psychiatric Association (1994). *Diagnostic and statistical manual of mental disorders*, 4th ed., 181. **F14** Kinney, J., & Leaton, G. (1987). *Loosening the grip: A handbook of alcohol information* (3rd ed.). St. Louis: Times Mirror/ Mosby, 153–8. **F15** The Twelve Steps are reprinted with permission of Alcoholics Anonymous World Services, Inc. Permission to reprint this material does not mean that AA has reviewed or approved the contents of this publication, nor that AA agrees with the views expressed herein. AA is a program of recovery from alcoholism—use of the Twelve Steps in connection with programs and activities which are patterned after AA, but which address other problems, does not imply otherwise.

CHAP. 9. **F4** Adapted from Starr, C., & Taggart, R. (1992). *Biology* (6th ed.). Belmont, CA: Wadsworth, 677; Creager, J. C. (1983). *Human anatomy and physiology.* Belmont, CA: Wadsworth, 521; and Martini, F. (1989). *Fundamentals of anatomy and physiology.* Englewood Cliffs, NJ: Prentice Hall, 606. **F5** Centers for Disease Control and Prevention. **F6** Top left: Centers for Disease Control and Prevention. Bottom and right: Adapted from Anonymous. (1992, October 11). Anatomy of a disease: A primer on tuberculosis. *The New York Times*, sec. 1, 20. **F7** Data from World Health Organization. Adapted from Gorman, C. (1992, August 3). Invincible AIDS. *Time*, 30–37. **F8** Centers for Disease Control and Prevention.

CHAP. 10. **F1** Adapted from Starr, C., & Taggart, R. (1992). *Biology* (6th ed.). Belmont, CA: Wadsworth, 664. Reprinted with permission of Wadsworth, Inc. **F2** Adapted from Curtis, H., & Barnes, N. S. (1989). *Biology* (5th ed.). New York: Worth, 755. **F3** Left: Adapted from Fowler, I. (1983). *Human anatomy.* Belmont, CA: Wadsworth, 408. Right: Starr, C., & Taggart, R. (1992). *Biology.* Belmont, CA: Wadsworth, 665–66; reprinted with permission of Wadsworth, Inc. and Joel Ito. **F5** Public Health Service (1990). *Healthy people 2000.* Washington, DC: U.S. Government Printing Office, 3. **F6** Starr, C., & Taggart, R. (1992). *Biology.* Belmont, CA: Wadsworth, 671; reprinted with permission of Wadsworth, Inc. **F7** Starr, C., & Taggart, R. (1992). *Biology.* Belmont, CA: Wadsworth, 672; reprinted with permission of Wadsworth, Inc. **SD1** Adapted from Luckmann, J. (1990). *Your health!* Englewood Cliffs, NJ: Prentice Hall, 337–38; American Heart Association, 1985. **F8** National Health and Nutrition Examination Survey II, 1976–80. **F10** American Cancer Society. (1993).

Cancer facts and figures. Atlanta: American Cancer Society. **F12** This excerpt first appeared in *Everyone's guide to cancer therapy: How cancer is diagnosed, treated, and managed day-to-day* by Malin Dollinger, M.D., Ernest H. Rosenbaum, M.D., and Greg Cable (adapted by The Canadian Medical Association, Richard Hasselback, M.D., editor) © 1992 Somerville House Books Limited and is published with the kind permission of Somerville House Books Limited.
F15, F18, F21 From *The American Medical Association family medical guide* by the American Medical Association. Copyright © 1987 by the American Medical Association. Reprinted by permission of Random House, Inc. **F16** Adapted from data from American Automobile Association, in Blyskal, J. (1993, January/February). Crash course. *American Health,* 74–79. **F17** Adapted from San Jose State University Police Department. (1989). *Safety & security.* San Jose, CA: San Jose State University, 26–27. **F23** Fingerhut, L. A., & Kleinman, J. C. (1990). International and interstate comparisons of homicide among young males. *Journal of the American Medical Association, 263,* 3292–95. Copyright 1990, American Medical Association.
SD3 Copyright © 1992 by The New York Times Company. Reprinted by permission.
F25 National Victim Center. Adapted from Anonymous. (1992, May 4). Unsettling report on an epidemic of rape. *Time,* 15.

CHAP. 11. SD1 Reprinted by permission of *Men's Health Magazine.* Copyright 1993 Rodale Press, Inc. All rights reserved.
SD2 Adapted with permission.
F2 Adapted from Luckmann, J. (1990). *Your health!* Englewood Cliffs, NJ: Prentice Hall, 523. **F4** The Garbage Project, University of Arizona. Adapted from Rathje, W. L. (1991, May). Once and future landfills. *National Geographic,* 123.
F5 United Nations, World Bank estimates.

CHAP. 12. F3 Roper Organization. Adapted from Robertson, I. (1987). *Sociology* (3rd ed.). New York: Worth, 337. **SD1** Reprinted with permission from *Psychology Today* magazine. Copyright © 1970 (Sussex Publishers, Inc.).
F6 Reprinted by permission of Choice In Dying, 200 Varick St., New York, NY 10014; 212/366-5540. **F7** Taken from a "Dear Abby" column by Abigail Van Buren © 1990. Distributed by Universal Press Syndicate.

Photo Credits

Credits are indicated by page numbers on which photos appear.

1 © David Lissy/Leo de Wys, Inc.; **4** © Jose Azel/Woodfin Camp & Associates; **16** © Ira Wyman/Monkmeyer Press Photo; **17** © David Joel/Tony Stone Images; **22** © Alon Reininger/Contact Stock Images; **29** © Walter Bibikov/The Image Bank; **32** © Chuck Savage/The Stock Market; **34** © Bob Daemmrich/Stock Boston; **37** © Ed Bock/The Stock Market; **38** © Bill Binzen/Fran Heyl Associates; **43** © Joanna McCarthy/The Image Bank; **44** © Gerd Ludwig/Woodfin Camp & Associates; **47** © Mike Kagan/Monkmeyer Press Photo; **49** © Steve Goldberg/Monkmeyer Press Photo; **50** © Jeffry Myers/Stock Boston; **56** © Frank Le Bua/Gamma Liaison Network; **62** © Gerard Vandystadt-Agence Vandystadt/Allsport; **63** © Richard Hutchings/Photo Researchers; **66** © Bob Daemmrich/Stock Boston; **73** © Erich Hartmann/Magnum Photos; **92** © 1993 Jerry Howard/Positive Images; **94** © Patricia J. Bruno/Positive Images; **99** © Robert Holland/The Image Bank; **101** © Charles Gupton/Stock Boston; **102** © Jon Feingersh/The Stock Market; **104** © David Lissy/Leo de Wys, Inc.; **129** © Roy Morsch/The Stock Market; **131** © Brian Williams and Stacey Sawyer/Sawyer & Williams; **136** © Bob Daemmrich/The Image Works; **160, 163, 171, 172, 173 top, 173 bottom, 174 left, 174 right, 175, 176 top, 176 bottom, 179** © Joel Gordon; **161** © Patricia Bruno/Positive Images; **209** © Momatiuk/Eastcott/Woodfin Camp & Associates; **177** Courtesy of The Upjohn Company, Communications Production Services; **183** © Francis Leroy/Biocosmos/Science Photo Library/Photo Researchers; **186 left** © Custom Medical Stock Photo; **186 right** © CNRI/Science Photo Library/Photo Researchers; **188** Courtesy of Stacey Sawyer; **190** © Michael Nichols/Magnum Photos; **197** © Gabe Palmer/The Stock Market; **211** © Patricia J. Bruno/Positive Images; **213** © Robert Cerri/The Stock Market; **217** © Renate Hiller/Monkmeyer Press Photo; **219** Copyright © Lennart Nilsson, from BEHOLD MAN, Little, Brown and Company; **228** © Patricia J. Bruno/Positive Images; **231 left** © Robert Frerck/Woodfin Camp & Associates; **231 right, 233** © Patricia J. Bruno/Positive Images; **239 top, bottom** © Fran Heyl Associates; **240** © Hugh Rogers/Monkmeyer Press Photo; **243** KL Jones/LLR Research; **247** © Bob Adelman/Magnum Photos; **252** © E. Sander/Frank Spooner/Gamma Liaison Network; **253** © Ogust/The Image Works; **257** © Mark Lawrence/The Stock Market; **263** © Cliff Feulner/The Image Bank; **269** © Patricia J. Bruno/Positive Images; **274** © Dann Coffey/The Image Bank; **276** © Jeffrey Duhn/Stock Boston; **283** © Jim Pickerell/The Image Works; **287** © Mario Ruiz/Picture Group; **311** © Ray Pfortner/Peter Arnold, Inc.; **313 top, 313 center, 313 bottom, 318, 319, 320** Centers for Disease Control and Prevention, Department of Health and Human Services; **324** © Mulvehill/The Image Works; **327** © Joe Carini/The Image Works; **329** © Richard Hutchings/Photo Researchers; **331** © Bob Daemmrich/The Image Works; **333** © Lori Adamski Peek/Tony Stone Images; **338** © Bob Daemmrich/The Image Works; **351** © Frank Siteman/Picture Cube; **358** © Bill Stanton/Rainbow; **370** © Jerry Howard/Positive Images; **371** © Lori Adamski Peek/Tony Stone Images; **373** © Fran Heyl Associates; **379** © Roy Morsch/The Stock Market; **383** © Freda Leinward/Monkmeyer Press Photo; **387** © Ovak Arslanian/Gamma Liaison Netowrk; **399** © Kirland/Sygma; **403** © Paul Fusco/Magnum Photos; **408** © Jon Ortner/Tony Stone Images; **412 left** The Bettmann Archive; **412 right** UPI/Bettmann Newsphotos; **415** © John Blaustein/Woodfin Camp & Associates; **421 top** © Dan McCoy/Rainbow; **421 bottom** © Ira Wyman/Sygma; **423** © Charles Gupton/Stock Boston; **428** © Jerome Friar/Impact Visuals; **433** © Patricia Woeber/Gamma Liaison Network; **439** © Joel Gordon; **411** © Fred Maroon/Photo Researchers, Inc.; **443** © Andrew Lichtenstein/Impact Visuals.

Learning How to Live: Making Health Decisions and Changes

How should one live?

All around us people *act* as though they know how they should live. But do they really? Is successful living something that just comes to us naturally, like breathing? Or is there an art to it, secrets that elude many people?

Perhaps living is indeed an art—the art of finding and using all the resources available to you to enhance your life. The art is not easily taught or learned—many people never learn it. But it is probably the most important subject that one can study.

This book represents a beginning to learning the *art of living*. This is the art of discovering who you are and your potential for growth and happiness. It is about expanding your knowledge of the great possibilities life has to offer and how to realize them. It is about learning to avoid rigid behavior that closes off new opportunities. It is about sharpening creative and critical thinking skills so that you can evaluate different authorities and situations. It is about determining the right action and taking responsibility for doing it.

Learning the art of living is nothing less than learning to develop our "genius, power, and magic." As Goethe, the German poet, wrote,

> *Whatever you can do, or dream you can begin, begin it. Boldness has genius, power, and magic in it.*

Health and the Art of Living

▶ Define health.

▶ Name and describe each of the five dimensions of health.

▶ Explain holistic health.

▶ Discuss high-level wellness and the concept of peak performance.

To be successful in life, one must first be successful in health. Health gives you the platform from which you can pursue all your other college and life goals. Health gives you the skills you need to apply lifelong, through the ups and downs in careers and relationships and personal fortunes.

Most people already sense this, if vaguely. They say, "If you have your health, you have everything." But do they really know what health is? And do you?

The Five Dimensions of Health: Five Kinds of Well-Being

Health is the achievement of physical, mental (intellectual), emotional, social, and spiritual well-being.

Many people think of *good health* in terms of its opposite. That is, they think of the absence of disease, of pain, of disability. Or they think in terms of vitality—being able to function with vigor. Or they consider health in terms of longevity—living to be at least 75, the average person's life expectancy in the United States. (The exact figure is 75.7 years. This is thirteenth in the world, behind Canada, which at 76.5 years is sixth. Japan at 79.1 years is first.)

Being without illness, having vitality, and living long are certainly all part of good health. But health is more than this. Indeed, we would say that health consists of attaining *well-being* in five areas, as we discuss next.

The Definition of Health In this book, we use the following definition:

> ***Health* is the achievement of physical, mental, social, emotional, and spiritual well-being.**

The first three aspects reflect the widely used definition of the Geneva-based World Health Organization (WHO), an arm of the United Nations. Health, they say, represents "complete physical, mental, and social well-being and not merely the absence of disease and infirmity." Note that true health involves not only your body but also your mind and your ability to interact with those around you.

The two final aspects draw on holistic health. The word *holism* refers to interacting wholes—the concern with complete systems rather than isolated parts. Holistic health looks at the *whole* person rather than the parts. Thus, ***holistic health* adds emotional and spiritual well-being to the physical, mental, and social dimensions of health.** In this view, a person's health is measured by his or her functioning in all areas of life. Hence, a person who is incapacitated physically may still be healthy in the other four of the five dimensions. Moreover, that person need not be consistently unhealthy in the physical dimension.

The Five Dimensions of Health Let us consider these five dimensions:

1. ***Physical: Physical health* means, first, functioning body systems and the absence of disease or disability; second, physical fitness; and, third, minimal exposure to abuse.** Examples of abuse are drugs, stress, and environmental hazards. One may be disabled or chronically ill, as with diabetes, but still healthy within one's limitations.

2. ***Mental or intellectual: Mental health, or *intellectual health,* means well-being in the area of thinking,** or cognition, as opposed to feeling. This area of health covers such activities as analyzing, judging, speaking, and writing. It involves our ability to learn and successfully meet intellectual challenges.

3. ***Emotional: Emotional health* is concerned with well-being in matters of feeling,** as opposed to thinking. It includes such aspects of life as self-esteem, love, and empathy. It involves our ability to recognize, control, and appropriately express our feelings.

4. ***Social: Social health* has to do with one's well-being in interactions with others.** It covers your comfort level with

others, your social skills, your concern for others, and your ability to accept differences. Social health involves making meaningful contributions to your family, community, and the world.

5. ***Spiritual: Spiritual health* could be defined as your ability to love and to accept love.** Spiritual health, says Richard Eberst of Adelphi University, "includes trust, integrity, principles and ethics, the purpose or drive in life, basic survival instincts, [and] feelings of selflessness." It also, he says, includes "commitment to some higher process or being and the ability to believe in concepts that are not subject to 'state of the art' [or customary] explanation."[1]

All five health dimensions overlap and affect one another. Thus, improvements in one area of well-being may affect several other areas. Exercise, for example, may improve your mood and give you energy that allows you to study more efficiently. This in turn may lessen your study worries and improve your social interactions and possibly your spiritual self.

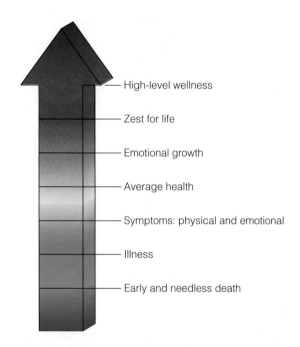

- High-level wellness
- Zest for life
- Emotional growth
- Average health
- Symptoms: physical and emotional
- Illness
- Early and needless death

● **Figure 1   The hierarchy of health.** Health may be ranked from early and needless death up to high-level wellness.

Toward High-Level Wellness and Peak Performance

Health may be considered on a hierarchy, with optimum health consisting of high-level wellness and peak performance.

Health, we said, is the attainment of physical, mental (intellectual), emotional, social, and spiritual well-being. All these together may be placed on a hierarchy. At the top end is *high-level wellness*. At the bottom end is *early and needless death*. (See ● *Figure 1.*)

Most people, of course, are somewhere in between. Moreover, their position in the hierarchy may vary depending on what experiences they are having in the five areas of health. Life and health are constantly undergoing change. Thus, the attainment of well-being in all dimensions of health is an ongoing, life-long, ever-changing process.

In this book, we are concerned not merely with avoiding disabling illness. We want to help you become engaged in the process of attaining

wellness and ultimately, if desired, to become a peak performer.

High-Level Wellness People who achieve a positive balance in the five dimensions of health are said to be holistically healthy. They are also said to have attained a high level of wellness. *Wellness* is the opposite of *illness*, of course. But wellness also suggests that people's health should not be measured just by the absence of disease. Rather, attaining **high-level *wellness* means that people are realizing themselves to the fullest.** That is, within their own limitations they are successful in achieving their human potential.

Peak Performance The phenomenon of ***peak performance* refers to repeatedly performing at the height of one's abilities to produce great individual accomplishments.** Psychologist Charles Garfield, author of *Peak Performers,* spent years studying top achievers in various fields.[2] He concluded that the qualities these achievers showed could be adopted by others to further their own development. "The differences between peak performers and ordinary performers do not stem primarily from the situations in which they operate," Garfield says. "The differences appear in the attitude and skills a peak performer brings to a situation."

Garfield found several qualities that characterize high-performing individuals. Peak performers tend to do the following: (1) They make an internal decision to excel. They have a sense of mission. (2) They consistently reach their goals, in both short and long time frames. (3) They are self-confident and able to see both the big and little picture. They are able to mentally rehearse the achievements they wish to attain. (4) They are team players, expanding their own potential by aligning themselves with others. (5) They are able to change course when they make mistakes. (6) They are able to anticipate difficulties and opportunities, adapt to them, and act to preserve what is best.

Do these sound like unattainable attributes? We would agree with Charles Garfield that peak performers are made, not born. As he says, searching for the peak performer within yourself means that you are always asking *What more can I be? (See ● Figure 2.)*

● **Figure 2   Peak performers are made, not born.**

❝*You recognize yourself as a person who was born not as a peak performer but as a learner. With the capacity to grow, change, and reach for the highest possibilities of human nature, you regard yourself as a person in process. Not perfect, but a person who keeps asking:* What more can I be? *And answering for yourself.* ❞

—Charles Garfield (1986). *Peak performers.* New York: Morrow, pp. 288–289.

5

*Taking
Responsibility,
Getting
Information, and
Mastering
Change*

Taking Responsibility, Getting Information, and Mastering Change

▶ Describe three stages of improvements that have increased life expectancy in the past century.

▶ Name the leading causes of death among those ages 15–24 and 25–65.

▶ Discuss the relationship between lifestyle and personal health status.

▶ Explain the principal sources of health information.

▶ Discuss how motivations and habits can be changed.

No doubt you know of someone who avoided all the standard advice for a healthy life and lived to a ripe old age. You may also know someone who did all the right things and still developed a severe illness. We need, then, to point out a fundamental fact: health-promoting habits *are not guarantees.* As health writer Jane Brody points out, "they do not offer 100% protection, like a vaccine against a disease. Good habits merely weight the odds in one's favor."[3]

Let us begin to take a look at habits and health.

Changing Lifestyles and Personal Responsibility

Life expectancy has risen because of improvements in public health, drugs and medical technology, and better lifestyle. Today most ill health is preventable with lifestyle changes.

More than a century ago, people were pretty much obliged to look after their own health. The "health authorities" themselves were not much more knowledgeable and were frequently unavailable or inaccessible. Then came the advances that have led to modern medicine.

From Public Health to Lifestyle Over the past century, the nature of problems that affect people in developed countries has changed dramatically. As result, death rates have declined through three stages, according to physician Donald M. Vickery.[4]

• *Age of Environment—improved public health:* From about 1885 until the 1930s, infectious diseases were a primary health problem. Focusing on this enemy, public health policies and improvements in the environment dramatically lowered death rates, especially those for infant mortality. During this period, city health departments were established, water supplies were cleaned up, milk became pasteurized, and public health campaigns were introduced.

• *Age of Medicine—improved drugs and technology:* In the 1930s, sulfa drugs, penicillin, and other antibiotics were introduced. These, too, controlled infectious disease, further accelerating the drop in death rates.

• *Age of Lifestyle—better living habits:* People began to live longer because the arrest of infectious diseases meant there were fewer deaths early in life. As a result, *chronic* diseases began to play the primary role in health. ***Chronic* means of long duration or recurring.** Chronic is distinguished from ***acute,* which is of short duration.**

In the early 1950s and 1960s, life expectancy leveled out. This occurred even though many high-tech innovations—open heart surgery, polio vaccine, and so on—continued to be introduced. Finally, in the 1970s, life expectancy rose again as people adopted healthier habits. The change reversed many ***lifestyle disorders*—ill health caused by unhealthy behavior** in eating, safety, drug use, and other areas.

The Importance of Prevention Today we are still living in the Age of Lifestyle—this despite a resurgence of infectious diseases. (New or mutated organisms such as HIV/AIDS, the rise in tuberculosis, and the declining effectiveness of antibiotics underscore the problem.) Unfortunately, people find assuming responsibility for their lifestyle choices a lot less fascinating than medical wizardry. Clearly, a lot of ill health is *preventable*. Consider the age group you are in, which most likely is either ages 15–24 (adolescents and young adults) or ages 25–64 (adults).[5]

- **Adolescents and young adults:** There are two categories of preventable health problems found among people between the ages of 15 and 24.

   (1) The first category of preventable health problems consists of *injuries and violence* that kill and disable. Far and away the leading cause of death for young people is unintentional injuries, three-quarters involving motor-vehicle crashes. (More than half of fatal motor-vehicle crashes involve alcohol.) The second leading cause of death in this group is homicide, and the third is suicide.

   (2) The second category consists of *emerging lifestyles*. Especially important are those having to do with diet, physical activity, safety, tobacco use, and sexual behavior. These are important because they affect one's health many years later. For example, AIDS is the leading cause of death among American men ages 25–44, according to the Centers for Disease Control and Prevention. Since AIDS takes up to 10 years to develop, the behaviors that led to infection with the virus occurred earlier.

- **Adults:** Many of the principal health problems for people 25–65 are also preventable in whole or in part through changes in lifestyle. Examples are changes in tobacco and alcohol use, diet, exercise, and safety matters.

   For this age group as a whole, the leading causes of death are cancer and heart disease. Cancer is actually not one but many diseases. Most significant are lung cancer, cancers of the colon and rectum, breast cancer, cervical cancer, and cancer of the mouth and throat. Other leading causes of death are heart disease and stroke (interruption of blood supply to the brain), and injuries, as from car crashes.

Health and Personal Responsibility Physician Gary Williams, director of medical sciences at the American Health Foundation, a health research organization, has ranked preventive health recommendations. He evaluated each for preventing particular illnesses, based on thousands of studies. *(See ● Figure 3.)* Although his analysis is not all-inclusive, it does show that lifestyle matters do make a difference.

The lesson is clear: *Your habits matter.* Taking responsibility for one's own health is a major part of the art of living. Having a strong foundation of knowledge is the key to taking responsibility for and making decisions about your life.

How Good Is Your Health Information?

People get health information from friends and family, folklore, the media, health practitioners, health groups, public and private consumer protection agencies, health educators, and other information sources.

You can't help but make decisions: *taking* action is a decision; so is *not* taking action. When it comes to your health, then, you're making decisions all the time. Considering that these can be life-and-death decisions, is the thinking going into the decisions proportional to their importance? For starters, let's consider the sources of information you may be relying on.

Sources of Health Information Some possible sources of information about health are the following:

- **Friends, family, and folklore:** If you're trying to find a good dentist, gynecologist, or psychotherapist, you likely start by asking people you know and have trusted in other matters. There's nothing wrong with this, at least as a beginning. Certainly some friends and family members can share accurate health information with you. They can, for instance, tell you if a health practitioner misdiagnosed them, caused them pain, or treated them with an uncaring manner.

7

*Taking
Responsibility,
Getting
Information, and
Mastering
Change*

	No tobacco	Low-fat diet	High-fiber diet	Avoid alcohol	Avoid salted, pickled foods	Diet high in vegetables and fruits	Exercise, weight control

Cancer
  Lung
  Breast
  Colon
  Liver
	✓✓✓	✓
		✓✓✓
		✓✓✓
			✓✓✓	✓✓✓	✓	✓
						✓✓
						✓✓✓
						✓✓
							✓
							✓

Heart attack	✓✓✓	✓✓✓				✓✓	✓✓
Stroke	✓				✓✓✓	✓✓	✓✓
Adult diabetes		✓✓✓	✓			✓✓	✓✓

Meaning of symbols:
✓✓✓ = Highly effective
✓✓ = Moderately effective
✓ = Somewhat effective

● **Figure 3   Preventing disease: a menu of health-saving tactics.** Dr. Gary Williams of the American Health Foundation has ranked various recommendations for healthy living. He studied their value in preventing certain cancers, heart attack, stroke, and adult diabetes. The analysis does not consider the harmful effects of high blood pressure, osteoporosis, and ulcers. Nor does it evaluate the benefits of stress reduction, regular breakfast eating, and 7 hours' sleep a night.

On the other hand, family, friends, and others may also simply pass along folklore, some old, some recent. Do you have a real itchy case of poison ivy? Go pick some jewelweed (wild touch-me-not), older relatives may advise, and rub the milky insides on your skin. Have a cold? Take megadoses of vitamin C, your friends may say.

• *Advertising and the mass media:* We are most comfortable with the familiar. Advertisers know this, so they bombard each of us with a staggering 400–3000 advertising messages *every day.*[6] That a product is familiar to us, however, does not make it superior to other products.

The mass media also present a great deal of health information as news, feature articles, books, or television or radio programs. A driving force in journalism, however, is the constant pressure to convert dry, technical material into interesting, readable stories. Relatively few journalists have special training in medicine or science. Consequently, they may be unable to evaluate the reliability of information from sources that may be biased. No wonder reporters unwittingly introduce inaccuracies, make important omissions, overemphasize the emotional side of scientific stories, or exaggerate or misinterpret risks.[7] On the positive side, however, the media may call attention to health developments that can lead you to information from credible sources.

• *Health practitioners and health groups:* If you look around your dentist's or doctor's office, you may see a variety of patient-education pamphlets. In addition, many professional associations, ranging from the American Heart Association to the American Dietetic Association, publish educational materials.

In general, these materials do contain reliable information. These professional associations can ill afford to be thought of as "inaccurate" or "crackpot." The same applies to informational inserts with pharmaceutical products, which are regulated by the Food and Drug Administration. Materials published by *unlicensed* health practitioners, however, are another matter.

- ***Public and private consumer protection agencies:*** Several federal and state agencies exist to educate the public in health matters and alert people to fraud and harm. The same is true of private consumer advocacy groups and voluntary health agencies. The principal consumer protection agencies are as follows:

  (1) Many *federal government* agencies provide accurate information to the public. One is the *Food and Drug Administration (FDA),* which regulates advertising of prescription drugs and labeling of nonprescription drugs. The FDA has an ongoing public information program, including a magazine on health and safety issues, *FDA Consumer.* Another agency is the *U.S. Department of Health and Human Services,* which issues many useful reports on health.

      Other sources for health information are the Federal Trade Commission, the U.S. Postal Service, the Environmental Protection Agency, and the departments of Agriculture and Education.

  (2) *State agencies* charged with health, education, environmental protection, and consumer safety offer a great deal of health information. So do many state-supported colleges and universities. State regulatory boards license physicians, nurses, and other health professionals and may investigate allegations of malpractice and other wrongdoings. State attorneys general are able to investigate and halt illegal advertising and services of unapproved drugs and health and safety matters.

  (3) *Consumer advocacy groups* are private organizations. Examples are Consumers Union, the National Consumers' League, and the Center for Science in the Public Interest.

- ***Health educators and health information sources:*** Health educators are employed not only in colleges and universities but also in hospitals, corporations, and community agencies. Generally they serve as a good resource for health information. Good information is also available in reference libraries and through reputable computer software programs and computerized databases.

Having correct information suggests you now have the tools to take correct action. But how difficult is it to make the moves you know you should take?

Strategy for Living: How to Change a Habit

Changing habits is an art that can be learned.

"Habits are simply things we create," notes one observer. "If you've created something, you can uncreate it."[8]

What habits would you like to change? Get more exercise or more sleep? Quit smoking? Lose weight? Change your diet? Stop procrastinating on your studies?

Changing a habit has two major parts to it: (1) developing the motivation, and (2) making the actual change.

The Importance of Motivation Often we tell ourselves we can't change "because that's just my nature," as though we were animals unable to be different. If people were as unable to change as other creatures, they would never get promoted, adjust to parenthood, or learn another language. We are not creatures but rather "creatures of habit"—which means we can change our habits.

Sometimes we do know how to change, but we don't know how to set realistic goals. Or we feel like failures if we set a goal and don't reach it. Or sometimes we compare ourselves to other

9

*Taking
Responsibility,
Getting
Information, and
Mastering
Change*

people, thinking we lack some kind of internal strength they have. "I don't have the self-discipline or willpower she has," we will say. Actually, self-discipline and willpower are just other words for *motivation*. To be motivated means that you (1) are clear about your goal, (2) make a promise to achieve that goal, and (3) keep your promise.

No doubt you are highly motivated to do some things. *The trick is to become motivated in areas you think you ought to change.* Some ways to increase your motivation are as follows:[9]

- *Clarify your goal:* Be very specific. What is it you want to achieve? How much time are you allowing yourself to do it? When will you do it? Break your goal down into smaller steps.

- *Write a plan of action:* Include enough variety in your plan to sustain your interest. Place the plan where you can see it every day, such as on the refrigerator.

- *Sweeten the task:* Think about the benefits you'll derive from making the change. Visualize yourself after the change. If some part of a task is putting you off, try changing just that part. For instance, if you resist exercise because it seems boring, do it while watching television or listening to music on a Walkman. Or do it after talking with friends and before going to a movie.

- *Adopt a model:* Another way to overcome resistance, as to doing exercise, is to do it with someone who can act as a model. For instance, join a friend who already jogs or lifts weights or whatever, and let him or her show you the ropes.

- *Get social support for yourself:* People learn to smoke because of social pressure. Joining an anti-smoking group or a running or climbing club can put positive pressures on you. So can talking to supportive people in your life.

- *Analyze the costs versus the benefits:* College can be difficult, with the ongoing pressure of studying, papers, and tests. Many students think a way to dispel the stress is by partying. However, heavy drink-ing adds to the stress by creating hangovers, jitters, and tiredness and makes the next day's studying even more difficult.

One way to deal with this and similar behaviors is first to acknowledge their benefits. Then compare these "benefits" with their costs. Maybe there is another way to get the same payoff—stress relief—without the costs (examples: going to movies, swimming, meditating).

- *Identify barriers and resources:* Obstacles to your goal might include limited time, lack of money, upcoming holidays, and non-supportive friends and family. Plan for ways to circumvent these barriers. Identify the people and activities that will help you overcome flagging motivation when it occurs.

- *Accept the discomfort:* If the prospect of discomfort puts you off, pay attention to the thoughts you have. For instance, you may hear your inner voice say, "I can't stand the idea of doing this." Reframe your negative statements to be more positive: "I will try this for 15 minutes and then reevaluate how I'm doing."

Also observe the reactions of your body, such as faster breathing, tight muscles, or terror in the stomach. Stay in contact with these feelings for a few minutes, judging them as neither good nor bad. As one writer points out, "Accepting the thoughts and body sensations robs them of their power. They may still be present, but in time they will stop being a barrier for you."[10]

- *Change your negative thoughts:* One way to lessen negative thoughts is simply to exaggerate them. Shut your eyes and imagine a negative statement, such as "People will laugh at me." Now exaggerate the statement to make it look ridiculous. "Then begin to intensify and enlarge it, making it more and more strident, perhaps flashing in brilliant neon lights," advises one book. "Then make the voice scream out in a tremendous echo chamber, with mile-high letters in view of thousands of people."[11]

Changing Habits "Success in school and life is largely a matter of cultivating effective habits," writes educator David Ellis. "Ineffective habits can be changed."[12]

Following are ways Ellis suggests we can change a habit:

- *Tell the truth:* The first task is to admit to the truth about any habit, whether it's continually oversleeping or cheating on diets. Facing the truth frees us. Once we admit the reality of our behavior, we are then open to receiving help to change that behavior.

- *Choose one new behavior at a time:* Don't try to remake yourself overnight, changing habits right and left. Start with just one. That makes the process of change more manageable. For instance, if you've decided to improve your study habits, don't try to quit smoking or lose weight at the same time.

- *Commit to using the new behavior:* Make a plan for when and how you will use the new habit. Ellis suggests you formulate your plan by answering questions such as these:

  (1) When will I apply the new habit?

  (2) Where will I be?

  (3) Who will be with me?

  (4) What will I be seeing, hearing, touching, saying, or doing?

  (5) How, exactly, will I think, speak, or act differently?

  For example, if you tend to drink too much at parties, you can make plans to replace alcohol with nonalcoholic beer. Or consider filling up your beer can with water after you've consumed the first one.

  By making a plan, you transform a vague idea into a true *intention*.

- *Affirm your intention:* Before you try to adopt your new behavior, make a mental picture in your mind of what actions you will take and in what order. Include all your senses, adding sounds, textures, and colors to your mental rehearsal. In your mind, *be* the change you want to see. Tennis players wanting to improve their serves, for instance, will imagine the ball in every detail, from fuzz to color. They rehearse in their mind's eye the path of the ball from start to finish.

- *Get feedback and support:* How many people have you known who have quit smoking for a few days but slipped back, saying "Just one cigarette after dinner won't hurt"? If you want a habit change to survive more than just a few days, alert lots of people and ask for support. The support can be as simple as a friend giving you gentle reminders from time to time. ("How many days have you been off cigarettes now?") Or you might join a quit-smoking self-help group that meets every week.

- *Practice, practice, practice . . . without reproach:* It may take a while for a habit change to feel comfortable. Accept the initial feelings of discomfort, but keep practicing. Expect that you will grow into your new behavior. If you momentarily slip (as in having a cigarette once), just note the behavior, without blame or guilt, and resume your program. A slip doesn't mean that you've failed, only that you've taken a step back for every two steps forward. In time, the new behavior will feel as natural as breathing.

Your Involvement Matters: Getting the Most Out of Health Care Services

- Describe the self-care movement and name two focuses of self-care.
- Discuss how health consumers can become active in and responsible for their own health care.
- Describe the roles of the primary-care physician and of specialist physicians. Summarize other health professionals who support them. Describe the various health care facilities available.
- Discuss how to prepare for and what to expect in a medical checkup, a dental checkup, a doctor's treatment recommendations, and surgery.
- Discuss what you need to be aware of for prescription and nonprescription drugs. Differentiate between the meaning of brand-name and generic drugs.
- Explain some of the more accepted therapeutic alternatives to traditional medicine.
- Identify and describe three categories of unconventional therapy.
- Discuss the hazards of quackery and health fads, list ways you can assess credibility, and explain how you can become your own expert.
- Explain what types of health insurance policies and health providers are available, and describe governmental health programs.

We have briefly considered *wellness,* which is what most of this book is about. However, before going further we need to briefly consider how to handle *illness*. After all, even the most conscientious followers of healthy practices fall ill sometimes. Let us therefore examine the conventional health care system and its alternatives and see how you can best advance your own interests.

Patient, Heal Thyself: Your Attitude Matters

Health consumers need to become active in and responsible for their own health care. As part of this, we need to learn preventive self-care and self-treatment.

"Consumers will be the primary practitioners in the new health care system," writes physician and medical editor Tom Ferguson. "Already, health-active, health-responsible individuals are improving and maintaining their own health and that of their families, actively seeking information on all the complex forces that make them ill or well."[13]

The Active and Responsible Health Consumer There are perhaps three groups or types of health consumers.[14] Which kind are you?

- ***Are you a passive health consumer?*** Are you passive in that you feel there is little you can do personally to improve your health? Do you rarely seek out information about your health?
- ***Are you a concerned consumer?*** Do you see yourself operating under the umbrella of—and compliant with—the doctor's authority? Do you rarely question your health care provider's decisions? Do you want to please your health provider? Although health practitioners may see you as a "model patient," you aren't taking an active role in decisions about your health care.
- ***Are you an active, responsible health consumer?*** Are you highly motivated to play an active role in your own health? Do you ask lots of questions? Do you insist on making key decisions about your care to others? Do you seek additional health information and advice—including obtaining second, third, or more opinions about a health problem, when indicated? If so, you want to not only understand your treatment but also to be an active participant in it.

Obviously, if you are the third type of health consumer, you are most assertive and involved in your health. You will thus be most likely to obtain quality health care and obtain high-level wellness.

Self-Care Comes First The foremost expression of the new health-active, health-responsible attitude is the self-care movement. **The *self-care movement* is the trend toward taking responsibility for managing one's health and preventing ill health.** Self-care focuses on two areas:

- ***Prevention:*** Preventive self-care is based on knowledge about health and on a healthful lifestyle. That includes activities recommended in this book, from avoiding tobacco to eating a low-fat diet to driving defensively to doing various self-examinations.

- ***Self-care treatment:*** Acute but nonserious conditions (colds, flu, sore throats) about which you have adequate knowledge can be treated on your own. You recognize, however, when you need the services of a health care professional.

Obviously, self-care means self-education. You should learn everything from the normal ranges for blood pressure, pulse rate, and respiration to how to buy nonprescription drugs. Most importantly, you must learn how to assess the health problems that arise and when to get assistance from health care providers.

Conventional Health Care: Practitioners and Facilities

The first doctor you see for a particular health problem is often a primary-care physician, who may refer you to specialist physicians. Other health care professionals include osteopaths, physician assistants, nurses (NPs, RNs, LPNs), and dentists. They are supported by audiologists, optometrists, podiatrists, pharmacists, and other medical specialists. Also available are a variety of conventional health care facilities, from hospitals to clinics to specialized "medicenters."

At some point even the most dedicated pursuer of self-care will need to seek professional advice. Who are the health professionals you might seek out? Let us consider those most likely to be found in the front line of your health defense. *(See ● Table 1.)*

Physicians By physicians we usually mean ***medical doctors,*** **health professionals who have earned M.D. (Doctor of Medicine) degrees.** An M.D. has 4 years of undergraduate education and has graduated from a 4-year accredited medical school.

A physician may also be an osteopath, who has received a D.O. (Doctor of Osteopathy) degree. ***Osteopathy*** **is based on the principle that the body, once correctly adjusted, can make its own remedies against disease and other disorders.** The adjustments include the same treatments available to conventional medicine—physical, medicinal, and surgical—but emphasize physical manipulation of the body.

Ideally, everyone should have a primary-care physician, although few people do. (Perhaps two-thirds of all women, for example, use their gynecologist as their primary-care physician.[15]) **A *primary-care physician* is the doctor who makes the primary evaluation. He or she also does the primary treatment for ordinary health problems.** Primary-care physicians will refer you to other M.D.s who specialize. Some, for example, specialize in a particular organ such as the heart (cardiology). Other examples of M.D.s' specialties are children (pediatrics) and emotional problems (psychiatry).

Physician Assistants ***Physician assistants (PAs)*** **perform about 80% of what physicians can do. Their duties range from basic primary care to high-technology surgical procedures.** A PA is a new class of health care practitioners operating under the direction of M.D.s.

Nurses **A *nurse* is trained in direct patient care, especially under the direction of a physician.** Not all nurses are alike, and their responsibilities usually depend upon their training. Nurse practitioners (NPs) and registered nurses (RNs) have more education than licensed practical nurses (LPNs) or licensed vocational nurses (LVNs).

● **Table 1   Principal health care providers**

Physician	
Medical Doctor (M.D.)	Health professional with M.D. (Doctor of Medicine) degree. Requirements: Bachelor's degree plus 4-year medical school, state examination, 1-year internship in hospital.
Primary-care physician	M.D. who does primary evaluation and treatment for ordinary health problems. May be one of three types: (1) *General Practitioner* (GP) treats full range of medical problems, referring patients to specialists for problems requiring ongoing care. (2) *Family practitioner* is a board-certified specialist with more training than GP: 3-year residency covering internal medicine, obstetrics, pediatrics, and orthopedics. (3) *Internist* is a board-certified specialist in diagnosis and nonsurgical treatment of adults with problems in their internal organs. Has more advanced training in such matters as heart disease, diabetes, and cancer compared to GPs and family practitioners.
Specialist	M.D. who has taken an additional 2–5 years of residency plus further examinations to qualify as "board-certified" in a medical specialty. Examples: cardiology (heart), pediatrics (children,) gynecology (women's reproductive health).
Osteopath (O.D.)	Physician with D.O. (Doctor of Osteopathy) degree. Uses same treatments as those used by M.D.s but emphasizes physical manipulation of the body. Requirements: bachelor's degree plus 4-year osteopathy school.
Physician assistant (PA)	Performs about 80% of what physicians do. Operates under direction of M.D. Duties range from basic primary care to surgical procedures. Requirements: 2-year training program, national certifying examination.
Nurse (RN, NP, LPN/LVN)	*Registered nurse (RN):* Provides or supervises direct patient care, educates patients, does research. Requirements: 2-year associate degree (technical nurse) or 4-year bachelor's degree (professional nurse), state examination. May specialize in various fields of medicine.
	Nurse practitioner (NP): Specialist in pediatrics, family health, public health, school health, etc. May prescribe drugs, have own clinic. Requirements: RN degree plus 2 years of graduate study.
	Licensed practical nurse (LPN), licensed vocational nurse (LVN): Provides direct patient care, such as bathing, oral hygiene, and change of dressings, under supervision of RN or physician; works in hospitals, nursing homes, and home health settings. Requirements: 2 or more years of high school, 12–18 months training in hospital-based program, state examination.
Dentist (D.D.S., D.M.D.)	Doctor of Dental Surgery (D.D.S.), Doctor of Medical Dentistry (D.M.D.): Diagnoses and treats impairments of teeth, gums, and oral cavity. Requirements: bachelor's degree plus 4-year dental school. Often followed by year of internship, written and clinical examination. Some go on to specialize in oral surgery, periodontics (gum disease), orthodontics (teeth straightening), or prosthodontics (dentures and other artificial appliances).
Other health specialties	Over 60 other health specialties exist. Some common ones:
Audiologist	Screens for hearing problems, fits hearing impaired with hearing aids.
Optometrist (O.D.)	Diagnoses vision problems and eye diseases, prescribes corrective lenses. Not a physician; holds O.D. (Doctor of Optometry) degree. (Treatment of complex eye problems and diseases is done by *ophthalmologist*, an M.D. specializing in the eye. Prescriptions for lenses are filled by *opticians*.)
Pharmacist	Trained and licensed to dispense medications according to physicians' prescriptions and give advice about medications.
Podiatrist (D.P.M.)	Specializes in disorders of feet and legs. May use drugs and surgery. Requirements: length of training similar to that for M.D.s, but degree is D.P.M. (Doctor of Podiatric Medicine).

Dentists **Dentists diagnose and treat impairments of the teeth and gums and oral cavity in general.** Some dentists go on to specialize in oral surgery, *periodontics* (gum disease), *orthodontics* (teeth straightening), or *prosthodontics* (dentures and other artificial appliances).

Other Health Specialists There are more than 60 other types of health specialties. However, those you are likely to deal with directly include the following:

- *Audiologists:* **An *audiologist* screens for hearing problems and can fit a hearing-impaired person with a hearing aid.**

- *Optometrists: Optometrists* **diagnose vision problems and diseases of the eye and can prescribe corrective lenses and glasses.** An optometrist is not a physician. Evidence of complex vision problems or eye disease may require a referral to an *ophthalmologist,* an M.D. specializing in the eye. Prescriptions for lenses are filled by *opticians.*

- *Pharmacists: Pharmacists* **are trained and licensed to dispense medications prescribed by a physician and to give advice about medications.**

- *Podiatrists:* **A *podiatrist* specializes in disorders of the feet and legs.** Podiatrists are the only health-care practitioners besides M.D.s and dentists who may use drugs and surgery in their practice.

There are a great many other *allied health care professionals* that a physician might refer you to. Some have the word "therapist" in their job title—occupational, physical, recreational, respiratory, speech. Other specialists are dietitians, nurse midwives (to assist in childbirth), radiologic technicians (for X-rays), social workers, and psychologists. Many are assisted by a variety of nurses' aides, orderlies, attendants, medical records personnel, and receptionists.

Conventional Health Care Facilities If you feel ill, where do you go? Health care facilities include the following:

- *College health service:* Many colleges and universities have a student health ser-

vice. Some health centers may be just small medical dispensaries; others are fully accredited clinics. If you're worried about costs, you may be pleasantly surprised; student health services are reasonably priced and sometimes included in student fees.

- *Hospitals:* There are approximately 6000 hospitals in the United States that principally offer **inpatient care, or in-hospital care for the ill and injured.** Many also have clinics offering **outpatient care, walk-in care for those whose illnesses or injuries do not require overnight stays.**

  There are three types of hospitals:

  (1) *Public hospitals,* such as large city or county hospitals or military or Veterans Administration hospitals, are supported by tax dollars. At the local level, such hospitals serve all comers.

  (2) *Private, for-profit hospitals,* in business to make money, generally accept only patients who can pay (or whose insurance company can). Some limit their services to specific disorders, such as drug and alcohol recovery.

  (3) *Voluntary, nonprofit hospitals* are operated by charitable organizations or religious orders and are supported by patient fees and contributions. They usually offer more services than private hospitals do.

- *Clinics:* Ambulatory clinics offer diagnosis and treatment for outpatient care. Although some are attached to hospitals or student health centers, others exist independently.

- *Specialized walk-in "medicenters":* A recent trend has been walk-in medicenters offering specialized services once found only in a hospital. Examples of these "doc-in-the-box" medicenters are freestanding emergency centers called *"urgicenters,"* which handle minor emergencies without appointment. Others are *"surgicenters,"* which offer same-day outpatient surgery (eye, ear, orthopedic, and the like). In addition, there are *women's centers,* specializing in health matters for women.

• *Home care and house calls:* The physician house call, which disappeared for a number of years, seems to have returned. As many as four-fifths of primary-care physicians see patients in their homes.[16] Nurses, health aides, and other health practitioners associated with home health agencies also provide home health care.

Physical Exams, Medical Tests, Dental Checkups, and Treatment

Before getting a medical checkup, you should make a few notes to help the physician. A physician makes a diagnosis based on three sources of information. They are the patient's medical history and description of symptoms, the physical examination, and the results of tests. Dental checkups should be done once or twice a year. Many patients don't follow medical treatment recommendations because they don't understand or are intimidated. If treatment includes surgery, you usually have time to make certain preparations.

You may expect certain things of your doctor or dentist, but he or she should also expect some things of you. The health care partnership doesn't work unless both participate. Let us see how this works during a physical exam, medical tests, and treatment.

Preparing for a Medical Checkup The American Medical Association recommends that healthy Americans over age 18 undergo a medical checkup every 5 years until age 40. After 40, one should have a physical every 1–3 years, depending on occupation, present health, medical history, and other characteristics.

An analysis by the American Society of Internal Medicine shows 70% of correct diagnoses *depend solely on what you tell your doctor.*[17] Thus, to prepare for a physical exam or any health care appointment, write down questions, worries, and symptoms and bring this "agenda" along. If it's your first visit, include your medical history and your family's, such as a history of heart disease, cancer, or genetic abnormalities.

Women should note the first day of their last menstrual period. Females who have reproductive health problems should bring a 6-month record of their menstrual cycles. In addition, it's wise to bring along any medications (prescription or nonprescription) you are taking. It's important that you be as complete as possible, even about something you think is insignificant or embarrassing.

Having a Physical Exam Whether you see a health care professional for a checkup or about a specific problem, he or she will obtain information via three avenues. These are your medical history, a physical examination, and medical tests.

• *Your medical history:* The traditional medical checkup is called a "history and a physical." In the first part, the health care provider will document your health history. **Your *history* includes past and present illnesses, allergies, and immunizations; prior hospitalizations and operations; and present medications.** He or she may also ask about your "chief complaint." **Your *chief complaint* is the primary concern that caused you to seek medical care in the first place.**

• *Physical examination:* The health provider will next perform a physical examination. *(See ● Figure 4.)* He or she will first look at your *vital signs,* **which include temperature, blood pressure, pulse rate, and breathing rate.** The health provider will then look at your skin, hair, and extremities. He or she will next check your head and throat area; neck and chest; breasts; abdomen; and ankles, feet, and joints. Finally, the provider will look at your rectum, genital, and pelvic areas.

Males will be given a prostate examination. Females may be given a pelvic examination, depending on the nature of the chief complaint. This examination includes a Pap test. **In a *Pap test*, cells are gently scraped from the cervix. These are sent to a laboratory to be examined under a microscope for signs of abnormal cells, including evidence of cervical cancer.**

● **Figure 4   The physical examination.** A complete physical examination includes these parts.

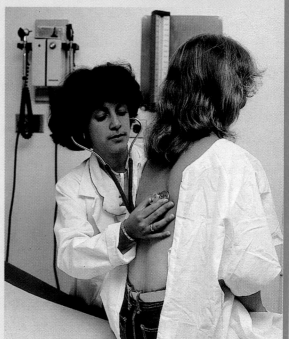

- **Vital signs:** Vital signs include temperature, blood pressure, pulse rate, and breathing rate. Your temperature should be about 98.2; blood pressure 120/70–138/88, depending on sex and age; pulse rate 72 beats per minute; and breathing rate about 12–20 breaths per minute. Irregularities may suggest the presence of heart or blood vessel disease, thyroid disorders, kidney damage, or other problems.

- **Head and throat area:** The provider will examine eyes, ears, nose, and throat.

  The exterior of the eye is checked for signs of redness (indicating possible infection) or paleness (indicating possible anemia). The provider uses a special lighted instrument (ophthalmoscope) to look at the interior of the eye for irregularities in the blood vessels that may indicate disease.

  The provider may do a minimal screening for vision problems, such as asking you to read a line or two from an eye chart. You may be referred to an ophthalmologist or optometrist for a more thorough eye examination. This may include a test for glaucoma if you are over age 20 and have a family history of this disease. *Glaucoma* involves increased pressure within the eyeball that can lead to gradual loss of vision.

  Using another lighted instrument (otoscope), the provider will look into your ears for signs of blockage or infection. He or she may also use a tuning fork or other device to get a rough idea of your hearing.

  Asking you to say "Ahhh," the health care provider will examine your throat, as well as your tongue, gums, and mouth in general, to check for any problems.

- **Neck and chest:** The health care professional will feel the front and sides of your neck to check for enlarged lymph glands (signaling infection) and abnormalities in the thyroid gland. With a stethoscope, he or she may listen to the arteries in the neck for signs of stroke, or blockage of blood flow.

  Also with the stethoscope, the provider will listen to your chest. First he or she checks for abnormal heart sounds and rhythms, then for irregularities in lung sounds. Tapping on the chest with fingers will also signal whether there is fluid in the lungs, a sign of pneumonia. In addition, if you're a woman, the provider will check your breasts for lumps or other abnormalities.

- **Abdomen:** The health care provider will probe the area around your stomach, feeling for the presence of masses or tenderness. These might indicate an enlarged liver, hernias (rupture of the intestines' abdominal wall), or other disorders.

- **Rectum, genital, and pelvic areas:** The provider will gently insert a gloved finger into the rectum to check for abnormal growths and hemorrhoids. In males, this can reveal an enlarged prostate gland, a sign of possible prostate cancer.

  The provider will check a male's genitals for sores or growths. By feeling the lower abdomen and scrotum and asking you to cough, the physician may detect whether or not a hernia is present.

  Females will be given a pelvic examination, including a *Pap test*. In this test, cells gently scraped from the cervix are sent to a laboratory to be examined under a microscope for signs of cervical cancer.

- **Skin, hair, and extremities:** The doctor or other health care provider will examine your skin for signs of rashes, sores, lumps, discoloration, and other abnormalities. Hair and nails will be examined for clues to blood disorders.

  Ankles and feet will be scrutinized for signs of swelling that would suggest heart, liver, or kidney disorders. Pulses in feet and wrists will be checked for blood flow. Joints will be checked for redness, swelling, or deformity that suggests the existence of arthritis. Your kneecap may be tapped with a rubber hammer to check your reflexes, showing whether there are problems in your muscle or nervous systems.

- **Is there pain?** If the health provider's probing produces any pain or you feel some unusual sensations, point it out. Don't hesitate to say, "Oh, by the way, I noticed . . ." if the examination triggers a memory of something unusual. All these clues may provide significant information.

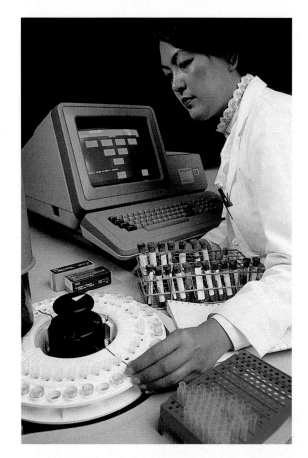

- *Medical tests:* You may be able to have medical tests done at the same time and in the same facility in which you have the physical exam. The principal medical tests are blood tests, urinalysis, chest X-ray, mammography for women, and electrocardiogram. *(See ● Figure 5.)*

  A *urinalysis* is an examination of a sample of your urine. This may show signs of bacteria, diabetes, or disorders of the urinary tract, kidneys, pancreas, or thyroid. **Mammograms are X-rays designed to detect breast abnormalities early. An *electrocardiogram (ECG or EKG)* can detect an enlarged heart, abnormal heart rhythms, and/or blood-vessel disease.**

● **Figure 5   Medical tests.** The principal medical tests include blood tests, urinalysis, chest X-ray, mammography for women, and electrocardiogram.

- **Blood tests:** Blood may be taken from a vein in your arm or from a finger prick. The sample is sent to a laboratory for analysis. Blood tests are of three principal types:

  (1) The most commonly performed blood test, the *complete blood count (CBC)* is used to diagnose anemia, leukemia, and other illnesses.

  (2) The *blood-chemistry panel* is a test for diabetes, gout, kidney stones, and other diseases. The word "panel" means that a group of different tests is done using one sample of blood.

  (3) The *cholesterol test* may indicate your risk of heart and blood-vessel disease. An optimum cholesterol level is below 200 mg/ml, with the level of "bad cholesterol" (low-density lipoprotein, or LDL) under 130. If yours is optimum, you are advised to repeat the test every 5 years. If it is borderline, you should repeat it every year.

- **Urinalysis:** A *urinalysis* is an examination of a sample of your urine. The tester checks for signs of bacteria, diabetes, or disorders of the urinary tract, kidneys, pancreas, or thyroid.

- **Chest X-ray:** The chest X-ray can detect an enlarged heart, pneumonia, or sinus infection. It can also detect lung cancer, and your physician will probably insist on this test if you are a smoker. X-rays aren't done routinely for healthy patients because every amount of radiation adds to lifetime risk of genetic and immune system damage. Two exceptions, however, are mammograms (breast X-rays) and dental X-rays.

- **Mammography:** *Mammograms* are X-rays designed to detect breast abnormalities early. Although authorities do not agree on this, it is suggested that women should have mammograms annually after age 40. (Some suggest every 1–2 years between 40 and 49, then annually thereafter.)

- **Electrocardiogram:** An *electrocardiogram (ECG or EKG)* can detect an enlarged heart, abnormal heart rhythms, blood-vessel disease, and other heart-related problems. Electrodes attached to your chest transmit electrical impulses from your heart to a stylus that then records the impulses on paper. A routine ECG is sometimes called a *resting ECG*. A variation, the *exercise stress test*, is conducted while you walk or run on a treadmill. It can assess heart function under conditions of stress, when the demand for oxygen to the heart muscle is increased.

18

Chapter 1
Learning How to
Live: Making
Health Decisions
and Changes

Dental Checkups The American Dental Association recommends that adults have a dental exam at least once a year. Teeth should be professionally cleaned at least twice a year. A dental checkup should include a screening for four primary problems: oral cancer, jaw disorders, gum disease, and cavities and existing fillings. A full set of dental X-rays should be taken every 5 years. Bitewing X-rays—to show the tops of your teeth and under the gumline, where bone loss from gum disease occurs—should be taken yearly. Additional X-rays should be done as needed.

Medical and Surgical Treatment After the history and physical exam, the health care provider will discuss any immediate findings with you. Some things may not be known until your lab results come back, probably a few days later. At that point, the provider will call you if there are any abnormalities and recommend a plan of action.

Two issues about treatment are particularly worth noting:

- *Noncompliance—the deadly epidemic:* Probably 125,000 people die in the U.S. every year simply because they don't take their prescribed medication properly or at all.[18] *Noncompliance,* or ignoring the doctor's orders, has become a very expensive and unnecessary epidemic in the United States. *Half of all patients don't take their medication or take it incorrectly.*

- *Preparing for surgery:* Four-fifths of all surgeries performed are elective. *Elective surgery* means the procedure is not an emergency and you can generally choose when and where to have the operation. Having time to get ready means you can decide what to take, make financial arrangements, and complete organ-donation and living-will forms. You can appoint a relative or friend to see that your wishes are carried out. You might also "pre-donate" your own blood for use during surgery.

Prescription and Nonprescription Medications

Medications may require a doctor's or dentist's prescription or may be available "over-the-counter." Generic-named prescription drugs are less expensive than brand-name drugs. Be aware that prescription mistakes sometimes occur. Also realize that misusing drugs means risking side effects, allergies, and drug interactions and that addiction to some drugs is possible. Nonprescription drugs can be powerful agents, especially the pain relievers (aspirin, acetaminophen, and ibuprofen) and cold-and-allergy medications (antihistamines and decongestants). Pharmacists can be good sources of advice about the handling and hazards of medications.

Medications are of two types:

- *Prescription: Prescription drugs* **must be ordered by a licensed practitioner, most likely a medical doctor, osteopathic physician, or dentist.** There are 2500 prescription drugs, ranging from tranquilizers to *antibiotics,* **drugs for destroying bacteria.**

- *Nonprescription: Nonprescription,* **or** *over-the-counter (OTC) drugs,* **are medications that can be obtained legally without a prescription.** There are 300,000 different nonprescription products (classified into 26 families), ranging from antacids to cold remedies.

In addition, there are medical and health *devices,* ranging from canes to heart pacemakers. Drugs are regulated by the Food and Drug Administration (FDA). Other medical devices and health products are regulated by the Federal Trade Commission (FTC). Drug-related problems are reported to these agencies.

Prescription Drugs Be aware of the following about prescription drugs:

- *Generic versus brand-name drugs:* For the first 17 years after FDA approval, a drug has patent protection. That is, it may be sold only under its *brand name,* **the specific patented name assigned to a drug**

by its manufacturer. *Inderal,* for example, is the brand name of a leading blood-pressure drug. *Valium* is the name of a leading tranquilizer. After the patent expires, other drug companies may market their own versions. These use the drug's **generic name, the common or nonproprietary name** for the drug. The generic name for *Inderal,* for example, is propranolol.

The significance to you as a consumer is this: *the same chemical can have an incredible price spread.* For instance, a few years ago 100 tablets of Inderal (the brand name) could cost as much as $43.25. At the same time, 100 tablets of propranolol (the generic name) cost as little as $1.99—a price 21 times cheaper![19]

• *Be aware of prescription mistakes:* The most common serious mistake made by physicians is prescribing a drug to which the patient is allergic. Other errors include prescribing antibiotics for the wrong patient, ordering overdoses or underdoses of drugs, and mixing up the names of drugs. Pharmacists can also sometimes make mistakes.

Clearly, it's important to inform your doctor about any allergies, dietary restrictions (including reactions to alcohol), and other drugs you're taking. It's equally important to mention pre-existing health conditions such as pregnancy, breast-feeding, or diabetes.

• *Be aware of the dangers of drug misuse:* If you had a bacterial infection, would you borrow a friend's antibiotic, or if depressed, a roommate's Valium? Some people may see nothing wrong with doing this. However, there is a reason that particular drugs are written in particular dosages for a particular person—that is, *prescribed.* The reason is that drug use can produce important consequences, as follows:

(1) *Side effects* **are secondary, and usually adverse, reactions produced by a drug.** Examples of side effects are nausea and dizziness, but more serious responses are possible. FDA approval does not guarantee that drugs are free of risk. Indeed, over half the new drugs approved by the FDA in a 10-year period had seriously adverse side effects. These included heart, kidney, or liver failure; blindness; and birth defects.[20]

(2) **An *allergy* is a hypersensitivity to a particular substance.** Some drugs, including penicillin and other antibiotics, barbiturates, anticonvulsants, and others—can produce allergic reactions. An extreme allergic reaction is known as anaphylaxis. ***Anaphylaxis* results in shock, blood pressure drop, nausea and vomiting, unconsciousness, and possible life-threatening collapse.** This is a medical emergency that requires immediate intervention by a health care professional.

(3) ***Drug interactions* may occur when two drugs (prescription and/or nonprescription) mix in ways that one might not expect.** One powerful—and often tragic—example of this is the mixture of tranquilizers or other depressant drugs and alcohol. This can produce unconsciousness, coma, and even death. Another example is the interaction between tranquilizers and cold medications, which may cause extreme drowsiness.

• *Be aware of inadvertent addiction:* Thousands of Americans have become hooked on drugs that are perfectly legal—and prescribed by their doctors. This seems to be particularly true for older people. One federal report estimated that 2 million older adults were addicted or at risk of addiction to sleeping pills or tranquilizers.[21]

Nonprescription Drugs Prescription drugs are powerful, but so are many nonprescription drugs. Indeed, the FDA has permitted marketers to repackage active ingredients formerly available only by prescription to be for sale as over-the-counter (OTC) drugs. This has been the case, for example, with the pain-killer Advil, the antihistamine Benadryl, and the athlete's-foot remedy Tinactin.[22] Although perfectly legal, this might suggest something about OTC drugs: they are not to be taken lightly.

Although nonprescription medications have a reputation for being harmless, they are not. Every year hundreds of thousands of Americans are hospitalized because of adverse reactions to OTC drugs, and many die. The dangers of the principal OTC medications are as follows:

- **Pain relievers:** There may be more than 100 brands of pain relievers, but they are of just three types: *aspirin, acetaminophen,* and *ibuprofen*. For occasional relief of minor aches, pains, and headaches, a medication containing any one of these drugs should suffice. However, each works better for some purposes than others, and all three have potential side effects.

  (1) *Aspirin* (generic name acetylsalicylic acid; example brand names Anacin, Bayer, Bufferin) is effective against minor pains and low fevers. It also has an anti-inflammatory effect that makes it effective against arthritis. The alleviation of pain and inflammation works because aspirin blocks the action of chemical messengers called *prostaglandins*. One purpose of prostaglandins is to maintain a protective mucous lining in the stomach. Many heavy users of aspirin suffer stomach irritation, including some of the 20 million Americans who take daily doses for arthritis. Some 20% develop severe gastric ulcers, and many die from hemorrhages each year.[23]

    Aspirin can also cause kidney and liver damage among elderly users. It should not be given to children or adolescents with the flu. In such a case, aspirin can trigger *Reye's syndrome,* a rare disorder that can result in severe brain damage. Some people take aspirin before drinking to avoid a hangover afterward, but it's not a good idea: aspirin actually *increases* blood-alcohol concentrations.[24]

  (2) *Acetaminophen* (brand names Tylenol, Datril, Panadol) causes fewer complications than aspirin. Instead of suppressing prostaglandins, it simply blocks pain receptors in the brain. Thus, it is useful for relieving minor to moderate headache and muscle pains and reducing fever. But acetaminophen does not reduce inflammation and so may not relieve arthritis or other conditions in which patients want to decrease inflammation. Overuse, and use by alcoholics, may lead to irreversible liver damage.[25,26]

  (3) *Ibuprofen* (Advil, Motril, Nuprin) works the same way aspirin does, suppressing the output of prostaglandins. It relieves mild to moderate pain, including headache and muscle pain. It is especially useful against menstrual pain, dental pain, and soft-tissue strains and sprains. In high doses under a doctor's supervision, it can be used as an anti-inflammatory agent against arthritis. The possible side effects, however, are the same as for aspirin. Children should not take ibuprofen at all, unless a physician approves.

- **Cold-and-allergy medications:** Two types of cold-and-allergy medications, *antihistamines* and *decongestants,* have some potent side effects.

  (1) **Antihistamines are useful medications against hay fever and similar allergies.** They are not, however, useful against the common cold. Antihistamines block the chemical messenger histamine, which is released by cells in the nasal tissues and makes the nose itch and run. However, histamine also has another purpose—as an alerting agent within the central nervous system. When you take an antihistamine, therefore, you fight alertness. Indeed, driving with a 50-milligram dose of antihistamine can make your reaction times more than twice as slow.[27] Other important side effects include dizziness, poor coordination, and impaired judgment—exactly what a driver should avoid. Alcohol combined with antihistamines can create severe drowsiness and impaired coordination.

    Antihistamines containing diphenhydramine (found in Actifed, Allerest, Benadryl, and Dimetapp) also have a dehydrating (drying) effect. People with asthma, glaucoma, hypertension, or cardiovascular disease should use antihistamines with caution.

(2) ***Decongestants* are intended to fight mucus production by constricting the blood vessels in the nose.** Spray decongestants, if used sparingly, are considered the most effective. Oral decongestants constrict blood vessels throughout the body, making such drugs unsafe for people with high blood pressure, thyroid disease, or diabetes. Additional side effects include anxiety, restlessness, and hallucinations.

Pharmacist Assistance Pharmacists are not just glorified clerks who hand out drugs on doctors' orders. They can provide a valuable service when you've forgotten (or been reluctant) to ask your physician about medications.

When you are buying a drug, whether prescription or nonprescription, ask your pharmacist the following:

- *Purpose:* What does this drug do? Can I substitute a generic for a brand name? How long will it take to get favorable results? What if I don't take it?
- *Hazards:* What are the side effects and possible adverse reactions? How will it react with other medications, alcohol, or foods?
- *Handling:* What time of day should I take it? How should it be stored? How long should I take it? How do I get refills?

Some Accepted Alternatives to Conventional Medicine

Alternative therapies to conventional medicine range from the helpful to the dangerous. Some more accepted alternative therapies are chiropractic, acupuncture and acupressure, biofeedback, hypnosis, and mental imagery.

Traditional medicine, it has been pointed out, works best for crisis intervention.[28] When you are stricken with a disease, found to have a tumor, or pulled from a car wreck, the drugs, surgery, and high technology of conventional medicine are exactly what you want. However, physicians with traditional training seem less

equipped for the illnesses related to lifestyle and aging—stresses, back pain, obesity, osteoporosis. *(See ● Figure 6.)*

What alternative therapies share, says one writer, "is an emphasis on wellness over disease, prevention over treatment, and a belief that they can heal the mind and spirit as well as the body."[29] Here let us consider some of the more accepted alternative therapies: chiropractic, acupuncture, biofeedback, hypnosis, and mental imagery.

Chiropractic *Chiropractic* **is a therapy that consists principally of spinal manipulation.** Chiropractors may use X-rays in making diagnoses, but they may not use drugs or surgery in treatment. Chiropractic technique is considered unorthodox for treatment of anything other than acute low-back pain present for 3 weeks or less. Other treatment is needed if X-rays reveal any fractures, tumors, or abnormalities.[30]

Acupuncture and Acupressure Traditional in China, ***acupuncture* is a therapy in which fine-gauge needles are inserted at specific points in the body. *Acupressure* uses gentle finger pressure instead of needles.** Both rely on the belief that the body's "acupuncture points," where healthful energy (*chi*) flows, connect to specific organs and body functions. The main role of acupuncture in the United States is the management of pain. Stimulating the acupuncture points triggers the release of ***endorphins*, mood-elevating, painkilling chemicals produced by the brain.**

Biofeedback *Biofeedback* **is the process of using an electronic device to teach you how to monitor and modify your physiological and mental state.** With some training, subjects can learn to use the technique to produce relaxation and to slow the heart rate through breathing control. Biofeedback is used to treat dozens of ailments, from hypertension to chronic pain, from asthma to drug addiction.

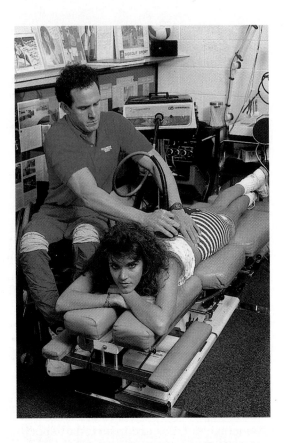

Hypnosis Hypnosis, or more specifically *hypnotherapy,* has been found to reduce pain, as in dentistry, and to diminish fears and phobias. It can help overcome smoking, overeating, and nail biting and ease the breathing of asthmatics and the tremors of Parkinson's disease. It's recommended the hypnotist have professional credentials in psychology, medicine, or dentistry, using hypnotherapy as part of a larger practice.

Mental Imagery ***Mental imagery* is the process of visualizing or daydreaming your condition and any desired change you wish to make.** It's also referred to as *guided imagery* or *creative visualization*. Sometimes a therapist or a tape recording helps guide the imagery. Mental imagery can help people reduce their muscle tension and focus on their problems without heightening their anxiety. It has also been used by patients battling serious illness, such as cancer, to try to improve their immune response. Whether it actually improves survival chances isn't certain.

Health Fads, Alternative Healing, and Quackery

One must be careful about health information based on fads or on alternative therapies. One must also be wary of health fraud, or quackery, and learn to tell if a health information source is credible. As a patient, you may need to become your own expert. That is, you need to know when to get a second opinion, learn the language of medicine, find organizations to help you, and learn how to use research tools.

The very human desire to be well and free of pain has a long history. It has been matched only by the answers provided by faddists, alternative healers, and out-and-out frauds.

Let us consider health fads, alternative healers, and frauds.

Health Fads Appearing on magazine covers with regularity, **health *fads* are practices followed for a time with excessive zeal.** A fad may or may not be dangerous. It also may or may not be new; many are simply old ideas with a different spin.

● **Figure 6   Why the popularity of alternative therapies?**

❝ *... Our health expectations have risen to heights that are perhaps impossible to satisfy. The steady lengthening of life expectancy, the banishment of numerous lethal infectious diseases, the development of cures for several cancers, the breakthroughs in surgery—all great triumphs of medicine and public health—have encouraged us to think there must be a fix for whatever ails us.*

And, yes, modern doctoring has failed to keep many of its promises. A visit to any hospital is an unsettling reminder that scientific medicine remains virtually helpless in the face of a great deal of human suffering. Even ordinary problems are sometimes beyond the reach of the ordinary M.D. And if stress really causes or aggravates all the disorders currently blamed on it, the typical annual visit to a harried physician is hardly the cure—especially when the doctor first keeps you waiting for an appointment, then forgets your name, yet expects you to write a sizable check on your way out. ❞

—Sharon Begley (1992 April). Alternative medicine, a cure for what ails us? *American Health*, p. 10.

Some recent health fads have been basically good, although their flaws weren't immediately apparent. For example, the running and jogging craze, which developed into the aerobic-dance fad, may have produced a lot of fit cardiovascular systems. Yet these exercises also created a lot of shin splints and cracked bones in the feet caused by repeated impact. We now have a greater understanding of the need for *moderate* life-long exercise.

Alternative Healing Therapies It is one thing to see a licensed acupuncturist or biofeedback therapist on the recommendation of your doctor. It is quite another to try to assess the bewildering number of claims by unconventional schools of healing. The schools range from homeopathy and herbalism to crystal healing and psychic surgery. In general, alternative medicine may be grouped under one of three approaches:

- *Bodywork or hands-on approaches:* These approaches include chiropractic, acupuncture and acupressure, and all forms of manipulation or massage. They also include less familiar approaches, such as the Alexander technique, shiatsu, Feldenkrais, Rolfing, and reflexology. Behind most bodywork treatments is the idea that manipulating your body can also bring harmony to your mind. Most such therapies lack the science to back up their claims, although their supporters point to plenty of testimonials and anecdotal evidence.

- *Chemical, herbal, and dietary approaches:* These approaches include a number of alternative therapies, some of which may have some basis in fact. Herbs used in Eastern medicine, for instance, contain some of the active ingredients used in the conventional drugs of Western medicine. Examples of this second category are homeopathy, naturopathy, herbal medicine, Ayurvedic medicine, Zen macrobiotics, iridology, and aromatherapy.

- *Mind-over-matter approaches:* These approaches include some therapies found to be useful by conventional medicine: biofeedback, hypnotherapy, and mental imagery. Others are a variety of stress-reduction techniques, from transcendental meditation

to yoga, a 6000-year-old Indian philosophy combining meditation, posture, exercise, and diet. Beyond these, however, are a whole range of alternative therapies that many conventional health professionals find useless or even dangerous. These range from crystal healing to color therapy to faith healing.

Health Fraud Also known as **quackery, health fraud is the practice of fake solutions or cures to health problems.** Quacks promise to cure what doctors cannot, and the claims are too good to be true. The facts of medical science are often dry, uninteresting, and inconclusive. The promises of quacks, however, are usually dramatic, eye-catching, and billed as quick, easy, and safe. Health frauds frequently use words such as "effortless," "guaranteed," "miraculous," "magical," "exotic," "secret," "exclusive," or "ancient." The problem is that these promises cost money, may be dangerous—and seldom deliver the change or cure being sought.

Quackery includes breast developers, steroids and growth hormones, tanning pills, hair removal/hair growth practices, fake pharmaceuticals, and some weight-loss programs. Other frauds include certain self-esteem-boosting and performance-enhancing techniques, such as self-help "subliminal learning" tapes.

Strategy for Living: Avoiding Being Victimized by Health Fraud Perhaps the best way to guard against being victimized by fads and frauds is to rely on *credible* sources of health information and care. Then employ strategies such as the following suggested by psychiatrist and health-fraud expert Stephen Barrett:[31]

- *Take a close look at the practitioner:* Not all diplomas and certificates are valid, nor are all scientific-sounding groups respectable.

- *Turn on your hype detector:* Be wary of advertising hype, testimonials, medical endorsements (reputable physicians rarely endorse commercial products), talk-show guests, and health-food industry propaganda.

- *Know your own needs:* Don't let desperation cloud your judgment. Be wary of pseudomedical jargon, paranoid accusations against the medical establishment, and methods characterized as "alternative."

Health knowledge essentially comes down to a question of authority or *credibility*. When trying to determine whether a particular source—whether person or written material—is credible or legitimate, you need to ask:[32]

1. Does this source have the information or judgment you need, according to the record? That is, does the source have an acceptable reputation, affiliation, educational background, or proven expertise in this area?

2. If so, can you trust a personal source to give you an honest, accurate assessment of your problem?

3. Do you have the time, desire, and ability to understand the expert's reasoning so you don't have to merely accept the conclusion?

When experts disagree or when matters become complex, you may need to become your own expert by doing your own research. This is particularly true for a decision that could have a problematic outcome—whether to have back surgery, for example.

Power to the Patient: Becoming Your Own Expert Suppose the doctor says that surgery to "fuse your spine" *may* relieve the back pain that has given you agony for years. However, the physician cautions, there are no guarantees, and the surgery offers the risk of possible paralysis. The pain in your back is so great that it has profoundly diminished your enjoyment of life. On the other hand, you certainly don't want to *worsen* the situation by developing other problems. What do you do?

Your ally here is information, the more the better. When faced with major medical decisions, you need to gather as much information as you can from credible sources.

- **Make sure you understand your health care provider:** According to one study, physicians spend less than 2 minutes of a 20-minute session giving information. As a result, 60% of patients leave a doctor's office confused about instructions for medication or other aspects of their care.[33] Be sure your physician takes time to answer all your questions in understandable terms.

- ***Get a second opinion:*** When facing an important decision, you need a second opinion—and maybe a third or fourth—from another specialist in the same field. Get a second opinion for surgery, cancer treatments, treatment for heart disease, and questions involving extended hospitalization.

- ***Don't let the technical language stop you:*** Don't be afraid of medical mumbo-jumbo. There is lots of medical information available in language written for lay people. There are also medical dictionaries to help you interpret technical terms.

- ***Learn how to find helpful organizations:*** We won't go so far as to say that for every disease there's an organization, but there are many—probably 200 or more.[34] The American Cancer Society and the American Heart Association are among the best known. In addition, there are support groups and self-help groups, libraries and databases.

- ***Learn to use research tools:*** The telephone book and library give you access to information you need. You can also use a computer with a modem that connects to all kinds of networks of computerized libraries and databases. To check your doctor's background, use the *American Medical Directory* or the *Directory of Medical Specialists*. Or look in *9,479 Questionable Doctors,* a directory compiled from public files by the Public Citizen Health Research Group.

Paying for Health Care

U.S. health insurance covers either fee-for-service medicine or prepaid medicine. Three types of insurance policies covering fees for service are basic protection, major medical, and comprehensive major medical. Individual and group insurance policies are available. Some health organizations offer "managed care," which limits fees; two types are health-maintenance organizations, with most fees prepaid, and preferred provider organizations. Government programs offer Medicaid and Medicare.

Can you *afford* quality health care? Are you covered in the event you should fall seriously ill? One of the most consequential matters you may have to confront is paying for health care. Here we consider the various types of health insurance, types of health organizations, and government-financed insurance plans.

Health Insurance If you get sick, *really* sick, without health insurance you may end up owing thousands of dollars to doctors and hospitals. Students who finish or drop out of school—or who cut back their course loads to part time—should take note. They may find themselves no longer covered by their parents' or partner's health plan and exposed to considerable financial risks. Health insurance is too important to ignore.

There are two basic approaches to paying for health care:

- *Fee-for-service:* This used to be the most common arrangement in the United States. **Fee-for-service medicine means that the physician or hospital performs treatment and presents you and/or the insurance company with a bill.**

- *Prepaid:* This arrangement is gaining favor with insurance buyers. **Prepaid medicine means that you or your employer pay for specified kinds of medical services ahead of time.** This form is characteristic of *managed-care organizations: health maintenance organizations (HMOs)* and *preferred provider organizations (PPOs).*

Three Types of Insurance Policies Assuming for the moment that you are interested in fee-for-service medicine, there are three kinds of coverage:

- *Basic protection:* **A basic-protection health-insurance policy covers hospital, surgical, and medical care.** It usually does not cover visits to physicians' offices and may exclude other items, such as paying for prescription drugs. **An exclusion refers to conditions or circumstances for which the policy does not pay benefits.** An example of an exclusion is a *pre-existing condition,* **a health problem you had before becoming insured.**

A basic-protection policy is a good choice if you're healthy and rarely need medical attention. In addition, you can get regular medical insurance, which covers physicians' fees for nonsurgical care.

One form of basic-protection policy reimburses you for 80% of covered charges after the deductible. **The *deductible* is the amount you must pay before the insurance company starts paying.** For instance, you might have to pay $2500 for medical bills in one year. But for the rest of the year the policy pays for 80% of the charges covered by the policy. The higher the deductible, the lower your insurance premiums.

The arrangement whereby you and the insurance company share the costs is *co-insurance,* as when you pay 20% and they pay 80%.

- *Major medical or catastrophic:* **A *major medical* or *catastrophic* policy is for those who can't afford basic coverage.** Everyone should *at least* have one of these, to keep a medical catastrophe from also being a financial catastrophe. These policies protect against medical expenses arising from serious injury or prolonged illness.

The deductible for such policies is apt to be high. You may have to pay the first $10,000 or more before the insurance company pays. However, hospitals are likely to arrange credit terms for you to pay off the $10,000 if they know insurance covers the rest.

- *Comprehensive major medical insurance:* **A *comprehensive major medical insurance* policy combines both the basic-care and the major-medical features into one policy.**

Individual Versus Group Policies Health insurance may be purchased as an *individual policy* or as a *group plan.*

- *Individual policies:* Individual policies are arranged directly between you and an insurance company. They are usually (but not necessarily) more expensive than group plans and provide less coverage.

- **Group policies:** Groups plans are available through the organization you work for. They are usually cheaper and offer more coverage than individual policies. Their main drawback is they expire when you leave the job. However, you have the legal right to continue coverage under your old plan for up to 18 months if you pay the premium.

Managed Care: HMOs and PPOs ***Managed care* means fees charged by health care providers are limited, but the use of medical services is controlled.** The result is that health care costs less, but there is less flexibility than under the old fee-for-service medicine. Two types of managed care are HMOs and PPOs.

- **Health-maintenance organizations: A health-maintenance organization (HMO) is an organization in which patients or their employers pay a fixed monthly fee. In return, salaried physicians and other health professionals deliver medical services,** usually under one roof. Because the HMO receives the fees whether members are sick or well, it emphasizes keeping people healthy by providing preventive services. HMOs also try to deliver care less expensively by controlling use of hospitals and surgery and limiting referrals to specialists. If you join an HMO, you get to choose your primary-care physician from a list of participating doctors. To see a specialist, you need a referral by this physician. If you go outside the HMO, you have to pay all the costs yourself.

- **Preferred-provider organizations: A preferred-provider organization (PPO) is a network of doctors and hospitals. Each has agreed to treat patients of a sponsoring organization at a discount from the usual charges,** perhaps 15–20% less. The sponsoring organization may be a union, employer, or insurance company. If you join a PPO, you can go to any physician in the network you want. If you go outside the network, the sponsor will not reimburse you for as much.

Government Programs: Medicaid and Medicare Two government programs (outside those for civilian and military government employees) are available to those who qualify— Medicaid and Medicare.

***Medicaid* offers a range of health services for people receiving public assistance.** The program is run by each state but subsidized by the federal government. ***Medicare* is a federal program of health care financing for those 65 and over or people who are chronically disabled.**

Onward: The Art of Living in the Here and Now

This book is about your life.

We spend much of our lives waiting—waiting for tomorrow to become today while the goals we sought so avidly pass into yesterday.

For instance, you may consider the course for which you are reading this book "just another course" to be checked off en route to the college degree. There is one important difference, however. This course is not just about giving you a well-rounded education, or teaching you how to think. It's not only about preparing you for a career or for graduate or professional training. It is about your *life*. It is about learning how to analyze the way you live and learning habits of body, mind, and spirit that will affect you in important ways in all the years ahead. It is about being healthy for life.

Suggestions for Further Reading

Editors of the University of California, Berkeley, *Wellness Letter*. (1991). *The wellness encyclopedia: The comprehensive family resource for safeguarding health and preventing illness.* Boston: Houghton Mifflin. A well-written guide for health consumers and patients.

Charles Garfield. (1986). *Peak performers: The new heroes of American business.* New York: Morrow. An interesting, well-researched book on personal high achievement and how to attain it.

United States Department of Health and Human Services, Public Health Service (1990). *Healthy people 2000: National health promotion and disease prevention objectives.* DHHS Publication No. (PHS) 91-50213. Washington, DC: U.S. Department of Health and Human Services.

Andrew Weil. (1992). *Natural health, natural medicine: A comprehensive manual for wellness and self-care.* Boston: Houghton Mifflin. A Harvard-trained M.D. blends the conventional and exotic, promoting alternative medicine for maintaining wellness.

800-HELP

Health Reference Center. 800-227-8431. A commercial database of 4000 consumer and medical publications. Call to find the center nearest to you and ask about fees.

Information Center for Individuals with Disabilities. 800-462-5015.

National Health Information Center. 800-336-4797. Refers callers to appropriate organizations for information about every disease and disability, including rare ones. Also offers toll-free 800 numbers for other hotlines.

National Organization for Rare Disorders. 800-999-NORD. Supplies the public with reports on any of 950 diseases, including current research and new clinical trials.

People Who Prevail

"The highest art," goes a Tibetan saying, "is living an ordinary life in an extraordinary manner." Here are people who have met this challenge—people we might call "ordinary heroes."

Some Ordinary Extraordinary Women

Valerie Pida, a student at the University of Nevada, Las Vegas, survived a bone-marrow transplant operation in which doctors had given her a 30% chance. Seven years earlier, she was found to have Hodgkin's disease. Despite regular radiation and chemotherapy treatment she never quit school. "You go to chemotherapy and be sick all week long and then go back to school on Monday," she said. At age 20 she was a cheerleader. "I never wanted [illness] to interfere with things I wanted to do," Pida said.[43]

Maria Foscarinis grew up as a privileged only child on Manhattan's Upper East Side, attended private schools, and received a law degree at Columbia Law School. At age 28, she left a prestigious New York law firm to open an office for the National Coalition for the Homeless, even though it meant reducing her $70,000 salary to $10,000. "At the time, $10,000 was the poverty level for a family of four," she said, "so it was instructive."[44]

Born in Batesville, Mississippi, one of 12 children, Oral Brown handled two children of her own, jobs, and night classes before finally earning a bachelor's degree in her mid-30s from the University of San Francisco. Later she started her own real estate firm in East Oakland, California. One day, when an 8-year-old boy tried to sell her some crack cocaine, she decided to do something to give children of the tough neighborhood a chance. She contacted a nearby elementary school and arranged to "adopt" a kindergarten class by placing $10,000 in a special savings account. Although not wealthy, every year Brown has attempted to add $10,000 to the account. The money will go for tuition for those of the 27 kindergarteners who graduate from high school and go on to college. "It not just the money that I'm offering them," she said. "A lot of these kids just need to know someone is there for them."[45]

Some Ordinary Extraordinary Men

Ralf Hotchkiss was an engineering student in Berkeley, Calif., when a motorcycle accident left him unable to walk. The wheelchairs available were expensive and unsuitable for 80% of the paralyzed people of the world. In the following years, Hotchkiss traveled to many primitive workshops. As he put it, "I visited people who make wheelchairs in remote regions, and stole their ideas." Today his wheelchairs are found in villages in 24 developing countries.[46]

Walter Littlemoon, a 6-foot-3 South Dakota Sioux, was in his late twenties in 1973 when federal marshals were called in to Wounded Knee to end a dispute with the American Indian movement. In the following years, as the village disintegrated, Littlemoon managed to overcome a drinking problem and return to school. Later he went back to Wounded Knee to help rebuild it. Working without pay, he has raised money for food, clothing, medical equipment, and a new community center.[47]

"He works as if each person in need were a member of his own family," says an admirer of Amos Wampler, retired. In Carroll County, Maryland, Wampler delivers food to the elderly. He also frequently visits those needing help, such as an elderly woman and her blind, mentally retarded daughter, and a deaf couple, for whom he installed a flashing light "doorbell." "Some people say when they retire they can't find enough to do," he says, "but I haven't found time enough to do it all!"[48]

Psychological Health: The Power of the Mind

2

"Is there a split between mind and body? And if so, which is better to have?"

The joke touches on one of people's most fundamental beliefs: we tend to think of mind and body as being separate. In fact, mind and body are interrelated. For instance, your body reacts the same whether a threat is real or imagined. Whether it's the terror when you swerve to avoid a collision or the anxiety when a deadline approaches, your heart races.

Understanding how your mind can be the enemy or the ally of your body is a vital lesson. Indeed, it is central to the art of living.

In Search of Psychological Well-Being

▶ Discuss the concept of psychological health.

▶ Describe Menninger's hierarchy of health and Maslow's hierarchy of needs.

▶ Explain the importance to psychological health of goal orientation, self-worth, self-efficacy, optimism, enjoyment and happiness, creativity, risk-taking and self-reinvention, and love.

Some days are diamonds, some days are duds. And some days are both, a roller coaster of moods. If this is a normal range of emotions, how can we identify emotional and mental health?

The Meaning of Psychological Health

Psychological health includes mental (intellectual) health and emotional health. Mental or intellectual health refers to thoughts, emotional health to feelings. Psychological health may be pictured as a hierarchy, such as Menninger's hierarchy of psychological health or Maslow's hierarchy of needs. Psychological health has these components: goal orientation, self-worth, self-efficacy, optimism, capacity for enjoyment, happiness, creativity, risk-taking, self-reinventing, and giving and receiving love.

One often hears the expressions "mental health" and "emotional health." However, we prefer the term *psychological health,* **which refers to the state of** *both* **mental and emotional well-being.**

In our usage, "mental" refers to *thoughts.* Having good *mental health* or *intellectual health* **means one can think reasonably clearly**—without wildly distorting reality. The word "emotional" refers to *feelings.* Having good *emotional health* **means one is aware of and expresses one's feelings in an appropriate way.**

What Is Psychological Health? Think of psychological health as falling into a hierarchy or range. Two hierarchies that have been proposed are these:

- *Menninger's hierarchy of psychological health:* Psychiatrist Karl Menninger has proposed a hierarchy of psychological health. Here psychological states range from severe psychological illness to optimal psychological well-being. *(See ● Figure 1.)*

- *Maslow's hierarchy of needs:* Humanistic psychologist Abraham Maslow theorized that people strive to achieve their "human potential" through a hierarchy of needs. In the *hierarchy of needs,* only when physiological, safety, affection, and self-esteem needs are fulfilled can people then try to achieve self-actualization. Self-actualization is the highest need of wellness or fulfillment. *(See ● Figure 2.)* According to one writer, *self-actualization* **is "the tendency of every human being . . . to** *make real* **his or her full potential,** to become everything that he or she can be."[1]

We will consider several components of psychological well-being. These are goal orientation, self-worth, self-efficacy, optimism, happiness and enjoyment, creativity, risk-taking and self-reinventing, and giving and receiving love.

Goal Orientation According to Maslow, an attribute of psychologically healthy people is a sense of self-direction.[2, 3] What are the goals of *your* life? Perhaps you burn with serious purpose—to become a doctor, to travel the world, to excel in business or art or politics. On the other hand, many people are serious searchers for meaning. A college or university is not designed solely to train people to make a living. It is also an arena for satisfying curiosity about yourself and the workings of the world.

Self-Worth To formulate a serious purpose for one's life, one must have a sense of self-worth. *Self-worth,* **or** *self-esteem,* **is the extent to which you believe yourself to be significant, capable, and worthy.**[4] *(See Self Discovery 1 on page 33.)* Self-worth comes in great part from one's upbringing and early childhood experiences. Learning academic subjects, for instance, requires basic emotional strengths. In

Optimal mental health

Normal coping devices and ego control

Level 1

Hyperreactions

Anxiety

Nervousness

Minor physical symptoms

Level 2

Personality disorders

Phobias

Level of Dysfunction

Level 3

Social offenses

Open aggression

Violent acts

Level 4

Severe depression and despondency

Psychotic and bizarre behavior

Level 5

Severe psychological deterioration

Loss of will to live

children whose families are unable or unwilling to provide financial support and nurturing, these strengths may be undermined.[5]

Self-Efficacy A big part of self-worth comes from a sense of self-efficacy. ***Self-efficacy* is the perception that you can perform certain tasks successfully.** Self-efficacy stems from a belief that success is possible; it gives you the sense of empowerment to overcome obstacles. This belief may arise from some of your previous successes. For instance, studying hard in the past has helped you raise your grades; therefore, you believe that studying hard can help again.

Optimism Pessimists may be overwhelmed by their problems. Optimists are challenged by them, according to therapist Alan McGinnis.[6] Optimists "think of themselves as problem-solvers, as trouble-shooters," he says. This does not mean they see everything through rose-colored glasses. Rather they have several qualities that help them have a positive attitude while remaining realistic and tough-minded. *(See ● Figure 3.)*

Happiness and Enjoyment Happiness is defined as the capacity to enjoy life. Make pleasures (the good kind, like touching, music, and good scents) a personal priority, say psychologist Robert Ornstein and physician David Sobel.[7] "Enjoying food, sex, work, and family is the innate guide to health," they say. "Good feelings and pleasures reward us twice: in immediate enjoyment and improved health."[8]

● **Figure 1 Menninger's hierarchy of psychological health.** Psychiatrist Karl Menninger has suggested ranking psychological states by decline in coping ability.

● **Figure 2   The hierarchy of needs.** Once basic needs are satisfied, according to Maslow, one can live to his or her full potential, achieving a state of wellness and fulfillment.

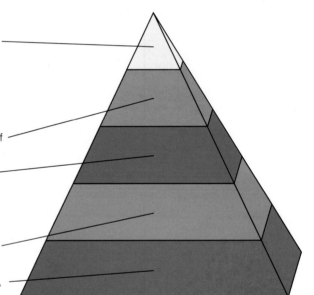

Self-fulfillment needs

Self-actualization need: Fulfillment of one's potential, including satisfaction of creative needs, needs for order and beauty, and needs for knowledge and understanding

Psychological needs

Esteem needs: Achievement and gaining of recognition

Belongingness and love needs: Social interaction, affiliation, and acceptance

Basic needs

Safety needs: Long-term security, survival, stability

Physiological needs: Hunger, thirst, shelter, sleep, sex

Creativity *Creativity* **is the human capacity to express ourselves in original or imaginative ways.** It is built into all of us, not just some supposed artistic class of people. Creativity may also be thought of as the process of discovery. As Nobel Prize-winning physician Albert Szent-Györgyi said, "Discovery consists of looking at the same thing as everyone else and thinking something different."[9] Being creative means having to resist pressure to be in step with the world. It means looking for several answers, not the "one right answer," as might be true of solving a specific math problem.

Risk-Taking and Self-Reinvention Positive risk-taking is having the courage to feel the fear and then proceeding anyway. Such risks are the type that pose threats not to your health (such as taking drugs) but to your pride. They are the kind where the consequences of failure are personal embarrassment or disappointment.

SELF DISCOVERY 1

Your Self-Image: How Do You Feel About Yourself?

This scale is designed to assist you in understanding your self-image. Positive attitudes toward oneself are important components of maturation and emotional well-being.

Self-image aspect	Strongly agree	Agree	Disagree	Strongly disagree
1. I feel that I'm a person of worth, at least on an equal plane with others.	A	B	C	D
2. I feel that I have a number of good qualities.	A	B	C	D
3. All in all, I am inclined to feel that I am a failure.	A	B	C	D
4. I am able to do things as well as most other people.	A	B	C	D
5. I feel I do not have as much to be proud of as others.	A	B	C	D
6. I take a positive attitude toward myself.	A	B	C	D
7. On the whole, I am satisfied with myself.	A	B	C	D
8. I wish I could have more respect for myself.	A	B	C	D
9. I certainly feel useless at times.	A	B	C	D
10. At times I think I am no good at all.	A	B	C	D

How to Score

Use the following table to determine the number of points to assign to each of your answers. To determine your total score, add up all the numbers that match the letter (A, B, C, or D) you circled for each statement.

Statement	A	B	C	D
1.	4	3	2	1
2.	4	3	2	1
3.	1	2	3	4
4.	4	3	2	1
5.	1	2	3	4
6.	4	3	2	1
7.	4	3	3	1
8.	1	2	2	4
9.	1	2	3	4
10.	1	2	3	4

Total: _____ This is your self-esteem score.

Interpreting Your Score

Classify your score in the appropriate score range.

Score range	Current self-esteem level
Less than 20	Low self-esteem
20–29	Below-average self-esteem
30–34	Above-average self-esteem
35–39	High self-esteem
40	Highest self-esteem

The higher your score, the more positive your self-esteem.

High self-esteem means that individuals respect themselves, consider themselves worthy, but do not necessarily consider themselves better than others. They do not feel themselves to be the ultimate in perfection; on the contrary, they recognize their limitations and expect to grow and improve.

Self-esteem is the most important variable in regard to human development and maturation. It is the master key that can open the door to the actualization of an individual's human potential.

Source: Rosenburg, M. (1986). *Society and the adolescent self-image.* Hanover, NH: Wesleyan University Press.

● **Figure 3   Optimist traits.** Optimism, which can be both born and bred in a person, is one of the attributes of psychological well-being.

" *Twelve characteristics of tough-minded optimists are as follows. Optimists . . .*

1. *Are seldom surprised by trouble.*
2. *Look for partial solutions.*
3. *Believe they have control over their future.*
4. *Allow for regular renewal.*
5. *Interrupt their negative trains of thought.*
6. *Heighten their powers of appreciation.*
7. *Use their imaginations to rehearse success.*
8. *Are cheerful even when they can't be happy.*
9. *Believe they have an almost unlimited capacity for stretching.*
10. *Build lots of love into their lives.*
11. *Like to swap good news.*
12. *Accept what cannot be changed.* "

—Psychologist Alan Loy McGinnis (1990). *The power of optimism.* San Francisco: Harper & Row.

What is failure, exactly? First, according to Carole Hyatt and Linda Gottlieb, authors of *When Smart People Fail,* it is a term for an event, such as the loss of a job. This kind of failure you may not be able to do anything about. More important, however, it is a *judgment you make about yourself*—"so that 'failure' may also mean not living up to your own expectations."[10] This second kind of failure you *can* do something about. For instance, you can use your own inner voice—your "self-talk"—to interpret an event more favorably. ("I didn't fit in there because I'm better suited to working alone than with a group.")

One characteristic of many peak performers, says Charles Garfield, is that of continually *reinventing* themselves, striving for new achievements and new definitions of themselves.[11] This can only be done by taking emotional chances and risking failure.

Giving and Receiving Love *Love* **is "an act of full attention and giving that accepts and attaches to someone as he or she is, thereby enhancing the potential of what that person can become,"** in one definition.[12] It's clear that we need to receive love. If we have grown into complete human beings, we also need to *give* love.

"Love" and "like" are, of course, part of the same emotional continuum. Why do some people seem to like us and some people not? The answer may lie in the observation that people we believe will like us generally will do so, and those whose rejection we fear will reject us.[13] When we *believe* someone likes us, we respond warmly. We are more disclosing, less disagreeable, and speak in a more positive tone. These behaviors lead the other person to like us even more.

The Art of Living Day by Day: Handling Stress and Other Emotions

▶ Define *stress* and *stressor.*

▶ Differentiate among hassles, crises, and strong stressors.

▶ Contrast the terms *eustress* and *distress.*

▶ Identify and describe each of the stages of the General Adaptation Syndrome.

▶ Discuss possible physical reactions to stress.

▶ Discuss possible psychological reactions to stress.

▶ Describe various strategies for overcoming stress, loneliness, shyness, sadness, anxieties, fears, anger, and aggression.

We are not, of course, blessed with ideally fulfilling lives. The states of happiness we strive for come up against expectations we cannot fulfill. What are the emotional states that prevent us from always being on top of our form? How can we deal with them?

We will consider six principal areas. They are stress, loneliness, shyness, sadness, anxieties and fears, and anger and aggression.

Stress

Stress is the body's reaction to stressors, which are the source of stress. Stressors can be either negative, causing "distress," or positive, causing "eustress." The physical response to stress may take the form of a three-stage General Adaptation Syndrome. Physical reactions to stress may be expressed as particular problems, such as skin problems, headache, or gastrointestinal problems. Your psychological response to stress depends in part on the number, kinds, and magnitude of stressors. Other factors are your emotional predisposition, intensity of feeling, self-esteem, and personality type—hurried and hostile "Type A" or unhurried "Type B." Psychological reactions include nervousness and anxiety, burnout, and post-traumatic stress disorder. You can adapt to or cope with stress. Adaptation is not changing the stressor or stress, such as escaping into drugs, TV watching, sleeping, or eating. Coping is changing the stressor or your reaction to it.

If you look around you, you can see that enormous industries exist because of the notion that stress is bad and should be prevented or relieved. Why do tobacco, alcohol, and other drugs legal and illegal continue to sell? Because millions of nervous people think they provide the principal means of relaxing their tensions.

But stress is not always unpleasant. Sometimes stress is associated with *positive* events and challenges and energizes us. We see this, for example, when we are competing at a sport or playing a musical instrument. Let us, then, take a closer look at the mechanism of stress.

How Stress Works: Body and Mind **Stress is the reaction of our bodies to an event. The source of stress is called a *stressor.*** Stressors may be specific, ranging from a flat tire to a death in the family. But the physical reaction is nonspecific and generalized, being felt throughout the entire body.

Life in modern society requires that we continually adapt to a variety of events. The human body constantly strives to maintain a state of balance known as homeostasis. **In *homeostasis*, physiological and psychological systems are stable, or in equilibrium.** Stressors may disturb this homeostasis by causing one's body to become unbalanced. If the stress is too great for too long, the lack of balance eventually causes illness and potentially death.

There are three things to be aware of about stress. First, there are different types of stressors. Second, stressors can be good and bad. Third, stressors produce both physical and psychological reactions. Let us consider these:

- *Types of stressors—hassles, crises, or strong stressors:* Stressors range in intensity and duration from hassles to crises to strong stressors.

  Hassles **are simply frustrating irritants,** but their cumulative effect can be significant. College students are most hassled by (1) anxiety over wasting time, (2) meeting high standards, and (3) being lonely.[14]

  A *crisis* **may appear suddenly and be of short duration but have long-lasting effects.** For instance, a horrible auto accident, an incident of childhood abuse, or a wartime experience can have a tremendous biological impact.[15]

  A *strong stressor* **is a strong source of stress of continuing duration,** which can dramatically strain a person's ability to adapt. A strong stressor can be extreme mental or physical discomfort. For example, a person who has suffered a fall may have pain as a constant companion.

- *Stressors, good and bad:* Stress researcher Hans Selye points out that stressors can be negative or positive—distressors and eustressors.[16]

  A *distressor* **is a negative source of stress,** such as being rejected in love or flunking a test. **The effect of a negative stressor is called** *distress.* Distress can be helpful when one is facing a physical threat. However, ongoing or high levels of distress may result in illness.

  A *eustressor* **is a positive source of stress,** such as falling in love or getting an A on a test. **The effect of a positive stressor is called** *eustress* (pronounced "*you*-stress"). Eustress can stimulate a person to greater adaptation—to become a peak performer.

- *Physical and emotional components:* Stress has both physical and emotional components. Physically, according to Selye, stress is "The nonspecific response of the body to any demand made upon it."[17] Emotionally, stress has been defined as the feeling of being overwhelmed. It is "the perception that events or circumstances have challenged, or exceeded a person's ability to cope."[18]

Next we consider the physical and emotional reactions in detail.

Physical Stress Reactions: The General Adaptation Syndrome Selye described the response to a stressor as a three-stage **general adaptation syndrome.**[19] The stages are *alarm, resistance,* and *exhaustion.* These reactions can occur to various degrees in many circumstances. They may happen if you meet a mugger in an alley, get a terse note from the boss ("See me!"), or hear the starting gun in a race.

- *Stage 1—alarm:* The alarm phase is often called the *fight-or-flight response.* This is the stage in which the brain rapidly and subconsciously perceives the stressor. Almost instantly the brain mobilizes your body's defensive forces to stand and fight or turn and flee. These forces (hormones) shift some blood supply from kidneys and intestines to brain and muscles and increase breathing and heart rate. They also increase sweating to reduce body heat, increase the blood's clotting ability, increase muscle tension, and make the brain fully alert. In addition, they release glucose, a type of sugar stored in the liver, for use as energy for muscular exertion.

- *Stage 2—resistance:* In this stage, you begin to concentrate more on psychological coping and defensive behavior rather than continuing the physical fight-or-flight response.

- *Stage 3—exhaustion:* If the stress goes on long enough, your physical and psychological energy will be depleted, and your body and mind will need to rest. If stressors cause wear and tear over a long period, they may lead to illness or even death. *It's important, therefore, for you to find ways to counter long-sustained stress.*

Physical Stress Reactions: Your "Stress Site" and Other Matters Would you admit that you occasionally suffer from **psychosomatic illnesses, physical disorders caused by or worsened by psychological factors?** Probably not, if you're like most people.

Most of us will go to great lengths to avoid having others think we are **malingering,** or **pretending sickness.** Nor do we want anyone to think that we suffer from **hypochondria, imaginary illnesses.** "Our society has taught us not to be weak without a cause," says clinical psychologist Ivy Walker Wittmeyer.[20] *(See ● Figure 4.)* Actually, we should take our "psychosomatic disorders" more seriously. Such symptoms as chronic headaches, abdominal pain, low back pain, chest pain, and severe eye-strain often are stress-related conditions—and they affect almost everyone at one time or another.

Doctors sometimes talk about a person's *stress site* (or stress organ)—the body part or area most prone to the effects of tension. After considering the examples below, think about your own primary stress site.

- **Skin:** If your skin develops a problem, the cause may be temperature, humidity, or cosmetics, but it may also be stress. Acne, hives, eczema, psoriasis, and herpes (caused by a virus) are examples of stress-related skin conditions.

- **Headaches:** Headaches are of two major types—tension and migraine.

  The most common kind of headaches, **tension headaches are caused by involuntary contractions of muscles in the neck, head, and scalp.**

  With *migraine headaches,* blood vessels expand (dilate) in the brain. Chemicals leak through the blood vessel walls and inflame nearby tissues, sending pain signals. Migraine headaches often run in families.

- **Gastrointestinal problems:** The gastrointestinal tract is the site of some common stress-related reactions. **The gastrointestinal (GI) tract consists of the stomach and large and small intestines.** *(See ● Figure 5.)* One stress-related reaction is **heartburn, a burning discomfort in the lower part of the chest.** Others are **gastritis, an inflammation of the lining of the stomach,** and **diarrhea, frequent watery bowel movements.**

● **Figure 4   The reality of psychosomatic illness.**

"*Ask someone if he or she ever suffers from psychosomatic illness and bet on a flat-out 'no' for an answer.*

But people always seem to know someone else who experiences these so-called all-in-your-head diseases—conditions that make us feel awful even though doctors can't pinpoint why. Those ailments that seem to strike just when we're pressured to the limit.

Wary of being labeled hypochondriacs or malingerers, most of us closet our own psychosomatic aches and pains. . . .

Professionals who specialize in treating psychosomatic conditions hope this attitude will soon disappear. The ailments are as real as a clogged blood vessel or a wound, they say. "

—Kathleen Doheny, Health & Fitness News Service. (1990, October 3). Illness "all in your head"? Maybe not. *San Francisco Chronicle,* p. B3.

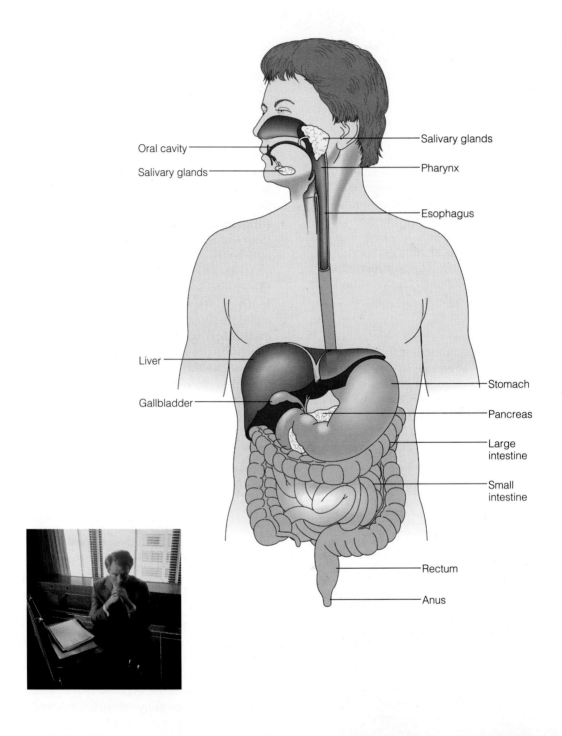

Oral cavity

Salivary glands

Salivary glands

Pharynx

Esophagus

Liver

Gallbladder

Stomach

Pancreas

Large
intestine

Small
intestine

Rectum

Anus

● **Figure 5 The gastrointestinal system.** The entire system includes the mouth, esophagus, stomach, and small and large intestines. Many people show stress-related reactions in the gastrointestinal system.

Another stress-related difficulty is ***irritable bowel syndrome (IBS), often characterized by chronic diarrhea or constipation accompanied by abdominal pain.*** IBS can be a highly inconvenient and embarrassing kind of distress. If this is an ongoing difficulty for you, you should definitely see a physician.

Many people still think of stomach ulcers as being stress-induced, as in the case of hard-driving business executives. ***Ulcers are open sores,*** sometimes caused by acidic juices or a bacterial infection. Ulcers may be aggravated by stress but are not caused by stress itself.

- ***Changes in the immune system:*** It is not clear why stress directly affects the immune system. **The *immune system* is the group of organs and tissues that protects your body against disease.** Nevertheless, certain kinds of behavior and experiences can impair this system. The body becomes more susceptible to disorders ranging from colds to cancer.[21, 22] For example, students faced with exam-related stress show a higher rate of infections than usual.[23, 24]

- ***High blood pressure and heart disease:*** High blood pressure (hypertension), which affects perhaps 35 million Americans, is a serious risk factor in heart disease.[25] Some people appear to react to stress with a rise in blood pressure—sometimes several times a day.[26]

Psychological Stress Reactions: What Affects Your Response How you respond psychologically to stress is an individual matter. Among the factors that influence your response are the following.

- ***Number, kind, and magnitude of stressors:*** In the early 1960s, physicians Thomas Holmes and Richard Rahe devised a "future illness" scale known as the Holmes-Rahe Life Events scale.[27] Stressors (life events) may be both positive and negative. At the most stressful end, they include death of a spouse, divorce, jail term, marriage, and sex difficulties. At the least stressful end, they include change in sleeping habits, vacation, Christmas, and minor violations of the law.

Adding up a year's stressful events shows how much adapting one has had to do and what the health implications are. The higher the stress score, the greater the likelihood the person will experience a future physical illness. A variation on the Holmes-Rahe scale has also been devised for students. *(See Self Discovery 2.)*

- ***Emotional predisposition and self-esteem:*** Emotional predisposition—your sensitivity or intensity of feeling—can influence how you perceive stressors and react to stress. When the source of the stress is other people, your reactions depend partly on the level of your self-esteem. By self-esteem we mean how you feel about yourself in relation to other people.

Emotional predisposition and level of self-esteem are, at least in part, learned behavior. A person may have been taught that expressing anger is "impolite" or "bad." Another may avoid criticism by not directing anger toward its source. Both may turn their anger inward. Lacking the self-esteem to direct the anger appropriately, a person may express it in unhealthy ways. Some use escapist activities, attempting to erase the stress, as with alcohol, drugs, or binge eating. Others overreact to the stress with expressions of fly-off-the-handle rage and even violence.

- ***"Type A" versus "Type B" personalities:*** Do you become extremely irritated if you have to wait in line? Do you always feel you should be working or studying when you're supposed to be relaxing? Do you often do two things at once—for example, study while eating, pay bills while talking on the phone? People who answer yes may be ***Type A personalities—hurried, time-urgent, deadline-ridden, and competitive.*** People who answer no may be ***Type B personalities—relaxed, unhurried, and carefree.*** Actually, Type A and Type B represent two ends of a range of hurried–unhurried behavior. Most of us fall somewhere between the two extremes.

In 1974, two San Francisco physicians linked Type A behavior to stress-related heart disease.[28] The more laid-back Type B personalities seemed less prone to heart

SELF DISCOVERY 2

The Student Stress Survey

The Student Stress Scale represents an adaptation of Holmes's and Rahe's Life Event Scale. It has been modified for teaching purposes to apply to college-age adults and should be considered a rough indication of stress levels and health consequences.

In the Student Stress Scale, each event, such as beginning or ending school, is given a score that represents the amount of adjustment a person has to make in life as a result of the change. In some studies, people with serious illnesses have been found to have high scores on similiar scales.

To determine your stress score, add up the number of points corresponding to the events you have experienced in the past 12 months.

1. Death of a close family member	_____	100	18. Outstanding personal achievement	_____	36
2. Death of a close friend	_____	73	19. First quarter/semester in school	_____	36
3. Divorce of parents	_____	65	20. Change in living conditions	_____	31
4. Jail term	_____	63	21. Serious argument with an instructor	_____	30
5. Major personal injury or illness	_____	63	22. Lower grades than expected	_____	29
6. Marriage	_____	58	23. Change in sleeping habits	_____	29
7. Firing from a job	_____	50	24. Change in social activities	_____	29
8. Failure of an important course	_____	47	25. Change in eating habits	_____	28
9. Change in health of a family member	_____	45	26. Chronic car trouble	_____	26
10. Pregnancy	_____	45	27. Change in the number of family get-togethers	_____	26
11. Sex problems	_____	44	28. Too many missed classes	_____	25
12. Serious argument with close friend	_____	40	29. Change of college	_____	24
13. Change in financial status	_____	39	30. Dropping of more than one class	_____	23
14. Change of scholastic major	_____	39	31. Minor traffic violations	_____	20
15. Trouble with parents	_____	39	TOTAL _____		
16. New girl- or boyfriend	_____	37			
17. Increase in workload at school	_____	37			

Here's how to interpret your score. If your score is 300 or higher, you are at high risk for developing a health problem. If your score is between 150 and 300, you have a 50–50 chance of experiencing a serious health change within two years. If your score is below 150, you have a 1-in-3 chance of a serious health change.

The following can help you reduce your risk:

1. Watch for early signs of stress, such as stomachaches or compulsive overeating.
2. Avoid negative thinking.
3. Arm your body against stress by eating nutritiously and exercising regularly.
4. Practice a relaxation technique regularly.
5. Turn to friends and relatives for support when you need it.

Source: Mullen, K., & Costello, G. (1981). *Health Awareness Through Self-Discovery.* Edina, MN: Burgess International Group.

disease. A 4½-year study of 862 people found health gains among those who received counseling and were able to reduce their Type A behavior. They had half the number of heart attacks as those who received only advice about diet, exercise, and treatments.[29]

It's important to note some important qualifications about Type A behavior. Hostility—especially an antagonistic style of interaction—seems to be an important component in putting one at risk for heart disease.[30, 31] Also, Type A people are more likely to smoke and less likely to exercise, adding two important risk factors for heart disease. Finally, *some* Type A people direct their competitive, hurried attributes to their advantage and do not suffer ill health.

- *Social resources:* Social support systems, or their absence, may make a vast difference in how well one reacts psychologically to stress.[32] For example, the single, the divorced, and the widowed have higher death rates in general than married people do. In addition, people who are uninvolved with other people or organizations are more vulnerable to chronic disease.

Psychological Reactions to Stress Some of the emotional and behavioral reactions to stress are as follows.

- *Nervousness and anxiety:* Are you constantly keyed up, startled by small sounds, and distracted? Do you feel a strong urge to cry or run away? Do you experience vague fears and feelings of dread without any obvious reason for them? These can be symptoms of too much stress.

    Such negative feelings may express themselves in certain negative behaviors. These may be sleep disturbances (such as insomnia and nightmares), speech difficulties (such as stuttering), sexual problems, quarrels, job mistakes, and accidents. Negative feelings may also be expressed through various dependencies, including television, food, alcohol, or other drugs.

- *Burnout:* Repeated emotional pressure can eventually cause **burnout, a state of physical, emotional, and mental exhaustion.** Burnout on the job seems to be

associated with three external factors: repeated deadlines, too many demands, and too much responsibility.[33]

- *Violence and victimization:* Violence is a special kind of stressor—ugly, brutal, often sudden and terrifying. Violence can leave lifelong psychological as well as physical scars. The stress can be pronounced even if the violence is witnessed rather than experienced. Boys who have seen violence, for instance, have a pattern of adjustment problems similar to those of abused boys.[34] Women battered by abusive men experience feelings of anxiety, depression, helplessness, and fear similar to those suffered by prisoners of war.[35] Victims of crime are 10 times more likely than average to be depressed even a decade or more later.[36]

- *Post-traumatic stress disorder:* **In post-traumatic stress disorder (PTSD), the victim has suffered unusual violence, continually relives the event mentally (flashbacks), and avoids anything resembling the event.** The victim also shows residual effects such as sleep disturbances, anger, and difficulty concentrating.[37]

    PTSD was first observed as combat-related stress. However, it has also been found among rape victims, abused children, and police officers involved in shootings. Other PTSD sufferers have been terrorist-hijacking victims, parents of murdered children, and mothers of AIDS victims.[38–42]

Strategy for Living: Coping with Stress
Regardless of your age, you are already finding ways to deal with stress in your life. The question is, Can your methods of reducing stress be improved?

The two principal methods of dealing with stress are *adaptation* and *coping.* **Adaptation is *not* changing the stressor or the stress. Coping, by contrast, *is* changing either the stressor or your reaction to it.**

A common adaptation for dealing with stress is drug use—for example, caffeine, cigarettes, alcohol, tranquilizers, and marijuana. Another escapist activity is television watching, although it has been found TV does *not* relax you. Other adaptations are overeating and junk-food snacking, sleeping too much, and withdrawing from others.

Coping consists of five aspects of a strategy for living, as follows:

- ***Reduce the stressors:*** It's surprising how long we can let something go on being a source of stress—usually because dealing with it is so uncomfortable. For example, you fall behind in your work, but you can't bring yourself to tell your instructor or boss. Or you have a misunderstanding with your family, your lover, or your roommate. It may not be easy, but these are matters you can do something about. Getting the advice of a counselor may help. Avoidance and procrastination only make things worse.

- ***Manage your emotional response:*** Quite often you can't do anything about a stressor—being stuck behind a slow-moving truck on a mountain road, for example. But you can do something about your *reaction* to it. Some techniques for managing your emotional response are the following: (1) Understand and express your feelings (for example, crying makes people feel better, regardless of gender). (2) Feel and act positively (such as giving yourself positive messages). (3) Keep your sense of humor and have hope.

- ***Develop a support system:*** Some forms of emotional support to which you might reach out are the following: (1) Talk to and do things with friends or family, so you fight the temptation to isolate yourself. (2) Talk to counselors, such as those at the college health service. (3) Join a support group, whether self-help or group-therapy.

- ***Take care of your body:*** When you're stressed, mistreating your body will only make your mind feel worse. Taking care of your body includes eating well, exercising, sleeping right, and avoiding drugs.

- ***Develop relaxation techniques:*** Various techniques can be used to achieve what is called the relaxation response. **The *relaxation response* consists of predictable, beneficial physiological changes that occur in both body and mind when one is truly relaxed.**[43, 44] Five relaxation

techniques for de-stressing yourself are as follows:

(1) Deep, slow breathing consists of inhaling through your nose, then slowly breathing out through your nose, while telling yourself, "Relax."

(2) ***Progressive muscular relaxation*** **consists of tightening and relaxing major muscle groups throughout your body.** Part of this procedure is used in mental imagery, described next.

(3) **In *mental imagery*—also known as *guided imagery* or *visualization*— you essentially daydream an image or desired change.** Anticipate that your body will respond as if the image were real. *(See ● Figure 6.)* Mental imagery is used not only for de-stressing but also for changing habits, such as quitting smoking. In addition, it is used to enhance performance, as when a tennis player imagines the outcome of the serve.

(4) An age-old technique, ***meditation* is concerned with directing a person's attention to a single, unchanging or repetitive stimulus. The point is to eliminate mental distractions.** When the religious and philosophical connotations are stripped away, the act of meditation itself is not mysterious at all. Its purpose is simply to eliminate the "mind chatter" that goes on in the heads of all of us and to relax the body. *(See ● Figure 7.)*

(5) ***Biofeedback* is using an electronic instrument to self-monitor and modify your physiological performance.** The electronic instrument can detect internal changes in your body and communicate them back to you through a light, tone, or meter. Biofeedback techniques help people relax "by signaling lowered muscle tension, improved blood flow in the extremities, or reduced sweat gland activity," says clinical psychologist Laurence Miller.[45]

● **Figure 6   Mental imagery.** To use visualization effectively, it's recommended you devote 10–20 minutes to this procedure, daily or several times a week.

To practice mental imagery, do the following:

- Get comfortable and quiet: *Remove your shoes, loosen your clothes, and sit down or lie in a comfortable setting, with the lights dimmed. Close your eyes.*

- Breathe deeply and concentrate on a word or phrase: *Breathe deeply, filling your chest, and slowly let the air out. With each breath, concentrate on a simple word or phrase (such as "One," or "Good," or a prayer). Focus your mind on this phrase to get rid of distracting thoughts. Repeat.*

- Clench and release your muscles: *Tense and relax each part of your body, proceeding from fist to face to stomach to toes.*

- Visualize a vivid image: *Create a tranquil, pleasant image in your mind—lying beside a mountain stream, floating on a raft in a pool, stretched out on a beach. Try to involve all 5 senses, from sight to taste.*

- Visualize a desired change: *If you're trying to improve some aspect of your performance, such as improving a tennis serve, visualize the act in detail: the fuzz and seam on the ball, the exact motion of the serve, the path of the ball, all in slow detail.*

● **Figure 7 Meditation.** Meditation includes the repetition of a word, sound, phrase, or prayer. Whenever everyday thoughts interrupt, they should be disregarded, and you should return to the repetition. The exercise should be continued for 10–20 minutes and practiced once or twice daily.

❝ *Pick a focus word or short phrase that is firmly rooted in your personal belief system. For example, a Christian person might choose the opening words of Psalm 23, "The Lord is my shepherd"; a Jewish person, "Shalom"; a nonreligious individual, a neutral word like "One" or "Peace."*

- *Sit quietly in a comfortable position.*

- *Close your eyes.*

- *Relax your muscles.*

- *Breathe slowly and naturally, and as you do, repeat your focus word or phrase as you exhale.*

- *Assume a passive attitude. Don't worry about how well you're doing. When other thoughts come to mind, simply say to yourself, "Oh, well," and gently return to the repetition.* ❞

—Herbert Benson, M.D. (1989). Editorial: Hypnosis and the relaxation response. *Gastroenterology, 96,* 1610.

Loneliness

Loneliness is the feeling that arises from a mismatch between one's desire for social contact and the actual contact one has. People who feel lonely frequently have less healthy behaviors. Overcoming loneliness means taking chances.

All of us experience loneliness at one time or another. ***Loneliness* is the discomfort you feel because of a discrepancy between the social relationships you want and the relationships you actually have.**
     People who feel truly lonely most of the time have different health behaviors than the not-lonely. For instance, a study of lonely adolescents found that they were more likely to use marijuana than not-lonely adolescents.[46]

The Feeling of Loneliness College students may first experience the pangs of isolation when they leave home for college. Then or thereafter, you might feel one of four types of loneliness. (1) You might feel *excluded* from a community you wish to be part of. (2) You might feel *unloved*—meaning uncared for—by people near you. (3) You might feel *constricted* about being able to share your feelings and worries with someone. (4) You might feel *alienated*—meaning isolated or distant from—people in your group.[47]

Strategy for Living: Overcoming Loneliness
Lonely people find it difficult to participate in groups, introduce themselves, or make telephone calls.[48] Overcoming loneliness means beginning to take chances. That is, it means giving the task of establishing friendly connections the same importance that you do to other priorities in your life. Thus, you might join groups with interests similar to yours or become a volunteer for a cause or activity you believe in. You can also pursue solo interests (such as music, photography, fishing, or jogging) that are absorbing enough that you can be happy with your own company.

Shyness

Shyness can range from occasional awkwardness in social situations to a complex condition that can disrupt a person's life. About 80% of people say they are shy at some point in their lives. Shy people need to take steps to build self-confidence and social skills.

Some shy students stare down at their notebooks to avoid making eye contact with the instructor, hoping to escape the instructor's attention. Sooner or later, however, most people are called upon to speak in public—and, for many, this can be an anxious, even terrifying experience.

The Experience of Shyness For many, shyness is situation-specific. Common situations include interactions with the other sex, meeting strangers, being the focus of attention, and interacting in large group settings. Some people, however, find themselves consistently tormented by feelings of shyness, regardless of the situation in which they find themselves.

Shyness, **then, can range from occasional awkwardness in social situations to a complex fear of people that completely disrupts a person's life.** According to one study, about 80% of those questioned reported they were shy at some point in their lives.[49]

Shy people may be of two types. The *publicly shy* are those who stutter, slouch, blush, avoid eye contact, and are otherwise unable to conceal their shyness. The *privately shy* cover up their shyness and may actually seem somewhat outgoing. Or, alternatively, they may seem bored or aloof. Still, they suffer the same inhibitions and fearfulness as the publicly shy.

Strategy for Living: Overcoming Shyness
There are three key elements to coping with shyness:

- *Analyze your shyness:* Identify the situation in which you feel most shy and try to understand what is causing your anxiety.
- *Take steps to build self-confidence:* Making use of the college counseling center is a good way to start. A good technique for conquering shyness is to put yourself directly into situations that make you uncomfortable. For instance, one can gain social confidence and skills by introducing oneself to classmates or to other guests at a party.
- *Build your social skills:* Building communication skills will help here. Learn to be a great listener or to be an expert in one of your personal areas of interest.

Sadness

Ordinary sadness is experienced as the "blues," as opposed to more serious clinical depression, which can go on for 2 weeks or more. Dealing with sadness sometimes means changing your thinking and finding enjoyable distractions. It also means being able to recognize and acknowledge the need for additional help if symptoms persist or increase in intensity.

The word *depression* has a clinical meaning, as we shall discuss later. Here we are concerned simply with *sadness*—"the blahs," "the blues," the troubling thoughts and down moods that we all sometimes get.

Is It Sadness or Worse? It's important to distinguish between sadness (or disappointment or grief) and genuine clinical depression. It may be depression if for at least 2 weeks you've felt sad, worthless, and fatigued and thought life isn't worth living. The National Foundation for Depressive Illness recommends that you see a physician or therapist about possible clinical depression in that case.[50]

Strategy for Living: Overcoming Sadness
The best thing you can do to overcome sadness is to break the pattern of negative thoughts that are bringing on the emotional lows. This means finding enjoyable distractions, such as being with friends or going on outings. Engaging in pleasant exercise such as walking or bicycling also helps. You can also, of course, seek the solace of talking to someone who cares.

Anxieties and Fears

Anxiety refers to generalized worry or apprehension that has no specific source. Fear, on the other hand, is a feeling of apprehension about something specific. In their mild forms, both can sometimes be alleviated by stress-reduction measures and positive "self-talk."

Are Sunday nights an agonizing time when you worry about what's in store for you on Monday? Are you sometimes so afraid that you don't even answer the phone? Anxieties and fears can be so severe as to be incapacitating, as we describe elsewhere. Here, however, we are concerned about normal worries and apprehensions that are simply part of the process of being alive.

Normal Worries Anxiety is *general*. You may have heard the term "free-floating anxiety." Fear, on the other hand, is *specific*. It is associated with something in particular, such as fear of examinations, of insects, of making a speech. Consider the Sunday-night dread about returning to school or work. It may be a mild to almost paralyzing general sense that something awful and unknown is about to happen. Or it may be a mild to deep discomfort about a specific matter, such as a speech you're giving. Feelings of both anxiety and fear may include physical symptoms, such as sweating, constriction in the chest, or pounding heart.

Strategy for Living: Overcoming Normal Anxieties and Fears One of the most important strategies for coping with anxiety is to pinpoint its source and then apply steps in the problem-solving process. In addition, stress-reduction techniques—relaxation, meditation, physical exercise, distraction, or positive "self-talk"—can help.

Find a comfortable, dimly lighted place where you can sit and try to determine the feeling. Listen to your "Voice of Judgment."[51] This is your negative "mind chatter," your internal voice that broadcasts inhibiting pronouncements. If it's general (meaning it's anxiety), the Voice of Judgment's messages may begin, "You never . . . ," "You always . . . ," "You should . . . ," "You shouldn't. . . . ," (Example:

"You never do well in school.") If it's specific (meaning it's a fear), you'll probably be able to hear a particular apprehension. (Example: "Your speech is going to bomb.")

Changing diet, cutting drug intake (including caffeine and nicotine), and increasing exercise level are all ways to lower discomfort. If you feel particularly overwhelmed, you may need to seek professional help. However, you can also use your own inner resources to counter the Voice of Judgment. You can use positive self-talk to confront your anxiety or fear and lessen its effect. *(See ● Figure 8.)*

Anger, Aggression, and Assertiveness

Anger can sometimes be cooled by being expressed. Sometimes, however, giving voice to anger can do more harm than good. Often, not expressing anger or expressing it in a civilized way is best. Anger is distinct from aggression, which is behavior designed to inflict hurt. Anger is also distinct from assertiveness, which is simply standing up for one's rights.

How often do you get angry? In one study that asked people to recall or record such incidents, most reported at least mild anger several times a week. Some people were angry several times a day.[52] More than half the time, the anger was in response to the perceived wrongful act of a family member or friend. Anger was particularly likely when the incident was considered avoidable and unjustified.

Expressing Anger The work environment is often a stimulus to anger, but it is also frequently an inappropriate setting for expressing it. "Men and women who are employed full time cited work twice as often as all other locations combined for occasions of feeling angry but remaining silent," writes Carol Tavris in *Anger: The Misunderstood Emotion.* "Conversely, the most popular location for screaming arguments and physical violence is—as you might expect—the home."[53]

But is an angry outburst the best way to handle your rage? Some people believe that

● **Figure 8 Using self-talk.** You can use positive "self-talk" to confront your fear and reduce its emotional significance.

"*Confront your fear.*

Once you locate your fear, say hello to it. Remember that you created it. You have invited it to live inside you. So get to know your guest. Talk to your fear, preferably out loud.

Say: Hello. Since you are staying here in my house, let's get clear what your chores are.

It is your job to make my life unpleasant. It is your job to give me an excuse not to try new things. It is your job to prevent me from feeling confident and free.

Thanks. You are doing a good job at this. Just remember, you are my guest. I can kick you out whenever I so choose."

—Psychologists Angela B. Miller & Richard Miller (1989, March 15). Phobias and free-floating anxieties. *San Francisco Chronicle*, Briefing section, p. 9.

expression of feeling (catharsis) produces emotional release, reducing the emotion. In the case of anger, this is sometimes true—provided the target deserved retaliation and the result doesn't cause the other person physical or emotional harm or leave you feeling guilty or anxious. However, expressing anger *while you feel angry* often makes you feel angrier and can be destructive to a relationship.

Two quite different ways of expressing anger are with aggression and with assertiveness.

- *Aggression:* Although the word sometimes has a positive meaning, here **aggression refers to intentional acts of hostility and violence.** That is, aggression is physical or verbal behavior designed to inflict hurt.

  Aggression is not the same as anger. You may feel anger and express it in several ways, some positive, such as cleaning the house energetically. You can also act aggressively without feeling anger, as professional soldiers do.

- *Assertiveness: Assertiveness* **is simply standing up for one's rights, stating one's feelings frankly and calmly,** without being angry or provocative.

Strategy for Living: Handling Anger How, then, can you best handle anger? Silent brooding and sulking (for supposed sake of harmony) is not useful. Nor is outspoken rage and cruelty (supposedly in the name of honesty) useful. Often the best response is nothing at all. "Let it go, and half the time it will turn out to be an unimportant, momentary shudder," says Tavris. "The other half of the time, keeping quiet gives you time to cool down and decide whether the matter is worth discussing or not."[54]

A first step, then, is to cool your rising temper and disengage from argument (perhaps by saying, "This is becoming a fight"). A second step is to learn to deal with anger with *civility.* Civility means knowing when to keep quiet about trivial irritations and when to discuss important matters clearly and assertively. Telling the other person how his or her aggravations make you *feel*, rather than leveling an accusation, will invariably get better results. For example, say "I get upset when you leave the laundry for me to do," not "You *never* do anything about the dirty clothes."

Understanding Abnormal Behavior

▶ Define psychological disorder and cite at least four examples.

▶ Discuss the causes of abnormal behavior.

▶ Distinguish among mood disorders, anxiety disorders, personality disorders, and schizophrenic disorders.

▶ Recognize the source of criteria for identifying psychological disorders.

Psychological illness can occur as suddenly and be as devastating as any physical illness. Clinical depression, for instance, is a disorder that affects 1 out of 20 Americans at some time. It's important to understand that mental and emotional disorders are commonplace, that they are exaggerations of normal behaviors. One of the most important skills in the art of living, then, is learning that we can live through psychological illness—and help is available.

Types of Psychological Disorders

A psychological disorder is a pattern of behavior associated with distress, disability, or risk of pain, death, or loss of freedom. Psychological disorders can have biological, early-life, and environmental causes. Common psychological disorders are mood disorders, anxiety disorders, personality disorders, and schizophrenic disorders.

The American Psychiatric Association (APA) defines a *psychological disorder* as a pattern of behavior associated with distress (pain), disability (impaired functioning), or risk of pain, death, or loss of freedom.[55]

Possible Causes of Abnormal Behavior
There are three possible causes of abnormal behavior:[56]

- *Biological causes:* Brain damage, biochemical abnormalities, faulty nutrition, disease, and various legal and illegal drugs may cause psychological disorders. Heredity may also be a cause, as it may be in schizophrenia and major depression.

- *Early-life causes:* Distorted thinking may be caused by traumatic experiences in infancy and childhood.

- *Environmental causes:* Instead of having causes originating within the person, psychological disorders may be caused by reactions to difficulties in the environment. The abnormal behavior may be the person's attempt to cope with problems such as in the family or at work.

Classifications of Psychological Disorders
In the past, two classes of psychological disorders were identified—neurosis and psychosis. A *neurosis* is a relatively minor psychological disturbance, such as anxiety and depression. A *psychosis* is a severe psychological disturbance that grossly impairs contact with reality.

Nowadays professional therapists find these two terms too vague to be useful. Instead, they rely on a reference book by the American Psychiatric Association, *Diagnosis and Statistical Manual of Mental Disorders* (Fourth Edition), commonly abbreviated DSM-IV. *DSM-IV* lists symptoms characteristic of almost 300 different psychological problems.

Among the many mental disorders described in DSM-IV are the following:

- Mood disorders, which include depression and suicide

- Anxiety disorders

- Personality disorders

- Schizophrenic disorders

We describe these next. Other commonly experienced problems, such as substance-abuse and eating disorders, are described in other chapters.

Mood Disorders, Including Depression and Suicide

Mood disorders are characterized by severe depression, mania (elation), or swings between. Serious mood disorders include depression and suicide. Depression refers to exaggerated feelings of sadness, hopelessness, and worthlessness. Several kinds of depression have been identified, including major depression, seasonal affective disorder, and bipolar disorder. Clues to likelihood of attempting suicide include changes in mood and behavior, stressful life events, previous suicide attempts, and talk of suicide.

Mood disorders are characterized by prolonged or severe depression, *mania* or elation, or swings between these extremes. The most common mood disorder is depression. Suicide is also considered a mood disorder.

Depression Being sad is part of the human condition. However, when sadness becomes one's constant outlook, it has another name: depression. This applies, for example, to someone lamenting a lost love not just a year later but 5 or more years after the loss.

Depression generally lasts more than 2 weeks and involves exaggerated feelings of sadness, hopelessness, anxiety, irritability, despair, worthlessness, low self-esteem, and guilt. It is also characterized by loss of energy and motivation; unrelenting fatigue; and change in appetite, body weight, sex drive, and sleep habits. Other symptoms are difficulty concentrating and thoughts of death and suicide.

Depression takes several forms, including the following:

- *Major depression:* **A *major depression* is a severe depression that lasts 2 weeks or longer.** Some people suffer recurring depressions throughout their lives.

- *Seasonal affective disorder:* To some extent, seasonal fluctuations in mood are common among many people living in the northern latitudes. However, it is particularly true for those suffering from ***seasonal affective disorder (SAD)*. People with SAD become seriously depressed in**

● **Figure 9   The SAD season.** People with seasonal affective disorder swing from severe depression in winter months to normal or manic (excitable) mood in summer months because of changes in daylight. Exposing SAD patients to 45–60 minutes of high-intensity light can relieve depression after only 2–3 days of treatment.

winter and normal or slightly manic (excitable) in summer. Such people are apparently more sensitive to sunlight. The earth's daily dark-light cycle influences the hormone melatonin, which affects mood and how energetic one feels.[57] Treatment consists of exposing SAD patients to a high-intensity light for a short time each morning. (See ● *Figure 9.*)

- *Bipolar disorder:* **Bipolar disorder, or *manic-depressive disorder*, is marked by moods alternating between the two extremes, or poles (hence, "bipolar"), of depression and mania. *Mania* is**

● **Figure 10   Behold the stars: delivery from depression.**
Eventually, after experimenting with a variety of kinds of healing,
including "seclusion and time," novelist William Styron overcame
his depression. He depicts the relief as resembling the emergence
from hell in the last line of Dante's poem *The Inferno.*

❝*For those who have dwelt in depression's dark wood, and
known its inexplicable agony, their return from the abyss is
not unlike the ascent of the poet, trudging upward and upward
out of hell's black depths and at last emerging into what he saw
as 'the shining world.' There, whoever has been restored to
health has almost always been restored to the capacity for
serenity and joy, and this may be indemnity enough for having endured the despair beyond despair . . . .*
     And so we came forth, and once again beheld the stars.❞

—William Styron (1990). *Darkness visible: A memoir of
madness.* New York: Random House, p. 84.

**characterized by constant, driven activ-
ity and lack of inhibitions.** People with
bipolar disorder are periodically in a slow,
inactive, inhibited state characterized by a
sense of helplessness and extreme sadness
(depression). Then they swing to an energetic, active, uninhibited state characterized
by elation or anger (mania). Mood swings
may take place over the course of a day or
over several months.

Strategy for Living: Fighting Depression
Depression is often treatable. Psychotherapy,
medication (such as Prozac), and finally time
can ease the pain of most sufferers. *(See ● Figure 10.)*

For many depressed people, one study indicates, a way out is to break the cycle of gloomy
thoughts. Psychologist Richard M. Wenzlaff recommends that depressed people do something
enjoyable. "Force yourself to get out, even if you
feel like crawling into a hole," he says. "If you're
obsessing about your rotten social life, for example, don't go to a bar if you hate that scene.
Choose a comfortable activity that also holds the
possibility of meeting someone."[58]

Suicide: "The Forever Decision" Choosing
to take one's own life signifies not just the death
of self but also the death of hope.

How do you know if someone will attempt
suicide? The answer is that there are no dependably predictable patterns. Here are some
considerations:

• *Look for changes in mood and habit:*
We mentioned several of the signs for depression, including sadness, hopelessness,
helplessness, apathy. In addition, studies of
adolescents suggest looking for school problems, antisocial behavior, social isolation, running away, and preoccupation with death.[59]

• *Look for changes in life events:* People
experiencing very stressful life events are at
a higher risk for suicide, examples being
divorce or death of a parent.[60]

• *Beware of previous attempts:* A prior
suicide attempt is always significant: about
one-third of people who survive a suicide
attempt eventually do kill themselves.[61]

• *Talkers may be doers:* If a person talks
about suicide, *always* take it seriously. It's a
myth that the people who talk about suicide
are not the ones who commit it. Such talk
may be about life not being worth living or
about the suicide of someone else. Or it may
be about how others will or will not miss
them when they are gone.

• *Warnings versus no warnings:* Usually
people contemplating suicide send out
warning signals in advance. However, one
study found that more than half the people

who attempt suicide do so on the spur of the moment. That is, they make a decision less than 24 hours before making the attempt.[62]

Strategy for Living: Helping Prevent Suicide If you think that someone is contemplating suicide, don't be afraid to get involved.

- *Encourage talk, and listen:* Be direct: Ask, "Are you feeling really depressed? Have you had thoughts of suicide?" Don't be afraid that he or she is too fragile to hear the word "suicide." Encourage the person to talk, then *listen* to his or her response. You can't know the type or depth of that person's pain unless you listen carefully.

- *Suggest solutions:* Be reassuring, but don't stop there. Suggest alternative solutions to the person's problems, if you can think of them. Most especially, urge him or her to get professional help. Offer to accompany the person to get help.

- *Show caring and be watchful:* Show you care by staying with the distraught person until you can get help. If you have to leave, make a pact that he or she will do nothing in the way of self-harm without calling you. And when you are called, get to the person's side right away.

- *Get help:* If you feel events are beyond your control, call a suicide hotline, a counselor, or the police. Don't stop being involved until the person has the support and assistance of a trained professional.

Anxiety Disorders

Anxiety disorders include several conditions characterized by irrational fears and worries. General anxiety disorder is marked by excessive or unrealistic worries. Panic disorder is a moderate level of anxiety interspersed by panic attacks, episodes of intense fear. Phobias are specific fears so intense they interfere with normal living. They may be treated by gradual exposure (systematic desensitization) or sudden exposure (flooding). Obsessive-compulsive disorder consists of an unwanted, repetitive stream of thought (the obsession) or a repetitive, irresistible action (the compulsion).

Anxiety disorders **are a class of disorders marked by feelings of excessive apprehension and anxiety.** Anxiety disorders include the following:

- Generalized anxiety disorder
- Panic disorder
- Phobias
- Obsessive-compulsive disorder

Generalized Anxiety Disorder A *generalized anxiety disorder* **is characterized by excessive or unrealistic worries that extend over a period of 6 months or more.** People suffering from this condition have no more basis for their concerns than anyone else, but they are constantly anxious. They worry, for example, "I might flunk out of school," "I might run out of money," "My kids might get sick." This anxiety is often manifested in physical symptoms such as irritability, nervousness, sleeping difficulties, and concentration problems.

Panic Disorder *Panic disorders* **involve recurrent attacks of severe anxiety that often occur suddenly and without provocation.** People with panic disorder live constantly with a moderate level of anxiety interspersed with panic attacks. *Panic attacks* **are episodes experienced as intense fear or terror.** This attack, lasting a few minutes to an hour or more, often occurs at night. Symptoms include pounding heart, racing pulse, shortness of breath, sweating, faintness, and fears about going crazy or dying.

Many people deal with anxiety by taking a couple of deep breaths, a useful way to calm oneself down. However, those who continue to do prolonged deep breathing, thinking more is better, may end up actually *increasing* their distress.[63] **Abnormal or rapid deep breathing, called** *hyperventilating,* **causes excessive loss of carbon dioxide in the blood.** This produces numbness in the extremities, faintness, and a sense of an inability to take a full breath. The effect of this reaction is to increase the already existing feelings of anxiety.

Strategy for Living: Coping with Panic Attacks Teaching people to do deep breathing but to avoid hyperventilation can help them deal with panic episodes.[64] Psychotherapy and medications such as antidepressants and antianxiety drugs are also helpful.

Phobias Anxiety is a mild to immobilizing *general* form of fear. Phobia, by contrast, is a *specific* fear—and not just a garden-variety fear. **A *phobia* is an unrealistic, irrational, disproportionate fear associated with a particular person, place, or thing.** The fear is so powerful, so beyond the person's voluntary control, that it interferes with normal living. People in the grip of a phobia experience trembling, sweating, rapid breathing, and pounding heart. In addition, they often have the feeling that the fear itself may kill them with a heart attack. However, unlike panic attacks, the level of anxiety is so high in a phobia that it is immobilizing.

Phobias are the most widespread form of anxiety disorders, affecting 5–13% of all Americans.[65] The most common phobia is ***agoraphobia*, the fear of being in open or public places or in crowds. *Simple phobias* are fears of specific objects,** such as snakes or spiders, or situations, such as flying in planes or crossing bridges. After agoraphobia, the most prevalent phobias are of closed spaces (*claustrophobia*), public places, heights (*acrophobia*), lightning and thunder, animals (*zoophobia*), and illness.

Strategy for Living: Coping with Phobias There are two kinds of treatment for phobias, both requiring therapeutic help:

- ***Systematic desensitization: Systematic desensitization* works to reduce fear by gradually exposing a person to the object that arouses the fear.**[66] Example: People with a fear of snakes are first trained in relaxation. Then they lie on a couch while soft music plays. Once relaxed, they are asked to imagine a black-and-white photo of snakes, then a full-color photo, then a real snake. Later they are given real photos, and finally a real snake.

- ***Flooding: Flooding* diminishes the fear by exposing persons to the object of the phobia suddenly instead of gradually**—"flooding" them with fear. This is done in the presence of a therapist. Example: People afraid of snakes are instructed to imagine themselves being crawled over and being bitten by snakes. Such images first stimulate the patients' breathing and heart rates to high levels. However, such physical responses cannot remain high for long, and the patients begin to feel relaxed despite the continuing presence of the snake images.

Obsessive-Compulsive Disorder "Everybody carries germs around with them," said anxiety-ridden billionaire Howard Hughes. "I want to live longer than my parents, so I avoid germs."[67]

Hughes's insistence on elaborate hand-washing rituals and fear of being touched was an extreme example of obsessive-compulsive disorder. ***Obsessive-compulsive disorder* is a condition marked by repetitive thought patterns and actions.** Actually, this disorder has two parts:

- ***Obsession:* An *obsession* is a repetitive, unwanted stream of thought.** An example is when you continue to hear a person's rebuke in your mind over and over years later.

- ***Compulsion:* A *compulsion* is a repetitive, almost irresistible action.** An example is when you constantly nibble on your fingernails.

People with obsessive-compulsive disorder often worry about the "right way" to do things. One frequent compulsion is cleaning, as was the case with Howard Hughes. Another is "double-checking," as of someone who repeatedly checks to see that a house is locked up before going to bed.

Strategy for Living: Coping with Obsessive-Compulsive Disorder Those with an obsessive-compulsive disorder can sometimes be treated with systematic desensitization, as we mentioned, for phobias. By exposing the obsessive person to the anxiety-provoking thought while restraining the compulsive behavior, therapists may be able to extinguish the repetitive behavior. In addition, certain medications may be effective, such as antidepressants that lessen anxiety.

Personality Disorders

Personality disorders are maladaptive, inflexible ways of dealing with the world and other people. Examples are personality disorders characterized by excessive dependence on others or extreme self-centeredness.

A *personality disorder* **is defined as a poorly adaptive, inflexible way of dealing with the environment and other people.** There are many personality disorders listed in DSM-IV.

Common Personality Disorders Some common disorders are found in people who are

- *Dependent: Dependent personality disorder* **is characterized by a lack of initiative and self-confidence** and by a preference for letting other people make decisions.
- *Self-defeating: Self-defeating personality disorder* **is characterized by a fear of achieving success,** as expressed in self-handicapping symptoms.
- *Histrionic: Histrionic personality disorder* **is characterized by excessive emotionality and attention-seeking,** and a constant demand for praise.
- *Narcissistic: Narcissistic personality disorder* **is characterized by an exaggerated self-centeredness** that can interfere with one's ability to form attachments to others. People with this disorder actually have a deep sense of worthlessness, so they need attention and admiration to bolster their self-esteem.
- *Borderline: Borderline personality disorder* **is characterized by the lack of a stable sense of self and feelings of inadequacy.** Such people have trouble making decisions about values, careers, and

even sexual orientation and they find it hard to establish lasting relationships. They repeat self-destructive behaviors, such as shoplifting or drug abuse.

Strategy for Living: Therapy for Personality Disorders Individual psychotherapy may help treat some forms of personality disorders. For example, therapy can help narcissistic patients develop more realistic concepts of themselves as neither extremely special nor completely worthless. In some instances, medication can be helpful.

Schizophrenic Disorders

Schizophrenia is characterized by personal deterioration, disturbed perceptions—including hallucinations, delusions of persecution, and delusions of grandeur—thought disorders, and inappropriate emotions. Causes are uncertain, and the disorder cannot be cured, although the condition can be alleviated with antipsychotic drugs.

In our dreams, we see ourselves hovering in the air, standing naked in a crowd, acting heroically, or being chased by phantoms. Our minds also leap from one event to another, defying time and space and logic. When we wake up, however, we know that we have been experiencing fantasy. Schizophrenics do not.

The Symptoms of Schizophrenia The word *schizophrenia* means "split mind"—not in the Jekyll-and-Hyde sense of split personality, but rather as a "split from reality." **Schizophrenia is characterized by various kinds of disturbed thinking, behavior, and feelings—particularly hallucinations, delusions, disorganized speech, and grossly disorganized behavior.** This definition from DSM-IV is a bit imprecise because the symptoms of schizophrenia are a *range* of emotional and cognitive disorders. No one who has schizophrenia has all the symptoms of the disease at a given time or even during the course of his or her illness.

The symptoms associated with schizophrenia include the following:

- **Personal deterioration:** Over 6 months' time, one's work performance, social relations, and personal appearance deteriorate. A schizophrenic finds he or she can't concentrate, relax, or sleep and withdraws from social relationships.

- **Disturbed perceptions:** Schizophrenics typically suffer from hallucinations and delusions. ***Hallucinations are sensory experiences—sights and sounds—that don't exist in reality.*** Sometimes they become exaggerated visual experiences.

  ***Delusions* are unfounded beliefs.** Three types of delusions are as follows. ***Delusions of grandeur* are a person's false belief that he or she is supremely important** ("I'm the Son of God"). ***Delusions of persecution* are the unrealistic belief that people are trying to harm him or her** ("The CIA is after me"). ***Delusions of reference* are beliefs that many messages personally refer to oneself** ("That TV announcer was talking about me").

- ***Thought disorders:*** The thoughts of schizophrenics often show a loose, bizarre association and difficulty with abstract concepts. Indeed, psychologists often refer to the verbal thoughts of schizophrenics as "word salad."

- ***Inappropriate emotions:*** Schizophrenics generally display little emotion in their faces. Or when they do, the expressions are inappropriate, such as laughter when the circumstances don't warrant it. Some patients fall into a state called **catatonia, being motionless or constantly in motion,** neither condition being triggered by outside stimuli.

Strategy for Living: Treatment for Schizophrenia Schizophrenia cannot be cured, but with medication it can be controlled. About half of all psychiatric hospital patients in the United States are schizophrenics. Still, antipsychotic drugs can help reduce the thought disorders, disturbed perceptions, and tormenting voices. With such help, many schizophrenics can live with their families and hold jobs.

Getting Help: Kinds of Therapy

▶ Discuss the criteria for determining when you need professional help.

▶ Identify sources of professional help for mental health disorders.

▶ Explain the various kinds of talking therapies, both individual and group.

▶ Name and describe the various kinds of nonverbal therapies.

Anxiety, headaches, panic attacks, anger, loneliness, and other kinds of major distress may be too overwhelming to be successfully overcome by sharing such problems with friends. Sometimes professional help is needed to relieve the pain and resolve underlying issues.

When and Where to Get Professional Help

You may need professional help if your present state is detrimental to yourself or others. Examples are depression and anxiety, a crisis, communication problems, addiction problems, and early-life problems. You might find a therapist through campus student services. Also check services listed in the phone book—community services, crisis intervention services, and organizations that deal with specific problems. After determining the initial treatment that you want, establish a level of comfort with your therapist and set goals for treatment. Therapies are of two basic types—talking therapies and nonverbal therapies.

Many people wonder, "Does therapy really help?" In general, it does, especially for specific, clear-cut problems.[68–70] Regardless of method, effective therapists offer patients *empathy*—understanding of their experiences. They are able to convey their care and concern in a way that enables them to earn their patients' trust.

When to Get Help There are several kinds of trouble for which you might seek professional help. All are essentially conditions that answer the question: "Is my present condition damaging to me or others?"

- *Depression and anxiety:* Have you felt several weeks of despair, helplessness, hopelessness, fearfulness, or sleeplessness?
- *Crisis:* Are you unable to cope with the loss or death of someone close, a major disruption such as job loss, physical illness, or an abusive relationship?
- *Communication problems:* Do you have problems with shyness, assertiveness, loneliness, intimacy, or relationship conflicts?
- *Addiction problems:* Are you unable to stop drinking, smoking, drugs, gambling, or shoplifting?
- *Early-life problems:* Were you neglected or emotionally, physically, or sexually abused as a child?

How to Get Help The first thing most people want when they go to a therapist is to have someone relieve the pain—whatever it is. Here are some ways to connect with a therapist quickly.

- *Student services:* If you are a college student, campus student-health centers, health-education instructors, or the dean of student affairs can direct you to college and community health services.
- *Community services:* Look at the following categories in the telephone book Yellow Pages: COUNSELING; ALCOHOL AND DRUG ABUSE; CHILD ABUSE AND FAMILY VIOLENCE; HEALTH CARE; MENTAL HEALTH AND CRISIS INTERVENTION; MOTHER AND INFANT HEALTH; RAPE AND SEXUAL ASSAULT; SUICIDE PREVENTION.
- *Crisis intervention:* Whatever the specific crisis, there is probably a crisis hotline for it in the telephone book. Examples: suicide prevention, violence prevention, sexual trauma, rape, battered women, drug abuse.
- *Specific organizations for specific problems:* Many kinds of self-help groups exist for specific ills. Examples: Alcoholics Anonymous, Narcotics Anonymous, Gamblers Anonymous, Adult Children of Alco-

holics, Overeaters Anonymous, and Parents of Murdered Children.

Once your immediate distress is relieved, you need to see how comfortable you are with your therapist. This means being satisfied with the therapist's credentials, experience, and methods (such as biofeedback compared to hypnosis). It also means being comfortable with whether the therapist seems to take you seriously. After all, although this is a *paid* relationship, it is also a very *personal* relationship. Compatibility is important; you don't want to feel mistrustful or intimidated. Once you are satisfied with the basics, you can then begin to set goals for therapy. *(See ● Figure 11.)*

Therapies are of two types—*talking* and *nonverbal.* We discuss both types below.

Talking Therapies

Talking therapies include different types of individual psychotherapy and group therapy. Psychotherapy is the interaction between therapist and patient to try to change psychological problems. Seven types of psychotherapy are psychoanalysis, personal-centered therapy, Gestalt therapy, rational-emotive therapy, cognitive therapy, transactional analysis, and brief therapy. Group therapy, which is less expensive than individual psychotherapy, includes couples or family therapy and self-help and support groups.

In *talking therapies,* **a patient interacts in a confiding way either individually with a trained therapist or in a group led by a therapist.** The purpose of the talking is to help patients achieve insight into the reasons for their behavior. Therefore, talking therapies are often called *insight-oriented therapies.*

Talking therapies may be *individual psychotherapy* or *group therapy.*

● **Figure 11   Early goals of therapy.**

❝*Here's how to start deciding what you want your therapy to accomplish:*

1. As best you can, jot down what you think is causing you distress. This list of events, relationships, or stresses can be long or short, but simply writing them down can help you understand better what has been going on, and going wrong.

*   . . . Your insight reveals a lot about how you think and how you understand the way life works. Left to their own devices and theories, therapists will come up with all sorts of reasons their clients are suffering. . . .*

2. After the first visit, consider carefully how comfortable you felt. Will you and the therapist be able to work together week after week? . . .

3. As you work with your chosen therapist in setting early goals, try to make them measurable in some way. This isn't always easy, but when the changes you want can be measured, it's a lot easier to tell, down the road, how well the therapy is working.❞

—Psychotherapist Paul G. Quinnett (1989, April). The key to successful therapy. *Psychology Today*, p. 46.

Some Types of Individual Psychotherapies

Broadly speaking, **psychotherapy is treatment designed to make changes by psychological rather than physical means, using persuasion, reassurance, and support.** It is principally thought of as the interaction between a trained therapist and an individual suffering a psychological difficulty. Most psychotherapy is done by psychiatrists; clinical psychologists; clinical or psychiatric social workers; pastoral, marital, abuse, and school counselors; and psychiatric nurses. *(See ● Table 1.)*

There are many types of psychotherapy, seven of which we describe here. It's important to point out that half of all therapists say they are eclectic. **Eclectic means they use a combination of methods and approaches.**[71] The seven best known types of psychotherapy are as follows:

- **Psychoanalysis:** Pioneered by Sigmund Freud, psychoanalysis was the first of the talking therapies. In **psychoanalysis, treatment focuses on the patient's unconscious motives and thoughts, releasing previously repressed thoughts** to give the patient self-insight. This method made famous the use of the psychoanalytic couch, where the patient lies down and the psychoanalyst sits out of view.

   Because its goal is a major reorganization of personality, psychoanalysis can require two or three sessions a week for several years.

- **Person-centered therapy:** Growing out of theories developed by Carl Rogers, **person-centered—or client-centered—therapy has the therapist focus on the patient's own conscious self-insights.** Self-insights are valued more than the therapist's interpretations. Therapists do not guide or offer judgments but mainly listen, like a loving parent. They restate the client's verbalizations and acknowledge the feelings being expressed.

- **Gestalt therapy: Gestalt therapy aims to help patients become aware of and express their feelings and take responsibility for their feelings and actions.** It combines the emphasis of psychoanalysis on becoming aware of unconscious feelings

● **Table 1   Different types of therapists.**
Some therapists adjust their fees to a sliding
scale, depending on the patient's income.

Type of therapist	Description
Psychiatrist	M.D. (medical doctor) degree required. Physician specializing in treating psychological disorders. Only therapist able to prescribe medications. Most expensive hourly rate.
Clinical psychologist or counseling psychologist	Ph.D. (doctor of philosophy) degree. Trained in therapy, testing, or research. Generally next highest hourly rate.
Psychoanalyst	M.D. or Ph.D. degree. Therapist trained in psychoanalytic (Freudian) methods. Hourly rate similar to preceding.
Psychiatric social worker	M.A., M.S., or M.S.W. (Master of Arts, Science, or Social Work) degree. Trained in individual and group therapy; may specialize in family therapy. Usually affordable hourly rate.
Other therapists	Other counselors include: (1) abuse counselors, (2) alcohol and drug counselors, (3) marriage and family counselors, (4) registered nurses, and (5) pastoral counselors. Hourly rates vary.

with the person-centered emphasis on immediate experience and current behavior. Besides concentrating on spoken language, therapists also focus on **body language— the gestures and expressions patients make with their bodies.**

• ***Rational-emotive therapy: Rational-emotive therapy* concentrates on the thoughts and beliefs that lead to people's emotions. It tries to replace *irrational* thoughts and beliefs with rational ones.** The theory is called "rational-emotive" because it assumes that thoughts, or rationality, lead to emotions. Rational-emotive therapists believe that people are governed by self-defeating ideas about "oughts" and "shoulds." The purpose of the therapist, they suggest, is to reveal the "absurdity" of these ideas.

• ***Cognitive therapy:* Practitioners of *cognitive therapy* use gentle questioning to help people discover their irrationalities for themselves.** This approach differs from that of rational-emotive therapists, who try to tell patients what to think. To improve people's well-being, cognitive therapists encourage their patients to find evidence that supports positive beliefs and refutes negative beliefs.

• ***Transactional analysis: Transactional analysis (TA)* is a form of therapy concerned with how people communicate, or "transact," with one another.** TA theory assumes we have three sides to our personality: instinctive childlike, rational adultlike, and judgmental parentlike. A transaction is considered problematic if you are communicating with someone at different levels (for example, your child to their parent). The purpose of therapy is to teach patients to be aware of how they are communicating with others.

• ***Brief therapy:*** Patients in brief therapy go for a much shorter time than those in other therapies. **In *brief therapy* the patient and therapist make a contract about length of treatment (generally 2–6 months) and problems to concentrate on.**

Group Therapy   Like individual therapy, ***group therapy*—therapy given to a group of people at the same time—aims to provide self-understanding and behavior change.** Most of the individual psychotherapies we described are also practiced within therapist-led groups of 8–10 people. Such methods have the advantage of being less expensive than individual therapeautic sessions. They also show people they are not alone in the problems they have.

Variants on group therapy are the following:

- ***Couples therapy:* In *couples therapy,* also known as *marital therapy,* the treatment focuses on the relationship problems between couples.** Couples may range from married heterosexuals to homosexuals to any other pair of people.

- ***Family therapy: Family therapy* expands the treatment of couples therapy to include members of one family.** Often the problems that bring the family to the attention of the therapist are those of one individual. However, family therapists proceed on the assumption that those problems may stem from problems of interaction within the family.

- ***Self-help and support groups:*** A therapist may organize a group whose members all suffer from a similar problem (such as alcohol abuse). However, **a *self-help group* is organized around a similar problem but is not led by a therapist.** Such tasks as those of chair, secretary, and treasurer are generally rotated among the members. Fees are far less than those for conventional group therapy (perhaps only a dollar). Members are available to each other for help in ways that a professional therapist may not be after office hours.

Nonverbal Therapies

Nonverbal therapies include behavioral therapies, hypnosis, and medical therapies. Behavior modification and aversion therapy are behavioral therapies. Medical therapies include drug therapies, electroconvulsive therapy, and psychosurgery.

Some psychological treatments rely on methods other than talk to try to help solve patients' emotional problems. Three general categories of nonverbal therapies are *behavioral therapies, hypnosis,* and *medical therapies.*

Behavioral Therapies Unlike the talking therapies, behavior therapies assume that psychological problems do not necessarily diminish with self-awareness. Instead of treating psychological distress by finding underlying problems, ***behavior therapy* holds that because negative behavior is learned, it can be unlearned.** The behavior therapies work best for achieving very specific purposes, such as conquering phobias and quitting behaviors such as smoking. We already mentioned desensitization. Two other types of behavioral therapies are:

- ***Behavioral modification:* In *behavior modification,* rewards are given for desirable behaviors, and the rewards are withheld for undesirable behaviors.** Behavior modification is a five-step process: (1) Specify your target behavior, the behavior you want to change, such as smoking cigarettes. (2) Gather baseline data describing your present behavior, such as how many cigarettes you smoke and under what conditions. (3) Design your program. (4) Execute and evaluate your program. (5) Bring your program to an end.

- ***Aversion therapy:*** Systematic desensitization attempts to substitute a positive reaction instead of a negative one. That is, a patient is taught to be relaxed instead of fearful around a harmless object such as dogs. In aversion therapy, the reverse is true. ***Aversion therapy* substitutes a negative response for a positive response to an undesirable behavior** such as smoking. For example, someone who is trying to quit smoking may be instructed to smoke under very unpleasant conditions. In a small room, the smoker is surrounded by overflowing ash trays and perhaps given mild electric shocks upon lifting a cigarette. The idea, of course, is to create an aversion to the particular habit.

Hypnosis ***Hypnosis* is a condition of heightened suggestibility that enables the subject to experience imaginary happenings as if they were real.** Hypnotists put their subject into a "trance." First, the hypnotist asks the subject to concentrate on a spot on the wall or a moving object. Then the hypnotist talks the subject into a hypnotic state ("Your eyelids are growing heavy . . .").

Although hypnosis does not work for everyone, it has had some success in reinforcing people's resolve to change certain habits. These include losing weight, stopping nail biting, giving up tobacco or alcohol, or becoming more sexually responsive.[72, 73] The device for doing this is the posthypnotic suggestion. **Through a *posthypnotic suggestion,* the hypnotist suggests to the subject something the subject will do after coming out of hypnosis.**

Medical Therapies Sometimes talking and behavior therapies aren't enough. The only hope is to alter the brain's functioning through direct medical intervention, therapies requiring the supervision of a medical doctor. These are some medical therapies:

- *Drug therapies:* Examples of mental disorders sometimes treated with drugs are *anxiety, depression,* and *schizophrenia.* For anxiety, Valium and Librium are among the most heavily prescribed drugs in the world. For bipolar disorder, lithium levels out the mood swings. Drugs such as chlorpromazine and haloperidol can arrest the deterioration of behavior in schizophrenics.

- *Electroconvulsive therapy:* Sometimes called "electroshock therapy" or "shock treatment," *electroconvulsive therapy (ECT)* **consists of administering a brief electrical shock to a patient's brain. The shock induces a convulsion similar to epilepsy.** Despite its horror movie reputation, ECT has been successful for treatment of severe depression that has not responded to drug therapy.

- *Psychosurgery:* The medical intervention of last resort, *psychosurgery* **attempts to change behavior through the surgical removal or destruction of brain tissue.**

Strategy for Living: Developing Resilience

Learning not just to endure but to prevail in life means developing qualities of resilience.

A task of all human beings is to learn to endure. However, the real challenge is not just to endure but to *prevail.* Prevailing means you are able to go forward despite pain, uncertainty, and limitations and to overcome the obstacles.

To prevail requires *resilience*—the ability to bounce back from life's travails. **Resilience is your ability to cope with disruptive, stressful, or challenging events so that you gain additional protective and coping skills.**[74]

Resilient people share six qualities.[75, 76] (1) They are *committed*—they understand and pursue their goals and values. (2) They are *challenged*—they take charge of and even seek out and solve problem situations. (3) They maintain a *sense of humor.* (4) They make *sensible lifestyle choices,* in diet, exercise, and relaxation. (5) They are guided by *principles* of the great religions of the world, such as the Golden Rule, even if they don't go to church. (6) They gain emotional *support* from being with others.

How can you develop these qualities of resilience? Consider this statement: *Feelings can't be controlled, behavior can be.* This statement reflects part of a Japanese philosophy known as Morita, or Constructive Living, a "lifeway" or practical strategy for dealing with difficulties. Constructive Living is based on three action-oriented principles: (1) Accept your feelings. (2) Know your purpose. (3) Do what needs to be done.[77, 78] In other words, do what needs to be done regardless of how you're feeling. After all, if we only did what we felt like doing, we'd never get anything done. Or, as the Nike slogan suggests: *Just do it!*

800-HELP

Crisis Line. 800-866-9600. Available 24 hours. Provides counseling on suicide, pregnancy, substance abuse, domestic violence, child abuse, sexual abuse, and other crisis situations. Also provides local referrals.

National Domestic Violence Hotline. 800-333-SAFE. (For hearing impaired: 800/873-6363.) Available 24 hours. National organization of shelters and support services for battered women and their children.

National Mental Health Association. 800-969-6642. (In Virginia, 703-643-7722.) Gives information on depression, schizophrenia, and other psychological disorders. Provides local referrals.

Suggestions for Further Reading

American Health editors, with Daniel Goleman and Tara Bennett-Goleman (1986). *The relaxed body book*. New York: Doubleday.

Girdano, Daniel A., & Everly, George S., Jr. (1986). *Controlling stress and tension*. Englewood Cliffs, NJ: Prentice-Hall.

Martorano, J. T., & Kildahl, J. P. (1989). *Beyond negative thinking*. New York: Insight Books. A New York psychiatrist and a psychotherapist describe cognitive therapy's techniques for changing negative thoughts to fight depression.

Seligman, Martin E. P. (1990). *Learned optimism*. New York: Knopf. Discusses using cognitive therapy to replace a pessimistic outlook with an optimistic one.

Selye, Hans (1976). *Stress in health and disease*. Reading, MA: Butterworths.

Tavris, Carol (1982). *Anger: The misunderstood emotion*. New York: Touchstone.

Zimbardo, Philip (1977). *Shyness: What it is; What to do about it*. Reading, MA: Addison-Wesley.

Eating Right: Nutrition and Weight Management

CHAPTER

3

Don't eat this. Don't drink that.

Do more of this, do less of that.

We are beset by conflicting messages influencing how and what we eat. Some of these messages are unhealthy, such as the dazzling advertising campaigns urging us to greater consumption of wonderful-taste, awful-nutrient foods. Some of the messages seem healthy, such as the advice of recognized scientists and health experts. The trouble is, however, *their* advice is often contradictory. What, then, are we to believe?

Despite nutritional controversies and conflicting research findings, a great deal of agreement exists about many aspects of nutritional health. Although knowledge about nutrition is continually evolving, there *is* a consensus of nutritional advice. This advice is based on two things: (1) studies of *available data,* and (2) the *probabilities* suggested by that data.

Although the data we have now suggests certain conclusions, other data may surface later to change those conclusions. Moreover, the present knowledge allows us only to suggest probabilities: certain health and lifestyle habits *probably* will produce well-being and longevity. However, there can be no guarantees.

Right Eating for Right Living

▶ Define food and identify three major categories of food.

▶ Explain the meaning of essential nutrients.

▶ Name the six essential nutrients for body growth and maintenance.

▶ Explain the types of carbohydrates, protein, and fat; their uses; their best sources; and the amount of energy that each generates. Discuss some of the controversies about sugar, sugar substitutes, fiber, protein, vegetarianism, and the health consequences of high-fat diets.

▶ Explain the different types of vitamins and minerals, their uses, sources, and controversies about megadoses, vitamin C, and sodium, and the importance of calcium, iron, and fluoride.

▶ Describe the uses and sources of water and controversies about tap water versus bottled water and water substitutes.

▶ Discuss how to read food labels; controversies over additives, irradiation, and explain processed versus "organic" food; and the Food Guide Pyramid.

▶ Discuss guidelines for healthful eating.

erhaps, like 1 out of 5 Americans, you know you could improve the way you eat but feel it's just too much work and sacrifice.[1] However, since eating is something you will do all your life, you might as well become good at it. Eating right will not extend your life beyond what your heredity has determined. But it can help you live a healthier, more active life.

What Food Is: Nutrients and Other Substances

Food consists of six essential nutrients for the body's growth and maintenance: carbohydrates, proteins, fats (lipids), vitamins, minerals, and water. Energy-yielding nutrients, measured in Calories, are carbohydrates, proteins, and fats. In addition, food consists of nonnutrients, microorganisms, additives, and other chemicals.

Our bodies are constantly changing. Many parts of them must be renewed, and the only way to do that is by eating food. ***Food*** **is the material—solid, liquid, or both—you take into the body that provides the** ***nutrients*** **you need to stay alive.** Besides nutrients, food contains other substances, including nonnutrients, microorganisms, and contaminants. Processed foods may also include additives, such as colors or nutrients. Some of these other substances give the food flavor, odor, and texture. Some are good and some are bad, and some are simply of no benefit to human beings but also of no harm.

Let us describe food according to three principal categories: *essential nutrients, energy-yielding nutrients,* and *other food substances.*

The Essential Nutrients ***Nutrients*** **are the substances obtained from food that the body uses to provide energy and promote its maintenance, growth, and repair.** Some nutrients are called *essential nutrients.* In nutrition, ***essential*** **means a substance that the body requires for energy, growth, and maintenance but cannot make in sufficient amounts.** Thus, ***essential nutrients*** **are those chemicals your body needs for growth, maintenance, and repair and which it must obtain from food.**

Research suggests that the number of essential nutrients you need to survive is 46. These 46 essential nutrients, none produced by the body, fall into six categories: *carbohydrates, proteins, fats* (or *lipids*), *vitamins, minerals,* and *water. (See ● Figure 1.)*

Any single mouthful of food will contain something from at least one of the major categories. We describe each of the essential nutrients in this chapter.

Energy-Yielding Nutrients and Calories
Three of the six categories of essential nutrients are energy-yielding nutrients. ***Energy-yielding*** ***nutrients*—carbohydrates, proteins, and fats—produce energy when they are used (oxidized or burned) by the body for movement, heat, or growth.** They may also be stored in the body for later use. As stated on every food label, fat provides the largest number of Calories per gram (9 Calories) compared to carbohydrates (4) and protein (4).

Energy **is the capacity to do work.** The cells in our bodies can survive only with a fairly constant and adequate supply of energy. The energy potential of food is measured in units of heat called *Calories:*

- *Calorie (kilocalorie): A Calorie is a measure of the heat potential of food.* (Actually, a Calorie with a capital C is called a *kilocalorie,* abbreviated *kcalorie.*) Technically a Calorie is the amount of heat required to raise the temperature of 1 kilogram of water 1 degree Celsius.

- *calorie:* The word *calorie* (no capital C) is one-thousandth of a Calorie (kilocalorie).

The word *Calorie* is, of course, one of the major themes in contemporary food advertising ("Low in calories!"). Most adults in the United States and Canada consume between 1500 and 3000 Calories a day. How many Calories you need depends on your age, gender, size, activity level, and metabolism. If you are 19–24 and engage in moderate activity, you will require about 3000 Calories if male, 2100 Calories if female.

Other Food Substances Some of the substances found in food include nonnutrients, microorganisms, additives, and environmental toxins:

- *Nonnutrients: Nonnutrients are not required by the body for its growth, maintenance, and repair, but some of them may serve other healthful purposes.* An example is *fiber,* found in plant foods. One type of fiber serves the purpose of helping digestion and elimination, but it is not in itself required by the body. Other examples of nonnutrients are naturally occurring chemicals that provide the color, odor, and flavor of food.

- *Microorganisms: Microorganisms are molds, fungi, and bacteria.* These occur naturally if a food is stored under conditions that encourage them. Some of these microorganisms are desirable; indeed, we would not have yogurt, cheese, or wine without them. Others are undesirable, such as salmonella, which causes food poisoning, and botulism, which is lethal.

- *Additives: Additives are various chemicals that may be added during food production to change color, enhance flavor,*

Categories of essential nutrients	Major food sources
1. Carbohydrates	Cereals, fruits, milk, some vegetables
2. Proteins	Meats, fish, legumes, nuts, eggs, dairy products, cereals
3. Fats (lipids)	Fats, oils, meats, fish, dairy products, some seeds & nuts
4. Vitamins	Variety of foods
5. Minerals	Variety of foods
6. Water	Liquids and water-containing solid foods

● **Figure 1 The essential nutrients.**

or extend storage life. One of the oldest known additives is salt, frequently used as a preservative.

- *Environmental toxins:* As a result of careless human intervention in nature, high levels of *environmental toxins, or certain contaminants,* have crept into some foods. Examples are mercury in fish, lead in water, and antibiotics in farm animals.

Carbohydrates: Energy Providers

Carbohydrates provide energy, help elimination, and help fat turn into energy. Derived mostly from plants, carbohydrates are either simple (sugars) or complex (starches and fibers). Half our daily energy should come from carbohydrates, preferably the complex type. Sugar has few benefits, fiber has many.

The principal nutritional function of carbohydrates is simple: to provide energy. Indeed, carbohydrates usually satisfy half of a person's energy needs.

The Types of Carbohydrates: Simple and Complex The class of nutrients known as **carbohydrates are of two types: simple carbohydrates and complex carbohydrates.** *(See* ● *Figure 2.)*

- *Simple carbohydrates: Simple carbohydrates* **provide the body with short-term energy and consist mainly of sugars.** They are found primarily in fruits, maple sugar, honey, corn syrup, and molasses. Simple carbohydrates include two kinds of sugars—*monosaccharides* (single sugars, such as glucose) and *dissacharides* (double sugars, such as sucrose, lactose, and maltose). The monosaccharide **glucose is your body's main energy source.** If you don't get glucose from carbohydrates, your body will have to start using fat and protein to make the glucose.

- *Complex carbohydrates:* **The *complex carbohydrates* provide the body with sustained (rather than short-term) energy and primarily include starches and fibers.** Complex carbohydrates are found mainly in fruits, grains, and in the seeds, roots, stems, and leaves of vegetables.

Types of carbohydrates	Common food sources
SIMPLE CARBOHYDRATES	
Monosaccharides (single sugars)	
Glucose (dextrose)	Fruits, honey, molasses, maple sugar, traces in most plant foods
Fructose 	Honey, fruits, berries, corn syrup, traces in most plant foods
Galactose	Found mainly as lactose (milk sugar)
Disaccharides (double sugars)	
Sucrose	Table sugar, fruits, maple sugar
Lactose 	Milk and other dairy products
Maltose	Sprouted seeds; produced in digestion of starch
COMPLEX CARBOHYDRATES (POLYSACCHARIDES)	
Starches and dextrins	Starchy plants, grains
Glycogen 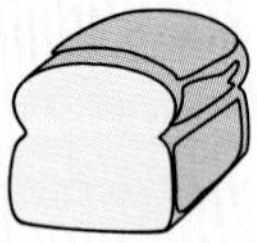	Liver (in very small amounts)
Fiber	
Cellulose	Wheat bran, part of plant-cell walls, whole-grain products
Hemicellulose	Part of plant-cell walls
Pectins and gums	Fruits, oat bran, legumes

● **Figure 2   Carbohydrates.** Foods containing carbohydrates.

Complex carbohydrates are *polysaccharides*—large molecules made of hundreds of monosaccharides linked together—which include starches and dextrins, glycogen, and cellulose. *Starch* is found in cereals and other plant goods. *Glycogen* is found only in animal tissues, such as oysters or liver, and provides glucose for cells. *Cellulose* is a source of *fiber* and is found in the walls and skins of plants, the peels of fruits, and the outer layer of whole grains.

The Uses of Carbohydrates Carbohydrates have several functions in the body. (1) Sugars and starches (though not fiber) are major sources of energy. (2) Fiber stimulates movement of the gastrointestinal tract and aids in elimination. (3) Some carbohydrates turn fat into energy.

Controversy: How Bad Is Sugar? Today Americans eat about 128 pounds of sugar per person per year—more than three times as much as a century ago.[2] More than 70% of this is sucrose—table sugar—found in processed foods of all kinds.

The major problem with sugar is that it leads to tooth decay. Sticky-sweet foods that adhere to tooth enamel make teeth a target for mouth-dwelling bacteria.[3] As these bacteria metabolize sugars in the mouth, they produce acids that gradually destroy tooth enamel. Eventually these lesions become **cavities or dental caries—that is, pockets of tooth decay.**

It is not true, however, that too much sugar leads to "sugar blues"—low blood sugar (hypoglycemia). Nor does it lead to diabetes, hyperactivity, or criminal behavior.

Controversy: Are Sugar Substitutes Safe? In the last two decades, an array of artificial sweeteners has come on the market and made sweeping changes in food products. Many of these are called *high-intensity sweeteners,* because their sweetness is so much more intense than natural sugars. For example, *aspartame (Nutrasweet)* is 300 times sweeter than sucrose, and *saccharin* is 500 times sweeter.

But are such artificial sweeteners safe? The answer would seem to be "yes." Saccharin has been tentatively linked to bladder cancer in laboratory rats. However, it has been found by the

Food and Drug Administration (FDA) to be safe for use in a variety of foods. Questions have been raised about whether aspartame (Nutrasweet) poses health risks, such as headaches or seizures.[4] However, the present evidence suggests it is safe. (The exception is for individuals suffering from *phenylketonuria.*)

Controversy: The Fervor Over Fiber You can survive without fiber in your diet. However, recently it has been argued that the lack of "roughage" in the diet contributes to gastrointestinal disorders common in North America and Europe. This has not been proven, but claims about fiber consumption are as follows:[5]

- *Fiber diminishes the risk of colon cancer:* Because dietary fiber holds water, it may help the contents of the intestine move along faster. Thus, cancer-causing substances spend less time in the colon.

- *Fiber diminishes diverticulosis: Diverticulosis* **is a condition in which the intestinal wall develops outpouchings called diverticula.** Fiber may exercise the muscles of the intestinal tract so these pockets are less likely to develop.

- *Fiber reduces constipation and hemorrhoids: Constipation* **is a condition of hard, dry, and sometimes painful bowel movements.** *Hemorrhoids* **are swollen veins in the rectum and anal area** similar to varicose veins. They are often caused by pressure resulting from constipation, heavy lifting, obesity, prolonged sitting or standing, or pregnancy. Fiber attracts water into the digestive tract, thereby softening stools and easing pressure on the bowel.

- *Fiber helps to keep weight down:* Foods containing dietary fiber are low in fat. Yet their bulking effect in the stomach helps ease hunger and gives a sense of fullness. These factors aid weight-loss efforts.

But does fiber lower cholesterol? Can it prevent gallstones? Does it help to manage diabetes? Unfortunately, we do not yet know the full impact of fiber on these health matters.

Strategy for Living: Getting the Right Kind of Carbohydrates For people in the United States and Canada, the problem is not so much getting the right amount of carbohydrates as getting the right *kind*. Most of us tend to eat too much sugar and sweeteners and not enough grain products, fruits, and vegetables. A recommended diet would have at least half its Calories in carbohydrates, and more starch and fiber and less sugar than most diets. *(See ● Figure 3.)*

Protein: Of Prime Importance?

Protein is important to the structure of the body. It helps growth and maintenance, regulates body processes, helps build important compounds, and provides a source of energy. Protein consists of amino acids—9 are essential and derived from the diet; 11 are nonessential and are made by the body. Most people get too much protein or too little of the right kind. Too much protein can lead to increased body fat, obesity, calcium loss, and dehydration.

Think of all those ads showing steak on the barbecue, chicken fresh from the oven, a roast on the dining table. Consider how many meals are planned with large portions of meat, fish, or fowl—in a word, *protein*—as the central dish.

In the United States, about two-thirds of the protein we eat comes from meat (including poultry and fish) and dairy products. Yet there are acceptable alternatives, such as pasta and beans. *(See ● Figure 4.)* Unfortunately, many meats and dairy products are also high in fat. Ground beef, for instance, may be more than 20% fat.

The Types of Proteins: Essential and Nonessential Amino Acids **Proteins are thousands of different combinations of amino acids. *Amino acids* are building blocks found in all living things.**

Amino acids are of two types, nine essential and eleven nonessential.

- ***Essential:*** The nine ***essential amino acids*** **are indispensable to life and growth and must come from the diet.** In general, you need to consume foods that provide the *nitrogen* your body needs to synthesize its own amino acids.

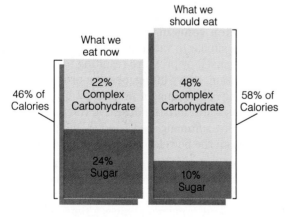

● **Figure 3** **How much carbohydrate should we eat?** We are advised to increase our intake of complex carbohydrates—starch and fiber—and decrease the amount of simple carbohydrates such as sugar.

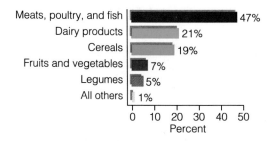

Meats, poultry, and fish — 47%
Dairy products — 21%
Cereals — 19%
Fruits and vegetables — 7%
Legumes — 5%
All others — 1%

● **Figure 4   Sources of protein in the
United States.** Most Americans get their
protein from meats and dairy products—
both sources often high in fat.

- *Nonessential:* The eleven **nonessential
amino acids are the ones the body can
manufacture itself**—assuming you are
eating an adequate diet in general.

The Uses of Protein Protein has some important purposes, as follows: (1) Protein gives the
body structure and assists in growth and maintenance. (2) Protein affects and regulates several body processes. Specifically, it helps provide
enzymes and hormones. **Enzymes are cata-
lysts that help speed up chemical reactions
in cells. Hormones are substances produced in one part of the body that affect
processes in another part.** (3) Protein helps
the body manufacture important compounds.
Among these are **hemoglobin, which carries
both oxygen and carbon dioxide in the
blood.** Other compounds are substances that
are responsible for blood clotting and that transport nutrients into tissues. (4) Protein provides
a backup source of energy. The body first uses
carbohydrates and fat for energy, but if these
sources are lacking (as during starvation) it
then uses protein.

**Controversy: What's So Bad About Too
Much Protein?** The average American consumes more than twice the recommended
amount of protein. The health consequences of
this can be quite serious:

- *Extra protein leads to more body fat:*
If you take in more Calories of protein than
you need, you will convert the extra protein
to body fat.

- *Meat and dairy products can produce
high fat intake:* Protein-rich foods also
tend to be high-fat foods, which can lead to
problems with weight control and obesity.

- *Too much protein can produce a possible loss of calcium:* Some researchers believe that if your protein intake is double the
recommended levels, it can lead to calcium
loss. The result can be fragile bones (osteoporosis) in older adults.

- *High protein consumption can lead to
dehydration:* Protein requires about *seven
times* more water for metabolism than does
carbohydrate or fat. Thus, high-protein
weight-loss diets and high-protein athletic
programs—neither of which are recommended—stress that you must drink a lot of
water. If you don't, you may be in danger of
dehydration and consequent fluid imbalance.

Controversy: Vegetarian Diets Two billion
people in the world are vegetarians, 10 million of
them in the United States. Some avoid meat for
religious reasons, others because they abhor the
slaughter of animals. Still others are concerned
that a heavy meat diet raises dietary cholesterol
and saturated fat, two possible risk factors in
heart disease.

Vegetarians actually consume a range of
foods. Some people eat no meat (including fish
and poultry) but do eat eggs and dairy products.
Others eat dairy products but not eggs. Still others eat foods of plant origin only. The only truly
unsafe vegetarian diets are those of fruitarians
and macrobiotic vegetarians. *Fruitarians* eat
only fruits and nuts. *Macrobiotic vegetarians*
follow 10 dietary stages ending with a mostly
grain diet.

To obtain adequate nutrition, vegetarians
must observe two principles—*complementation* and *diversity.*

- *The principle of complementation:*
People who avoid all foods of animal origin,
including milk and milk products, can find
themselves short on certain amino acids.

They must plan carefully to eat complementary proteins together so the body has the right amino acids available together. The solution, then, is to apply the ***principle of complementation,* in which two or more of the right plant foods are eaten together to provide essential amino acids needed by the body.**

Complementary protein combinations generally involve *legumes plus grains* or *legumes plus nuts and/or seeds.* Combining corn (a grain) with beans (a legume), for example, will provide both methionine and the lysine. This is why a Latin American meal of corn tortillas and refried beans is a successful complementary protein combination. Some other popular combinations of complementary proteins are peanut butter on whole-wheat bread, macaroni and cheese, pizza, and rice and black-eyed peas.

- ***The principle of diversity:*** In order to avoid vitamin and mineral deficiencies, vegetarians need to follow a principle of *diversity* in eating. That is, they must be sure to eat a variety of foods.

Strategy for Living: Getting the Right Kind of Protein In general, the more Calories one takes in per day, the more protein. Most of us, however, don't need to take in more protein. Increased amounts of protein are needed only for certain people. Pregnant women need more protein to help the growth of the fetus. Lactating women need it to help manufacture milk for breastfeeding. Infants and children need extra protein to help them with bone and tissue growth. People recovering from malnutrition or injuries need more protein, whatever their age.

For the rest of us, what's important is not how much protein we eat but *what kind.* The finest quality sources of essential amino acids are foods of animal origin. However, as we discussed, a meatless diet need not be a deficient diet, if the principles of complementation and diversity are followed.

Fat: What Good Is It?

Fat provides energy, body protection, and essential fatty acids and carries vitamins A, D, E, and K. Fatty acids, the basic chemical units of fat, may be saturated (harmful in excess), monounsaturated (mostly beneficial), or polyunsaturated (both). How hard a fat is at room temperature tells you how saturated it is. The presence of fat in food is not always obvious. High levels of cholesterol, considered harmful, are found only in foods of animal origin.

Fat makes food taste good—makes it more palatable, flavorful, juicy. No wonder so many people prefer a hamburger that is 30% fat rather than the lean ground meat of 5–10% fat available in a supermarket. *(See Self Discovery 1.)* And no wonder the average American adult currently consumes about 34% of his or her total Calories from fat.[6] However, the national health objectives for the year 2000 recommend limiting fat to 30% or less of our total intake and saturated fat to less than 10%. Some experts suggest even less.[7]

Most of us know what fat is. Some obvious sources are butter, margarine, shortening, cheese, and salad dressings. Fat also comes from the "marbling" (white streaks) in meat such as steaks and from chicken and turkey skin, ice cream, and fried foods. *(See ● Figure 5.)*

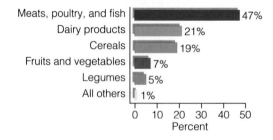

● **Figure 5 Sources of fat in the U.S. diet.** Contribution of different food groups to the fat content in the American diet.

Types of Fat: Saturated, Monounsaturated, Polyunsaturated What we commonly call "fat" may be divided into *fats* and *oils*. **Fats are solid, fatty substances at room temperature,** such as a cube of butter. **Oils are fats in liquid form,** such as corn oil. Both are called **lipids, the general term for fatty substances.** Some words pertaining to fat are splashed across food packages: "Low cholesterol!" "No saturated fats!" "High in *un*saturated fats!" Let us see what these phrases mean.

There are several types of lipids; however, here we are principally concerned with fatty acids. **Fatty acids are the basic chemical units of fat and are of two types—saturated and unsaturated.** *Unsaturated fats in turn are also of two kinds—monounsaturated and polyunsaturated. (See* ● *Figure 6.)*

- *Saturated fats:* **Saturated fats, considered harmful to health, generally come from foods of animal origin.** For example, saturated fats are in meat, milk, and cheese, but also in two oils: palm and coconut. Research shows that saturated fat elevates blood cholesterol, an indicator for high risk of heart disease in some people.

- *Monunsaturated fats:* **Monounsaturated fats, which are largely beneficial, come from foods of both animal and plant origin,** such as peanut butter and many margarines.

- *Polyunsaturated fats:* **Polyunsaturated fats, which may be good for hearts but have been implicated in breast cancer, come from vegetable oils and some fish.** Vegetable oils with polyunsaturated fats include safflower, soybean, and corn oils.

Two forms of beneficial polyunsaturated fats are omega-3 fatty acids and omega-6 fatty acids. **Omega-3 fatty acids may decrease the risk of heart and blood-vessel disease and cancer.** They are found in fish oils, Chinook salmon, and albacore. **Omega-6 fatty acids are important for growth.** They are found in plant oils such as corn and peanut oil.

SELF DISCOVERY 1

How Do You Score on Fat?

Do the foods you eat provide more fat than is good for you? Answer the questions below, then see how your diet stacks up.

How often do you eat:	Seldom or never	1–2 times a week	3–5 times a week	Almost daily
1. Fried, deep-fat fried, or breaded foods?	___	___	___	___
2. Meats such as bacon, sausage, luncheon meats, and heavily marbled steaks and roasts?	___	___	___	___
3. Whole milk, cheese, and ice cream?	___	___	___	___
4. Desserts such as pies, pastries, and cakes?	___	___	___	___
5. Cream sauces and gravies?	___	___	___	___
6. Oily salad dressings or mayonnaise?	___	___	___	___
7. Whipped cream, table cream, sour cream, and cream cheese?	___	___	___	___
8. Butter or margarine on vegetables, dinner rolls, and toast?	___	___	___	___

What the Results Mean

If you checked several responses under "3–5 times a week" or "Almost daily," you may have a high fat intake. It's time to cut back on foods high in fat, starting today.

Source: Adapted from *Home and Garden Bulletin,* no. 232–3 (April 1986), pp. 1, 8. Published by Human Nutrition Information Service, U.S. Department of Agriculture.

Recall that fatty acids are the basic chemical units in fats. Most (95%) of the fats and oils in our bodies and in our foods consist of *triglyc-erides,* **three fatty acids joined to a molecule of glycerol.** Research indicates that high triglyceride levels in a person's blood may be a warning of heart and blood-vessel disease, the number 1 cause of death in the United States.

Cholesterol Another kind of fat is the often-mentioned substance cholesterol. Let us clarify one point that confuses many people: the word *cholesterol* has two meanings.

- *Dietary cholesterol is found in food:* **Dietary cholesterol is a type of fat found principally in egg yolks and in organ meats** such as liver. It is not found in foods of plant origin, such as fruits and vegetables.

- *Blood cholesterol is produced by your body: Blood cholesterol,* **also called** *serum cholesterol,* **is a compound produced by our own bodies.** It is needed to form bile acids (which aid in the digestion and absorption of fats), and hormones (such as sex hormones). Cholesterol is also essential for cell membranes (which selectively allow the entry and exit of materials), and other body substances.

High blood cholesterol levels have been implicated in heart disease, as we will describe. It is important to note that *the most significant factor in food that affects blood cholesterol is not dietary cholesterol but total fat in the diet.*

Type of fat	Food source	Effect on heart	Effect on breast
Saturated fats	Meat Milk Cheese Butter Egg yolk Vegetable shortening Coconut and coconut oil	Bad 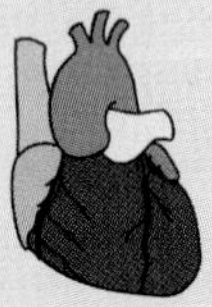	Bad
Unsaturated fats			
Monounsaturated fats	Peanut butter Peanuts and peanut oil Olives and olive oil Avocado Cashews Many margarines	Good	Good 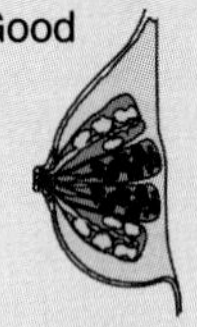
Polyunsaturated fats	Fish oils Corn oil Safflower oil Soybean oil Albacore tuna Chinook salmon	Good	Probably bad

● **Figure 6   Foods containing fat.** Saturated fats have been implicated in both heart disease and breast cancer, polyunsaturated fats in breast cancer but not heart disease.

The Uses of Fat Does fat do you any good? Surprisingly, considering its negative image, the answer is yes—at least in reasonable amounts. Fat does the following: (1) It provides energy—indeed, fat delivers twice as much energy as either carbohydrates or protein. (2) It protects your internal organs from shocks and bruises and insulates your body against extremes in outside temperature. (3) It provides essential fatty acids. (4) It provides a means of absorbing into the body vitamins A, D, E, and K (known as the fat-soluble vitamins). (5) It provides building materials for several important compounds, such as those that help blood clotting.

When carbohydrates, protein, and fat are consumed beyond body needs, they are stored as fat. This assures that we are able to provide our body with a constant supply of energy without having to eat constantly. However, if we are not physically active, the fat ends up being added to our waistlines, abdomens, or hips.

Controversy: Fat, Cholesterol, and Heart Disease Heart and blood-vessel disease kills more Americans than all other causes of death combined—about half of all deaths. A high-fat diet may be one of the principal risk factors for ***cardiovascular disease,* or impairment of the heart and blood vessels.** When the impairment is so severe that it interrupts the blood flow, it may cause either of two life-shattering events:

- *Heart attack:* **A *heart attack* occurs when interrupted blood flow to the heart muscle deprives the heart of oxygen and nutrients, killing the tissue.**

- *Stroke:* **A *stroke* is the interruption of blood to the brain, resulting in the death of brain tissue.**

Several factors can cause these events, including a blood clot, which obstructs the flow of blood through blood vessels. The blockage may occur because fatty material, cholesterol, and other matter collect on the inside of a blood vessel. It's not entirely clear what role fat and dietary cholesterol play in heart and blood-vessel disease. However, it is generally agreed that these substances in our diet need to be reduced.

Controversy: Fat and Cancer Studies of laboratory animals suggest that fat in the diet can raise the risk of certain cancers. These include cancers of the breast, colon, and prostate. The incidence of these cancers in Japan, which did not have a high-fat diet until recently, has been quite low. However, it rose among the children and grandchildren of Japanese immigrants who were exposed to the typical American diet. Also, cancer rates have risen in Japan since 1949, at the same time the Japanese have learned to like more American-style fatty foods.[8, 9]

Can we say, then, that a Westernized, fat-heavy diet causes cancer? Not necessarily, for the Japanese are also heavy smokers. Yet the United States and Canada show correlations between consumption of fat and cancer deaths.[10] Still, cancer rates in other countries have been similar to U.S. rates despite differing levels of fat consumption. So the link between cancer and diet remains controversial.

Controversy: Do Fish Oils Reduce Heart Disease? Greenland Eskimos have been found to have low rates of heart and blood-vessel disease *despite* a high-fat diet. Yet Eskimos also eat an average of ¾ pound of fish a day, compared to only 13 pounds a year for most Americans.[11] A closer look at the fish intake by Eskimos revealed that polyunsaturated fats called omega-3 fatty acids in the fish oil changed the blood's chemistry and reduced the risk of heart disease.[12] In the United States, a 20-year study of 852 middle-aged men also found less heart disease among fish-eaters. The group of men who ate an ounce of fish a day had half the rate of heart disease of men who ate little or no fish.[13]

How do fish oils accomplish this? Research shows that apparently they alter the relationship between "bad" and "good" cholesterol (called lipoproteins). That is, they lower the "bad" cholesterol (low-density lipoproteins), which blocks arteries, and possibly raise the "good" cholesterol (high-density lipoproteins), which reduces such blockages. Certain fish oils also produce substances that make the blood less likely to clump together and form clots. They also reduce triglycerides, which have been implicated in heart disease.[14]

Fish-oil supplements have become a popular item in health-food stores. However, it takes many pills, perhaps 15–20 a day, to get the effects the Eskimo studies have shown. The long-term effects of these pills are unknown.

Rather than taking such supplements, consider simply increasing the number of servings of fish in your weekly diet.[15]

Unfortunately, the presence of fats and oils in meat and other foods is not always obvious. If you really want to reduce the amount of fat in your diet, you need to know how to identify sources of invisible as well as visible fat:

- *Visible fats:* Visible fats are fairly easy to spot: they are almost anything greasy—butter, margarine, shortening, and cooking and salad oils.

- *Invisible fats:* Invisible fats are harder to identify, although nowadays people in North America get more fats from this source than from visible fats. The major sources of invisible fats are meat, poultry, fish, and dairy products.

Fat is frequently added during the preparation of food. If you often eat at restaurants, remember that many dishes use fat. Examples are fried foods, butter on baked potatoes, cream sauces, or anything deep-fried in batter. Order foods that are broiled or baked. Ask to have sauces and dressing served on the side. Ask questions if you are not sure about how a dish is prepared.

When shopping for food, read labels to help you identify products with fat added. When cooking, avoid fried foods and cream sauces. Also avoid using cooking oils; use nonstick pans or a spray instead. Remove the skin from chicken before cooking. Some dishes can be cooked ahead of time, chilled so that fat can be skimmed off the top, and then reheated in a microwave when ready to serve.

Vitamins: Mighty Micronutrients

There are 13 known vitamins, four of which are fat-soluble (A, D, E, and K) and nine of which are water-soluble nutrients (8 B-complex vitamins and C). Vitamins put major nutrients to use in the body, help growth, and maintain many body activities. To ensure adequate vitamin intake, eat a variety of foods. Megadosing can be wasteful or dangerous.

Vitamins are organic substances derived from animals and plants. Vitamins are *micronutrients*, **organic compounds that are essential in very small (trace) amounts every day and that do not supply energy.**

Although vitamins are derived from animals and plants, not all are usable by the body in the form they are received. The body has to convert some vitamins from *precursors*—**compounds that are not nutrients but from which a nutrient can be formed.** *Provitamin* **is the name given to vitamin precursors.** For example, a substance known as carotene is the provitamin for vitamin A.

Types of Vitamins: Fat Soluble and Water Soluble There are 13 vitamins, divided into those that are *fat soluble* and those that are *water soluble*. *(See • Figure 7.)*

- *The fat-soluble vitamins—A, D, E, and K: Soluble* **means a substance can be dissolved. The** *fat-soluble vitamins* **are vitamins A, D, E, and K, which are soluble (dissolvable) in fat.** Fat-soluble vitamins need not be consumed every day (unless your diet is unbalanced) because they are stored in your liver. Fat-soluble vitamins are found in fatty foods: meat, fish, dairy products, vegetable oils. In addition, certain precursors (called carotenoids) are in green and yellow vegetables.

- *The water-soluble vitamins—the eight B-complex vitamins and vitamin C:* The eight B or B-complex vitamins were so named because they were originally thought to be one vitamin. These vitamins now go principally by other names: *thiamin, riboflavin, niacin, pantothenic acid, folacin (folic acid), biotin,* and *vitamin B_6* and *vitamin B_{12}*. Vitamin C is the remaining water-soluble vitamin.

Water-soluble vitamins **do not need fat or bile to be absorbed by the body.** Moreover, the body has only small reserves of them—hence, such vitamins are more perishable. They are constantly disappearing from your body in urine and sweat. As a rule, then, you should take in these vitamins every day (for example, drink a glass of orange juice for vitamin C).

Fat-soluble vitamins
  Vitamin A
  Vitamin D
  Vitamin E
  Vitamin K

Water-soluble vitamins
  B-complex vitamins
    Thiamin
    Riboflavin
    Niacin
    Pantothenic acid
    Biotin
    Vitamin B_6
    Folacin
    Vitamin B_{12}
  Vitamin C

● **Figure 7   The vitamins.**

The Uses of Vitamins Vitamins perform many tasks. (1) They help nutrients release energy. (2) They promote growth of cells, bones, and teeth. (3) They help regulate body functions, such as blood clotting. (4) Some vitamins, such as vitamins A, C, E, and beta-carotene (called the *antioxidants*), have been strongly implicated in disease prevention.

Controversy: Is Vitamin C a Miracle Vitamin? **Vitamin C is also known as *ascorbic acid.*** Some people today have attributed special powers to vitamin C. It has been suggested, for instance, that taking high doses of vitamin C helps fight the common cold.[16] However, numerous studies have failed to demonstrate this.[17] Some people also take larges doses of vitamin C to try to relieve stress, allergies, arthritis, and diabetes and to reduce blood cholesterol levels. However, the vitamin does not seem to do any of these things. Some scientists think that vitamin C builds the body's defenses against cancer or that it prolongs the survival rate of cancer patients, but these claims are also unproven.[18–20]

Controversy: Should You Be Taking Vitamin Supplements? ***Vitamin supplements* are sold in the form of tablets, capsules, and even powders and liquids.** Water-soluble vitamins are also marketed as ***time-release supplements,* in which the vitamin is released slowly into the bloodstream**. Release occurs over a 6- or 12-hour period because water-soluble vitamins cannot be stored in the body long. Certain breakfast cereals are also classified as vitamin supplements because they are heavily fortified with vitamins.

In theory, healthy adults consuming the average requirement of 2000–3000 Calories of food a day should get all the vitamins they need. This should be particularly true in North America, where a variety of foods are available, including vitamin-fortified cereals and breads. Indeed, extreme vitamin deficiency in North America is rare. But some people have special nutritional needs or simply don't eat enough of the right foods. These include the elderly, pregnant or nursing mothers and their infants, and those in low-income families (particularly children). Cigarette smokers, alcoholics, and users of certain legal and illegal drugs also need special nutrition. For these people, vitamin supplements may be advisable.

What kind of supplements are important? Some studies suggest that vitamins A, C, E, and beta-carotene (the antioxidants) may inhibit damage to the body that relates to cancer and heart disease. However, the data are not conclusive.[21] Use of some other vitamin supplements have had some positive outcomes.[22] Niacin may decrease the risk of heart and blood-vessel disease. Vitamin B_6 may prevent a type of damage to nerves and tendons in the hands (carpal tunnel syndrome) characteristic of heavy computer users. Supplements of folic acid reduces the risk of certain birth defects (neural tube defects) when taken during pregnancy.

Controversy: Do Megadoses Work? As it turns out, a third or more of American adults are already regularly taking some vitamin supplement. This is the case even though most supplement users tend to be healthy people already.[23] Some people wonder, if vitamins are good, aren't more vitamins—megadoses—even better?

The term *megadose* **refers to a vitamin dose that is more than 10 times the recommended dietary allowance (RDA).** The problem with megadoses is that they are often either wasteful or dangerous:

- *Wasteful:* Megadoses of water-soluble vitamins (the Bs and C) are wasteful because they are simply flushed out rapidly by the body. Thus, they don't stay around long enough to provide long-term results, as fat-soluble vitamins do.

- *Dangerous:* Megadoses of fat-soluble vitamins (A, D, E, and K) are dangerous. Because they are stored in the body, they can build up to toxic levels. People who take exceptionally large doses of vitamins risk toxicity or unpleasant side effects.

Strategy for Living: The Best Sources of Vitamins The best way to get the amount and kinds of vitamins you need is to eat a *variety* of foods. You cannot rely on vitamin pills or vitamin-fortified foods (such as breakfast cereals) to make up for faulty nutrition. Recommended dietary allowances (RDA) and estimated safe and adequate dietary intake have been determined for the 13 vitamins. The Food and Nutrition Board of the National Academy of Sciences/National Research Council established these. *(See* ● *Table 1.)*

Minerals: The "Significant Seven" and the "Mighty Mites"

Minerals are inorganic substances classified as seven macrominerals and 14 microminerals. Macrominerals help maintain fluid balance in the cells and assist with the growth of bones and teeth. The macrominerals are calcium, phosphorus, sulfur, potassium, sodium, choloride, magnesium. Microminerals are essential components of enzymes and help the body handle oxygen. Microminerals are divided into trace elements (iron, zinc, copper) and ultratrace elements (all others). We tend to get too much sodium (salt), but many women do not get enough iron and calcium.

People often think of "vitamins and minerals" as if they were one nutrient group. There are, however, differences between the two. The basic distinction is that vitamins are *organic* compounds; they contain carbon. By contrast, **minerals are inorganic; they are chemical elements *other than* carbon, hydrogen, oxygen, and nitrogen.**

Types of Minerals: Macrominerals and Microminerals Minerals are classified as *macrominerals* and *microminerals,* organized according to the amounts needed by the body, from large to small. *(See* ● *Figure 8.)*

- *Macrominerals—the "significant seven":* **Macrominerals consist of seven elements: calcium, phosphorus, sulfur, potassium, sodium, chloride, and magnesium.** What is distinctive about these minerals is that they should be consumed in amounts *greater than 100 milligrams per day.*

Each day about half of all the minerals you take in should be calcium, and about a quarter should be phosphorus. The other 25% should be distributed among the several other minerals.

● **Table 1   Vitamins: What you need, where you get them**

Vitamin	Recommended Daily Allowance	Best Sources	Some Known Functions
Fat Soluble			
A	5000 IU*	Dairy products; liver; orange and deep green vegetables	Required for night vision, bone and tooth development
D	400 IU	Dairy products, egg yolk	Promotes absorption and use of calcium and phosphorus
E	30 IU	Vegetable oils and their products; nuts, seeds	Prevents cell membrane damage
K	Not established	Green vegetables; tea, meats	Aids blood clotting
Water Soluble			
Thiamin (B$_2$)	1.7 mg	Dairy products, meats, eggs, enriched grain products, green leafy vegetables	Used in energy metabolism
Riboflavin (B$_1$)	1.5 mg	Pork, legumes, pea-nuts, enriched or whole-grain products	Used in energy metabolism
Niacin	20 mg	Nuts, meats, and other proteins	Used in energy metabolism
B$_6$	2.0 mg	High protein foods in general, bananas, some vegetables	Used in amino acid metabolism
Folacin (folic acid)	0.4 mg	Green vegetables, orange juice, nuts, legumes, grain products	Used in DNA and RNA metabolism
B$_{12}$	0.6 mg	Animal products	Used in DNA and RNA metabolism; single carbon utilization
Pantothenic acid	4–7 mg	Widely distributed in foods	Used in energy metabolism
Biotin		Widely distributed in foods	Used in energy metabolism
C	60 mg	Fruits and vegetables, especially broccoli, cabbage, cantaloupe, cauliflower, citrus fruits, green pepper, strawberries	Maintains collagen; is an antioxidant; aids in detoxification; still under intense study

*IU = International Units. Less accurate than RE values; to be used only until food composition tables are converted to RE values.

Sources: Adapted from Christian, J. L., & Greger, J. L. (1991). *Nutrition for living* (3rd ed.). Redwood City, CA: Benjamin/Cummings; Hegarty, V. (1988). *Decisions in nutrition.* St. Louis: Times Mirror/Mosby; Whitney, E. N., & Hamilton, E. M. (1987). *Understanding nutrition* (4th ed.). St. Paul: West.

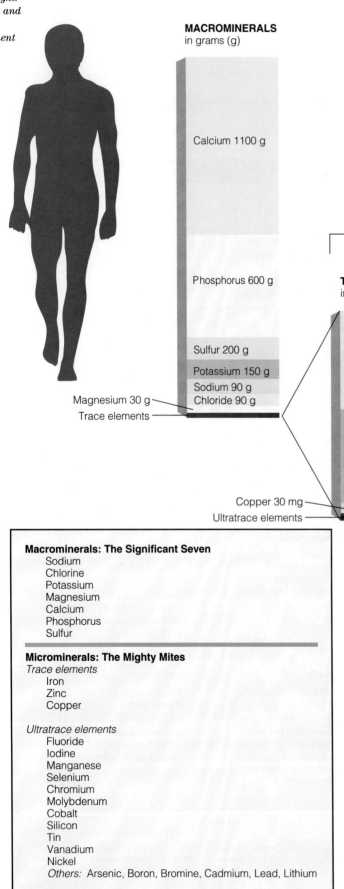

MACROMINERALS
in grams (g)

Calcium 1100 g

Phosphorus 600 g

Sulfur 200 g

Potassium 150 g

Sodium 90 g

Chloride 90 g

Magnesium 30 g

Trace elements

MICROMINERALS

Trace elements
in milligrams (mg)

Iron 2000 mg

Zinc 2000 mg

Copper 30 mg

Ultratrace elements

Ultratrace elements
in milligrams (mg)

Iodine 30 mg

Manganese 20 mg

Selenium 15 mg

Boron
Chromium
Molybdenum
Nickel
Silicon

Other minerals

Macrominerals: The Significant Seven
Sodium
Chlorine
Potassium
Magnesium
Calcium
Phosphorus
Sulfur

Microminerals: The Mighty Mites
Trace elements
Iron
Zinc
Copper

Ultratrace elements
Fluoride
Iodine
Manganese
Selenium
Chromium
Molybdenum
Cobalt
Silicon
Tin
Vanadium
Nickel
Others: Arsenic, Boron, Bromine, Cadmium, Lead, Lithium

● **Figure 8   Macrominerals and microminerals.** This is the approximate mineral composition of a 132-pound (60-kilogram) person. About 50% of a person's mineral composition is calcium and 25% is phosphorus. Values vary depending on bone mass and stores of minerals such as iron. Some ultratrace elements (boron, chromium, and so on) are present in such small amounts that good estimates are not available.

- ***Microminerals—"mighty mites":***
  Microminerals are minerals for which it is recommended you take in *less than 20 milligrams each day.* **Microminerals consist of about 14 minerals.** These include iron, zinc, and copper (called the *trace elements*) and iodine, manganese, selenium, and other microminerals (called the *ultratrace elements*).

The Uses of Minerals As you might suspect, even though some minerals are present in minuscule amounts, their presence is essential to health.

Among the tasks the seven *macrominerals* perform are the following: (1) Sodium, chloride, and potassium (called *electrolytes* when dissolved) help maintain fluid balance among the body's cells. (2) Calcium, phosphorus, and magnesium help build bones and teeth. (3) Sulfur helps form joint lubricants.

Among the tasks the 14 *microminerals* perform are these: (1) They assist enzymes in speeding up chemical reactions in cells. (2) They help the body use oxygen or protect it from oxygen damage. (3) They may serve in place of other minerals temporarily.

Controversy: Is Sodium Linked to Heart Disease? Sodium is important, but you don't need as much of it as people tend to consume. Next time you find yourself filling up on potato chips or beer nuts, you might want to remember the powerful craving that some people develop for salt (sodium). Reducing the amount of salt in the diet results in people having less and less a taste for it.[24]

The safe and adequate intake per day for adults is considered to be 1.1–3.3 grams (1100–3300 milligrams). To get an idea what this means, consider that just a teaspoon of salt provides 2 grams of sodium. Most Americans take in 6–18 grams a day—way too much. People in the United States and Canada get most of their sodium from **table salt, which is 40% sodium and 60% chloride.**

Although sodium is often restricted for people with hypertension, we now know that controlling blood pressure is more complicated than was previously thought. Some people are not salt sensitive at all. In addition, other minerals (chloride, potassium, calcium), hormones, and other factors also play a role in regulating blood pressure.

All About Iron Iron is the body's principal oxygen handler; one of its most important purposes is to transport and distribute oxygen to the cells. Nearly three-quarters of the iron in your body is in hemoglobin, the blood's second major component after water. **Hemoglobin is the blood protein that picks up oxygen inhaled into the lungs and transports it to the body's cells. It also transports carbon dioxide from the cells through the bloodstream to the lungs,** to be exhaled.

Too little iron can produce a type of anemia. **Anemia is a decreased ability of the blood to carry oxygen because levels of red blood cells or hemoglobin are low.** In people with iron-deficiency anemia, less oxygen is transported to the cells, and carbon dioxide is not removed as efficiently. The result is continual fatigue, lack of appetite, shortness of breath, and cold fingers and toes. People who complain of feeling "run down" may well be suffering from anemia. Iron-deficiency anemia is second only to obesity as the leading nutritional disorder in the United States.

The adult recommended daily intake for iron is 10 milligrams for men, 15 milligrams for women. The reason it is higher for women is that they lose iron from their bodies during menstruation and childbirth.

All About Calcium Calcium is the most abundant mineral in the body. About 99% of the calcium is in the bones and teeth. Bones are not like the wood of a dead tree; they are constantly in the process of building or renewal. Among children and adolescents, of course, bones must enlarge as the person grows. Even in adults the nutrients going to the bone must be continually replenished. Calcium and other minerals are brought in by the blood and crystallize around the connective framework of bone.

Many women do not get enough calcium, which puts them at risk for problems related to calcium deficiencies, including osteoporosis. **Osteoporosis is a condition of porous or brittle bones,** especially common among postmenopausal women. Beginning at age 30 or 40, many women (and some men) lose bone mass because of calcium deficiency. After a while skeletal strength declines, and the slightest impact can produce bone fractures. Many elderly women suffer hip fractures (150,000 a year in the United States alone) owing to osteoporosis.[25]

For adults, the recommended daily intake for calcium is 800 milligrams; for adolescents, it is 1200 milligrams. Today a man on the average consumes 1143 milligrams of calcium, but many women and adolescents have low intakes—a problem because maximum bone density is generally attained by age 20. Failure to "bank" calcium in bone may lead to osteoporosis. In general, pregnant and breast-feeding women have a higher need for calcium and may need to take calcium supplements.

Who Needs Fluoride? Tooth decay (dental caries) still affects many children and some adults. If community water systems do not contain the mineral fluoride (fluorine) for preventing tooth decay, fluoride tablets or other sources are useful. This is especially important during the years of primary and secondary tooth formation and growth. Brushing teeth with fluoride-containing toothpaste also helps.

Strategy for Living: The Best Sources of Minerals Many people are "at risk" for developing certain mineral deficiencies because of their low intakes over long periods. Infants and young children are at risk for not getting enough iron and zinc; so are women of childbearing years. Women in general are at risk for not getting enough calcium. People with low incomes may have calcium, iron, and zinc deficiencies. Getting too little zinc can lead to mental or physical retardation in children. The elderly may have some general mineral deficiencies, owing to past eating habits or physiological changes with age.

For other people, a diet that includes a variety of foods will probably include plenty of minerals. *(See ● Table 2.)* Sources for sodium, iron, and calcium are as follows:

- **Sodium:** Sodium occurs naturally in some foods and is added to many others during processing. So you rarely need to add any salt to your food. By and large, there is more sodium in meat than in vegetables and grains, though canned vegetables are an im-

portant exception. Fruits contain little or no sodium. Many nonprescription drugs also contain significant amounts of sodium.

- **Iron:** Dietary iron can be obtained from both animal and plant sources. The best animal sources are liver—pork liver is best, followed by calf, beef, and chicken liver. Other sources include fish, poultry, red meats, kidneys, and eggs. The best sources from plant foods are dried beans and peas; nuts; green, leafy vegetables; and enriched and whole-grain cereals. People who eat only nonmeat sources of iron should consume vitamin C (ascorbic acid) in the same meal to enhance iron absorption.

  It is difficult to get more than 6–7 milligrams of iron per 1000 Calories. Thus, people who routinely eat only 1200–1800 Calories a day—infants, children, and many premenopausal women—may find an iron supplement useful. Pregnant women are routinely advised to take an iron supplement.

- **Calcium:** The best dietary sources of calcium are lowfat or nonfat milk and milk products: yogurt, milk, cheddar cheese, ice cream, and cottage cheese. One cup of milk provides about 300 milligrams of calcium. Calcium may also be obtained from eggs, shrimp, sardines, canned salmon eaten with bones, clams, and oysters. Some dark green, leafy vegetables and citrus fruits are also calcium sources.

Water: The Life Fluid

Water acts as a transporter and lubricant and regulates body temperature. Water quality varies in many areas, but bottled water may be no better than tap water. Milk is superior to water in some ways, not in others. Soft drinks and coffee provide water but don't advance health. Fruit juices are the best substitute for water.

How much water does your body consume? Anywhere from a pint to 6 quarts daily, although the average is about 2½ to 3 quarts a day.[26]

● **Table 2   Minerals: What you need, where you get them**

Mineral	Recommended Daily Allowance	Best Sources	Some Known Functions
Major Minerals			
Calcium	800 mg	Milk, cheese, dark green vegetables, beans or peas	Aids in bone and tooth formation; blood clotting; nerve transmission
Phosphorus	800 mg	Milk, cheese, meat, poultry, whole grains	Bone and tooth formation; acid-base balance; part of enzymes
Magnesium	300–350 mg	Whole grains, green leafy vegetables	Part of enzymes; building bones
Iron	Males: 10 mg Females: 18 mg	Meats, eggs, beans, peas, whole grains, green leafy vegetables	Part of hemoglobin and enzymes
Iodine	150 mg	Marine fish and shellfish; dairy products; iodized salt; some breads	Part of thyroid hormones
Copper	2–3 mg*	Seafood, nuts, beans, peas, organ meats	Enzyme formation
Zinc	15 mg	Meats, seafood, whole grains	Enzyme formation

* Estimated safe and adequate daily dietary intake

Sources: Adapted from Christian, J. L., & Greger, J. L. (1991). *Nutrition for living* (3rd ed.). Redwood City, CA: Benjamin/Cummings; Hegarty, V. (1988). *Decisions in nutrition.* St. Louis: Times Mirror/Mosby; Brody, J. (1982). *Jane Brody's nutrition book.* New York: Bantam Books.

Sources and Losses of Body Water   Body fluids come from what you drink every day as well as the solid foods you eat. They also come from the body itself—from ***water of metabolism, which is produced during many chemical reactions in the body.*** Once water has been used by the body, it must be disposed of. Water disposal happens mainly in the urine, through the skin and lungs, and in the feces.

You can lose water almost without knowing it. On a 3½-hour plane flight, for instance, the dry air can cause you to lose up to 2 pounds of water. On a marathon run (about 26 miles), a person might lose 10–20 pounds of water. ***Dehydration—abnormal depletion of body fluids***—occurs when not enough water is taken in to make up for the amount lost. A loss of only 10% of the body's usual water intake can cause severe disorders; a loss of 20% may cause death.

The Uses of Water An adult female is 55% water, by weight; an adult male 60%. Water is in every part of one's body. This "life fluid" performs many functions. (1) It transports nutrients and wastes. (2) It lubricates eyeballs and joints. (3) It regulates body temperature by helping to dissipate heat from the body.

Controversy: Is Bottled Water Better Than Tap Water? Tap water quality varies in many areas. Since 1908, chlorine has been added to water supplies in the United States to kill disease-causing bacteria and viruses. As a result, cholera, typhoid, and dysentery, which have caused epidemics in the past, are rare diseases in the United States today. Nevertheless, contaminants do enter the water supply—whether from decay of vegetation or collection of chemicals from agricultural runoffs and industrial wastes.

Bottled water, many people believe, is healthier than tap water. However, a great deal of it is probably no better than your local tap water, and certainly more expensive. Most bottled water sold in the United States and Canada is not natural spring water but simply reprocessed from local community water supplies. Some bottled waters contain sodium, which may raise blood pressure in certain people and consequently the risk of heart disease.

Controversy: Can Other Beverages Replace Water? Water itself is no longer the biggest source of liquid for most of us. Is this a healthy development? Consider some of the replacements:

- **Soft drinks:** Today Americans drink more *soft drinks* than they do water. Most soft drinks contain Calories and no nutrients. During periods of physical growth, when people need all the nutrients they can get, soft drinks offer nothing. Moreover, because so many have artificial sweeteners and caffeine, they may negatively affect health. Finally, sweetened drinks don't really quench your thirst: indeed, they actually increase the body's need for water.

- **Caffeine drinks:** Coffee, tea, cocoa, and many cola drinks contain **caffeine, a mild stimulant** with a "pick-me-up" effect that keeps us awake and alert. However, caffeine is also a **diuretic, which means it causes you to actually *lose* fluids.** Thus, when you drink coffee, instead of replenishing your body fluids you may be further dehydrating yourself.

- **Milk:** There is no doubt that—with the exception of fruit and vegetable juices—milk is the most healthful alternative to water. Milk is high in protein and calcium, a good source of riboflavin and (when fortified) vitamins A and D.

  Despite milk industry slogans, not Every Body Needs Milk. After the age of 2, many of the peoples of the world—two-thirds, in fact—cannot digest the milk sugar lactose, a condition called *lactose intolerance*. Eighty percent of Asian and Middle Eastern peoples and 70% of African-Americans and American Jews, for instance, suffer great discomfort—gas, cramps, and diarrhea—if they consume much lactose.[27] This is because they do not have the enzyme necessary to digest it. A substance called *lactaid* can be used to enable people to benefit from calcium-rich food sources in their diet.

- **Fruit juices and fruit drinks:** Probably the best alternative to plain water is a fruit juice, which is apt to be low in sodium and high in potassium.[28] Oranges and other citrus fruits provide juices with high amounts of vitamin C. Tomato juice is a good source of vitamins A and C; moreover it contains only 35 Calories in a 6-ounce glass.

  You must be careful, however, to distinguish between a fruit *juice* and a fruit *drink*. Fruit drinks include fruit juices, but they usually are not as nutritious because they are diluted. Still, they do provide water—something many people have trouble getting enough of.

Strategy for Living: Getting the Right Kind of Fluids The thirst mechanism, it turns out, is not perfect. Sometimes it fails to cue a person to replenish needed water, particularly if one is sick or is performing strenuous physical activity. Indeed, following only your thirst instinct, you may replace only 60–70% of the water you lose.[29] Thus, it's recommended—particularly if you are physically active—that you drink *beyond* the point of quenching thirst. Any excess water will simply be excreted from the body. In general, nutritionists recommend that you drink at least six (and preferably eight) 8-ounce glasses of liquid a day. An 8-ounce glass is equivalent to 1 cup.

If you are physically active you should drink fluids not only during and after workouts and competitions but also before. Exercise physiologists usually recommend water rather than sports beverages, such as Gatorade. The high concentration of sugar in many sports beverages can keep the fluid in the stomach rather than speeding it where it is needed.[30] If you use sports drinks, dilute them by adding an equal amount of water.

How to Read a Food Label

Food labels define serving size, the amount of Calories per serving, and Calories from fat per serving. Labels also express the Daily Value for particular nutrients and the Percent Daily Value that a serving contributes toward the daily need for that nutrient, based on a daily requirement of 2000 Calories. Food labels are particularly focused on total fat, saturated fat, cholesterol, sodium, total carbohydrate, dietary fiber, protein, and a few vitamins and minerals.

If you still have some older food packages in the back of a cupboard, it is an illuminating exercise to compare old and new food labels. The old label was often misleading and confusing. The new Nutrition Facts label, which went into effect May 1994, uses larger, boldface type to make numbers more revealing. The old label was designed to help Americans choose foods that would reduce their risk of getting vitamin deficiencies. The new label deals with today's major issues—fat, cholesterol, sugar, sodium, and fiber. *(See ● Figure 9.)*

The old label had a laundry list of 8–12 vitamins and minerals. Today's Nutrition Facts label focuses on vitamins A and C, sodium, calcium, and iron. Other vitamins and minerals have been omitted because they are found in many foods regularly consumed by Americans. In place of the vitamin panel are guidelines for consuming substances we are advised to minimize: fat,

cholesterol, sodium, and sugars. Also indicated are guidelines for more beneficial nutrients, such as carbohydrates, dietary fiber, and protein. Despite the improvements, the Nutrition Facts label still takes some getting used to. Let us explain how it works.

What Foods Are Covered Most packaged foods—including processed meat and poultry products—now require labeling, which was once not the case. Not covered are food sold in restaurants or cafeterias and genetically engineered and irradiated foods.

Serving Size In the past, food manufacturers would minimize the serving size in order to mislead consumers about the number of Calories or grams of fat contained in certain foods. With today's label the serving size is set by federal regulators to more closely reflect how much people actually eat. This serving size is also used to compute the number of servings per container.

Calories and Calories from Fat This line, which has "Calories" and "Calories from Fat," is crucial. The number at left indicates the amount of Calories (kilocalories) you will consume for each serving. The number at right indicates how many of these Calories come from fat. A serving of oat meal (without milk) and a serving of "artificially flavored" potato chips may each have 150 Calories. However, the serving of oat meal has 25 Calories, or only 17%, from fat. The serving of potato chips, on the other hand, has 90 Calories, or a hefty 60%, from fat. You should beware of any product in which fat Calories are more than a third.

Percent Daily Value The column heading *% Daily Value* applies to all the percent figures that fall below it. Although the term is not exactly self-evident, ***Percent Daily Value (or % Daily Value or %DV) states what percentage of a day's worth of a nutrient the item contains, based on a recommended diet.*** Daily Values replaced the old U.S. Recommended Daily Allowances (U.S. RDAs). **The *Daily Values (DVs)* set government recommendations for total fat, saturated fat, cholesterol, sodium, total carbohydrate, dietary fiber, protein, and some vitamins and minerals.**

① **Serving size:** Defined by Food and Drug Administration to more closely reflect how much people actually eat.
② **Calories:** Number of Calories (kilocalories) in a serving.
③ **Calories from fat:** Number of Calories from fat in a serving. Watch out for products in which fat Calories are more than a third.
④ **% Daily Value:** Daily Value replaces old U.S. Recommended Daily Allowances. % Daily Value shows percentage of a day's worth of particular nutrient, based on a diet of 2000 Calories a day.
⑤ **Saturated fat:** The % Daily Value of Saturated Fat shows percentage of artery-clogging saturated fat in a serving; compare grams (g) in serving with 20g below for recommended saturated fat for a 2000-Calorie daily diet.
⑥ **Cholesterol:** Shows amount and percentage of cholesterol in a serving. Plant foods don't have cholesterol.
⑦ **Sodium:** Some people's blood pressure is affected by sodium levels.
⑧ **Total Carbohydrate:** Fiber is considered beneficial. So far there is no Daily Value for sugars.
⑨ **Protein:** There's no recommended Daily Value for protein.
⑩ **Vitamins and Minerals:** A % Daily Value of 10% or more makes the food a good source for vitamin or mineral.
⑪ **Percent Daily Values Table:** Larger packages may carry this information, which includes Daily Values for these 6 nutrients based on 2000- and 2500-Calorie diets.

OATMEAL

POTATO CHIPS

Figure 9 Reading a food label. Two labels are compared—one for oatmeal (without milk), one for potato chips. Differences are especially marked for fat, sodium, and dietary fiber.

The *% Daily Value* heading on the food container contains an asterisk (*) that refers to a note lower down in the label. This note states: "Percent Daily Values are based on a 2000 calorie [Calorie] diet. Your daily values may be higher or lower depending on your calorie needs." This note is then followed by a table (on larger packages), which does not vary. This table expresses the Daily Values for six items, based on both 2000-Calorie and 2500-Calorie diets. (Recall that if you are 19–24 and engage in moderate activity, you will require about 3000 Calories a day if male and 2100 Calories if female. Most food labels assume the person is over age 4 and is not pregnant or breast-feeding.)

For example, health authorities hold that if you have a 2000-Calorie daily diet, you should have no more than 65g (grams) of total fat. If this is your diet, you can then look back up to the "Total Fat" line in the table to see how much a single serving of the particular food product will contribute toward the Daily Value, or daily recommended allowance. In the case of oatmeal, it might be 5g (grams), or only 5%. In the case of potato chips, it might be 10g, or 15%.

Of course, you may not need to consume 2000 Calories of food in a day, considered 100% DV on food labels. In that case, you need to adjust your Calorie count and use a calculator to compute the nutrient amounts for total fat, saturated fat, total carbohydrate, dietary fiber, and protein. (A 1600-Calorie diet is 20% smaller than the 2000-Calorie diet; a 2400-Calorie diet is 20% larger.)[31]

Controversy: Are Additives Safe? **A *food additive* is a substance that is added to food to enhance qualities such as taste, appearance, or freshness.** For instance, chemicals may be added during food production to change color, to enhance flavor, or to ensure longer storage life. Additives are reviewed by the Food and Drug Administration to make sure they are safe. Nevertheless, people worry about the effects of some additives.

Hot dogs and other cured meats, for example, are made with sodium nitrite. This is an important additive, for which there is presently no useful substitute. Sodium nitrite has caused controversy because it converts in the human body to nitrosamines—and nitrosamines cause cancer in laboratory animals. Yet sodium nitrite

preserves a hot dog's color (pink) and enhances its flavor (by slowing the rate at which it becomes rancid). It also protects against bacteria growth (especially the deadly toxin that produces *botulism,* a form of food poisoning).

Such tradeoffs are typical of certain food additives. However, with over 3000 different substances commonly added to food, it is difficult to make generalizations about these substances.

Controversy: Is Irradiation Safe? A newer processing method, ***irradiation* consists of exposing food to low doses of ionizing radiation, ultraviolet light, gamma rays, or high-energy electrons.** It does not make the food radioactive. However, there are some safety concerns about the process; irradiation in the United States is currently approved for only a few uses. These include killing insect eggs in wheat grain and flour and preventing insect growth on fruits and vegetables. It is also approved for sterilizing spices, herbs, and similar dehydrated foods. It can also be used to inhibit sprouting in grains and in root crops such as carrots, onions, and potatoes. All irradiated products must be labeled ("Treated with radiation" or "Treated by irradiation") and carry the international symbol for irradiated foods.

Controversy: Processed Food and Fast Food Versus "Natural" or "Organic" Food There are no legal definitions of "natural" or "organic" foods. Used on food labels, ***"natural food"* implies the food has been altered as little as possible from its farm-grown state. *Organic food* seems to mean that the food is produced without chemical fertilizers, pesticides, or additives.** Both terms also misleadingly suggest that the food has unusual power to promote health. Organic foods are often grown using "natural" fertilizers such as manure and compost, although the plant can't tell those from chemical fertilizers. Also, organic foods undergo less processing than usual (as in the case of whole-grain flours, for instance) and so have fewer additives. Whether this enhances nutritional value or increases safety isn't proved.

However, processed foods are not necessarily worse than "natural" food, and often may be better. **A *processed food* is food that has gone through a process in which it is**

cooked, mixed with additives, or altered in texture. For instance, during processing, nonfat milk is pasteurized (sterilized to destroy objectionable organisms) and fortified (enriched with vitamins and minerals), and loses Calories. But other foods are deprived of their nutritional advantages. Potato chips, for example, lose nutrients, gain fat and salt, and gain Calories during processing.

Fast foods **usually refer to the convenience foods available in drive-in or drive-through restaurants,** ranging from McDonald's to Pizza Hut. Fast foods are often high in Calories, fat, sugar, and salt, but they need not be. Pizza, for instance, provides a reasonably balanced meal, and many fast-food restaurants have salad bars and provide reduced-fat selections. Thus, you *can* eat reasonably healthily in fast-food restaurants by avoiding high-sugar, high-fat foods.

Probably a more useful distinction than that between natural and conventional grocery-store foods are those between *whole foods* and *partitioned foods*.[32] **Whole foods are unaltered from their farm-grown state.** *Partitioned foods* **are composed of only** *parts* **of the plant and animal tissues we need to eat to obtain nutrients.** They are foods that have been altered from their farm-grown state and packed in boxes, bags, bottles, or cans. An apple is a whole food; a jar of apple juice or apple jelly (whether labeled "natural" or not) is partitioned. In general, it is better to choose whole foods than partitioned foods, regardless of any promotion labels such as "natural" or "organic."

The Basic Food Groups and the Food Guide Pyramid

There are five basic food groups: (1) breads and cereals; (2) fruits and vegetables; (3) milk, yogurt, and cheese; (4) meat, poultry, fish, and eggs; and (5) fats, oils, and sweets. These are shown in the Food Guide Pyramid.

Nutritionists in the United States and Canada base their recommendations on five principal food groups:

- Bread, cereal, rice, and pasta group
- Fruit and vegetable group
- Milk, yogurt, and cheese group
- Mealt, poultry, fish, dry beans, eggs, and nuts group
- Fats, oils, and sweets group

These five food groups are shown in the Food Guide Pyramid. *(See ● Figure 10.)* This pyramid emphasizes the importance of some categories over others, based on government nutrition guidelines developed over a decade. At the top of the pyramid is the least important group: fats, oils, and sweets. The pyramid gives more space and emphasis at the bottom to bread, cereal, rice, and pasta.

1. Bread, Cereal, Rice, and Pasta Group—6 or More Servings Daily This group includes breads, cereals, and pasta. Enriched and whole-grain breads and cereals are sources of protein, B vitamins, and iron.

The U.S. Department of Agriculture (USDA) offers the following recommendations.

- Eat breads, but avoid spreads, such as butter and jams, that are high in fat and sugar.
- Eat breakfast cereals, but add little or no sugar. Try raisins, grapes, or bananas instead.
- Eat rice and pasta, but watch out for sauces (especially cream sauces), which tend to be heavy in fats and sugars.

2. Fruit and Vegetable Group—2–4 Servings Fruit and 3–5 Servings Vegetables Daily Besides being low in fat and high in fiber, fruits and vegetables are important sources of vitamins A and C. They also contain many minerals, including iron, calcium, and magnesium.

USDA suggestions are as follows.

- Eat any fruits you like—except avocados and olives, because they are high fat. Don't add sugar or whipped cream to fruits.
- Eat any vegetables, except those that are fried. Go easy on butter, margarine, and other sauces or toppings that are high in fat.

3. Milk, Yogurt, and Cheese Group—2–3 Servings Daily This group includes milk, cheese, yogurt, and ice cream and contributes protein, calcium, riboflavin, and vitamins A, B_6, and B_{12}.

Some suggestions:

- Drink nonfat or low-fat milk. Eat low-fat cheeses.
- Eat low-fat, plain yogurt.

4. Meat, Poultry, Fish, Dry Beans, Eggs, and Nuts Group—2–3 Servings Daily This group includes more than just beef, veal, lamb, pork, fish, shellfish, chicken, turkey, and eggs. It also includes all kinds of beans: dry beans, dry peas, soybeans, as well as lentils, seeds, nuts, and peanuts. These foods are good sources of protein, vitamin B_6, and such minerals as iron, zinc, and phosphorus.

You need to be cautious about consuming too much in the way of meat and eggs. Suggestions:

- Eat only the lean parts of meat. Eat poultry only without the skin. Fish is preferable to either meat or poultry.
- Avoid fried or breaded meat dishes. Meat is best broiled, roasted, or simmered. Choose lower grade meats because they contain less fat. Use a portion size no larger than a deck of cards.
- Substitute good alternatives to meat, such as dried beans, dried peas, and tofu.
- Eat eggs sparingly.

5. Fats, Oils, and Sweets—Use Sparingly This group also includes alcohol. Watch out for the foods in this group. They provide Calories, which add weight but very little else. Suggestions:

- Eat fresh fruit as an alternate to sweet snacks and desserts.
- Eat baked products made with less fat and sugar, such as angel food cake.

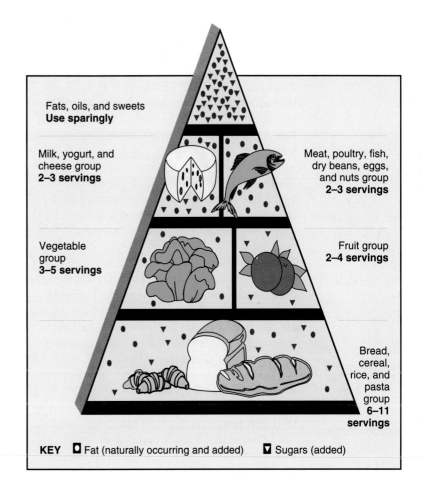

Fats, oils, and sweets
Use sparingly

Milk, yogurt, and cheese group
2–3 servings

Meat, poultry, fish, dry beans, eggs, and nuts group
2–3 servings

Vegetable group
3–5 servings

Fruit group
2–4 servings

Bread, cereal, rice, and pasta group
6–11 servings

KEY ☐ Fat (naturally occurring and added)   ▽ Sugars (added)

● **Figure 10   The Food Guide Pyramid.** The pyramid emphasizes the importance of making fruits, vegetables, and grains the basis of the diet.

Strategy for Living: What the Experts Say About Eating

Experts suggest we eat a variety of foods, including more vegetables and fruits. They recommend consuming less fat, sugar, salt, and alcohol and maintaining desirable weight.

Eating right—whether it's a defensive diet to avoid illness or a power diet to improve performance—comes down to a handful of rules. Here they are, as taken from numerous reports:[33–37]

1. Eat a Variety of Foods Following the daily servings in the Food Guide Pyramid will provide the essential nutrients you need, including all vitamins and minerals. It will also reduce sugar and fat in your diet. (These food components are thought to increase the risk of cancer and cardiovascular disease.)

2. Avoid Too Much Fat, Saturated Fat, and Dietary Cholesterol The point of this advice is to lower your exposure to the risk of heart and blood vessel disease and cancer. In general, it means eating less meat, whole-milk dairy products, and cooking oil and more lean poultry and fish.

3. Eat Foods with Adequate Starch and Fiber High-fiber foods may help prevent and alleviate constipation and certain intestinal disorders, such as diverticulosis (inflammation of the colon). Getting more fiber means eating more whole fruits and vegetables as well as pasta, rice, whole-wheat products, and the like.

4. Avoid Too Much Sugar and Salt (Sodium) Sugar provides energy but not many nutrients other than carbohydrate. Moderate sugar intake with meals is all right. However, most of it should come not from high-sugar foods such as candy but from "natural sugar" sources, such as fruits. Too much salt may raise blood pressure in certain sodium-sensitive people (there is presently no way of telling who they are). High blood pressure is an indicator of potential heart disease. Taste your food before you salt it, since it may already be salty enough; also try using pepper or herbs for seasoning.

Since 75% of sodium intake is from processed and canned foods, buy low-sodium versions of these products.

5. Drink Alcohol in Moderation, If at All How moderate is "moderate"? The current thinking is: probably 1–2 drinks a day, depending on gender. Heavy drinkers may suffer from nutritional deficiencies, since alcohol has no nutritional value. They also run the risk of certain cancers (especially if they smoke) and other serious diseases, such as cirrhosis of the liver. Alcohol use increases women's risk of breast cancer. In addition, pregnant women should avoid all alcohol.

6. Avoid Excess Vitamin or Mineral Supplements, but Watch Calcium, Iron, and Folic Acid Intake Be wary of vitamin and mineral supplements that exceed government Daily Values and other supplements (such as protein powders, single amino acids, fiber, and lecithin). These "not only have no known health benefits for the population," says *Diet and Health*, "but their use may be detrimental to health. The desirable way for the general public to obtain recommended levels of nutrients is by eating a variety of foods."[38] Women, however, should increase their calcium intake, to avoid the bone-weakening disorder osteoporosis. Children, adolescents, and women of childbearing age should eat foods that are good sources of iron. Women of childbearing age should also ensure an adequate folic acid intake.

7. Maintain Desirable Weight In this context, "desirable" means "appropriate for your height and build." In the United States, more people need to lose weight than to gain it. It is important to maintain appropriate body weight by balancing food intake and physical activity. Excess weight is associated with increased risk of several chronic disorders, among them high blood pressure and heart and blood-vessel disease. Other risks include gallbladder disease and types of bone and joint arthritis.[39]

Weight Management

- ▶ Identify appropriate criterion for assessing body weight.

- ▶ Name the percentage of body fat appropriate for males and females and describe at least four ways to determine body fat.

- ▶ Explain the concept of energy balance.

- ▶ Distinguish between overweight and obesity. Discuss the possible causes of obesity and describe treatments for various forms of obesity.

- ▶ Describe the symptoms and treatments of the eating disorders anorexia and bulimia.

- ▶ Discuss the pros and cons of various kinds of weight-loss diets.

- ▶ Describe a healthful strategy for losing weight and reducing body fat that involves behavioral change.

Standards of attractiveness change over time, particularly for women. A generation ago, reports writer Naomi Wolf in *The Beauty Myth*, models weighed 8% less than the average American woman. Today they weigh 23% less. Put another way, the average model—and dancer and actress—is thinner than 95% of women.[40] What effect does that have on our feelings about our own attractiveness? According to one study, 75% of women aged 12–23 are dissatisfied with their weight, 50% with their shape.[41]

How Much Weight and Fat Is Desirable?

New guidelines replace "cosmetically desirable" weight with "healthy weight" standards. Various techniques are available for determining body fat percentage. The concept of energy balance is that either the amount of energy consumed in food equals energy used or weight increases or decreases.

If you're like most people, you think you're less than perfectly attractive. Indeed, even handsome people feel they are flawed. There are a great many other areas of sensitivity—baldness, eyeglasses, teeth—that bear on the matter of body image. However, it is very clear that *size and weight* are considered important—indeed, almost overriding—issues for many people. A 1990 Gallup survey revealed that *half* of all Americans, particularly women, view themselves as overweight. Yet only about a quarter of males and females are actually considered so.[42]

How you feel about your body can influence your eating and exercise habits, particularly in adolescence but probably throughout your life. No doubt about it, for both men and women, the pursuit of a beautiful body rather than good health is what drives the powerful $33-billion-a-year diet industry.[43] Ironically, however, even with 1 out of 4 Americans now dieting, the nation continues to gain weight. Before we consider how you can achieve your optimum weight, let's consider how much you *should* weigh.

The New Ideal: Healthy, Not Cosmetic Weight From the standpoint of attractiveness, there is probably some elusive—and often-changing—cultural ideal of how much a person should weigh. Probably the closest codification of what was considered "cosmetically desirable" have been the Metropolitan Life Insurance Company tables. *(See ● Table 3.)* These tables were supposed to roughly predict people's insurability by relating their weight to their height and frame size (small, medium, large).

In November 1990, however, the U.S. Food and Drug Administration and the Health and Human Services Department came out with new guidelines. *(See ● Table 4.)* Unlike the Metropolitan Life tables, these new "healthy weight" guidelines combine both sexes into one table. Higher weights generally apply to men and lower weights to women. They also allow for weight gain as one grows older.

Body Composition: Measures of Fat Percentage Number of pounds isn't the only critical number. More important is the *percentage of body fat,* which should be in the range of 15–19% for men and 22–26% for women. You'll

● **Table 3   1983 Metropolitan Life Insurance Company height and weight tables.** Weights and heights are without clothes or shoes. Weight ranges are based on lowest mortality for people ages 25–29.

Men						Women			
Height		Small Frame	Medium Frame	Large Frame	Height		Small Frame	Medium Frame	Large Frame
Feet	Inches				Feet	Inches			
5	2	128–134	131–141	138–150	4	10	102–111	109–121	118–131
5	3	130–136	133–143	140–153	4	11	103–113	111–123	120–134
5	4	132–138	135–145	142–156	5	0	104–115	113–126	122–137
5	5	134–140	137–148	144–160	5	1	106–118	115–129	125–140
5	6	136–142	139–151	146–164	5	2	108–121	118–132	128–143
5	7	138–145	142–154	149–168	5	3	111–124	121–135	131–147
5	8	140–148	145–157	152–172	5	4	114–127	124–138	134–151
5	9	142–151	148–160	155–176	5	5	117–130	127–141	137–155
5	10	144–154	151–163	158–180	5	6	120–133	130–144	140–159
5	11	146–157	154–166	161–184	5	7	123–136	133–147	143–163
6	0	149–160	157–170	164–188	5	8	126–139	136–150	146–167
6	1	152–164	160–174	168–192	5	9	129–142	139–153	149–170
6	2	155–168	164–178	172–197	5	10	132–145	142–156	152–173
6	3	158–172	167–182	176–202	5	11	135–148	145–159	155–176
6	4	162–176	171–187	181–207	6	0	138–151	148–162	158–179

Source: Reproduced with permission of Metropolitan Life Insurance Company. Source of basic data: *1979 Build Study*, Society of Actuaries and Association of Life Insurance Medical Directors of America, 1980.

note from this that women are, in fact, *supposed* to have more fat than men. This is because women naturally store fat in the hips and abdomen for extra energy needs during pregnancy and breast-feeding.

There are a number of ways of determining your fat percentage. For instance, physicians and fitness experts use the **body-density test, or underwater weighing, to distinguish dense muscle from buoyant fat.** Another test is the *fatfold test*, **or skinfold test, using a pincer-like instrument called** *skin calipers* **to measure the percentage of body fat.**

Two tests that you can do yourself are as follows:

- *Pinch test:* In the **pinch test, you simply pinch the loose skin on the underside of your upper arm** between thumb and forefinger. If you can pinch more than an inch of skin, you have too much body fat. The pinch is the least accurate means of assessing body fat.

- *Girth test:* The *girth test* was developed by exercise physiologist Jack Wilmore of the University of Texas at Austin. Men measure their waist circumference and women their hip circumference to arrive, via Wilmore's tables, at their percentage of body fat. A tape measure is required to perform this test. *(See Self Discovery 2.)*

● **Table 4   1990 Guidelines for suggested weight.** Weights and heights are without clothes or shoes. Higher weights generally apply to men, lower to women. These guidelines allow for weight gain as you grow older.

Height	19–34 Years	35 Years and Over
5'0"	97–128	108–138
5'1"	101–132	111–143
5'2"	104–137	115–148
5'3"	107–141	119–152
5'4"	111–146	122–157
5'5"	114–150	126–162
5'6"	118–155	130–167
5'7"	121–160	134–172
5'8"	125–161	138–178
5'9"	129–169	142–183
5'10"	132–174	146–188
5'11"	136–179	151–194
6'0"	140–184	155–199
6'1"	144–189	159–205
6'2"	148–195	164–210
6'3"	152–200	168–216
6'4"	156–205	173–222

Source: U.S. Food and Drug Administration and U.S. Department of Health and Human Services. Reprinted in: Anonymous (1991). Great bodies come in many shapes. *University of California, Berkeley Wellness Letter, 7,* 1–2.

SELF DISCOVERY 2

The Girth Test: What Is Your Percentage of Body Fat?

This self-evaluation requires a tape measure.

Directions for Men

Measure your waist at your navel, keeping the tape level. In the chart below, draw a straight line from your "Body Weight" (left) to your "Waist Girth" (right). At the point where it crosses the "Percent fat" line, read your body-fat percentage. You are fit if the figure is between 12 and 17.

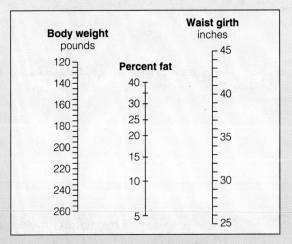

Directions for Women

Measure your hips at the widest point, keeping the tape level. In the chart below, draw a straight line from your "Hip girth" (left) to your height (right). At the point where it crosses the "Percent fat" line, read your body-fat percentage. You are fit if the figure is between 19 and 24.

Source: Adapted from Wilmore, J. H. (1986). *Sensible fitness* (2nd Ed.). Champaign, IL: Leisure Press.

● **Table 5 How many Calories do you need?**

Category	Age	Light Activity	Moderate Activity	Heavy Activity
Children	4–6		1800	
	7–10		2000	
Males	11–14		2500	
	15–18		3000	3600
	19–24	2700	3000	4000
	25–50	3000	3200	
	50+		2300	
Females	11–18		2200	
	19–24	2000	2100	2600
	25–50	2200	2300	2800
	51+		1900	

Pregnant women: Add 300 Calories during second, third trimesters. Breast-feeding women: Add 500 Calories.
Source: *FDA Consumer.*

The Concept of Energy Balance How many Calories you need depends on your sex, age, frame, percentage of body fat, and level of activity. *(See* ● *Table 5.)* Two examples of U.S. recommendations for 20-year-olds are as follows:

- *For women:* Say you are 5 feet 4 inches tall, weigh about 120 pounds, and generally engage in only light activity. You would need 1700–2500 Calories a day to maintain your weight.

- *For men:* If you are 5 feet 10 inches tall, weigh 154 pounds, and engage in only light activity, you need 2500–3300 Calories daily.

It is interesting to compute how many Calories a day you *consume* in food and compare it to the Calories you *expend.* **If the Calories expended are the same as those consumed, you have what is called *energy balance.*** If the Calories you eat are not expended in activity, you will gain weight. If you don't consume enough Calories for the energy you expend, you will lose weight.

Actually, energy expenditure is principally affected by two factors—physical activity and metabolism.

- *Voluntary physical activity:* About one-third of the energy you expend daily is in voluntary physical activity, mostly using your muscles. You may be writing a paper (little energy expenditure) or lifting barbells (great energy expenditure).

- *Metabolic processes:* About two-thirds of the energy you expend each day is devoted to metabolic processes, the basic work of your body's cells. **The *basal metabolic rate* refers to the energy spent to sustain your life when you are in a resting position.**

To compute your *energy consumption,* keep a "food diary" for a week or two. Do this during a period when your activities are typical for your life style. Record *all* food and beverages consumed and the amounts. With the help of "calorie counter" books or nutrition texts, you can then determine the Calories consumed. Computing your daily *energy expenditure* is a little easier, because you can use formulas to approximate your basal metabolic rate and your voluntary physical activity. *(See Self Discovery 3.)*

The Heavy, the Overweight, the Obese

Being overweight (10% over normal weight) is not unhealthy, but obesity is. Obesity is a condition of being 20% or more over normal body weight. Among the theories of obesity are fat-cell, setpoint, and external cue, but lack of activity is certainly a contributor.

Can you be simply "heavy" rather than overweight? The new weight tables shown in Table 4, representing the United States' official nutrition policy, allow for a certain amount of overweight. The exception is for people with hypertension, diabetes, or other weight-aggravated health problems. Even health officials, however, don't agree at what point healthy weight becomes unhealthy overweight.

SELF DISCOVERY 3

Evaluating Your Calorie Needs

The following is a method of roughly estimating caloric needs for healthy, nonpregnant adults 18–50 years old.

A. Calculate your ideal body weight.

Height: _____ feet _____ inches

Women: Allow 100 pounds for first 5 feet of height
           plus 5 pounds for each additional inch

Men: Allow 106 pounds for first 5 feet of height
           plus 6 pounds for each additional inch

Example:
Woman 5′2″

_____	100
+ _____	+ 10
Ideal body weight _____	110

Man 5′7″

_____	106
_____	+ 42
Ideal body weight _____	148

B. Classify yourself by lifestyle and activity level.

Sedentary _____   Active _____   Very active _____

C. Determine your energy needs.

Multiply your ideal body weight by your activity level:

Sedentary = 13   Active = 15   Very active = 17

_____ × _____ = _____ Calories/day
(Ideal body weight)   (Activity level)

D. Adjust for weight gain or weight loss.

_____ − 500   = _____ To LOSE 1 pound a week
(Calories from section C)

_____ + 500   = _____ To GAIN 1 pound a week

E. DAILY CALORIC GOAL = _____ Calories

Source: Zaret, B. L., Moser, M., Cohen, L. S., & Subak-Sharpe, G. J. (Eds.) (1992). *Yale University School of Medicine heart book.* New York: Hearst Books, p. 58.

Weight, Obesity, and Health In general, health professionals define underweight, overweight, and obesity in relation to the Metropolitan Life tables we showed in Table 3:

- *Underweight:* **If people are 10% below the Metropolitan Life table values, they are** *underweight.*
- *Overweight:* **If people are 10% above the table values, they are** *overweight.*
- *Obese:* **If they are 20% above the tables, they are** *obese.*

Being a few pounds overweight or having moderate body fat seems to pose no real threat to long-term health.[44] Obesity, however, is a devastating risk factor. The dangers include not only back and knee problems and hernias but a whole host of other troubles.[45–47] Obesity seems to contribute to or aggravate high blood pressure and heart and blood-vessel problems. It is also linked to liver disorders, gallbladder disease, arthritis, respiratory problems, diabetes, and surgical complications. Obesity also appears to be related to certain types of cancer. These are cancer of the breast, uterus, and cervix for women, and of the colon, rectum, and prostate for men. In addition, there are dangers that derive from misguided kinds of diets. The bottom line, then, is that the obese tend to die at a younger age. In addition, the obese experience social and psychological problems as a result of rejection or their own lack of self-esteem. *(See* ● *Figure 11.)*

With all these hazards, one might think obesity is an uncommon occurrence. We need only look around us to see that it is not. In the United States, *15%* of adolescents are obese and, astonishingly, *26%* of adults are also obese—about 1 out of 4 Americans.[48]

Some Possible Causes of Obesity Is obesity caused by circumstances inside the body, outside the body, or both? Actually, there are probably many causes, and there may also be different types of obesity. Besides genetic predisposition or endocrine system disorders, some possible explanations are the following.

- ***The fat-cell theory:*** Studies show that obese people have more fat cells than other people do.[49, 50] **The *fat-cell theory* suggests that overfeeding in early childhood increases the numbers of fat cells.** The number of fat cells becomes fixed and these cells then cause the person to be abnormally hungry as an adult. The theory has been disputed, because it is hard to determine numbers of fat cells. Even so, once people become obese, they have a tendency to remain so.

- ***The setpoint theory:*** The *setpoint theory* assumes that the body instinctually "chooses" its weight range. The *setpoint* represents the body's natural point of stability in body weight.[51] According to this theory, everyone has a built-in control system that determines how much fat he or she should carry. This system may result from the body's metabolism compensating for increases or decreases in eating or physical activity. Setpoint theory may explain why people tend to get stuck at certain plateaus when losing weight.

● **Figure 11 The agony of obesity.**

❝*Social and economic disadvantages . . . plague the fat person. Obese people are less often sought after for marriage, pay higher insurance premiums, meet discrimination when applying for college admission and jobs, can't find attractive clothes so easily, and are limited in their choice of sports. For many, guilt, depression, withdrawal, and self-blame are inevitable psychological accompaniments to obesity.*❞

—Eleanor Noss Whitney & Eva May Nunnelley Hamilton (1987). *Understanding nutrition.* (4th ed.). St. Paul, MN: West, p. 253.

- **The external cue theory:** Some scientists theorize that eating is a response to *internal cues*—**hunger, the physiological need to eat, and** *appetite,* **the desire to eat.** By contrast, **the** *external cue theory* **holds that the body eats in response to external cues.** External cues include time of day (noon signifies lunch) or the presence of food (a chance offering of potato chips). The external cue theory suggests that food is its own reward. For example, obese people often show signs of "stress eating"—some try to alleviate anxiety by eating more.

- **Lack of activity:** No doubt some people are obese because they eat too much. But that's only half the story. As we saw from the concept of energy balance, the Calories expended are as important as the Calories consumed. Not being physically active enough may be *the* most important reason that 1 out of 4 adults in the United States is obese.[52]

  We describe exercise and activity at length in another chapter.

Treating Obesity Despite the bad news about obesity, the good news is that, for many people, it can be reversed. Indeed, when it is, the mortality risk for the formerly obese is no more than that for those who have never been obese.

The treatment for obesity depends on how mild or severe the obesity is.

- **For mild obesity:** *Mild obesity* is 20–40% above the ideal weight in the Metropolitan Life Insurance tables. *(Refer back to Table 3.)* This overweight can be treated by changing eating and exercise habits so you can *maintain* your desirable weight once it is achieved. Useful weight-reduction techniques emphasize behavior change and include support groups, such as Weight Watchers, Take Off Pounds Sensibly (TOPS), or Overeaters Anonymous.

- **For moderate obesity:** *Moderate obesity* is 41–100% above the weight in the Metropolitan Life tables. This weight problem can be treated in part as mild obesity is. Treatment also includes education in better nutrition, and counseling and support groups to

help practice assertiveness and raise self-esteem levels.

- **For severe obesity:** *Severe obesity* is weight 100% or more above the weight in the Metropolitan Life tables and that requires assistance by a health care professional. This condition is so threatening to health that it may require extraordinary measures. One radical solution is *bypass surgery,* which involves shortening the small intestine to reduce absorption. Another is *gastric stapling,* in which the stomach is stapled to make it smaller.

  We describe a course of weight loss in another few pages.

Eating Disorders: Anorexia and Bulimia

Eating disorders consist of anorexia, or self-starvation, and bulimia, or binge-eating and purging.

Eating disorders **involve hazardous food consumption behaviors.** In this section, we discuss two types of eating disorders: *anorexia nervosa* and *bulimia nervosa.* Many also suffer from a combination of these disorders called *bulimarexia.*

Anorexia Nervosa *Anorexia nervosa* **is self-starvation.** Anorexia involves self-imposed starvation that leads to potential problems with malnutrition and mortality rates of 15–21%— among the highest levels recorded for psychiatric disorders.[53]

Anorexia characteristically develops during the teen years or the 20s, although it is even being encountered among people in their 50s and 60s.[54] It most frequently affects women. The principal symptoms are the following: (1) Anorexics refuse to maintain normal body weight (they are often 15% below their minimal normal weight). (2) They have a fear of fatness or weight gain—even when they are *underweight.* (3) They have a distorted body image, so that they perceive themselves as fat even when they are emaciated. (4) Women show *amenorrhea,* **the abnormal absence or suppression of**

● **Figure 12   The bulimia cycle.** Bulimia is
a cycle of binge-eating and purging.

❝*The pain in my left side was so severe I
couldn't stand straight. I made my way to
the bathroom, pushed my finger down my
throat, and forced myself to vomit out the
enormous amount of food I had just
eaten—a box of sugared cereal, a half-gal-
lon of milk, a loaf of bread, a jar of peanut
butter, a dozen donuts, and a package of
Oreos.*

*When I finished vomiting, the pain in
my side was gone, but my throat burned,
my abdominal muscles ached, and I felt
hot, sweaty, smelly, dizzy, and exhausted. I
wanted to die, yet I still felt driven to eat
and vomit disgusting amounts of food
night after night.*❞

—Dianne-Jo Moore (1989, November/
December). I invented bulimia. *Medical Self Care*, p. 30.

menstruation, for at least three consecutive
monthly menstrual cycles. Women who are
anorexic are often perfectionistic, achievement-
oriented, model students and daughters. They
fear a loss of control in their lives and gain a
sense of control and achievement thorough their
weight-loss efforts.

Many anorexics develop eccentric behaviors
about food. They may eat only a narrow range of
foods, eat only alone, secretly throw food away,
and hoard small amounts of food to eat later.
They show an obsessive interest in food and
calorie-counting. Some anorexics exercise compulsively and force themselves to vomit (particularly after eating binges, when large amounts of
food are consumed in a short time). They may
also use ***laxatives,* drugs that act to loosen
the bowels,** or ***diuretics,* drugs that increase the elimination of body fluid via
urination.**

Clearly, an important goal of treatment is to
improve nutrition. Other therapies include psychotherapy and behavior therapy to control
food-consumption behavior. Some drug therapy
has been successful, including use of antidepressants and antipsychotic drugs.

Bulimia Nervosa ***Bulimia nervosa* consists
of episodes of binge eating alternating
with purging**—that is, self-induced vomiting or
use of laxatives or diuretics. *(See ● Figure 12.)*
Like anorexia, bulimia occurs mostly among
women in their teens and 20s, but it is also
found among females middle-aged and older. It
affects about 5% of males. Unlike anorexia,
those with bulimia appear to be normal weight
or slightly overweight.

The main symptoms are as follows: (1) Bulimics binge, or consume great amounts of food
in short periods of time—perhaps three to five
times the normal quantities of a meal. (2) They
feel a lack of control over their eating behavior.
"After a substantial dinner," writes one former
bulimic, "I'd drive to the grocery store and buy
all kinds of high-calorie junk foods. . . . The next
night, I'd shop at a different grocery store and
do the same thing. I'd often go to three or four
drive-in restaurants—Burger Kings and McDon-
alds—in one evening. . . ."[55] (3) They regularly
engage in self-induced vomiting, use of laxatives
or diuretics, strict dieting or fasting, or vigorous

exercise to prevent weight gain. Some bulimics build up a tolerance to laxatives and need larger quantities to achieve the same effect. Exercise addiction may be hard to detect as a component of an individual's problem because it is considered "healthy." (4) Bulimics engage in an average of two or more binge-eating episodes a week for at least 3 months. (5) They show depressive symptoms and express self-deprecation about their weight and their looks.

Behavior-modification techniques can help bulimics relearn eating patterns. Psychotherapy is particularly important, and a therapist experienced in treating eating disorders may be best. Some studies indicate that a significant proportion of those who have bulimia have been sexually abused.[56] Antidepressant drugs may help. Self-help groups, such as Overeaters Anonymous, are useful to help bulimics overcome their sense of isolation.

Diets: What's Wrong with Them?

Types of diets include fasting and partial fasting with the use of appetite suppressants or liquid supplements. Two other classes of weight-loss programs should be avoided—high-protein diets and food-combining diets. "Yo-yo" or repetitious dieting is especially harmful.

You've made up your mind that you want to be thinner. What's the best way to get to your desired weight level? Let's consider some principal kinds of dieting.

Fasting *Fasting,* **or semistarvation, consists of eating little or nothing** for a certain length of time. Unfortunately, it takes a long time to lose weight with this method, because the body's metabolism slows down to conserve energy. In addition, the fasting body may lose lean body mass—muscle—rather than use up all its fat for energy first. Moreover, it may produce heart-rhythm abnormalities that can be fatal. Finally, once your reducing program is over, your metabolism will remain slowed down, using up fewer Calories. So you may actually *gain* weight while eating *less.*

Modified Fasting: Appetite Suppressants Some appetite suppressants are available by prescription (mazindol, phentermine, diethylpropion). However, they are not very effective and can cause dizziness, palpitations, hypertension, nausea, insomnia, irritability, and other adverse side effects.[57]

Nonprescription appetite suppressants are considered safer, but they are not necessarily more effective. These include the following: (1) *Diet candies and gum* contain a local anesthetic that numbs the taste buds. (2) *Diuretics,* or "water pills," help you take off weight quickly. But because the lost weight is mainly water, the weight is gained back almost immediately. (3) *Fiber fillers* are agents containing fiber (methylcellulose, glucomannan) that may produce a feeling of fullness in the stomach. None of these help you with the behavioral changes needed to attain and sustain a desirable body weight level.

Modified Fasting: Liquid Supplements Liquid (or powder) low-calorie supplements include enough essential nutrients in 600 Calories to prevent the body from using muscle tissue for energy. These supplements may be useful for *medically supervised* diets for moderate or severe obesity, or even to get other weight-loss programs started. However, they can increase the risk of heart attack by altering one's fluid (electrolyte) balance or damaging the heart muscle.

Diets to Avoid There are so many diets that we cannot list them all here. However, since most new diets are simply variations on old diets, we can make a few general assertions.

- *Avoid low-carbohydrate, high-protein diets:* Dr. Atkins' Diet Revolution and the Complete Scarsdale Medical Diet are examples of low-carbohydrate, high-protein diets. Such diets seem to work fast because they cause one to rapidly lose water and hence weight—at least at first. In addition, the lack of carbohydrates makes food so unappetizing that people tend to eat less. Ultimately, however, surplus protein (amino acids) is stored as body fat.

- *Avoid food-combining diets:* Food-combining diets include the Fit for Life Diet and the Beverly Hills Diet. They claim that eating certain foods at certain times or in combination with other foods can produce weight loss. For instance, the Beverly Hills Diet has you eat meat and fruit at separate times during the day, and vary the fruits. There is no scientific basis for such diets.

The Dangers of Yo-Yo Dieting The thinness obsession has come to this: On any day, 50% of American women—half of them not overweight—and 25% of American men are dieting to lose weight.[58] A Gallup poll revealed that nearly a third of American women ages 19–39 diet *at least once a month.*[59] Meanwhile, many of the rest are *putting on* weight: up to 95% of dieters are unable to keep their weight off. **The unhealthy, ineffective cycle of weight loss and weight gain is called the yo-yo syndrome.** According to one study, repeated weight changes are linked to an increased death rate overall and to a doubled death rate from the chance of heart disease.[60] Moreover, yo-yo dieters tend to have more difficulty losing weight on subsequent tries. Finally, although such dieters may lose fat from one part of the body, they gain it back somewhere else.[61]

Strategy for Living: Behavior Change for Permanent Weight Loss

We describe seven steps to permanent weight loss.

New diet gimmicks are introduced every year, and it's easy to believe that the latest is the ultimate key to weight loss. Unfortunately, most are simply flashy variations on old ideas. What is important is not diets but *behavior change.*

How's Your Diet Readiness? It's not impossible to lose weight and keep it off. However, *it's essential not to diet at the wrong time for the wrong reasons.* Disliking how you look or wanting to be more successful at work are not great motivators for holding your weight down. Instead, think of the positive things: self-esteem, energy, health, sexual vitality.[62] Relapsers, according to one survey, were by and large unhappy with their bodies; most maintainers view themselves as thin or of average weight.[63] Relapsers are also more likely to try to escape from stressful issues by eating, sleeping more, or wishing problems would disappear. Maintainers usually seek social support or professional help and actively try to confront and solve their problems.[64]

It's important, then, to assess your *diet readiness.* Your diet readiness is your state of mind, your motivation, your commitment, and your life circumstances. Also consider your attitude toward exercise and your reasons for eating at various times.[65] How realistic your assessment is can significantly increase your chances of lasting weight loss—regardless of the weight-loss program you follow.

The "Beyond Diets" Diet Let us propose a program of behavior change that reflects the latest consensus among health care professionals about taking weight off. *It involves a combination of doing physical exercise and modifying food-related choices (especially fats) and behavior.* To give it a come-hither title like many diet programs, we call it The "Beyond Diets" Diet. One must look beyond dieting, after all, for a successful program.

Here, then, is a seven-step program recommended by psychologist Kelly Brownell for losing weight. It will also initiate attitude changes and a way of life that will keep you from regaining those pounds.[66]

1. *Set reasonable goals:* Compare your weight with the Metropolitan Life height/weight tables. *(Refer back to Table 3.)* Bear in mind, however, that the tables focus on weight, not fat. For instance, some muscular individuals may weigh in as too heavy even though they are not carrying excess fat. If you can, you might go through a college health center or fitness club to find an expert to determine your percentage of body fat.

2. ***Do a reality check:*** Your expectations should be realistic. Many people who start a diet want the pounds off next week. However, rapid weight loss produces mainly losses of water and muscle, not fat, so weight is easily regained. People who expect quick weight loss are setting themselves up for disappointment and relapse. Slow and gradual weight loss is better—no more than 1–2 pounds a week.

   To compute how long you should diet, Brownell suggests that (a) you calculate the number of weeks it will take to reach your goal if you lose 1 pound a week. Then (b) do the same calculation for losing 2 pounds a week. Look ahead to the number of weeks it will take for both figures. Then set a date for reaching your goal that is midway between those two projected dates.

3. ***Follow a balanced, low-fat diet:*** Whatever diet program you follow, good nutrition is essential. Eat a variety of foods to ensure you get the necessary vitamins and nutrients (including calcium, iron, and protein), while limiting Calories. To lose 1 pound a week, you need to take in about 500 Calories a day less than the amount you expend. Avoid fat, but eat lots of fruits, vegetables, and grains to provide both fullness and nutrition. *Limiting fat is particularly important.* Learn to recognize both "visible" and "invisible" fats.

4. ***Reshape bad eating habits:*** Get an understanding of your eating patterns by keeping a 2-week record of what you eat. Note the amount and Calories, the time, location, what you are doing, and how you feel. This will suggest to you the conditions under which you eat too much. From these you can devise strategies for lifestyle change—for instance, avoiding situations that cause eating. It's important to become aware of the link between eating and feelings.

5. ***Exercise:*** Exercise can help control your appetite. Also, dieters who exercise are more apt to lose weight and keep it off than those who do not. Brownell says exercise gives people the confidence to make positive changes. Exercise also increases one's basal metabolic rate, thus making it easier to sustain desired weight levels.

The trick is to find an exercise program you enjoy so you will stay with it. Begin by making small changes (such as walking instead of riding, and climbing stairs instead of taking the elevator). Explore a variety of activities to find ones you enjoy. Begin doing physical activity on a regular basis, exercising 3–5 times a week. Vary your workout routine to avoid boredom.

6. ***Track your progress:*** You should weigh yourself no more than once a week, so that transient changes will even out. Or, using a tape measure, you can measure your thighs, hips, and waist every 3–4 weeks.

7. ***Celebrate your success:*** Brownell points out that rewarding yourself for your achievements is an important part of all programs that produce lasting change. Thus, when you reach the midway point of your weight loss, you should give yourself something you want. (Examples are a new CD, tickets to a show, a weekend away.) For the end of the program, do something really special. For example, give all your old clothes to charity, then "indulge in new ones that show you off as you now are."

800-HELP

American Institute for Cancer Research Nutrition Hotline. 800-843-8114. Registered dietitians answer questions on how diet affects health.

Bulimia/Anorexia Self-Help Hotline. 800-227-4785. M–F 10 A.M.–5 P.M. Eastern time.

Food Allergy Center. 800-937-7354. Offers advice on reactions to various foods.

National Center for Nutrition and Dietetics. 800-366-1655. Hotline to correct misconceptions and myths about nutrition and diet.

Suggestions for Further Reading

Applegate, Liz (1991). *Power foods: High-performance nutrition for high-performance people*. Emmaus, PA: Rodale. The nutrition editor of *Runner's World* magazine offers a guide to food for the semi-active and athletic. Her "60-15-25 Power Diet" takes 60% of its Calories from carbohydrates, 15% from protein, and 25% from fat to provide an ideal amount of energy and nutrients.

Brody, Jane (1987). *Jane Brody's nutrition book*. Revised Edition. New York: Bantam. Written by the "Personal Health" columnist for *The New York Times*, this well-researched, well-written book discusses eating for health and weight control.

Jacobson, Michael F., Lefferts, Lisa Y., & Garland, Ann W. (1991). *Safe food: Eating wisely in a risky world*. Los Angeles: Living Planet Press. Written by the executive director of the advocacy group Center for Science in the Public Interest and two coauthors. They attempt an even-handed evaluation of the risks related to what we eat.

Physical Fitness: Activity and Rest

4

Use it or lose it.

You may have heard this expression, but what does it mean? Simply this: By age 40, most people have lost 30–35% of the range of motion in their hips. However, if one walks 10 or so minutes a day and stretches the hips, this loss will likely never happen.[1] In other words, *you have to move it or lose it.*

Physical Fitness

▶ Name a major risk factor in heart disease.

▶ Define sedentary living.

▶ Discuss the benefits of physical activity.

▶ Discuss the importance of motivation in exercise.

▶ Name and describe three principal areas of physical fitness.

▶ Discuss the benefits and activities for each of the following: flexibility, aerobic endurance, and muscular strength and endurance.

▶ Differentiate among isometric, isotonic, and isokinetic exercises.

▶ List the guidelines for performing isotonic and isokinetic exercises.

▶ Identify the principal exercise-related injuries and mechanisms to prevent them.

▶ Recall the meaning of R-I-C-E.

Do you have to push hard, get sweaty, run, or do high-impact aerobic dance in order to deliver benefits to the body? This is a myth. As psychologist Robert Ornstein and physician David Sobel state, "Even the most dedicated sloth can make great gains in health and well-being merely by increasing activity from none to some."[2]

A lot of people, they point out, have *exercise* and *physical activity* confused. "Exercise is usually a deliberate, sometimes odious, sweat-soaked endeavor . . . ," they write, "whereas physical activity can be any daily undertaking, work or play, that involves movement."[3]

Even a little regular physical activity can help give the body a new lease on life—literally.

The Sedentary Society

Inactivity, not high cholesterol, is one of the most important risk factors for heart attacks. Unfortunately, only a third of Americans engage in a regular program of physical activity. One enemy of fitness is television: people who watch 4 or more hours of TV a day are more apt to be fat. Some healthy people are not necessarily athletic but engage in daily physical activity.

In the 1970s and 1980s, people by the millions throughout North America began adopting healthier ways of living. They gave up smoking, started eating less cholesterol-rich eggs and red meat, and began exercising regularly. By now, you would think, these healthy habits must have affected every part of life. Unfortunately, there is one exception: exercise. The percentage of adult Americans who exercise regularly was found in one 1991 survey to be unchanged since 1983—just 34%.[4]

This is a tremendously important fact because lack of physical activity is a health risk. Despite all the publicity about cholesterol causing coronary heart disease, this fatty substance is not the most important factor. Rather, the principal cause of deaths from heart attacks in the U.S. is a way of life characterized by little or no physical activity. This is ***sedentary living*, defined as being physically active fewer than three times per week and less than 20 minutes per session**.[5] *(See ● Figure 1.)*

The moral: A regular program of physical activity won't just help you look better or feel better. It may save your life.

TV or Not TV: Does Television Make You Fat? How do you spend your time? For most American adults, when it comes to devoting their waking hours, television watching is second only to working for a living.[6,7] Ninety-eight percent of Americans watch some TV every day. Women ages 18-34 watch an average of 25 hours of TV a week, men of the same age 22 hours. Television viewing tends to increase with age.[8] When teenagers today reach the age of 70, most will have watched *7 years* worth of television![9] With so much time spent before the tube, no wonder so many people are overweight and out of shape.

Strategy for Living: Breaking the TV Habit If you decide that you are pouring too much of your time into television watching, there are a number of things you can do.[10] (1) You can plan your viewing. Watch only previously selected programs, and turn off the set when they are over. (2) You can avoid channel hopping to decrease mindless viewing. (3) You can get away from the TV set and go do something else when you are not following your TV viewing plan. (For instance, try spending about 15 minutes getting some exercise.)

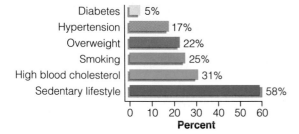

Diabetes	5%
Hypertension	17%
Overweight	22%
Smoking	25%
High blood cholesterol	31%
Sedentary lifestyle	58%

Percent

● **Figure 1   The hazards of the inactive life.** Modifiable risk factors for coronary heart disease and their prevalence among Americans. People with a sedentary, or inactive, lifestyle are twice as likely as active people to die from heart disease. The risks of sitting still are higher than those of cigarette smoking or high blood cholesterol.

The Benefits of Physical Activity

Physical activity can enhance your mood, energy, and creativity; keep weight down; and reduce heart disease risk. It may also reduce risk of cancer and diabetes; protect against bone loss in women; make you sexier; and slow aging.

As we shall show, physical fitness can be derived from a wide range of activities. The important point is to realize that the benefits of physical activity are substantial. Among them are the following.

Enhance Mood and Creativity Physical activity or exercise can improve our mood in several ways.

- **It releases "feel good" brain chemicals:** Exercise promotes the release of endorphins and serotonin.

  Endorphins are naturally occurring painkillers that make the mind feel anywhere from mildly better to ecstatic. These chemicals are produced in the brain and spinal cord to minimize pain in the body. However, researchers believe endorphins also produce the "runner's high"—the feeling of euphoria said to energize long-distance runners.[11]

  Serotonin is a brain chemical associated with a sense of well-being and impulse control. Depletion of serotonin results in depression. Serotonin is one of the brain's principal neurotransmitters. (A *neurotransmitter* is a chemical that transmits nerve impulses.)

- **It can prevent or alleviate mild to moderate depression:** Physical activity can help alleviate the blues. One group of mildly and moderately depressed patients who were assigned to do running felt better after only a week. They were declared "virtually well" within 3 weeks, with the benefits lasting at least a year.[12–15]

- **It can relieve feelings of anger, anxiety, and tension:** Physical activity may provide a way to release anger and anxiety and physical tension.[16–18]

- **It can distract you and stimulate creative thinking:** Some people who exercise experience *disassociation*—the brain "takes a vacation" from the task at hand, providing mental refreshment.[19] Indeed, studies suggest that exercise can sharpen mental skills and enhance creativity.[20]

Increase Energy and Keep Weight Down Physical activity can boost your energy level and help you control your weight. *(See ● Figure 2.)* For instance, a brisk 10-minute walk can increase energy and decrease fatigue for as long as 2 hours afterward.[21] Thus, when you have an afternoon slump in energy, a short, vigorous walk is a better picker-upper than a candy bar.[22]

● **Figure 2   Workouts, energy, and weight loss.**

❝*Studies show that aerobically fit people have more mitochondria, the tiny 'boiler rooms' inside muscle cells where fat is turned into energy, than do people who are out of shape. That means they can work harder and longer without huffing and puffing and feeling exhausted. It also means that, if they continue eating about the same amount, they're likely to burn more calories than they take in. So it's easier for them to lose fat.*❞

—Kathleen McCleary (1992, December/January). The no-gimmick weight-loss plan. *In Health*, p. 83.

In addition, physical activity "helps you lose weight by turning your body into a calorie-guzzling machine," as one writer puts it.[23] How does this work? Although you may burn relatively few Calories during a workout, your body burns much more throughout the day *following* the activity.

Reduce Heart-Disease Risk It seems that it doesn't take a great deal of physical activity to help your heart. This conclusion was supported by findings from a long-term study of nearly 17,000 Harvard alumni, men ages 30–79. The study analyzed the relationship between heart-disease deaths and exercise and found that most of the benefits came from expending 500–2000 Calories a week.[24] There were some added benefits for those expending up to 3500 Calories. Spending 500 Calories a week reduced death rates 20% and is easily achieved. All it takes is a 15-minute walk a day.

More physical exercise may be even more helpful—but only up to a point, according to one study of 12,000 middle-aged men. The study found that those who burned 1600 Calories a week had 40% fewer deaths from heart attacks than those who expended under 500 Calories a week. However, increasing the exercise level to expend 4500 Calories a week did not further reduce fatal heart attacks.[25]

Reduce Risk of Cancer and Diabetes Does exercise help diminish the risk of cancer and diabetes? Women who were involved in varsity sports in college were found to be less likely to develop breast cancer or cancers of the reproductive system in later life. A study of nearly 5400 college alumnae also found such women experienced lower risk of bone fractures and diabetes.[26]

The Harvard alumni study mentioned earlier found that regular vigorous exercise in middle age and beyond reduced colon and rectal cancer rates. Those who were moderately or highly active exercisers had half the risk of colon cancer compared to men who were inactive. The protection against cancer appeared to diminish or disappear if the subjects stopped exercising.[27]

At least 20% of the adult population is at risk for adult onset diabetes.[28] **Adult onset diabetes** is a disorder in which the body does not effectively process insulin. *Insulin* is a hormone produced by the body to regulate blood sugar levels. A study of nearly 6000 male graduates of the University of Pennsylvania found that exercise reduces the chances of acquiring this disease. This is especially true among those who are overweight, have high blood pressure, or have a family history of the disease. Exercising 4 or more hours a week could reduce the risk by more than 40%.[29]

Protect Against Bone Loss in Women
Every woman should be concerned about *osteoporosis*, **a disorder in which the bones become porous, brittle, and easily fractured.** Indeed, osteoporosis occurs in 1 out of 4 women above 65 years of age.[30] This condition may cause the bones to become so weak that even a simple fall can break them. In women, osteoporosis may occur following menopause and seems to be related to decreased estrogen levels. As a result, women in later life frequently experience hip fractures.

To prevent these painful problems in later life, women need to take steps early in life. Besides ensuring an adequate daily intake of calcium, young women should engage in regular, weight-bearing physical activity to stimulate new bone formation.

There are two forms of physical activity that all women can use to strengthen their bones. The first consists of weight-bearing, moderate-impact, aerobic exercises (which require high oxygen intake). Examples are jumping or running activities (jogging, dancing, tennis, volleyball) that produce enough impact on the legs and feet to stimulate bone development. The second form is weight-bearing, strength-training exercises such as weight training with Nautilus-type machines.

Make You Sexier Moderate exercise can dramatically improve a person's love life, even with increasing age. For example, men and women swimmers aged 40 and over reported a frequency of sexual activity of about seven times a month.[31] That frequency is the same reported by many people in their 20s and 30s. The reasons may include the social and personal reinforcement for looking attractive and fit.

Slow Aging Says physician Walter Bortz II, author of *We Live Too Short and Die Too Long*, "We now know that a very fit body of 70 can be the same as a moderately fit body of 30."[32] Among the things that a lifelong program of physical activity can do to slow the aging process are the following:

- *Retain muscle mass:* As they age, most people lose their body muscle, primarily through nonuse. Even minimal exercise can allow you to hang on to most of your muscle mass well into old age. Walking 20 minutes a day or lifting weights twice a week will do the job.

- *Strengthen immune system:* A health science professor found that compared to no exercise, moderate exercise improved immunity, shown by fewer cases of colds and flu. He also found that moderate exercisers had fewer colds and flu bouts than those who overexerted (running 60 miles per week versus 20).[33]

- *Keep you independent:* Exercise does not necessarily help people live longer. But it can help people stay independent longer—that is, live alone into their 80s and 90s, rather than needing custodial care.

Fitness for Fun and Feeling Good

Motivation is important, so exercise should be fun. Physical fitness consists of three parts: flexibility, aerobic endurance, and muscular strength and endurance. Guidelines for achieving fitness can help.

"No pain, no gain." If you hear people say this, ignore them.

Sacrificing for physical fitness may be required of competitive athletes at times, who may have to push themselves through pain to win. For other people, however, physical activity should not add stress to their lives. True, activity may cause your body to protest somewhat, but *stop* doing what you're doing when you experience discomfort or pain. *(See ● Figure 3.)*

● **Figure 3   Pain versus challenge.** How hard should you exercise?

"My simple rule of thumb is as follows. If I am exercising so vigorously that I cannot talk easily (without gasping and panting), then I am probably exercising too vigorously. On the other hand, if my body does not feel some stimulation or challenge (an 'alive feeling'), then I probably am not exercising vigorously enough."

—Howard S. Friedman, Ph.D. (1991). *The self-healing personality: Why some people achieve health and others succumb to illness.* New York: Henry Holt, p. 193.

Physical Activity Versus Exercise As we suggested earlier, physical fitness may be achieved in two ways:

- ***Physical activity: Physical activity refers to any behavior that involves moving your muscles,*** from house cleaning and gardening to running and weightlifting.
- ***Exercise: Exercise is a particular kind of physical activity involving conscious participation in activities that promote physical fitness.*** Such activity can range from walking to competitive sports.

Any activity is better than no activity, and regular movement better than infrequent movement. The point of exercise, however, is that it builds physical fitness in specific areas that are challenged during your workouts.

The Important Question of Motivation Personal fitness is not about punishment; it's about *fun* and *feeling good*. The idea is not to train for "how far, how fast." Instead, build in a strong component of fun and remind yourself that exercise not only improves your health but also makes you feel better.

There are three points during physical activity where your motivation is important: when starting, while continuing, and when you're tempted to quit.[34]

- ***Getting started:*** To get going, three factors are important. (1) Your *attitude* toward a specific activity (running, lifting weights) determines whether you think the activity is too uncomfortable or is worth doing. In other words, you must find an activity that's right for you. (2) You need to have social support by friends or family. (3) You need to feel you're in control, able to make time for the activity.
- ***Maintaining participation:*** Continuing physical activity can depend on three motivators. First is feeling good while you exercise. Second is having goals and self-reinforcement to accomplish them, such as jogging a certain distance. Third is having an exercise leader who is positive and effective (for activities with a leader).
- ***Preventing the "I quit" mentality:*** To resist dropping out, do the following:

---

(1) Prepare to resist the urge to quit. (2) Identify what caused the desire to quit when it happens. (3) Mobilize your support group and reset your goals to get started again.

Above all, follow this rule: *try to make exercise fun.* Sometimes it *will* be fun, sometimes it won't. In any case, the point is to enjoy it most of the time and to feel better afterward.

The Three Parts of Physical Fitness The purpose of fitness is to enhance your body, mind, and spirit. *Total fitness* has mental, emotional, social, medical, nutritional, and physical elements. Here we are concerned about **physical fitness, defined as having above-average (1) flexibility, (2) aerobic endurance, and (3) muscle strength and endurance.** Let's consider these three parts:

- *Flexibility: Flexibility* **is the suppleness of movement, your ability to move through the full range of motion allowed by your joints.** This describes, for instance, your ability to touch your toes or twist your body without discomfort or injury.

- *Aerobic endurance: Aerobic endurance* **describes how efficiently your body uses oxygen.** An indicator is how out of breath you become while climbing stairs, riding a bicycle, or any other aerobic activity. **In an *aerobic* activity the oxygen taken in is equal to or slightly more than the oxygen used by the body.**

  You need aerobic endurance to give yourself *cardiovascular fitness*—**the ability to pump blood through your heart and blood vessels efficiently.**

- *Muscle strength and muscular endurance:* The fitness of your muscles is measured in two ways—by strength, and by endurance.

  (1) *Muscle strength* **is the ability to exert force against resistance,** whether standing up from a chair or lifting a free weight.

  (2) *Muscular endurance* **is the ability to keep repeating those muscle exertions,** to scoop not one but several shovels full of snow.

Ideally, your physical activity or exercise program will address these three major areas.

Guidelines for Improving Fitness The American College of Sports Medicine offers physical fitness recommendations. These recommendations are intended not just to keep people *healthy* (which even moderate levels of activity will do) but to achieve *fitness.* The guidelines are as follows:[35–37]

- *How often:* Exercise 3–5 days a week. Resistance training, such as weight lifting, should be at least two of those days.

- *How long:* Exercise at least 20–60 minutes per session at your recommended heart-rate level. (This is target heart rate, not maximum heart rate.) To avoid injury, nonathletes should exercise at lower intensities for a longer period.

- *How much:* Exercise at an intensity level of 60–90% of maximum heart rate. Estimate your maximum heart rate by subtracting your age from the number 220.

Training should be of three kinds: *aerobic, resistance,* and *flexibility.*

- *Aerobic training:* Exercise should be rhythmic and aerobic, using large muscle groups. Examples are walking, jogging, stair-climbing, bicycling, and rowing.

- *Resistance training:* Exercise should consist of 8–12 repetitions of 8–10 specific exercises that condition the major muscle groups. Weight machines, free weights, or calisthenics can be used for resistance training.

- *Flexibility:* No official guidelines exist—apparently, the jury is still out on how much stretching is enough. But flexibility exercises that involve stretching should be performed regularly, at least twice a week.

The College of Sports Medicine points out that lower-intensity, longer-duration workouts offer less chance of injury. Moreover, it has been shown that people maintain these programs longer than those that involve higher-intensity, shorter-duration workouts. Finally, exercising beyond these limits doesn't really improve fitness.

In the next three sections we discuss the three important elements of physical fitness:

- Flexibility
- Aerobic endurance
- Muscular strength and endurance

Flexibility Test: Sit-and-Stretch

You will need a yardstick for this activity.

Directions

1. Sit on the floor with a yardstick between your outstretched legs. Slide the stick forward so that the 15-inch mark is even with your heels. Tape it to the floor, if you like.
2. Slowly lean and reach with both hands, touching the yardstick as far forward as possible with your fingertips.
3. Don't bounce or lunge. Hold for 3 seconds. Repeat three times, and record your best mark.

How you shape up for flexibility

The following are general guidelines indicating how flexible you are for your age.

Women

Age	Inches stretched				
	Excellent	High	Average	Low	Very Low
Under 30	24+	20–23	18–19	14–17	0–13
30–39	24+	20–23	18–19	14–17	0–13
40–49	23+	19–22	17–18	12–16	0–11
50–59	23+	19–22	17–18	11–16	0–10
60 and older	23+	19–22	17–18	10–16	0–9

Men

Age	Inches stretched				
	Excellent	High	Average	Low	Very Low
Under 30	23+	19–22	12–18	9–11	0–8
30–39	23+	19–22	12–18	9–11	0–8
40–49	22+	18–21	12–17	8–11	0–7
50–59	22+	18–21	11–17	8–9	0–7
60 and older	22+	18–21	11–17	8–9	0–7

Source: The President's Council on Fitness and Sports, YMCA.

Flexibility

Staying flexible prevents soreness and injuries and reduces stress. Stretching should be slow and relaxed. Flexibility activities should be done twice weekly.

Flexibility is suppleness of movement, your ability to move through the full range of motion allowed by your joints. How flexible you are depends in great part on the joint in question. Even so, a test in one area can indicate your general flexibility.

You may wish to stop and test your flexibility before reading on. *(See Self Discovery 1.)*

The Benefits of Flexibility In general, flexibility exercises consist of *stretching*. There are three benefits to stretching. (1) It decreases muscle stiffness and soreness. (2) It reduces the risk of injury and improves coordination by extending the range of motion. (3) It reduces stress by loosening up tight muscles and helping you to relax.

Activities for Flexibility The most important areas for maintaining flexibility are your hips, chest, hamstring muscles, shoulders, and neck. *(See ● Figure 4.)*

Procedures for enhancing flexibility are as follows:

- **Warm up for 5–10 minutes before stretching:** A warm-up should involve jogging in place, a brisk walk, or calisthenics. This will help you increase your temperature and circulation. This in turn increases the pliability of your muscles and helps you avoid injuries that come with using cold muscles.

- **Do slow, "static" (no-bounce) stretching:** Stretch gradually, while breathing deeply. Stretch until you feel slight resistance—a pulling sensation, not a pain. Hold the position for 30–60 seconds, then let go slowly. Relax for 20–30 seconds. **This gradual, no-bounce stretching and holding is called *static stretching*.**

- **Don't do bouncing, "ballistic" stretching:** Never bounce as you stretch. **Ballistic stretching is bouncing on the balls of your feet, repeatedly forcing yourself**

Upper calves
Stand about 18 inches from a wall with your feet apart and your hands on the wall for balance. With your legs straight and your toes pointed ahead, lean toward the wall as you would in a pushup. Keep your body straight during the stretch. Good for: *any activity requiring walking or running.*

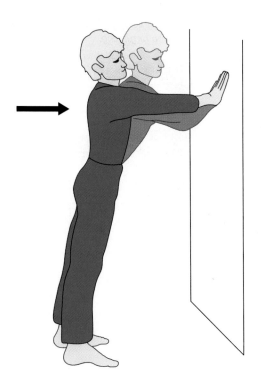

Spine rotation
Sit on the floor with your legs stretched out flat in front of you. (If you can't straighten your legs, bend them cross-legged.) With your arms folded across your chest, slowly turn your entire upper torso to the right, then to the left, keeping your legs and hips in place. Good for: *any activity requiring turning, twisting, or reaching.*

Overall stretch
Lie on the floor with your back flat, arms and hands on the floor above your head. Keeping your arms and legs as flat against the mat or carpet as possible, stretch your body in opposite directions by reaching up with your arms and down with your legs. Good for: *overall flexibility.*

Hips
Lie flat on the floor. Pull one knee up toward your chest, keeping the opposite leg flat on the floor. Slowly return the bent leg to the start position. Repeat with the other leg. Good for: *walking, tennis, golf, or any activity requiring hip flexibility.*

● **Figure 4   Stretches for flexibility.**

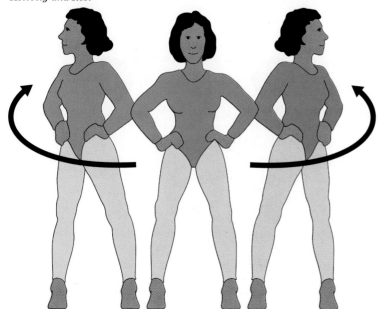

Achilles tendons

Do the same exercise as for upper calves, but bend your knees. Good for: *any activity requiring walking or running.*

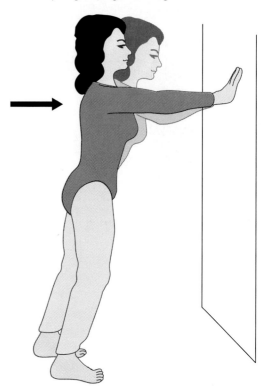

Spine and hip rotation

Stand with your hands on your hips. Do the same twisting motion as in the spine rotation exercise, but include the hips as you rotate. Keep your knees in place and your feet pointing straight ahead approximately your shoulders' width apart. Good for: *walking, golf, tennis, or any activity requiring reaching or hip rotation.*

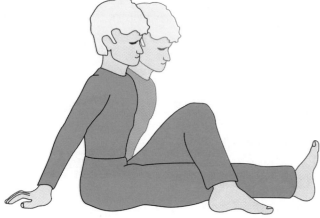

Shoulders

Lie flat on the floor with your arms straight down at your sides, palms down. Bend your knees and slide your feet up close to your buttocks. Keep your lower back flat and elbows straight as you raise your arms in the air, then slowly lower them until the backs of your hands touch the mat above your head. Good for: *tennis, golf, or any activity that uses the shoulders.*

Hamstrings

Sit on the floor with one leg stretched out in front of you. Bend the other leg and cross it above the stretched leg's knee. Planting your hands on the mat next to your hips for support, bend forward from the hips, keeping your arms straight. Make sure you bend from the hips and not the upper back. Focusing attention on an object directly in front of you may help you do this properly. Good for: *most activities that require walking or running.*

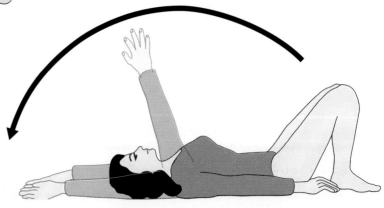

to touch your toes, and the like. It can tear muscle fibers and cause injuries.

- *Do at least 5 minutes of flexibility exercises twice a week:* Do stretching or range-of-motion exercises for 5–60 minutes at least twice a week. Do them after every aerobic endurance or muscular strength/endurance workout.

Besides stretching exercises, certain kinds of sports or activities are particularly useful for enhancing flexibility. Activities for flexibility range from such pastimes as gardening, golf, and swimming to yoga, martial arts, and rock climbing.

Aerobic Endurance

Aerobic activity, unlike anaerobic and nonaerobic activity, is effort without breathlessness. It reduces body fat, heart disease, and some cancers. Aerobic exercises such as running or rowing, should be done three times weekly or more. You should monitor your efforts by checking your target heart rate or rate of perceived exertion.

Aerobic endurance describes how efficiently your body uses oxygen. To appreciate how aerobic activities differ from other kinds of activities, consider these three categories:

1. *Aerobic activity—effort without breathlessness:* In aerobic activity, the oxygen taken in is equal to or slightly more than the oxygen used by the body. Brisk walking, jogging, or long-distance bicycling or swimming are examples of aerobic exercise. The workout is strenuous, but you never become breathless to the point that you can't talk while engaging in the activity.

2. *Anaerobic activity—effort that leaves you gasping:* In *anaerobic* activity, the oxygen taken in is less than the oxygen required, leaving an "oxygen deficit" to be made up later. Sprinting, as in track, football, or speed skating, is an example of anaerobic exercise. You expend tremendous effort for a short period, then are left gasping for air.

3. *Nonaerobic activity—some effort with frequent rest:* In *nonaerobic* activity, the oxygen taken in always meets the need, so the lungs and heart don't put out much effort. Bowling, golf, tennis, and softball are examples of nonaerobic exercise, where the body gets frequent rests.

Anaerobic and nonaerobic activities are fine, except that they don't deliver the important health benefits that aerobic exercise does.

Before proceeding, you may wish to test your aerobic endurance. *(See Self Discovery 2.)*

The Benefits of Aerobic Endurance The payoffs of aerobic physical activity are great. (1) It seems to reduce your risk of heart disease, the No. 1 cause of death in the United States. Aerobic exercise can lower blood pressure and raise the "good" (HDL) cholesterol, counteracting two risk factors in heart disease. It can also strengthen the heart muscle. (2) It can reduce body fat and increase lean muscle mass. (3) It may help reduce the risk of breast and reproductive cancers in women and colon and rectal cancers in men. (4) It can reduce stress, relieve depression, and perhaps stimulate creativity.

Activities for Aerobic Endurance Unlike stretching, aerobic activities usually build physical fitness in more than one area at the same time. For instance, bicycling benefits your leg muscles, canoeing your arm muscles, and both strengthen your heart and lungs.

The trick to doing aerobic activity is to go about it in the right way. Here's how:

- *Before—do warm-up exercises:* Do calisthenics or jog in place for 5 minutes, followed by 5 minutes of stretching before you walk, run, or whatever. The warm-up will help you avoid injury and smooth out your form. For example, before running, do some calisthenics followed by stretching the Achilles tendon and heel. *(See ● Figure 5.)*

- *After—do cool-down exercises:* The purpose of the cool-down is to return the blood to the heart from the body's extremities. Five to 10 minutes of walking and/or stretching is sufficient. Two good cool-down exercises are stretching for the front of your legs and behind-the-back or hands-over-

Aerobic-Endurance Test: 3-Minute Step Test

For this activity you will need a watch and a 12-inch-high step.

Directions

1. Don't practice before you time yourself, but do stretch.
2. For 3 minutes, step up and down on the step in a four-part movement: (a) up with the left foot, (b) up with the right foot, (c) down with the left foot, (d) down with the right foot.
3. You can alternate your lead foot, but try to keep pace at 24 steps a minute. (One step is a complete, four-part, up-and-down movement.)
4. Immediately after the 3 minutes, sit down and check your pulse. Count the number of heartbeats for 10 seconds, then multiply by 6 to get your exercising heart rate in beats per minute.

How You Shape Up for Aerobic Endurance

The following are general guidelines indicating how much aerobic endurance you have for your age.

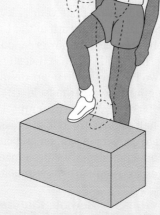

Women

Age	Step test—heart rate				
	Excellent	High	Average	Low	Very Low
Under 30	72–84	85–108	109–116	117–135	136–155
30–39	74–86	87–107	108–117	118–136	137–154
40–49	74–90	91–112	113–118	119–131	132–152
50–59	76–92	93–112	113–120	121–134	135–152
60 and older	74–90	91–109	110–119	120–133	134–151

Men

Age	Step test—heart rate				
	Excellent	High	Average	Low	Very Low
Under 30	70–78	79–97	98–105	106–126	127–164
30–39	72–80	81–100	101–109	110–126	127–168
40–49	74–82	83–103	104–113	114–128	129–168
50–59	72–84	85–104	105–115	116–130	131–154
60 and older	72–86	87–101	102–110	111–128	129–150

Source: The President's Council on Physical Fitness, YMCA.

head stretching to prevent shoulders from slumping. *(Refer to Figure 5.)*

- ***Exercise at least 20 minutes three times a week, and up to 60 minutes four or five times a week:*** For people starting out, 20 minutes three times a week of brisk walking, dancing, bicycling, stair-climbing, swimming, and the like is sufficient. An optimal exercise level might be 35–45 minutes of moderate exercise three to five times a week, such as jogging, brisk walking, bicycling, or swimming. A peak level would be 45–60 minutes four or five times a week of strenuous exercise, such as running, rowing, or cross-country skiing.

During your workouts you should always monitor how hard you are pushing yourself. One way is to stop your workout and place your finger on your pulse to measure your heart rate. Another way is to visualize how hard you're working, using the Rate of Perceived Exertion (RPE) scale. We explain both methods next.

Monitoring Your Efforts: Target Heart Rates Your heart rate is one indicator of how hard to exercise and the level at which you are currently exercising. (It is not, however, an accurate or infallible measure of exertion.) Here's how to use heart rate.

- ***Step 1—Determine your maximum heart rate:*** The ***maximum heart rate is the rate beyond which you do not want to push yourself during aerobic training.*** Overdoing it carries danger of putting too great a strain on your heart.

One formula for finding your maximum heart rate is simple: *subtract your current age from 220.*

- ***Step 2—Determine your target heart rate:*** The ***target heart rate is the rate at which you derive maximum benefit from aerobic exercise.***

One formula for determining your target heart rate is as follows: *find 60% and 80% of your maximum heart rate.* Twenty-year-olds, for example, have a maximum heart rate of 200. They need to push their heart rate to between 120 (which is 60% of 200) and 160 (which is 80% of 200). The lower target rate is sufficient for those just starting out. They may then work toward achieving the higher rate over a period of 6 months or more of training.

- **Step 3—Learn how to determine your pulse rate:** To monitor your heart rate, you simply take your pulse. You can do this by placing two or three fingers (your forefinger and middle finger, not your thumb) as follows: (a) on your *radial artery,* located just below the base of your thumb on the inner side of your opposite wrist, or (b) on your *carotid artery,* located on the side of your neck below the angle of your jaw bone. *(See ● Figure 6.)*

  To determine your heart rate per minute, count the number of beats in 10 seconds, then multiply by 6. (Or count the number in 30 seconds, and multiply by 2.)

  Try taking your pulse now. Your heart rate is called your **resting heart rate when you are sitting or lying down.** When you are doing aerobic exercise, you use the same pulse-taking method to determine your target rate.

  An average heart rate is 80 beats per minute, with a range of 60–80 beats per minute. People who have efficient cardiovascular systems owing to regular exercise may have a resting heart rate of 50 beats per minute or less.

Monitoring Your Efforts: Rate of Perceived Exertion The American College of Sports Medicine suggests the Rate of Perceived Exertion scale is preferable to pulse-taking. However, anyone with a history of heart disease should use pulse-taking. **The *Rate of Perceived Exertion (RPE) scale* assumes you can subjectively *feel* how strenuous your workout is. That feeling can be expressed as a number corresponding to your heart rate.**[38,39] The RPE provides a means of quantifying subjective exercise intensity. *(See ● Figure 7.)*

Aerobic Cross-Training for Variety One way to make exercise pleasant and fun is to add *variety.* Try doing **cross-training, which combines several different exercise activities** to prevent boredom and increase fitness. Cross-training also helps you avoid injuries stemming from overuse and provides benefits to more than one part of your body. For example, you might

1 **Before your run:** Stand leaning against a solid support with one foot forward and knee bent to stretch the Achilles tendon. Now bend the back knee slightly, keeping the foot flat, until you feel a gentle stretching in the heel. Repeat on the opposite leg.

2 **After your run:** Get down on one knee, so that the other knee is aligned directly above the ankle. Lower your hips until you feel a stretching sensation in the front of your rear leg.

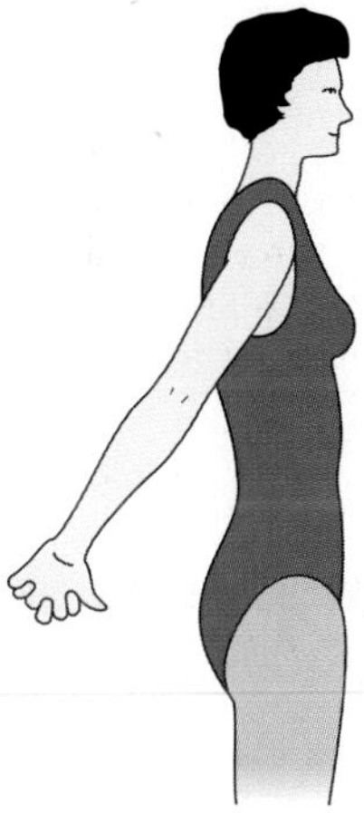

3 **After your run:** To stop your shoulders from slumping, lace your fingers together behind your back, palms in. Slowly turn your elbows inward while straightening your arms to stretch in your shoulders and chest.

● **Figure 5 Warm-up and cool-down stretches.** Several minutes of daily stretching will smooth out your form and help you avoid injury. Stretch slowly, without bouncing, to the point where you feel an easy stretching sensation. Hold this position for 5-30 seconds, until the tension diminishes, then stretch slightly farther and hold again.

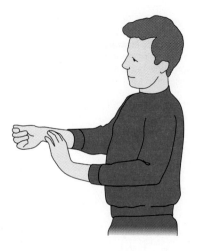

Wrist pulse
Two or three fingers on the radial artery, just below the base of the thumb, on the inner side of the wrist.

Neck pulse
The tips of two or three fingers on the carotid artery on the side of the neck below the angle of the jawbone.

● **Figure 6** **Pulse-taking.**

mix running, bicycling, and swimming on alternate days, depending on your mood, the weather, and the facilities available.

Many health clubs have rooms for aerobic *circuit training*, **in which you follow a course using different equipment for different aerobic activities.** Thus, you might begin with a treadmill, then climb on an exercise bike, then a few minutes later get on a rowing machine, and so on.[40]

Types of Aerobic Activities Some popular categories of aerobic activities are as follows:

- *Walking:* Walking should be done three or four times a week 20–30 minutes at a time, at a brisk pace.

- *Jogging and running:* Jogging or running should be done 25-30 minutes three times a week. The aim is to achieve and sustain your target heart rate for 20 minutes. **In jogging, one moves at a pace slower than 9 minutes per mile. In running, one goes faster than that.** Both jogging and running can be done on the same outing (or on a stair-climbing machine).

  Another variation is *interval training*, **which combines running with intervals of sprinting.** Typically you alternate several minutes of aerobic running with 30–60 seconds of anaerobic sprinting. During the sprinting part, you push to the point of being breathless.[41]

- *Bicycling:* Pedaling can build aerobic endurance and burn off 450–800 Calories per hour if a brisk intensity is maintained. Pedaling can be done outside on a touring or mountain bike or inside on a stationary bike.

- *Swimming:* Swimming is one of the best aerobic fitness activities because it uses many of the body's muscles and produces gentle stretching. An hour of vigorous swimming can burn 660 Calories.

- *Skating, "blading," and skiing:* Both skating and skiing have made some advances over the last few years as all-weather sports. Ice skating and rolling skating can provide excellent aerobic conditioning. Rollerblade-style *in-line skates*, **which put the wheels in a row,** are used in the popular activity of "blading." A half hour of blading can burn up 285–450 Calories, compared to 300–350 Calories for runners and bicyclists.[42] Blading also strengthens hip, thigh, and lower back muscles that are not well developed by running or bicycling. However, the use of protective gear is essential, as injuries are a problem.

Downhill skiing is a reasonably good aerobic sport. Cross-country skiing is an exceptionally good cardiovascular exercise, particularly when done correctly, with a long diagonal stride.

- *Aerobics and dancing:* Hard-impact, jump-around aerobics has resulted in injuries. Now **nonimpact aerobics combine the grace of modern dance and yoga with the fluidity of martial-arts movements. Step aerobics involves stepping on and off a 4- or 12-inch-high platform while making coinciding arm movements.** It provides a high-intensity, low-impact workout set to a slower tempo of music than regular aerobic dancing.[43]

Even ballroom dancing, with the cha-cha, polka, samba, and the like, can help people who have trouble sticking to a workout schedule.

- *Other—rowing, stair climbing, treadmill, jump rope:* These indoor activities are great fat-burning routines if you have access to a health club or gym.

These are a few of many possible exercise options. The key is to select some activity that you might enjoy and do it.

Muscular Strength and Endurance

Muscle strength is the measure of the force you are able to exert against resistance. Muscle endurance is the ability to keep repeating those exertions. Such muscular activity makes you feel and look good, reduces heart disease and cancer risk, and strengthens bones. Resistance-training exercises, which should be done twice weekly or more, are specialized, involving use of free weights, weight machines, or calisthenics. Circuit training can be helpful.

6	
7 Very, very light	How you should feel when warming up or cooling
8	down — but not when aerobically exercising
9 Very light	
10	Between 10 and 15 is your aerobic workout zone.
11 Fairly light	
12	
13 Somewhat hard	13 is your ideal. You should be sweating but still able
14	to talk without effort.
15 Hard	Here you have trouble talking.
16	Here you're beyond
17 Very hard	aerobic and into anaerobic. You can't talk.
18	Muscles are aching!
19 Very, very hard	This is like sprinting as hard as you can!
20	

- **Figure 7   Rate of perceived exertion.** The Rate of Perceived Exertion (RPE) scale is an attempt to quantify how you *feel* about how strenuous your workout is. Assuming good health, if you judge you're doing an aerobic task "Somewhat hard" (13), you're probably at the right level.

People who get lots of aerobic exercise often have strong legs, but they may lack upper-body strength. When muscles are not used, they fall into a condition called **atrophy, a state of wasting away.** Conversely, when they are used regularly, they achieve a state called **hypertrophy, a state of increased size.**

The fitness of your muscles is measured in two ways—muscle strength and endurance. *Muscle strength* is the ability to exert force against resistance, as when you lift a box of books. To increase strength, you need to do a few repetitions with heavy loads. *Muscle endurance* is the ability to keep repeating those muscle exertions, so you can move not just a box of books into your house but several other boxes before resting. To increase endurance, you need to do many repetitions with light loads.

You may wish to test your muscular strength and endurance before reading on. *(See Self Discovery 3.)*

SELF DISCOVERY 3

Muscular Strength and Endurance Test: Push-Ups for Upper Body Strength and Sit-Ups and Curl-Ups for Abdominal Strength

Directions: Push-Ups—Upper Body Strength

1. Lie face down on the floor with your hands directly beneath your shoulders. Then, keeping your back rigid, push your body off the floor until your arms are straight.
2. If full push-ups are too difficult, lower your knees to the floor for support, but keep your back straight.
3. Stop 2 inches above the floor in the down position in standard push-ups. Touch your chest in the modified, knees-down version.
4. Down and up is one push-up. Do as many as you can without breaking form or resting.

Push-ups

Directions: Sit-Ups and Curl-Ups—Abdominal Strength

1. Lie flat on your back, legs bent, with heels 6 inches from your buttocks. Cross your arms over your chest for sit-ups or extend them along your sides for curl-ups.
2. Keeping your feet on the floor, curl your upper torso upward. Touch your crossed arms to your knees for sit-ups. For curl-ups, make sure your hands slide 3 inches forward.
3. Do as many as you can in 1½ minutes.

Sit-ups and curl-ups

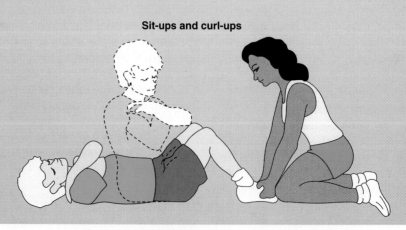

Push-Ups: How You Shape Up for Upper Body Strength

The following are general guidelines indicating how much upper-body muscular strength you have for your age based on number of push-ups.

Women

Age	Push-ups—number completed				
	Excellent	High	Average	Low	Very Low
Under 30	49+	34–48	17–33	6–16	0–5
30–39	40+	25–39	12–24	4–11	0–3
40–49	35+	20–34	8–19	3–7	0–2
50–59	30+	15–29	6–14	2–5	0–1
60 and older	20+	5–19	3–4	1–2	0

Men

Age	Push-ups—number completed				
	Excellent	High	Average	Low	Very Low
Under 30	55+	45–64	35–44	20–34	0–19
30–39	45+	35–44	25–34	15–24	0–14
40–49	40+	30–39	20–29	12–19	0–11
50–59	35+	25–34	15–24	8–14	0–7
60 and older	30+	20–29	10–19	5–9	0–4

Sit-Ups and Curl-Ups: How You Shape Up for Abdominal Strength

The following are general guidelines indicating how much abdominal strength you have for your age based on number of sit-ups and curl-ups.

Women

Age	Sit-ups—number completed				
	Excellent	High	Average	Low	Very Low
Under 30	45+	35–44	25–34	15–24	0–14
30–39	45+	35–44	25–34	15–24	0–14
40–49	40+	30–39	20–29	14–19	0–13
50–59	35+	25–34	15–24	10–14	0–9
60 and older	35+	25–34	15–24	8–14	0–7

Men

Age	Sit-ups—number completed				
	Excellent	High	Average	Low	Very Low
Under 30	50+	40–49	30–39	20–29	0–19
30–39	50+	40–49	30–39	20–29	0–19
40–49	45+	34–44	25–43	19–24	0–18
50–59	40+	30–39	20–29	15–19	0–14
60 and older	40+	28–39	19–27	14–18	0–13

Source: The President's Council on Physical Fitness, YMCA.

The Benefits of Muscular Strength and Endurance The benefits of strength training are as follows: (1) It makes you look and feel good, since it can tone up muscles and slow down sagging. Posture improves, and so does breathing.[44] As you look better, your self-confidence also increases. (2) Developing your muscles will decrease body fat and increase lean body mass. It also opens up tiny blood vessels (capillaries) to increase the flow of blood and nutrients to the muscles and increases efficient metabolism. The result is a decreased risk of heart disease, some cancers, and adult diabetes. (3) Strengthening the bones along with the muscles improves posture, prevents back pain, and enables you to remain active as you grow older.[45]

Activities for Muscular Strength and Endurance The important muscle groups that need to be strengthened are your chest, back, legs, buttocks, arms, shoulders, and stomach. The key to fitness is to avoid emphasizing one group over another and to keep several principles in mind for developing the properties of muscular strength and endurance:

- *General versus specialized exercises:* Certain activities such as swimming, cross-country skiing, and rock-climbing can help flexibility and aerobic fitness along with muscular strength and endurance. However, the development of large muscle groups requires strength training—namely, exercises with weight machines, free weights, or calisthenics.

- *Resistance training for strength versus endurance:* All muscle-development training is based on the principle of resistance. During training you need to demand more of the muscles than they are accustomed to doing; in short, you must overload them.

  Building *strength* requires *few* repetitions with *heavy* loads. Building *endurance* requires *more* repetitions with *light* loads. In the beginning, you should strive to build up strength. As the muscles become developed, strive for endurance.

- *Isometric, isotonic, and isokinetic exercises:* Resistance training takes various forms—isometric, isotonic, and isokinetic. The idea behind all three is to apply the principle of overload to the muscles. To do this, increase the resistance or load,

increase the number of repetitions, or increase the number of sets (consecutive repetitions).

Isometric exercises consist of pushing (without noticeable movement of a body part) against an immovable object such as a wall. Each muscle contraction is held for a few seconds. The exercise is repeated 5–10 times. Isometric exercises are *not* recommended because they can raise blood pressure in some people.

Isotonic exercises use free weights, weight machines, or calisthenics to strengthen muscles by creating muscular tension through shortening or lengthening the muscle. An example is using heavy weights with a low number of repetitions.

Isokinetic exercises use specialized weight machines to put tension on a particular set of muscles through an entire range of motion. For instance, Nautilus machines are built with cams that vary the load to match muscle strength in different joint positions.

- *Free weights, weight machines, and calisthenics:* The three principal methods of resistance training are with free weights, weight machines, or calisthenics. *(See ● Figure 8.)*

  Free weights are a type of isotonic exercise generally using dumbbells and barbells. These two weights are different. **A *dumbbell* consists of a short bar joining two weighted spheres** or sometimes adjustable weighted disks. **A *barbell* consists of a long bar connecting adjustable weighted disks at each end.** Beginners need special training to use free weights because of the safety risks they pose if dropped or lifted incorrectly.

  Weight machines are Nautilus-type machines that are used for isokinetic exercises. They are easier and safer to use than free weights because they control the range of motion and can't be dropped. People often call these machines "Nautilus machines," but Nautilus is only one brand. (Some others are Universal, Paramount, Keiser, Hydrafitness, and Cybex Eagle.) Some weight machines are single-purpose, others can be adjusted for different exercises.

For developing chest and triceps
Bench press using free weights: Keep hands 6–10 inches apart, push away

Bench press using weight machine: Back flat on bench, feet on floor, push away

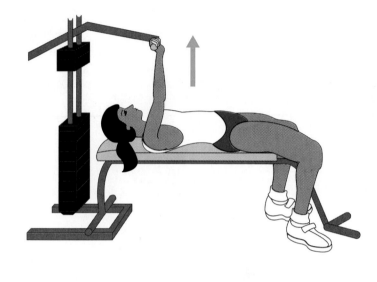

For developing biceps
Concentration curl using free weights: Sit with knees apart, bring weight toward chin

● **Figure 8   Exercises with free weights, weight machines, and calisthenics.** *(continued on pages 118–119)*

For developing back muscles Bent-over row, using free weights: Pull weights straight up to the sides of the chest

Bent arm curl Using weight machine: Shoulders should be slightly raised between lifts

For developing leg muscles Lunge using free weights: Take a large step forward, then reverse

Lateral pulldown using weight machine: Pull bar down behind the neck

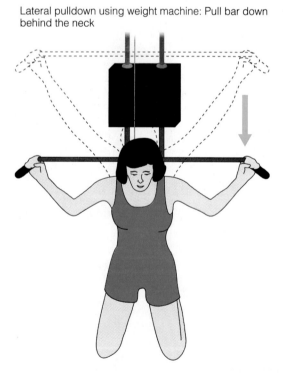

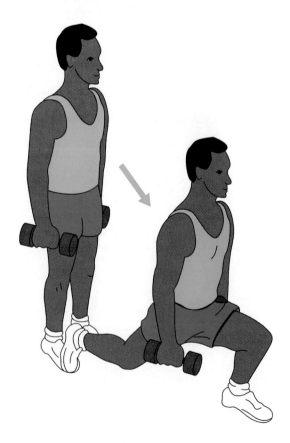

Knee extension (top) and leg curls, using weight machine

Calisthenic Alternatives to Equipment Exercises

Equipment exercise	Calisthenic alternatives
Bench press	Push-ups (full)
	Push-ups (modified)
Overhead press	Lateral raise (with jugs)
	Arm stretch (with bands)
Lateral pulldown	Pull-ups (with spotter)
	Arm pulls (with bands)
Seated leg press	Standing squats
	Standing squats (with jugs)

Calisthenics **are systematic rhythmic exercises, such as push-ups and pull-ups.** These activities are usually performed without any apparatus, except perhaps for stretch bands or surgical tubing for light resistance exercises. Calisthenics are useful especially when one cannot get to a gym and does not wish to miss a training session.

- *Warm up:* Before lifting weights, be sure to warm up with a few minutes of walking, stretching, and light calisthenics.

- *Exercise from 20 minutes two times a week up to 90 minutes five times a week—or do 1–3 sets of 8–12 exercises:* These recommendations should be thought of in terms of *sets of repetitions.*

    A *set* is the number of times the same movement has been completed. A *repetition* ("rep") is the single execu-tion of a movement—for example, lifting a barbell once. According to the American College of Sports Medicine, a set consists of 8–12 repetitions. Each exercise is for one or more of the important muscle groups: back, chest (pectorals), backs of legs, front thigh (quadriceps), buttocks (gluteus maximus), fronts and backs of upper arms (biceps and triceps), shoulders (deltoids), and stomach (abdomen).

    Beginners should start out with a set of 8 repetitions for each of 8–10 resistance exercises. The whole routine should be done within 20–30 minutes twice a week. As you build your strength and endurance, increase to 2 sets of 10–12 repetitions for 12 exercises. These are done in 45–60 minutes three times a week. People pursuing maximum fitness may do 3 sets of 12 repetitions for 15 exercises, for 90 minutes 3–5 days a week.

• *Concentrate on form and technique:* When starting out on a weight-training program, you should work hard enough to feel some muscle fatigue. You should not, however, try to "go for the burn"—pain in the muscles—which may signal that you are overdoing it. Use enough weight to tax your muscles on the last few repetitions of each set.

If you're using weight machines, make sure they're adjusted to fit your body's dimensions. Hold rather than squeeze the handgrips as you lift. Move through the full range of motion for each exercise, concentrating on the specific muscles used in the exercise.[46]

If you're using free weights (dumbbells and barbells), do each exercise in a slow, controlled manner, concentrating on feeling each contraction.[47] Don't let the weight drop between lifts.

Breathing and timing are important. Breathe *out* when you are doing the hardest part of the lifting, counting "one, two." Breathe *in* during recovery, counting "one, two, three, four."

Be sure to rest a few seconds between machines or sets. Allow your breath to return to normal.

• *Give your muscles time to rest:* It's important to avoid overtraining. In general, allow 48 hours for your muscles to recover from a workout. It's a good idea to schedule training for aerobic endurance on alternate days from training for muscle strength and endurance.

Circuit Training and Fitness Trails (Parcours) Many health clubs offer **circuit training, a logical sequence of exercises performed at different stations of free weights or weight machines.** The idea is to perform the exercises in order so no one muscle group is overworked and fatigue does not limit lifting ability.[48] For example, the first exercise might be for arm muscles, the second for stomach, the third for thighs, and so on.

Some community park departments and colleges offer fitness trails. These *fitness trails,* or *parcours,* consist of a marked path composed of separate exercise stations** set at various distances. Each station has equipment (such as a bar for chin-ups) and posted instructions for self-paced exercises. The ideal distance for the trails is 1 mile, but they can be much shorter or longer. A parcours provides self-tailored programs for walking or running between stations, then opportunities for stretching movements and endurance training.

Fitness trails provide ways of developing all three kinds of fitness—flexibility, aerobic endurance, and muscular strength and endurance. Do them on a regular basis, such as two or three times a week.

Exercise Dependency: How Much Is Too Much?

Overtraining, or "exercise dependency," can lead to injuries and mood disorders.

Called *exercise addiction* by laypeople, ***exercise dependency* is a compulsion to overexercise.** When this occurs, exercise displaces other areas of life in importance, such as family, friends, sex, hobbies, and job.[49] A study of New York City Marathon runners found that several characteristics especially predicted exercise dependency. These included avoiding people after missing a workout, obsessing over missing exercise, worrying about injuries disrupting the program, and feeling depressed after a workout.[50]

Even if you are not exercise dependent, overtraining can lead to a variety of problems:[51] (1) High on the list are bone and muscle injuries. Continuing to work out despite injuries can also lead to arthritis and other problems. (2) Moderate exercise may relieve depression, but too much exercise can *cause* depression.[52] (3) Some women who overtrain may lower their estrogen levels, which disrupts their menstrual cycles. **The absence or suppression of menstrual cycles is called *amenorrhea,*** and it can reduce fertility in the short run and perhaps produce osteoporosis in the long run. (4) Among men who overtrain, some show "sports anemia"—fatigue, weakness, and irritability. Some show lowered sperm count, testosterone levels, and sex drive.

How much exercise is too much? Probably going beyond the guidelines set forth by the

American College on Sports Medicine is excessive. However, because major variations exist, what would be exercise dependence or overtraining for one person would not be for another. The main thing is to listen to your body's signals. Remember that rest and restoration are necessary and that persistent soreness or fatigue means you're overextending yourself.

Strategy for Living: Preventing and Managing Injuries and Pain

Avoiding injuries starts with getting medical clearance and dressing right. Know the hazards of hot weather, such as dehydration, and cold weather, such as hypothermia. Make adjustments for smog, dim light, or high altitude. Treat soreness and mishaps appropriately.

There are a lot of ways to keep from putting yourself *out of* action when performing any physical activity. Let's consider some of them.

Getting Medical Clearance Nearly every article or book on exercise suggests you get a physician's approval before starting an activity program. This is particularly true if you are overweight, over 40, have not exercised in many months, are taking any prescription medicines, or are a smoker. Also be sure to tell the physician if you have any congenital or chronic condition that could cause concern. These include heart murmur, asthma, sickle-cell anemia, high blood pressure, or extreme tiredness.

Dressing Right Clearly, there are some activities where having the right clothes and gear is a must—rock climbing, for instance, or skiing. For most workouts and sports, however, what counts are correct, properly fitting shoes and clothing to suit the weather. Also, men need athletic supporters (jockstraps) and women need sports bras. The clothes should be comfortable and loose-fitting to allow freedom of movement. Here are a few specifics:

- **Shoes:** Choose the shoe for the specific activity you engage in. Be sure to shop for shoes at the end of the day while wearing the socks that are appropriate for your activity. Try on both shoes, being sure to allow ¼ inch between the end of your longest toe and the shoe. Be sure the shoe doesn't gap when you walk or run in it. Buy for your larger foot.

- **Dress for the weather:** Loose-fitting, light-colored T-shirts and shorts are the best clothing for many summer activities, such as running. Cotton is preferable to nylon because cotton absorbs water quickly and is nonirritating. During cold-weather activities you want to retain your body heat and slow heat loss. But you don't want to prevent perspiration from evaporating. Wear two or three loose-fitting layers of dark clothing (dark colors help retain heat), which can be removed. Avoid wearing waterproof outer garments to avoid trapping body heat. Wool is a good choice because it dries from the inside out, allowing sweat to evaporate. Be sure to wear mittens, wool socks, and a hat (50% of body heat escapes from your head).[53]

Hot Weather Hazards A hot day or heavy exercise leads to increased body heat. That makes more blood circulate near the cooler surface of your skin to release excess body heat to the outside. The heat is dissipated by the evaporation of sweat, in which water vaporizes from the skin, causing a cooling effect. The greatest risk of heat problems occurs when the weather is high in both temperature and humidity, because the high water content of the air prevents the water on your skin from evaporating. *(See ● Figure 9.)*

The problems associated with exercising in hot weather range in severity from dehydration to heat stroke.

- **Dehydration: Dehydration, or abnormal depletion of body fluids,** occurs when not enough water is taken in to replace the amount lost. A loss of 10–20% of usual water intake may be serious and sometimes life-threatening.

- **Heat cramps and heat stress: Heat cramps are painful muscle spasms in the arms, legs, and abdomen** caused by body fluid loss. Heat cramps are frequently accompanied by **heat stress, consisting**

Heat and humidity chart

Numbers within the chart show equivalent temperatures. Shaded areas indicate when exertion may be dangerous.

Air temperature (F°)

	70°	75°	80°	85°	90°	95°	100°	105°	110°	115°	120°
30%	67	73	78	84	90	96	104	113	123	135	148
40%	68	74	79	86	93	101	110	123	137	151	
50%	69	75	81	88	96	107	120	135	150		
60%	70	76	82	90	100	114	132	149			
70%	70	77	85	93	106	124	144				
80%	71	78	86	97	113	136					
90%	71	79	88	102	122						
100%	72	80	91	108							

Relative humidity

☐ Risk of heat exhaustion   ▨ Risk of heat stroke   ▦ High risk of heat stroke

Wind chill chart

Temperatures assume dry conditions. The greater the moisture, the higher the temperature at which your skin may be in danger.

Estimated wind speed (mph)   **Air temperature (°F)**
50   40   30   20   10   0   −10   −20   −30   −40

Equivalent temperature (°F)										
Calm	50	40	30	20	10	0	−10	−20	−30	−40
5	48	37	27	16	6	−5	−15	−26	−36	−47
10	40	28	16	4	29	−21	−33	−46	−58	−70
15	36	22	9	25	−18	−36	−45	−58	−72	−85
20	32	18	4	−10	−25	−39	−53	−67	−82	−96
25	30	16	0	−15	−29	−44	−59	−74	−88	−104
30	28	13	−2	−18	−33	−48	−63	−79	−94	−109
35	27	11	−4	−20	−35	−49	−67	−83	−98	−113
40	26	10	−6	−21	−37	−53	−69	−85	−100	−116

Wind speeds over 40 mph have little additional effect

Little danger for properly clothed person

Increasing danger   **Great danger**
DANGER OF FREEZING EXPOSED FLESH

● **Figure 9   Weather warnings.** The dangers of too much heat (and humidity) and too much cold.

of a drop in blood pressure, dizziness, and blurred vision.

- **Heat exhaustion: Heat exhaustion is prostration caused by excessive fluid loss.** It is characterized by increased sweating, higher body temperature, cool wet skin, and lack of coordination.

- **Heat stroke: Heat stroke is a life-threatening problem characterized by elevated body temperatures above 107°F (42°C), *lack* of perspiration, hot and dry skin, rapid breathing, seizures—and coma.** This requires *immediate* medical attention. The outcome may be poor if diagnosis and treatment is delayed as little as 2 hours.

For heat cramps and heat stress, stop activity, sit down in a cool place, and drink lots of water. Don't move until you've recovered. For heat exhaustion, you should do the same but also get medical treatment. Heat stroke is a medical emergency; until help comes, try to cool the victim's body down. Apply ice to the back of the neck and armpits. Sponge him or her continuously with cool water. Don't try putting the victim in the bathtub or pool of cold water as this may cause shock.

Strategy for Living: Exercising in Hot Weather Exercising safely in the heat is mostly a matter of drinking lots of fluids and following common sense. Some recommended actions are avoid strenuous exercise and don't exercise during the hottest part of the day. Drink more water than you think you need rather than what simply satisfies your thirst. If you are getting used to a new, hot climate, give yourself a chance to become acclimatized or adjusted (10–14 days).[54] To prevent heat disorders, you should drink 2 or more cups of water 2 hours before an event and another 2 cups 15 minutes before. During the activity, you should drink ½–1 cup of water about every 15 minutes. Water or diluted fruit juices are considered better than commercially available sports beverages, such as Gatorade, which often have a high sugar content.

Cold Weather Hazards You can exercise at temperatures as low as −22°F (−30°C) without heavy clothing.[55] However, the ***wind-chill factor,* which expresses the absolute tem-**perature combined with the wind velocity, is a temperature measurement that is a lot colder than the thermometer indicates. *(Refer back to Figure 9.)*

The dangers of overexposure to cold weather range from frost nip and frostbite to hypothermia:

- **Frost nip and frostbite: Frostnip is painless and is signaled principally by a lightening of the skin.** It can progress to ***frostbite,* where the affected part of the body becomes frozen and underlying tissue may be destroyed.** One of the first signs of frostbite is a white, grayish yellow, or blue discoloration of the skin. Pain may or may not be present. As frostbite progresses, affected body parts become numb, the skin becomes glossy and pale, and thawing produces great pain.

- **Hypothermia:** Hypothermia is the result of prolonged exposure to cold owing to inappropriate clothing or inadequate protection from the weather. It also results from immersion in cold water. **In hypothermia, the body's temperature drops below 95°F (35°C). One experiences shivering, slurring of speech, poor coordination, blue skin, and slowed pulse and respiration.** Hypothermia is a life-threatening condition. In extreme cases, the person may be disoriented, in shock, perhaps unconscious, and will stop breathing.

For both frostbite and hypothermia, get victims indoors, give them a warm drink (not alcohol), and get quick medical attention.[56] For frostbite, if no professional help will be available, place the affected part in lukewarm (not hot) water to rewarm it. (Don't rub snow on it or massage it.) The rewarming process takes about 30 minutes and is very painful.

For hypothermia, the victim should be wrapped in warm blankets. In serious cases, the person may be confused or comatose and no longer shivering. In such instances, heat must be applied, as with a hot water bottle, but gradually and gently. Don't rub the affected area or put the person in a warm bath.

Strategy for Living: Exercising in Cold Weather As with hot weather, exercising safely in cold weather is mostly a matter of common sense. Consider the wind as well as the cold.

124

Chapter 4
Physical Fitness:
Activity and Rest

The wind-chill factor can make all the difference. A 20-mile-per-hour wind can transform 10°F air temperature into an equivalent temperature of −25°F—within the zone of increasing danger. Layer clothing and always cover your head. Remove wet clothing right away. To decrease heat loss from lips, cheeks, and nose, apply an oil-based ointment.

Avoid alcohol and cigarettes. Alcohol makes you *feel* warmer, because it expands (dilates) the blood vessels in the hands and feet, but it actually increases the escape of heat from the body, making you colder. Smoking (nicotine) constricts these same blood vessels, thereby reducing the body temperature and blood supply in these areas.

What to Do About Strains and Sprains Different sports have different common injuries, which require different strategies for preventing them and ways of treating them. Strains and sprains are two of the most common injuries in athletics. **A *strain* is a stretch or tear in a muscle or in a tendon,** the tissue connecting muscles with bones. **A *sprain* is a stretch or tear of a ligament,** the connective tissue attaching bones together at the joints.[57]

The treatment for strains and sprains, as well as for most other unexposed injuries affecting tissue, is with *R-I-C-E,* or *R*est, *I*ce, *C*ompression, *E*levation:

- ***Rest:*** Rest the injured area; 48 hours is a reasonable length of time.
- ***Ice:*** Ice wrapped in a towel should be applied for 20 minutes to the injured area to reduce swelling and pain, then removed for 20 minutes. Apply more ice for the next 20 minutes, and so on, up to several hours.
- ***Compression:*** Compress the injury by wrapping the area in an elastic bandage; this will help to reduce pain and build-up of fluid around the affected area.
- ***Elevation:*** Elevate the injury above the level of your heart, to prevent swelling.

Sleep and Rest

▶ Distinguish between REM and non-REM sleep.

▶ Discuss the sleep problems of insomnia and narcolepsy.

▶ Identify strategies for maximizing sleep.

▶ Describe problems associated with snoring and ways to remedy it.

Most animals follow natural sleep cycles, and don't vary from them. But many humans—the 7 million Americans who work nights, for instance—ignore their natural rhythms, staying awake nights and sleeping days. This and other variations cause people to have problems getting enough sleep. Indeed, you may find you have some sleep problems yourself.

Sleep

Understanding sleep stages and daily circadian, or sleep/wake, cycles can help fitness. Many people have sleep problems, from insomnia to narcolepsy.

One of the most widespread problems with sleep in North America is that most people get 60–90 minutes less sleep each night than they should. Let's see the significance of this and what can be done about it.

The Cycles and Uses of Sleep During a normal night's rest, your body may go through four or five sleep cycles. Each cycle involves different stages of brain-wave activity that reflect REM and non-REM sleep. ***REM, for rapid-eye movement,* refers to times during the night when the eyes shift rapidly back and forth beneath the closed lids. It is during REM sleep that most vivid dreaming occurs. *Non-REM* sleep is quieter, mainly nondreaming sleep,** and it accounts for the majority of a night's sleep.

There seems to be no doubt about the importance of sleep and its effect on our performance. Going without sleep even one night seems to diminish people's ability to think creatively the following day.[58] And after 5–6 nights of shortened sleep, the way we work and feel is definitely affected. Researchers also may have evidence that sleep boosts the immune response against disease.

Sleep Disorders Although there are many sleep disorders, two of the most important are *insomnia* and *narcolepsy*.[59]

- ***Insomnia: Insomnia* is an inability to achieve adequate or restful sleep.** Inadequate sleep is a major cause of the errors that people make. One leading sleep researcher, Stanford University's William Dement, says that sleep is such an important factor in accidents that someday "driving or going to work while sleepy may be as reprehensible and even as criminally negligent as driving or going to work while drunk."[60]

  Insomnia may be of three types—*transient* (occasional), *short-term* (3–6 weeks' duration), and *chronic* (long-term). Any sleep problem that lasts 3 or more weeks should be assessed by a health care professional.

- ***Narcolepsy:*** The opposite of insomnia, ***narcolepsy* is an ongoing condition characterized by an irresistible urge to fall asleep.** It differs from normal sleepiness in that it cannot be fully relieved by any amount of sleep. A second symptom of narcolepsy is a sudden muscle weakness known as *cataplexy*. Usually brought about by excitement or high emotions such as laughter, anger, or fear, cataplexy causes one to collapse and be unable to move.[61] Narcoleptics number between 1 in 1000 and 1 in 10,000 people in the United States.[62,63] Narcolepsy is a treatable disorder.

Strategy for Living: Improving Your Sleep Performance

Strategies are available to take advantage of circadian rhythms; pull a study all-nighter; improve your sleep performance; and stop snoring.

Because sleep is so vital to your performance, it's important to know what things you can do to enhance your sleep quality. Here we present some strategies.

Understanding Your Circadian Rhythms An important physiological cycle is your ***circadian rhythm*, the body's built-in daily, or circadian, clock that determines the sleep-wake cycle.** The cycle also affects blood pressure, body temperature, hormone output, and cell division. Circadian rhythms can be the reason you get sleepy after lunch, and why you get those Sunday afternoon blues. It's also why your performance declines when you start night-shift work.

Consider some of these instances:

- ***Afternoon sluggishness:*** Afternoon sleepiness can be remedied by short naps. On the other hand, what you eat for lunch can also make a difference. A meal high in carbohydrates will make you sleepier than one high in protein, because the carbohydrates release sleep-related chemicals in your brain. Exercising during your lunch hour can also lessen the likelihood of your wanting to take an afternoon snooze.[64]

- ***The Sunday afternoon blues:*** Many people experience a downward mood swing midafternoon as they contemplate Monday morning's return to work or school. Part of this mild depression—which may extend to Monday morning—may derive from more than the end of the weekend's bright promise. Another cause, as one writer describes it, is "the imbalance between weekend sleep-wake cycles and the internal biological clock set by evolution to the cycle of day and night."[65] People often stay up late and rise later on weekends, and this disruption of the circadian rhythms may affect people's moods.

- *Night-shift work:* Many of the 7 million Americans who work at night have difficulty adjusting to a night schedule. Not only does sleepiness lead to accidents, but the upset in body rhythms also produces insomnia and gastrointestinal disorders. There are also more cases of heart disease and, in women, infertility. Many people working at night apparently never adjust to their schedule, no matter how many years they work the night shift.[66] Treatment using special lights may be helpful.

Circadian rhythms also manifest themselves in other ways, such as "jet lag" or tiredness after one flies across several time zones. In addition, many people feel they are "night people," who do their best work at night. It's worth paying attention to your inner body rhythms so you can use your high-energy time for work and study.

When you must pull an all-nighter, as when you've let studying slide, one helpful strategy is to take a nap *before* you light the midnight oil. "Prophylactic napping," as it has been called, will prevent sleepiness. A short nap before staying awake all night will enhance your performance more than a deeper nap later.[67]

How Much Sleep Do You Need? Do you *need* to sleep the 8 hours that everyone seems to consider standard? Sleep researchers say that people's sleep needs range from 2–3 hours a night to 10 or more. Most adults seem to do their best work by sleeping 7–8 hours.

Most people get less sleep than they want to or need, rather than more. Indeed, sleep scientists say there is virtually an epidemic of sleepiness in the nation. More than 100 million Americans get by with insufficient sleep—nearly every other adult and teenager.[68] Most short themselves 1–2 hours of sleep a night. But even one night's loss of 2 hours sleep is not made up during the following 5–6 days of normal sleep, says sleep researcher James Maas. "There are some people who are literally walking zombies," Maas says. "If you need an alarm clock to get up in the morning, or if you feel more than a minor sag in the middle of the day, you need more sleep."[69]

Assuming you don't have chronic insomnia, in which case you should see a doctor (or con-

tact the National Sleep Disorders Foundation), here are some tips on how to sleep better:

- *Follow a regular sleep schedule—7 days a week:* You don't have to go to bed at the same time every night, but you should get up at the same time every morning, even on the weekends.

- *Save your bed for sleeping and sex:* The idea is to associate bed with these activities and not with such activities as studying or afternoon snacks.

- *Develop a bedtime routine:* Develop bedtime rituals to allow yourself to wind down before sleep. Soak in a bath or read a book. After turning out the light, give yourself 15 minutes to drift off to sleep. If you don't become drowsy, don't stay in bed; go into another room and do something else until you feel sleepy.[70]

- *Watch what and when you drink and smoke:* Caffeine is a stimulant, so drinking coffee or caffeinated soft drinks after midday may affect your sleep. Nicotine is also a stimulant and won't help you sleep. Also, there is the danger of fire if you fall asleep with a lit cigarette. Alcohol, even in small amounts, can make you sleep less soundly. A glass of warm milk before bedtime may help you relax.

- *Deal with worries before you go to bed:* If you find yourself lying awake worrying about a problem, write down what you can do about it in the morning. List the reasons why it's not worth being upset about it now. Earlier in the day you can take time for a "worry session," writing down how you will handle any upcoming events. Talk over your problems with someone else.

- *Exercise at regular times:* Try to get at least some exercise every day. Although vigorous exercise just before bedtime doesn't encourage sleep, a short evening walk may be helpful.

- *Minimize distractions:* Try to eliminate distracting bedtime noises, or mask them with a soothing noise, such as music or the hum of a fan.

- *Avoid sleeping pills:* The effects achieved by most sleeping pills usually stop after 2–4 weeks of use. Moreover, sleeping pills only help you fall asleep faster; they do not help you achieve deep sleep. They leave a hangover in the morning and decrease your alertness. If you must take a sleeping pill, try to limit yourself to one per week.[71]

Help for Snoring Snoring is caused by the vibration of tissues of the throat and soft palate that become relaxed during sleep. Maybe your own snoring doesn't bother you, but it may bother your bed partner or roommate. Your snoring could be a signal of the sleep disorder known as apnea. **In *apnea*, one stops breathing for brief periods each night, and the lack of oxygen causes the sleeper to wake up.** Stopping breathing is usually caused by the closure of throat tissues. As though one were awakened by the phone ringing every 15 minutes throughout the night, the resulting sleep deprivation can cause daytime sleepiness.

Serious cases of snoring should be treated by a physician. However, there are several changes in lifestyle and sleeping habits that may help.[72] Some of these are health habits that will benefit you in other ways as well.

- *Alter drug use:* Don't smoke, avoid or reduce alcohol and other drug consumption, and use over-the-counter medications cautiously.

- *Change sleep habits:* Sleeping on a firm mattress with a low pillow can help reduce airway obstruction. If you snore only while sleeping on your back, try changing sleeping positions or sleeping without a pillow.

800-HELP

American Running and Fitness Association. 800-776-2732. Furnishes information on aerobic sports. Offers referrals to orthopedists, coaches, trainers, sports-medicine clinics, podiatrists, and chiropractors.

Nutrition for Athletes. 800-231-3438. Registered dietitians at the University of Alabama at Birmingham offer advice on high-performance nutrition.

Running Injuries. 800-843-8664. The American Running and Fitness Association offers free pamphlets on runners' injuries and tips on treatment.

Suggestions for Further Reading

American College of Sports Medicine. (1992). *ACSM fitness book*. Champaign, IL: Leisure Press. Comprehensive, easy-to-understand guide to physical fitness for people of all levels.

Bryant A. Stamford & Porter Shimer. (1990). *Fitness without exercise*. New York: Warner Books. Shows how to use small, nonstructured bouts of activity to develop and maintain fitness.

People and Physical Activity

Whatever you can do, or dream you can begin," Goethe said, "begin it." The challenges faced and overcome by the following men and women, of various races, ages, and abilities, are those faced by millions of people. Whatever your dream about athletics, begin it.

The Blader[73]

Casey Pieretti was 18 when he was hit by a drunk driver while pushing a disabled car off the road. That accident cost him the lower part of his right leg.

In June 1993, at age 26, he rollerbladed into Washington, D.C., ending a 3100-mile skate that began in San Diego 87 days earlier. The purpose of the trip was to raise $3 million for a national limb bank for children.

Rollerblading across the country on one good leg and a prosthesis wasn't easy, but the last 110 miles were especially difficult. He had to skate with one arm in a sling, having broken a clavicle in Richmond, Virginia. "It was pretty tough," Pieretti said. "I think that was the hardest part."

The accident happened while he was doing stunts. Pieretti does back flips, car jumps, and other tricks as a professional skater.

The Swimmer[74]

When Sybyl Smith went to Boston University to major in psychology and to join the swim team, she left her support system behind her. Back in Fresno, California, she was often the only African-American swimmer in a sport overwhelmingly dominated by whites. Nevertheless, she had felt encouraged, and by the time she was 10 had held seven national age-group records.

In college, however, "it was like, 'Who is this black girl?'" she said. "I had no friends. I was terribly lonely."

She almost retired from competitive swimming, but "I was determined to be on top." As a result, she became the first African-American woman to win N.C.A.A. Division 1 All American honors in swimming.

After college, as the director of the International Swimming Hall of Fame Minority Enrichment and Recruitment Program, Smith traveled around the country, speaking of the emotional ups and downs of her career and encouraging others to swim. Talking to youngsters in a New York City elementary school, she said: "Being different is not bad, it's unique."

The Bronco Buster[75]

Though he had a degree in business administration from UCLA, Wayne Orme had a lifelong love of horses, and at age 27 he decided to become a professional rodeo cowboy.

"For years, I was looked at as a freak," he said. "People came to point and laugh at the funny-looking cowboy with the black face." For Orme and other African-American rodeo contestants, the idea wasn't to impress the fans or even the judges but the other cowboys, who were mainly white.

Today Orme is known as one of the most graceful steer ropers on the rodeo circuit. He is also a successful businessman and Hollywood stuntman.

The Track and Field Star[76]

Berta Gray played basketball and baseball in high school and college, but for most of her life she has owned a printing business.

She learned about the Senior Games, open to people as youthful as 55, and became Northern California champion of the discus, javelin, and high jump in the 75–79 age category.

With sports, she says, age is not relevant. "They say you're as young as you feel," she said. "That's a bunch of baloney. You're as young as you *think*."

Intimacy, Sexuality, and Safer Sex

Learning to like and love yourself is the key to intimacy.

So says psychiatrist David Burns.[1] A great many people, he points out, feel unattached, lonely, unlovable. Even some of those who for all appearances are handsome, poised, and outgoing are actually in great despair. They mistakenly believe that only a loving partner will deliver them from depression and boredom and make them feel happy and secure. However, one's feelings of loneliness and inadequacy may actually drive others away. People look not for needy partners but for partners who are self-confident enough that they bring excitement and contentment to others' lives. Love, then, begins with self-love—a matter you can probably do something about.

Relationships

▶ Discuss the importance of self-love.

▶ Define intimacy and describe five forms of intimate relationships.

▶ Differentiate between love that is romantic, erotic, friendship, altruistic, and dependent.

▶ Discuss strategies for coping with the loss of love.

▶ Explain how one's family of origin affects the quality of future relationships.

▶ Name and describe three types of committed relationships.

▶ Identify the advantages and disadvantages of marriage and the attributes that strengthen or undermine a marriage.

Self-love does not mean being selfish or conceited. It means appreciating who you are and your potential. To stop feeling inferior and rejected and project the self-confidence that will attract other people, Burns suggests taking four steps: Stop abusing yourself and get involved in life. Stop putting yourself down and think about yourself in a compassionate manner. Drop self-defeating attitudes and develop a more positive value system. Confront and conquer your fear of being alone.

When you include yourself in your positive feelings you can then include others, and they will include you.

Intimate Relationships: From Being Alone to Being in Love

The capacity for love starts with self-love and the rewards of being alone. Intimate relationships include friendship but also various kinds of intimacy—recreational, social, intellectual, emotional, and physical. Love may be of five types: passionate or romantic, erotic or sexual, dependent or addictive, friendship or companionate, and altruistic or unselfish. Loss of love means having to deal with feelings of rejection and rebuilding self-esteem.

Many psychologists seem to measure mental well-being by the success of our relationships with others. But being able to be comfortably alone is also a sign of strength. In contrast, there is love that is actually not love but neediness. Let us examine the range of relationship possibilities.

Being Alone Twenty million Americans currently live alone, some by choice, others by circumstance. Regardless of how we feel about it, all of us are alone at some period in our lives. Being alone, however, need not mean feeling lonely. Indeed, it is important to discover what the rewards of being alone are. *(See* ● *Figure 1.)*

Friendship *Friendship* **is a relationship between two people that involves a high degree of trust and mutual support.**

Friendship is important throughout your life. The well-being of adults in all age groups seems to be related to the quality of social interaction they have with friends as well as with family.[2] Numerous studies find better health among people who can turn to friends or family for advice, empathy, assistance, and affirmation as well as affection. They are more likely to survive major life challenges such as heart attacks and major surgery than those without such support. They are also less likely to develop cancer, respiratory infections, and other diseases.[3] Friends can help reaffirm your self-worth when you lose a job or relationship or your good opinion of yourself is otherwise challenged.

Intimacy Friendships can be close and may or may not involve intimacy. To some people, the word "intimate" means having sex. However, *intimacy* **is defined as a close, familiar, affectionate, and loving relationship with another person.**[4] Intimacy can take five forms:[5]

- *Recreational intimacy: Recreational intimacy* **is the sharing of interests, hobbies, and recreational activities** with another person.

- *Social intimacy:* **The experience of having common friends and similar social networks is called** *social intimacy.* An example is when you and your partner enjoy spending time with other couples or share the same close friends.

- *Intellectual intimacy: Intellectual intimacy* **is the closeness developed by sharing ideas,** as when you find an endless number of things to talk about together. This intimacy is important for free communication of feelings and desires through words and body language. *Body language* **is nonverbal communication through body posture and gestures.** Effective communication has a great deal to do with sustaining a couple's satisfaction with their relationship.[6]

- **Emotional intimacy: Emotional intimacy is closeness of feeling.** This kind of intimacy occurs, for example, when partners feel they can understand each other's joys and pains. Also, both feel they can discuss their feelings without causing the other person to become defensive.

- **Physical intimacy: Closeness developed through physical contact—from touching to hugging to caressing to kissing, and so on—is *physical intimacy*.** This kind of intimacy includes all forms of physical and sexual contact.

Love   What is love? The reason there is so much confusion about love is that this one word is used for a multitude of feelings.

Professor F. Philip Rice describes five types of love—romantic, erotic, dependent, friendship, and altruistic. Together they make up what he calls *complete love:*[7]

- **Infatuation, passionate, or romantic love:** When we experience that dizzying ecstasy and joy known as "falling in love" we are infatuated. **Infatuation is passionate love, or romantic love: passionate, strong feelings of affection for another person.** This kind of love is real enough in its physiological manifestations: pounding heart, breathlessness, sometimes the inability to eat or sleep.[8]

    The reasons people fall in love are probably proximity, commonality, and perceived attractiveness. People become attracted to those they see frequently and who share similar attributes.[9] Physical attractiveness is also often important at first. Attractiveness is sometimes heightened by the perception of dangerous circumstances (which is why secret love may be so intense).[10,11]

    In the end, infatuation or romantic love cannot be sustained. It becomes less wildly romantic and more rational, although feelings of love may continue to grow. Wildly emotional love evolves into the more low-keyed **companionate love or friendship love, with feelings of friendly affection and deep attachment.**[12]

● **Figure 1   The joy of being alone.**

“*Living alone can be a positive experience at any age. It needn't be equated with loneliness.*

Many people who live alone are lonely. And statistics indicate that loneliness leads to an increased risk of physical and psychological illness, including depression so severe that it can result in suicide. But what these statistics fail to point out is that there are thousands and thousands of people who are alone, alive, and well.

For every miserable, pathetic, and lonely individual who lives alone, there are many others who are healthy, involved in interesting, productive activities, and enjoying life.”

—Barbara Powell. (1985). *Alone, alive, and well.* Emmaus, PA: Rodale, p. 2.

- *Erotic love: Erotic love* **is sexual love,** but not necessarily romantic love. Many people can have sex without romantic love; indeed, some are unable to handle emotional involvement. Others find that having sex actually diminishes the feelings of romantic love. Yet others find that tensions that diminish loving feelings also adversely affect the sexual aspect of their relationship. Many couples, however, discover that their sexual and loving feelings blend and enhance their relationship.

- *Dependent love: Dependent love* **is love that develops in response to previously unmet psychological needs.** For instance, someone who got little praise as a child may have an intense psychological need for appreciation met by the beloved. Or a studious person may welcome appreciation for his or her playfulness.[13]

  At its extreme, this kind of love can become an addiction to another person as a source of security. Then love becomes a "mutual protection racket" between two people hanging on to avoid loneliness or to meet an extreme need for approval.

- *Friendship love:* As mentioned, *friendship* or *companionate love* is more low-key than romantic love is. Friendship love is genuine *liking* for the other person, which results in a desire to be together. Despite the mass media's emphasis on romance and sexuality, companionate love may be the most common and frequently experienced aspect of love.[14]

- *Altruistic love: Altruistic love* **is unselfish concern for the welfare of another.** An example is a parent willingly and happily assuming care for a child. In a relationship such as marriage, altruistic love means accepting the beloved without insisting that he or she change.

The End of Love Relationships can be a source of great joy, their loss a source of great pain. One difficulty in coping with the end of love is dealing with *rejection.* Rejection can be unreciprocated love in an attempted relationship or love that "grows old and waxes cold."

In *How to Fall Out of Love,* Debora Phillips suggests some steps for recovering from the loss of love, using methods of behavioral therapy:[15]

- *Stop thoughts of the person:* You can learn to spend less and less time thinking about the loved one. Make a list of positive scenes and pleasures that do not involve the former beloved. When a thought about the person enters your mind, say "Stop," then think about one of the best scenes on your list.

- *Build self-esteem:* Just as a love relationship can build self-esteem, being rejected can lower it. To raise your self-esteem, Phillips suggests you use index cards on which every day you write two good things about yourself. For example, write down things you have done recently or in the past that are positive. When negative thoughts creep in, say "Stop," and think one of these good thoughts about yourself.

If you are the one being let down, don't spend a lot of time speculating *why*. The other person may not even know why he or she is no longer in love, and it doesn't help to torture yourself trying to figure it out. A helpful strategy may be to simply put some distance between yourself and the other person.

If you are the one trying to disengage from the relationship, remember how it feels to be rejected. Try to be honest but gentle: "I no longer feel the way I once did about you." Don't promise to try to "work things out," and don't try to take care of or "rescue" the other person. Do try to mobilize your support group and get involved with activities you enjoy.

You and Your Committed Relationships

How well you were treated by others early in life affects your emotional availability and ability to have intimate relationships with others. Some people are happy with singlehood, others get involved with dating and courtship. Among the types of committed, or monogamous, relationships people have are living together or cohabitation, whether heterosexual or homosexual, and marriage. Without positive interaction and good problem-solving skills, many marriages will end in divorce.

In the beginning, when you were a newborn, everything outside of you, from baby toys to mother, seemed simply a part of you. The messages and treatment you received from others, particularly adults who were your primary caretakers, deeply influenced your ability to love yourself. Perceptions about yourself established during childhood form the basis for how you relate to others today. Positive feelings of self-love often result in the ability to love others and to be loved by them.

Families, Dysfunctional Families, and Emotional Availability Your emotional training began, most likely, with your family of origin. **Your *family of origin* consists of those in your immediate family who had the most direct influence on your life.** These included adults who parented you and your brothers and sisters. You may also have been emotionally affected by people in your *extended family*—**grandparents, aunts and uncles, cousins, and so on.** Extended families are characteristic of multi-generational households, such as those of Asian and Latin American families.

The best that could be hoped for any child is to be raised in an atmosphere of openness, support, trust, and sharing. Far too often this is not the case. Many of us grow up in dysfunctional families. **In *dysfunctional families*, the interactions between family members restrict rather than foster emotional expression, individual growth, and self-love.** Sometimes a family is dysfunctional because of the presence of someone with a dependency problem (alcohol, drugs, gambling, workaholism, religion, violence). In dysfunctional families, people are dishonest and distrustful of each other because one or more members try compulsively to control others. Some members also have unrealistic expectations about how they and others ought to be, and constantly seek to further their own self-gratification. The result is that the family suffers emotional and social isolation (for example, in keeping outsiders away from an alcoholic family). They also tend to suffer a continuing cycle of pain.[16]

Another damaging kind of upbringing is sexual abuse in childhood. This may consist of molestations—ranging from sexually suggestive remarks to fondling of breasts and genitals to intercourse or oral sex. The molester may be someone inside the immediate family or another such as a relative, neighbor, or babysitter. One form of sexual abuse is ***incest,* sexual relations between two people too closely related to legally marry,** such as father and daughter or brother and sister. Some survivors of sexual abuse are so traumatized that they may actually not remember the abusive incidents. However, they may be supremely wary and uncomfortable about opening themselves emotionally to prospective lovers.

How you have been treated by others, then, is the basis of your emotional availability. ***Emotional availability* is your ability to give and receive emotionally from another person without the fear of being hurt or taken advantage of.** Clearly, it has much to do with how you handle relationships and intimacy, now and in the future.

The Single Life Being single is fairly common. Sixty-six million people (37% of all American adults) are not involved in an intimate relationship, never married, or "newly single"—the divorced and widowed.[17] More people are choosing to live alone, people are marrying for the first time later in life, and divorce rates are high. Although adult men are more likely than women to live alone, women live longer, so they outnumber men in later years.

Do people *like* being single? Some do, for a variety of reasons. Many find it as appealing as being married. Also, many committed relationships do not involve marriage. Others, both men and women, say they have not found the right person but would like to get married some day. Psychologist Florence Kaslow reported other reasons for staying single that people gave in a survey of several states. Some men said they don't want to marry because they are putting their independence and the resolution of personal issues first. Women, especially those over 30, often put their careers and quests for financial independence first.[18]

Dating and Mating The 20s are an age when most **people are seriously on the lookout**

for prospective mates—a time described by that old-fashioned word *courtship*. Courtship includes the ritual known as *dating* and may take the form of actively pursuing relationship possibilities (such as going to dances). Other means are getting friends to "fix you up," running personal ads, and so on.

The dating experience itself can be extremely difficult for many people. Indeed, one study found that problems in dating relationships were the most frequent complaints voiced by undergraduates using a college counseling center.[19] Says one writer, "Interaction with the opposite sex is a major factor in our development, and scars acquired during dating encounters may have long-lasting effects on later adjustment."[20] Anxiety may come from feeling awkward about what to say and do on a date. Being uncomfortable about encounters of a potentially sexual nature and being overcritical of one's own abilities may also lead to high anxiety. Anyone experiencing these kinds of worries about dating can get help by going to a college counseling center or getting similar assistance.

Contrary to popular belief, however, extensive dating does not predict success in terms of choosing a mate with whom one will live "happily ever after." According to the author of one study, "The length of the dating experience, the number of dating partners, the length of the relationship with the eventual first husband, and the degree of sexual intimacy with that husband—none of these predictors had any significant independent influence on the fate of the marriage."[21] Rather, according to this particular study, marital success corresponded more with the degree of romantic love the woman felt at the moment of marriage. Other important influences were shared family values, leisure activities, and control of family finances.

The Committed Relationship: Living Together Once upon a time, the phrase "committed relationship" meant a long betrothal or courtship or being married. It still includes those things, but today it also describes ***monogamous* relationships, in which two people are sexually faithful to each other.** That is, there may be a committed relationship between an *unmarried heterosexual couple* living together as "domestic partners." A committed

relationship may also be between a *homosexual couple*, male or female, sharing living quarters.

A heterosexual couple living intimately together in the same household outside of marriage is said to be *cohabiting*. The Census Bureau recorded 2.7 million of these couples in 1990. The average length of cohabitation is only about 12 months.[22] However, **if the relationship continues longer than 7 years, some states consider it a *common-law marriage*** for real estate or financial purposes.

Is living together in a "trial marriage" a good way to practice for the real thing? Some see cohabitation as simply a new development in the American courtship process. According to sociology professor Ronald Rindfuss, "In an earlier time, they would have gotten married or simply continued dating."[23] Yet some studies show that people who live together and then marry are *more* likely to divorce than people who did not live together first.[24,25] There may be several reasons for this: Long-term cohabitors who are unsure about or ideologically opposed to marriage may be pressured by friends or relatives to tie the knot. Cohabitors who marry may be less likely to pool incomes, own joint property, and share activities, values, and interests, which help a marriage.[26]

Committed Relationships: Homosexual Couples Same-sex relationships are every bit as strong as opposite-sex relationships. In fact, **couples' rights and family issues are a focus for many** people with a *homosexual* orientation—sexually attracted to members of the same sex. **Many *lesbians*, or female homosexuals,** are in long-term relationships and are more likely than ***gays*, or male homosexuals,** to settle down with one partner. About one-third of lesbians are mothers, from heterosexual relationships, artificial insemination, or adoption.[27,28] However, there are also many gay men who have long-term relationships and some who raise children.

Children growing up in a gay home clearly are being raised in somewhat unconventional circumstances. Some suffer insults from peers in early adolescence if their same-sex parents' sexual orientation is known or suspected by others in the community. On the other hand, studies suggest that most children of gay parents are well-adjusted.[29] Indeed, some experts compare them with children of interracial marriages, where confronting prejudice in early adolescence builds character and enriches later life.[30]

Committed Relationships: Marriage The traditional committed relationship in Western society is *marriage,* **the legal, and often religious, union of two people of the opposite sex.** Most people get married—70% of Americans at least once, although not necessarily "so long as ye both shall live," as the marriage oath has it.[31]

In general, marriage is beneficial: married people are happier and healthier than people who are never married, divorced, or widowed.[32] Married people also live longer: the average mortality rate for unmarried men is twice as high as for married men, and 1½ times higher for unmarried women. Divorced people, especially men, generally have the highest death rates.[33,34]

Interestingly, although members of both sexes benefit psychologically from marriage, men seem to benefit more than women.[35] The reason may have to do with gender roles: whether they work outside the home or not, being married is probably harder on women. They generally find themselves carrying a larger share of housework and childcare, making them feel stressed or unappreciated.

The longer couples stay married, the more likely they are to become like each other, eventually sharing many of the same thoughts and perceptions. However, women are more likely to change than their husbands are.[36]

Can science predict which marriages will survive and which will not? One psychological study has found that the husband's disappointment with the marriage is the single most potent predictor of divorce.[37] Frequent arguing is not a liability—provided it is outweighed by praise. *In couples who stay together, about five times more positive things are said to and about one another than negative ones.* In couples who divorce, there are about 1½ times more negative things said than positive ones. In addition, the couple's approach to problem solving—specifically whether or not the husband tended to withdraw from arguments—is predictive of divorce. This corresponds with findings from another study that communication difficulties were the leading cause of divorce.[38]

Divorce When film star Elizabeth Taylor married construction worker Larry Fortensky in 1991, it was her eighth marriage and his third. Taylor had long since joined the club of 2 million American women ages 15–65 who have been married three or more times. Another 10 million have been married twice (and 50 million once).[39] One divorce occurs for every two marriages in the United States, and at present 8% of Americans age 15 or over are currently divorced. (This compares with 7% who are widowed, 26% who haven't been married, and 59% who are married.)[40] Almost 80% of people who divorce will take a chance and marry again, usually within 3 years. Indeed, divorced people are more likely than singles to take the plunge, according to the National Center for Health Statistics.[41,42]

Many states now have *no-fault divorce* laws, which assume that no blame exists (or the blame is shared). With earlier laws, one party had to prove the other "at fault." Under no-fault laws, any alimony, spousal support, and child support are supposedly tailored by the court or mutual agreement to the circumstances.

Despite attempts to bring civility to the end of a marriage, the loss can be comparable to the death of a spouse. *(See ● Figure 2.)* "In both cases the person undergoes a grieving process," write sexuality authors Robert Crooks and Karla Baur. "There are important differences, however. When the grief is caused by death, there are rituals and social support available, which may be helpful to the survivor. In contrast, there are no recognized grief rituals to help the divorced person."[43]

Strategy for Living: The Importance of Communication Becoming one-half of a committed couple may end one search, but it begins another. It is said that no married couple hasn't thought about divorce; likewise no other committed couple hasn't thought about splitting up. The number of subjects over which two people can disagree is awesome. But some principal areas where couples must adjust are as follows:[44]

- *Unrealistic expectations:* Many people enter a committed relationship with unrealistic expectations about how it's going to be dealing with jobs, bills, housework, and so on. Confusion about roles—who will do which chores, for example—may strain these expectations.

● **Figure 2   The pain of divorce.**

❝*Initially, a person may experience shock: 'This cannot be happening to me.' Disorganization may follow, a sense that one's entire world has turned upside down. Volatile emotions may unexpectedly surface. Feelings of guilt may become strong. Loneliness is common. Finally (usually not for several months or a year), a sense of relief and acceptance may come. . . . If after several months of separation a person is not developing a sense of acceptance, she or he may need professional help. Although many of the feelings triggered by divorce are uncomfortable, even painful, they can be steps toward resolving the loss so that a person can reestablish intimate relationships. Grieving can lead to healing.***❞**

—Robert Crooks & Karla Baur. (1990). *Our sexuality* (4th ed.). Redwood City, CA: Benjamin/Cummings, p. 522.

- ***Work and career issues:*** Especially with both partners working outside the home, there can be a great deal of work/family conflict and adjustments about parental and other family roles.
- ***Financial difficulties:*** Having money does not ensure partners' stability, but not having it can produce serious problems. Even when money is plentiful, however, there can be quarrels over how to spend it.
- ***Problems with in-laws:*** Mobility may have reduced problems with in-laws—each other's family—but they can still be a source of "interference" in some relationships.
- ***Sexual problems:*** Sexual problems are often entwined with couple problems, but it's difficult to know which causes which. Inhibited communication about sexual issues can be a source of great distress.
- ***Commitment:*** It may be acceptable to imagine having a passionate love affair outside the committed relationship, but having one almost always changes the relationship. Perhaps infidelities are best left inside the mind—just as it is better to covet your neighbor's car than it is to steal it.

Most of the foregoing problems can be overcome with effective communication. Indeed, good communication—to handle conflict and wants—is critical to a successful marriage or other committed relationship.

Your Sexuality

▶ Name the principal parts of the male and female reproductive systems and describe the function, location, and problems associated with each.

▶ Name and describe the three phases of the fertility cycle and the role of relevant hormones. Discuss the major menstrual-cycle-related problems.

▶ Differentiate between sex and gender and discuss the determinants of each.

▶ Discuss the kinds of sexual orientation and the continuum of sexual orientation described by Kinsey.

▶ Identify the stages of human sexual response described by Masters and Johnson and the changes that occur within each stage.

▶ Discuss the different varieties of sexual expression and the concept of "normality."

▶ Describe the sexual problems that are commonly experienced by men and women.

Do men and women have different feelings and fears? It might seem so: Men report fears of physical weakness, discomfort with any strong emotion except anger, powerful women, intellectual inferiority, and failure. Women report fears of being unattractive, victimized, and inadequate; mismanaging a relationship; and being estranged from close personal connections. At least these are the his-and-her concerns unearthed in research by Richard Eisler and others.[45,46]

Or do these fears really only reflect **stereotypes, oversimplified ideas and opinions about how men and women ought to be?** Today our society is struggling to transcend traditional and stereotypical notions of masculinity and femininity. Changes in perception are not only of childhood but also of adult areas such as workplace, bedroom, and family life. Indeed, for many people the ideal of what it is to be a man or a woman contains few of the old notions of maleness and femaleness. They find it more

useful to use ideas of **androgyny, a word meaning "having characteristics of both sexes."** This ability of either sex to express both masculine and feminine traits represents a profound liberation for both.

Sexuality is a private matter, yet it is given vast importance by the mass media. For both these reasons, it's difficult to assess what's *real* and appropriate about male and female roles, sex and sexuality. How much do you know about sex? Before proceeding you might wish to take the accompanying Self Discovery. *(See Self Discovery 1.)*

The Male Reproductive System

The visible, external parts of the male reproductive anatomy include the penis and scrotum. The penis contains the urethra for carrying sperm and semen, and the scrotum holds the testes. Reproductive organs inside the body are the testicles, epidymis, vas deferens, seminal vesicles, prostate gland, ejaculatory ducts, and Cowper's glands. In middle age, men may experience prostate enlargement and a decline in production of the male sex hormone, testosterone.

Many notions about gender start with anatomy, most particularly sexual anatomy. We consider the reproductive system for males first.

Male Reproductive Anatomy The male sexual organs consist of two parts visible outside the body, the *penis* and the *scrotum*. The rest of the male reproductive system is inside the body. *(See ● Figure 3.)* Let us consider these.

● *Outside and inside the penis:* **The penis has a double function—urination and sexual intercourse.** The penis contains no bones or muscle. An erection occurs when the spongy cylinders of tissue within the penis become engorged with blood during sexual arousal. A nonerect (flaccid) penis has spongy cylinders that contain little blood. Penis length is a concern to many men, but the size of a man's penis is not related to women's sexual satisfaction.

SELF DISCOVERY 1

How Much Do You Know About Sex?

The Kinsey Institute/Roper Organization National Sex Knowledge Test

Circle one answer after reading each question carefully.

1. Nowadays, what do you think is the age at which the *average* or *typical* American *first* has sexual intercourse?
   a. 11 or younger   c. 13   e. 15   g. 17   i. 19   k. 21 or older
   b. 12   d. 14   f. 16   h. 18   j. 20   l. Don't know

2. Out of every 10 married American men, how many would you estimate have had an extramarital affair—that is, have been sexually unfaithful to their wives?
   a. Less than 1 out of 10   d. 3 out of 10 (30%)   g. 6 out of 10 (60%)   j. 9 out of 10 (90%)
   b. 1 out of 10 (10%)   e. 4 out of 10 (40%)   h. 7 out of 10 (70%)   k. More than 9 out of 10
   c. 2 out of 10 (20%)   f. 5 out of 10 (50%)   i. 8 out of 10 (80%)   l. Don't know

3. Out of every 10 American women, how many would you estimate have had anal (rectal) intercourse?
   a. Less than 1 out of 10   d. 3 out of 10 (30%)   g. 6 out of 10 (60%)   j. 9 out of 10 (90%)
   b. 1 out of 10 (10%)   e. 4 out of 10 (40%)   h. 7 out of 10 (70%)   k. More than 9 out of 10
   c. 2 out of 10 (20%)   f. 5 out of 10 (50%)   i. 8 out of 10 (80%)   l. Don't know

4. A person can get AIDS by having anal (rectal) intercourse even if neither partner is infected with the virus that causes AIDS.
   True   False   Don't know

5. There are over-the-counter spermicides people can buy at the drugstore that will kill the virus that causes AIDS.
   True   False   Don't know

6. Petroleum jelly, Vaseline Intensive Care, baby oil, and Nivea are *not* good lubricants to use with a condom or a diaphragm.
   True   False   Don't know

7. More than 1 out of 4 (25 percent) of American men have had a sexual experience with another male during either their teens or adult years.
   True   False   Don't know

8. It is usually difficult to tell whether people *are* or *are not* homosexual just by their appearance or gestures.
   True   False   Don't know

9. A woman or teenage girl can get pregnant during her menstrual flow (her period).
   True   False   Don't know

10. A woman or teenage girl can get pregnant even if the man withdraws his penis before he ejaculates.
    True   False   Don't know

11. Unless they are having sex, women do not need to have regular gynecological examinations.
    True   False   Don't know

12. Teenage boys should examine their testicles regularly just as women self-examine their breasts for lumps.
    True   False   Don't know

13. Problems with erection are most often started by a physical problem.
    True   False   Don't know

14. Almost all erection problems can be successfully treated.
    True   False   Don't know

15. Menopause, or change of life as it is often called, does *not* cause most women to lose interest in having sex.
    True   False   Don't know

16. Out of every 10 American women, how many would you estimate have masturbated either as children or after they were grown up?
    a. Less than 1 out of 10   d. 3 out of 10 (30%)   g. 6 out of 10 (60%)   j. 9 out of 10 (90%)
    b. 1 out of 10 (10%)   e. 4 out of 10 (40%)   h. 7 out of 10 (70%)   k. More than 9 out of 10
    c. 2 out of 10 (20%)   f. 5 out of 10 (50%)   i. 8 out of 10 (80%)   l. Don't know

17. What do you think is the length of the average man's *erect* penis?
    a. 2 inches   d. 5 inches   g. 8 inches   j. 11 inches
    b. 3 inches   e. 6 inches   h. 9 inches   k. 12 inches
    c. 4 inches   f. 7 inches   i. 10 inches   l. Don't know

18. Most women prefer a sexual partner with a larger-than-average penis.
    True   False   Don't know

SELF DISCOVERY 1

(*continued*)

Scoring the Test

Each question is worth 1 point, so the total possible number of points you can get is 18. Using this chart, score each item and then add up your total number of points. When a range of possible answers is correct, according to currently available research data, all respondents choosing one of the answers in the correct range are given a point.

Question Number	Give yourself a point if you circled any of the following answers	Circle the number of points you received
1	f,g	0 1
2	d,e	0 1
3	d,e	0 1
4	False	0 1
5	(any answer; everyone gets a point)	1
6	True	0 1
7	True	0 1
8	True	0 1
9	True	0 1
10	True	0 1
11	False	0 1
12	True	0 1
13	True	0 1
14	True	0 1
15	True	0 1
16	g,h,l	0 1
17	d,e,f	0 1
18	False	0 1

Total Number of Points: _____

Now look up the grade you received:

If you got this number of points	You receive this grade
16–18	A
14–15	B
12–13	C
10–11	D
1–9	F

Compare yourself to other Americans: America's report card

Grade	Number of correct answers required to receive this grade	Number of participants receiving this grade	Percent of participants receiving this grade
A	16–18	5	<1
B	14–15	68	4
C	12–13	239	14
D	10–11	463	27
F	1–9	936	55

Note: Of the 1974 survey participants, 263 (12%) completed 10 or fewer of the 18 test items and were not included in the computation of these overall test scores. However, all those answering a question were included in the item-by-item analyses.

Source: Adapted from Reinisch, J., & Beasley, B. (1990). *The Kinsey Institute new report on sex.* New York: St. Martin's Press.

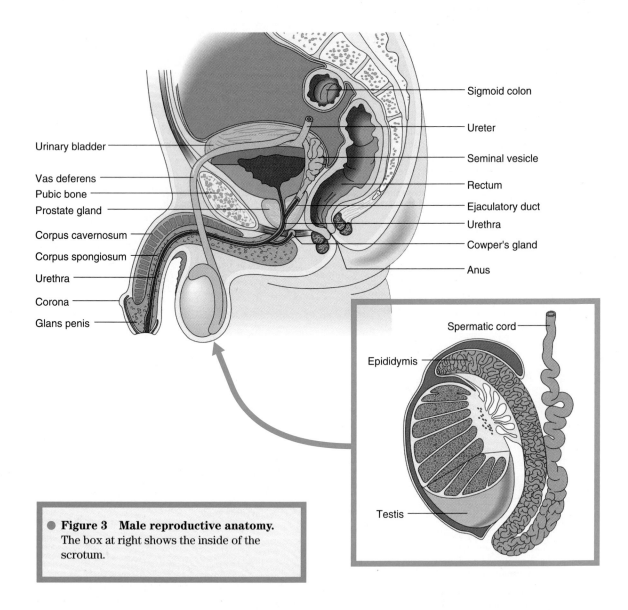

Urinary bladder

Vas deferens
Pubic bone
Prostate gland

Corpus cavernosum

Corpus spongiosum

Urethra

Corona

Glans penis

Sigmoid colon

Ureter

Seminal vesicle

Rectum

Ejaculatory duct

Urethra

Cowper's gland

Anus

Spermatic cord

Epididymis

Testis

● **Figure 3   Male reproductive anatomy.**
The box at right shows the inside of the
scrotum.

**At the head of the penis is the
glans, a particularly sensitive part.**
(Refer back to Figure 3.) On newborn male
babies, the skin of the penis shaft extends
past the glans, forming the ***foreskin* (pre-
puce), a cap of skin covering the glans.**
In the United States, 3 out of 5 infant boys
currently undergo ***circumcision*, the
surgical removal of the foreskin,** for
religious, cosmetic, or perceived health
reasons. The American Academy of Pediatrics contends that while there may be
some medical advantages to circumcision,
there are also some risks (as we describe in
a later chapter).[47]

Inside the penis is the ***urethra*, the
main canal through which urine and
semen is passed. *Semen* is the whitish
ejaculatory fluid that carries *sperm*,
the male reproductive cells.**

• *Inside the scrotum:* **The *scrotum* is a
pouch that holds the testicles and
other structures.** *(Refer back to Figure
3.)* The scrotum keeps the temperature of
the testicles about 5°F below normal body
temperature. It does this by contracting and
relaxing muscles that move the testicles
closer or farther away from the body.

The pair of *testicles,* **or** *testes,* **have two functions: (1) to produce sperm and (2) to produce about 95% of the body's** *testosterone,* **the male sex hormone that stimulates male secondary sex characteristics** such as facial hair. (The adrenal glands on top of the kidneys produce the other 5% of testosterone.)

Also within the scrotum are **coiled tubes called** *seminiferous tubules,* **located in the testicles, in which sperm are produced. Sperm maturation occurs in the** *epididymis,* a comma-shaped structure attached to the testicle. **Two 18-inch tubes called the** *vas deferens* **carry sperm from the epididymis to the urethra.** (It is these tubes that are cut during a sterilization procedure called *vasectomy.*)

- *Inside the body: Sperm* are produced by the testicles, but *semen*—the whitish fluid that carries sperm and that appears during ejaculation—is produced by three other glands. These are the seminal vesicles, the prostate gland, and Cowper's glands (bulbo-urethral glands). *(Refer back to Figure 3.)*

  (1) The *seminal vesicles* **are two glands that secrete fluid containing nutrients for sperm.** (The nutrients are fructose and protein.) The seminal vesicles join with the vas deferens to form a pair of ejaculatory ducts. **The** *ejaculatory ducts* **are 1-inch-long passageways that empty into the part of the urethra that passes through the prostate gland.**

  (2) **The** *prostate* **gland is a walnut-sized gland located beneath the bladder and surrounding the urethra.** It secretes a thin, milky fluid that makes the semen more alkaline and thus more life-sustaining for sperm.

  (3) The pea-sized *Cowper's glands* **(bulbo-urethral glands) secrete a fluid that alkalinizes the normally acid environment of the urethra before ejaculation.** Sometimes called pre-ejaculatory fluid, this often appears during sexual arousal as clear droplets on the tip of the penis. Since fluid from Cowper's glands may contain sperm, pregnancy can occur even though the

penis is withdrawn from the vagina before ejaculation. Withdrawal therefore is not a reliable means of contraception. (Nor does it offer protection against sexually transmitted diseases.)

The male reproductive system coexists with the system of elimination (bladder, rectum, anus) but does not intermingle with it. For instance, during sexual arousal the sphincter, a muscle at the base of the bladder, closes. This prevents semen from getting into the bladder and urine from getting into the urethra.

During *ejaculation* **the male releases about a teaspoon of semen through the urethra to the outside.** *Semen* **contains sperm and fluid from the seminal vesicles, prostate gland, and a tiny amount from Cowper's gland.** *Orgasm* **is the highly pleasurable feeling at the height of sexual arousal,** accompanied by a series of contractions of the pelvic muscles.

Prostate and Other Problems Like anything that is complex, the male reproductive system can develop problems. *Prostatitis,* **which can occur in men of all ages, is an inflammation of the prostate,** often following a bacterial or viral infection. Its symptoms include pain in the pelvic area, urinary complications, and backache. In the case of infection, medical treatment using antibiotics is often required.

Another important prostate problem is prostate enlargement. *Prostate enlargement,* **called** *benign prostatic hypertrophy (BPH),* **is a condition in which the prostate enlarges and presses on the urethra.** This noncancerous condition happens to most men over 40. It can often lead to symptoms such as a need to urinate at night, a change in size and force of the urinary stream, and a sensation of incomplete emptying. The problem may require surgery.[48,49] Indeed, a 40-year-old American male has a 30–40% chance of undergoing such surgery if he survives to age 80.[50]

Older men may also develop benign or malignant tumors of the prostate. This is one reason all men over 40 should have yearly prostate evaluations. Surgical removal of the prostate or other forms of treatment may be required.

The production of testosterone declines after age 40, but this need not diminish sexual pleasure. However, older men may take longer to become sexually aroused, to achieve an erection, to have an ejaculation, and to resume intercourse after ejaculation.

The Female Reproductive System

Much of the female reproductive anatomy is inside the body. Externally, the vulva includes the mons pubis, labia, clitoris, and vaginal and urethral openings. Internal organs include the vagina, cervix, uterus or womb, fallopian tubes, and ovaries. A woman's menstrual cycle has three phases. Menstrual problems may include menstrual cramps, premenstrual syndrome, and amenorrhea. In midlife, a woman's fertility cycle gradually ends, a process called menopause that is associated with a decline in estrogen production.

Human males produce sperm continuously from puberty on. The reproductive capacity of human females, however, is cyclical and intermittent.

Female Reproductive Anatomy In the following paragraphs, we describe first those parts of the female reproductive anatomy that are on the outside, then those on the inside. *(See ● Figure 4.)*

- *The outside anatomy—from mons pubis to perineum:* The external organs of the female reproductive system, or genitalia, are collectively called the *vulva.* These parts include the *mons pubis,* the *labia majora,* the *labia minora,* the *clitoris,* the *urethral opening,* and the *vaginal opening.* We will also describe the *perineum. (Refer back to Figure 4.)*

  (1) **The *mons pubis* is the mound of fatty tissue that cushions the pubic bone.** Starting in puberty it becomes covered with pubic hair.

  (2) Below the mons pubis and covering the opening to the vagina and urethra are the vulva's outer and inner lips. **The outer lips, the fleshy outer folds, are called the *labia majora.* The hairless inner lips, called the *labia minora,* surround and protect the**

urethral and vaginal openings. They come together to form the protective hood of the clitoris.

  (3) **The *clitoris* is the most sexually sensitive portion of the external female genitals,** because it contains many nerves. The clitoris is composed of spongy cylinders of tissue that become filled with blood during sexual excitement. When stimulated, it is a source of much of a woman's sexual excitement. However, it can be extremely sensitive to direct touch.

  (4) **The tube through which urine is expelled from the bladder is the *urethra.*** The urethra has a separate opening located above the vaginal opening. Women's urinary and reproductive systems are thus separate.

  (5) Beneath the urethra is a larger opening, the vaginal opening. Before adolescence **the vaginal opening *may* be protected by the *hymen,* a thin fold of mucous membrane** that partly (rarely completely) covers the opening. It was once thought that a broken hymen indicated a woman was no longer a *virgin*—**had not had sex**—but this is a myth. An intact hymen usually has openings through which vaginal secretions are discharged.

  (6) The *perineum* is the sensitive area of skin between the vagina and the anus, the opening of the rectum.

- *The anatomy within—from vaginal opening to cervix:* Beyond the vaginal opening is the vagina. **The *vagina* is an elastic muscular tube through which sperm must travel** to fertilize an egg. It is also through the vagina that a baby passes into the world (unless the infant is delivered by surgery). At the far end of the vagina is the *cervix,* **the opening to the uterus.** *(Refer back to Figure 4.)* The opening of the cervix is tightly closed, but when a baby is being born, the cervix must dilate (enlarge) considerably. The process of dilation accounts for much of the pain of childbirth. During a pelvic exam, cells from the cervix are obtained to check

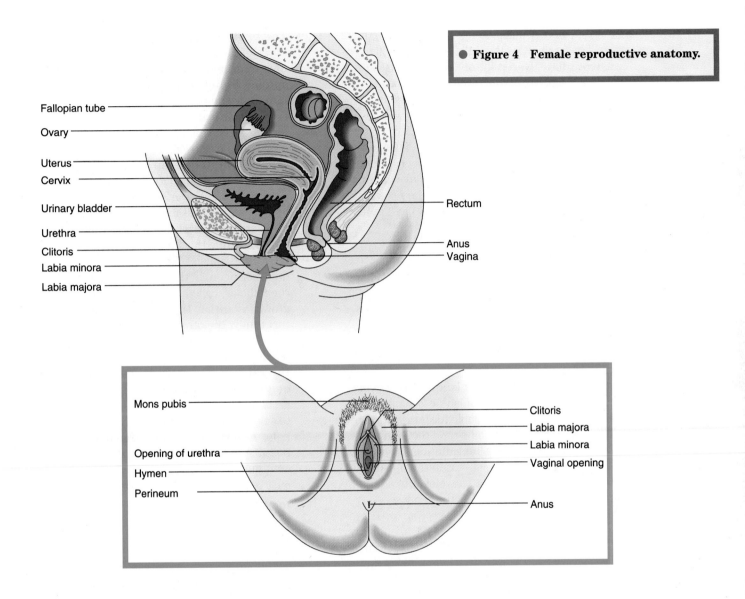

● **Figure 4   Female reproductive anatomy.**

Fallopian tube

Ovary

Uterus

Cervix

Urinary bladder

Urethra

Clitoris

Labia minora

Labia majora

Rectum

Anus

Vagina

Mons pubis

Opening of urethra

Hymen

Perineum

Clitoris

Labia majora

Labia minora

Vaginal opening

Anus

for changes and problems such as cancer. This is called a *Pap test.*

- *The internal anatomy—from uterus to ovaries:* Beyond the cervix, inside the body and inaccessible except by medical means, are the *uterus, fallopian tubes,* and *ovaries. (Refer back to Figure 4.)*

  (1) **The *uterus,* or *womb,* is the pear-shaped and pear-sized muscle that contains and nurtures a fetus** until it is born. **The internal lining of the uterus is called the *endometrium.*** It is into the endometrium that the human embryo implants itself and develops. In adult women, the endometrium changes

in response to the menstrual cycle and is shed during menstruation.

(2) Extending from the upper uterus is a pair of 4-inch-long fallopian tubes. **The *fallopian tubes* are the small tubes through which eggs (ova) pass from the ovaries to the uterus.** It is in the fallopian tubes that fertilization takes place.

(3) Near the end of each fallopian tube is an ovary. Analogous to the testes in the male, **the *ovaries* are the pair of female reproductive glands that contain the eggs. The eggs are called**

ova. Women do not produce eggs; they are born with all the eggs they will ever have. Generally, one ovary releases **an egg, or *ovum,*** one month, and the other ovary releases an egg the following month. The egg moves down the fallopian tube into the uterus.

The ovaries also produce female sex hormones, estrogen and progesterone. These two hormones are important in the development of secondary sex characteristics (such as breasts) and in the menstrual cycle.

The Menstrual Cycle Understanding the menstrual cycle provides insight into conception, pregnancy, menopause, contraception, and other vital aspects of a woman's health. The cycle begins about age 12–14; **the first menstruation is called *menarche.*** The cyclical shedding of the endometrium continues until menopause, around ages 45–55.

The *menstrual cycle* is a fertility cycle. About once a month, a woman's body matures an egg (ovum) to be available for fertilization by a male's sperm. At the same time the lining of her uterus prepares for implantation, or embedding, of that fertilized egg. It is in the uterus that the fertilized egg begins to develop into a fetus.

The menstrual cycle has three phases— *menstrual, proliferative,* and *secretory.* These phases take place over *approximately* a 28-day period. We say "approximately" because normal cycles vary from 21 days to 34 days, averaging 28. The menstrual cycle is counted from day 1 of one menstrual period to day 1 of the next menstrual period. Let us consider these three phases:

- *The menstrual phase:* **The *menstrual phase* is the phase of *menstruation* or menstrual bleeding.** *(See* ● *Figure 5, top.)* If a pregnancy does not occur, the endometrium—the lining of the uterus, composed of blood, cells, and tissue—is shed as menstrual fluid. The muscle of the uterus contracts in order to expel this tissue (due to the action of substances called *prostaglandins*). This contraction often produces the cramps that so often cause women discomfort during this time.

- *The proliferative phase:* After menstruation and during the ***proliferative phase,* a new endometrium develops into a thick spongy lining composed of blood and mucous.** The purpose of the endometrium is to establish an environment in which a fertilized egg can implant and develop. *(Refer back to Figure 5, top.)*

During this time, an egg cell begins to mature in the ovary. *(Refer back to Figure 5, middle.)* The ovaries in every woman's body contain thousands of ***ovarian follicles,* sacs in which individual eggs develop.** During this phase of the cycle, about 20 ovarian follicles begin to grow and produce estrogen. In the following days, *one* of the follicles, called the *graafian follicle,* grows faster than the others. This follicle matures fully; the other follicles degenerate.

The graafian follicle finally ruptures and releases a mature egg. This one-time event, **the release of a mature egg, is called *ovulation.*** The ruptured follicle left behind is called the *corpus luteum.* Its purpose is to secrete progesterone. The progesterone helps maintain the endometrial lining for possible implantation of a fertilized egg and continues during pregnancy.

- *The secretory phase:* During the ***secretory phase,* roughly the second half of the menstrual cycle, the released ovum enters and moves down the fallopian tube.** *(Refer back to Figure 5, bottom.)* It is in the fallopian tube that fertilization by the sperm takes place. The ovum can be fertilized during a 24- to 36-hour period. If fertilization does not take place, the egg begins to disintegrate.

Simultaneously, the endometrium continues its buildup, ready to receive a fertilized egg. At the end of the cycle, if the egg has not been fertilized, the uterine lining is shed during menstruation. Thus, the menstrual cycle begins again at day 1.

All three phases of the menstrual cycle are controlled by changes in ***hormones,* substances in the blood that regulate specific body functions.** Thus, the monthly menstrual cycle is also called the *monthly hormonal cycle.* Changing levels of four hormones regulate

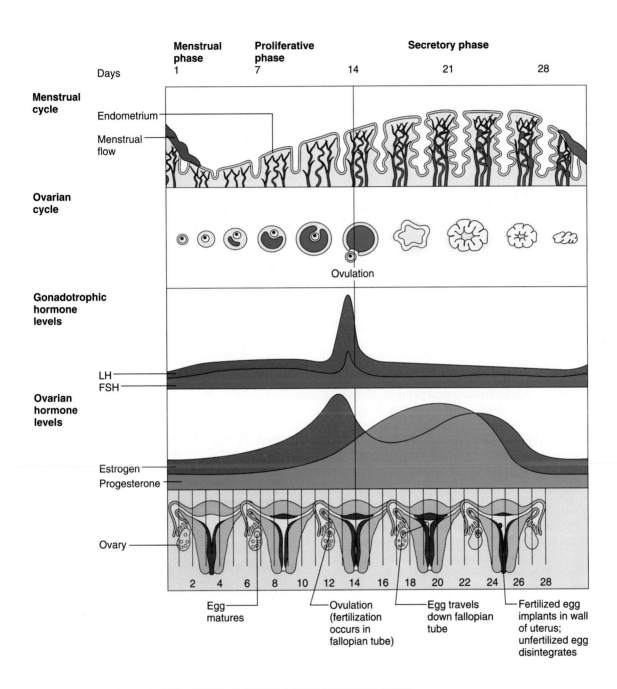

Days 1 7 14 21 28

Menstrual phase | Proliferative phase | Secretory phase

Menstrual cycle

Endometrium

Menstrual flow

Ovarian cycle

Ovulation

Gonadotrophic hormone levels

LH
FSH

Ovarian hormone levels

Estrogen
Progesterone

Ovary

2 4 6 8 10 12 14 16 18 20 22 24 26 28

Egg matures

Ovulation (fertilization occurs in fallopian tube)

Egg travels down fallopian tube

Fertilized egg implants in wall of uterus; unfertilized egg disintegrates

● **Figure 5   The menstrual cycle.**

the cycle throughout the 28 days: *FSH, LH, estrogen,* and *progesterone.*

- **FSH: FSH, an abbreviation for *follicle-stimulating hormone*, is produced by the pituitary gland and stimulates the growth of ovarian follicles. The *pitu-***

***itary gland* is a gland located within the brain which controls reproductive functions.** Thus, FSH levels are elevated in the bloodstream during the second (proliferative) phase of the menstrual cycle. *(Refer to Figure 5, middle.)*

In males, FSH stimulates the production of sperm.

- ***LH:*** LH is also produced by the pituitary gland. **The principal function of *LH,* an abbreviation for *luteinizing hormone,* is to stimulate ovulation.** Thus, there is a surge of LH level in the blood toward the end of the second (proliferative) phase of the menstrual cycle. *(Refer back to Figure 5, middle.)*

  In males, LH stimulates the production of testosterone.

- ***Estrogen: Estrogen* is a female sex hormone secreted by the ovaries.** Estrogen has many functions, including control of the menstrual cycle. An estrogen surge toward the end of the second phase of the menstrual cycle triggers more buildup of the endometrium. *(Refer back to Figure 5, middle.)*

- ***Progesterone: Progesterone* is another female sex hormone secreted by the ovaries,** especially after ovulation. Its purpose is to maintain the endometrium in the event of pregnancy. *(Refer back to Figure 5, middle.)*

If pregnancy does not occur, blood levels of estrogen and progesterone drop, and the menstruation phase of the cycle begins.

Do these hormonal ups and downs affect how a woman feels? Indeed they do. In some cases, they cause significant physical and psychological changes, as we describe next.

Menstrual Problems: Menstrual Cramps, PMS, and Others Most physical and psychological symptoms related to the menstrual cycle are minor. However, *menstrual cramps, premenstrual syndrome,* and *amenorrhea* are not for some women.

- ***Menstrual cramps: Dysmenorrhea* refers to discomfort or pain during menstruation.** Pelvic cramping, the most common symptom of dysmenorrhea, is caused by too-high levels of *prostaglandins.* These hormones cause uterine muscles to contract. Dysmenorrhea somewhat affects about half of menstruating women and may incapacitate another 10–20% for a day or two.[51]

In some women, the condition may be relieved with over-the-counter medication, heat to the lower abdomen, and exercise.[52] Those with severe discomfort require an assessment by a health care professional and possible prescription medication. Oral contraceptive use reduces dysmenorrhea in some women.

- ***Premenstrual syndrome: Premenstrual syndrome,* or *PMS,* may occur during the week or so before the onset of the menstrual period. It creates severe physical and psychological distress** in up to 15% of women.[53] The cause of PMS is not currently known. Some women experience extreme discomfort, including mood swings, concentration problems, irritability, and hostility. They may also experience muscle aches, pelvic cramps, breast tenderness, dizziness, bloating, fatigue, and diarrhea. Other women are less affected.

  PMS may be relieved with medication, relaxation techniques, exercise, and eating a wholesome diet, with limited salt, sugar, alcohol, and caffeine. However, no single remedy seems to work for all women. An assessment by a health care professional is recommended for any troubling symptoms.

- ***Amenorrhea: Amenorrhea* is the absence of menstruation that normally occurs during pregnancy and after menopause.** It is also a symptom of other problems, such as eating disorders, strenuous exercise, environmental changes, and hormonal changes. If amenorrhea continues for a prolonged period of time, it may lead to the bone-weakening disorder known as osteoporosis.

Menopause: The End of Female Fertility Eventually, usually around ages 45–55, **a woman's cycles of ovulation and menstruation come to an end, a process called the *menopause.*** This is aptly described as "the change of life." This process is foreshadowed by increasingly irregular periods and decreasing amounts of estrogen and progesterone, to the ending of ovulation.

Some women experience problems linked to declining levels of hormones, especially estrogen. One problem is vaginal dryness that makes intercourse painful. "Hot flashes," surges of heat and perspiration that cause physical reddening, may occur, and so may headaches, irritability, and depression. But the years following menopause are viewed as the best years of life by many women. With current life expectancy, women may expect to spend about one-third of their lives in the postmenopausal period.

Sex and Gender: Your Sexuality and Sexual Orientation

The male or female sex is determined by biology—genetic instructions and sex hormones. Male and female gender identity and gender role are largely determined by social learning and culture. Sexual orientations include heterosexuality (attraction to other sex), homosexuality (to same sex), bisexuality (to both), and transsexuality (gender identity opposite of biological sex). Homosexual and bisexual orientations may have both social-learning and genetic bases.

Your maleness or femaleness begins with your biology and is shaped by your experience. That is, your *sex,* **male or female, is determined by genetic and other biological factors.** Your *gender* **refers to how you perceive yourself as male or female** and is determined by physiological, psychological, and sociological factors.

The Biological Bases of Sexuality Becoming a male or female depends on many factors, especially your chromosomes and hormones. We mentioned the sex hormones earlier, but the important ones that determine your sexual identity are three: *estrogen, progesterone,* and *testosterone.* Both sexes have these hormones, but *differences in their relative amounts significantly influence whether one is male or female.* Men have more testosterone than estrogen and progesterone, women more estrogen and progesterone than testosterone.

Immediately after conception, human embryos do not have *gonads—***testes or ovaries** that indicate they are male or female. However,

the embryos already contain genetic instructions (in the form of X and Y chromosomes, as we describe elsewhere). By the 7th week these genetic instructions cause an embryo to begin developing testes, if male, or by the 8th week ovaries, if female. The testes produce testosterone in males, creating the male genitals. The absence of a Y chromosome or testosterone leads to the formation of female genitals.

At *puberty,* **the beginning of sexual maturity,** the sex hormones trigger development of *secondary sex characteristics,* **physical changes related to maleness and femaleness.** Both boys and girls show rapid skeletal growth (as much as 6 inches in a year) and produce pubic hair and underarm hair. They may experience hormonally influenced skin changes such as acne. Boys develop hair on their faces and bodies, their voices deepen, their muscles become stronger, their penises become longer. Girls develop wider hips, nipples enlarge and breasts fill out, external genitals become larger, and they begin to menstruate and later ovulate. Although humans are sexual beings throughout life, the sex hormones spur the *sex drive,* **the desire to engage in sexual behavior.** However, the extent of the desire varies with individuals. Finally, at about ages 18–21, as the bones stop growing, puberty comes to an end.

The Social-Learning Bases of Sexuality Whatever the biological basis of your sexuality, the psychological and social influences on your sexuality are incredibly strong. Perhaps they start in the hospital bassinette with the pink card ("I'M A GIRL!") or blue card ("I'M A BOY!") on it. Which set of genitals you have is the beginning of your destiny.

Your *gender identity* **refers to how you psychologically perceive yourself as either male or female.** Children develop a strong sense of gender identity by 18 months.[54] *Gender role,* **or sex role, is the collection of attitudes and behaviors considered appropriate within a given culture for each sex.** For example, children in many parts of North America are told it is not "masculine" for males to kiss each other on the cheek. (However, they may consider it acceptable for males to slap each other on the bottom.) But a greeting kiss between men is a custom in European cultures.[55] Social learning also affects the expression of aggression (not innately masculine behavior), nurturing (not innately feminine behavior), and what we have come to perceive as "normal" behavior.

People can and do express their sexuality in a variety of ways, which often do not involve sexual intercourse. Perhaps the principal form of sexual exploration is self-stimulation (masturbation), engaged in by two-thirds of females and nearly all males.[56]

Some people express themselves sexually by kissing, hand-holding, and touching of genitals and other erotically sensitive areas but not sexual intercourse. Others, sometimes as a consequence of peer-group pressure, engage in sexual intercourse. According to the federal Centers for Disease Control and Prevention, 54% of teenagers surveyed in 1991 said they had had sexual intercourse. That percentage was down from 59% in 1989. Thirty-five percent said they had had two or more sexual partners (versus 40% in 1989). Nineteen percent reported four or more partners (down from 24% earlier).[57]

Even by young adulthood we may still be trying to clarify the forms that sexual expression can and should take. Indeed, our sexuality and means of sexual expression may change throughout life, and many people remain sexually active in old age.

Sexual Orientation: Heterosexual, Homosexual, Bisexual, Transsexual As we stated, your gender identity results from a combination of biological, social, and psychological factors. What is it, then, that determines our ***sexual orientation,*** **our attraction to a particular sex or both sexes?**

Four sexual orientations have been described:

- ***Heterosexual:*** A person with a ***heterosexual*** **orientation is sexually, emotionally, and socially attracted to members of the other sex.** This is the orientation of the majority of North American adults: 75% of men and 85% of women in the United States.[58]

- ***Homosexual:*** People with a ***homosexual*** **orientation are sexually, emotionally, and socially attracted to members of the same sex. Male homosexuals prefer the term *gay;* female homosexuals use the term *lesbian*** to describe themselves.

(The term *gay* is sometimes used to refer to homosexual people of both sexes.) About 2% of American men and 1% of American women have an exclusively homosexual orientation.[59]

- ***Bisexual:*** **People who are attracted to members of both sexes have a *bisexual* orientation.** An estimated 23% of men and 14% of women in the United States have had bisexual experiences.[60]

However, isolated sexual experiences—a few same-sex sexual experiences in adolescence, for example—do not accurately indicate true sexual orientation. What seems to matter is *repeated* sexual and emotional attraction to members of either or both sexes during one's life.

- ***Transsexual:*** A small percentage of people are transsexual. **In *transsexuals* gender identity, or feelings about whether they are male or female, is the opposite of their biological sex.**[61] It is not clear what causes transsexualism.[62,63]

Psychotherapy has not been successful in helping transsexuals adjust to their biological sex. Thus, following careful psychological assessment and preparation, sex-change operations that alter genitals and hormone injections that alter breasts and body hair are often performed.[64,65]

Many of us are tempted to view our sexual orientation as solely heterosexual or homosexual. However, pioneer sex researcher Alfred Kinsey contended that sexual orientation is not an either/or phenomenon. Instead, he suggested, an individual's sexual orientation falls somewhere along a continuum. Kinsey developed a model of sexual behavior, with 0 representing no homosexual desire or behavior and 6 representing no heterosexual desire or behavior.[66] Many people, he discovered, are not at 0 or 6 but somewhere in between. *(See ● Figure 6.)*

Bisexuality, Homosexuality, and Homophobia Are homosexual and bisexual people "born that way" or is the behavior learned? The debate about the origin of homosexuality continues. Bisexuality occurs among many male and female adolescents in many cultures. In some Latin and Muslim societies, it is reportedly a common but

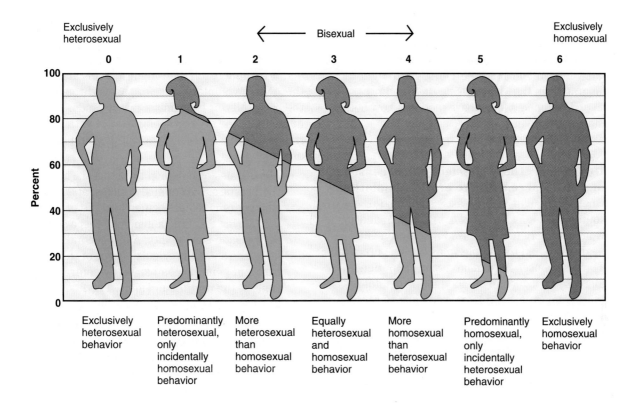

Exclusively heterosexual   ←   Bisexual   →   Exclusively homosexual

0   1   2   3   4   5   6

| Exclusively heterosexual behavior | Predominantly heterosexual, only incidentally homosexual behavior | More heterosexual than homosexual behavior | Equally heterosexual and homosexual behavior | More homosexual than heterosexual behavior | Predominantly homosexual, only incidentally heterosexual behavior | Exclusively homosexual behavior |

● **Figure 6   The continuum of sexual orientation.** The continuum ranges from exclusively heterosexual (0) to exclusively homosexual (6).

unspoken practice among men.[67] This seems to suggest a strong social-learning component.

Yet scientists have also discovered physiological differences between those who are homosexual and heterosexual, suggesting that homosexuality may be genetic.[68] For instance, one study of identical-twin brothers (the two have identical genes) of homosexual men found that a high percentage, 52%, were also homosexual. Only 22% of fraternal-twin brothers (who do not have identical genes) of homosexual men in the study were gay.[69] Other studies found anatomical differences between the brains of homosexual and heterosexual men, suggesting that homosexuality is at least partly inborn.[70,71]

***Homophobia* is the irrational fear of homosexuality in others and of homosexual feelings within oneself.** Public acceptance of homosexuality seems to have increased in one way and decreased in another. A 1992 Gallup Poll found that 74% (up from 56% 15 years earlier) of American adults supported equal work rights for homosexuals. On the other hand, the poll also found that 57% think homosexuality is an unacceptable lifestyle. Less than half (48%) seemed willing to make homosexual relations legal (many states continue to carry laws making it a crime).[72] Still, the poll does suggest that the backlash toward gays seen in earlier polls is subsiding.

The Human Sexual Response

The human sexual response proceeds through four stages—excitement, plateau, orgasm, and resolution. There are marked similarities and some differences between the sexes and among individuals, including the frequency of orgasm.

People have been having sex for thousands of years, of course. But the *study* of sex was considered off-limits until William Masters and Virginia Johnson began researching sex in their laboratory in the 1950s. Using their findings, they developed a four-phase model of how both men and women respond to sex physiologically: *excitement, plateau, orgasm, resolution.*[73]

Excitement The *excitement phase* **consists of a physical reaction to erotic stimulation,** whether thought, touch, taste, sight, and/or sound. *(See ● Figure 7, left.)* Both men and women experience increased respiration and heart rates and the nipples may become erect. Their responses are similar as they experience increased congestion of blood in the genital area (vasocongestion) and increased muscular tension (myotonia).

- **Men:** The penis becomes erect, although the erection may subside and return several times. The testes lift and increase in size. A man's initial physical response to sexual arousal is erection.

- **Women:** The clitoris swells, as do the labia minora; the labia majora flatten and separate away from the vaginal opening. The vaginal walls begin to lubricate. The uterus enlarges. A woman's initial physical response to sexual arousal is believed to be vaginal lubrication.

Plateau During the *plateau phase,* **sexual excitement and muscle tension continue to build.** Blood pressure and heart rate continue to rise, and breathing becomes faster. *(Refer back to Figure 7, middle.)* (The word *plateau* does not mean it is an unchanging state, only that no *new* behaviors can be observed.)

- **Men:** The penis becomes fully erect and testes continue to swell and elevate.

- **Women:** The clitoris retracts under its hood. The inner two-thirds of the vagina enlarges and the muscles in the outer third of the vagina tighten.

Orgasm The third stage observed by Masters and Johnson, the *orgasmic phase,* **is the most ecstatic** for those who experience it. *(Refer back to Figure 7, middle.)* Here, rhythmic contractions cause the release of neuromuscular

tension and feelings of intense pleasure. This experience is an orgasm (also known as a "climax" or "coming"). Blood pressure, heart rate, and breathing reach their highest levels and there are involuntary muscle spasms throughout the body. All this lasts only a few seconds. The intensity of the orgasm seems to vary with experience, setting, partner, expectations, and level of anxiety.

- **Men:** Males ejaculate in two stages. First, the prostate, the seminal vesicles, and the vas deferens release semen into the urethra. It is during this time a man may feel a sense of orgasmic inevitability. A few seconds later, the semen is ejaculated out of the urethra and penis, accompanied by contractions of the urethra and anus. The first two or three contractions are most intense.

- **Women:** Contractions occur in the uterus, the vaginal opening, and anal areas. Masters and Johnson identified three patterns: (1) one or more orgasms without dropping below the plateau level; (2) extended plateau with no orgasms; and (3) a rapid rise to orgasm with no plateau.[74]

  Some research suggests the presence of a *G-spot (Grafenberg spot)* that, when stimulated, causes orgasm. It is possible that some females ejaculate fluid (not urine) from their urethras during orgasm. This type of intense orgasm may follow stimulation of the G-spot, located in the ceiling and toward the front of the vagina. The G-spot is not noticeable until it is stimulated, when it may swell to the size of a dime or quarter.

Resolution The *resolution phase* **is the return of the body to its unaroused state.** Heart rate, blood pressure, breathing, muscle tension, and nipple erection all subside. *(Refer to Figure 7, right.)*

- **Men:** The penis returns to its nonerect or nonaroused state, and the testes return to normal. Most men are unable to resume erection and ejaculation for a period that may range from seconds to hours. With age, the recovery period is considerably longer, up to several hours.

- **Women:** The clitoris, uterus, vagina, and vaginal lips return to their normal unaroused positions.

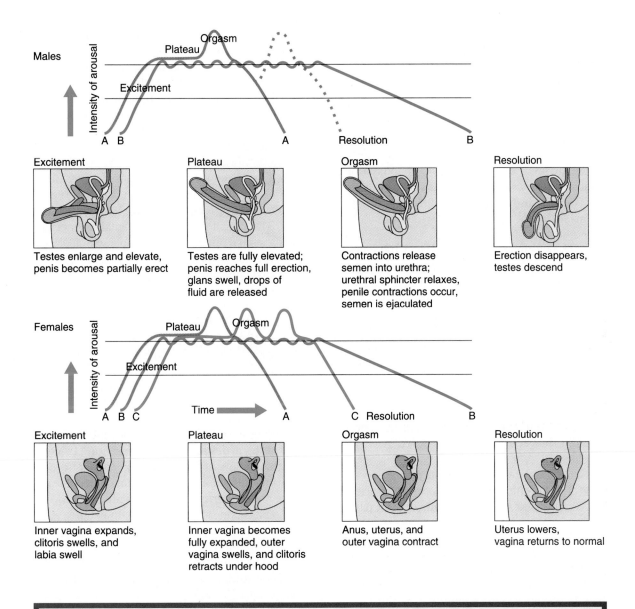

Males

Intensity of arousal

Orgasm

Plateau

Excitement

A B   A   Resolution   B

Excitement	Plateau	Orgasm	Resolution
Testes enlarge and elevate, penis becomes partially erect	Testes are fully elevated; penis reaches full erection, glans swell, drops of fluid are released	Contractions release semen into urethra; urethral sphincter relaxes, penile contractions occur, semen is ejaculated	Erection disappears, testes descend

Females

Intensity of arousal

Plateau   Orgasm

Excitement

A B C   Time   A   C Resolution   B

Excitement	Plateau	Orgasm	Resolution
Inner vagina expands, clitoris swells, and labia swell	Inner vagina becomes fully expanded, outer vagina swells, and clitoris retracts under hood	Anus, uterus, and outer vagina contract	Uterus lowers, vagina returns to normal

● **Figure 7   Human sexual response.** The four phases of the sexual response cycle as described by sex researchers Masters and Johnson. The graphs (letters) indicate different basic patterns of sexual response.

The Varieties of Orgasm We owe much to Masters and Johnson in gaining insight into many of the physiological mysteries of sex. For example, they found that most men are not *multiorgasmic*—**able to have multiple orgasms within a single period of sexual arousal.** However, 10–30% of adult females are routinely able to have multiple orgasms. On the other hand, they found, some 10% of females are *anorgasmic*, **unable to have an orgasm.** Or they can experience orgasms during masturbation but not during conventional sexual intercourse.[75] (We discuss erectile and orgasm problems later.)

The Varieties of Sexual Expression: "Am I Normal?"

Sexual expression takes many forms and covers a wide range of possibilities: sexual fantasies and dreams, masturbation, caressing and genital play, oral-genital stimulation, anal stimulation, and sexual intercourse or coitus in different positions. Some people are celibate—they don't have sex. Others indulge in pornography or prostitution or become sex workers.

Sexual intercourse occurs more than 100 million times around the world *every day,* according to the World Health Organization.[76] For all its frequency, however, sex remains basically a private matter. As one sex therapist notes, "We don't observe others having sex, don't hear anyone discussing sexual experiences seriously, and don't have access to reliable information about what other people feel and do."[77] The result, he says, is that many people have *normality anxiety:* they wonder if what they are thinking or feeling or even doing about sex is normal. Let us consider the varieties of sexual experience.

Sexual Fantasies and Dreams Many questions about normality have to do with fantasies. Sex is not just genitals and glands; a great part of it is the mind. For instance, a 24-year-old woman who had never had intercourse, interviewed by Nancy Friday, stated "I am an extremely sexual person. I think about sex a lot and can become horny if just the right word, sound, or suggestion is made."[78]

A *sexual fantasy* **is any mental representation of any kind of sexual activity.**[79] It may be a single act, such as oral sex. Or it may tell a story from beginning to end (for example, starting with a kiss and ending with orgasm). The fantasy may be stimulated by one's experience, imagination, or words or pictures. A *sexual dream* occurs during sleep, without a person's conscious control, and may produce a ***nocturnal orgasm,* an involuntary orgasm during sleep.** In males, this is also called a "wet dream," because ejaculation occurs while one is asleep.

Perhaps the principal purpose of sexual fantasies, when they occur during masturbation or sexual intercourse, is to help sexual arousal. Both men and women report fantasizing about one person—a former or imaginary lover—while making love to another.[80] Sexual fantasies also help overcome anxiety or boredom, rehearse new sexual experiences, and express forbidden wishes (such as forced sex or same-sex encounters).[81]

How "normal" is sexual fantasizing? Research by Alfred Kinsey and his associates found that nearly all the males and two-thirds of the females studied reported having sexual dreams. Also, 84% of males and 67% of females reported having sexual fantasies.[82,83] People who feel more guilt about sex are less apt to be aroused by sexual fantasies than are people who feel less guilt about sex.[84]

Masturbation *Masturbation* **is self-stimulation of the genitals for sexual pleasure,** as with one's hand or with a vibrator, resulting in orgasm.

Do people in committed relations or those with regular sexual partners masturbate? The answer seems to be yes, as shown in one study of couples in their 20s and 30s. Seventy-two percent of the males reported masturbating twice a month and 68% of the females once a month.[85] The practice is not considered abnormal unless it somehow interferes with one's life or with enjoyable sexual sharing in a relationship.[86] As might be expected, single and divorced people masturbate more often than people who are married or living together.[87]

Is masturbation normal? One study of young people ages 15–18 found that 80% of males and 59% of females masturbated.[88] The Kinsey studies in the 1950s found that males ages 16–20 masturbated an average of 57 times a year. Males 21–25 reported an average of 42 times a year, and females ages 18–24 an average of 21 times a year.[89] However, men masturbate less as they approach age 30, whereas women masturbate more in their 20s and 30s.

Kissing, Touching, Genital Play—and the Importance of Setting Kissing and touching need not, of course, be preliminary steps toward sexual arousal or intercourse. When they are, however, they are considered part of ***foreplay,* or sex play.** Foreplay is stimulating activity that may or may not culminate in sexual intercourse.

Touching or kissing **sexually sensitive, or erogenous,** areas—genitals, breasts, the anal area in some people—can build sexual excitement and even lead to orgasm.

Setting and cleanliness seem to be important for many lovers. Interestingly, heavy doses of cologne, perfume, and douches may actually work against sexual arousal—advertising to the contrary.

Oral-Genital Stimulation *Oral-genital stimulation* **consists of mouth-to-genital contact** to stimulate sexual pleasure. Three basic forms are practiced by both heterosexual and homosexual couples.

- *Fellatio: Fellatio* **is oral stimulation of the penis** (and perhaps the scrotum) by the partner. Fellatio risks the exchange of bodily fluids, and hence the passage of sexually transmitted diseases (STDs), including HIV. This can occur through small openings in the skin of the mouth or genitals. Thus, couples not in a long-term mutually monogamous relationship should either avoid fellatio or always use a condom.

- *Cunnilingus: Cunnilingus* **is oral stimulation of the clitoris, labia, and vaginal opening.** To avoid the risk of STDs, couples not in mutually monogamous relationships should avoid practicing cunnilingus. Or the woman receiving oral sex should cover her vulva with a *dental dam,* a latex square available in pharmacies and some dentists' offices.

- *Mutual oral-genital stimulation:* Couples sometimes practice simultaneous oral-genital stimulation by facing each other while lying in opposite directions. This arrangement is known as the "69 position."

How commonplace is oral-genital sex? One 1974 study found that 90% of married couples under 25 years old had experienced it within the year.[90] A 1983 study of 203 Canadian college women found that 61% had performed fellatio and 68% had experienced cunnilingus.[91]

Anal Stimulation Some people don't care to do anything sexual with the anus, associating it with matters of excretion or "unnatural" acts. Others find touching of the anus to be highly erotic sex play. *Anal intercourse* **consists of inserting the penis into the anus** and is a sexual behavior engaged in by people regardless of sexual orientation.

Anal sex is one of the riskiest activities for transmission of sexual diseases, including HIV. The risk level is high because the lining of the rectum tears easily during penetration. Using a condom would seem to be mandatory for all but the most monogamous of sexual partners, whether homosexual or heterosexual. However, one should be aware that condoms have a higher breakage rate (1 in 105) for anal sex than for vaginal sex (1 in 165).[92]

Anal intercourse can be uncomfortable or painful for the recipient. Thus, the anus and penis (or other object) should be well lubricated before insertion, and penetration should be slow and gentle. Under no circumstances should anything inserted into the anus then be inserted into the vagina without thorough washing. Otherwise, infection is apt to occur.

How frequently does anal intercourse occur among heterosexual partners? One survey found that 25% of married couples under age 35 said they performed it occasionally.[93]

Sexual Intercourse or Coitus The terms *sexual intercourse* and *coitus* **usually mean penetration of the vagina by the penis.** *(See ● Figure 8.)* This is the only sexual act designed for *procreation* **or reproduction.** It may or may not produce orgasm in one or both partners. Indeed, many females have difficulty experiencing a vaginal orgasm during certain coital positions in which the clitoris is not readily stimulated.

What is the normal frequency of sexual intercourse? The answer is: there is no normal frequency. A 1974 study found that couples in their 20s and 30s *average* sex 2–3 times a week.[94] However, the frequency for any couple tends to decrease over the years. The demands of work and child-rearing may leave partners fatigued, and interest may decline due to a familiar sexual routine.[95,96] In a 1990 study, married and unmarried adults on average reported 57.4 instances of sexual intercourse in the preceding year—about once a week.[97] In sum: a wide range of frequency of intercourse is considered normal.

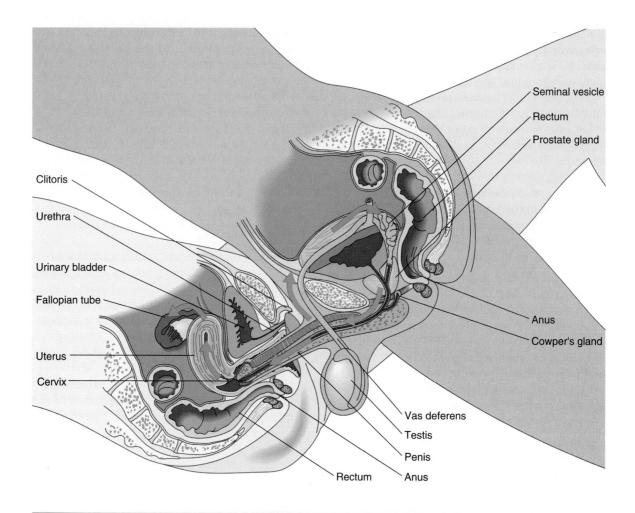

Clitoris

Urethra

Urinary bladder

Fallopian tube

Uterus

Cervix

Rectum

Seminal vesicle

Rectum

Prostate gland

Anus

Cowper's gland

Vas deferens

Testis

Penis

Anus

● **Figure 8   Sexual intercourse.**

Celibacy *Celibacy* **may either be complete—a person has no sex at all—or partial. In partial celibacy, a person masturbates but has no sexual relations with others.** Being celibate is not done just for religious reasons or for lack of sexual partners. Some people choose to "renew their virginity" because of concern about sexually transmitted diseases. Others are celibate while they recover from a broken relationship or a health problem, including chemical dependency. How common is celibacy? A 1990 survey found that 22% of people—including 9% of married people—said they had no sex partners at all during the previous year.[98]

Pornography and Prostitution Pornography and prostitution are two aspects of "commercial sex"—which includes everything from phone sex (dial-a-porn) to child prostitution. Paying for sex—or for sexual fantasies—seems to be as old as history. In the late 20th century, however, sex has also been exploited commercially and used to sell products. In other words, sex has shifted from the private world to the public world: it has become popularized.[99]

Here, however, let us consider just two aspects of commercialized sex—pornography and prostitution.

• *Pornography: Pornography* **is depiction through words or pictures of**

sexual conduct involving same-sex or
opposite-sex partners designed to
cause sexual excitement. Most pur-
chasers of pornography use it as a stimulus
for masturbation. By identifying with the
people in pornographic fantasies, some people may deny their fears about sexual inadequacy, sexual fatigue, or failing sexual
interest.[100]

Some pornography is simply explicit
portrayal of sexual acts such as we have described so far. Couples sometimes use it as
an adjunct or stimulus for lovemaking. Some
pornography, however, is violent, involving
acts of rape, humiliation, and pain, often
with female victims.

Even in some countries that prohibit
pornography (such as Saudi Arabia),
women are not immune from violence by
men.[101] Although there *may* be some link
between violence in the media and violence
in real life, it is complicated and difficult to
prove. Moreover, anti-pornography legislation might drive pornography deeper underground and make it more difficult to protect
women in the porn industry.

- *Prostitution: Prostitution* **is the exchange of sexual services for money,** or
sometimes drugs. The reality of prostitution
is not as depicted glamorously in some
movies. The reality, as one writer puts it, is
"about drugs and bad mistakes, and it's
sometimes about violence."[102]

Some men sentimentally believe that
sex workers (prostitutes) enjoy their work.
However, there seems to be no "happy
hooker," say ex-prostitutes and psychological experts; the business kills body and
soul.[103] Even in enlightened countries such
as Holland, Norway, and Sweden, where
prostitution is often legal, most prostitutes
express a wish to quit. The life after prostitution is often equally sad, however: the
emotional damage of having one's body used
as a sex object remains. Self-esteem and
sexual pleasure are often replaced by self-
hatred and depression.[104]

Many people are split over legalization of
pornography and prostitution. Some feminists,
for instance, believe the practices degrade not
just the participants but all women. Others say

that outlawing them may reduce but never stop
them, and if they have to exist they are better
done safely and hygienically.[105] However, in an
era of HIV infection and other sexually transmitted diseases, is it possible to have "safe sex"
even as a legal prostitute?

**Strategy for Living: Don't Worry So Much
About Normality** The range of sexual activity
is tremendous, as we have seen, from touching,
to kissing, to sexual intercourse, to all the variations. It is not useful to constantly try to compare ourselves with others. *Assuming one's
sexual behavior is not exploitative, coercive,
violent, or self-destructive and occurs between consenting adults,* what does it matter
how "normal" it is? In sexuality, as in many
other aspects of life, we can celebrate individual
differences.

Sexual Difficulties and What to Do About Them

**For both men and women, commonly expe-
rienced sexual problems include inhibited
sexual desire or lack of interest, or compulsive sexual behavior. Men may experience erection difficulties and premature
ejaculation. Women may be unable to have
an orgasm or experience pain during intercourse or spasms of the vaginal muscles.**

Our society raises all kinds of sexual expectations that promote an unrealistic view of sex.
Even so, when real-life problems occur, we may
perceive them as personal failures instead of
talking about or seeking help for them.

Inhibited Sexual Desire Perhaps the greatest
sexual complaint of couples is that one or both
individuals experience inhibited sexual desire.
***Inhibited sexual desire (ISD)* is a lack of
interest in sex, or an inability to feel sexual** or get sexually aroused.[106] ISD may come
about for various reasons. Perhaps the relationship has become too close for comfort; for a
partner feeling suffocated, ISD can be a way of
getting some space. Or one person may feel
pushed around by a domineering partner, and

ISD is a means of retaining some power in the relationship. There may be a lack of trust, fear of intimacy or rejection, or unresolved issues, anger, or resentment. Or ISD may result from frustration over lack of sexual arousal and orgasm. Or stress outside the relationship—jobs, children, the consumption of drugs, including alcohol—may turn a couple into roommates more than lovers. Indeed, some couples in long-term relationships have asexual partnerships—they haven't had sex in years.[107] A variation on ISD is dissatisfaction with the frequency or kind of sexual activity. One partner may want more (or less) sex than the other or different varieties of sex.

How do you maintain a vital sexual relationship within a committed partnership or how do you rekindle the flame? Assuming there is no physical problem, therapists suggest various techniques to break the cycle of routine sex. These include having sex in a different place (the living room instead of the bedroom), and setting aside time when you're not stressed. Try different sexual positions, increase daily physical contact with each other (more touching and hugging), and have getaway weekends. Other ideas: buy sexy lingerie, watch erotic videotapes, and voice the desires you have been afraid to bring up.[108] If problems persist, see a marriage counselor or sex therapist to help you sort out the problem and develop strategies to solve it.

Sex Addiction: Compulsive Sexual Behavior The obsessive compulsive person may wash his or her hands 100 times. The sexual compulsive may take sex to a similar extreme, such as compulsive masturbation or insatiable sexual demands within a relationship. Other signs are feverish interest in pornography or phone sex, frenzied anonymous sex, or multiple affairs. ***Sexual addiction, or compulsive sexual behavior (CSB), is an intense preoccupation with sex. It makes having a satisfying sexual relationship with just one lover difficult.***

Often sexual compulsives were emotionally or physically abused as children and learned that sex was not a nurturing, natural experience. Thus, they alternate between profound anxiety and self-loathing. Like the alcoholic they are mainly intent on diverting their pain but use

sex.[109] Psychologists and other health professionals are uncertain what the condition is and how to treat it, but psychotherapy seems the best course. In addition, those who are sexually compulsive may find support by joining such organizations as Sexaholics Anonymous or Sexual Addicts Anonymous.

Sexual Dysfunctions in Men Common sexual problems in men include *erection difficulties* and *premature ejaculation.*

- ***Erection difficulties:*** Sexual adequacy is important to men, so they can be devastated by erection dysfunction. ***Erection dysfunction, or impotence, is failure to achieve or maintain an erection.*** Actually, the problem affects almost every man at some time. Only when an erection cannot be maintained in 1 out of 4 sexual encounters is the problem considered serious. Problems may come from "performance anxiety" (self-consciousness about having an erection), tension, or too much to eat or drink. Other factors are marital strife, prescription or "street" drugs, fatigue, lack of privacy, or a new partner. Sometimes there are physical causes, such as diabetes or blood-vessel disorders when the body cannot deliver enough blood to engorge the penis. Impotence can also be a medication side effect.

  A man cannot simply *will* an erection to happen. Thus, therapists recommend that couples try non-demanding techniques, such as massage or simply lying together 10–20 minutes. These can reduce anxiety and allow sexual arousal to occur naturally.

- ***Premature ejaculation:*** After a period of abstinence, almost any man will ejaculate rapidly. However, ***premature ejaculation is the inability of a man to *reasonably* control his ejaculatory reflex on a regular basis.*** That is, he reaches orgasm so quickly that his partner may consistently have trouble achieving orgasm. This is usually a psychological rather than physical problem.

  Sometimes a condom can dull sensation and boost staying power. Sometimes masturbating before sex will make the second ejaculation occur less rapidly. There is also a squeeze-and-release technique suggested by Masters and Johnson: When the man is about to ejaculate, he withdraws his penis. The partner squeezes the neck of the penis between thumb and first and second fingers for 4 seconds. After 15–30 seconds stimulation of the penis is resumed.

Sometimes men are unable to ejaculate. This temporary condition is usually caused by fatigue, stress, alcohol, illness, or lack of emotional involvement with the partner.

Sexual Dysfunction in Women Sexual enjoyment is now expected of women, although once it was not. So women, too, have sexual expectations that they sometimes can't meet, such as pressure to achieve multiple or simultaneous orgasms. Chief among the female dysfunctions are *inability to have an orgasm, painful intercourse,* and *spasms of the vaginal muscles.*

- *Inability to have an orgasm: Anorgasmia or inhibited female orgasm* **are terms now used instead of "frigidity" to describe an inability to reach orgasm.** Perhaps 7% of women have never experienced orgasm.[110] Others have orgasms infrequently.

  One reason a woman may not achieve orgasm is that her partner experiences premature ejaculation. Another is that orgasm is difficult to accomplish through sexual intercourse: what is required is additional, direct stimulation of the clitoris.

Therapists may help a woman give herself permission to express her sexual feelings and eliminate inhibitions. Learning how to explore her body, masturbate, and tell her partner how to touch and stimulate her in a pleasurable way may help.

- *Painful intercourse:* **Painful or difficult sexual intercourse is called** *dyspareunia.* Occasionally, women experience a burning or sharp pain when the penis is inserted into the vagina. Causes include inadequate lubrication or infection of the vagina, a tight hymen, irritation by contraceptive creams, and the penis touching the cervix. If dyspareunia persists, the woman should see a health care professional.

- *Vaginismus: Vaginismus* **consists of involuntary spasms of the muscles surrounding the lower third of the vagina** so the penis cannot enter. Sometimes it is a normal response when a woman is expecting pain (as on first intercourse). Or she may not want sex, perhaps as a reaction to sexual trauma such as rape. When the problem is chronic, a woman needs to seek assistance from her health care provider. After exploring the underlying problem, some therapists may teach a woman to explore her genital area and learn to relax her vaginal muscles.

Safer Sex

▶ Discuss the primary elements in reducing the risks of sexually transmitted diseases.

▶ Differentiate between saved sex, safer sex, and high-risk sex.

Know your sexual partner," medical authorities advise. Many young adults have taken the advice to heart. They are rightly concerned about getting ***sexually transmitted diseases (STDs), diseases transmitted by sexual contact,*** such as HIV. ***HIV, the human immunodeficiency virus, is the organism that causes AIDS.***

Unfortunately, says psychologist Jeffrey D. Fisher, they may go about it the wrong way.[111] College students may ask other students about home town, family, and major. Or they make judgments on the basis of perceived "social class" or the other person's educational level, attractiveness, and the like.[112] Do such external clues work? No, says Fisher. These are useless and irrelevant facts, not guides to safe sex.

How can you be sure that sex is really safe? The answer is: you can't. However, there are things that you can do to reduce your risks.

Unsafe Sex and Knowing Your Partner

To reduce your risk of exposure to sexually transmitted organisms such as HIV, ask the right questions of prospective sexual partners. However, the answers are no guarantees. You need to make the right decisions regarding your own behavior independent of the responses of others.

AIDS, or acquired immunodeficiency syndrome, the final and fatal stages of HIV infection, appeared in North America sometime around 1975. In the years following, it has become a disease to which all who are sexually active are vulnerable. The fastest-growing group of HIV-infected people worldwide is heterosexual women, and women account for half of new AIDS cases. An official for the World Health Organization (WHO) says that by the year 2000 most new AIDS infections worldwide will be among women.[113]

The Concerns About Unsafe Sex HIV is only one of several STDs that have shown an alarming rise. The rates are up for syphilis, chlamydia, genital warts, genital herpes, and other STDs. Gonorrhea, pelvic inflammatory disease due to gonorrhea or chlamydia, genital warts, and hepatitis B continue to pose serious problems. A 1993 report by the Alan Guttmacher Institute says *more than 1 in 5 of all Americans is infected by a sexually caused viral disease.*[114] About 12 million new sexually transmitted infections occur every year, two-thirds of them to people under 25 and one-quarter to teenagers.[115]

The sexually transmitted diseases caused by viruses cannot be cured, although they can in many cases be controlled. Viral STDs include hepatitis B, genital herpes, genital warts, and HIV infection. Some, such as genital warts, have been linked with an increased risk of cervical cancer in women. STDs caused by bacteria (such as gonorrhea, chlamydia, and syphilis) can be cured. Unfortunately, many have no obvious symptoms. Thus, they continue to cause serious health problems and continue to be transmitted to other sexual partners. Untreated infections can lead to serious complications particularly for women of childbearing age. Examples are infertility, tubal pregnancies, chronic pain, and fetal problems.

Asking Partners About Their Sexual History However embarrassing the conversation, it can be helpful for people to explore their prospective partners' sexual histories before getting involved. Here are some questions to ask:[116]

- ***STD tests:*** "Have you ever been tested for HIV or for other STDs? Would you be willing to have an HIV test?"
- ***Previous partners:*** "How many sexual partners have you had?" (The more partners, the higher the STD risk.)

- **Prostitution:** "Have you ever had sex with a prostitute?" Or, "Have you ever exchanged sex for money or drugs?" (If so, was protection used?)
- **Bisexuality:** For a woman to ask a man: "Have you ever had a male sexual partner?" For a man to ask a woman: "Have you ever had a sexual partner who was bisexual?"
- **IV drug use:** "Have you—*or your sexual partners*—ever injected drugs?" (A previous sexual partner can transmit HIV or hepatitis by sharing needles.)
- **Blood transfusion:** "Have you ever had a transfusion of blood or blood products?" (This fact is particularly important if the transfusion occurred before 1985, when blood wasn't screened for HIV.)

Even if you ask all the right questions, however, you still can't be sure of the answers. Someone may state with absolute honesty and sincerity that he or she has never had a genital infection or HIV. But that person may have an infection and not know it. Even people who have had an HIV test can't prove they are HIV negative. The test measures the presence of antibodies (which fight HIV) that can take 6 months or more to develop. So a person can become infected and infect others during the time it takes to show antibodies, as well as after the test.

Truth is the first casualty in war, it is said. Some think it is also the first casualty in sexual behavior.[117] Clearly, the bottom line is that simply *asking* a prospective sexual partner about HIV does not by itself guarantee safer sex.[118]

Reducing Risks of Acquiring Sexually Transmitted Diseases

The safest form of sex for preventing transmission of STDs is abstinence and other behavior in which body fluids are not exchanged. The next least risky is protected sex, such as that using condoms and dental dams. High-risk behavior involves the exchange of body fluids or use of intravenous needles. Long-term mutually monogamous relationships are an especially important consideration.

So how *should* one pursue sexual relationships? There are two principal pieces of advice:

- **Use precautions universally:** If you choose to have sex, then CONSISTENTLY use safer-sex measures (such as a condom and spermicide) with ALL partners. This means *all* sexual partners, not just those you don't know well or those you think may be higher risk. This means learning to overcome any embarrassment you may feel associated with condom use.
- **Keep your head clear:** Be careful about using alcohol and other drugs with a prospective sexual partner. Drugs cloud your judgment, placing you in a position of increased vulnerability.

No doubt you have heard the phrase "safe sex." However, only abstinence is considered safe. Abstinence is no sexual contact at all, or no contact with a partner's body fluids, including semen, vaginal secretions, saliva, or blood. Actually, some STDs such as genital herpes and pubic lice can sometimes be transmitted by skin-to-skin contact.

In general, then, there are three levels of risk in sexual behavior: "saved sex," "safer sex," and high-risk sex.

Lower Risk: "Saved" Sex, Including Abstinence The safest kind of sex avoids the exchange of semen, vaginal secretions, saliva, or blood. The principal kind of "saved sex" is **abstinence, defined as the voluntary avoidance of sexual intercourse.** Saved sex includes massage, hugging, rubbing of bodies, dry kissing (not exchanging saliva), masturbation, and mutual manual stimulation of the genitals. (In all cases, contact with body fluids is avoided.)

Thus, abstinence can mean anything from avoiding all sexual activity to avoiding only those, such as intercourse or oral sex, in which fluids are exchanged. The trick in practicing only safe sexual activity is not to get swept away and end up practicing unsafe sex.

Somewhat Risky: "Safer" Sex, Including Use of Condoms The next best step to ensuring safe sex—actually, only saf*er* sex—is to use *latex:* condoms and dental dams. "Safer" sex is still somewhat risky, but at least it minimizes the exchange of body fluids (semen, vaginal secretions, saliva, or blood). Examples of safer-sex behavior include deep (French) kissing and vaginal intercourse using latex condoms with the spermicide nonoxynol-9 (which kills STD organisms). Other examples are fellatio with the male wearing a condom, and cunnilingus with a nonmenstruating female using a latex dental dam.

Let us consider the two principal means of protection, condoms and dental dams:

• ***Condoms:*** **A *condom* ("prophylactic," "rubber") is a thin sheath made of latex rubber or lamb intestine.** (Though called "natural skin," lamb intestine is not as safe as latex.) Packaged in rolled-up form,

the condom is unrolled over a male's erect penis, leaving a little room at the top to catch the semen. Some condoms are marketed with a "reservoir" at the end for this purpose. *(See ● Figure 9.)*

A latex condom provides protection for both partners during vaginal, oral, or anal intercourse. It keeps semen from being transmitted to a man's sexual partner and shields against contact with any infection on his penis. It also protects the male's penis and urethra from contact with his partner's secretions, blood, and saliva.

• ***Dental dams:*** Every major sexually transmitted disease can be acquired during oral sex, although not as easily as during inter-

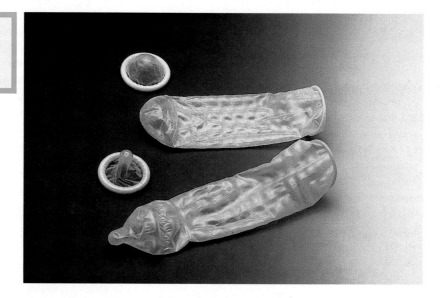

● **Figure 9   Putting on a condom.** *(Right)* Two kinds of condoms, one with a "reservoir" tip. *(Below)* How to put on a condom.

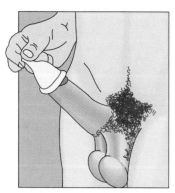

Pinch or twist the tip of the condom, leaving one-half inch at the tip to catch the semen.

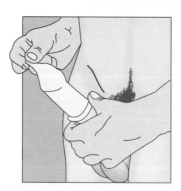

Holding the tip, unroll the condom.

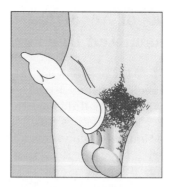

Unroll the condom until it reaches the pubic hairs.

course. Males receiving oral sex should wear a condom. If a female is the recipient, she should use a dental dam. Sold in medical supply stores and pharmacies, **a *dental dam* (designed for use in dental surgery) is a flat 5-inch-square piece of latex. It may be placed over the vaginal opening and surrounding area.** *(See ● Figure 10.)* Some people use plastic wrap (for example, Saran Wrap) for the same purpose, although this has not been tested.

Unfortunately, *condoms are not perfect protection.* They only *reduce* the risk of acquiring HIV infection and other STDs. Note that *reducing the risk is not the same as eliminating the risk.* If the condom is flawed or it slips off or breaks during intercourse, there is suddenly 100% exposure—possibly to a disease that is 100% fatal.

Condoms break most frequently when couples use oil-based lubricants or engage in prolonged sex. A condom may also be weakened if couples attempt their own "quality testing" (such as blowing up condoms to test for leaks). There are several precautions people can take to ensure that condoms are used properly. *(See ● Figure 11.)*

Condoms, whether made by U.S. or overseas manufacturers, are tested for leakage by the Food and Drug Administration. As of February 1988, 12% of the samples of domestically produced condoms and 21% of foreign-made condoms failed the FDA tests.[119] In March 1989, Consumers Union tested condoms and listed 43 brands and models and their features and performance in resisting breaking. Planned Parenthood will also answer questions about condoms.

Very Risky: Unprotected Sex and Other Behavior Behavior that is high-risk for the transmission of STDs includes unprotected sex or any behavior that involves sharing intravenous needles. This includes vaginal or anal intercourse without a condom, fellatio without a condom, cunnilingus without a dental dam, and unprotected oral-anal contact. It includes all forms of sex in which body fluids may be exchanged: semen in the mouth or contact with a partner's blood (including menstrual blood). Any sexual behavior that leads to bleeding or tissue damage also risks fluid exchange.

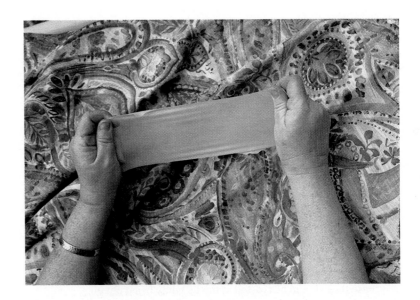

● **Figure 10   A dental dam.** Sold in medical supply stores and pharmacies, the dental dam is a thin latex square. It is used to cover the vagina when the couple is engaging in cunnilingus (the woman is the recipient of oral sex).

Finally, high risks include people or behavior having to do with the intravenous injection of drugs, a prime means of transmitting some STDs. Don't share IV needles yourself, and avoid sexual contact with an injectable-drug user or someone whose previous partner was. Avoid having sexual contact with people who sell or buy sex, who are often injectable-drug users.

Mutual Monogamy Having multiple sexual partners is one of the leading risk factors for the transmission of STDs. Clearly, mutual monogamy is one way to avoid infection. However, even apparent monogamy *may* have its risks:

- ***"Cheating hearts":*** If one partner secretly has a sexual adventure outside the supposedly monogamous relationship, especially not using condoms, it does not just breach a trust. It endangers the other's life, whether the outside relationship is heterosexual, bisexual, or homosexual.

● **Figure 11   How to buy and use condoms.**

How to Buy

Materials: Buy latex, not natural membrane or lambskin. Latex is less apt to leak and better able to protect against HIV transmission. Inexpensive foreign brands are suspect.

Sizes: The Food and Drug Administration (FDA) says condoms must be between 6 and 8 inches in length when unrolled. (The average erect penis is 6½ inches.)

Condoms labeled *Regular* are 7½ inches.

Instead of "Small" for condoms under 7½ inches, manufacturers use labels such as *Snug Fit.*

Instead of "Large" for condoms over 7½ inches, manufacturers use labels such as *Max* or *Magnum.*

Shapes: Most condoms are *straight-walled.* Some are labeled *contoured,* which means they are anatomically shaped to fit the penis and thus are more comfortable.

Tips: Some condoms have a *reservoir* at the end to catch semen upon ejaculation. Others do not have a reservoir, in which case they should be twisted at the tip while being put on.

Plain or Lubricated: Condoms can be purchased *plain* (unlubricated) or *lubricated,* which means they feel more slippery to the touch. There are four options:

1. Buy a plain condom and don't use a lubricant.

2. Buy a plain condom and use your own lubricant, preferably water-based (such as K-Y Jelly or Astroglide).

3. Buy a lubricated condom pregreased with silicone-, jelly-, or water-based lubricants.

4. Buy a *spermicidally lubricated* condom, which contains *nonoxynol-9,* a chemical that kills sperm and HIV. This is probably the best option.

Strength: A standard condom will do for vaginal and oral sex. Some people believe an *"extra-strength"* condom is less apt to break during anal sex, although this is debatable.

Gimmicks: In addition, condoms come with all kinds of other features:

1. *Colors:* Red, blue, green, and yellow are safe. Avoid black and "glow in the dark," says the FDA, since dyes may rub off.

2. *Smell and taste:* Latex smells and tastes rubbery, but some fragranced condoms mask this odor.

3. *Adhesive:* Condoms are available with adhesive to hold them in place so they won't slip off during withdrawal.

4. *Marketing gimmicks:* Condoms are sold with ribs, nubs, bumps, and so on, but unless the additions are at the tip and can reach the clitoris they do no good whatsoever.

How to Use

Storage: Condoms should be stored in a cool, dry place. Keeping them in a hot glove compartment or wallet in the back pocket for weeks can cause the latex to fail.

Opening package: Look to see that the foil or plastic packaging is not broken; if it is, don't use the condom. Open the package carefully. Fingernails can easily damage a condom.

Inspection: Make sure a condom is soft and pliable. Don't use it if it's brittle, sticky, or discolored. Don't try to test it for leaks by unrolling, stretching, or blowing it up, which will only weaken it.

Putting on: Put the condom on before any genital contact to prevent exposure to fluids. Hold the tip of the condom and unroll it directly onto the erect penis. (If the man is not circumcised, pull back the foreskin before rolling on the condom.) Gently pinch the tip to remove air bubbles, which can cause the condom to break. Condoms without a reservoir tip need a half-inch free at the tip.

Lubricants: *Important!* If you're using a lubricant of your own, *don't use an oil-based lubricant.* Oil-based lubricants—examples are hand lotion, baby oil, mineral oil, and Vaseline—can reduce a latex condom's strength by 90% in as little as 60 seconds. Saliva is not recommended either.

Use a water-based or silicone-based product designed for such use, such as K-Y Jelly or spermicidal compounds containing nonoxynol-9.

Add lubricant to the outside of the condom before entry. If not enough lubricant is used, the condom can tear or pull off.

Slippage and breakage: If the condom begins to slip, hold your fingers around the base to make it stay on. If a condom breaks, it should be replaced immediately.

If ejaculation occurs after a condom breaks, apply a foam spermicide to the vagina at once.

After ejaculation: After sex, hold the base of the condom to prevent it from slipping off and to avoid spillage during withdrawal. Withdraw while the penis is still erect. Throw the used condom away. (Never reuse condoms.) Wash the genitals.

- *The AIDS time bomb:* A person can be infected with HIV for perhaps 10 years before AIDS itself begins to appear. *And there may be no outward signs or symptoms at all during that time.* This poses a dilemma, for you could be in a monogamous relationship but have no idea if your partner was infected previously. You can wait several months while remaining faithful to each other and then take a test to see if HIV antibodies are present. This gives some indication (though not absolutely) that the partner is currently free of infection.

Having extramarital affairs or otherwise "cheating" outside the relationship means, of course, that the commitment is not truly monogamous. Despite AIDS and the rise of other STDs, many of our cultural images remain the same. Movies and magazines still celebrate the glories of passion, of losing oneself in sexual ecstasy, of having relationships with exciting strangers. But clearly the world itself has changed.

800-HELP

AIDS Hotline. 800-533-AIDS (U.S.), 899-668-AIDS (Canada)

Impotence Information Center. 800-843-4315.

Suggestions for Further Reading

Barbach, Lonnie. (1975). *For yourself: The fulfillment of female sexuality*. Garden City, NY: Doubleday. A classic self-help book for women by the innovator of a sex-therapy treatment for women.

Comfort, Alex. (1991). *The new joy of sex: A gourmet guide to lovemaking for the '90s*. New York: Crown. An update of the phenomenal bestseller on "advanced lovemaking" first published in 1972, which reflected the spirit of the era that sex is fun.

Zilbergeld, Bernie. (1978). *Male sexuality*. Boston: Little, Brown. A classic self-help book for men.

CHAPTER

6

Birth Control, Pregnancy, and Childbirth

Love and passion are among the most powerful human forces.

Love, or the belief in love, sometimes leads people to take chances. Even if her boyfriend was also seeing other women, a San Francisco 17-year-old says, "nothing would happen because he says he'll never do anything that would mess me up, and I believe him." They don't need a condom, she states, "because he says he loves me."[1]

We are surrounded by words and images about sex. However, a great many people, regardless of education, are surprisingly uninformed about the subject. For instance, the *majority* of women and men in the United States do not know the most likely time in the monthly menstrual cycle when a woman can become pregnant.[2] However, in sexual matters, ignorance can no longer be considered bliss, if it ever could.

Birth Control

▶ Define conception, and describe how conception works.

▶ Discuss the changes a fertilized egg undergoes after conception.

▶ Differentiate between the terms *fetus* and *embryo*.

▶ Discuss the various types of contraception and rate them for effectiveness.

▶ Describe possible future forms of contraception.

The human motivation for sex has evolved over 500 million years and shows no sign of abating. If anything, human fertility seems to be escalating out of control, with 1.7 million new infants born worldwide *each week*. An understanding of conception and contraception can be helpful in planning and preparing for your children.

165

Conception: The Merging of Sperm and Ovum

Contraception, or birth control, begins with understanding conception—how sperm and ovum merge to form a fertilized egg or zygote. The fertilized egg then implants itself in the lining of the uterus, where it grows into an embryo and then a fetus.

Following sexual intercourse (or artificial insemination) **the male reproductive cell, the *sperm*,** may meet the **female reproductive cell, the egg or *ovum*. When the two merge, it is known as the moment of *conception*, or *fertilization*.** *(See ● Figure 1.)* Let us explore the process by which sperm and ovum produce a human being.

The Ovum Eggs are stored in the **two *ovaries*, the female reproductive glands, or gonads.** The ovaries are located near the ends of the ***fallopian tubes*, channels whose opposite ends connect with the uterus.** *(Refer back to Figure 1.)* As a consequence of the hormonal changes associated with the menstrual cycle, one egg usually matures every month. **The release of a mature ovum from an ovary (approximately 14 days before the onset of menstruation) is called *ovulation*.** In most cases, once a month one egg becomes available for fertilization. Sometimes multiple eggs are released, and the subsequent fertilization produces multiple births.

Women are born with all the eggs they will ever have. In most women, only 300–400 eggs mature during their lifetime.

The Sperm A single ejaculation contains as many as 500 million sperm. Each sperm resembles a tiny tadpole that moves by means of whip-like motions of its tail. The life span of sperm is about 2–5 days, or perhaps a week once they enter the fallopian tubes.

Each sperm released into the vagina attempts to move through the cervix, through the uterus, and up into the fallopian tubes. *(Refer back to Figure 1.)* Most never make it. Of the 1% that do, most find themselves in the wrong tube or their timing is wrong. An egg can be fertilized only within 24–48 hours of ovulation. If conception fails to occur, the unfertilized egg is reabsorbed or passes out of the vagina unnoticed, sometimes during menstruation.

Fertilization and Implantation If a sperm and an ovum meet, it will probably happen in the fallopian tube, in the part closest to the ovary. *(Refer back to Figure 1.)* The sperm that reach this point probably number less than 250, and they have already undergone changes that make fertilization possible. They cluster around the egg, each contributing an enzyme that works to dissolve the outer layer of the ovum. When one sperm finally penetrates the ovum, the lining of the ovum immediately changes, preventing additional sperm from entering. Thus, only one sperm combines its genetic material with the egg.

The initial fertilized egg is called a *zygote*. Within about 36 hours of fertilization, cell division begins. While division continues, hair-like structures (called *cilia*) move the egg down through the fallopian tube. The destination is **the *uterus*, the site where the baby grows and is nourished until birth.** The trip is a relatively slow one, taking 3–5 days.

Once in the uterus, the fertilized egg (now called a *blastocyst*) floats around for a day or two. Finally it burrows itself into the ***endometrium*, the lining of the uterus. This burrowing is called *implantation*.** *(Refer back to Figure 1.)*

For the first 8 weeks after fertilization, the product of conception is called an *embryo*. From the beginning of the ninth week on, it is called a *fetus*. In most cases, a fetus cannot sustain life outside the uterus before the 24th week.

The Gambling Casino of Reproduction As we have described it, conception might seem to be a fairly unusual occurrence, a hit-and-miss proposition. It probably seems this way to the many couples who want to have a child and discover they cannot conceive. In general, however, the chances of pregnancy for a couple having unprotected intercourse over a 1-year period is 85–90%. As the number of unplanned pregnancies in the United States indicates, the gambling casino of reproduction is rigged in nature's favor. About 1 million unplanned adolescent pregnancies occur every year and 1.5 million abortions are performed annually. Recognizing the possibilitiy of pregnancy, almost all U.S. women— 95% of those who have ever had sex—use contraceptives at some time.[3] (Many also use condoms and spermicides also to decrease their risk of contracting a sexually transmitted disease.)

Avoidance of unwanted pregnancies requires the practice of **contraception or birth control, the prevention of fertilization.**

Choosing a Contraceptive Method

Methods of contraception vary greatly in effectiveness, side effects, cost, and other matters. Here we consider abstinence, douching, withdrawal, vaginal spermicides, vaginal sponges, condoms, diaphragms, cervical caps, IUDs, oral contraceptives, implants, injectable contraceptives, tubal sterilization, and vasectomy.

There are many different contraceptive methods, and no one can tell others which method is best for them. Today, however, concerns about preventing pregnancy often have to be linked with concerns about protection from sexually transmitted diseases (STDs). In general, for anyone who is sexually active and outside a long-term, mutually monogamous relationship,

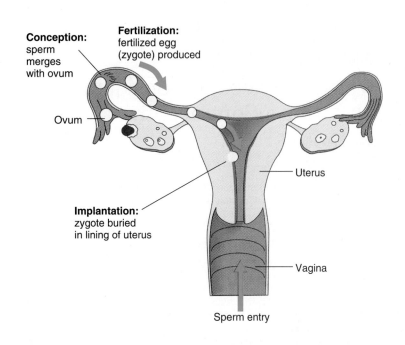

Figure 1 Conception.

there is a single method of contraception and protection. That method is *condoms,* especially combined with **nonoxynol-9, an antiviral, antibacterial spermicidal agent.** Heterosexual couples who need not worry about STDs, however, have a great many choices in contraception.

Choices Available: Five Categories of Birth Control There are many criteria for choosing a method of contraception. These criteria range from availability, to effectiveness, to cost, to considerations of personal comfort, health, and religious beliefs. *(See Self Discovery 1.)* Many people also recognize the benefits of combining methods, which increases effectiveness.

The five categories of birth control are the following:

- *Natural family planning methods:* Various kinds of periodic abstinence, such as fertility awareness, the rhythm method, and withdrawal are examples of natural family planning methods of preventing conception.

- *Barrier methods:* Condoms, diaphragms, and vaginal contraceptive sponges are

SELF DISCOVERY 1

What Do I Need to Consider in Choosing a Contraceptive Method?

If you are considering choosing a method of contraception, apply the following criteria to see if that method seems right for you. Answer the following yes or no:

	Yes	No
1. *Effectiveness:* Am I satisfied this method is effective enough in preventing pregnancy?	___	___
2. *Comfort:* Will I find this method personally acceptable and comfortable? (For example, women uncomfortable with touching themselves may find a diaphragm difficult to use.)	___	___
3. *Safety:* Do I consider this method safe enough for me? (For example, although oral contraceptives are relatively safe for nonsmokers under age 35, they do have potentially serious side effects.)	___	___
4. *Cost:* Is this method affordable on an annual basis?	___	___
5. *STDs:* Are my sexual relationships such that I should be concerned that the contraceptive method be effective against sexually transmitted diseases?	___	___
6. *Protection:* Does the method I am considering offer protection against STDs?	___	___
7. *Access:* Do I have access to the kind of health care that will make this method and follow-up available to me? (For example, oral contraceptives, the IUD, and Norplant require a prescription and regular follow-up appointments.)	___	___
8. *Health:* Do I have existing health problems that would prohibit use of this method?	___	___
9. *Religion:* Is this method compatible with my religious beliefs?	___	___
10. *Partner:* Are there concerns about this method I must consider with my sexual partner? (Examples are cost, personal preference, issues of shared responsibility.)	___	___

examples of contraceptive devices that put physical barriers between egg and sperm.

- *Chemical methods:* Vaginal spermicides are examples of chemical contraceptives that destroy sperm. Contraceptive sponges, which also contain spermicides, are both barrier and chemical contraceptives. Oral contraceptives—The Pill—are hormonal contraceptives that prevent ovulation or implantation.

- *Invasive methods:* With intrauterine devices (IUDs), male sterilization (vasectomy), and female sterilization (tubal sterilization), the body is entered by insertion of a device or by surgery.

- *After-intercourse methods:* The morning-after pill is an example of an after-intercourse contraceptive option.

In this chapter, we will describe various contraceptive methods from these five categories. We proceed from contraceptive methods that are *least effective* to those that are *most effective*. (See ● *Figure 2.*)

No Method at All Using no method of contraception at all has the highest failure rate for birth control. In one study, 85% of fertile women were estimated to have become pregnant within 1 year.[4] This was at least four times as high as the rate among those using *any* method of birth control.

Breastfeeding Nursing delays fertility in many women after childbirth. However, it is an unreliable form of birth control, since no one can predict in whom ovulation is suppressed and for how long. About 80% of women ovulate before their menstrual periods return after childbirth. Nursing mothers should therefore use other methods of contraception.

Douching *Douching* **is the practice of rinsing out the vagina with a chemical solution right after sexual intercourse.** From the standpoint of birth control, it is almost worthless. Although douching is an attempt to "wash out" the ejaculate, it actually often brings the sperm into contact with the cervix. Moreover, some sperm are able to enter the uterus within seconds of ejaculation, before a woman has a chance to begin douching.[5]

Periodic Abstinence *Abstinence* **is the voluntary avoidance of sexual intercourse. Periodic abstinence goes under the names of** *fertility awareness, natural family planning,* **and the** *rhythm method.* All three terms refer to the avoidance of sexual intercourse during perceived fertile periods of the woman's menstrual cycle.

This method cannot be used by women who have irregular menstrual cycles or who are at risk for STD exposure. Using this method to prevent pregnancy requires a motivated, knowledgeable couple who has undergone training. They must be able to abstain or use another contraceptive method during those times the woman is likely to be fertile. Actually, the method has been successfully used by some couples who are trying to *become* pregnant.

The time in a woman's cycle when she is at increased risk of ovulation is assessed in four ways: by the *calendar method,* the *basal-body-temperature method,* the *cervical mucus method,* and the *sympto-thermal method:*

- *Calendar method:* **The** *calendar method* **involves counting days.** Each month for 6–12 months the beginning and end of the menstrual period is charted on a calendar. At the end of this time, the shortest and longest cycles are determined. *(See ● Figure 3.)* A cycle ranges from day 1 of one menstrual period to day 1 of the next menstrual period. A formula then is used to estimate the days of the month a woman is most likely to be fertile. Needless to say, this method alone is not particularly reliable, given that women can ovulate at unpredictable times.

- *Basal-body-temperature (BBT) method:* **In the** *basal-body-temperature (BBT) method,* **a woman uses a special thermometer to record her body temperature daily.** She takes her temperature *immediately* upon waking (before going to the bathroom or any physical activity). Records are kept for 6–12 months. The pattern that many women experience includes a slight drop in *basal body temperature* 1–3 days before ovulation. Then a sharp rise at the beginning of ovulation. *(See ● Figure 4.)* Ovulation is confirmed if the rise is sustained at least 3

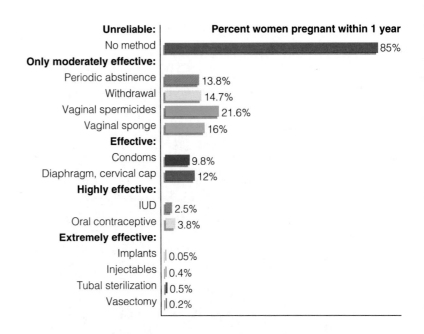

● **Figure 2   Effectiveness of contraceptive methods.**

days. It is unsafe to have intercourse from the day the temperature drops until 3 days after it rises.

- *Cervical mucus method:* **The** *cervical mucus method* **requires that a woman evaluate the appearance, amount, and consistency of the daily mucus discharge from her cervix.** Unsafe days for intercourse are indicated by a discharge that is clear, thin, and elastic rather than cloudy and thick. The woman generally has to abstain from intercourse about 9 days in each 28-day cycle. Also called the *Billings method* or the *fertility awareness method,* this method must be learned from a family-planning professional or physician.

- *Sympto-thermal method:* **The** *sympto-thermal method* **combines all three previous methods—calendar, BBT, and the cervical mucus—and provides the** most reliable means of determining high- and low-risk times for sexual intercourse.

Days	Risk of conception
1	
2	
3	*Menstruation:* low-risk days for unprotected intercourse
4	
5	
6	Low-risk days for unprotected intercourse
7	
8	Possibly risky days,
9	if 28-day cycle varies by 8–9 days
10	
11	Risky days for unprotected intercourse
12	
13	
14	*Ovulation:* risky days for unprotected intercourse
15	
16	
17	Risky: ovum may still be present
18	
19	Risky days for unprotected intercourse
20	
21	
22	
23	
24	
25	Low-risk days for unprotected intercourse
26	
27	
28	

● **Figure 3 The calendar method.** Most women's cycles are not a consistent 28 days but may vary as much as 8 or 9 days (21–35) days).

One of the problems with the methods described above is that ovulation is difficult to accurately and consistently predict. The only relatively accurate way to determine ovulation is by hindsight: on day 1 of the menstrual period one can look *back* and say that 2 weeks *ago* ovulation probably occurred. The problem, however, is in trying to predict ovulation *ahead* of time.

Withdrawal The birth-control technique known as ***withdrawal, or coitus interruptus,* consists of removing the penis from the vagina before ejaculation.** The theory, which dates back to biblical times, is that withdrawal prevents sperm from being deposited in or around the vagina. This method is flawed: 14.7% of women using the technique are estimated to become pregnant. Probably one reason is that withdrawal requires unusual willpower. In any case, all it takes is the little bit of fluid (from Cowper's glands) released from the penis *before* ejaculation to send sperm into the vagina.

Vaginal Spermicides Alone ***Vaginal spermicides* are sperm-killing chemicals, such as spermicidal foam, cream, jelly, film, or suppositories. These are placed in the vagina within 30 minutes before intercourse.** *(See* ● *Figure 5.)* Some require the use of an applicator. Others, such as the suppositories, require a waiting time after insertion of 10–15 minutes before intercourse can take place. (Read the product's directions before using it.)

Spermicides can be effectively used as lubricants during sexual intercourse. Those that contain nonoxynol-9 kill bacteria and viruses in addition to sperm. It is recommended that these agents be used with other methods such as male and female condoms, diaphragms, and cervical caps. Spermicides can be purchased without a physician's prescription in many drugstores and supermarkets. Some people are sensitive or allergic to these agents. If burning or itching occurs, switching to another brand will often alleviate the problem.

One of the newer spermicide contraceptives is the ***vaginal contraceptive film (VCF). This is a thin, small (2-inch × 2-inch) film impregnated with nonoxynol-9.*** From 5 to 90 minutes before intercourse, the woman inserts the VCF into her vagina. There it dissolves into a gel-like material over the cervix. It is effective for up to 2 hours. One of the chief benefits is that it can be used by people who are allergic to foams and jellies.

Vaginal Sponge The ***vaginal contraceptive sponge* is a soft, mushroom-shaped spongy disk saturated with spermicide (nonoxynol-9).** *(See* ● *Figure 6.)* The sponge is moistened and inserted into the vagina over the cervix up to 24 hours before intercourse. The device blocks sperm from entering the uterus and kills the sperm. The sponge must be left in place for 6–8 hours after intercourse.

The vaginal sponge is a one-size-fits-all method that is available in pharmacies without prescription. However, users must be able to feel that the sponge is properly placed so it covers the cervix.

Condoms Condoms present a physical barrier between sperm and egg. These thin, tight-fitting sheaths of latex rubber or animal skin are available in all kinds of colors, shapes, and textures, with or without a reservoir tip, dry or lubricated. Spermicide-coated condoms, including those with nonoxynol-9, have been shown to be effective in killing sperm.[6] When buying condoms, always check the expiration date. Don't store them in places where they might be exposed to heat (wallets, glove compartments), which causes latex to deteriorate.

Special note: Natural skin condoms do not effectively prevent the transmission of some STDs, in particular HIV. They do provide effective contraception and increased sensitivity during intercourse.[7]

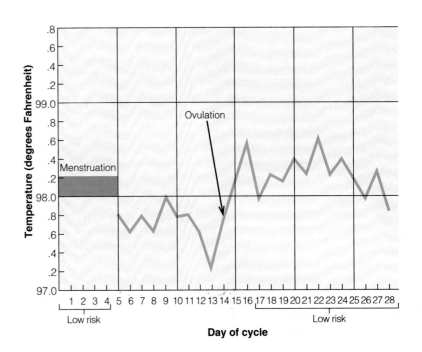

● **Figure 4   The BBT method.**

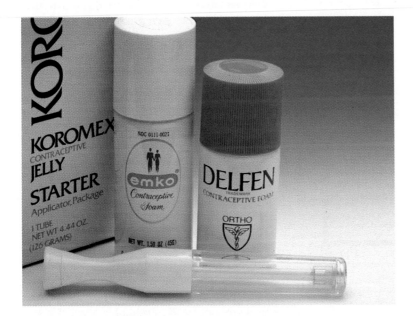

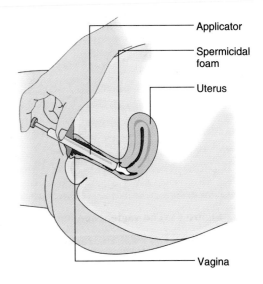

● **Figure 5 Vaginal spermicides.** Among the sperm-killing chemicals offered are foams, jellies, creams, suppositories, and films.

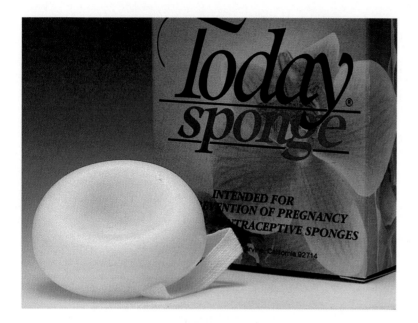

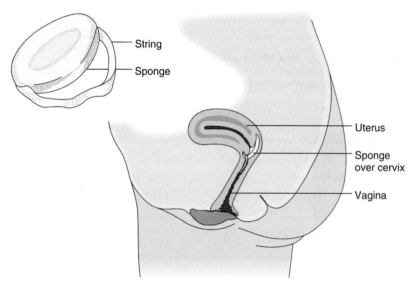

- String
- Sponge

- Uterus
- Sponge over cervix
- Vagina

● **Figure 6**   **The vaginal sponge.**

Diaphragm and Cervical Cap   Diaphragms and cervical caps are barrier contraceptives that are always used with spermicidal creams or jellies. They are available only by prescription. Both come in various sizes and require a fitting by a health care professional to determine correct size and style.

Diaphragms and cervical caps can be inserted up to 6 hours before intercourse and must remain in place for 6–8 hours afterward. Insertion closer to the time of intercourse may afford better protection. Both should be checked for holes after every use (just hold them up to the light). Both increase the woman's risk of *toxic shock syndrome*—a severe, potentially life-threatening bacterial infection—if they remain in the vagina for prolonged periods.

Let us now distinguish between the two devices:

- **Diaphragms: A *diaphragm* is made of a soft latex rubber dome stretched over a flexible metal spring or ring. The size varies from 2 inches to 4 inches, depending on the length of the vagina. When in place, the diaphragm covers the ceiling of the vagina, including the cervix.** *(See ● Figure 7.)* It works primarily by holding spermicide in contact with the cervix and by blocking sperm from entering the cervix. If possible, diaphragms should be removed before 24 hours has elapsed from the time of insertion. They should not, however, be removed within 6 hours of the last act of intercourse. Diaphragms can be reused up to 1 year.

- **Cervical caps: The *cervical cap* operates in much the same way as the diaphragm. This is a much smaller, thimble-shaped rubber or plastic cap that fits directly onto the cervix.** *(See ● Figure 8.)* Insertion of the cervical cap may present more of a challenge to first-time users than does the diaphragm.

 Unlike diaphragm users, cervical cap users do not need to reapply spermicide with each subsequent intercourse after insertion. In addition, they can leave the cap in place for up to 48 hours. Not all women can use the cap, owing to fitting problems or problems with cervical damage.

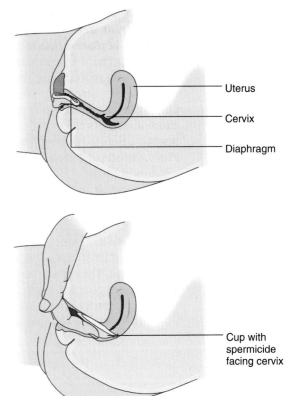

Uterus

Cervix

Diaphragm

Cup with
spermicide
facing cervix

● **Figure 7 The diaphragm.** Users must be able to feel the
cervix to ensure that it is covered by the diaphragm.

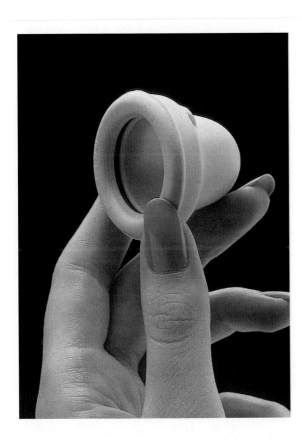

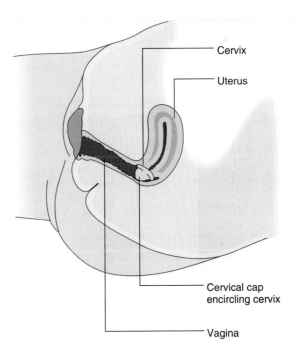

Cervix

Uterus

Cervical cap
encircling cervix

Vagina

● **Figure 8 The cervical cap.**

The IUD **The *IUD,* the abbreviation for the *intrauterine device,* is a small plastic device that is placed inside the uterus.** *(See ● Figure 9.)* The IUD, which must be inserted by a health care professional, may prevent fertilization in some women. Or, if fertilization takes place, the IUD interferes with implantation because it changes the lining of the uterus. Once inserted, the IUD's string must be located after every menstrual period to be sure the device remains in place.

Depending on the type used, an IUD may remain in the uterus for 1–6 years. Presently two principal types are:

- ***Copper-T:*** The *copper* (Paragard) IUD is made of plastic and covered with fine copper wire. The copper seems to cause a biochemical reaction in the uterine lining, which interferes with implantation. The IUD may be worn for as long as 6 years, when it

must be replaced because the copper is completely dissolved.

- ***Medicated:*** The *medicated* (Progestasert) IUD contains the hormone progesterone, which inhibits implantation and also reduces cramping. The device must be replaced after 1 year, when the hormone has run out.

Oral Contraceptives **The *oral contraceptive* or *birth-control pill,* commonly known as simply The Pill, consists of synthetic female hormones that prevent ovulation or implantation.** *(See ● Figure 10.)* It is the most effective *reversible* birth control method available (surgery, for instance, may not be reversible). Nearly 14 million women use the pill in the United States. It appears to be the contraceptive of choice among U.S. women ages 15–24.[7]

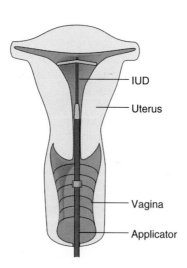
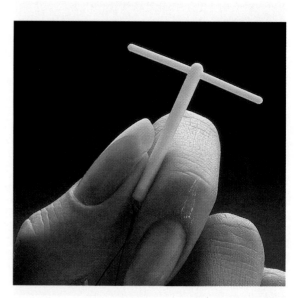

● **Figure 9   The IUD.** Two types of intrauterine devices are shown: copper (Paragard T 380A) and medicated (Progestasert).

There are three basic types of pills—the combination, the multiphasic, and the minipill.

- *Combination pill:* **The *combination pill* contains two hormones, estrogen and progesterone. These hormones, independently or together, prevent pregnancy in three ways:**

    (1) They primarily prevent ovulation.

    (2) They change cervical mucus, making it difficult for the sperm to enter the cervix.

    (3) They change the lining of the uterus (endometrium), preventing implantation.

The combination pill provides a steady dosage of estrogen and progesterone. This type of pill is taken for 21 days, with 7 days off.

- *Multiphasic pill:* The multiphasic pill is a variation on the combination pill, which provides a steady dosage of estrogen and progesterone. **The *multiphasic pill* provides a changing dosage of estrogen and progesterone that more nearly mimics the body's natural cycle of hormones.** Like the combination pill, the multiphasic pill is taken for 21 days, with 7 days off.

- *Minipill:* **The *minipill* contains progesterone only.** It thus has fewer side effects than the other two, but it is also less effective in preventing pregnancy. Because it contains no estrogen, the minipill does not consistently prevent ovulation. It does, however, offer pregnancy protection by changing cervical mucus and changing the lining of the uterus. Unlike the combination and multiphasic pills, the minipill is taken every day.

Users should check with their health care practitioner regarding their pill-taking schedule and find out what to do in the event a pill is missed.

Although oral contraceptives have several advantages, any prospective user must also weigh certain disadvantages: (1) One of the biggest is that they do not protect the user against STDs, including HIV. (2) They increase the risk of blood clots (especially in the legs), stroke, migraine headaches, gallbladder disease, and benign liver tumors. (3) They cause 1 in 20 pill users to develop hypertension, a risk factor

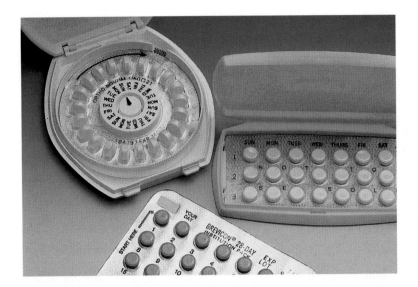

● **Figure 10   Oral contraceptives.** Some pills are taken daily for 3 weeks, then stopped during the fourth week to allow menstruation to occur (though "reminder" pills that contain no hormones may be taken during the fourth week). Others, such as the mini-pill, are taken daily.

in heart disease.[8] (4) For smokers, they cause increased cardiovascular risks. Users of combination pills in particular have an increased risk of heart attacks, especially women over the age of 35 who smoke. (5) They may cause swollen, tender breasts, nausea, and weight gain, especially among new users. However, these symptoms often subside after 1–3 months of use. (6) Users may experience acne, a change in sex drive, mood swings or depression, spotting between menstrual periods, and vaginal yeast infections. (7) Women are often concerned about the risk of breast cancer with use of the pill. Evidence about the association between the two is inconclusive. Users of oral contraceptives may simply be screened for breast cancer more frequently than nonusers, so their breast cancers are detected earlier.[9]

Women who should avoid oral contraceptives are those with a history of blood clots, stroke, heart disease, impaired liver function, or

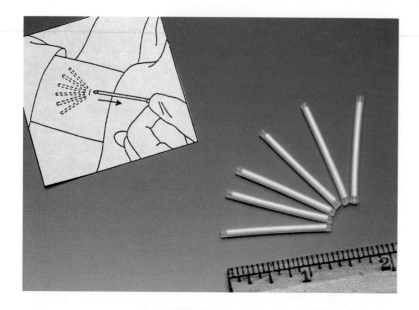

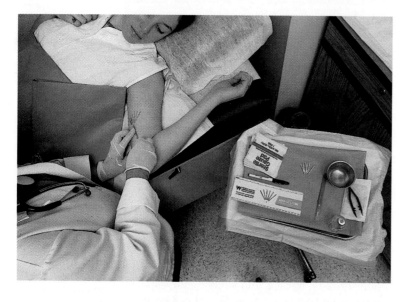

● **Figure 11   Implants.** Norplant silicone rods surgically implanted in a woman's arm release progestin over a 5-year period.

cancer. Those with diabetes, migraine headaches, hypertension, mononucleosis, or other problems should discuss the risks with a health care practitioner.

Despite the side effects, oral contraceptives are relatively safe if the user understands the risks and is carefully monitored by a health care professional. It may help to realize that *any* method of contraception, including use of the pill, is safer than pregnancy. For pregnancy, the risk of death is 1 in 10,000. For a pill user who is a smoker the risk is 1 in 16,000, and for a non-smoker it is 1 in 63,000.[10]

Implant Contraceptive (Norplant) In 1990, the FDA approved for use in the United States a contraceptive called an *implant,* marketed under the brand name *Norplant.* Norplant consists of small, removable silicone-rubber rods or capsules filled with synthetic progestin, a form of progesterone, which are embedded in a woman's arm or leg. *(See ● Figure 11.)* The capsules can be implanted surgically by a physician in 15 minutes using a local anesthetic. They release low levels of synthetic progestin, preventing ovulation and thickening the cervical mucus to prevent sperm from entering the uterus. The implants may stay in place for 5 years and can be removed surgically if a woman wants to become pregnant or discontinue use.

Some women experience irregular patterns of menstrual bleeding, but otherwise side effects appear minimal. Implants are considered extremely effective, with only an estimated 0.05% of women becoming pregnant in the first year.

Injectable Contraceptive (Depo-Provera)
An *injectable contraceptive* known as *Depo-Provera* was approved for use in the United States in 1992 by the FDA. It consists of a long-lasting progestin that is administered once every 3 months. *(See ● Figure 12.)* During the time between injections, a woman has no menstrual periods or irregular ones. Fertility returns after the use of injectables is discontinued.

The risk of pregnancy from injectable contraceptives is extremely low—only 0.4% of women are estimated to become pregnant within the first year.

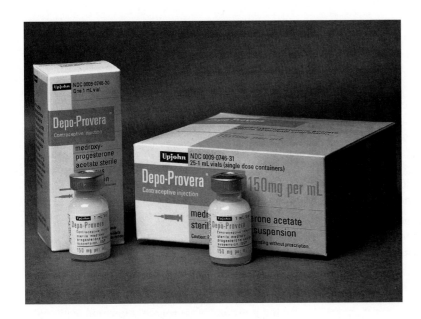

• **Figure 12   Injectable contraceptive.**
Depo-Provera is injected once every 3
months.

Tubal Sterilization—Female Sterilization

Sterilization **is the surgical—and generally permanent—interruption of a person's reproductive capacity,** whether male or female. Sterilization prevents the normal passage of sperm or ova. It is the most popular contraceptive method among American couples. In females, the procedure is called *tubal sterilization* **and is accomplished by blocking or cutting the fallopian tubes. This prevents the passage of the egg through the fallopian tube** to the uterus. *(See ● Figure 13.)* There are two types of tubal sterilization: (1) *tubal ligation,* **the cutting and tying of the fallopian tubes;** (2) *tubal occlusion,* **the blocking of the tubes by cauterizing (burning) or by use of a clamp, clip, or band of silicone.**

There are three procedures for accomplishing tubal sterilization: *laparotomy, laparoscopy,* and *colpotomy.* The choice of method often has to do with the place and extent of the incision, and the anticipated anesthesia and length of hospitalization needed. Other factors are the surgeon's skill and the potential for reversibility (in case a woman later decides she wants to have children).

• *Laparotomy:* **In a** *laparotomy,* **a surgeon makes a 2-inch-long incision in**

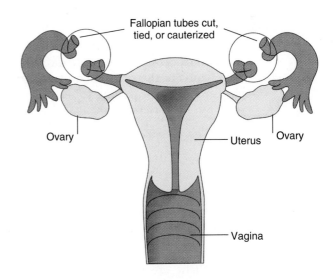

• **Figure 13   Female sterilization: tubal sterilization.** The fallopian tubes are interrupted surgically—cut and tied or blocked. This prevents passage of the eggs from the ovaries to the uterus.

the woman's abdomen and cuts the fallopian tubes. The procedure is performed with anesthesia in a hospital. It requires up to 5 days' stay in the hospital and several weeks of recovery at home.

A laparotomy leaves a 2-inch scar. **A *minilaparotomy* attempts to make the scar less visible by making a 1-inch-long incision just above the pubic hairline.** Often the minilaparotomy can be done under local anesthesia in just 30 minutes, and the patient can go home the same day.

- *Laparoscopy:* **In a *laparoscopy*, a tube-like instrument called a *laparoscope* is inserted through a half-inch incision in the area of the navel. This is the most common means of female sterilization.** After the abdomen is filled with carbon dioxide, the fallopian tubes are closed using instruments inserted through the laparoscope. The operation may be performed in 30 minutes and the patient discharged in a few hours.

- *Colpotomy:* **In a *colpotomy*, an incision is made through the back of the vagina.** Though the operation leaves no outside scar, it is somewhat more difficult and hazardous.

Vasectomy—Male Sterilization Male sterilization is accomplished by ***vasectomy*. This surgical procedure involves making a pair of incisions in the scrotum and cutting and tying two sperm-carrying tubes** called the *vas deferens. (See ● Figure 14.)* The vas deferens connect the testes, which produce the sperm, with the urethra, through which semen is ejaculated. After vasectomy, sperm continue to form, but are absorbed by the body. The man continues to be able to have erections, enjoy orgasms, and produce semen, but the ejaculate contains no sperm cells.

Vasectomies, which can be performed as a 20-minute procedure in a doctor's office with local anesthetic, are considered extremely effective. Only 0.2% of women whose mates have had vasectomies are estimated to become pregnant in the first year. A man contemplating a vasectomy should proceed as though the procedure were irreversible. Although 90% of the operations to reopen the tubes are successful, through a procedure called *vasovasectomy,* only 40-70% result in the ability to father children.[11]

New Directions

Methods of birth control that are relatively recent or still under development include the female condom, vaginal ring, and RU 486 pill.

Numerous new contraceptives and barrier devices against STDs are in development, but the approval process by the Food and Drug Administration puts the United States behind Europe in releasing these for use.[12,13] Some of the following methods have recently become available.

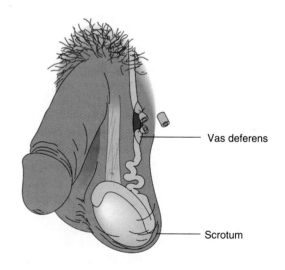

Vas deferens

Scrotum

● **Figure 14   Male sterilization: vasectomy.** A pair of incisions are made in the scrotum, and the vas deferens are cut, tied, and sometimes cauterized. Interrupting the vas deferens—the tubes connecting the testes and the urethra—prevents the passage of sperm to the urethra.

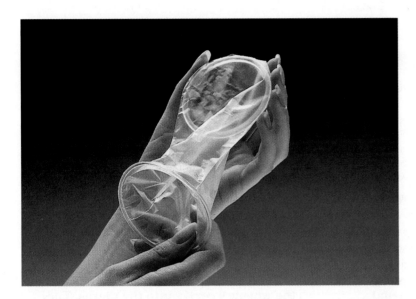

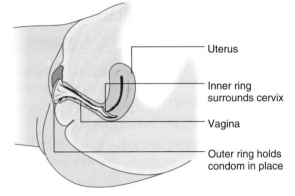

Uterus

Inner ring surrounds cervix

Vagina

Outer ring holds condom in place

● **Figure 15   The female condom.** The 6½-inch-long sheath lines the vagina, held in place by two plastic rings.

Female Condom One of the more promising contraceptive devices is the female condom. Now available in the United States, the *female condom* or *vaginal pouch* (brand name: Reality) is a soft, loose-fitting polyurethane sheath, about 6½ inches long, that lines the vagina.[14] It is held in place by two flexible plastic rings, a 2-inch-diameter ring outside the body and a 1½-inch-diameter ring at the cervix. *(See ● Figure 15.)* The device is inserted much like a diaphragm. The condom must be discarded after one act of intercourse.

Vaginal Ring The *vaginal ring* is something like a diaphragm, but is worn for 3 months before being replaced. Each ring slowly releases estrogen and progestin (or progestin alone), and the hormones are slowly absorbed into the blood through the vagina. The vaginal ring has been found to be comparable in safety to other low-dose, progesterone-like contraceptives.[15]

RU 486 Pill Developed in France, **RU 486 is a hormonal compound available in pill form that can be used to terminate a pregnancy within 5 weeks of conception.** The pill works by blocking the action of progesterone, a hormone that maintains the endometrial lining during pregnancy and prevents uterine contractions. By blocking progesterone, RU 486 induces menstrual bleeding and uterine contractions, thus expelling the fertilized egg. Women experience some discomfort, which has been compared to menstrual cramps. One study found that RU 486 was effective 96% of the time when taken within 49 days of a missed period.[16]

Abortion

▶ Differentiate between spontaneous abortion and induced abortion.

▶ Name and describe five principal types of induced abortion.

▶ Describe the emotional effects of abortion on women with unintended pregnancy.

Abortion is the removal or expulsion of an embryo or fetus from the uterus before it can survive on its own. An abortion can happen spontaneously, owing to medical, hormonal, genetic, or other problems; this is called a *spontaneous abortion* or *miscarriage*. A spontaneous abortion is a miscarriage that occurs within the first 20 weeks of pregnancy. About 20% of all pregnancies end in a spontaneous abortion, usually during the first 3 months (trimester) of pregnancy. A miscarriage often represents a significant loss to the woman and her partner that must be grieved for.

In contrast with spontaneous abortions, **in induced or elective abortions a decision has been made to purposefully terminate a pregnancy.** Every year over a million women terminate their pregnancies by means of abortion.

Types of Induced Abortion

Five principal methods of induced abortion range from those appropriate earlier in pregnancy to those late in pregnancy. In order, they are suction curettage, D and C, D and E, saline induction or use of prostaglandins, and hysterotomy.

Five principal methods of induced abortion that we will describe (there are others as well) are as follows:

- Suction curettage
- D and C
- D and E
- Saline induction/use of prostaglandins
- Hysterotomy

Each method is appropriate for a different stage or stages of pregnancy. From a medical standpoint, abortions are least risky during the first 3 months of pregnancy. During the second 3 months, the woman is more apt to suffer complications. Abortions are generally not performed after the 24th week of pregnancy.

Suction Curettage: Performed in First 12 Weeks The most common method of abortion—used for 96% of all abortions—is suction curettage, usually performed during weeks 6–12.[17] The procedure itself usually takes about 10–15 minutes. **In *suction curettage,* after the cervix is numbed with a local anesthetic, the cervix is dilated. A small, plastic tube called a *curette* is then inserted through the woman's cervix into the uterus. The curette is attached to a suction pump, and the contents of the uterus are then drawn out into the vacuum system.** *(See ● Figure 16.)*

When performed during the first trimester, this kind of abortion usually takes place in a clinic or physician's office. Although suction curettage is one of the safest surgical procedures when performed by a trained, experienced health care professional, side effects can occur. Side effects include perforation of the uterus, bleeding, uterine cramping, or incomplete evacuation of the uterine contents.

D and C, Dilation and Curettage: Performed in Weeks 9–14 A benefit of suction curettage is that it reduces the risk of the physician accidentally perforating the uterus. From the 9th to 14th weeks, however, a physician may use the ***D and C*** technique, which stands for *dilation and curettage.* **In this surgical procedure, after general anesthesia has been administered, the cervical canal is *dilated*—that is, gradually expanded. The physician then uses a small, spoon-shaped curette to scrape the uterine wall of fetal tissue.** Hospitalization is usually required for a D and C because of the risk of perforation of the uterus and bleeding and infection.

D and E, Dilation and Evacuation: Performed in Weeks 13–20 Similar to the D and C method, ***D and E*** stands for *dilation and evacuation.* **Performed with general anes-**

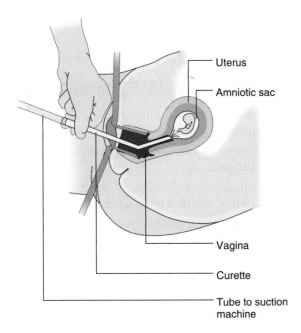

Uterus

Amniotic sac

Vagina

Curette

Tube to suction machine

● **Figure 16 Suction curettage.** The contents of the uterus are removed with a suction machine. This method is most often used during the first 3 months of pregnancy.

thesia in a hospital, because of the risk of perforation, the D and E starts with dilation of the cervix. The physician then uses a combination of suction curettage and forceps (an instrument for grasping) to extract fetal tissue.

Saline Induction/Use of Prostaglandins: Performed in Weeks 16–20 The *saline-induction method*, or *instillation*, uses a hypertonic saline (salt) solution. A physician instills the solution by needle through the abdominal wall and into the amniotic sac surrounding the fetus. This induces the uterus to contract and thus simulate labor, which results in the expulsion of the fetus within 24 hours.

Instead of using salt solutions, physicians may use ***prostaglandins*, naturally occurring hormonelike substances.** These produce labor contractions faster but may also cause vomiting and diarrhea.

Hysterotomy: Performed in Weeks 16–24 A hysterotomy is a surgical procedure performed late in a woman's pregnancy, in weeks 16–24. A hysterotomy is used mainly when the woman's life is in danger and other abortion methods are considered too risky. Called a "small cesarean section," this procedure requires hospitalization and general anesthesia. **In a *hysterotomy* the physician makes a surgical incision in the abdomen and uterus and removes the fetus.** A hysterotomy should not be confused with a hysterectomy (removal of the uterus).

After the 24th Week After week 24, abortion by any method is not considered advisable, or at least will not be performed by very many doctors. This creates hardship for parents who learn late in the pregnancy that the fetus is severely deformed or brain-damaged and would like to consider having an abortion.[18]

Abortion, Psychological Health, and Moral Issues

Abortion is only one alternative; bringing the baby to term is another. Abortion may be emotionally difficult for the woman if the child is wanted but is often not if the child is not wanted. Some women denied abortions experience difficulties in later life. Abortion is an issue about which there is much debate in the United States.

There are, of course, alternatives to abortion. Assuming absence of a serious threat to a woman's life or health, the pregnancy can be carried to term. The child can then be kept, put up for adoption, or placed in a foster home.

Some women and couples who have planned or wanted pregnancies but lose their babies through a spontaneous abortion (miscarriage) may become quite distraught and may have to grieve for their loss, although some feel little effect.[19] How, then, might women be expected to react psychologically to an *induced* abortion?

In some ways, the reactions are predictable: The more a pregnancy is wanted and personally meaningful to the woman, and often her partner, the more difficult emotionally abortion may be for her or them. But if a pregnancy is unintended, women seem not to experience negative psychological responses, under two conditions. Those are that the idea of abortion does not violate their deeply held values or beliefs, and it does not have a perceived social stigma. In fact, emotional distress is usually greatest *before* an abortion rather than afterward, when women frequently report relief and other positive emotions.[20,21]

Equally important, at least one study reports that women who are denied abortions only rarely give up their unwanted babies for adoption. Many harbor resentment and anger toward their children for years. Also, the study found, children born to women whose abortion requests were denied are much more likely to have problems than wanted offspring. They are more likely to be troubled and depressed, to have drug and alcohol problems, to drop out of school, and to commit crimes. More of them suffer from serious illnesses and express dissatisfaction with life.[22]

Abortion is an issue about which many Americans profoundly disagree, which is why laws about it vary from state to state. Strictly from a public-health standpoint, however, when abortions are illegal, maternal deaths increase because of botched illegal abortions by unqualified practitioners. In 1972, there were probably thousands of deaths from illegal abortions in the United States. The next year the U.S. Supreme Court upheld the decision in *Roe v. Wade*. That decision stated that an abortion in the first 3 months of pregnancy is a matter to be determined by a woman and her physician. (It said that abortions in later months can be performed on the basis of health risks and the danger to the mother's health.) By 1985, there were only six deaths from abortion—making it safer than pregnancy or childbirth.

One writer points out that in all of human history, no culture has been able to satisfactorily answer three questions: When is a fetus a person? What circumstances justify abortion? Who decides? And in our time abortion continues to polarize the political dialogue.[23]

Preparing to Be a Parent

▶ Describe the key components and mechanisms of heredity.

▶ Identify and describe four common genetic disorders.

▶ Explain the importance of genetics in considering whether to be a parent.

▶ Describe preconception care and discuss the health strategies associated with such care.

With parenting, there is not just one of you or two of you. Even if you have been with your partner for some time, the arrival of a baby is a new family experience. Now you don't just *come* from a **family, a group in the same household united by marriage, blood, or adoption.** Now you *are* a family yourselves. You become conscious of life being a process and yourself as part of it.

Deciding to Be a Parent: What Is Your Genetic Legacy?

Through sperm and egg, the biological information from each parent is passed along to the offspring as chromosomes. These structures, composed of DNA, carry the organism's hereditary information in units called *genes*. Biological sex and related traits are determined by X and Y chromosomes. Inherited birth defects include Down syndrome, sickle-cell disease, cystic fibrosis, and PKU, some of which can be detected by genetic testing. The risk of some inherited disorders can be considered with genetic counseling techniques.

Your heredity determines some important things about you, and it will determine some important characteristics of your children.

The Master Plan for Your Body: Chromosomes, DNA, Genes At a certain moment, **the male reproductive cell, the *sperm*,** from your father and **the female reproductive cell, the *ovum*,** from your mother met. At that moment of conception, they fused to create **a new cell, the *zygote*, the beginning of life** for you. *(See ● Figure 17.)* Amazingly, that one cell—which divided and later diversified into all the others—contained all the biologically inherited information from each of your parents. That information determined most of your principal characteristics: hair color, foot size, heart shape, blood type, and so on, as well as mental and personality characteristics.

The biological information from each parent was passed along as *chromosomes, DNA,* and *genes.* Let's explain how these work.

- *Chromosomes:* Within the nucleus of each of your cells are *chromosomes,* **which contain the master life plan for your body.** *(See ● Figure 18.)* When egg and sperm unite, the 23 chromosomes carried in the egg are paired with the 23 chromosomes in the sperm. Every human cell (including the first one, the zygote) contains 46 chromosomes in the form of 23 chromosome pairs. Each pair has a member from each parent. A chromosome is composed of long threads containing *DNA,* which transmit genetic information from generation to generation.

- *DNA:* **DNA, which stands for *deoxyribonucleic acid*, is considered the basic unit of control of human life, the carrier of hereditary information.** *(Refer back to Figure 18.)* Each strand of DNA contains thousands of segments called *genes.*

- *Genes:* **Genes are the units of heredity, the transmitters of hereditary information**—your sex, your eye color, and so on. Genes direct the manufacture of proteins that determine biological traits. Genes "specialize" in carrying specific biochemical instructions that produce a particular physical characteristic or trait.

Dominant and Recessive Genes A particular pair of genes, one from each parent, may determine a specific inherited characteristic.

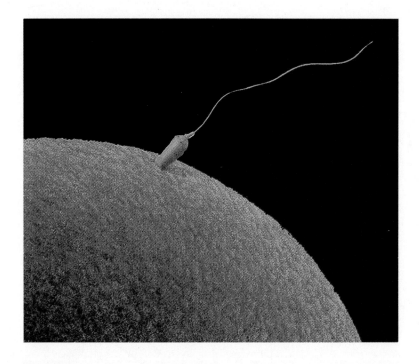

● **Figure 17   The moment of conception: when a sperm unites with an egg.**

❝*Like space voyagers approaching a huge planet, the sperm approach a cell 85,000 times bigger than themselves. The relatively few sperm that make it to the egg release digestive enzymes that eat away the egg's protective coating, allowing one sperm to penetrate. . . . As it does so, an electrical charge shoots across the ovum's surface, blocking out other sperm during the minute or so that it takes the egg to form a barrier. Meanwhile, fingerlike projections sprout around the successful sperm and pull it inward. The egg nucleus and the sperm nucleus move toward each other and, before half a day has elapsed, they fuse. The two have become one.*

But even at that moment, when one lucky sperm has won the 1 in 300 million lottery, an individual's destiny is not assured. Fewer than half of fertilized eggs, called zygotes, survive beyond the first week . . . and only a fourth survive to birth. . . . If human life begins at conception, then most people die without being born. ❞

—David G. Myers (1989). *Psychology* (2nd ed.). New York: Worth, pp. 59–60.

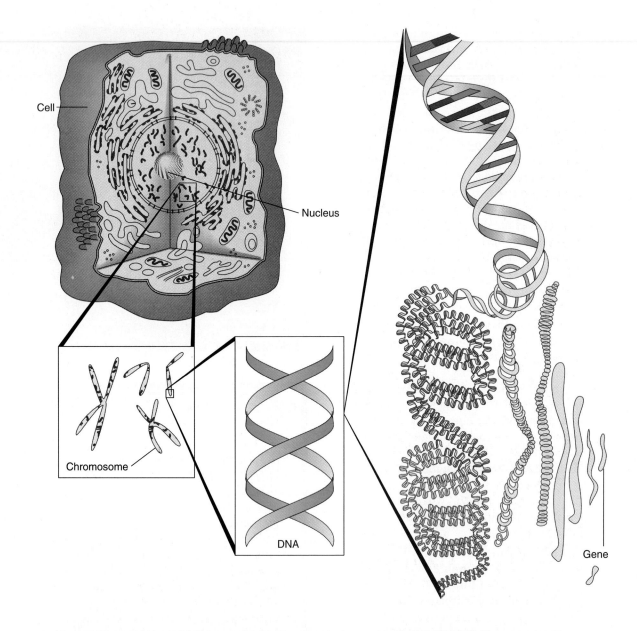

● **Figure 18   Your genetic heritage.** Within the nucleus of each of your cells are chromosomes, which contain the master plan for your body. Each chromosome is composed of long threads of the molecule DNA. Genes, which are segments of DNA, direct the production of proteins that determine specific biological characteristics or traits.

When the actions of the two genes are
alike, they are said to be *homozygous
genes.* However, **sometimes the actions of
the two genes are different, in which case
they are said to be *heterozygous genes.***
That is, one gene is a ***dominant gene,* having
greater influence in determining a particular characteristic.** Such a gene is more powerful than a ***recessive gene,* whose influence is
not as great.**

Many physical characteristics follow the rule
of dominant-recessive genes, but one in particular is eye color. Brown is dominant over blue. If
one parent has two genes for brown eyes, and
the other has two genes for blue eyes, they will
produce brown-eyed children. However, if both
parents are brown-eyed but both carry the
recessive blue gene, they will have one blue-
eyed child for every three brown-eyed children.
(See ● Figure 19.)

Sex Chromosomes: Is It a Boy or a Girl? Of
your 23 pairs of chromosomes, 22 (called *auto-
somes*) control the development and functioning of most of the body. The remaining pair
determine a person's sex and are called the sex
chromosomes or *gametes.*

The sex chromosomes are of two types, X
and Y. *(See ● Figure 20.)* The sex of an offspring is determined by the sperm that fertilizes
the ovum.

- ***X sex chromosome:* The *X* chromosome
  is found in both males and females.** Men
  have one X chromosome; women have two
  X chromosomes. If the sperm is carrying an
  X chromosome, fusion of the sperm (X) and
  the ovum (X) results in the development of
  a female (XX).

- ***Y sex chromosome:* The *Y* chromosome
  is found only in males.** If the sperm is
  carrying a Y chromosome, fusion of the
  sperm (Y) and the ovum (X) results in the
  development of a male (XY).

Inherited Birth Defects Several diseases and
disorders have been linked to, or have a suspected link with, hereditary causes or defective
genes. *(See ● Table 1.)* Some of the most common are the following:

- ***Down syndrome:* Down syndrome occurs
  in 1 out of every 650 births.** The most com-

Brown is dominant over blue. Thus, if a parent with 2 genes for brown eyes joins
with a parent who has 2 genes for blue eyes, all possible combinations are for
brown eyes; no matter how many children they have, all will have brown eyes.

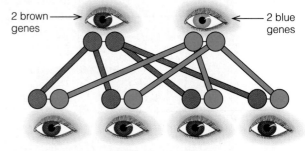

If a brown-eyed parent with a recessive blue gene joins with another brown-eyed
parent with a recessive blue gene, and they have 4 children, then each child has
only a 1 in 4 chance of having 2 recessive blue genes and thus blue eyes.

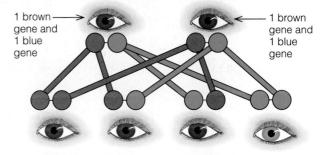

● **Figure 19   Eye color.**

mon condition caused by a chromosomal abnormality, ***Down syndrome* leads to various degrees of mental retardation and
physical deformity.**

- ***Sickle-cell anemia: Sickle-cell anemia
  is a genetic disorder of the blood characterized by sickle-shaped red blood
  cells.*** About 10% of African-Americans in
  the United States carry sickle-cell trait, and
  1 in 500 has sickle-cell anemia.[24,25] The
  sickled cells can't transport enough oxygen
  to important organs, causing tiredness,
  weakness, irritability, shortness of breath,
  and severe pain. Half the victims of the disorder die before the age of 20.

- ***Cystic fibrosis:* At least 30,000 Americans
  have *cystic fibrosis,* a severe abnormality of the respiratory system and sweat**

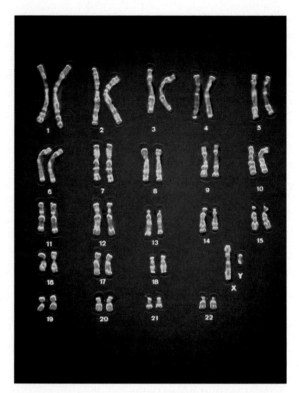

● **Figure 20   46 chromosomes—including the sex chromosomes, X and Y.** *Left:* The 46 chromosomes as they appear under a microscope. *Right:* The 46 chromosomes arranged in pairs. Note the X and Y sex chromosomes.

and mucous glands. It is one of the most common genetic diseases, with 12 million people thought to be carriers.[26] The symptoms are digestive and respiratory problems caused by a sticky mucus that clogs the lungs and leads to chronic infections. The average life span of victims is 26, and few live beyond 40.

● *Phenylketonuria (PKU): Phenylketonuria,* **or** *PKU,* **is a condition that leads to severe retardation unless preventive steps are taken soon after birth. The condition is caused by the absence of a crucial liver enzyme (phenylalanine).** Most newborns are screened for PKU, and those found to have

it are put on a strict phenylalanine-free diet that prevents brain damage.

The chances of having a baby with chromosome abnormalities, such as Down syndrome, increase as the mother gets older. More than 1 in 4 women who gave birth in 1988 were over 30, according to the National Center for Health Statistics.[27] *(See ● Figure 21.)*

Strategy for Living: Genetic Counseling
Because of rapid advances in medicine and biotechnology, it makes sense to analyze your family's "health tree." **The** *family health tree* **is like any genealogical family tree but with health information added. Besides your parents', grandparents', and other**

● **Table 1 Some genetic disorders.**

Disease	Description
Alcoholism	In April 1990, researchers announced a suspected link. The connection is still not confirmed as a genetic disorder.
"Bubble boy" disease	ADA deficiency is rare disorder called "bubble boy" disease, because child lacks a working immune system and must live in a bubble-like enclosure to protect against infection.
Colon cancer	Researchers have discovered one major gene that contributes to it.
Coronary atherosclerosis, premature	Hardening of the arteries.
Cystic fibrosis	Mucus in the lungs is so thick it cannot be cleared, killing most victims by age 27.
Down syndrome	Physical and mental retardation; occurs in 1 of 650 births.
Duchenne muscular dystrophy	Wasting muscle disease, affecting 1 in 5000 males.
Emphysema, premature	A breathing disorder usually associated with smoking, emphysema can also strike early in life. Found in people with genetic defect known as alpha 1-antitrypsin deficiency.
Fragile-X syndrome	Common genetic form of mental retardation, striking more than 1 in 1000 males.
Hemophilia	Disorder in which blood fails to clot.
Huntington's chorea	A lethal degenerative brain disease that strikes between ages 15 and 80.
Lesch Nyhan syndrome	Disorder causing spasticity and self-mutilation, affecting 1 in 100,000 babies.
Neurofibromatosis	A hereditary disease of the nervous system that produces birthmarks, tumors of the skin and nerve cells, and learning disabilities in about 100,000 Americans.
Phenylketonuria (PKU)	Genetic disorder in which crucial liver enzyme, phenylalanine, is absent. Produces severe mental retardation if not treated.
Polycystic kidney disease	Genetic disease causing kidney cysts, leading to kidney failure; it affects 1 in 1000.
Retinoblastoma	Eye cancer.
Sickle-cell anemia	Severe anemia brought about by abnormal form of hemoglobin, the molecule that carries oxygen to the blood. It affects 8–10% of African-Americans.
Tay-Sachs disease	Fatal enzyme deficiency, affecting 1 in 3600 Ashkenazi Jews.
Thalassemia	Forms of blood disease (anemias) found in people of Mediterranean, African, and Southeast Asian descent.

Source: Adapted from Gladstone Foundation Laboratories, San Francisco General Hospital, San Francisco, CA.

relatives' birth and death dates, it includes diseases they may have died of. If known, the age at which the diseases were diagnosed is shown. The family health tree can point out not only possible genetic disorders but also cancers, heart disease, diabetes, and other "familial" conditions. *(See Self Discovery 2.)* Whether or not you contemplate having children, if you suspect that a disorder runs in your family, a genetic counselor may help.

Strategy for Living: Preconception Care for Parenthood

Preconception care is care prospective parents take before even conceiving a child. This includes not smoking, not consuming alcohol or other drugs, eating right, and being careful about pollution and radiation.

SELF DISCOVERY 2

Your Family Health Tree

The purpose of the family health tree is to help you establish any genetic disorders or familial diseases for which you or your children may be at risk. Besides genetic diseases such as sickle-cell anemia, PKU, Down syndrome, and cystic fibrosis, you should try to establish any patterns for various types of cancers, heart disease, diabetes, addictions, and mental disorders (depression, schizophrenia, "senility"). You can get information by interviewing parents and close relatives.

Once your information is as complete as you can get it, look for similar diseases (such as cancers or heart disease) among your parents and brothers and sisters (your *primary relatives*), then among your grandparents and aunts and uncles (your *secondary relatives*), then among your great-grandparents and your cousins (your *tertiary relatives*). If similar disorders or diseases exist in your primary and secondary relatives particularly, that may be a warning sign to be discussed with a health care professional.

In each area below, include *name*, *date of birth*, *age at death*, *cause of death*, *incidence and type of disease*, and *age of diagnosis of disease*. Of course, not all this information may be available to you, but complete as much as you can.

Explanation

Squares = male relatives   Red = primary relatives
Circles = female relatives Blue = secondary relatives
                            Yellow = tertiary relatives

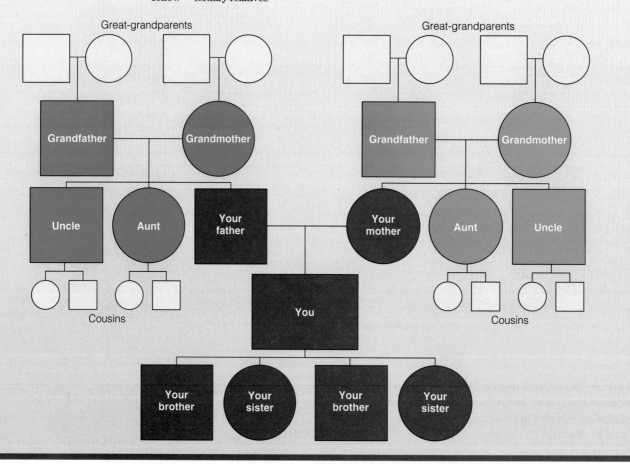

When the mother's age is . . .	20	25	30	35	40	45	49
Her chances of having a baby born with Down syndrome is 1 out of . . .	1667	1250	952	378	106	30	11
And her chances of having a baby born with some chromosomal abnormality is 1 out of . . .	526	476	385	192	66	21	8

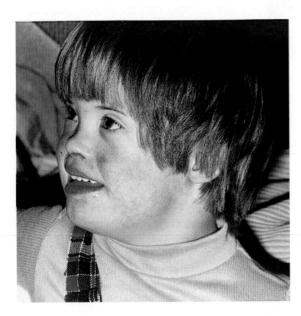

● **Figure 21　The older mother and risk of genetic abnormalities.** The chances of having a baby with chromosomal abnormalities, such as Down syndrome, increase with age, as this table shows.

Aside from knowing their genetic heritage, prospective parents can take other steps to improve their chances of having a healthy baby. These steps are ***preconception care, the care you take before conceiving a child to ensure its health.*** Preconception care can be valuable for both women and men. Indeed, the lifestyles and occupations of fathers can be as important as those of mothers in affecting the health of future offspring.

The Mother's Self-Care If you are a woman who has thought about "getting in shape," plans to become pregnant should give you plenty of reasons. Smoking, alcohol, drugs, and nonnutritious diet are not only bad *during* pregnancy but also *before* the baby is even conceived. So is being overweight or underweight and being exposed to radiation and various fumes and solvents.[28–30]

Some diseases contracted by the mother are particularly risky for the baby. All women of childbearing age should be vaccinated against rubella (German measles), which can cause birth defects ranging from deafness to congenital heart disease. Women should also be tested for genital herpes. One study found that 32% of 277 pregnant women had herpes, although two-thirds reported no history of symptoms.[31]

The U.S. Public Health Service has also recommended that all women of childbearing age take folic acid supplements (a B vitamin). This can prevent such birth defects as spina bifida (the spinal cord protrudes from the spinal column) and anencephaly (missing most of the brain). The government recommends that *all* women of childbearing age take 400 micrograms (0.4 milligrams) of folic acid a day.[32,33]

The Father's Self-Care The man who really wants healthy children has two pieces of business to take care of. He should do nothing that reduces the potency of his sperm and avoid environmental and lifestyle hazards that could lead to birth defects.

● ***Creating healthy sperm:*** Men may already have a problem. One study indicates a significant reduction in men's average sperm

● **Figure 22   Fathers' jobs and habits and babies' health.**

❝ *Men who work in the glass, clay, stone, textile, and mining industries have twice the average risk of fathering premature infants.*

* *Fathers who smoke have above-average rates of low-birth-weight babies and children with brain cancer and leukemia.*

* *The wives of men exposed to vinyl chloride, an ingredient in plastic, and water treatment materials have elevated miscarriage rates.*

* *Men exposed to low levels of radiation in a British nuclear power plant fathered children with increased rates of leukemia.*

* *Firemen exposed to the wide variety of poisons in smoke have an increased risk of having children with heart defects.*

* *Children of men who work with hydrocarbons, solvents, spray paints, and toxic metal fumes have increased rates of cancer and birth defects.*

* *Children of male aerospace workers have higher rates of brain tumors.* ❞

—Sandra Blakeslee (1991, April). Father figures: The male link to birth defects. *American Health*, pp. 54–57.

count in the past 50 years, possibly because of environmental pollution.[34] Starting with this possible disadvantage, men must try to avoid worsening the situation.

Men who have an unbalanced diet or who smoke may have low levels of vitamin C. This may increase the likelihood of producing children with birth defects and certain types of cancer (leukemia and lymphoma).[35] It is recommended that they include more fruit and vegetables in their diet or take a vitamin C supplement every day.

Men who are heavy drinkers are known to have comparatively low sperm counts. Alcohol, particularly binge drinking, also suppresses the body's ability to produce sperm, research on rats shows.[36] Indeed, drinking a six-pack of beer in less than 2 hours blocks the genetic messenger that orders the testicles to produce sperm. (But don't rely on this phenomenon for contraception!)

* ***Habits and working conditions:*** The male reproductive tract is extremely vulnerable to poisons and gene-damaging substances. Yet men may be exposed to some of these in their work. *(See* ● *Figure 22.)* Among the sperm-damaging substances are lead, paint thinners and other industrial solvents, pesticides, and ionizing radiation. Alcohol and marijuana smoke are also dangerous.[37] One study suggests that men in certain jobs—janitors and certain mill workers, for instance—have a higher risk of fathering children with birth defects.[38]

Pregnancy, Childbirth, and Homecoming

▶ Explain the experience of pregnancy from the baby's, mother's, and father's points of view.

▶ Differentiate between presumptive, probable, and positive signs of pregnancy.

▶ Describe the kind of prenatal care a mother-to-be should concern herself with.

▶ Identify and explain common pregnancy-related complications.

▶ Describe the 3-stage process of labor and delivery.

▶ Discuss the kinds of decisions about childbirth that must be made by prospective parents.

▶ Describe the causes of infertility.

▶ Identify and explain infertility treatment options.

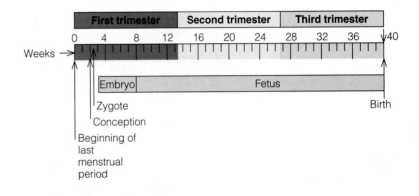

● **Figure 23   The three trimesters of pregnancy.**

At what time of year are obstetricians least likely to take their vacations? Late summer, especially September, says one report.[39] That's when most babies are born—at least in the United States.

Pregnancy: The Inside Story

The 9 months of pregnancy are divided into three parts called *trimesters.* The first trimester consists of conception, implantation, and early growth of the embryo and fetus. At the end of the second trimester the infant has a small chance of surviving outside the womb. In the third trimester the infant develops surfactant, which enables it to breathe on its own.

If your mother's pregnancy was full term, your stay inside her body lasted on average 266 days from conception to birth, about 9 months. **These 9 months are divided into thirds called *trimesters*.** (*See* ● *Figure 23.*) Actually,

the first trimester is dated from the beginning of the last menstrual period, about 2 weeks before conception.

The First Trimester: Conception, Implantation, and Early Growth You began life with conception. **Conception, or *fertilization,*** was the uniting of the ovum or egg from your mother with a sperm cell from your father. This occurred in one of the two *fallopian tubes,* attached to the uterus. The *ovum* is the female reproductive cell, the *sperm* the male reproductive cell, and the fertilized ovum is called a *zygote.*

Moved along by hairlike projections called *cilia,* which line the fallopian tube, the zygote was propelled into the *uterus,* or *womb.* There the baby grew and was nourished until birth. (*See* ● *Figure 24.*) As it moved, the zygote underwent cell division—one cell divided into two cells, two into four, four into eight, and so on. The subdivided cells were smaller, so the total zygote remained the same size as the fertilized ovum. Three to four days after conception, the zygote entered the uterus. In another three or four days it buried itself within the uterine lining, called the *endometrium.* The process of the zygote burying itself is called *implantation.* At this point, from the second through the eighth week, the growing baby is called an *embryo.*

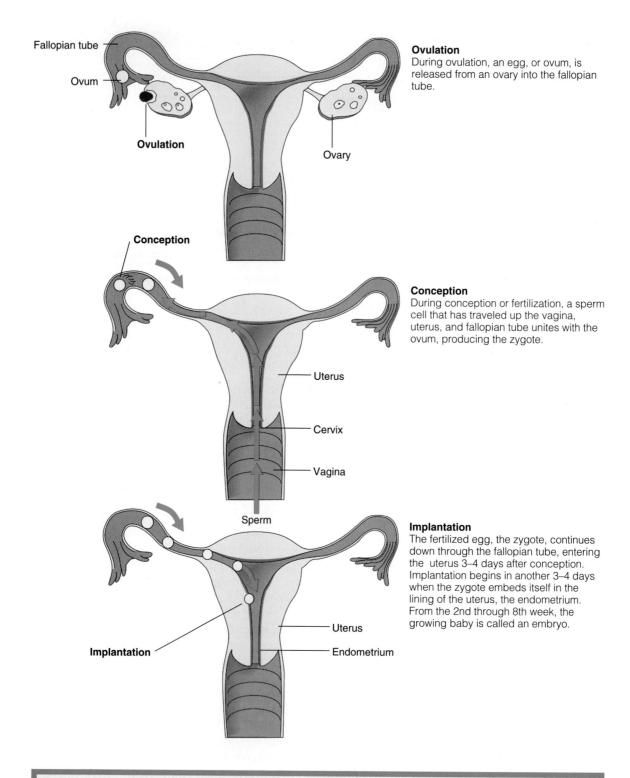

Ovulation
During ovulation, an egg, or ovum, is released from an ovary into the fallopian tube.

Conception
During conception or fertilization, a sperm cell that has traveled up the vagina, uterus, and fallopian tube unites with the ovum, producing the zygote.

Implantation
The fertilized egg, the zygote, continues down through the fallopian tube, entering the uterus 3–4 days after conception. Implantation begins in another 3–4 days when the zygote embeds itself in the lining of the uterus, the endometrium. From the 2nd through 8th week, the growing baby is called an embryo.

● **Figure 24   Conception and implantation.**

Chorionic villi, **small fingerlike growths from the embryo,** began to burrow into the endometrium, the uterine blood supply. From these villi and the uterine wall, a placenta began to form. *(See ● Figure 25.)* Beginning about 4 weeks after conception, the ***placenta* supplied you, the growing infant, with nourishment and oxygen from your mother's blood. It returned wastes back to your mother's body for disposal.** This was accomplished through the ***umbilical cord,* which contained two arteries and a vein to carry blood between you and the placenta.** Inside the uterus, you floated in **a sac of liquid called *amniotic fluid,*** also called the "bag of waters."

By the end of your first month, you had multiplied to 10,000 times your original size. Yet you were still only about a quarter-inch long and weighed only one-seventh of an ounce. *(See ● Figure 26.)* Did you look like a person? Barely. Your head was disproportionately large, because of brain development. The forerunners of your throat, jaw, and mouth had developed, but they looked like gills. You had only the rudiments of eyes, ears, and nose. A fold called the neural groove had appeared, which would later become your nervous system.

By the end of the second month, you were called a *fetus.* You were now 1.2 inches long, had fingers and toes in human form, and had developed a circulatory system.

By the end of the third month—the end of the first trimester—you were about 3 inches long. Most major organs were present, a heartbeat could be detected with a stethoscope, and your face and head were formed. Your sex was also apparent. You probably also were moving a bit within your watery environment, although your mother could not feel it yet.

The Second Trimester By the end of the fourth month, you had become more than 6 inches long and weighed perhaps 5 ounces. Your skeleton developed and your skin was covered with a **fine hair, called *lanugo,*** which is usually shed before birth.

At the end of the fifth month, you could have been as much as 12 inches long and weighed about a pound. You had developed nails on your fingers and toes, and your ears were able to hear sounds. You were capable of grasping and sucking and took turns sleeping and

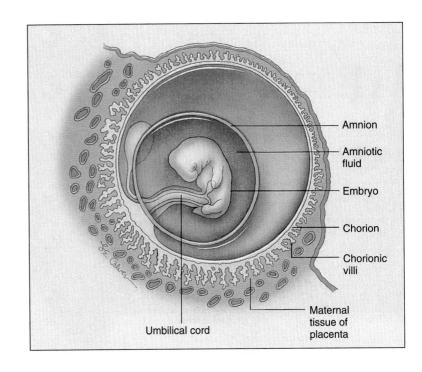

● **Figure 25 The protected infant.** Formed by the embryo's chorionic villi and the mother's uterine wall, the placenta feeds and protects the growing infant. Through the umbilical cord it provides nutrients from the mother's bloodstream and removes wastes. The infant floats in a liquid environment called amniotic fluid.

waking. Your mother could feel you kicking and moving about in her womb. **Your skin was covered by a cheeselike coating called the *vernix caseosa.*** This coating remained until it was absorbed into your skin within the first 24 hours after you were born.

By the end of the sixth month, you were perhaps 13 inches long and your eyes had become light sensitive. Eyebrows and eyelashes were formed. You were sucking your thumb and perhaps even had hiccups. If you were born at this age, you appeared thin and scrawny. In addition, you had a 10% chance of surviving, in part because your organs, including your lungs, remained immature.

A critical matter during the second trimester was your brain development, which is essential to your attaining the ***age of viability.* This is a point between the 20th and 26th weeks after conception when you would**

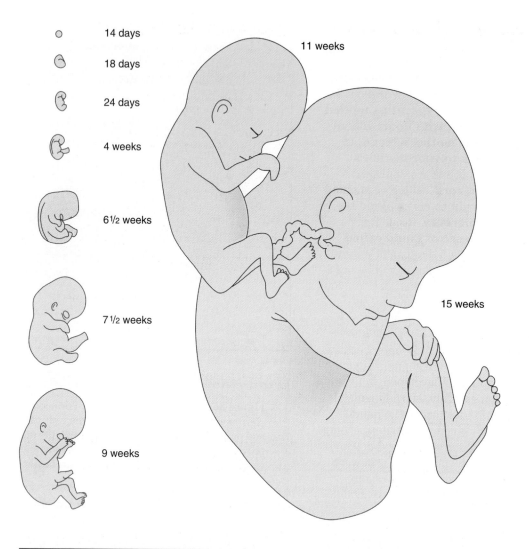

14 days

18 days

24 days

4 weeks

6½ weeks

7½ weeks

9 weeks

11 weeks

15 weeks

● **Figure 26   Actual size.** Growth of the embryo and fetus from 2 to 15 weeks after conception.

have some chance of survival outside the womb. Expert care would be required.

The Third Trimester At the end of the seventh month inside your mother, you had reached 14 or 15 inches in length. You had gained weight, mainly as fat layers under your skin, so that you weighed perhaps 3 pounds. Your head had abundant hair, your eyelids were open, and—particularly critical—you probably had developed surfactant. ***Surfactant* is a substance produced in your lungs that enabled you to breathe on your own.**

By the end of the eighth month, you may have reached 18 inches long and weighed about 5 pounds. Your skin had a wrinkled appearance. By this time, you had also probably assumed a head-down position in your mother's uterus.

By the end of your third trimester, you had reached about 19 inches and weighed 6 or 7 pounds. Your limbs were proportional, your face had features, your skin was smooth, the bones of your skull had hardened.

Ready or not, here you came—into the world.

Pregnancy: The Mother's Story

Pregnancy detection begins in the first trimester with presumptive signs leading a woman to guess she's pregnant, such as a missed menstrual period. A physician looks for probable signs, such as the placental hormone HCG, detected by a laboratory test. Later the physician looks for positive signs, such as hearing a fetal heartbeat. In the second trimester, the woman gains weight, experiences changes in body secretions, and feels the baby move inside her. The third trimester may be a period of increasing discomfort as the infant gains weight, putting pressure on the mother's organs. At last the baby is ready to be born.

Nearly any pregnancy can be an uncomfortable experience, characterized by such complaints as fatigue, nausea, indigestion, constipation, breathlessness, and trouble sleeping. On the other hand, there are few thrills to compare with those of feeling the stirrings of a new life within.[40]

The First Trimester: Pregnancy Detection

Pregnancy detection depends on three signs:

- *Presumptive signs: Presumptive signs* **are the subjective signs by which the woman herself guesses she may be pregnant.** The classic presumptive sign is a missed menstrual period. Another common symptom is *morning sickness*—**nausea and vomiting that occur on rising** in the morning. Other symptoms are frequent need to urinate owing to the pressure of the fetus on the bladder, and fatigue. The breasts become enlarged and more tender as milk glands develop.

- *Probable signs: Probable signs* **are those by which a physician determines that pregnancy is probable.** Probable signs include a positive pregnancy test, slight increase in body temperature, softening and enlargement of the uterus, and bluish discoloration of the cervix.

    Pregnancy tests are based on detecting the presence of *human chorionic gonadotropin (HCG),* which is secreted by the placenta. Home pregnancy tests, which test urine for HCG, are inexpensive and easy to use. However, they are not always accurate (they are in error 20% of the time), especially in the early weeks of pregnancy. Laboratory pregnancy tests, by contrast, have only a 1% error rate.[41]

- *Positive signs: Positive signs* **are those detected by the physician that definitely indicate pregnancy.** There are five positive signs: The examiner (1) feels the fetus move, (2) hears the fetal heartbeat, (3) detects the fetal skeleton through an X-ray, (4) obtains an electrical tracing of the fetal heart rate, and (5) sees an outline of the fetus through use of ultrasonic equipment.[42]

To calculate the expected date of childbirth, subtract 3 months from the first day of the last menstrual period and add 7 days. This is called *Naegele's formula.* The calculation works out to 9 months and 7 days from the beginning of a woman's last menstrual period.[43]

The Second Trimester

This is a time of many adjustments. The mother may find herself craving certain foods. She may experience indigestion, constipation, and hemorrhoids. The pigment around her nipples will darken further, and a dark line will appear down the center of her abdomen. Body secretions increase: perspiration, salivation, and vaginal fluids. Her breasts may build **colostrum, a yellowish milk that exists for a few days following childbirth.**

The Third Trimester

During months 7 through 9, the mother-to-be may experience increasing discomfort as the growing infant puts pressure on her internal organs. Pressure on her bladder causes frequent urination, pressure on her lungs and diaphragm causes breathlessness, and pressure on her stomach causes heartburn. About 2–4 weeks before birth, the baby "drops" its head and settles low in her pelvis. Then one day—or, often, one night—the time she thought would never come finally does. The baby signals it is ready to be born.

Pregnancy: The Father's Story

If fathers-to-be often get less attention than prospective mothers, many are still excited participants. Some even experience "couvade," completely identifying with the woman's physical symptoms.

The father's story is mainly an emotional one. Even the most involved father, however, is less apt to get attention than the prospective mother. *(See ●Figure 27.)*

Some fathers are excited participants, identifying with all the stages of pregnancy.[44] Indeed, there are men who so completely identify with the woman's pregnancy that they even experience some of the same physical symptoms.[45] The name given to this psychosomatic behavior, *couvade*, from a French word meaning "to sit on or to hatch," may affect a great many fathers.[46,47] Some fathers-to-be become preoccupied with themselves, overexercising or overeating.[48] Others become so resentful that they harm their partners; in fact, the incidence of wife-beating actually increases during pregnancy.[49] Many couples, however, find that the event brings them closer together than they have ever been before.[50]

Mother Care: Prenatal Care for Mother and Infant

Prenatal care is care the expectant mother takes of herself and her infant during pregnancy. This includes medical care, a well-balanced diet, exercise and rest, and stress reduction. Pregnant women who smoke risk having premature or low-birth-weight babies. Those who drink alcohol risk producing babies with fetal alcohol syndrome, a cause of retardation, or other problems called *fetal alcohol effects*. Marijuana, cocaine, and other drugs also cause trouble. Pregnant women should also avoid radiation and environmental pollution.

***Prenatal care* means a new mother-to-be should take care of herself and the baby before birth.** Poor health care for expectant mothers leads to many potentially preventable problems. Of the 3.8 million infants born in the United States in 1987, 38,408 died before their first birthday.[51,52] In addition, more than 250,000 low-birth-weight infants are born each year. Low birth weight is associated with increased risk of death and a wide range of disorders. These include nervous system disorders, cerebral palsy, low IQ, learning disorders, behavior problems, and lower respiratory tract infections.[53]

Among the things an expectant mother must think about are:

- Medical care
- Nutrition
- Exercise and rest
- Stress
- Caffeine, tobacco, alcohol, and other drug use
- Environmental hazards

Of course, all these factors affect her own health, but now she has the added responsibility of thinking about her baby's health.

Prenatal Medical Care As soon as a woman suspects she may be pregnant, she should see a health care professional and have a complete physical examination. This is important because the first trimester of pregnancy is critical to the fetus's health and well-being. The health care professional may be a physician assistant or nurse-midwife. Or it may be a physician such as a general practitioner or family practitioner. Most often it is an ***obstetrician/gynecologist (OB/GYN)*, a doctor who specializes in the female reproductive system and pregnancy.**

Nutrition: Eating for Two If indeed "You are what you eat," as the saying goes, so is your baby if you're pregnant. Some physicians will prescribe special vitamin supplements during pregnancy. But the expectant mother also needs *increased* amounts of vitamins and minerals from a well-balanced diet, as well as increased protein.

An important part of prenatal nutrition is appropriate *weight gain*—25–35 pounds, according to the National Academy of Sciences'

● **Figure 27   The overlooked father.**

" . . . Although fathers-to-be may need as much social support as mothers-to-be, they are less likely to get it. For one thing, their imminent parenthood is not visible, so their friends, family, and co-workers are less likely to express interest in the pregnancy. For another, men at all points of the life span are less likely to reveal their need for help. Especially as fatherhood approaches, many men make a special effort to appear strong and protective, frequently camouflaging their understandable feelings of panic by springing into action. Some build a crib, a room, or even a house; others become intensely involved in physical fitness or sports; others eat too much or develop physical symptoms of their own."

—Kathleen Stassen Berger (1988). *The developing person through the life span* (2nd ed.). New York: Worth, p. 94.

Food and Nutrition Board.[54] It is particularly important to gain enough weight in the first and second trimesters, to lower the risk of low-birth-weight babies.[55]

Exercise and Rest "Pregnancy is like an athletic event," says obstetrician Douglas Hall. "A woman should prepare for it the way an athlete would."[56] Expectant women can continue doing the kinds of activities they're used to—although they shouldn't *take up* strenuous new activities while pregnant.

Rest is important, and women who find the baby's exertions and the bladder pressure keeping them awake nights are advised to take day naps.

Caffeine, Tobacco, Alcohol, and Other Drugs All drugs, whether available in a pharmacy, liquor store, or on the street, should be avoided unless prescribed by a doctor. The reason, of course, is that any drug taken by the mother may readily cross the placenta and enter the baby's bloodsteam. This means that if the mother is dependent on some drug, the baby will be too.

Some of the most common drugs to think about are the following:

- *Caffeine:* Is a cup of coffee, tea, or Coke harmful? In moderation, probably not. However, research suggests that mothers who usually consume caffeine fairly heavily may produce low-birth-weight babies.[57,58] "Heavily" is 300 milligrams or more a day—3 cups of coffee or 6 cans of cola.

- *Tobacco:* Smoking reduces the flow of blood to the infant and reduces the amount of oxygen carried by the blood.[59] As a result, smoking mothers have increased rates of miscarriage, stillbirths, and premature babies. They often produce smaller, low-weight babies and have babies with higher infant death rates.[60–62] Lower birth weight does not mean merely a smaller baby. Cigarette smoking deprives the fetus of essential growth of *all* its body organs, including the brain. This can lead to permanent developmental delays in children.[63]

- *Alcohol:* Pregnancy and alcohol is always a dangerous combination. The leading known cause of preventable mental retardation and birth defects in the United States is ***fetal alcohol syndrome (FAS). Babies born with FAS have a common pattern of mental retardation and other central nervous system problems. More specifically, they have delayed language development, low IQ, and malformations of various organ systems (heart, urinary, genital, and skeletal). They also have growth deficiency and facial abnormalities*** (small heads, small eyes, and abnormal facial features, including an underdeveloped midface).[64]

  About 1 in every 750 babies born has FAS, and many more have a condition known as ***fetal alcohol effects (FAE). The symptoms of FAE include low birth weight, abnormalities of the mouth and the genital and urinary systems, and altered behavioral patterns.***[65]

- *Street drugs:* If street drugs (illegal drugs) are trouble for adults, they are trouble for babies, too. Babies whose mothers are addicted to heroin and methadone, for instance, are born addicted. They may die of withdrawal symptoms if they do not receive the drug shortly after birth. Those who survive are apt to be of low birth weight and suffer a variety of problems.[66]

  Moderate consumption of marijuana can also lead to complications, some of them resembling those produced by alcohol.[67-69] Cocaine can lead to spontaneous abortions, stillbirths, and premature births.[70-72]

- *Prescription drugs:* Several physician-prescribed drugs have been shown to be harmful to the fetus: streptomycin, tetracycline, anticoagulants, and bromides. Tran-

quilizers and barbiturates such as Valium, chlorpromazine, and phenobarbital are also dangerous.[73,74]

Environmental Hazards: Radiation and Pollution Two environmental hazards that a pregnant woman should be aware of are *radiation* and *pollution.*

- ***Radiation:*** The largest dosage of radiation a pregnant woman is apt to receive is during a pelvic X-ray. The X-ray may be in conjunction with a medical emergency or radiation therapy (as for cancer). In most cases, the dosages are low enough that the fetus will not be harmed.[75] However, especially during the first trimester, X-rays slightly increase the risk of leukemia during childhood.[76] An expectant mother thus should consult with her doctor about the benefits of any X-rays and risks to her baby.

- ***Pollution:*** A likely source of environmental pollution harmful to the fetus is automobile emissions, such as carbon monoxide and lead. Exposure may occur, for example, if a woman lives near a heavily traveled street with lots of stop-and-go traffic. Such circumstances have been associated with low birth weight and slow neurological development.[77]

With all the possible hazards, it's easy for pregnant women to worry that they run the risk of doing *something* wrong. However, we need to point out that *most* women are exposed to some of these risks, yet have healthy babies anyway. What is important is the interaction among hazards: the more hazards and the longer the mother's exposure to them, the greater the possibility of harm to the infant.

Coping with Complications: "Will My Baby and I Be All Right?"

Expectant women need to be aware of possible pregnancy-related complications. These include premature labor, preterm births, miscarriage, stillbirth, and ectopic pregnancy. Other possible complications are placenta previa, premature separation

of the placenta, and high blood pressure and toxemia. Diseases that might endanger the unborn baby are rubella, cytomegalovirus, toxoplasmosis, and sexually transmitted diseases. Rh disease may occur in second and later pregnancies. Prenatal tests may help to detect birth defects and other problems. Types of prenatal tests are ultrasound, amniocentesis, the AFP plus test, chorionic villus sampling, and percutaneous umbilical blood sampling.

In 1987, for every 100 deliveries there were 22 hospitalizations for pregnancy-related complications—*before* delivery.[78] Expectant women need to be aware of what some of these common complications are. Here we describe:

- Premature labor and preterm births
- Miscarriages and stillbirths
- Ectopic pregnancy
- Placentia previa
- High blood pressure, toxemia, and eclampsia
- Exposure to infections, such as rubella, cytomegalovirus, toxoplasmosis, and STDs, which can result in birth defects
- Rh disease

Premature Labor and Preterm Births About 27% of the hospitalizations for pregnancy complications are for premature labor.[79] **Premature labor is defined as labor occurring before 36 weeks' gestation.** A *mature infant* at birth or near full term (40 weeks) averages about 7.5 pounds. An *immature infant* is born before the 28th week and weighs less than 2.2 pounds. A *premature infant* is born after the 27th week and before full term and weighs 2.2–5.5 pounds. Depending on the weight, the chances of a premature infant's survival range from poor to good. The earlier a baby is born during pregnancy and the less it weighs, the less its chances for survival.

Sometimes pregnant women will experience early uterine contractions that turn out to be false labor, which usually stops spontaneously. **In *false labor*, the contractions of the uterus are brief and irregular, and the pain is limited to the groin and lower abdomen.**

Miscarriages and Stillbirths **A *miscarriage*, or *spontaneous abortion*, is the expulsion of the fetus when it is too young to live outside the womb.** The term *miscarriage* is usually applied to occurrences between the 12th and 28th weeks. **A *stillbirth* is the delivery of a dead fetus.** Most miscarriages and stillbirths result from chromosome abnormalities, bacterial or viral infections, and rejection by the immune system.[80] About 1 in 6 pregnancies is miscarried, most early in the pregnancy; often the woman does not even realize she is pregnant.[81] Miscarriages are twice as apt to occur in women over age 35 as in women under age 24, because of the increase in chromosomal abnormalities with age. This is why there is considerable anxiety about miscarriages the older the woman trying to become pregnant. Miscarriages do not result from physical exercise, sexual activity, or any psychological matters.

Ectopic Pregnancy Ectopic pregnancy is a potentially fatal (to the mother, as well as fetus) pregnancy complication. **Ectopic pregnancy occurs when a fertilized egg becomes implanted somewhere other than the lining of the uterus.** A growing embryo that is implanted in the fallopian tubes (through which eggs move from the ovaries to the uterus) may rupture surrounding tubes and blood vessels. The heavy bleeding that results can be fatal to the woman. Ninety percent of ectopic pregnancies take place in the fallopian tubes and are called *tubal pregnancies*.[82] Other ectopic pregnancies take place in the abdomen, cervix, or ovary. Tubal ectopic pregnancies usually occur during the first eight weeks of pregnancy.

The diagnosis of ectopic pregnancy continues to be challenging. Signs and symptoms include a blood pregnancy test, missed period, abnormal vaginal bleeding, pelvic pain, and sometimes dizziness and nausea. Earlier diagnosis, including the use of ultrasound, have helped physicians to treat the problem before it becomes life-threatening.

Placenta Previa This disorder, which usually occurs in the third trimester, affects 1 in 200 pregnant women. **Placenta previa is the premature separation of the placenta from the wall of the uterus.** This usually occurs because the placenta has grown over all or part of the cervical opening. About 80–85% of the infants survive, if treated properly.

High Blood Pressure and Toxemia High blood pressure can occur because of the extra weight gain of pregnancy and the strains on the circulatory system. Women are more apt to develop high blood pressure—hypertension—during pregnancy than at any other time. In the early stage of a health problem called **toxemia, the mother experiences high blood pressure and sudden weight gain. Other symptoms are swollen fingers and ankles (owing to increased water retention), protein in the urine, blurring vision, and headaches.** If the problem is not treated, it can lead to convulsions, which can be fatal to the mother and child.

Exposure to Infectious Diseases: Rubella, Cytomegalovirus, Toxoplasmosis, and STDs It's difficult enough having a disease for oneself; it's even worse when the disease affects the unborn. Some of the most important are the following:

- **Rubella (German measles): Rubella, or German measles, is a virus that is reasonably mild outside of pregnancy. However, if contracted during pregnancy, it can cause the fetus to develop serious handicaps, including blindness and deafness.**

  Fortunately, this is one disease that can be prevented. Immunity to the organism that causes rubella is conferred by previous exposure to rubella or by a vaccine. A rubella vaccination is one of the standard immunizations that one receives in childhood and its protection is usually lifelong. All women of childbearing age should be certain they are immune to rubella.

- **Toxoplasmosis: Toxoplasmosis is a disease caused by a parasite found in uncooked or undercooked meat and in dust or water contaminated by cat feces. Although healthy adults rarely experience symptoms, the disease can cause blindness and serious brain damage to the infant.**

  A blood test early in pregnancy may determine whether the mother is vulnerable to toxoplasmosis. If she is, she should avoid eating rare meat and should avoid any contact with a cat's litter box.[83]

- **Cytomegalovirus (CMV) infection:** Like rubella, **cytomegalovirus (CMV) infection has only a mild effect on healthy adults, but may have severe consequences for the fetus. Some infants experience brain damage, mental retardation, blindness, deafness, cerebral palsy, seizures, and liver damage.**

  Adults usually get CMV by such intimate contact as kissing, sexual contact, or handling infected children's diapers. A transmission to the newborn can occur during childbirth if CMV is present in cervical secretions and during breast-feeding. Pregnant women who are around other children should wash their hands frequently.

- **Sexually transmitted diseases (STDs): Once called venereal diseases, sexually transmitted diseases (STDs) include all diseases spread by sexual contact:** HIV, chlamydia, gonorrhea, genital herpes, human papilloma viruses, syphilis, and others. STDs can harm fetuses and infants.

  In an infected woman, the virus that causes AIDS—human immunodeficiency virus (HIV)—can cross the placenta into the blood of the fetus. A woman with undetected genital herpes virus may pass it to her infant during the birth process, possibly causing central nervous system infection and other problems in the baby.

Rh Disease **Rh disease, or erythroblastosis, is a condition that occurs when antibodies produced by the mother's blood damage and destroy fetal blood cells. The fetus will possibly be stillborn or suffer severe brain damage.** Rh disease can occur when a woman whose blood type is Rh-negative conceives a child with a man whose blood is Rh-positive. This combination exists in about 12% of marriages;[84] it is not a problem until antibodies from a first pregnancy attack during the second.

Fortunately, this problem is now preventable by giving such mothers Rhogam, Rh-negative blood that already contains antibodies. Rhogam prevents the mother's body from forming its own antibodies. The antibodies disappear, and when the woman becomes pregnant the second time no antibodies attack the blood of the Rh-negative baby.

Prenatal Tests "Will my baby and I be all right?" a pregnant woman may ask. The odds of a positive outcome are generally good, particularly if she has followed the kind of prenatal program we described above. If she seems at risk for any of the conditions we've just described, she should be closely monitored by a physician. There are a number of prenatal tests that can be used to identify more than 250 diseases and disorders. The most common are the following:

- *Ultrasound:* In *ultrasound*, **also known as *ultrasonography* or *prenatal sonography*, a physician passes a hand-held instrument over the pregnant woman's abdomen. Sound waves beam into the body, make contact with the fetus, and send back echoes. The echoes are translated into an image on a television monitor.**[85] There is no danger from radiation (ultrasound is not an X-ray). Ultrasound can be used to count the number of fetuses during pregnancy, check for fetal anomalies, and monitor the infant's growth.

- *The AFP Plus test:* A combination of three blood tests, the ***AFP Plus test* offers an improvement over past tests (including amniocentesis) in detecting Down syndrome.** The tests look for three substances (alpha-fetoprotein [AFP], unconjugated estriol and chorionic gonadotropin). Levels of these compounds can determine which women are at risk for bearing afflicted children. The test predicts Down syndrome correctly 60% of the time.[86] A similar test developed in England is called *Bart's Triple Test.*[87]

- *Amniocentesis:* If fetal abnormalities are suspected, *amniocentesis* **may be used during the 14th–16th weeks of pregnancy to discover if they are present.** Using ultrasound for guidance, **the physician inserts a needle through the woman's abdominal wall into the amniotic sac surrounding the fetus. A small amount of amniotic fluid is removed.** *(See ● Figure 28.)* The fluid contains fetal skin cells, which are grown as a culture in a laboratory and analyzed for genetic defects. Results take up to 4 weeks.

Because it is an invasive procedure, amniocentesis poses some risk to the fetus, so it is not recommended for every pregnancy. Also, because it is conducted relatively late in pregnancy, certain abortion techniques will not be available to people who decide to choose this option.

- *Chorionic villus sampling (CVS):* In ***chorionic villus sampling (CVS)*, the physician, guided by an ultrasound device, inserts a tube into the cervix. A sample of the developing placenta is suctioned out. *(An alternative method is to insert a needle through the abdomen, as in amniocentesis.)* (Refer back to Figure 28.)** Genetic tests can be performed on the tissue sample, and results of the analysis can be available within 5 days.

- *Percutaneous umbilical blood sampling (PUBS):* The procedure called ***percutaneous umbilical blood sampling* is a technique for getting a blood sample from a fetus.** Guided by ultrasound, the physician inserts a needle into a blood vessel in the umbilical cord of a fetus. A blood sample is drawn that may be analyzed for diseases and disorders. Because the cells come directly from the fetus's bloodstream, they need not be cultured and can produce results in about 2 days.

Childbirth: Labor and Delivery

Labor consists of regular muscular contractions to propel the baby through the birth canal. Labor takes place in three stages: (1) dilation of the cervix; (2) passage of the baby through the birth canal; (3) expulsion of the placenta, or afterbirth.

Labor begins when a woman experiences regular contractions and expels the mucous plug from her cervix (called "bloody show"). The "breaking of the waters" is when the amniotic sac (bag of water) ruptures, causing fluid to

Amniocentesis

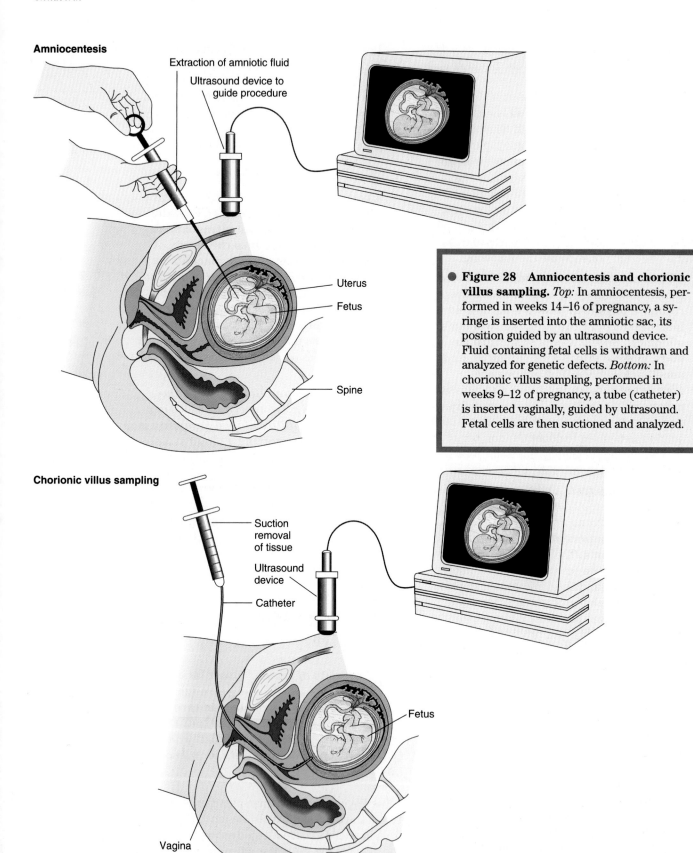

Extraction of amniotic fluid

Ultrasound device to guide procedure

Uterus

Fetus

Spine

● **Figure 28   Amniocentesis and chorionic villus sampling.** *Top:* In amniocentesis, performed in weeks 14–16 of pregnancy, a syringe is inserted into the amniotic sac, its position guided by an ultrasound device. Fluid containing fetal cells is withdrawn and analyzed for genetic defects. *Bottom:* In chorionic villus sampling, performed in weeks 9–12 of pregnancy, a tube (catheter) is inserted vaginally, guided by ultrasound. Fetal cells are then suctioned and analyzed.

Chorionic villus sampling

Suction removal of tissue

Ultrasound device

Catheter

Fetus

Vagina

rush or leak from the vagina. In one-eighth of all pregnancies, especially first pregnancies, the breaking of the amniotic sac happens before labor begins. Labor usually follows within 6–24 hours. However, the amniotic sac often does not break until the last hours of labor.

***Labor* is defined as the rhythmic muscular contractions of the uterus that dilate the cervix and ultimately propel the baby through the birth canal.** At the beginning of labor, the time between contractions may be 15–20 minutes and irregular. As labor progresses, the contractions become regular, more frequent, and longer lasting. The contractions themselves may progress from half a minute to a minute or more in duration.

The Three Stages of Labor Labor takes place in three stages. The first stage begins with the appearance of the first contraction and the third stage ends with the delivery of the placenta (afterbirth). *(See ● Figure 29.)* For women experiencing their first labor, the average (median) number of hours is 10.6. But 1 in 9 take more than 24 hours and 1 in 100 requires less than 3 hours. For women giving birth to their second or subsequent child, the average number of hours is 6.2.[88]

- ***First stage—dilation of cervix:*** The first stage of labor is the longest. The *early* first stage begins with the **dilation, or opening up, of the *cervix*, the opening between the vagina and the uterus.** The cervix also undergoes thinning (*effacement*). *(Refer back to Figure 29.)* The mother is not supposed to bear down at this point. She should only to try to relax and let the contractions do their work and use breathing exercises to help control discomfort.

  The dilation continues until the opening is equivalent to the width of five fingers (4 inches or 10 centimeters). At this point the baby is ready to enter the birth canal. The *transition* stage occurs during the *late* first stage of labor. At this point the contractions become more frequent and more painful, and the woman must concentrate on each contraction. Fortunately, this stage averages only 30-60 minutes. Dilation is complete when the baby's head can start to pass through the cervix.

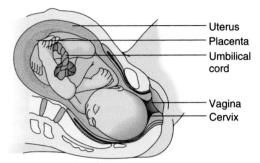

First stage
Dilation of cervix, followed by transition phase, when baby's head can start to pass through the cervix

Uterus
Placenta
Umbilical cord
Vagina
Cervix

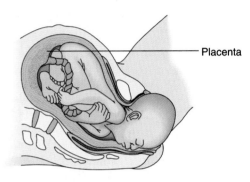

Second stage
Passage of the baby through the birth canal, or vagina, and delivery into the world

Placenta

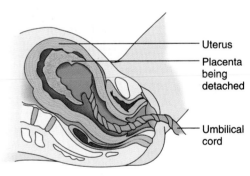

Third stage
Expulsion of the placenta, blood, and fluid ("afterbirth")

Uterus
Placenta being detached
Umbilical cord

● **Figure 29   The three stages of labor.**

- ***Second stage—passage of baby through birth canal:*** The second stage of labor begins when the cervix is fully open. The baby moves through the cervix into the birth canal, or vagina. *(Refer back to Figure 29.)* In this stage, which may last an hour or more, the contractions will occur every 2–3 minutes and will be quite strong. At this point, the woman needs to alternately push and relax to help the baby move through the birth canal.

Each contraction moves the baby farther down the birth canal. First the head emerges, then the neck and shoulders, then the body is quickly expelled. At this point, the baby's umbilical cord is clamped a few inches from the navel. Mucus covering the baby's nose and mouth, which came from the birth canal and amniotic fluid, is cleaned out.

Most babies begin crying automatically after their oxygen stops when the umbilical cord connecting the placenta is clamped. Sometimes they may need to be gently rubbed or have oxygen blown in their faces to stimulate breathing. Now, unless there is an emergency, the umbilical cord is cut and the baby is usually given to its mother. Putting the baby to the mother's breast stimulates breast-feeding and contraction of the uterus, beginning to return the uterus to its normal size.

- *Third stage—expulsion of placenta:* Within about half an hour of the birth of the baby, the contractions of the uterus begin again. They continue until the placenta or *afterbirth* is separated and expelled, a process that may take about 10 minutes. *(Refer back to Figure 29.)*

After the delivery, mother and child may be together in the hospital or the mother may have help with the baby. If there are difficulties, the infant may be kept for a time in a separate nursery. This occurs, for example, when the baby is born prematurely or with low birth weight.

Decisions About Childbirth

Prospective parents have many decisions to make regarding childbirth. Should the baby be delivered by an obstetrician or a midwife? Should the baby be born in a hospital, a birthing center inside or outside a hospital, or at home? Should an episiotomy be done? Should a woman opt for anesthesia or try natural childbirth (no medication) or prepared childbirth (using Lamaze or Leboyer methods)? Under what circumstances should cesarean sections be performed?

There is more than one way to deliver a baby, more than one kind of "birth style." Thus, expectant parents, both fathers and mothers, should be aware of the the options available to them.

Choice of Birth Attendants Expectant parents should anticipate being part of a team in terms of preparing for childbirth. One of the most important decisions they make is who will be the primary health care provider. They will work with this provider both during the pregnancy and at the time of labor and delivery. Who should deliver the baby, where, and how much will it cost?

The choices of birth attendants are as follows:

- *Obstetrician/gynecologist:* An obstetrician/gynecologist (OB/GYN) is a physician who specializes in female reproductive health and pregnancy. Some physicians limit their practice to *gynecology,* **which deals with the reproductive health of women and related diseases.** A physician will be required if the pregnancy is considered high-risk to either mother or child. High risk exists when a physical examination shows poor nutrition, inadequate prenatal care, unwanted pregnancy, genetic abnormalities, multiple pregnancy, and similar problems.[89]

- *Midwives: Midwives* **are specialists who are not medical doctors but who assist in uncomplicated pregnancies and deliveries.** Midwives may be of two types, *certified nurse-midwives* and *lay midwives.*[90,91]

  Certified nurse-midwives (CNMs) **are registered nurses. They have also completed graduate programs in normal pregnancy and birth, are state-licensed, and practice primarily in hospitals.**

  Lay midwives **lack nursing education, are often trained by other lay midwives, and primarily do home deliveries.** Lay midwives do not use medications and technology and are not able to legally practice in many states.

  In the five European countries with the lowest infant mortality rates, midwives preside at more than 70% of all births.[92] For many reasons, many of them having to do with liability and malpractice coverage, midwifery has been slow to catch on in the United States.

The Birthplace In 1988, about 99% of births in the United States occurred in hospitals.[93] More than 96% of these deliveries were attended by physicians. If the expectant mother chooses the services of a physician, she will no doubt have her baby in a hospital. A hospital delivery will be necessary if the woman or child seems to be high-risk. However, for uncomplicated pregnancies, there are a number of alternatives. One is a *hospital-based birthing center,* with a more homelike atmosphere than the traditional hospital delivery room yet with immediate emergency care. Another is a *free-standing birth center,* which is not in a hospital but may be near one. It provides a comfortable environment in which family and friends can participate in uncomplicated deliveries. Childbirths are generally supervised by certified nurse-midwives. A third possibility is a *home birth,* a somewhat uncommon event today. Still, some studies show that under certain circumstances home births attended by lay midwives can be as safe as physician-attended hospital deliveries; they also offer less intervention.[94–96]

Controversy: Should Episiotomies Be Performed? Although the procedure is no longer performed routinely, a hospital physician may do an *episiotomy.* **This is a small, straight surgical incision in the *perineum,* the area of skin between the anus and the vagina.** The theory here is that the episiotomy allows room for the baby's head to emerge without tearing the mother's vaginal tissue. This may prevent certain complications.[97,98]

The American College of Obstetrics and Gynecology does not recommend episiotomy in normal deliveries. An expectant mother should let the delivering physician or midwife know if she does not want this surgical procedure except in an emergency.

Pain Management Some birth practitioners believe that for many women pain during childbirth can be reduced without medication. Instead, prepared childbirth techniques can often be used for pain management. However, effective painkilling drugs are commonly available.

Drugs used for pain control are generally administered in two ways:

- *General anesthesia: General anesthesia* **affects the whole body, rendering the mother unconscious.** The problem is that general anesthesia can actually slow or stop labor and may decrease the responsiveness of the newborn.[99] Today general anesthesia during childbirth is used only in emergencies or when there is no time to administer a regional anesthetic.

- *Regional or local anesthesia: Regional anesthesia,* **or** *local anesthesia,* **involves injecting a drug into a localized area or region to alleviate pain confined to that area.** This kind of anesthesia rarely affects the baby. Among the kinds of regional anesthesia available are these:

  (1) *pudendal block,* in which an anesthetic is injected into the pudendal nerves inside the vagina

  (2) *paracervical block,* in which anesthesia is injected into the cervical area

  (3) *epidural block,* in which an anesthetic is injected slowly into the lower back, numbing the lower half of the body and easing the pain of contractions

  (4) *spinal block,* a short-acting anesthetic that is injected into the lower back

Natural Childbirth and Prepared Childbirth The term *natural childbirth* **means a normal vaginal delivery during which the mother uses no medication.** *Prepared childbirth,* **or** *participatory childbirth,* **uses classes to prepare the expectant mother to actively participate in the delivery of her baby. The preparation often helps her avoid pain-killing drugs.** Sometimes "natural childbirth" and "prepared childbirth" are used interchangeably. The difference, however, is that in prepared childbirth the mother *may* use medication if she wishes.

Prepared childbirth stresses the preparation of the woman and the partner (referred to as the "coach") who will accompany her during the delivery in special classes. These classes teach not only about nutrition and exercise during pregnancy but also about the birth process. The woman and her partner are also taught how breathing and pushing (coached by the partner) can help in the delivery and reduce the pain.

Two variations on prepared childbirth are the *Lamaze* and the *Leboyer* methods.[100,101]

- **The Lamaze method: The *Lamaze method* involves teaching women breathing, massage, and pushing techniques so they learn not to focus on the pain during labor.** The partner offers emotional support and helps the woman to focus on her breathing and to release muscular tension that causes pain. Lamaze classes may begin as early as the first trimester or as late as the seventh month. They attempt to teach the expectant mother that she can be in control during labor and delivery.[102,103]

- **The Leboyer method: The *Leboyer method* attempts to make the birth as nontraumatic as possible for the infant.**[104] A Leboyer delivery includes dim lights, lowered voices, and caressing of the infant. Cutting the umbilical cord is delayed while the newborn rests on the mother's abdomen, followed by bathing in soothing water.

The Lamaze method in particular has won a great deal of acceptance among obstetricians in North America.

Father Participation In the Lamaze method, the "coach" is the father or a partner allowed to participate in the birthing process. Fathers who participate in prenatal classes and are present at the delivery may show more interest in their babies than other fathers who do not.[105]

Controversy: Are Cesarean Sections Done Too Often? A *cesarean section* is a procedure in which the obstetrician makes a surgical incision in the abdominal and uterine walls to remove the baby. Cesarean (or Caesarean—the name comes from Caesar, who was said to have been plucked from the womb) section has become the most common operation in the United States. Nearly one million babies a year are born by "C-section" rather than by normal vaginal delivery—18–25% of all U.S. births, the highest rate in the world.[106,107]

The four most common reasons given for cesareans are these: (1) the woman had a prior cesarean delivery (35.6%). (2) Labor did not progress normally (28.9%). (3) It was a **breech birth, where the baby is positioned buttocks or feet first rather than head down** (12.3%). (4) There was fetal distress (9.9%).[108]

Maternal deaths from cesareans are rare, less than 2%.[109] Even so, the risk is two to four times higher than that for vaginal delivery. Moreover, there are medical complications, such as infection (of the uterus, urinary tract, or surgical wound), in perhaps 40% of cesarean mothers.[110]

We do not mean that cesareans should be avoided, should an emergency arise. But the expectant mother should understand that it is major abdominal surgery, with all the complications such surgery entails.

After the Baby Is Born

After the baby is delivered, she or he may be placed with the mother in a rooming-in arrangement at the hospital or taken home. New parents need to think about diapers (cloth or disposable) and safety matters. They need to be aware of the phenomenon of sudden infant death syndrome. They may wish to become knowledgeable about the pros and cons of breast-feeding versus bottle-feeding. New mothers need to be aware of the difference between postpartum blues and postpartum depression.

Sometimes separation between mother and child immediately after birth cannot be avoided, although if it is prolonged it can have important effects. In general, however, the more time the family spends together after the birth, the better the **emotional attachment or *bonding*** between them.[111,112] Indeed, frequent contact with both parents and the baby is important in developing future attachments.[113]

Rooming-In Many hospitals now offer ***rooming-in* arrangements, a room or place where the mother can stay and take care of her baby.** The father and other members of the family can visit there. Besides letting the new family be together, rooming-in allows the mother to learn from the hospital staff some fundamentals of baby care.

Sudden Infant Death Syndrome *Sudden Infant Death Syndrome (SIDS),* **commonly known as "crib death," is the unexpected death of an apparently healthy baby.** It usually occurs between the ages of 1 week and 1 year (most likely between 2 and 4 months). It is the second leading cause of infant death in the United States.[114] The cause remains unexplained, even after an autopsy. SIDS is not a diagnosis; it is simply medicine's way of saying "We don't know what the cause is." It is not caused by suffocation, aspiration, regurgitation, immunization, or child abuse, and it cannot be predicted.

Breast-Feeding or Bottle-Feeding? Most authorities agree that breast-feeding is better than bottle-feeding, at least for the first 6 months. In recent years, there was first an increase in mothers breast-feeding their young, then in the early 1980s a steep decline. The drop-off signals a possible public-health crisis in protecting infants from infection. Some reasons for the decline are that breast-feeding is no longer considered fashionable, and the popular media promote it less now. Also, infant formula is marketed aggressively.[115]

Babies who are breast-fed get better nutrition, develop fewer allergies, and have fewer intestinal infections.[116] Indeed, some physicians are of the opinion that the benefits of breast-feeding extend even into adulthood. People breast-fed as infants have fewer cases of allergies and are less likely to develop inflammatory bowel disease, a painful intestinal disorder.[117] They are also less apt to develop a bad dental bite compared to bottle-fed babies.[118] A British study of premature infants found that those fed breast milk scored significantly higher on intelligence tests than those who were not.[119] Nursing also helps the mother shrink the uterus back to normal and return to her pre-pregnancy shape. Recently, research suggests that drinking cow's milk during infancy may trigger juvenile diabetes in some people later in life.[120]

Infertility: Medical Solutions and Adoption

Infertility is when a sexually active couple is unable to conceive after trying for a year. Most causes are physiological, although some are psychological. Alternatives include artificial insemination, ovulation-stimulating hormones, in vitro fertilization, embryo transfer, or use of surrogate mothers. Another option is adoption.

For about a third of all couples in the United States, having a child is difficult. Either they cannot conceive or the woman is physiologically unable to carry the child to term. About one couple in 10 cannot ever have children.[121]

The Causes of Infertility. Although definitions vary, **by** *infertility* **we mean the failure to conceive after 1 year of regular sexual intercourse without contraception. It is differentiated from** *sterility,* **the total inability to conceive.**[122,123] Infertility is a couple's problem that requires an evaluation of both partners.

- *Causes of infertility in couples:* A couple's inability to conceive can have any number of causes:[124] (1) not enough intercourse (once or less per week); (2) too much intercourse (several times a day or over the course of several days, which prohibits sperm from building up); (3) intercourse during times of the month when the woman is less apt to conceive; (4) use of vaginal lubricants such as Vaseline, which may prevent sperm from entering the cervix; and (5) anemia, fatigue, emotional stress, poor nutrition, or general poor health in either one of the couple.
- *Causes of infertility in males:* Principal causes of infertility in men are the following:[125] (1) reduced number of sperm or defective sperm, owing to untreated sexually transmitted diseases and environmental toxins; (2) blockage somewhere between testicle and end of the penis; and (3) inability to ejaculate or to sustain an erection.
- *Causes of infertility in females:* Some of the main causes of infertility in women are as follows:[126] (1) age of the mother, since fertility decreases slightly as women become older; (2) failure to ovulate, owing to such factors as hormonal deficiencies, defective ovaries, metabolic imbalances,

genetic factors, various medical conditions, cigarettes or other drugs; (3) blockage of fallopian tubes; (4) abnormalities of the uterus, such as **endometriosis, in which some cells of the inner lining of the uterus grow in the pelvic and abdominal cavities;** and (5) an immune response or acidic chemical climate in the vagina, which may immobilize sperm.

If none of these problems occur and the sperm and egg are united, there is still no guarantee of full-term pregnancy. About 30% of pregnancies end in *miscarriages,* or spontaneous abortions.[127]

Treating Infertility: High-Tech Baby Making After a couple has tried to conceive for a year or more, they may seek alternative methods of conception. Physicians cannot manipulate every aspect of the reproductive cycle, but here are some techniques they do try:

- *Artificial insemination:* Sometimes sperm don't have the strength, mobility, necessary enzymes, or ability to bypass hostile vaginal secretions and pierce the outer shell of the egg (ovum). Or a man may be unable to produce sperm at all. **In artificial insemination, sperm are collected from the male partner—or an anonymous male donor—by masturbation. With the help of a powerful microscope, the sperm cells are injected by syringe directly into the woman's vagina or uterus.**

- *Ovulation-stimulating hormones:* Some women have difficulty ovulating naturally. Others produce eggs that cannot be fertilized. When large doses of ovulation-stimulating hormones (clomiphene or Pergonal) are administered, an ovary may produce dozens of eggs. One common result of this treatment is multiple births—twins, triplets, even quadruplets. Unfortunately, many multiple births are premature and low-birth-weight babies, which puts them at risk for many problems.[128,129]

- *In vitro fertilization:* The term *in vitro* means "in glass," and thus the origin of the term "test-tube babies." During an **in vitro fertilization (IVF) procedure, the egg**

and sperm are taken from the parents and kept in a laboratory setting until the mother's uterus is hormonally ready, then the fertilized egg is implanted in the wall of the uterus. This procedure is particularly useful when the woman's fallopian tubes are blocked or otherwise unable to transport an ovum.

- *GIFT and ZIFT: Gamete intrafallopian transfer (GIFT)* **involves collecting the woman's egg and the man's sperm and uniting them inside the woman's fallopian tubes.** The procedure, which has a 50–60% success rate, is often tried when the cause of the infertility is unclear.

  In *zygote intrafallopian transfer (ZIFT),* **the mother's egg and father's sperm are collected and placed in a laboratory dish. Then, 1 day after fertilization takes place, the zygote, or single-celled fertilized egg, is placed in the woman's fallopian tubes.**

- *Embryo transfer:* In an embryo transfer, the sperm of a male partner of an infertile woman is placed in another woman's uterus during ovulation. Five days later, the embryo is transferred to the uterus of the infertile woman, who carries the embryo and delivers the baby. Sometimes, in a technique known as *frozen embryo transfer,* the embryo is frozen and later implanted in an unfertile woman's uterus.

- *Surrogate mothers:* A surrogate mother is a consenting woman who is artificially inseminated with the sperm of the male partner of a woman who is infertile. For a fee, the surrogate mother carries the child through pregnancy and gives the newborn to the couple with whom she contracted.

High-tech baby making can be quite expensive and usually is not covered by health insurance. IVF, for instance, may cost about $10,000 a try, and several tries may be necessary to achieve a single pregnancy.[130]

Adoption Adults who cannot become biological parents may still become parents by adopting children. The children may have been relinquished by their birth parents or orphaned. Most adoptions are arranged through public or nonprofit agencies or private counselors. In recent years, however, adoptions have become more difficult in the United States as relinquishment rates have declined. This may be a consequence of more single parents keeping their babies. For instance, over one-quarter of all children are born to single mothers today, four times the percentage of just 25 years ago.[131] There now is an imbalance between prospective parents and adoptable children. As a consequence, some American adults seek to arrange adoptions of babies from other countries, principally South Korea, Romania, Latin America, and India.[132]

800-HELP

AASK-America (Aid to Adoption of Special Kids). 800-232-2751. Nonprofit adoption program that places so-called "unadoptable" children—e.g., drug-addicted children, fetal alcohol syndrome infants, those with AIDS, and older, abused, abandoned children.

Alliance of Genetic Support Groups. 800-336-GENE. An umbrella organization of support groups for people or parents of children with genetic disorders.

American College of Obstetricians and Gynecologists. 800-INTENDS.

Childhelp USA/IOF Foresters National Child Abuse Hotline. 800-4-A-CHILD. Provides crisis counseling and referrals for child abusers and their victims.

National Abortion Federation Consumer Hotline. 800-772-9100. Provides information and referrals to local organizations and answers questions on pregnancy and abortion.

National SIDS Foundation. 800-221-SIDS. (In Maryland, 301-459-3388.) Hotline for Sudden Infant Death Syndrome (crib death).

Planned Parenthood Federation of America. 800-829-7732. Information on contraception and abortion.

RESOLVE. 800-662-1016. Nonprofit, nationwide information network serving needs of infertile couples; gives support-group referrals for people coping with infertility.

STD National Hotline. 800-634-3662. (In California, 800-982-5883.)

Suggestions for Further Reading

Robert M. Baird & Stuart E. Rosenbaum (Eds.). (1989). *The ethics of abortion: Pro-life vs. pro-choice*. Buffalo, NY: Prometheus. Twelve essays on both sides of the complex issue of abortion.

Ferdnand Lamaze. (1970). *Painless childbirth*. Chicago: Regency. French obstetrician's techniques for controlled breathing and concentration to release muscular tension during childbirth.

Frederick Leboyer. (1975). *Birth without violence*. New York: Alfred Knopf. French obstetrician emphasizes gentle, loving treatment for newborns to introduce them to the world gradually.

Benjamin Spock & Michael Rothenberg (1992). *Dr. Spock's baby and child care* (6th ed.). New York: Pocket Books. The famous bible of baby and child care that has served parents for five decades. The latest edition breaks new ground with discussion of medical updates on injuries, AIDS, immunizations, headaches, choking, as well as treatment of step-family dynamics, homosexuality, and open adoptions.

Carolyn Pape Cowan & Philip A. Cowan (1992). *When partners become parents: The big life change for couples*. New York: Basic Books. Two University of California at Berkeley professors, married to each other, report on a 10-year project tracking parent and nonparent couples. They conclude parenthood is more difficult now than in the past and that it is easy to fall into traditional mom-and-dad roles, however egalitarian one's ideals.

Female Breakers of Boundaries

I think one of the most positive qualities any individual can have is what I call the phoenix syndrome," said Dianne Feinstein. The phoenix is the mystical bird that has become the symbol of rising from one's own ashes. "That's the challenge of life," she said. "You've got to recover from your own ashes many, many times."

Phoenix Rising

Feinstein is the former mayor of San Francisco and a U.S. Senator from California. She herself has often overcome death, loss, and defeat. Although born to affluence, her childhood was nightmarish because her mother had an undiagnosed brain malady that made her act violent. Five close members of her family, including her second husband, died within a five-year period. She was defeated twice in attempts to become mayor, defeated in a race for California's governorship, then was elected senator.

"My whole fundamental philosophy is that we're here just for an instant in eternity," she said, "and the only thing that matters is what we're able to do with that instant."[133]

The Homeless Freshman

Maria Lupe Vasquez always liked school, and her mother, a Spanish-speaking farmworker, always urged her to try her best. But she found it hard to study when in her senior year of high school she and her family were evicted from their quarters and had to move into an Oxnard, California, shelter for the homeless. Still, even with seven sharing one room, she managed to shut out distractions and study. She graduated second in a class of 397 in her high school.

She applied to and was accepted by six colleges, and chose Stanford University, where she studied engineering. She financed her education through a combination of federal grants, private scholarships, and a loan. Her message to other young people in difficult circumstances is simple: "Always believe in yourself. That's what kept me going."[134]

The Aspiring Cadet

When Shannon Faulkner was admitted to the Citadel, the South's 152-year-old all-male military college, her role was limited to that of day student—the only one. All areas reserved for cadets, from barracks to parking lot, were off-limits to her. However, she continued her legal fight to become the first female full cadet.

Shannon gained strength from her mother and grandmother, the latter of whom said: "A woman can do anything a man can do. . . . You take charge when you have to. And that's what Shannon's doing."[135]

The Black Astronaut

Growing up on the South Side of Chicago, Mae Carol Jemison watched space flights on television and knew that she would be a space traveler. No matter that the astronauts were male and white and that she was female and black. In September 1992, by then a 35-year-old physician and engineer, she realized her dream when she launched into orbit as part of the crew of the shuttle Endeavor—and became the first African-American woman to go into space.

There is a need, she said, for all people, not just blacks, to realize that people of color can excel in all areas, if given a chance. "It's important not only for a little black girl growing up to know, yeah, you can become an astronaut because here's Mae Jemison," she said. "But it's important for older white males who sometimes make decisions on those careers of those little black girls."[136]

7 Caffeine, Tobacco, and Alcohol

Is there a human need to alter consciousness?

Caffeine and nicotine are *stimulants*—they stimulate the central nervous system, speed up brain activity, increase the level of nervous system arousal. Alcohol is a *depressant*—it slows down the central nervous system, makes one feel relaxed, sleepy, even anesthetized. No wonder sometimes we hear people talking about being on a "coffee-wine cycle." They start by drinking coffee all morning and afternoon. Then they are so wound up they decide to have several glasses of wine or other drinks to calm themselves down.

Of course there are many other mind-altering substances of all sorts all around us, all the time, all part of our lives. Every day the newspapers and television are filled with news about drugs—about cocaine smuggling, marijuana busts, an upsurge in heroin use. But three drugs, some researchers say, have had a greater effect on human civilization than all the other mood-altering drugs combined. These three are caffeine, nicotine, and alcohol.[1]

Caffeine: The National Wake-Up Drug

▶ Name the drug category to which caffeine belongs.

▶ Identify common sources of caffeine.

▶ Define caffeinism and recall the symptoms associated with it.

▶ Discuss the health consequences of caffeine use.

▶ Identify those who should avoid caffeine.

Caffeine, it has been suggested, is the drug that keeps our society running, with its lift that fights boredom and fatigue. Consider coffee, which in the United States is what caffeine means to most people.[2] Although it is used worldwide, the United States, with one-twentieth of the world's population, drinks a third of the planet's coffee. We drink some 360 million cups per day. Indeed, imported coffee (2 billion pounds costing $6 billion a year) ranks second only to petroleum in value of imported products.[3]

Caffeine: How You Get It, What It Does

Caffeine appears in coffee, soft drinks, tea, chocolate, some prescription and nonprescription drugs, and some processed foods. People often use caffeine to keep alert and to alleviate boredom. Some people develop a dependency on this drug and experience withdrawal when they stop taking it. Too much caffeine can produce caffeinism—anxiety, headache, irregular heartbeat. Caffeine use is associated with several potential health risks and should be avoided by pregnant and breast-feeding women and people with a history of heart disease.

Caffeine, a bitter alkaloid, is the principal drug found in coffee. Until recently, coffee was the most significant source of caffeine for Americans. But now caffeine-containing soft drinks have overtaken coffee as primary sources of dietary caffeine, particularly among young adults, those ages 18–24.[4,5] Indeed, the caffeine *taken out of* coffee to make decaffeinated coffee is principally used as an additive for soft drinks.[6]

It is hard to avoid this drug. Besides coffee and soft drinks, it also appears in tea, cocoa, chocolate, and a number of prescription drugs. Caffeine is also in many nonprescription drugs used for alertness (NoDoz), for pain relief (Anacin, Excedrin), for weight loss, and as decongestants. *(See ● Figure 1.)* Aside from its use as a mild painkiller, caffeine has no purpose except to help people be more alert and avoid boredom.

The lift that most people expect requires 150–250 milligrams (mg) of caffeine, about 1–2 cups of coffee. *(See ● Table 1, p. 214, for an explanation of milligrams.)* On average, each American consumes caffeine from all sources equivalent to 4 or 5 cups of coffee a day.

The Effects of Caffeine Ninety-nine percent of the caffeine you consume is absorbed and distributed to all your body organs and tissues.[7] The effects of caffeine are similar to those of other stimulants such as amphetamines. Physiologically, caffeine works because the chemical somewhat resembles **a brain chemical called *adenosine*. This chemical depresses (slows down) the activity of the central nervous system and the brain.** Caffeine fits into the brain's receptor sites intended for adenosine and blocks them. The adenosine can no longer do its work of slowing down nervous system activity; thus, one feels stimulated.[8]

How much stimulation depends on the person, including his or her age, use, level of tolerance, and use of other drugs.[9] People vary widely in their sensitivity to the drug—and caffeine *is* a drug. In general, someone who drinks one or two cups of coffee in succession would likely notice increased attentiveness and decreased drowsiness. However, caffeine does not noticeably enhance one's ability to perform complex intellectual tasks.[10] In fact, one study of college students showed an association between *high* intakes of caffeine and *lower* academic performance.[11]

Too Many Cups of Coffee: Caffeinism *Caffeinism*—**caffeine intoxication, sometimes called "coffee nerves"—is characterized by anxiety, lightheadedness, breathlessness, headache, tremulousness, and irregular heartbeat.** Generally, 4–6 cups (600 milligrams) of coffee a day are considered enough to produce some caffeinism.[12] But many coffee drinkers, it must be noted, do not use the standard 5-ounce coffee *cups* found in restaurants. Rather, they favor 12-ounce coffee *mugs,* which hold as much liquid as a soft-drink can.

High doses of caffeine do more than make people feel nervous, irritable, and unable to sleep. They also produce pronounced physiolog-

Food and beverages	Caffeine in milligrams
Coffee (5-oz. cup)	
Drip method	110–150
Percolated	64–124
Instant	40–108
Decaf	2–5
Instant decaf	2
Tea, loose or bags (5-oz. cup)	
1-minute brew	9–33
3-minute brew	20–46
5-minute brew	20–50
Tea Products	
Instant (5-oz. cup)	12–28
Iced tea (12-oz. can)	22–36
Chocolate Products	
Hot cocoa (6 oz.)	2–8
Dry cocoa (1 oz.)	6
Milk chocolate (1 oz.)	1–15
Baking chocolate (1 oz.)	35
Sweet dark chocolate (1 oz.)	5–35
Chocolate milk (8 oz.)	2–7
Chocolate-flavored syrup (2 tbsp.)	4
Soft Drinks, per 12-oz. serving, by flavor type	
Cola or pepper	30–48
Diet cola or pepper	0–59
Cherry cola	12–46
Citrus	0–64

● **Figure 1   Caffeine content.**

Over-the-counter drugs	Caffeine in milligrams per tablet
Stimulants	
NoDoz	100
Vivarin	200
Pain Relievers	
Anacin	32
Excedrin	65
Excedrin P.M.	0
Midol (for cramps)	32
Midol P.M.S.	0
Plain aspirin	0
Vanquish	33
Diuretics	
Aqua-Ban	100
Cold Remedies	
Coryban-D	30
Dristan	0
Diet Pills	
Dexatrim	200
Dietac	200

ical effects: increased heart rate, respiratory rate, body temperature, blood pressure, urine production, and stomach acid secretions. A study of college students revealed that moderate and high consumers of caffeine were more likely to be depressed and anxious than those who abstained.[13] Caffeine should be avoided by those with a history of panic attacks, because its use can trigger the problem in some people.

Caffeine Dependence and Withdrawal Caffeine use can lead to psychological and physical dependence. Stopping the drug after long-term heavy or even moderate use can result in a number of withdrawal symptoms. These include headache, nervousness, poor concentration, irritability, lethargy, restlessness, and nausea.

Headache is an especially common problem for people quitting caffeine. The headache usually begins about 18 hours after stopping the drug and gradually subsides within 2–6 days.[14,15]

● **Table 1   Metric Units**

Units of weight:

The meaning of 1 gram: 1 gram = 0.035 ounce, the weight of 2 paper clips or 1 shirt button

1 kilogram (kg) = 1000 grams (or 2.2046 pounds)
1 gram (g) = 1000 milligrams
1 milligram (mg) = 1000 micrograms (µg)

Units of liquid volume:

The meaning of 1 liter: 1 liter = 1.057 quarts, slightly more than a standard quart of milk

1 liter (l) = 1000 milliliters (ml)

Risks: Has the Up Drug a Down Side?

It is not clear whether caffeine increases risk of heart disease, infertility, low-birth-weight infants, or premenstrual syndrome. Pregnant women, nursing mothers, and those with a history of heart disease should avoid this drug.

What about long-term effects? Over the years there has been back-and-forth debate about the harmfulness of caffeine. The results to date are as follows.

Possible, Unproven Link to Heart Disease Caffeine increases the heart rate and blood pressure, but whether it increases long-term risk of heart and blood-vessel disease is unclear. Several major studies show an association of heavy caffeine consumption (5 or more cups per day) with heightened risk of heart disease.[16–19] However, a 1990 study of over 45,500 men ages 40–75 who were followed by Harvard researchers for 2 years differed. It revealed no association between total coffee consumption—even 6 cups a day—and risk of heart disease or stroke.[20,21]

Possible, Unproven Link to Infertility The question of fertility, too, has different answers. One study was of women during 12 months of trying to conceive. Women who had daily caffeine equal to 1 cup of coffee were less able to conceive than women who consumed less.[22] However, another study found no difference among the two groups regarding likelihood of conceiving.[23]

Possible, Unproven Link to Low-Birth-Weight Infants Caffeine does not seem to cause birth defects, but health professionals nevertheless worry, particularly because research has been inconclusive. They are concerned that the drug may have some effect on fetal development.[24] Some research suggests that mothers who usually consume caffeine fairly heavily may produce low-birth-weight babies.[25,26] The study considered "fairly heavily" to be 300 milligrams or more a day—3 cups of coffee or 6 cans of cola. Other studies say it may not be caffeine use but rather *cigarette smoking* that is associated with the delivery of low-birth-weight infants.[27]

Because of the uncertainty, women who are trying to become pregnant, are pregnant, or are breast-feeding are advised to avoid caffeine.

Caffeine and PMS and Breast Changes Though the link is not proven, there is some evidence that caffeinated beverages may aggravate ***premenstrual syndrome (PMS)*. PMS is a disorder many women suffer, characterized by physical and psychological discomfort prior to menstruation.**[28]

There appears to be no link between coffee and other caffeine-containing beverages and breast cancer.[29,30] However, women who find **noncancerous (benign) breast lumps, a condition called *fibrocystic breast disease,*** might eliminate caffeine to see if the condition improves.

Caffeine and Osteoporosis According to a study of 980 California women ages 50–98 years, lifetime intake of caffeinated coffee equivalent to 2 cups a day was associated with decreased bone density of the hip and spine, except in women who reported drinking at least one glass of milk per day most of their adult lives.

Strategy for Living: Cutting Down and Quitting Caffeine

Cutting down caffeine is not difficult. Cutting it out, however, is a process that should be done gradually and with an eye on hidden sources of caffeine.

Cutting down on caffeine intake is usually not difficult; cutting *out* caffeine, however, takes more effort. Some suggestions:

- **Quit gradually, not outright:** Quitting "cold turkey" can lead to caffeine-withdrawal headache (often lasting days) and other mischief, such as depression, lethargy, and nausea. It's best to ease off over a week or two.

- **Watch out for hidden sources of caffeine:** Soft drinks, candy, baked goods, and over-the-counter drugs may contain caffeine.

  Many former coffee drinkers have switched to decaffeinated coffee in hopes of avoiding the effects and hazards we've mentioned. However, concern has been raised about the decaffeination process itself. The removal of caffeine from coffee beans is sometimes done using an organic solvent that can leave some residue.[31] Some studies also suggest that decaffeinated coffee may be related to health problems including infertility, impaired fetal development, and heart disease.[32–34]

Tobacco: A Habit Under Fire

▶ Name the drug category to which nicotine belongs.

▶ Identify those U.S. residents at risk for smoking.

▶ Discuss possible reasons for smoking.

▶ Identify the additive element in tobacco, and describe the process of addiction.

▶ Name the main constituents of tobacco smoke and describe their effects.

▶ Discuss the health hazards of cigarette smoking.

▶ Describe the health consequences of using tobacco products other than cigarettes.

▶ Discuss the problem of passive smoking.

▶ Describe the keys to successful smoking cessation.

▶ Discuss strategies for quitting smoking.

Today most smokers in North America have at least an inkling that what they are doing is unhealthy. They certainly are beginning to find that it is unpopular and prohibited in many enclosed areas.

Who Smokes?

In North America, the largest categories of smokers include children and teenagers, the poorly educated, and those with lower incomes. The number of women smokers is growing fast. Many smokers are addicted to other substances.

If in North America smoking is so unpopular these days, who's buying those 270 brands of cigarettes available? Let's consider this question.

Children and Teenagers Forty-five states prohibit selling tobacco to minors, but Americans ages 8–18 still consume around 1 billion packs of cigarettes every year. This fact is important because many smokers—nearly half of those now under age 60—started before age 18. Among 24-year-old smokers, 68% began smoking before age 18.[35] The good news, however, is that the number of 20- to 24-year-olds who smoke is down considerably from 25 years previously. Even so, a third of this group smokes.[36]

Women Catching Up to Men In the United States, more men (31%) smoke than women (26%). However, women today are smoking more than they used to and are now starting to smoke at younger ages than in the past. Among high-school seniors, more females than males smoke.[37] An estimated 23–30% of adolescent female users will become regular smokers by the time they are 18.[38]

Less-Well-Educated, Lower-Income People College students are less likely to smoke than other people of the same age.[39] So also are college graduates: only 18% of college graduates smoke, compared with 34% of those who never went to college.[40] Of people living in households earning more than $40,000, only 22% smoke. In households earning a quarter that amount or less, 29% smoke.[41]

People Addicted to Other Substances People who are heavy users of alcohol, cocaine, and similar substances tend to smoke cigarettes as well.[42] Smokers are also more likely than nonsmokers to drink and drive and consequently have more traffic violations and auto accidents.[43] As some experts on addiction observe, "smoking is very often a sign of heedlessness toward health and safety. Cigarette addicts are more antisocial and less concerned for their physical well-being than nonsmokers."[44]

Why Smoke?

The reasons for smoking include the need for stimulation, handling something, and relaxation; tension reduction; the wish to be different; and a desire to be slim. Also, many smoke because they are addicted.

Cigarettes are not only a legal recreational drug but an aggressively promoted one. The tobacco industry spends $2.7 billion dollars a year (tax deductible) on advertising and promotion. A good part of that promotion, of course, is concerned with giving people reasons to smoke or reinforcing these reasons.[45] Some of the reasons for smoking behavior are as follows.

Stimulation, Handling, and Relaxation Because nicotine is a stimulant, smokers often begin to depend on the lift of the drug to get going in the morning. They continue smoking to ease boredom on the job and to keep themselves going through the day. Cigarettes (and pipes particularly) also give one a "prop" to handle or manipulate, something to toy with in social and work situations. Smokers also say that cigarettes provide a means of pleasurable relaxation, as when completing a job or ending a delicious meal.[46]

The Tension Reducer: Maintaining Emotional Balance According to psychologist Paul Nesbitt, smokers are more anxious than nonsmokers, but they feel more calm when they are smoking.[47] Stress has also been cited by the U.S. Surgeon General as a reason for increased cigarette consumption among smokers.[48] Researchers suggest that smoking masks the tension a smoker would otherwise feel. That is, by using nicotine to maintain their internal stimulation, smokers may protect themselves from the ups and downs of external stimulation.[49]

Adolescents in particular find cigarettes a tension reducer. As British researcher Alan Marsh says about teenagers who take up smoking: "A cigarette covers embarrassment, lifts depression, restores youthful cool. What the smoking adolescent never has the chance to learn is that, like his nonsmoking friends, he would have acquired that knack of affect [emotional] control anyway. It is called growing up and nearly everyone does it, with or without the help of cigarettes."[50] *(See ● Figure 2.)*

The Wish to Be Different Advertisements try to appeal to smokers' sense of being adventurous, independent, and otherwise different from others. "Research indicates that smokers are more often risk-takers, extroverted, defiant, and impulsive," writes Jean Kilbourne. "It is no coincidence that cigarette companies are the leading sponsors of events that appeal to risk-taking and rebellious teenagers: races of motorcycles, dirt bikes, hot rods, rodeos, and ballooning."[51]

The Wish to Be Slim Many advertisements aimed at women try to reinforce the idea of cigarettes as a form of weight control. This pitch may be a major reason why cigarette smoking is increasing among teenage females, a group especially susceptible to concerns about weight.[52] Cigarettes may, in fact, suppress appetite, deadening the taste buds, decrease the stomach's hunger contractions, and slightly increase the body's blood sugar level. In addition, cigarette smoking seems to speed up oxygen consumption in the body, producing a higher metabolic rate and consequent weight control.

The Process of Addiction Cigarettes are highly addictive, or at least the nicotine in them is. The 1988 report by the U.S. Surgeon General states that cigarette smoking is as addictive as alcohol, cocaine, and heroin.[53]

Becoming addicted to cigarettes is not an immediate process; one has to work at it. Most people inhaling on their very first cigarette experience dizziness, palpitations, coughing, sweating, even nausea and vomiting. It usually does not take long, however, for a person to become a seasoned smoker. Indeed, 85% of teenagers who smoke more than two or three cigarettes on occasion go on to become dependent on nicotine.[54] People who are "puffers"—who smoke occasionally or only a couple cigarettes a day—are rare, only 2% of all smokers.

As with other mood-altering drugs, cessation of cigarettes produces withdrawal symptoms. Within 24 hours of stopping, a smoker who has become dependent typically experiences irritability, anxiety, difficulty concentrating, restlessness, increased appetite, impatience, and insomnia. Of course, they also have a strong craving for tobacco.[55] No wonder one of the most powerful incentives to smoke is to prevent the unpleasantness of withdrawal. One reason some smokers greatly enjoy the first cigarette of the day is they begin to overcome the previous 8 or so hours' withdrawal.

● **Figure 2   Smoking: the artificial means of emotional regulation.**

"*All people experience fear, insecurity, discomfort, weariness. More is expected of us than we can fulfill, and our energy and attention levels are not always up to the demands of our jobs or families. We are not blessed with ideally fulfilling lives. For some, smoking has been a device for negotiating the gap between human frailty and a fast-paced, sometimes emotionally draining world. The more a person relies on artificial means of emotional regulation, however, the less practiced he or she becomes at regulating tension and anxiety naturally. Thus begins the cycle of dependence on nicotine, parallel to that which people experience with alcohol or drugs, in which the psychoactive [mood-altering] effects of a substance become for a time an essential means of gaining a desired emotional state.*"

—Stanton Peele, Ph.D., Archie Brodsky, with Mary Arnold (1991). *The truth about addiction and recovery.* New York: Simon & Schuster, p. 102.

The Inside Story of Tobacco: What Goes In

The principal constituents of tobacco are nicotine, tar, and carbon monoxide. Nicotine, the addictive element, can seriously damage the heart and blood vessels. Tar can cause cancerous growths. Carbon monoxide interferes with the transport of oxygen.

It would be almost impossible to create tobacco in a laboratory. There are over 4000 chemical compounds in tobacco smoke. Benzene, for example, is not a chemical one associates with cigarettes. Yet cigarettes reportedly have over 2000 times as much benzene as the Perrier water that was recalled in 1990 for contamination.[56] Let us consider the principal constituents of cigarettes: nicotine, tar, and carbon monoxide.

Nicotine *Nicotine* **is a colorless, oily compound that is the principal and addictive element in tobacco.** Actually, nicotine is a poison, one of the most toxic of all drugs. Nicotine can reach the brain from the lungs in only 7 seconds. That is twice as fast as the rush of heroin to the brain when it's injected into the arm. When people simply take smoke into their mouths, 20–30% of the nicotine is absorbed into the body. But when they inhale, 90% of the nicotine in the smoke is taken in. Thus, pipe and cigar smokers, who generally do not inhale, take in nicotine, but less than cigarette smokers do.

Nicotine is a *stimulant,* **which means that it stimulates the central nervous system, producing an aroused, alert mental state.** It speeds up the heart rate 15–20 beats a minute, raises blood pressure, increases the respiration rate, and stimulates adrenaline production. Nicotine also constricts the blood vessels, causing the heart to have to work harder to pump the blood. As a result, there can be serious damage to the heart and blood vessel system.

Tar Produced when tobacco is burned, *tar* **is a sticky, dark fluid made up of several hundred different chemicals, many poisonous.** The chemicals in tar can damage the bronchial tubes, branch-like tubes in the lungs, making them less able to remove unwanted materials.

These chemicals are also responsible for the development of cancerous growth in the respiratory system.

Carbon Monoxide The same gas found in car exhaust, *carbon monoxide* **is an odorless, colorless gas** that is a by-product of burning tobacco. Smokers who find themselves short of breath are feeling the effects of carbon monoxide. It interferes with the blood's ability to transport oxygen.

What Smoking Does to Smokers

One-fifth of all deaths in the United States are attributable to smoking. Cigarette smoking raises the risk of lung cancer and chronic obstructive lung disease (pulmonary emphysema and chronic bronchitis). It also increases the risk of heart and blood-vessel disease and stroke, wrinkled skin, diminished sexuality in men, cervical cancer in women. Cigarette smoking is also related to hazards during pregnancy and to healthy fetal development.

Smoking causes more preventable illness than any other form of drug addiction.[57] In the United States, smoking is a leading cause of diseases associated with premature death.[58] One-fifth of all deaths in the United States are attributable to smoking. In personal terms, what it comes down to is this: if you are a deep-inhaling smoker who started before age 15, you are essentially giving up a minute of life for every minute you smoke.

Smoker's Odds Many smokers simply don't ever see themselves as being statistics. There are all kinds of excuses and rationalizations: "It'll never happen to me, I'm the lucky type." "I have a lot of years left to kick it." "I could get hit by a bus before I get cancer." "Grandma's still smoking, and she's all right." How true are they?

If you commute by car 27 miles a day, the odds of death from an accident are 1 in 4000 in a year, or 1 in 60 over a lifetime.[59] If you smoke a pack a day, the odds of death within a given year are 1 in 200.[60] If you smoke a pack a day for 50 years, the odds of dying from this behavior are 1 in 6.[61]

Lung Cancer Smokers are actually more likely to die of heart disease than of lung cancer. But cancer of the lung is a serious matter for a very important reason. When smokers quit, their risk of heart disease decreases very quickly. However, the relative risk of lung cancer remains high for 10–20 years compared to the risk of people who have never smoked.[62]

Knowing this, a smoker might ask, "Why bother to quit? What difference could it make now?" However, it is never too late to stop. In fact, the risk for lung cancer drops year by year after one quits smoking.[63] *(See ● Figure 3.)*

Lung cancer is the leading kind of cancer death in the United States, and most cases could be avoided by not smoking.[64] Lung cancer is difficult to detect early enough to treat it effectively. Symptoms do not appear until the cancer has progressed. Thus, despite technological advances in treatment, the survival rate—people

alive 10 years after detection—has not changed much over the years.[65]

In recent years there has been some evidence that genetic factors make some people more likely to develop lung cancer than others. This gene would explain why some people are more likely than others to get lung cancer if they smoke. It also explains why the sooner one quits smoking, the less the chance of triggering the lung cancer gene.[66]

Respiratory Disorders: Chronic Obstructive Lung Disease Among the principal respiratory disorders are *pulmonary emphysema* and *chronic bronchitis*. **Pulmonary emphysema and chronic bronchitis often occur together and are referred to jointly as *chronic obstructive lung disease*, abbreviated *COLD*. This is characterized by the slow, progressive interruption of air flow within the lungs.** Cigarette smoking is the most important cause of COLD.

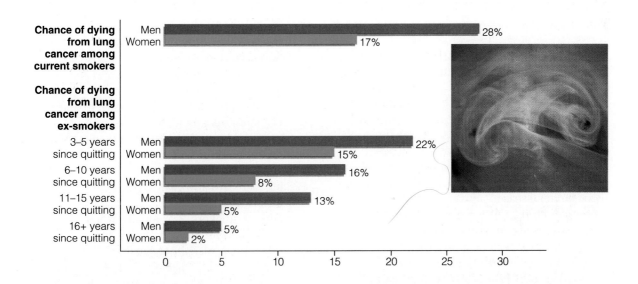

Chance of dying from lung cancer among current smokers	Men	28%
	Women	17%

Chance of dying from lung cancer among ex-smokers

3–5 years since quitting	Men	22%
	Women	15%
6–10 years since quitting	Men	16%
	Women	8%
11–15 years since quitting	Men	13%
	Women	5%
16+ years since quitting	Men	5%
	Women	2%

0   5   10   15   20   25   30

● **Figure 3   Lessened lung cancer risks.** The 1990 U.S. Surgeon General's report concluded that smokers who quit significantly reduce their risks of dying from lung cancer. *Photo:* Smoke being inhaled.

- *Pulmonary emphysema:* Pulmonary emphysema is one of the sadder consequences of smoking, because the person has such great difficulty breathing.

  In *pulmonary emphysema,* over the years cigarette smoke causes the *alveoli,* the tiny air sacs of the lung, to lose elasticity. In time many of them are stretched to the point that they rupture and are destroyed. In addition, the chest cage becomes enlarged as the body tries to accommodate overstretched lungs, which makes the diaphragm work less efficiently. That in turn interferes with the lungs' ability to exchange oxygen and carbon dioxide. This leads to continual shortness of breath and an overworked heart.

- *Chronic bronchitis:* The bronchial tubes, or bronchi, are large passageways that deliver air into the lungs. The bronchi become smaller passageways, the smallest being called bronchioles. ***Chronic bronchitis* consists of inflamed bronchi and increased mucus production, which narrows the air passages.**

Cigarette smokers also suffer from other chronic lung diseases such as pneumonia and take longer to recover from respiratory infections. Quitting seems to reduce the risk of dying from these lung diseases.

Heart Disease and Stroke Heart disease is the No. 1 cause of death among smokers. Nicotine stimulates the heart rate, constricts the blood vessels, and raises the blood pressure, all of which force the heart to work harder. The result is that smokers are two or three times as likely to die of heart disease as nonsmokers. Even smoking one to four cigarettes a day is associated with a twofold risk of fatal heart and blood vessel disease.[67] For smokers consuming more than 25 cigarettes a day, the risk of heart attack is 10-fold compared to nonsmokers.[68] Moreover, smokers are two to three times more likely than nonsmokers to have a ***stroke,* an interruption of bloodflow to the brain.**[69]

There is good news, however: the risk for heart disease drops in half within a year after smokers quit. It keeps dropping the longer they abstain.[70] This is true even for people who have been smoking for decades. The risk of stroke is also reduced to only slightly more than that for nonsmokers.

Smoking, Diminished Sexuality, and Risks to Women To judge by the advertising, smokers like to think they look sexy. Unfortunately, the evidence is all the other way. Consider:

- ***Increased facial wrinkles:*** People who smoke are more susceptible to premature facial wrinkling than nonsmokers are. Smokers who are heavily exposed to the sun show the most wrinkles, apparently because smoking multiplies the wrinkling effects of sunlight.[71]

- ***For men—decreased sexual arousal and possible damage to sperm:*** Smoking can reduce sexual motivation and performance in men. It constricts the blood vessels, slowing the body's response to sexual stimulation, and reduces testosterone (the male sex hormone) levels in the blood.[72] Men who smoke also have an increased risk of damaged sperm and of fathering children with brain cancer and leukemia.[73]

- ***For women—increased risk of early menopause, osteoporosis, cervical cancer, and (for oral contraceptive users) heart disease:*** In women, smoking increases the chance of early ***menopause,* the process during which the monthly menstrual cycle ends.** Menopause normally occurs between ages 45 and 55.[74] It may also be a risk factor in the development of *osteoporosis,* "brittle-bone disease." **Osteoporosis is a condition of decreased bone density, which results in easily broken bones.**[75]

  Evidence suggests that cigarette smoking increases a woman's risk of cervical cancer, particularly among those who are current smokers.[76–78] Finally, women who smoke and use oral contraceptives ("The Pill") are at vastly increased risk for heart and blood vessel diseases.[79] These diseases include heart attack and stroke. The risk is so serious that women over 35 are strongly advised to stop using one or the other—quit smoking or use another contraceptive.

Smoking and Pregnancy Smoking presents a significant risk to pregnancy, to the growing fetus, and to the newborn. Women who have been smoking at the time of conception have a higher risk of a potentially fatal kind of **pregnancy complication. This is *ectopic pregnancy*, when a fertilized egg becomes implanted somewhere other than the lining of the uterus.** Often the growing embryo is implanted in the fallopian tubes (which carry the eggs from the ovaries to the uterus). There it may rupture surrounding tubes and blood vessels, putting the woman at risk of bleeding to death.[80] Smokers have twice the risk of nonsmokers for ectopic pregnancy. In addition, smoking women are more apt to experience spontaneous abortion, fetal death during pregnancy, and premature birth.[81]

In newborns, the negative effects of the mother's smoking may show themselves in the infant's low birth weight and reduced body length. These are probably the result of poor development because of reduced availability of oxygen during pregnancy. This does not mean merely a smaller baby. Cigarette smoking deprives the fetus of essential growth of *all* its body organs. This includes the brain, and permanent developmental delays can result.[82] The more cigarettes a woman smokes during pregnancy, the more the baby's weight is reduced and the smaller the circumference of the baby's head. Conversely, the earlier a woman quits smoking during her pregnancy, the more positive the effect on her baby's birth weight.[83]

Other Hazards Smokers experience less pain relief from pain-killer drugs because the constituents of tobacco interact negatively with other drugs.[84] Smokers need more time to recover from anesthesia after surgery than nonsmokers do.[85] They are also apt to develop oral cancer.[86] Women smokers who take oral contraceptives are more apt to develop inflammatory bowel disease.[87] Men smokers with human immunodeficiency virus (HIV) are more apt to develop full-blown AIDS than HIV-positive men who are nonsmokers.[88] Finally, there are the great number of smokers who fall asleep with a cigarette in their hands and set fire to themselves and others.[89,90]

Other Tobacco Products

Greater awareness of the hazards of cigarette smoking has led many people to switch to other tobacco products. These offer their own sets of problems. Pipes and cigars lead to oral cancers. Smokeless tobacco—snuff and chewing tobacco—leads to nicotine effects and dependency, oral and dental problems, and various cancers. Clove cigarettes are 60% tobacco and generate even more nicotine, tar, and carbon monoxide than all-tobacco cigarettes. They also produce respiratory illnesses.

Let us examine some other tobacco and related products—pipes and cigars, smokeless tobacco, and clove cigarettes.

Pipes and Cigars Smokers who *start* smoking by using pipes or cigars are less likely to develop lung cancer and heart disease than cigarette smokers. There is a simple reason: most pipe and cigar smokers don't inhale. They are, however, putting themselves at risk for an assortment of oral cancers—cancer of the mouth, larynx, throat, and esophagus.

Cigarette smokers who *switch* to pipes and cigars, on the other hand, are likely to continue to inhale. If they do so, they are inhaling more throat- and lung-irritating tobaccos than cigarettes contain.

Smokeless Tobacco: Snuff and Chewing Tobacco Some people think that switching to smokeless tobacco—snuff and chewing tobacco—can give them some of cigarettes' pleasures without the risks. **Snuff is finely shredded or powdered tobacco that is sold in cans or tea-bag-like packets. The user absorbs nicotine through the mucous membranes in the nose or the mouth.** Most American users "dip" snuff out of the can and place it between their lower lip and gum. **Chewing tobacco consists of loose-leaf tobacco mixed with molasses or other flavors and pressed into cakes (called "plugs") or twisted into ropelike strands. A portion of loose-leaf tobacco, plug, or strand can be chewed or placed between the gum and cheek or lower lip.** The nicotine is absorbed through the mucous membranes in the mouth.

An estimated 10 to 12 million Americans use smokeless tobacco.[91] College students' use of smokeless tobacco is not unusual, particularly among males. One national survey found that 22% of college males and 2% of college females reported that they currently use smokeless tobacco.[92]

The major smokeless tobacco risks are (1) nicotine effects and dependency, (2) oral and dental problems, and (3) cancer, especially oral cancer. These risks tend to increase as dose and frequency increase.[93]

- ***Nicotine effects and dependency:*** Some researchers say smokeless tobacco has even *more* of an effect on the heart and blood-vessel system than does cigarette smoking. Holding tobacco in the mouth results in nicotine exposure that is twice that of cigarette smokers.[94]

  The addictive potential of smokeless tobacco is significant. In one study, adolescent male smokeless-tobacco users were found to be more addicted than male cigarette smokers.[95]

- ***Oral and dental effects:*** One study of National League baseball players found that 48% of the 386 smokeless tobacco users had developed leukoplakia.[96] **Leukoplakia refers to white-colored, thick, hardened, wrinkled patches on the mucous membrane lining of the mouth.** It usually occurs in the area where the smokeless tobacco product is held against the cheek or gum. The disorder is a serious cause for concern because it is considered a tissue change that may develop into cancer. The risk of leukoplakia in those who have used snuff has been observed to be 50 times that of nonusers.[97]

  In time most smokeless tobacco users develop other problems most snuff and chewing tobacco manufacturers won't tell you about. They include bad breath, tooth discoloration, tooth loss, excessive wearing away of tooth enamel, gum problems, and an impaired ability to smell and taste.[98]

- ***Cancer:*** Even though smokeless tobacco products are not burned, they still contain powerful ***carcinogens—cancer-causing agents.***[99] One of the most potent carcino-

gens is *TSNA* (for Tobacco-Specific-N-Nitrosamines). TSNA levels in snuff have been found to exceed those in any other consumer products known to contain carcinogenic nitrosamines.[100] Some of the newer products on the market contain the highest levels of TSNA ever found in smokeless tobacco.

In the end, smokeless tobacco is associated with most of the nicotine-related health hazards linked to smoking, including cancer. Long-term use of snuff and chewing tobacco has been associated with increased risk of cancer of the mouth, larynx, throat, and esophagus.[101] Long-term snuff users have a 50-fold increased risk of oral cancer.[102] Smokeless tobacco may also be related to other upper digestive tract cancers, such as cancer of the pancreas, kidneys, and bladder.[103,104] On the bright side, precancerous lesions in the mouth can heal quickly when people stop using smokeless tobacco.[105]

Clove Cigarettes In the 1980s, some cigarette smokers took up Indonesian-produced clove cigarettes in the mistaken belief that they were safer than regular cigarettes. Also called *kretek cigarettes,* **clove cigarettes contain about 60% tobacco and 40% shredded clove buds.**[106] Clove is the spice taken from the dried flower buds of East Indian evergreen trees.

Actually, clove cigarettes produce the same problems as all-tobacco cigarettes and generate even *more* nicotine, tar, and carbon monoxide.[107,108] They also can cause serious lung injury and respiratory illnesses in some users.

What Smoking Does to Nonsmokers: Passive Smoking

Passive smoking, when nonsmokers inhale surrounding cigarette smoke, is responsible for thousands of deaths. Infants and children are especially at risk. Separating smokers from nonsmokers in the same air space helps but does not eliminate the risk.

Maybe you don't smoke yourself, but have you lived with or are you living or working closely with a smoker? If so, you should be aware that you don't own the air you breathe—that you are engaging in passive smoking. **In *passive smoking*, you are breathing *secondhand smoke*, also known as *sidestream smoke* or *environmental tobacco smoke (ETS)*.**[109] A smoker inhaling *mainstream smoke*—**the smoke drawn directly from the cigarette**—may take in smoke for only about half a minute. However, everyone else in the room may be breathing in sidestream smoke for the entire 12 minutes or so that the cigarette is burning. Sidestream smoke contains a larger number of carcinogens than does mainstream smoke, perhaps because mainstream smoke is filtered.[110]

Should you treat this as just another annoyance, or are you right to think that you are being put at risk?

Here's what the research says:

- *Cigarette smoke kills nonsmokers too:* Secondhand smoke is responsible for thousands of deaths.[111] According to one report, it kills 53,000 nonsmokers every year—3700 from lung cancer, 37,000 from heart disease.[112,113] It may also increase breast cancer risk.[114] If these figures are true, secondhand smoking would be the third leading cause of preventable death, behind active smoking and alcohol abuse. It also means that cigarette smoking is causing *the death of 1 nonsmoker for every 8 smokers.*[115]

- *Children are especially at risk:* Researchers strongly recommend that contact be limited between smokers and children, particularly newborn infants.[116] The children of parents who smoke, compared with children of nonsmoking parents, have increased frequency of respiratory infections and increased respiratory symptoms.[117] Passive smoking is associated with pneumonia, wheezing, and middle-ear disease in children. Children of mothers who smoke have impaired lung growth and development.[118]

- *Separation helps only slightly:* The simple separation of smokers from nonsmokers within the same air space—say, an office—may reduce the exposure of nonsmokers to secondhand smoke. But it does not eliminate exposure.[119]

Strategy for Living: Quitting Cigarettes

It is never too late to quit smoking, even for older people. Although cigarette smoking is one of the toughest drug dependencies, it can be beaten by getting motivated and selecting the right quit-smoking techniques. Methods include tapering off, "cold turkey" (the most successful), stop-smoking groups, nicotine gum and patches, hypnosis, aversion therapy, acupuncture, and inpatient groups.

More than 50 million Americans are smokers today. However, an estimated 40 million others are ex-smokers.[120] "Almost half of all living adults in the United States who have ever smoked have quit," the U.S. Surgeon General pointed out in her 1990 report on smoking and health.[121]

Before people can begin the work of quitting, however, they need to believe that it is worthwhile.

Is It Too Late? Smoking is a killer, and no matter how long people smoke, real benefits to giving up cigarettes begin to appear quickly.[122]

"Older people who smoke can still do their health a lot of good by quitting," says researcher Andrea LaCroix. "A lot of older people believe that once you've smoked 40 or 50 years, you have nothing to gain from quitting. That's clearly not true."[123]

We do not mean to imply that the task of quitting cigarettes is simple or easy. Relapse rates for smokers who quit are high. Of the approximately 1.3 million smokers who quit every year between 1974 and 1985, 75–80% resumed smoking within 6 months of stopping.[124] Eventually, however, many smokers do quit. The key to stopping is two things:

- Motivation and persistence
- Finding the right technique and developing ways to deal with the difficulties of quitting

Understanding Yourself: How Badly Do You Want to Quit? The first order of business is to understand why you smoke, then to look at how much you want to change your smoking habits. *(See Self Discovery 1.)* It's important to know that change will also mean discomfort, so think about how prepared you are to endure the difficulties.

People quit for all kinds of reasons. Sometimes it has to do with what psychologists call "maturing out"—reaching a stage of life when substance abuse is simply outgrown. For instance, a new father, feeling the responsibilities of parenthood, might finally quit when his first child is born. Some quit when the stresses of life

level off. Others stop because of signals they cannot possibly disregard, such as having open-heart surgery. The health movement in North America has probably also helped motivate many to quit.

Once you have determined that you do, in fact, want to quit, you can choose among several methods. As one former smoker writes, "there's only one way to approach quitting smoking: do whatever it takes. Almost all those stop-smoking techniques you see and read about are useful for some people, useless for others."[125] Some smokers can successfully quit regardless of the techniques they use, others have great difficulty quitting regardless of what they try.[126]

SELF DISCOVERY 1

Why Do You Smoke?

Here are some statements made by people to describe what they get out of smoking cigarettes. How often do you feel this way when smoking? Choose one number for each statement.

5 = always   4 = frequently   3 = occasionally   2 = seldom   1 = never

A. I smoke cigarettes in order to keep myself from slowing down. _____

B. Handling a cigarette is part of the enjoyment of smoking. _____

C. Smoking cigarettes is pleasant and relaxing. _____

D. I light up a cigarette when I feel angry about something. _____

E. When I have run out of cigarettes, I find it almost unbearable until I can get more. _____

F. I smoke cigarettes automatically without even being aware of it. _____

G. I smoke cigarettes to stimulate me, to perk myself up. _____

H. Part of the enjoyment of smoking a cigarette comes from the steps I take to light up. _____

I. I find cigarettes pleasurable. _____

J. When I feel uncomfortable or upset about something, I light up a cigarette. _____

K. I am very much aware of the fact when I am not smoking a cigarette. _____

L. I light up a cigarette without realizing I still have one burning in the ashtray. _____

M. I smoke cigarettes to give me a "lift." _____

N. When I smoke a cigarette, part of the enjoyment is watching the smoke as I exhale it. _____

O. I want a cigarette most when I am comfortable and relaxed. _____

P. When I feel "blue" or want to take my mind off cares and worries, I smoke cigarettes. _____

Q. I get a real craving for a cigarette when I haven't smoked for a while. _____

R. I've found a cigarette in my mouth and didn't remember putting it there. _____

SELF DISCOVERY 1
(continued)

How to Score

1. Enter the numbers you have selected for the test questions in the spaces below, putting the number you have selected for question A over line A, for question B over line B, etc.

2. Total the three scores on each line to get your totals. For example, the sum of scores over lines A, G, and M

gives you your score on Stimulation. Scores 11 or above indicate that this factor is an important source of satisfaction for the smoker. Scores of 7 or less are low and probably indicate that this factor does not apply to you. Scores in between are marginal.

_____ (A)	+	_____ (G)	+	_____ (M)	=	Stimulation
_____ (B)	+	_____ (H)	+	_____ (N)	=	Handling
_____ (C)	+	_____ (I)	+	_____ (O)	=	Relaxation
_____ (D)	+	_____ (J)	+	_____ (P)	=	Crutch
_____ (E)	+	_____ (K)	+	_____ (Q)	=	Craving
_____ (F)	+	_____ (L)	+	_____ (R)	=	Habit

Interpreting Your Score

- *Stimulation:* You smoke because it gives you a lift. Substitute a brisk walk or a few simple exercises.

- *Handling:* You like the ritual and trappings of smoking. Find other ways to keep your hands busy.

- *Relaxation:* You get a real sense of pleasure out of smoking. An honest consideration of the harmful effects may help kill the "pleasure."

- *Crutch (or negative feelings):* If you mostly light up when you're angry or depressed, you're using smoking as a tranquilizer. In a tough situation, take a deep breath to relax, call a friend, and talk over your feelings. If you can learn new ways to cope, you're on your way to quitting.

- *Craving:* Quitting smoking is difficult for you if you feel you're psychologically dependent, but once you've stopped, it will be possible to resist the temptation to smoke because the withdrawal effort is too tough to face again.

- *Habit:* If you usually smoke without even realizing you're doing it, you should find it easy to break the habit pattern. Start by asking, "Do I really want this cigarette?" Change smoking patterns and make cigarettes hard to get at.

Source: Adapted from "Smoker's Self Test" by Daniel Horn, Ph.D., Director of the National Clearinghouse for Smoking and Health, Public Health Service, 1980; interpretation adapted from *Quitters' quide: 7-day plan to help you stop smoking cigarettes*, American Cancer Society, 1978.

The methods include:

- Tapering off
- Quitting cold turkey
- Stop-smoking groups
- Other methods—nicotine gum, nicotine patches, hypnosis, aversion therapy, acupuncture, and inpatient treatment

Self-Quitting: Tapering Off Gradual reduction may be a good starting place. For one thing, it can help you understand when and why you smoke. You discover your *conditioned association triggers,* the particular conditions associated with lighting up, such as talking on the telephone or drinking a beer. Then you can learn to perform each of these activities without a cigarette. *(See* ● *Figure 4.)* This cutting down can also help you through the first few days of withdrawal symptoms.

Daily Cigarette Count

Instructions: Attach a copy of this form to a pack of cigarettes. Complete the information each time you smoke a cigarette (those from someone else as well as your own). Note the time and evaluate the need for the cigarette (1 is for a cigarette you feel you could not do without; 2 is a less necessary one; 3 is one you could really go without). Make any other additional comments about the situation or your feelings. This record helps you understand when and why you smoke.

Time	Need (1 to 3)	Feelings/Situation

● **Figure 4   Daily cigarette count.**

Some smokers who are trying to quit do not experience any unpleasantness, but for others withdrawal is unquestionably difficult. The withdrawal pains may range from drowsiness and difficulty concentrating to nervousness, anxiety, irritability, and anger. Physical symptoms may include headaches and constipation. The worst of the withdrawal pangs usually peaks 1–3 days after quitting, although for some people withdrawal lingers up to 6 weeks.

Tapering off works well for some people down to the range of 10–15 cigarettes per day, says disease-prevention researcher Stephen Fortman. People may not only find it difficult to reduce their consumption below a certain level but also tend to inhale more deeply. That makes each remaining cigarette so precious that it becomes even harder to quit completely.[127]

Self-Quitting: Cold Turkey Some smokers prefer tapering off because they fear failure if they go "cold turkey"—stop outright. In fact, however, one analysis of 13,000 people discovered that 85% of the people who succeeded in quitting did so cold turkey. The rest gradually decreased the number of cigarettes they smoked, switched to low-tar and low-nicotine cigarettes, or substituted other tobacco products.[128]

For some smokers, quitting cold turkey works better than participating in formal stop-smoking programs. Among those who had smoked in the decade before one survey was done, 48% of those who tried to quit on their own succeeded. That compared with 24% of those who sought assistance, including counseling, hypnosis, and acupuncture.[129]

One reason that self-quitting cold turkey has a higher success rate is that some smokers who enter programs cannot quit on their own.[130] Also, those who can quit on their own often may not have been smoking as long or as much as those in programs.[131]

Stop-Smoking Clinics and Self-Help Programs If a smoker is motivated to quit but is having trouble doing so, he or she needs to try a treatment program. Different programs should be tried until one turns up that works. The most successful programs are those that use a variety of approaches.

Stop-smoking programs use a mixture of group support, behavior modification techniques, and counseling to help wean smokers of their habit. Some successful programs are nonprofit, such as those sponsored by the American Cancer Society, the American Lung Association, or the Seventh-Day Adventist Church. Others are profit-oriented groups, such as SmokEnders. Most of these involve some fees. Smokers Anonymous, a self-help program based on the Twelve Steps of Alcoholics Anonymous, has no fees and meets in some localities.

Other Methods There are at least six other methods that people can try in conjunction with giving up smoking, as follows:

- **Nicotine gum:** Nonprescription smoking-cessation aids currently available have not proven effective. A prescription drug, nicotine gum (such as Nicorette), has helped some people ease withdrawal symptoms and stop smoking, one study says. Results were best for smokers who are highly nicotine-dependent, who are motivated to quit, and who are involved in a support program.[132] However, another study found that the gum was minimally effective in helping people quit or had no effect at all.[133]

- **Nicotine patch:** Available by prescription, nicotine patches (Nicoderm, Habitrol) are patches that smokers apply daily to the skin anywhere on the upper body. Over the next few weeks, the amount of nicotine that seeps into the bloodstream decreases. Treatment is typically 10–12 weeks and works best when combined with other methods.

  One study found that the quit rate for cigarettes after 6 weeks among smokers who used the nicotine patch was 31%. That compared with 14% for those wearing a similar-looking patch (a placebo) that contained no nicotine.[134]

- **Hypnosis:** Hypnosis may be an effective technique for motivated smokers. The ex-smoker-to-be meets with a psychiatrist, psychologist, or social worker who is a licensed hypnotherapist. The client learns to practice self-hypnosis to strengthen the idea that

smoking is a poison and the body deserves more respect. Stanford University faculty psychiatrist David Spiegel and colleagues conducted one hypnosis study involving 226 heavy smokers. They were able to achieve a two-year abstinence rate of 23% after only one session of hypnosis.[135]

- **Aversion therapy: Aversion therapy tries to teach smokers to associate smoking with unpleasantness.** Sometimes this involves forcing the smoker to inhale so many cigarettes in rapid succession that he or she feels nauseous. Sometimes it involves administering mild electric shocks in conjunction with smoking. This approach is so unpleasant that it should not be considered the method of first choice. Anyone considering it—especially anyone with heart disease, diabetes, or respiratory problems—should consult a doctor before starting it.

- **Acupuncture: Acupuncture is an ancient Chinese technique in which a needle or a staple is inserted in a specific part of the body,** often the outer ear. The results of this technique, too, are mixed.

- **Inpatient treatment:** People with other drug dependencies are often treated in a hospital environment for recovery, and some programs now offer such treatment for nicotine addiction. Usually somewhat expensive, such programs follow the models of other drug-treatment programs with 7-day courses. They may offer group therapy, individual counseling, exercise, nutritional guidance, and meditation.

Several personal considerations apply to any stop-smoking effort. (See ● *Figure 5.*)

Worries About Weight Gain A great many people worry they will put on a lot of weight when they quit smoking. It is true that about one person in 10 who quits will gain 30 pounds or more, according to a survey of over 9000 people. However, the average smoker who gives up cigarettes gains only 6–8 pounds over the next 5 years. Those who stop smoking continue to gain weight at a faster rate than smokers for at least 7 years after they stop. Nevertheless, the study

concluded, the health benefits of giving up cigarettes far exceed any risk from gaining the few
extra pounds.[136]

Actually, weight gain should be viewed as a
sign of *success,* some researchers found. Those
who put on 20 pounds or more after they quit
are less likely to light up again. As Keilli Skoog, a
co-author of the study, said, "Abstinent smokers—those who quit—who gained more weight
were less likely to relapse than others."[137]

The Addiction Can Be Treated No one says
that quitting smoking is easy. Indeed, many patients questioned at a drug-addiction treatment
facility in Toronto said they thought cigarettes
would be harder to quit than the substance for
which they were treated. Yet they also said they
found cigarettes less pleasurable than alcohol or
other drugs.[138] Whether you are a smoker or
simply know people who smoke, it's important to
understand the power that tobacco holds. Realize, too, that the addiction can be broken.

● **Figure 5** **Tips for quitting smoking.**

- *Make a contract:* Analyze your personal
  commitment to change and state it in writing. A signed contract enhances your
  chances of success.

- *Set a quit day:* Determine the day you will
  stop—then do it.

- *Determine your resources:* Identify your
  personal resources and support for your
  plan. Tell people what you're trying to do.
  Going public with your intentions helps
  you activate your plan and enables others
  to support you.

- *Develop healthy habits:* Encourage
  healthy lifestyle behaviors such as exercising and relaxation techniques.

- *Don't despair:* View a relapse as a learning opportunity, not cause for despair. If
  you are among the four out of five smokers who have already quit at least once,
  you can draw on your quit-smoking experiences and resources for the next try. Remember that you stopped before and you
  can stop again.

- *Prepare for danger spots:* Identify high-
  risk situations—those that trigger a craving for a cigarette. Prepare by practicing
  how to deal with such occasions. Even after several years of not smoking, a personal crisis can make you want to reach
  for a cigarette.

Alcohol

▬▬▬▬▬▬▬▬▬▬▬▬▬▬

▶ Identify the category of drugs to which alcohol belongs.

▶ Define the terms *proof* and *standard alcoholic drink,* and identify the equivalent of a standard alcoholic drink of beer, wine, and distilled spirits.

▶ Differentiate between alcohol absorption and metabolism, and identify where each takes place and the rates at which they occur.

▶ Discuss the factors that affect alcohol absorption and metabolism.

▶ Discuss the risks and problems associated with alcohol consumption, including its effect on body senses and function, as well as the problem of hangovers.

▶ Explain the influences of biological, ethnic, and economic factors on people's experience of alcohol.

▶ Describe how people can avoid intoxication when they drink.

▶ Define *alcohol abuse* and *alcoholism.* Discuss the causes of alcoholism and Johnson's stages of progression.

▶ Discuss the effects of problem drinking and alcoholism on a person's health.

▶ Discuss the cause, manifestations, and prevention of Fetal Alcohol Syndrome.

▶ Discuss the effect of alcoholism on the family and society.

▶ Discuss intervention and the treatment options available to those who have an alcohol problem.

▬▬▬▬▬▬▬▬▬▬▬▬▬▬

People tend to equate drinking with relaxation, good times, fellowship, and the easing of pain and problems. In fact, we may attribute such properties to alcohol because drinking really *does* change behavior. We stop feeling shy or tense or anxious. As we begin to feel less tongue-tied and awkward, we find ourselves bolder and presumably wittier, quicker,

and more inspired. At the same time, the people we are drinking with become more relaxed and more receptive to us, our jokes, our astute opinions about almost everything. If one or two drinks makes us feel this good, we think, another —and another—would be even better.

Unfortunately, several thousand years of human experience say this isn't so.

How Alcohol Works: "Magic" in a Glass?

A can of beer, glass of wine, or shot glass of whiskey all equal a "standard drink:" ½ ounce of pure alcohol. Intoxication is determined by blood alcohol concentration (BAC), the ratio of alcohol to blood. Increased BACs, which are usually higher in women than in men for similar amounts consumed, can eventually produce comas and be fatal. Hangovers, caused by high BACs and fermentation by-products or additives called *congeners,* are mainly cured by time.

To explain what alcohol does to us, we need to explain (1) what a "drink" is, and (2) what blood alcohol level means.

What a Drink Is Beer, wine, and distilled spirits, the major types of alcoholic beverages, have different alcohol concentrations. However, a typical *serving* of any such beverage contains about the same amount of alcohol. That is, a **standard drink is defined as ½ ounce of pure alcohol.** This is equivalent to:

- *1 beer:* one standard-size can or bottle (12 ounces) of beer that is 5% alcohol; or

- *1 glass of table wine:* one standard wine glass (4 ounces) of table wine, such as chablis or burgundy, that is 12% alcohol; or

- *1 glass of fortified wine:* one small glass (2½ ounces) of fortified wine that is 20% alcohol, such as sherry or port; or

- *1 shot of distilled spirits ("hard liquor"):* one shot glass (1 ounce) of distilled spirits, such as whiskey, vodka, gin, rum, brandy, or tequila, that is 50% alcohol.

If you think of certain drinks as "stronger" ones, you may be surprised that all the serving sizes listed above contain about the same amount of alcohol. To prove it, multiply the percentage of alcohol by the number of ounces. For each drink listed, you will arrive at approximately ½ ounce of straight 100% pure alcohol. (See ● Figure 6.)

Pure alcohol of the kind used in alcoholic beverages is known as *ethanol* or *ethyl alcohol*. Other types, such as methyl (wood) alcohol or isopropyl (rubbing alcohol) are poisonous and should not be drunk. The alcohol percentage contained in "one drink" is based on fairly standard measures. However, alcohol content can range from 0.5% to 80%, and container sizes can also vary quite a bit. For instance, a tall, 16-ounce can of malt liquor with 9% alcohol is a more powerful "drink" than a standard can of "three-two" beer (3.2% alcohol). Table wines can vary from 10% to 13.5% alcohol. Fortified wines, such as certain dessert wines, are so called because the wines have been "fortified" (made stronger) by adding alcohol. Distilled liquors or spirits can range from 40% to 75% alcohol. **The alcohol content of distilled spirits is expressed in terms of *proof*, a number that is twice the percentage of alcohol.** Thus, 100-proof bourbon or rum contains 50% alcohol.

What Intoxication Is: Determining Blood Alcohol Concentration Consider a driver stopped at a checkpoint by the highway patrol a few hours past New Year's Eve. The police will try to determine if the driver is legally sober enough to drive. If in doubt, they can determine how much alcohol is in his or her bloodstream using a breathalyzer test on the spot. A breathalyzer is a device used to measure breath alcohol. A driver who refuses the breathalyzer may be taken to the police station for a blood or urine test.

What the police are looking for is the blood alcohol concentration. **The *blood alcohol concentration (BAC)* is the amount of alcohol in the blood. BAC is measured as a ratio of milligrams (mg) of alcohol per 100 milliliters (ml) of blood.** Thus, 10 drops of alco-

6 beers (12 oz)   15 ounces of fortified wine   24 ounces of table wine   6 glasses of liquor (1.3 oz 80 proof)

● **Figure 6   Six equivalent drinks.** These containers all have the same amount of alcohol, equivalent to 3 ounces of pure alcohol. When consumed within a 2-hour period, they would cause a 160-pound person to be considered legally intoxicated in most places. (Mixed drinks or poured drinks may have more alcohol than those in bottles or cans.)

hol, which is about 10 mg, in 1000 drops of blood, which is about 100 ml, is a BAC of .10%. This is the legal level of intoxication in most states (in some places it is lower). However, many people are significantly impaired at a lower BAC than this. *(See ● Figure 7.)*

● **Figure 7   Effects of blood alcohol concentrations.**

- *.02% BAC:* Relaxation, heightened mood, little behavior change.
- *.04% BAC:* More relaxed, sightly decreased muscular coordination, usually not intoxicated.
- *.06% BAC:* Impaired judgment, more boisterous, slurred speech, difficulty making decisions about ability to drive or operate machinery.
- *.08% BAC:* Legal intoxication in many states; impaired balance and vision, decreasing muscular coordination.
- *.10% BAC:* Distinctly impaired mental functioning and judgment; about 5 hours will be required for alcohol metabolism.
- *.12% BAC:* This is equivalent to the BAC a 160-pound male would have if he drank a six-pack of beer in an hour; loss of motor coordination, lack of judgment; vomiting may occur.
- *.14% BAC:* Staggering gait, very slurred speech, blurred vision.
- *.20% BAC:* Confusion, inability to walk without assistance.
- *.30% BAC:* No judgment or coordination; the senses don't register anything, and person may lose consciousness.
- *.40% BAC:* Loss of consciousness and coma; person will be dangerously close to death—perhaps even dead. At a blood alcohol level of *.40%–.50%,* a person is usually in a coma. At *.60%–.70%,* death occurs.

Someone of legal age has gone to a party and had some drinks. Is there any way he or she can tell—short of falling down, of course—whether it is safe to drive home? To some extent, there is, if the person can keep track of the number (and kinds) of drinks consumed and the number of hours he or she has been drinking. If you want to do this, you need to know how much you weigh and the number of drinks you've consumed in a 1- or 2-hour period. *(See ● Table 2.)* Find your weight on the table. Then look down the column to find your *approximate* (repeat: this is only approximate) blood alcohol concentration for a given number of drinks. For example, if you weigh 160 pounds and have 6 drinks within 2 hours—say, a six-pack of beer—your BAC will be .10%. That will make you legally drunk in most places. An important note:

for men and women of equal weight, *women* generally experience a higher BAC after the same number of drinks. We explain this difference shortly.

Drinking Rituals and Hangovers How much can you drink? Consider the ritual of "chug-a-lugging." Every year a number of deaths result from this "Let's see who can drink the most" activity. Normally, the body has a built-in safety mechanism in which too much alcohol produces gastric irritation, spasm of the pyloric sphincter (a valve between the stomach and the small intestine), and consequent vomiting. However, if alcohol is drunk too rapidly, as happens in drinking contests, the safety valve doesn't work, producing possible fatal results.

● **Table 2   Calculating the percentage of alcohol in your bloodstream**
This table presents the approximate blood alcohol concentration (BAC) according to weight and the number of drinks in 1 or 2 hours. Actual BAC is influenced by a number of factors, including gender. These values are only estimates.

Number of Drinks	Body weight, pounds							
	100	120	140	160	180	200	220	240
For 1 hour of drinking:								
1	0.03	0.03	0.02	0.02	0.02	0.01	0.01	—
2	0.06	0.05	0.04	0.04	0.03	0.03	0.03	0.02
3	0.10	0.08	0.07	0.06	0.05	0.05	0.04	0.04
4	0.13	0.10	0.09	0.08	0.07	0.06	0.06	0.05
5	0.16	0.13	0.11	0.10	0.09	0.08	0.07	0.07
6	0.19	0.16	0.13	0.12	0.11	0.10	0.09	0.08
7	0.23	0.19	0.16	0.14	0.13	0.11	0.10	0.09
8	0.26	0.22	0.18	0.16	0.14	0.13	0.12	0.11
For 2 hours of drinking:								
1	0.01	0.01	—	—	—	—	—	—
2	0.04	0.03	0.02	0.01	0.01	0.01	—	—
3	0.08	0.06	0.04	0.03	0.03	0.02	0.02	0.01
4	0.11	0.09	0.07	0.06	0.05	0.04	0.03	0.03
5	0.15	0.12	0.10	0.08	0.07	0.06	0.05	0.04
6	0.18	0.14	0.12	0.10	0.09	0.08	0.07	0.06
7	0.22	0.18	0.15	0.12	0.11	0.09	0.08	0.07
8	0.25	0.20	0.17	0.15	0.13	0.11	0.10	0.09

***Hangovers*—morning-after headache, fatigue, upset stomach, irritability, anxiety, and thirst—are believed to be the result of alcohol withdrawal.** The body is reacting to excessive alcohol intake. Two factors contribute significantly to hangovers:

- ***High BAC:*** As you might expect, a high blood alcohol level the night before produces alcohol withdrawal symptoms the next morning.

- ***Type of alcoholic beverage:*** Alcoholic beverages contain substances called ***congeners*, which are by-products of fermentation and preparation.** Distilled spirits such as bourbon are more frequently associated with hangovers than are beer or vodka. Liquors such as bourbon or scotch have more congeners (.1%–.2%) than do gin or wine (.04%), which in turn have more than vodka or beer (.01%).

Here are some of the symptoms of a hangover—and some things that can be done about it. *(See* • *Figure 8.)*

- ***Headache:*** Caused by alcohol's expansion of the blood vessels in the head, headaches can be relieved with aspirin. Coffee and a hot shower may also help. Note: Taking aspirin *before* you start drinking is *not* a good idea. Research has shown that aspirin significantly lowers the body's ability to break down alcohol in the stomach.[139]

- ***Nausea:*** Caused by irritation to the stomach, nausea can be eased by antacids and bland foods, such as toast.

- ***Thirst:*** Brought on by dehydration because of frequent urination while drinking, thirst can be abated with fluids, especially slightly salty ones.

The only way to get alcohol out of the body is the slow, steady, 1-speed metabolism of alcohol by the liver. We discuss this process next. For an adult, the average rate of metabolism is about ½ ounce per hour. That translates roughly to about 1 drink per hour. All alcohol that cannot be metabolized accumulates in the body until the liver can get to it. Hangovers often result from alcohol overdose—an intake of alcohol that exceeds the ability of the liver to immediately metabolize it. The only effective treatment for a hangover is time.

● **Figure 8   Any hangover remedies?**

"*Uncle Charlie's 'surefire miracle medicine' notwithstanding, there is no known cure or palliative for the morning-after miseries. . . . There seems little doubt, though, that the condition is an inherent part of the 'sobering up' process for some individuals. In that respect, although solid food, bed rest, and aspirin will make the discomfort somewhat more bearable, time and time alone will do the job. . . .*

Folklore dies hard, to be sure, but the fact remains that neither black coffee nor cold showers nor breaths of pure oxygen will hasten the sobering-up process. 'Give a drunk black coffee and a cold shower,' I've heard it said, 'and you end up with something really special—a wide-awake, soaking-wet, shivering drunk!"

—Jack B. Weiner (1976). *Drinking.* New York: W. W. Norton.

What Happens When You Drink: How Alcohol Affects You

Alcohol can be absorbed, or consumed, at a fast rate. But it can be metabolized, or processed by the body, at the rate of only about one drink an hour. Alcohol sedates and depresses the central nervous system. As alcohol levels increase, the drug dulls the senses, distorts perception, and interferes with sexual performance, creative activity, sleep, and memory.

Many people do not have a clear idea of how alcohol actually affects them. Indeed, alcohol acts unlike either food or other drugs, so it's worth taking a look at its distinctive effects.

Absorption Alcohol is a unique substance in that it does not need to be digested. Unlike food or pills, a small portion of alcohol is absorbed as soon as it is swallowed. A small amount is taken into the tiny blood vessels called *capillaries* as it passes through the mouth and esophagus. Although about 20% is absorbed into the bloodstream through the stomach walls, the majority of alcohol is absorbed from the small intestine. *(See ● Figure 9.)* The bloodstream delivers the alcohol throughout the body, including liver, heart, and brain. Indeed, alcohol is distributed so quickly that it can be detected in the bloodstream only 2 minutes after being swallowed.

How fast alcohol is absorbed and how significantly people feel the effects of alcohol depend on several factors, some of which are controllable and some of which are less so. Those factors over which people have control include:

1. Amount of alcohol and kind of alcoholic beverage consumed. Those that are carbonated speed absorption. They tend to move quickly out of the stomach into the small intestine, where more rapid absorption takes place.

2. Strength of the drinks. The more concentrated an alcoholic beverage, the faster it is absorbed.

3. Speed of drinking.

4. Presence of food in the stomach—especially milk products and foods high in protein—to delay the absorption of the alcohol.

Less controllable factors include:

1. **Gender:** Compared to men, women tend to have reduced amounts of stomach enzymes that break down some alcohol before it is absorbed. In addition, menstrual-cycle-related hormonal changes can affect alcohol absorption.

2. **Body size:** Heavier, larger people have more body fluids in which the alcohol is diluted.

3. **Body chemistry and emotions:** Such matters as condition of stomach tissues and presence of negative emotions affect emptying time of the stomach.

4. **Drinking history:** Long-term heavy drinkers develop tolerance—they require more alcohol to produce intoxication than less experienced drinkers.

5. **Genetic vulnerability:** Evidence suggests that those who have alcoholic parents or grandparents are at increased risk of becoming alcoholic. They may be less likely to feel the effects of alcohol than those who have no family history of alcohol dependency.

Metabolism An important fact to be aware of is this: although the body can *absorb* (consume) alcohol very fast, it can only *metabolize* (process) it at a fixed rate. This rate is about 1 drink per hour (equivalent to ½ ounce of pure alcohol). Say a person drinks a six-pack of beer in an hour. The body needs another 5 or more hours to get rid of all the alcohol. Alcohol, then, is metabolized at a relatively slow, constant rate that is independent of the amount you take in.

About 95% of the alcohol is metabolized by that unglamorous but essential workhorse organ, the liver. A small portion is metabolized by enzymes in the stomach (particularly in males). Less than 5% is expelled through our breath, urine, and sweat.

Effects on the Central Nervous System Many people look forward to winding down with a drink or two after work or when they're tired. The expression "winding down" is apt: alcohol is one of that class of drugs known as central nervous system *depressant.* Alcohol depresses the activity of the nerve cells (neurons) in the brain, gradually dulling their responses. Thus, at low dosages, one feels looser, less inhibited, relaxed.

At higher dosages, even more central nervous system activity is lost. At first, this is experienced as loss of concentration, sensory discrimination, and motor control. Later there are mood swings and memory loss. Eventually, there is sleep, general anesthesia, and, eventually, coma and death.

What happens to your sensations and behavior as the sedative and dulling consequence of alcohol take effect? Consider some of the things that might happen to people during an evening's drinking:

- *Hearing:* On arriving late at a party, you notice that the noise level has risen. In part, this is because people who drink alcohol lose their inhibitions and tend to talk and laugh more loudly. Alcohol has also affected their hearing: people's ability to judge the direction of sound and distinguish between sounds is impaired.

- *Taste and smell:* At first alcohol stimulates the taste but later, drinkers may notice their interest in food is reduced. Snacks with drinks may be one reason, but after a while alcohol interferes with the senses of taste and smell.

- *Time and space:* Drinkers may find themselves sitting in one place for several hours without knowing it, because alcohol distorts perceptions of time and space.

- *Touch, temperature, and pain:* Leaving the party, a drinker may step outside into freezing weather but be unaware of it. This is a real danger, because drinkers have been known to die of *hypothermia,* a reduction in body temperature. In part this is because alcohol expands (dilates) the blood vessels in the skin, releasing body heat. Although one feels warmer, alcohol actually reduces body temperature.

    The sense of touch is also affected, so that the drinker may not be able to distinguish between hot and cold. Indeed, alcohol diminishes one's perception of pain, adding further to risk of harm.

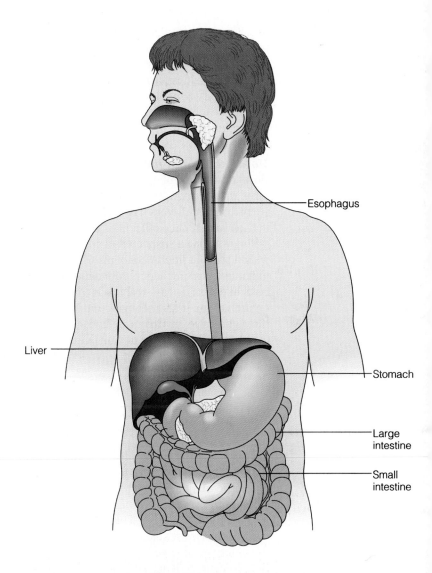

● **Figure 9   How alcohol is absorbed and metabolized.** Some alcohol is absorbed into small blood vessels as it passes through the mouth, esophagus, and stomach. Most of it passes through the small or upper intestine before it is absorbed into the bloodstream.

- **Vision:** If the drinker has been so unwise as to get behind the wheel of a car, he or she usually has problems due to "tunnel vision" (the visual field is narrowed), blurred vision, and difficulty adjusting to the glare of on-coming headlights. The sensitivity to color is also reduced, so that one sees a red light less quickly.

- **Motor skills and judgment:** Alcohol slows down control of muscles and inter-feres with reaction time and coordination, so intoxicated drivers have difficulty staying in their lane. Police officers often test motor skills by asking a suspected drunk driver to walk a straight line. Alcohol also affects judgment, making one more inclined to take risks like passing cars without having enough room. It also seems to unleash hos-tile, aggressive, or violent behavior. Many murders and other acts of violence are asso-ciated with heavy drinking.

- **Sexual performance:** Drinkers lose the ability to make rational decisions and use good judgment. They may thus find them-selves in situations that increase their vul-nerability to STDs, sexual assault, and other problems. Drinkers may also find that alco-hol is not the aphrodisiac they thought. As Shakespeare pointed out years ago about alcohol, "It provokes the desire but takes away the performance." That is, in men, al-cohol increases sexual interest but reduces the ability to achieve or maintain an erec-tion. Recent evidence suggests that, after drinking, women, too, perceive sexual inter-est and pleasure but experience a decrease in arousal and physiological response.[140]

- **Creative activity:** If a drinker spends the rest of the evening working on a project, he or she will be disappointed the next morn-ing. The work will be superficial, sloppy, and poorly organized. As with sex, so in art and in work: alcohol may release one from inhi-bitions but doesn't help imagination and productivity.

- **Sleep:** Alcohol may help a drinker get to sleep, but it does not give truly restorative sleep. Alcohol interferes with normal sleep rhythms.

- **Memory and blackouts:** A drinker may wake up the next morning unable to recall some of the evening's events—including parking the car. Yet no loss of consciousness occurred during that time. **This kind of am-nesia is called a *blackout*. It is thought to result from an interference in trans-ferring information from short-term to long-term memory.**

Strategy for Living: Deciding What to Do About Drinking

Learning how to drink or not drink means knowing who you are. That is, your individ-ual character, biology, and ethnic, family, and economic background affect your abil-ity to consume alcohol. The "drinker's toolkit" shows how to drink without getting drunk.

Deciding what to do about drinking involves un-derstanding how alcohol works in general and on you in particular.

Knowing Who You Are: Choice and Respon-sibility About 77% of men and 60% of women drink alcohol, making up 67% of the adult popu-lation.[141] This means that about one-third of Americans do not use alcohol at all. It's impor-tant to know that (except for alcoholics) most people have a choice: they do not *have* to drink. Nor do they have to drink as much as our soci-ety seems to encourage.

How much drinking is problematic? The Addiction Research Foundation in Toronto has suggested the following standards:[142]

- **Risk to good health:** more than 2 drinks a day
- **Hazardous:** 5–6 drinks a day
- **Harmful:** 7–8 drinks a day
- **Extremely dangerous:** 9 or more drinks a day

The difficulty with these standards is that they suggest the problem is *daily* drinking. In fact, many alcohol abusers go for long stretches without drinking. The American Psychiatric

Association gives some guidelines. It asks these questions to determine alcohol abuse.

1. Have you ever continued to use alcohol despite negative consequences?
2. Have you ever used alcohol in situations in which drinking is physically hazardous?
3. Have you had symptoms associated with #1 or #2 for 1 month or more?
4. Have you ever met the criteria for dependence? (We discuss dependence in the next section.) These criteria differentiate between alcohol abuse and dependence.

People are considered alcohol abusers who answer yes to *either* 1 or 2 *and* 3 but no to 4, which indicates dependency, not abuse. (The American Psychiatric Association's DSM-IV criteria for alcohol dependence are presented later in the chapter, in Figure 13.)

Knowing Who You Are Biologically Some of the factors that affect how people experience alcohol include the following:

- *Larger people can drink more than smaller people:* In an hour's time, a 100-pound person can attain a .10% BAC after three drinks whereas a 200-pound person may require 5–6 drinks. One reason for this is that heavier people have more water within their bodies (adult males are 55% water, adult females 45%). Water in the body dilutes alcohol.

- *Men have lower BACs than women for the same amount of alcohol:* Women can handle less alcohol than men can, but the fact that most women weigh less is only one reason. Even when men and women of the same weight are drinking the same amounts, the women will reach a higher BAC sooner.

  One reason is that women's bodies contain a higher proportion of fat to water and thus have less water to dilute the alcohol. Also, because alcohol is not very fat-soluble, women have more alcohol in their bloodstreams. In addition, women have less of a protective enzyme (alcohol dehydrogenase) that breaks down alcohol in the stomach.

  Yet another difference is that hormonal changes associated with women's menstrual cycles influence the absorption and/or metabolism rate of alcohol. Prior to their menstrual periods, women absorb alcohol faster than at other times during their menstrual cycles. In addition, women who take birth-control pills may absorb alcohol faster.[143]

- *Younger people tend to have lower BACs than older people do:* Younger people have more water in their bodies with which to dilute alcohol than older people do. Thus, a 20-year-old and a 50-year-old trying to match drinks will find that the older person reaches a higher BAC sooner. However, young people may experience more impairment than those who are older, despite similar BACs.

Knowing Your Ethnic and Economic Background Some people believe that some ethnic and economic groups are more vulnerable to alcohol abuse than others. Let us consider this.

- *Some ethnic groups are more prone to have drinking problems than others.* Some groups have higher alcoholism rates than others. This may be due, in part, to cultural norms and expectations, as well as genetics.

  Although African Americans and Hispanics are more likely to abstain than whites are, those who drink have higher rates of alcohol dependency than whites.[144,145] Irish Americans and Native Americans (Indians and Eskimos) have very high rates. (Among Native Americans, however, drinking practices differ significantly among tribal groups.) People of English and Slavic descent and some other American Protestant groups also have somewhat high rates. People of Italian, Jewish, Greek, and Chinese descent have very low rates.[146]

  Interestingly, high-alcoholism groups also show a high number of abstainers. Being from one of these ethnic backgrounds does not mean you personally are more disposed to develop or avoid a drinking problem. It only means you may have been raised in an environment that shows this kind of profile.

- *Economically deprived groups have a history of more drinking problems than affluent groups.*[147] This may explain why some ethnic groups are more disposed to develop drinking problems: many minorities experience economic deprivation.

- *Male groups have a history of more drinking problems than do female groups.* College fraternities, the armed forces, construction crews, and other groups of males have a history of heavy drinking. Even in those ethnic and socioeconomic groups that show more alcoholism, there are fewer female alcoholics than males. As Peele and Brodsky point out, being part of a hard-drinking social circle makes it difficult to control one's own drinking. The group is more powerful than the individual.[148]

With the "Children of Alcoholics" movement, many people worry that being offspring of alcoholics may cause them to be alcoholics. Alcoholism does indeed seem to run in families. The typical finding suggests that the offspring of alcoholics have *3–4 times greater risk* of developing the disease.[149] Current thinking is that heredity plays a significant part in the development of alcoholism, though such development is *not* inevitable. The majority of alcoholics' offspring do not become alcoholic. On the other hand, about 50% of alcoholics have an alcoholic parent.

The Drinker's Toolkit: How to Drink Without Getting Drunk A lot of what happens to drinkers develops out of expectations. For instance, people who believe they are drinking alcoholic drinks, but in fact are imbibing nonalcoholic drinks, may act more talkative and relaxed. Their behavior changes simply because they expect to be affected by alcohol in certain ways.

Many people, of course, deliberately drink to get drunk—to wipe out major pain, to really celebrate, or just to "party." Unfortunately, for some people, getting inebriated even *once* can be disastrous, even fatal. If you do choose to drink, the following will help you reduce your risks:

- *Don't mix alcohol with other drugs.* This rule is primary above all others, because it is literally a matter of life or death. Alcohol in combination with another mood-altering (psychoactive) drug can have several times the effect of each used alone. This is especially true of alcohol combined with another depressant, such as a tranquilizer, painkiller, or sleeping pill. Check with your pharmacist and read the warnings on any prescription or nonprescription drugs you are taking.

- *Eat before and while drinking.* Food in the stomach—particularly protein and fat, such as cheese, milk, and meat—slows down the absorption of alcohol. It coats the areas in the stomach and small intestine through which the alcohol is absorbed. There's a good reason, therefore, to attack the cheese dip if you're drinking alcohol.

- *Avoid fizzy drinks.* Carbonated beverages, like champagne, cola, club soda, tonic, and ginger ale, speed the delivery of alcohol through the bloodstream to the brain. Avoid bourbon-and-beer combinations ("boilermakers," "depth charges"), since they are a surefire way to get drunk fast.

- *Measure drinks, use ice, drink slowly.* These actions enable you to control the amount of alcohol you consume. Use a bartender's shot glass to measure the amount of alcohol added to a mixed drink (instead of just splashing in liquor). Let ice melt in your glass. Sip rather than gulp drinks. All these are ways to slow down the alcohol consumption.

- *Take care of your friends.* If you're hosting a party, you can help them—and yourself, because ultimately you're responsible for them. Measure drinks, offer snacks, but don't push drinks on people, and make nonalcoholic alternatives available.

In recent years, breweries and a handful of wineries have been making nonalcoholic or de-alcoholized beers and wines available. Some have even less alcohol than ordinary fruit juices and soft drinks (for example, Kaliber nonalcoholic beer is only .01%

alcohol). Taste tests reveal that some of these nonalcoholic drinks are an acceptable alternative to alcoholic beverages.[150,151] (See ● *Figure 10.*)

You are not out of place in setting drinking limits, politely expressing concern for your guest and offering a substitute like coffee. Above all, don't let an inebriated guest get behind the wheel of a car. That involves a threat to life—to your guest and to other people on the road. There is also the risk that you (or your parents) can be sued for negligence.

What Alcohol Does to People: Alcohol and Abuse

Alcohol *in moderation*—one or two drinks a day—may actually lower the risk of heart disease. However, heavy drinking has unfortunate consequences at different stages of life. Younger drinkers suffer injuries, especially from motor vehicle crashes, peaking at age 24; older drinkers suffer chronic diseases, peaking in the 60s.

Can alcohol in fact be good for you?

It has been reported that people who have less than two alcoholic drinks a day reduce their risk of heart disease. Their incidence of heart disease is lower than that of people who are either abstainers or heavy drinkers. For instance, a 1988 Harvard University study included women who regularly take a drink or two a day. That group has a reduced risk of heart attacks and some kinds of strokes compared to non-drinkers.[152]

What happens if you take three or four or more drinks a day? One study for the national Centers for Disease Control showed heavy drinking tends to be fatal for different reasons in two stages of life:

- In early adulthood, peaking at about age 24, due to injuries
- Later in life, peaking in the 60s, due to chronic disease

When victims' life expectancies were figured, the study found, alcohol had cheated them of *about 26 years apiece.*[153] (See ● *Figure 11.*)

● **Figure 10   Nonalcoholic beers and wines.** These are available mostly nationwide or in major urban areas. Other brands, both domestic and foreign, are also available.

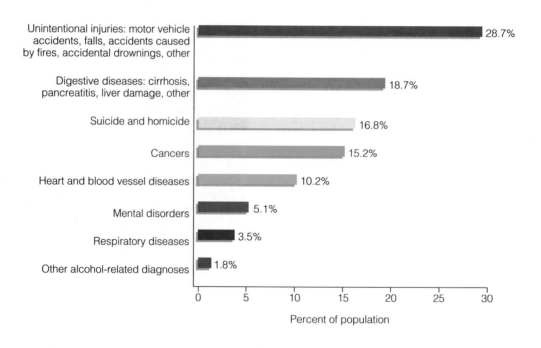

● **Figure 11 Alcohol-related deaths.**

Short Young Lives: Accidents, Suicides, and Homicides

Among young people, alcohol has been heavily implicated in accidents, particularly car crashes, as well as suicides and homicides.

Deaths from alcohol-related injuries, mainly automobile crashes, rise sharply through adolescence and peak at 6000 a year at ages 20–24, then fall off rapidly.[154] Increased public awareness, stiffer penalties, and an increase in the minimum drinking age to 21 have reduced drunk driving deaths somewhat.[155] Yet in a study of over 1500 tavern and nightclub goers, researcher Barry Caudill found that many heavy drinkers still drink and drive. According to his findings, 87% had driven while intoxicated an average of 30 times. Some 75% said they might be able to, or definitely could, drive safely while intoxicated.[156]

Alcohol also figures in accidents other than motor-vehicle fatalities. In deaths caused by fire, alcohol is involved in at least half the cases. It is also involved in half of home accidents and nearly 70% of drownings.[157]

Intentional injuries, primarily suicides and homicides, ran a close second to car crashes in 1987 alcohol-related deaths. More than 17,600 people, or 16.8% of the total, died in suicides or homicides.[158] In four out of five suicide attempts, the individual had been drinking; half of all successful suicides are alcoholics. In 67% of all homicides, either the killer or the victim or both had been drinking.[159]

Reduced Life Spans: Alcohol-Related Diseases

A lifetime of heavy drinking leads to sexual problems and brain problems such as Wernicke's syndrome and Korsakoff's syndrome. Liver problems from alcohol include acute fatty liver, hepatitis, and cirrhosis; gastrointestinal problems include pancreatitis. Drinking heavily also is linked to heart and blood-vessel problems and cancers, especially breast cancer.

The death toll from chronic alcohol-related diseases (such as cirrhosis of the liver and hepatitis) rises slowly from age 20 to age 60. By age 60, however, it accounts for three times as many deaths as accidents do. Cancer of the esophagus accounts for under 10% of total alcohol-related deaths, stroke for less than 10%, and cirrhosis for about 7%.[160]

Among the disorders that one can look forward to after a lifetime of heavy drinking are the following.

Sexual Problems Heavy drinking affects the male sex hormones, producing a loss of sexual desire and difficulty in sexual performance (including impotence). Male drinkers may develop breasts (gynecomastia) because of sex hormone imbalance, have decreased sperm production, sterility, and an increased risk of conceiving defective offspring.[161] In women, heavy drinking may produce impaired sexual functioning, menstrual disorders, and cessation of the menstrual period.[162] Finally, in both men and women, drinking is associated with high-risk sexual behavior, making it a risk factor for exposure to sexually transmitted diseases, such as HIV.[163] Unintended pregnancy and sexual assault may also be associated with such high-risk behavior.

Brain Problems After a while, heavy drinkers begin to show, even when sober, remnants of neuropsychological problems they experience when under the influence. They have memory loss, impaired motor skills, and difficulty in solving problems and learning. However, such impairments can be almost completely reversed (though some problems remain) if drinkers become abstinent.[164]

One characteristic of severe alcoholism is nutritional and vitamin deficiency, especially thiamine (vitamin B_{11}). Such a deficiency accompanied by heavy drinking may lead to *Wernicke's syndrome*. **It includes paralysis of eye nerves, mental confusion, loss of memory, and staggering gait.** *Korsakoff's syndrome* **may also have a nutritional basis but is caused primarily by alcohol. It is characterized by memory and learning dysfunction, mental confusion, and hallucinations.**

Liver Problems Some parts of the body can be damaged and in time will regenerate. The liver, however, is not one of them; at some point alcohol can cause irreversible damage to this organ. As the "detox center" of the body, the liver is the major metabolic, or processing, site of alcohol.

Alcohol dependence can cause three progressively serious kinds of damage to this essential organ:

- *Acute fatty liver:* Fat accumulates in the liver. The condition can be reversed by quitting alcohol.

- *Alcoholic hepatitis:* Patients have inflammation of liver cells and *jaundice,* **in which the skin appears yellow. The diseased liver's inability to remove a yellow pigment called** *bilirubin* **causes the yellow color.** This condition too can be reversed with abstinence and medical treatment, although it can be fatal if not treated.

- *Cirrhosis: Cirrhosis,* **irreversible scarring of the liver,** is the ninth leading cause of death in the United States.[165] At this point, the liver is unable to metabolize various toxins and drugs. These accumulate in the body, resulting in death.

Gastrointestinal Problems Besides liver disease, chronic alcohol use can cause irritation in the stomach. Thus heavy drinkers experience loss of appetite, morning nausea, frequent belching, and diarrhea alternating with constipation. Sometimes they also may experience hemorrhoids, abdominal pain, and bleeding from the gastrointestinal tract.

Pancreatitis **is inflammation of the pancreas, the gland that manufactures digestive juices. It is experienced as nausea, vomiting, diarrhea, and upper abdominal pain.** The disorder reduces the ability of the pancreas to make insulin, which can lead to diabetes.

Heart and Blood-Vessel Problems Heavy drinkers suffer increased risk of dying earlier than most people from heart and blood-vessel diseases. Many alcohol-dependent people have high blood pressure (hypertension), which has been linked to increased risk of strokes and heart attacks. Alcohol also elevates blood fat (or lipid) levels that may contribute to atherosclerosis, or hardening of the arteries. In addition, irregularities in heartbeat (arrhythmias) and an enlarged heart have been associated with heavy alcohol consumption.

Cancers—Especially Breast Cancer A long list of cancers is associated with heavy alcohol use, running, as it were, from the beginning to the end of the body. From the top, they are cancer of the oral cavity, tongue, pharynx, larynx, esophagus, stomach, liver, lung, pancreas, colon, and rectum.[166] Some of these may also be related to cigarette smoking, since so many heavy drinkers are also smokers. Indeed, alcohol may actually *increase* the cancer-causing effects of cigarettes.

Women who are heavy alcohol users have a special concern: breast cancer. A study of more than 89,000 female nurses found that women who have more than one drink a day have a higher risk of breast cancer.[167] In general, women with a family history of breast cancer or who are obese should be particularly alert for signs of breast cancer.[168]

The Effect on Others

Problem drinkers harm others, not just themselves. Pregnant women who drink may produce offspring suffering from fetal alcohol syndrome or fetal alcohol effects. Alcoholism is a family disease that tends to have an impact on all family members. Children and even grandchildren of alcoholics show difficulties in many areas. Society at large also suffers from the behavior of alcoholics.

One might argue that since alcohol-dependent persons are only doing damage to themselves, we should simply let them go to it. Unfortunately, there are a great many other unwilling and even unknowing participants in a heavy drinker's life. Let us look at them.

Unborn Children: Fetal Alcohol Syndrome and Fetal Alcohol Effects How much alcohol should you allow yourself if you're pregnant? The answer: none.

The leading known cause of preventable mental retardation and birth defects in the

Western world is fetal alcohol syndrome, caused by maternal drinking during pregnancy. **Babies born with *fetal alcohol syndrome (FAS)* have a common, recognizable pattern of birth defects and mental retardation.** The main characteristics are mental retardation and other central nervous system problems, growth deficiency, and facial abnormalities.[169] *(See ● Figure 12.)*

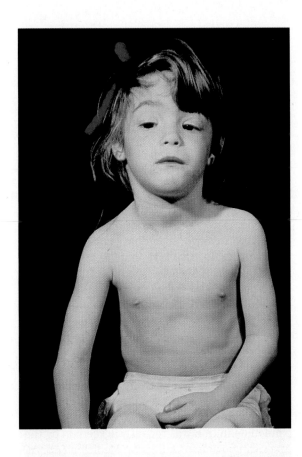

● **Figure 12   Child with fetal alcohol syndrome.** Children with FAS have mental retardation and physical abnormalities (including underdeveloped midface, as shown here). They are the offspring of alcohol-dependent mothers who drank during pregnancy.

About 1 in every 750 babies has FAS. Many more suffer from fetal alcohol effects. **The symptoms of *fetal alcohol effects (FAE)* include low birth weight; abnormalities of the mouth, the genitals, and the urinary system; and altered behavioral patterns.**[170]

Codependents and COAs: Families and Children of Alcoholics A 1988 national survey found that an astonishing number of American adults—76 million, or 43%—have been exposed to alcoholism in the family. They grew up with an alcoholic or problem drinker, married one, or had a blood relative who was one.[171]

Thus, alcoholism is now considered to be a *family illness,* signaling the tremendous impact that alcoholics have on those around them. As families react to alcoholic behavior with anger, confusion, and bewilderment, their behavior can become as impaired as that of the alcoholic. Accordingly, health professionals are now giving increasing attention to treating members of the alcoholic's household.

Two terms have emerged to describe some major groups greatly affected by alcoholics:

- *Codependents: Codependents,* or *coalcoholics,* **were originally considered to be spouses or partners of alcoholics. Now the term has been extended to children and others close to an alcoholic family member. The chief characteristic of codependents is that they tend to accommodate themselves to the alcoholic.** At first they may attempt to control the alcoholic, initially being "understanding," then being angry, then trying to ignore the situation. Eventually they give up and try to work around the alcoholic. Gradually they may take over many of the drinker's usual functions and responsibilities, such as meal preparation or bill-paying. They become *enablers,* **protecting the alcoholic from the negative consequences of addiction and thereby unintentionally promoting the alcoholic's drinking.**

- *Children of alcoholics: Children of alcoholics (COAs)* **are those who grow up in a family in which one or both parents is an alcoholic.** As you might imagine, children of alcoholics must often weather stress, family conflict, neglect, abuse, and divorce. In fact, such children are more likely than other youngsters to have mental and emotional problems, school problems, and physical problems.[172] Children of alcoholics are three to four times more likely to become alcoholics themselves.

COAs demonstrate why alcoholism is often called a "family disease." Alcohol interferes with the parents' ability to give their offspring the attention that is important for emotional growth. So the children often go to great lengths to gain attention from others or withdraw into a world of their own.[173] In hopes of coping with and surviving their dysfunctional families, they may also strive to be responsible for everyone in the family. For example, they may take care of the other children and do the cleaning and cooking.

Adults raised in alcoholic families report difficulties in several areas: expressing their needs to others, identifying and expressing their feelings, putting themselves first, trusting people, and dealing with issues of dependency and intimacy in relationships.[174] They may need to participate in their own recovery from growing up with this family disease.

Social Costs Alcohol is an enormous social problem—a factor in half of motor-vehicle fatalities and suicides and homicides. In about a third of homicides, drownings, and boating deaths the victims are intoxicated. Alcohol figures in a large number of spouse and child abuse cases and in more than four-fifths of police arrests. Its use during pregnancy is the leading preventable cause of birth defects. Alcohol also costs our society a great deal economically—$70 billion a year, mainly in reduced productivity.[175] No wonder it has been said that if alcohol were invented today it would immediately go on the government's controlled substances list.

Alcoholism

Alcoholism is a chronic, progressive, and potentially fatal disease characterized by continuing to drink despite negative consequences, loss of control over drinking, preoccupation with the drug, and thinking disorders, especially denial. The development of the disease may be influenced by genetic, psychosocial, and environmental factors. Alcoholism increases in severity through several stages. Some alcoholics "hit bottom" and voluntarily seek treatment. Others may require intervention.

Many readers of this book may need to address a fundamental question: How badly do you need alcohol to change your mood? Believing that it is necessary as a basic pleasure or as a stress and pain reliever may be the beginning of alcohol problems. Alcohol's role in your life is part of the accompanying self-survey. *(See Self Discovery 2.)*

What Is Alcoholism? People have all kinds of misguided notions about what an alcoholic is. Consider the stereotypical view of homeless people as society's castoffs who have failed in the competitive world and have sunk into alcoholic squalor. In fact, only about 3–5% of alcoholics become homeless. The majority have jobs and families. However, their ability to function productively in all areas of their lives progressively declines.[176] In actuality, alcoholics come from every social class and occupation, from students to college professors to priests to airline pilots.

Alcoholism **is a chronic, progressive, and potentially fatal disease characterized by a growing compulsion to drink.** An expanded definition was recently agreed on by the American Society of Addiction Medicine (ASAM) and the National Council on Alcoholism and Drug Dependence (NCADD). They say alcoholism is "characterized by continuous or periodic impaired control over drinking, preoccupation with the drug alcohol, use of alcohol despite adverse consequences, and distortions in thinking, most notably denial."[177]

SELF DISCOVERY 2

What Kind of Drinker Are You?

Answer each of the following questions by placing a check in the appropriate column.

	Yes	No

1. Do you feel you are a normal drinker? (If you are a total abstainer, check "Yes.")

2. Have you ever awakened the morning after some drinking the night before and found that you could not remember a part of the evening before?

3. Does your spouse (or a parent) ever worry or complain about your drinking?

4. Can you stop drinking without a struggle after one or two drinks?

5. Do you feel bad about your drinking?

6. Do friends or relatives think you are a normal drinker?

7. Do you ever try to limit your drinking to certain times of the day or to certain places?

8. Are you always able to stop drinking when you want to?

9. Have you ever attended a meeting of Alcoholics Anonymous (AA)?

10. Have you gotten into fights when drinking?

11. Has drinking ever created problems with you and your spouse?

12. Has your spouse (or other family member) ever gone to anyone for help about your drinking?

13. Have you ever lost friends or dates because of drinking?

14. Have you ever gotten into trouble at work because of drinking?

15. Have you ever lost a job because of drinking?

16. Have you ever neglected your obligations, your family, or your work for two or more days in a row because you were drinking?

17. Do you ever have a drink before noon?

18. Have you ever been told you have liver trouble? Cirrhosis?

19. Have you ever had delirium tremens (DTs) or severe shaking, heard voices or seen things that weren't there after heavy drinking?

20. Have you ever gone to anyone for help about your drinking?

21. Have you ever been in a hospital because of drinking?

22. Have you ever been in a psychiatric hospital or on a psychiatric ward of a general hospital where drinking was part of the problem?

23. Have you ever gone to a psychiatric or mental health clinic or to a doctor, social worker, or clergyman for help with an emotional problem in which drinking had played a part?

24. Have you ever been arrested, even for a few hours, because of drunk behavior?

25. Have you ever been arrested for drunk driving or driving after drinking?

SELF DISCOVERY 2
(continued)

Scoring

Give yourself points for your answers as follows:

Question	Yes	No		Question	Yes	No
1	0	2		14	2	0
2	2	0		15	2	0
3	1	0		16	2	0
4	0	2		17	1	0
5	1	0		18	2	0
6	0	2		19	2	0
7	0	0		20	5	0
8	0	2		21	5	0
9	5	0		22	2	0
10	1	0		23	2	0
11	2	0		24	2	0
12	2	0		25	2	0
13	2	0				

Interpretation

0–3	You are most likely a nonalcoholic.
4	You may be an alcoholic.
5 or more	You almost definitely are an alcoholic.

Source: Michigan Alcoholism Screen Test, adapted from Selzer, M. L. (1971). The M-A-S-T. *American Journal of Psychiatry, 127,* 1653. Copyright 1971, the American Psychiatric Association. Reprinted by permission.

***Denial* is a defense mechanism; one simply refuses to admit or to face unpleasant realities.** The American Psychiatric Association's *Diagnostic and Statistical Manual of Mental Disorders* (Fourth Edition, called *DSM-IV*) has published criteria for diagnosing alcoholism. (See ● *Figure 13.*)

The Causes of Alcoholism No one knows exactly what causes alcoholism. The ASAM-NCADD definition above notes that it has "genetic, psychosocial, and environmental factors influencing its development and manifestations." These are worth considering.

- ***The possible genetic basis:*** Over the years, there have been theories—none of them proven—that alcoholism has a biological basis. Specifically, it could be metabolic, biochemical, glandular, or allergic. Alcoholism may or may not be inherited. In April 1990, an experiment suggested that inheriting a common version of a gene may place people at risk for alcoholism.[178,179] Later studies suggest that the gene is only one of many genes that may increase an individual's susceptibility to alcoholism.[180]

Family studies also show that offspring of alcoholics are 3–4 times more likely to be alcoholic compared to people with nonalcoholic parents. Adopted children whose biological parents were alcohol-dependent also show more alcohol problems, even when raised in families without alcohol problems.[181] Such studies strengthen the argument for a genetic or biological predisposition to alcohol dependence.

- ***The psychosocial basis:*** Some researchers have tried to identify an "alcoholic personality" that might predispose people to alcohol dependence. The closest they have found is an "antisocial personality," showing "impulsivity, intensity of mood, unstable self-esteem, and alternating dependence on and independence from others."[182] Such traits *might* predispose people to dependence on alcohol and other drugs. By and large, however, the idea of an alcoholic personality is not accepted. Such traits seem to follow, rather than precede, the onset of alcoholism.

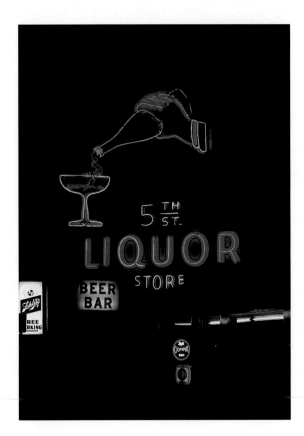

• **The environmental basis:** As we mentioned earlier, different cultural groups seem to be more disposed toward alcoholism than others. For instance, there seems to be less alcohol abuse in cultures that have clear messages about how and when to drink. These messages include significant sanctions against intoxication.

The Stages of Alcoholism The emergence of alcoholism has been described by Vernon Johnson, in *I'll Quit Tomorrow,* as a four-stage process along a pain-euphoria continuum.[183] (See ● *Figure 14.*)

• **Learning stage:** Stage 1 is *learning the mood swing.* People learn that if they are feeling "normal" and then have a drink, their mood will dependably and fairly quickly shift toward euphoria. Then it swings back to normal when the alcohol wears off.

• **Seeking stage:** Stage 2 is *seeking the mood swing.* People learn that, when they feel down, alcohol can be counted on to enhance their mood. Drinking now has a particular purpose, to make one feel better.

• **Harmful dependence stage:** Stage 3 is *harmful dependence.* People are unwilling to stop using alcohol to alter their moods and begin to rationalize their reasons for needing alcohol. They find that when the alcohol wears off it leaves them in a more uncomfortable place than before.

• **Drinking to feel normal stage:** In stage 4, people (who are by now alcoholic) *drink to feel normal.* They no longer drink to achieve euphoria but to escape the negative feelings from the "pain" end of the mood scale.

Stage 1: Learning about the mood swing
One learns that alcohol is a drug and if one is feeling "normal," alcohol will produce euphoria. After the alcohol wears off, one's mood returns to normal.

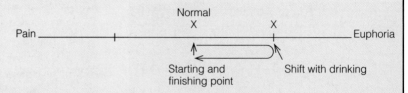

Stage 2: Deliberately seeking the mood swing
One learns to drink to make things better, so that when a person is "feeling a little down," alcohol will help. After drinking, one's mood returns to normal. Most people who experience a hangover or other unpleasantness will learn to avoid alcohol in excess in the future. However, alcohol-dependent persons will not, and will progress to Stage 3.

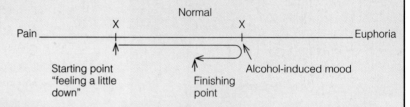

Stage 3: Developing harmful dependence
One becomes unwilling to stop using alcohol to achieve euphoria and begins to rationalize reasons for needing alcohol. When the alcohol wears off, the drinker is left in a more uncomfortable place than before.

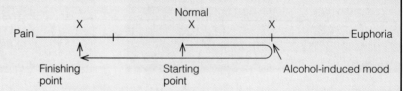

Stage 4: Drinking to feel normal
One drinks not to achieve euphoria but to escape negative feelings, such as withdrawal pangs, and to feel "normal." After a drinking experience, one's mood is at an even lower state than before. By now the drinker is an alcoholic in chronic pain.

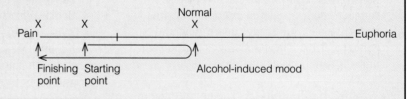

● **Figure 14   Four stages in the development of an alcohol-dependent person.** Vernon Johnson has described these four changes in the drinker's relationship to alcohol on a pain–euphoria scale.

The Recognition of Alcoholism: "Hitting Bottom" How do alcoholics get to the point of recognizing that they *are* alcoholics and accept treatment? Quite often it simply doesn't happen, so the death rate from alcohol-related disorders is very high. Because alcohol problems range from occasional misuse by social drinkers to continual misuse by the alcohol-dependent, it is easy to deny a serious problem. As the disorder worsens, so does judgment: alcoholics often view all attempts to interrupt their drinking as meddling.

Recovering alcoholics use the phrase "hitting bottom" to describe the point where they realize they must seek treatment. Usually the recognition is brought about by outside events that the alcoholic can no longer ignore. For some alcoholics the moment may come with the departure of a spouse, loss of a job, arrest, hospitalization, or the like. Other alcoholics may develop this realization before their lives have reached this level of destruction.

Among recovering alcoholics are those who have been reached through a process called intervention. Vernon Johnson describes **intervention as "presenting reality in a receivable way to a person out of touch with it."**[184] A team of concerned family members and friends, sometimes accompanied by an alcohol counselor or mental health professional, confront the sufferer. They state specific objective facts and observations or descriptions about that person's behavior in a nonjudgmental and caring way. The goal is to compel that person to seek recovery from chemical dependency. The process of intervention must be researched and rehearsed carefully. The team must also assemble a list of local treatment options for the alcoholic to use.

Getting Help for an Alcohol Problem

There are several kinds of treatment for alcoholism, some of which may be available through employers. There are programs for detoxification, individual rehabilitation, and family rehabilitation. Also available are self-help programs such as Alcoholics Anonymous for the alcoholic and AlAnon, Alateen, and Children of Alcoholics support groups for family members.

There seem to be two degrees of alcohol abuse that require attention, according to reports by the Institute of Medicine:[185,186]

- *Mild or moderate alcohol problems:* These problems occur in the 60% of the population that drinks lightly or moderately. Just by the weight of their numbers, these drinkers are responsible for a significant share of personal and societal alcohol-related problems.

- *Substantial or severe alcohol problems:* These are the 10% of the population that are considered alcoholics and require specialized treatment.

Those with mild or moderate alcohol problems, the Institute suggests, could be helped by brief treatment. This could be short-term counseling, discussions with clergy or family, or simply reading self-help materials. Those with substantial or severe alcohol problems may be helped with more specialized treatment, described below.

Employee Programs With many alcoholics, the job is one of the last things they lose, after the driver's license and after the spouse. Many employers are aware of the work-related problems caused by substance abuse. They have found that taking action can increase productivity and decrease job-related accidents and injuries significantly. Employers have discovered that, when threatened with firing, alcoholic employees can also be reached and persuaded to attend a treatment program.

Detoxification Programs Alcoholics who suddenly stop drinking develop withdrawal symptoms within 6–24 hours and may require 3–10 days of detoxification, or "drying out." **The alcohol withdrawal syndrome is a cluster of symptoms that include tremulousness, seizures, and hallucinations. Detoxification consists of putting affected persons in a hospital, preventing them from getting alcohol, and helping them get through any withdrawal symptoms.** (Symptoms can range from the unpleasant to the life-threatening.) A minority of alcoholics may have **delirium tremens (DTs)—trembling, fevers, hallucinations, and delusions.**

Individual Rehabilitation Programs
Whether or not they require detoxification, alcoholics have several inpatient and outpatient rehabilitation programs available. Inpatient residence programs are located in a hospital or alcohol rehabilitation facility. They provide 2–6 weeks of treatment, including various kinds of counseling and psychotherapies, drug therapy, and alcohol education. Following inpatient treatment, recovering alcoholics are directed toward various kinds of outpatient treatment programs. The outpatient status allows them to resume their lives while continuing their recovery.

Both inpatient and outpatient rehabilitation programs offer the following kinds of therapies:

- *Individual therapy:* Psychotherapy, or conversation between the patient and a specially trained therapist, is valuable in helping alcoholics understand their feelings. However, psychotherapy alone, without other methods, may be insufficient.

- *Group therapy:* Small groups consisting entirely of alcoholics led by a trained therapist are useful because members can brace each other about the truth of their addiction.

- *Drug therapy:* Used along with other therapy, drug therapy involves the drug disulfiram (trade name: Antabuse). It comes in tablet form and is taken by the alcoholic every day. Disulfiram acts as a deterrent to drinking because when alcohol is consumed it makes one nauseous.

 Other kinds of drug therapy involve the use of tranquilizers to help alcoholics overcome withdrawal symptoms and depression. If alcoholics suffer from malnutrition (as those in advanced stages often do), they may also be treated with vitamin supplements. Preliminary studies have found that a drug called naltrexone can help drinkers quit by lessening the pleasurable effects of alcohol.[187]

- *Behavior therapy:* Behavior therapy, or behavior modificaton, attempts to change alcoholic behavior so that people will not be as likely to drink. For instance, one procedure known as *aversion therapy* puts drinkers through a 10-day course using drugs that make them vomit after several drinks. According to one study, 35–60% of those in such a program were abstinent after a year.[188]

Family Rehabilitation Programs We mentioned that alcoholism is thought of as a "family disease." One writer, Sharon Wegscheider-Cruse, describes the family as similar to a mobile, which hangs in delicate balance. Like a mobile, the family is disrupted by the winds of alcoholic crises but comes back to rest when the storms subside. Alcoholic families maintain this kind of equilibrium as long as everyone supports the alcoholic's drinking. But when that person begins to recover, or some family members fail to support the drinking, the system becomes stressed and imbalanced.[189]

Sobriety cannot transform a family relationship; indeed, sobriety brings a whole new set of problems. Family therapy aims at helping both alcoholics and their families live together in new ways. There are also several self-help organizations dedicated to helping members of alcoholic families deal with their special problems. Three well-known organizations are Al-Anon, for anyone whose life has been affected by an alcoholic; Alateen, open to pre-teens through 20-year-olds; and Adult Children of Alcoholics.

Alcoholics Anonymous and Other Self-Help Programs Most alcoholism recovery programs are based on a policy of long-term, usually lifelong abstinence from drinking. However, because alcoholism is characterized by a strong tendency toward relapse, no program can claim to be entirely successful.

The principal self-help programs are the following:

- *Alcoholics Anonymous:* The world's oldest alcoholism recovery program was begun in 1935 by two alcoholics. Alcoholics Anonymous (AA) today has almost 2 million members in 63,000 groups in 114 countries. About half of all members are in the United States.[190] AA is a self-help organization, or "fellowship," of men and women whose aim is to help each other maintain sobriety. People who wish to begin to solve their drinking problems can find the AA number in any phone book. In recent years, more young people have poured into the organization, most of them addicted to other drugs as well as alcohol. In some areas, there are special-interest meetings: women only, men only, gays and lesbians, Spanish-speaking, and so on.

The program consists of the following: try to remain sober "one day at a time" (because it's easier than trying to think of quitting drinking for life). Attend meetings, which take place in nearly every city in the country, where recovering alcoholics share their experiences. Enlist the help of a "sponsor," another member who has been longer in sobriety, whom one can call during difficult times. "Working the steps"—the famous Twelve Step program. *(See • Figure 15.)*

• ***Women for Sobriety/Men for Sobriety:*** Established in 1975, Women for Sobriety (WAS) was founded on the premise that women alcoholics have different problems than male alcoholics. Their problems reflect the problems of women in general, such as low self-esteem. The WAS "New Life Program" is based on Thirteen Statements of Acceptance aimed at building self-confidence and self-responsibility.

The WAS New Life Program has been adapted for men, Men for Sobriety.

• ***Save Our Selves:*** Founded in 1986, Save Our Selves, or Secular Organizations for Sobriety (SOS), has 300 groups in the United States, Canada, Europe and Asia. SOS provides a "nonspiritual" alternative, or supplement, to AA for agnostics, atheists, and others who have difficulty with AA's spirituality. Instead of believing in a "higher power," members are encouraged to give themselves credit for their sobriety. They work to rebuild their self-esteem through group support and self-empowerment.

• ***Rational Recovery:*** Also founded in 1986, Rational Recovery (RR) grew to meetings in 150 cities by 1991. RR is based on Albert Ellis's rational emotive therapy model, which holds that if you change your thinking, your feelings and behavior will change as a result. Thus, if you convince yourself that life is much better without alcohol, RR proponents say, you will be able to stop

• **Figure 15   The Twelve Steps of Alcoholics Anonymous.**

 " 1. We admitted we were powerless over alcohol—that our lives had become unmanageable.

2. We came to believe that a Power greater than ourselves could restore us to sanity.

3. We made a decision to turn our will and our lives over to the care of God, as we understand God.

4. We made a searching and fearless moral inventory of ourselves.

5. We admitted to God, to ourselves, and to another human being the exact nature of our wrongs.

6. We were entirely ready to have God remove all these defects of character.

7. We humbly asked God to remove our shortcomings.

8. We made a list of all persons we had harmed and became willing to make amends to them all.

9. We made direct amends to such people wherever possible, except when to do so would injure them or others.

10. We continued to take personal inventory, and when we were wrong, we promptly admitted it.

11. We sought through prayer and meditation to improve our conscious contact with God, as we understand God, praying only for knowledge of God's will for us and the power to carry that out.

12. Having had a spiritual awakening as the result of these steps, we tried to carry this message to alcoholics and to practice these principles in all our affairs. "

—*Alcoholics Anonymous* (Third Edition) (1976), New York: Alcoholics Anonymous World Services, Inc., pp. 59–60.

drinking. Unlike AA, RR claims that no higher power is necessary for recovery, there is no need to admit that one is "powerless over alcohol," nor need one attend meetings after a year's time. Rational Recovery presents a positive approach meant to reach people who do not relate well to AA and to help train their minds to keep them free from alcohol.

800-HELP

Alcohol Abuse Emergency. 800-ALCOHOL. Available 24 hours.

Alcoholism and Drug Addiction Treatment Center. 800-477-3447. Available 24 hours. Provides phone counseling and local referrals.

American Council on Alcoholism. 800-527-5344. Available 24 hours. Provides referrals and treatment information.

Suggestions for Further Readings

Robert Ackerman (1986). *Growing in the shadow: Children of alcoholics.* Pompano Beach, FL: Health Communications. Addresses children of alcoholics from childhood to adulthood.

Timmen Cermak (1985). *A primer on adult children of alcoholics.* Pompano Beach, FL: Health Communications. Identifies issues and steps to recovery for adults who have grown up in alcoholic families.

J. W. Farquhar & G. A. Spiller (1990). *The last puff: Ex-smokers share the secrets of their success.* New York: Norton. Unlike the usual stop-smoking books, this book is a collection of over 30 interviews of smokers from truck drivers to poets to models for cigarette ads who tell how they kicked their habit.

F. S. Goulart (1984). *The caffeine book: A user's and abuser's guide.* Lexington, MA: Dodd, Mead. Covers sources, effects, and possible health hazards; includes a 10-step program for getting off of caffeine.

Vernon E. Johnson (1980). *I'll quit tomorrow: A practical guide to alcoholism treatment.* New York: Harper & Row.

Charlotte Davis Kasl (1992). *Many roads, one journey: Moving beyond the Twelve Steps.* New York: HarperCollins. An addiction expert offers a new look at addiction and codependency that goes beyond Twelve Step programs.

Drug and Other Dependencies: Lifestyles and Gratifications

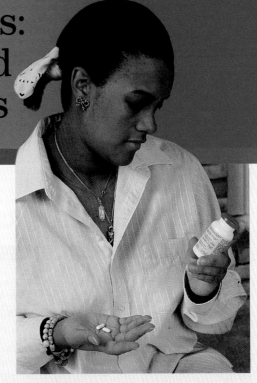

Are drugs an inevitable part of life?

People have been using and abusing substances for a long time. The European explorations of the world have in great part been driven by the search for profits from drugs—tea, tobacco, rum. We no longer hear the terms *Indian hemp* and *coca,* popular drugs in the mid-1800s, but that's only because they are better known today as *marijuana* and *cocaine.*

Society's drugs of choice seem to come in cycles. In the view of the late Harvard psychiatrist Norman Zinberg, for instance, the United States has recently gone through four major waves of drug use, beginning with LSD in the early 1960s, marijuana in the mid- to late-'60s, heroin from 1969 to 1971, and cocaine in the late '70s and '80s. In addition, choices about drug use vary from region to region. Some drugs of choice are frequently found within a particular social class structure, and some drugs will piggyback on others, as cocaine and alcohol became associated or amphetamines and heroin were linked to each other.

Whatever their patterns, it seems that drugs have always been with us. "History teaches that it is vain to hope that drugs will ever disappear and that any effort to eliminate them from society is doomed to failure," write physician and addiction researcher Andrew Weil and his coauthor.[1] The same might be said of other addictive habits, such as addiction to gambling, eating, sex, spending, and other compulsions. If indeed such strong areas of addiction are here to stay, the best defense is an understanding of how they work—and how you are affected. In this unit, then, we describe two principal areas of dependence—those of *substances,* such as drugs, and those of *processes,* such as gambling or spending.

Drugs and Dependence

- ▶ Evaluate the statement that adolescents who casually experiment with drugs are better adjusted than those who abstain from and those who abuse drugs.

- ▶ Define the terms *drug, medication*, and *psychoactive drugs*.

- ▶ Explain how psychoactive drugs work.

- ▶ Identify the factors that influence the effect of a particular drug.

- ▶ Differentiate between drug use, drug misuse, drug abuse, and chemical dependency.

- ▶ Describe the principal methods by which drugs are administered.

- ▶ Differentiate between local, systematic, selective, and cumulative drug actions.

- ▶ Describe three types of tolerance.

- ▶ Name and describe four drug interactions.

- ▶ Describe the differences among the main types of mood-altering drugs—stimulants, depressants, cannabis, hallucinogens, opiates, and designer drugs—and give examples of each.

- ▶ Name some of the treatment programs for overcoming drug dependency.

It is estimated that Americans spend $110 billion a year to buy cocaine, marijuana, heroin, and other illegal drugs. More than a third of Americans—74 million people—ages 12 and over has used an illicit drug at least once.[2] We could add to this a second group, the users of legal drugs—alcohol, cigarettes, caffeine, and tranquilizers. Then it seems that most people have at some time tried to find chemical ways to transcend ordinary consciousness and stresses. The largest group of users are those in the 18–25 age group.

Is There a Well-Adjusted Drug User?

The assertion that some "psychologically healthy" young people experiment with drugs is suspect.

Researchers Jonathan Shedler and Jack Block created an uproar with their 1990 release of a 15-year study of teenage drug use. The results suggested that teenagers who experimented casually with drugs were better adjusted than adolescents who either abstained or regularly abused drugs.[3, 4] The teenagers the researchers labeled "experimenters" used no drug more than once a month, and no more than one drug other than marijuana. The frequent users used marijuana regularly, at least once a week, and had tried several stronger drugs such as cocaine. The frequent users showed evidence early in life of psychological maladjustments, mood swings, inattentiveness, stubbornness, insecurity, and other signs of emotional distress.

Shedler and Block insisted that their research absolutely did not mean that they were advocating drug experimentation. Nor did it mean that using drugs could possibly be beneficial. Nevertheless, many drug counselors were horrified. One pointed out that the teenage drug use of the 101 boys and girls took place before the explosion of crack. Had that cheap and highly addictive form of cocaine been available, the results might have been different.

We draw three conclusions as follows.

Drug Experimenters and Health *Drug experimenters are not necessarily healthier.* Young people who experiment with drugs aren't necessarily psychologically healthier. Rather, the healthiest can survive the drug-experimentation years and are flexible enough to right themselves if they do experiment.

Drug Experimentation and Addiction *Drug experimentation CAN lead to addiction.* Unfortunately, some beginning users don't survive. After all, how do you *know* you're "psychologically healthy" when you start out using? Experimenting with "gateway drugs" such as alcohol and marijuana can lead to the addiction trap of these drugs or more powerful ones.

Drugs and Optimum Experience *Drug experimentation is unnecessary.* It is not necessary to explore drugs in order to explore life or to combat stress. Techniques for achieving the "optimal experience" and for escaping tension are available without drugs.

Types of Drugs

Drugs are chemical substances that alter an organism's function or structure. Psychoactive drugs are those that alter thinking, mood, and/or behavior. Categories of drugs are prescription drugs, over-the-counter drugs, and drugs both legal and illegal used for nonhealth purposes.

Is a drug the same as a medicine?

Sometimes it is. Consider the definition of drugs: **Drugs are chemical substances other than those required for the maintenance of normal health, such as food. The administration of these chemical substances alters a living organism's function or structure.**[5] The terms "medication" and "drug" are often used interchangeably. **Medications (or medicines) are drugs used for the purpose of diagnosing, preventing, or treating disease. They may also help in the care of an individual during illness,** such as drugs to relieve pain.[6]

Clearly, the basic definition of a drug, then, is that it includes medication such as prescription drugs and nonprescription drugs. The definition also includes illegal drugs, cigarettes, alcohol, food additives, and industrial chemicals. All drugs are risky for some people under some circumstances at some dosage levels. Some drugs are more hazardous than others. Importantly, some individuals are more susceptible to the effects of some drugs than they are to others.[7]

Drugs may be classified in several ways, including their origin, their effects, and their chemical structure. In this chapter we look at drugs whose effects are psychoactive. **Psychoactive drugs are mind-altering substances that are capable of changing people's moods, thinking, perceptions, and behavior.**

Psychoactive and other drugs are obtained in several ways:

- **Prescription drugs: Prescription drugs are substances that require a physician's prescription and are obtained from a pharmacy.** Examples are tranquilizers, major pain relievers, and antibiotics. Some of these drugs are considered psychoactive because they are mind-altering.

- **Over-the-counter drugs: Over-the-counter drugs,** or **nonprescription drugs, are substances that can be legally obtained without a prescription.** They are available in pharmacies, supermarkets, and convenience stores. Examples are aspirin, sunscreens, laxatives, and some cold remedies.

- **Legal psychoactive drugs for nonhealth purposes:** These are drugs that are marketed to people for no other reason than to supposedly help them have fun or be alert or relaxed. Some, such as chocolate, tea, and coffee, are available in stores even to minors. Some, such as tobacco and alcohol, are only legally available to those over age 18 or 21 (depending on the state). Though legal, some of these drugs are capable of doing great harm.

- **Illegal psychoactive drugs for nonhealth purposes:** These are the drugs that people think about when they hear about "the drug problem." The government has determined that they are harmful and has declared their cultivation, manufacture, sale, and use illegal. Examples are psychoactive drugs such as marijuana, cocaine, LSD, amphetamines, and heroin.

256

*Chapter 8
Drug and Other
Dependencies:
Lifestyles and
Gratifications*

How Psychoactive Drugs Work Psychoactive drugs work by altering chemicals in the central nervous system that affect one's ability to monitor, interpret, and respond to stimuli. **The *central nervous system* is a complex communication system made up of a vast network of specialized cells called *neurons*.** When the communication system is working well, messages are sent and received, and the person operates in expected ways.

Although there are millions of neurons in the brain, they are not directly connected. **Messages are transmitted from one neuron to another by chemicals called *neurotransmitters*. The space between any two neurons that these chemical messengers must cross is called a *synapse*.** About 50 different chemicals serve as neurotransmitters, but each neuron responds to only one or a few of them. Psychoactive drugs change the transmission of nerve impulses by affecting these neurotransmitters in some way. Thus they change behavior, mood, perception, and thought processes.

The Dynamics of Drug Use: Basic Training

Besides its chemical composition, a drug's effects depend on many factors, including its site of action, toxicity, tolerance, and means of administration. Effects can also change with interactions with other drugs, individual human factors, and setting.

We are all exposed to endless messages—from the mass media, family, or friends—enticing us to use legal and/or illegal drugs. It is one thing to use a drug, however, and quite another to misuse or abuse it. Consider these distinctions:

- ***Drug use:*** The Food and Drug Administration, or FDA, the main government regulator of drugs, defines the term narrowly. The FDA says **drug use is the use of a legal drug for the purposes and in the amounts for which it was intended or prescribed.**

- ***Drug misuse:*** According to the FDA, ***drug misuse* means a drug is not used in the ways for which it was intended or prescribed.** For example, it might mean drugs

taken in too great amounts or too frequently. This applies whether the drug is a vitamin, an aspirin, a tranquilizer or something else.

- ***Drug abuse:*** The FDA says that ***drug abuse*, or *illicit drug use*, is the use of a drug for nonmedical reasons in violation of legal restrictions.**

    The American Psychiatric Association defines drug abuse as a maladaptive pattern of psychoactive drug use. Abuse is indicated by at least one of the following over a period of at least 1 month: (1) Continued use despite problems associated with use. Such problems may be psychological, physical, occupational, or social. (2) Recurrent use in situations that are physically hazardous (such as operating machinery, driving a car, or placing oneself in socially risky situations).

The action of a drug on the body is called a *drug effect*. The use of marijuana, for example, increases the heart rate and causes dryness in the mouth. Besides its chemical composition, the effect of a drug depends on several factors:

- Method of administration
- Site of action
- Dosage
- Toxicity
- Tolerance
- Dependence
- Interaction with other drugs
- Individual human factors
- Setting

Method of Administration Drugs can be taken into the body in many ways. The principal methods of administration are as follows:

- ***Ingestion: Ingestion* is taking a drug by swallowing it.** This method is also called *oral administration*.

- ***Inhalation: Inhalation* is breathing or sniffing a drug into the lungs.**

- ***Injection: Injection* is using a hypodermic needle to insert a drug. Injection may be directly under the skin (subcutaneously), into a muscle (intramuscularly), or into a blood vessel (intravenously).**

• *Absorption: Absorption* **refers to the passing of substances into or across membranes or tissue.** One kind of absorption is placing a drug in contact with the skin (topical or dermal) or mucous membrane lining. Another way is via *suppositories* placed in the vagina or rectum. Some drugs are absorbed after placement under the tongue (*sublingual*) or on the conjunctiva of the eye.

The two fastest routes of administration are by inhalation and injection. *(See • Figure 1.)* The best or most effective method of administration depends on the specific drug. Some drugs, for example, are inactivated when swallowed; others cannot be injected. Some drugs can be effectively administered by several routes. Marijuana, for example, can be administered by inhalation and ingestion. Cocaine can be administered by injection, absorption, or inhalation.

Site of Action Once inside the body, a drug can affect the body to various extents:

• *Locally:* A drug can act **locally, affecting one part of the body but not others.** An example is when the dentist uses novocaine to deaden pain in just one part of your mouth.

• *Generally or systemically:* A drug can act *generally*—also called *systemically* —**affecting the body in general.** An example is when a patient is made unconscious with an anesthetic before surgery.

• *Selectively:* A drug can act **selectively, as when it affects one organ or body system more than others.** An example is with drugs used to control the speed and quality of a patient's heartbeat.

Some drugs act *cumulatively*—**they accumulate when they are taken in faster than the body can process and excrete them.** Alcohol is one such drug: the faster you drink, the more it accumulates in your body.

Dosage The *dosage* or amount of a drug dictates its effects. Some drugs have multiple or varying effects, depending on dosage.

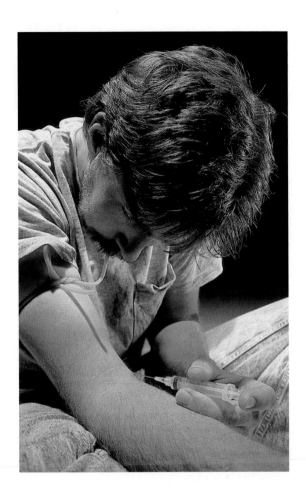

• **Figure 1   How fast drugs work.**

"*Cleopatra may have been one of the first to realize that a drug taken orally is slower to act than one that is injected through the skin.*

The relatively slow onset of an orally administered drug is partially because the medicine must first travel into the stomach and then usually pass through the lining of the small intestine before it enters into the circulation. That takes time.

A drug injected under the skin, as Cleopatra's snake demonstrated, has a much faster action simply because it avoids the barriers of the gut wall."

—Kenneth Jon Rose (1988). *The body in time.* New York: Wiley.

258

*Chapter 8
Drug and Other
Dependencies:
Lifestyles and
Gratifications*

Toxicity **The level at which a drug causes temporary or permanent damage to the body is referred to as *toxicity*.** The damage may be minor, such as the wakefulness caused by certain cold tablets. Or it may be major, as in some of alcohol's effects on the liver. The toxicity of a drug is influenced by several factors, including the amount used and how the drug is taken.

Tolerance **The word *tolerance* refers to the diminished effect of a drug as a person continues its use.** Tolerance occurs as a result of different mechanisms:

- ***Dispositional tolerance: Dispositional tolerance* means that the user's metabolism rate for a drug—the body's ability to break down and get rid of the drug—increases.** Thus, greater quantities of the drug are required to maintain a given level of the substance within the body.

- ***Functional tolerance: Functional tolerance* means that the user's brain and central nervous system become less sensitive to a drug's effect.** For instance, some people may find it takes six cans of beer to get the effects they formerly got with three cans.

- ***Cross tolerance: Cross tolerance* (or *cross addiction*) is tolerance for (or addiction to) drugs as a result of developing tolerance for a related drug.** For example, a tolerance to alcohol also results in tolerance to tranquilizers. Both alcohol and tranquilizers belong to the drug category of depressants.

Chemical Dependency ***Dependence* on a drug refers to the reliance on or need for a chemical substance.** Drug or chemical dependence is sometimes called *addiction*. It involves a loss of control over drug use, preoccupation with drug use, continued drug use despite negative consequences, and thought distortions, especially denial. The person uses the drug to experience the psychoactive effects and, in some cases, to avoid symptoms associated with withdrawal.

The dependence may be physical, psychological, or both.

- ***Physical dependence: Physical dependence* is (1) increased tolerance that requires increasing drug doses to achieve the same effect, and (2) withdrawal symptoms if the drug is discontinued.**[8]

- ***Psychological dependence: Psychological dependence* refers to a craving for a drug and a compulsive drive to use it.** The focus of activity by the person is on obtaining and using the drug. With psychological dependence, the person experiences no withdrawal symptoms when drug use ceases.

Psychoactive drugs such as tranquilizers, cocaine, or heroin can produce physical dependence—that is, addiction. Marijuana may create psychological dependence but does not seem to lead to physical dependence.

Interaction with Other Drugs There is a reason why so many prescription drugs carry a warning not to use them with other drugs, including alcohol. When mixed together, drugs that are safe individually can become harmful.

There are at least four possible ways drugs can interact with each other:

- ***Additive:*** In an ***additive interaction,*** **the effect is the same as the sum of the individual effects of the drugs used.**

- ***Synergistic:*** In a ***synergistic interaction,*** **the effect of two drugs together is *greater* than the effects of each drug used alone.** For instance, the combination of alcohol and barbiturates has *four times* the depressant effect of either used alone.

- ***Potentiating:*** In a ***potentiating interaction,*** **one drug can increase the effect of another.** For example, a drug called probenecid is given with penicillin to enhance the effects of the penicillin.

- ***Antagonistic:*** In an ***antagonistic interaction,*** **one drug neutralizes the effects of another.** The drug naloxone, for instance, will neutralize the effects of heroin.

Who You Are: Individual Human Factors There are, to be sure, physical and biological differences that determine how a drug will affect you. Among them:

- **Weight:** A person who weighs 100 pounds may experience greater effects from a certain amount of a drug than someone who weighs 200 pounds.

- **Gender:** For some drugs, a dose given to a woman produces greater effects than a dose given to a man. This is because women generally have a higher percentage of body fat, resulting in some drugs being active in their bodies longer.[9]

- **Age:** The very young and very old are more sensitive to drugs. Children are more sensitive because they do not have fully developed enzyme systems that metabolize drugs. An older person's system may be impaired.

- **Inherited characteristics:** Inherited differences may explain why some people are more apt to become dependent on drugs than others. This question has been particularly investigated for alcoholism.

- **General physical health:** A drug may affect you more intensely when you're weakened by flu or some other health problem than when you're not.

- **Emotional disposition:** One's mood influences the effects of a drug. If you already feel depressed, for instance, a depressant such as alcohol may make you feel worse.

- **Expectation: Drug expectancy—what one expects to occur when using a drug—**is an important factor in drug use. Expectations may derive from personal experience or exposure to friends' experiences, advertising, or other factors.

Setting In terms of drug effects, not only is your inner state of mind (called your *mindset*) important, so are the external influences. **The setting, the immediate environment in which you take drugs,** can profoundly alter the results. This includes the physical environment, such as room size; the features, such as music, lighting, temperature, furnishings, or cost of drinks; and companions.[10]

The Classes of Psychoactive Drugs Psychoactive drugs—mind-altering drugs, both legal and illegal—affect the body's central nervous system. Psychoactive drugs are classified into

the following general categories according to the primary effects they produce:

- **Stimulants**—for example, caffeine and nicotine (mild stimulants); amphetamines and cocaine (major stimulants)

- **Depressants**—for example, alcohol, sedative-hypnotics, and inhalants

- **Cannabis**—marijuana and hashish

- **Hallucinogens**—LSD, mescaline, psilocybin, phencyclidine (PCP)

- **Opiates** (narcotics)—opium, morphine, codeine, heroin

The accompanying table summarizes these categories. *(See ● Table 1.)*

Stimulants: Drugs That Arouse

Stimulants speed up brain activity, increasing arousal. Mild stimulants include caffeine and nicotine. Major stimulants include amphetamines and cocaine, both highly addictive. Amphetamines in small doses increase attention and counter sleep but in repeated large doses may lead to psychosis. Cocaine acts like amphetamines but is shorter-acting and is considered an extremely destructive drug. Types of cocaine are cocaine hydrochloride, freebase, and crack.

Stimulants excite the central nervous system, speeding up brain activity and body processes, increasing excitement and alertness. The stimulating characteristic of these drugs raises people's level of arousal so they feel "up"—more responsive to the world inside and outside.

Stimulants can be classified into two categories of drugs:

- **Mild stimulants: Mild stimulants are those that are legally and readily available.** They include caffeine and nicotine.

- **Major stimulants: Major stimulants are either closely regulated by the government or are illegal.** Examples are amphetamines and cocaine.

260

*Chapter 8
Drug and Other
Dependencies:
Lifestyles and
Gratifications*

● **Table 1   Categories of psychoactive drugs**

Drugs	Often-Prescribed Brand Names	Medical Uses	Dependence Potential Physical/Psychological
Narcotics			
Opium	Dover's Powder, Paregoric	Analgesic, antidiarrheal	High/high
Morphine	Morphine	Analgesic	High/high
Codeine	Codeine	Analgesic, antitussive	Moderate/moderate
Heroin	None	None	High/high
Meperidine (Pethidine)	Demerol, Pethadol	Analgesic	High/high
Methadone	Dolophine, Methadone, Methadose	Analgesic, heroin substitute	High/high
Other narcotics	Dilaudid, Leritine, Numorphan, Percodan	Analgesic antidiarrheal, antitussive	High/high
Depressants			
Chloral hydrate	Noctec, Somos	Hypnotic	Moderate/moderate
Barbiturates	Amytal, Butisol, Nembutal, Phenobarbital, Seconal, Tuinal	Anesthetic, anticonvulsant, sedation, sleep	High/high
Glutethimide	Doriden	Sedation, sleep	High/high
Methaqualone	Optimil, Parest, Quaalude, Somnafac, Sopor	Sedation, sleep	High/high
Tranquilizers	Equanil, Librium, Miltown, Serax, Tranxene, Valium	Anti-anxiety, muscle relaxant, sedation	Moderate/moderate
Other depressants	Clonopin, Dalmane, Dormate, Noludar, Placydil, Valmid	Anti-anxiety, sedation, sleep	Possible/possible
Stimulants			
Cocaine*	Cocaine	Local anesthetic	Possible/high
Amphetamines	Benzedrine, Biphetamine, Desoxyn, Dexedrine	Hyperkinesis, narcolepsy, weight control	Possible/high
Phenmetrazine	Preludin	Weight control	Possible/high
Methylphenidate	Ritalin	Hyperkinesis	Possible/high
Other stimulants	Bacarate, Cylert, Didrex, Ionamin, Plegine, Pondimin, Pre-Sate, Sanorex, Voranil	Weight control	Possible/possible
Hallucinogens			
LSD	None	None	None/unknown
Mescaline	None	None	None/unknown
Psilocybin-psilocyn	None	None	None/unknown
MDA	None	None	None/unknown
PCP†	Sernylan	Veterinary anesthetic	None/unknown
Other hallucinogens	None	None	None/unknown
Cannabis			
Marijuana Hashish Hashish oil	None	Antinausea for cancer patients; experimental for glaucoma	Unknown/moderate

*Designated a narcotic under the Controlled Substances Act.

†Designated a depressant under the Controlled Substances Act.

Source: Drug Enforcement Administration, *Drugs of abuse.*

Tolerance	Usual Methods of Administration	Possible Effects	Effects of Overdose	Withdrawal Syndrome
Yes	Oral, smoked			
Yes	Injected, smoked	Euphoria, drowsiness,	Slow and shallow	Watery eyes, running
Yes	Oral, injected	respiratory depres-	breathing, clammy	nose, yawning, loss of
Yes	Injected, sniffed	sion, constricted	skin, convulsions,	appetite, insomnia, ir-
Yes	Oral, injected	pupils, nausea	coma, possible death	ritability, tremors,
Yes	Oral, injected			panic, chills and
				sweating, cramps,
Yes	Oral, injected			nausea
Probable	Oral	Slurred speech, disori-	Shallow respiration,	Anxiety, tremors, delir-
Yes	Oral, injected	entation, drunken	cold and clammy	ium, convulsions, pos-
		behavior without	skin, dilated pupils,	sible death
Yes	Oral	odor of alcohol	weak and rapid pulse,	
Yes	Oral		coma, possible death	
Yes	Oral			
Yes	Oral			
Yes	Injected, sniffed	Increased alertness, ex-	Agitation, increase in	Apathy, long periods
Yes	Oral, injected	citation, euphoria,	body temperature,	of sleep, irritability,
		dilated pupils, in-	hallucinations, con-	depression,
Yes	Oral	creased pulse rate	vulsions, possible	disorientation
Yes	Oral	and blood pressure,	death	
Yes	Oral	insomnia, loss of		
		appetite		
Yes	Oral, injected	Illusions and hallucina-	Longer, more intense	Withdrawal syndrome
Yes	Oral, injected	tions (with exception	"trip" episodes, psy-	not reported
Yes	Oral	of MDA); poor per-	chosis, possible	
Yes	Oral, injected, sniffed	ception of time and	death	
Yes	Oral, injected, smoked	distance		
Yes	Oral, injected, sniffed			
Yes	Oral, smoked	Euphoria, relaxed inhi-	Fatigue, paranoia, pos-	Insomnia, hyperactivity,
		bitions, increased ap-	sible psychosis	and depressed ap-
		petite, disoriented		petite reported in a
		behavior, amotiva-		limited number of
		tional syndrome		individuals

262

Chapter 8
Drug and Other
Dependencies:
Lifestyles and
Gratifications

The mild stimulants of caffeine and nicotine are described in another chapter. We discuss the major stimulants of amphetamines and cocaine below.

Amphetamines Considered a major central nervous system stimulant, amphetamines have street names like "uppers" and "speed." ***Amphetamines* are laboratory-made (synthetic) drugs that lessen fatigue, improve concentration, and produce exaggerated feelings of well-being and elation.** The prescription drugs are marketed under a variety of names, and their illegal distribution has given rise to several street names:

- *Amphetamine*—brand name Benzedrine, street name "bennies"

- *Dextroamphetamine*—brand names Dexedrine and Biphetamine, street names "dexies," "black beauties," "Cadillacs"

- *Methamphetamine*—brand names Methedrine and Desoxyn, street names "meth," "crank"

Related stimulants are methylphenidate (Ritalin), phenmetrazine (Preludin—"bam"), and diethylpropion (Tenuate and Apisate).

In 1970, the Food and Drug Administration restricted amphetamines to the medical treatment of three problems. These are narcolepsy, attention-deficit hyperactivity disorder (ADHD), and short-term weight reduction for patients who are obese. Amphetamines have a strong stimulant effect that lasts for several hours after they have been taken orally.

Some people have begun taking amphetamines after discovering that in the short run the drug improves performance by counteracting fatigue and boredom. Amphetamine use may begin as an attempt to meet pressures in one's life. For instance, a new user might be a student with a deadline or a long-haul truck driver on a tight schedule.

In small amounts, amphetamines increase attentiveness and counter sleep, although they may also produce increased blood pressure, dizziness, and headaches. In larger amounts amphetamines can give people a momentary highly pleasurable feeling that is often described as a euphoric "rush." This is especially true when amphetamines are injected intravenously

("mainlined") rather than taken in pill form. Because the "rush" lasts only a few minutes, the user craves another one, and a series of injections often follows. Repeated use of these drugs leads to rapid tolerance and strong psychological dependence.

Because amphetamines not only prevent sleep but also suppress appetite, the user may go several days without sleep and with little food. The user may repeatedly do injections until the drug runs out or he or she finally has to "crash" (fall asleep for a long period). When taken repeatedly, particularly in high doses, amphetamines can produce a ***stimulant psychosis*, characterized by paranoid delusions, hallucinations, and disorganized behavior.**

Crystal methamphetamine ("Ice") can be smoked or injected. When smoked, its effects are felt in less than 10 seconds. Unlike other forms of amphetamine or cocaine, crystal methamphetamine has effects ranging from 8 to 14 hours. Chronic use can result in insomnia, restlessness, irritability, and nervousness. Dangers associated with use include the development of a schizophrenia-like psychosis and severe depression. In addition, overdoses may result in convulsions, coma, and death.

Cocaine Over the past several years, cocaine (street names: "coke," "snow," "blow"), in different forms, has become available to all levels of society. It is, says psychologist John Flynn, a drug of considerable power:

> *Even among drugs of considerable addiction potential, cocaine stands apart. It is, in its various forms, the most destructive drug in human history. Not heroin, not LSD, not marijuana, not alcohol, not PCP—none of these drugs is as capable as cocaine of grabbing on and not letting go. . . .*
>
> *The reason that cocaine can exert this powerful hold on people is the unique relationship of the drug to the pleasure centers of the brain. Cocaine acts, in effect, as a "key" that opens up these parts of the brain as no other drug can do.*[11]

Cocaine is so addictive because, unlike many other drugs, it *directly* stimulates the pleasure centers in the brain. People who are dependent on cocaine tend to ignore other needs—food, sleep, sex—in pursuit of the ultimate "feel-good" feeling. Cocaine users describe the experience as a burst of energy. They feel an astonishing surge in their physical and mental powers, that anything is possible and almost any task can be accomplished.

The high associated with cocaine is fleeting, followed by a severe depression (a "crash"). Next come anxiety, fatigue, shakiness, and other withdrawal symptoms. The quickest solution to this unhappiness? More cocaine—and the cycle begins again. However, as one uses cocaine more and more in an attempt to recover the feelings of ecstasy, more frequent and higher doses are required. As the use gets heavier, the highs get higher but the valleys get deeper.

Repeated use can produce a host of problems: headaches, shakiness, nausea, lack of appetite, loss of sexual interest, depression. People who "snort" the substance seem to constantly suffer from an inflamed, runny nose because of the irritation to their nasal passages. Freebasers and crack users may suffer lung damage from smoking, and freebase users risk setting themselves on fire. Cocaine users who share hypodermic needles risk hepatitis and, more seriously, HIV infection. Repeated use at increasingly high doses of cocaine can produce a *psychosis*—paranoid delusions, hallucinations, compulsive rocking, hyperactivity. High dosages can also cause seizures, heart attack, heart muscle damage, and stroke.

Cocaine is extracted from the coca plant (not to be confused with the cacao plant, from which chocolate is derived). The South American Indians first used coca as a stimulant, chewing the leaves to alleviate fatigue. The crude cocaine available in coca leaves, however, has nowhere near the addictive power of the products chemically extracted from them. These products are cocaine hydrochloride, freebase, and crack. *(See ● Figure 2.)*

- ***Cocaine hydrochloride:*** The form most used in the 1970s, ***cocaine hydrochloride*** **is what most people simply call *cocaine* ("coke," "blow"). It is a white, crystalline powder that is inhaled or injected.** Users who inhale ("snort") the powder through the nose experience intense effects within 10–15 minutes. Users who inject the

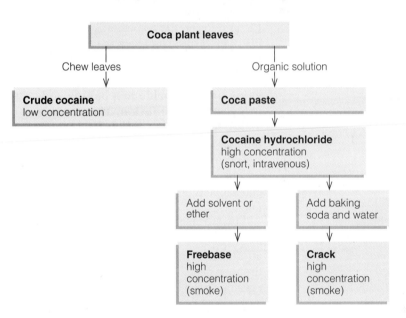

● **Figure 2   Forms of cocaine.** Various forms of cocaine obtained from the coca plant, and typical methods of use.

264

Chapter 8
Drug and Other
Dependencies:
Lifestyles and
Gratifications

powder mixed with water using a hypodermic syringe experience a quicker effect, beginning within 30 seconds. (Some users combine an injection of cocaine with heroin, an extremely dangerous practice known as "speedballing.")

- *Freebase: Freebase cocaine* **is made from cocaine hydrochloride by removing an acid (hydrochloric acid), leaving what chemists call a base, which can be smoked.** Smoking freebase cocaine delivers the drug to the body's system much more quickly than inhalation, producing a much more intense euphoria.

  Note: To "free the base," the cocaine hydrochloride must be treated with solvents, some of them highly flammable, such as ether. If the ether is not completely removed from the powder before one smokes it, it can literally blow up in one's face. Richard Pryor, the comedian, apparently discovered this when he was badly burned in 1980, allegedly in a freebase accident.

- *Crack: Crack* **involves dissolving cocaine hydrochloride in a baking soda or other alkaline solution. The product is small, hard lumps, or "rocks," which may be smoked in a pipe.** Compared to freebase, crack is less volatile and less expensive. It is a smokable, cocaine-containing substance that produces quick and intense euphoria.

  Unfortunately, the appearance of this cheap form of cocaine has made the drug affordable to nearly anyone (including children). When smoked, crack quickly delivers cocaine to the brain, producing a powerful rush, which is followed 10–20 minutes later by a crash. That is the beginning of a craving for more crack. Dependency develops rapidly with crack cocaine use.

Depressants: Drugs That Take You Down

Solvents and inhalants, sedatives/hypnotics, and tranquilizers are types of drugs categorized as depressants, which slow down or sedate brain activity. Solvents are chemicals found in cleaning products and adhesives. Inhalants are found in aerosols and many anesthetics. Sedatives induce relaxation, and hypnotics induce sleep; barbiturates and nonbarbiturates are sedative/hypnotics prescribed as sleeping aids and tension relievers. Tranquilizers, or anti-anxiety drugs, are minor and major. Minor tranquilizers are used to ease minor anxieties, muscle tension, and sleeplessness. Major tranquilizers are used to treat serious mental disorders.

Unlike the stimulants, which speed up brain activity, *depressants* **("downers") are drugs that slow down or sedate the central nervous system. They induce a feeling of relaxation, which progresses to a lessening of inhibitions and drowsiness as the dosage is increased.** Depending on the dosage, sedation can lead to anesthesia, then to coma and eventually death from respiratory failure.

The most widely used depressant drug is alcohol. Here we discuss three other types of depressants:

1. Solvents and inhalants
2. Sedatives/hypnotics
3. Tranquilizers

Solvents and Inhalants There is a vast world of highly dangerous depressants classed as inhalants. *Solvents* **are chemicals found in many cleaning products and adhesives.** *Inhalants* **are found in aerosols and many anesthetics.** When inhaled, these chemicals act as depressants and produce delirium.

Examples of these chemicals show just how readily available they are: gasoline, glue, paint, varnish, kerosene, butane, paint thinners, cleaning fluids, spot removers, rubber cement, nail polish remover, typewriter correction fluid, and aerosol propellants. Other inhalants include:

- *Butyl nitrate:* An over-the-counter drug, butyl nitrate (brand names: Locker Room, Rush) produces a brief period of euphoria.

- *Amyl nitrate:* A drug prescribed for heart patients, amyl nitrate is used to widen (dilate) the blood vessels and increase the heart rate. It has also found its way to the street (street names: "poppers," "snappers") where it is used to produce brief euphoria.

- *Nitrous oxide:* Nitrous oxide (laughing gas) also has a valid medical use, as a dental anesthetic, but has been diverted to illicit purposes.

The first problem with solvents and inhalants is the one common to all depressants. Regular use leads to tolerance, so that the user requires more and more to get the same effect. Initially, one experiences a euphoria that feels like a floating sensation and delirium. As more substances are inhaled, users begin to experience not just excitement but also confusion and headaches. Eventually, these chemicals can cause nausea, coughing, and abnormal heart rhythms. Worse, they can lead to hepatitis, liver or kidney failure, coma and brain damage, and an increased risk of death by asphyxiation.

Sedatives/Hypnotics: Barbiturates and Nonbarbiturates Depressants are chemical substances that can produce muscular relaxation and relief from tension and anxiety. **Depressants can also produce a calming effect and, as such, are called** *sedatives.* **At larger doses, some depressants, called** *hypnotics,* **are capable of inducing sleep or a trance-like state.**

The sedative/hypnotics include five classes of drugs:

1. Some inhalants
2. Barbiturates
3. Nonbarbiturate sedatives/hypnotics
4. Minor tranquilizers
5. Major tranquilizers

Barbiturates are chemical compounds that are dispensed by prescription in pill or liquid form to be used as sleeping aids and tension relievers and to control epileptic seizures. Barbiturates can also be used as general anesthetic agents, in which case they are injected intravenously. Barbiturates may be short-acting or long-acting.

- *Short-acting:* Short-acting barbiturates rapidly penetrate into the brain and can induce sleep very quickly. Examples are pentobarbital (brand name Nembutal, street name "yellow jackets") and secobarbital (Seconal; "reds").

- *Long-acting:* Longer-acting barbiturates take longer to be absorbed by the brain but can keep one sedated for several hours. Examples are amobarbital (Amytal; "blues") and phenobarbital (Luminal; "phennies").

Like other depressants in moderate doses, barbiturates act like alcohol and produce staggering, slurred speech, and loss of motor coordination. They also produce euphoria and disinhibition—in short, the characteristics of intoxication. Indeed, like alcohol, they produce hangovers. Increased doses lead to sedation and sleep, which is why barbiturates were once prescribed medically as sleeping pills. Higher doses produce anesthesia, and barbiturates are prescribed for this purpose as well as to control seizures, such as those of epilepsy.

Barbiturate use has caused so many problems that their medical use has been greatly reduced. For one thing, tolerance develops rapidly, so that higher doses are required to produce sleep. Attempting to withdraw from barbiturates after regular use will produce a syndrome similar to that found among those withdrawing from alcohol. The symptoms are shakes, perspiration, confusion, even delirium and convulsions. Indeed, barbiturates are one of the most dangerous drugs for withdrawal. There is also a subsequent danger of drug overdose, particularly—and this cannot be stressed enough—when barbiturates are used with another depressant such as alcohol. Combining depressants is so dangerous because these drugs interact synergistically. Barbiturates have often been used in suicides and unintentional deaths, including the case of film star Marilyn Monroe.

Some nonbarbiturate sedatives have been introduced for treating sleep disorders and anxiety. Perhaps the best known is methaqualone, marketed under such names as Quaalude (street name: "ludes") and Sopor ("sopors"). Methaqualone became known as "the love drug" because it was thought to enhance sexual performance, but there is no evidence that it has any aphrodisiac qualities.

Methaqualone and other nonbarbiturates have not lived up to their promise as a safe alternative to barbiturates. They are quite toxic at high doses, lead quickly to dependence, and produce withdrawal symptoms similar to those of alcohol and barbiturates.

266

Chapter 8
Drug and Other
Dependencies:
Lifestyles and
Gratifications

Minor and Major Tranquilizers *Tranquilizers* **are anti-anxiety drugs,** marketed under such brand names as Valium and Librium, until recently the most widely prescribed drugs in the United States. Tranquilizers may be classed as minor and major:

- *Minor tranquilizers:* Minor tranquilizers include benzodiazepines and nonbenzodiazepines. They are used primarily for three purposes: (1) to treat minor anxieties, (2) to ease muscle tension, and (3) to induce sleep.

- *Major tranquilizers:* Major tranquilizers, such as chlorpromazine (Thorazine) and haloperidol (Haldol), are used to treat people with serious mental disorders. Although major tranquilizers allow patients to remain conscious and will reduce hallucinations, they may also cause confusion and stupor.

Those minor tranquilizers called the *benzodiazepines* have had an enormous effect on our society. Four of them are among the top 30 most prescribed drugs in America. These are diazepam (Valium), flurazepam (Dalmane), lorazepam (Ativan), and chlorazepate (Tranxene).[12] The group of minor tranquilizers called the *nonbenzodiazepines* include meprobamate (brand name Equanil) and buspirone (BuSpar).

The benzodiazepines have become the drugs of choice for alleviating anxiety and insomnia.[13] However, using these drugs as the sole treatment for anxiety disorders, especially over the long term, merely masks the patients' symptoms; they do not cure anxiety or affect its origins. The main adverse effects of most minor tranquilizers are drowsiness and interference with people's memories—that is, blackouts. In addition, tolerance develops, albeit reasonably slowly, and there is cross tolerance between them and other depressants, particularly alcohol. The effects of benzodiazepines can last for several days. Withdrawal from these drugs is similar to that for barbiturates and for alcohol—insomnia, anxiety, tremors—although not as severe.

Cannabis: Marijuana and Hashish

The hemp plant produces marijuana and hashish, both of which contain the psychoactive agent THC. THC may be smoked or ingested. There are several harmful long-term effects from the drug.

Marijuana and hashish are both derived from the hemp plant **cannabis** (*Cannabis sativa*), which grows freely throughout the world. One species of this plant has also been widely used to provide fibers (hemp) for rope and clothes. *Marijuana* **("pot," "grass," "weed") is the leafy top portion of the plant.** *Hashish* **is made from gumlike secretions (resin) produced by the hemp plant, which are dried and compressed. The principal psychoactive agent in cannabis is** *THC* (short for delta-9-tetrahydrocannabinol). THC content can range from near zero to 8%, depending on the plant.

In general, the most efficient way to absorb THC is through smoking, either in a hand-rolled cigarette ("joint") or in a pipe. The effects depend upon the dosage: low doses typically produce mild analgesia and sedation, but high doses may produce hallucinations. Thus, effects vary not only according to the particular plant but also on how long a person can hold the inhaled marijuana in the lungs. Cigarette smokers or experienced marijuana smokers therefore tend to feel the effects more intensely than inexperienced users do. Peak drug concentrations occur 30–60 minutes after the first inhalation ("toke"), and the effects are experienced for about 2–4 hours. However, even nonsmokers sitting in the same room with pot smokers can experience some drug effect, a "contact high." THC has shown up in nonusers' urine tests hours and even days after the event.[14]

THC can also be administered orally, as when it has been baked in the form of marijuana brownies and ingested. For the same effect, the dose needed is about three times greater than when smoking. The onset of the high may be as long as 1 hour; however, the drug effects may last 4–6 hours. THC is also in *hash oil,* **a concentrated liquid extract that is more potent (up to 60% THC) than marijuana or hashish.**

In the short run, marijuana acts somewhat like alcohol or some tranquilizers. It produces feelings of relaxation and tranquility and, for some people, a heightened sense of perception, and impaired psychomotor performance. Some marijuana users experience panic reaction. It is probably unsafe to drive a car while under the influence of marijuana. Unlike users of the two legal drugs of alcohol and tobacco, marijuana users do not seem to develop significant physical dependence but do develop some tolerance to the drug. Few develop psychological dependence. Heavy users who stop the drug may experience sleep disturbances, chronic irritability, nausea, or other symptoms.[15]

Cannabis may be medically useful for several problems. It reduces pressure in the eye (intraocular pressure), which is a cause of glaucoma, the leading cause of blindness in the United States. It also has been found to reduce the nausea and vomiting associated with chemotherapy and some radiation treatments for cancer. Cannabis and THC synthetics have been tried in an attempt to treat pain, convulsions, hypertension, asthma, and depression, although the results are not certain.

That's the good news. The bad news is that marijuana smoking has been linked to respiratory disorders, such as chronic bronchitis and pulmonary disease. This is particularly likely if marijuana is used frequently and in heavy doses. Cigarettes made with marijuana contain more than 400 different chemicals. They have more tar than those made with tobacco, and the cannabis tar seems to contain more cancerous substances than tobacco tar.[16] Still, the long-term effects are unknown and are complicated by the fact that many cannabis smokers are also cigarette smokers. The short-term effects of increased heart rate and slight to moderate elevation in blood pressure seem to hold no danger for healthy people. But they might pose a risk for people with existing heart and blood-vessel problems. Men who are heavy marijuana users have been found to have decreased sperm production. Women who are continual users have been found to have nonovulatory menstrual cycles, although the effect on fertility is unclear.[17] As with nearly all drugs, however, pregnant women should abstain from cannabis use because of possible significant effects on the fetus.

Cannabis use decreases the activity of the immune system in animals, but there seems to be no long-range effect in human beings.

Hallucinogens

Hallucinogens, or "psychedelics," profoundly alter perceptions, producing hallucinations, scrambling of senses, depersonalization, and flashbacks. The most potent is LSD. Other hallucinogens are mescaline from the peyote cactus, psilocybin from certain mushrooms, and morning glory seeds. The extremely dangerous drug phencyclidine, or PCP, is classified as a hallucinogen, although it seldom causes visual hallucinations.

Hallucinogens **are drugs that can alter perceptions in profound ways.** In the 1960s, **they were also called** *"psychedelics,"* **because of their supposed "mind-expanding" or "mind-revealing" properties.** They alter the consciousness to produce not only the sensory disturbances called *hallucinations* but also changes in thinking, mood, and physiological processes.

Although we have discussed it separately, marijuana is sometimes classified as a hallucinogen. Other hallucinogens are LSD (lysergic acid diethylamide) and PCP (phencyclidine), which are synthesized in laboratories, and mescaline and psilocybin, derived from natural sources.

Among the principal effects of hallucinogens are the following:

- *Hallucinations:* Hallucinations are the vivid images that users have reported when under the influence of these drugs. Examples are spiral explosions, vortex patterns, lattice patterns, flashing lights, and a sense of movement around objects.

- *Scrambled senses: Synesthesia* **is the perception of a stimulus in a sense other than the one in which it is presented.** For example, one "sees music," "touches a taste," "hears colors."

- *Depersonalization: Depersonalization* **is the distortion in how people see their bodies and themselves.** Examples

268

Chapter 8
Drug and Other
Dependencies:
Lifestyles and
Gratifications

are the perception that one's legs are wriggling out of one's trousers or a feeling of "a oneness with the universe."

- ***Flashbacks: Flashbacks, unexpectedly re-experienced parts of a hallucination episode or perceptual distortions,*** can occur weeks, months, or even years after the drug was used. One study reported that 53% of LSD users reported flashbacks.[18]

Unlike other drugs we've discussed, hallucinogenic drugs do not seem to cause physical dependence or withdrawal symptoms. On the other hand, tolerance develops quickly, so that users find a drug's effects are quickly reduced with use. People develop a cross tolerance to drugs in this category, particularly LSD, mescaline, and psilocybin. Thus they cannot switch from one hallucinogenic drug to another in hopes of changing their level of tolerance.

LSD   One class of hallucinogenic drugs (*serotonergic hallucinogens*) includes LSD, mescaline, psilocybin, and morning glory seeds, all of which cause vivid visual hallucinations. We will describe the most potent of the hallucinogens first.

LSD (D-lysergic acid diethylamide, street name "acid") was originally derived from ergot, a fungus that infests grain. It was first synthesized in the laboratory in 1938, and now it is synthetically produced. It is colorless, odorless, and tasteless and extremely potent. Its discoverer, Swiss chemist Albert Hoffman, reported on the bizarre results of one of his initial experiences. *(See ● Figure 3.)*

Because it is so potent, extremely small doses of the drug are needed to produce effects. The drug is sold in a variety of forms, including on paper, in a gel, or in a sugar cube or tablet. The effects begin within 20–60 minutes of ingestion and last for 8–12 hours. During an "acid trip," heart rate and blood pressure increase slightly, the pupils dilate, and sweating and chills occur. The hallucinatory experience varies. Some people report many numerous pleasurable, ecstatic experiences followed by an occasional "bummer" or bad trip, associated with acute panic and paranoia. Setting, companions, and one's own feelings and expectations seem to greatly influence the character of the drug experience. So does the nature of the drug actually used, since adulterated street drugs lead to uncertain effects and potential dangers.

Hazards include flashbacks, the unpredictable recurrence of initial effects days to months after LSD was taken. Flashbacks occur most often before sleep, during periods of emotional stress, and while driving. Other problems are fear of losing one's mind, accidental injury, and panic reactions. Pregnant women should not take the drug because LSD causes contractions of the uterus. However, there is no evidence it causes chromosomal damage or birth defects.

The long-range effect of prolonged LSD use is not clear. Despite concerns that it might cause cancer, this has not been proven. There is speculation that heavy LSD use may produce psychiatric disorders, but this, too, has not been proven.

Mescaline, Psilocybin, Morning Glory Seeds   Originally these LSD-like hallucinogens were obtained from natural substances, although mescaline and psilocybin are now synthesized in laboratories. All these were used by native peoples in the New World for rituals of healing and worship. All produce vivid hallucinations, including bright colors and lights.

- ***Mescaline: Mescaline* is the major psychoactive ingredient in the small crown or button of the peyote cactus** of Mexico and the southwest United States. Members of the Native American Church have used peyote since the 19th century.

  Peyote buttons are eaten, boiled, and drunk as peyote tea, or smoked in cigarettes or pipes. When eaten, the effects of mescaline begin within 30–90 minutes and may last 8–12 hours. Although mescaline causes altered perceptions and other effects similar to LSD, it is only about 1/3000 as potent as LSD. Although no delirium or amnesia has been reported, the drug may produce nausea.

- ***Psilocybin: Psilocybin* is found in several kinds of "magic mushrooms" throughout the world** (among them mushrooms of the genus *Psilocybe*). The drug is only about 1% as potent as LSD and is eaten or drunk in a tea. Its effects last about 4–6 hours. Psilocybin is known for the strong visual distortions it produces.

- *Morning glory seeds: Morning glory seeds,* **pulverized seeds of the morning glory plant, contain a psychoactive substance that is similar to LSD but less potent.** It is only about 5–10% as strong as LSD. To discourage use of the seeds as a psychoactive drug, commercial morning glory seed producers apply a poisonous substance to the seeds. The poison causes nausea, vomiting, diarrhea, and dizziness.

Phencyclidine *Phencyclidine* **(street names: "PCP," "angel dust," "love boat," "lovely," "hog") has been classed as a hallucinogen, although it seldom causes visual hallucinations. Instead, users experience perceptual changes or distortions in body image.** They may feel, for example, as though parts of their bodies are extremely large or detached. The effects also resemble those of alcohol intoxication: euphoria, slurred speech, numbness, lack of motor coordination, and double vision.

Phencyclidine is a unique drug in that, depending on the dose and user, it has stimulant, depressant, hallucinogen, and anesthetic properties. The drug can be injected, but it is usually sprinkled as a powder on a cigarette and smoked. The drug effects generally take place 5–15 minutes after smoking and last 4–6 hours or even days with high doses.

PCP is an extremely dangerous drug, in part because its effects are unpredictable. More frequent use seems to produce a higher rate of negative reactions than other psychoactive drugs.[19] Overdoses may result in seizures, coma, or death from respiratory failure. Bad trips may occur in 50–80% of PCP users.[20] The drug may also produce paranoia and violence lasting several days and long-term psychotic episodes and depression. "In many cities," experts write, "PCP is responsible for more psychiatric emergencies than any other drug, and in some hospitals PCP psychoses exceed schizophrenia and alcoholism as a cause of psychiatric admission."[21]

● **Figure 3   One of the first LSD trips.** The discoverer of LSD reported the following experience as the result of ingesting a mere 250-microgram dose.

    After 40 minutes, I noted the following symptoms in my laboratory journal: slight giddiness, restlessness, difficulty in concentration, visual disturbances, laughing. . . . Later: I lost all count of time. I noticed with dismay that my environment was undergoing progressive changes. My visual field wavered and everything appeared deformed as in a faulty mirror. Space and time became more and more disorganized and I was overcome by a fear that I was going out of my mind. The worst part of it being that I was clearly aware of my condition. My power of observation was unimpaired. . . . Occasionally, I felt as if I were out of my body. I thought I had died. My ego seemed suspended somewhere in space, from where I saw my dead body lying on the sofa . . . . It was particularly striking how acoustic perceptions, such as the noise of water gushing from a tap or the spoken word, were transformed into optical illusions.

    —Albert Hoffman, Swiss discoverer of LSD

270

*Chapter 8
Drug and Other
Dependencies:
Lifestyles and
Gratifications*

Opiates

Opiates, or narcotics, are drugs derived from the opium poppy plant that provide pain relief and sedation. Major opiates include opium, morphine, codeine, heroin, and other synthetic opiates. All are addictive. Opium serves as a source of morphine, codeine, and heroin.

***Opiates,* also known as *narcotics,* include several drugs derived from the Oriental poppy plant that produce numbness, relieve pain, and induce sleep.** These sleep-inducing ***analgesic,* or painkilling,** effects give the opiates important, legitimate medical uses. They have also been used medically to treat diarrhea and coughing. What makes them popular as illicit drugs, however, is the euphoria they produce. The opiates include opium, morphine, codeine, heroin, meperidine, and methadone. These drugs are called *opiates* because they originated from the opium poppy plant. Natural derivatives of the plant are opium, morphine, and codeine. Modifying the chemicals in opium produces other opiates (heroin, Dilaudid, or Percodan). Some opiates are synthesized in the laboratory (meperidine, methadone, or Darvon). **Opiumlike substances called *endorphins* or *enkephalins* have also been found naturally in the body.** Tolerance, cross tolerance, and physical as well as psychological dependence characterize chronic use of the opiate drugs.

Opium **Dark brown chunks or powder from the dried sap from the seedpod of the Asian poppy plant is *opium.* When smoked it produces vivid, dreamlike experiences,** which has given rise to the expression "pipe dreams." In the 19th century, it was widely used in numerous patent medicines in the United States. It was also popular recreationally, as when it was smoked in China. Opium is still used in some parts of the world, but today it mainly provides morphine, codeine, and heroin.

Morphine **The active ingredient in opium, *morphine* is an extremely effective painkiller. It can be taken orally or smoked but is usually injected.** Morphine's effects last about 4–5 hours. Analgesics like morphine act

on the central nervous system, blocking out the messages of pain sent to the brain. Thus, morphine does not actually remove pain but changes a person's awareness so that he or she no longer cares about pain. When under the drug, one feels drowsy, tranquilized, and often euphoric.

Although euphoria is an attraction of the drug for many people, some people actually experience anxiety and fear. Other possible side effects include nausea and vomiting. Morphine depresses respiration, and too large a dosage can cause death because people stop breathing. The drug is extremely addictive, and tolerance develops after only a few injections. After a while, tolerance builds to the point that no amount of the drug will provide the desired effects. Withdrawal symptoms can be very unpleasant: chills, sweating, shaking, cramps, and nausea, to name a few.

Codeine **Principally derived from morphine, *codeine* is a less effective painkiller and sedative than morphine but in low doses does not have the addiction problems.** It is found in many medications, both prescription and nonprescription, such as cough medicines and combined forms of aspirin (Empirin, Tylenol).

Heroin **A semi-synthetic drug derived from morphine and four times as potent, *heroin* ("junk," "smack") is one of the most addictive drugs available.** "It's so good," one young middle-class addict said about it, "don't even try it once."[22]

Discovered in 1874, heroin was promoted as a nonaddictive substitute for morphine. Earlier, morphine had been hailed as a nonaddictive substitute for opium. Heroin was used medically in the United States as an analgesic early in the 20th century. Eventually it was banned for any nonmedical use. In Great Britain, however, physicians can use a ***Brompton's cocktail,* a mixture of heroin and cocaine, to ease the suffering of the terminally ill.**[23]

When injected, heroin produces euphoria and analgesia lasting 3–4 hours. Addicts experience the injection as a "rush" of ecstasy, although it may actually be simply the relief of withdrawal symptoms. These symptoms resemble those of morphine withdrawal: sweating, chills, cramps, nausea, shaking, restlessness, and anxiety. Goose bumps appear, perhaps the basis for the expression "going cold turkey." Tolerance to heroin increases rapidly, so that the effects diminish unless the user increases the dose, as often happens. Indeed, tolerance develops so quickly that users often speak lyrically of their first dose. They keep trying to find stronger blends of the drug in an attempt to re-create that experience. This escalation in turn increases the risk of overdose and death.

During the 1960s and 1970s, heroin, usually injected, became the scourge of the American streets. Its use dropped markedly in the 1980s as cocaine and crack became more available. In the early 1990s, however, the cocaine market became saturated with heavy law-enforcement attention. Heroin sellers began packaging the drug in potent blends that could be snorted or smoked rather than injected.[24, 25] An even more potent combination, heroin and crack ("moon rock," "speedball," "parachute"), also hit the streets.[26] The heroin-cocaine combination in a speedball was determined to be the cause of death of comedian John Belushi. Heroin and depressant drugs such as alcohol have also been found to potentiate one another. Rock singer Janis Joplin's death in 1970 was attributed to heroin that she injected into herself following an evening of heavy drinking.

Other Synthetic Opiates Besides codeine, several other legal opiates less powerful than morphine are available for pain relief: propoxyphene, meperidine, oxycodone, hydromorphone, and methadone.

Propoxyphene (Darvon) has in the past been widely prescribed for all kinds of pain, from menstrual cramps to cancer. However, it is actually less effective than aspirin in pain relief and half as potent as codeine. Because people develop tolerance to it quickly, they are apt to increase the dosage. The drug has been implicated in numerous deaths and suicides.

Meperidine (Demerol; street name: "demies"), a painkiller whose effects last 2–4 hours, is not only as potent as codeine but is addictive. *Oxycodone* (Percodan; "perkies") has a drug action of 4–5 hours. Somewhat less potent than morphine, it is slightly more potent than codeine. *Hydromorphone* (Dilaudid; "Little D") has about

five times the potency of a similar amount of morphine. Its action lasts about 4–5 hours.

Methadone (Dolophine; "meth," "dollies") is as potent as morphine and is used principally as a substitute drug to help addicts get off heroin. Whereas the duration of action is 4–5 hours for morphine and 3–4 hours for heroin (and both must be injected), the effects of methadone last for 24–48 hours (and it can be administered by mouth). Sometimes methadone is given in decreased doses over a two-week period, sometimes in regular doses over a 6-month period or even indefinitely. The doses are enough to reduce heroin withdrawal pains but not enough to produce much euphoria. The danger, however, is that methadone itself can become an addictive drug.

Some opiates are even more powerful than heroin. *Fentanyl* (Sublimaze, "China white") is *80–100 times* as potent as morphine, *20 times* as potent as heroin. This drug is used to produce anesthesia in surgery, but from time to time it has been sold on the street. In 1991 in the greater New York City area, several heroin addicts died after buying heroin that was apparently laced with fentanyl.

Designer Drugs: More Dangerous Than Heroin

Designer drugs are drugs that are chemically similar to other controlled substances. They were originally designed to circumvent the law banning dangerous addictive drugs. Designer drugs are highly unpredictable and dangerous.

Far more dangerous than heroin are the so-called **designer drugs**, also called **analog drugs**. In the 1970s and early 1980s, back-room chemists began making drugs closely related chemically to regulated or banned drugs (such as amphetamines). Thus, manufactured drugs produced similar effects in the body, but the makers could not be prosecuted. The law at the time had to specify the exact chemical architecture of illegal drugs.[27] In 1986, however, the Controlled Substance Analogue Act was passed, banning drugs similar to those classified as controlled substances.

272

*Chapter 8
Drug and Other
Dependencies:
Lifestyles and
Gratifications*

The earliest designer drugs to appear on the street were in a class of drugs called *methylated amphetamines*. These produced mild euphoria and a sense of openness and empathy. One was *MDA* ("Love drug," "Mellow Drug of America"), which supposedly helped users develop loving or positive feelings toward others. Next came *MDMA* ("Ecstasy," "Adam"), which some psychotherapists said could help patients achieve insight breakthroughs, although no studies support this contention. MDMA, DOM, and MDA are considered hallucinogenic amphetamines. Concerns about these drugs include fatal or nearly fatal toxic reactions that may result from hypersensitivity to the drug or an overdose. The drugs may also deplete neurochemicals essential to brain function. These drugs in turn were followed by *MDE* ("Eve").

A "designer heroin" known as *MPPP* or *MPTP* has produced brain damage and associated neurological disorders that have left people seriously crippled. Derivatives of the above-mentioned fentanyl have been developed that may be 10–1000 times more potent than heroin. Such potency means a great risk of death from overdose. The greatest danger is that makers of designer drugs will develop substances that are more addicting or have more serious side effects.

Strategy for Living: Managing Drug Use and Abuse

Overcoming drug dependency means first admitting the problem—overcoming denial. This may require intervention by others. Mild or moderate drug problems may be handled with brief treatment. Severe drug problems may require detoxification, inpatient or outpatient treatment, and the help of other support programs. Family members of those who are chemically dependent need to participate in their own recovery, regardless of whether or not the affected person seeks treatment.

We live in a society that offers constant inducements to medicate oneself to escape life's pain. It starts with aspirin, alcohol, tranquilizers, and then—the logical next step for many people—

illegal drugs. People may go for months or years using drugs moderately, then increase their use as dependence on these addictive substances occurs. Progression to drug dependence is often gradual. But there may come a time when drug use begins to interfere with sleep, memory, peace of mind, interest in sex, and performance in all areas of life. Family members may be the first to notice the signs of addiction. There may be conflicts in relationships, financial problems, absences from work or school, and trouble with the law. If any of these are happening in your life or the life of someone you know, help is needed. *(See Self Discovery 1.)*

Admitting the Problem: Overcoming Denial
At some point a drug user may "hit bottom." This is the point when he or she finally realizes the addiction and the need to change. Sometimes this is a natural development as people mature and realize that their drug use is no longer satisfying but rather life-disturbing. Sometimes the realization comes about through *intervention,* **as family members or friends, often accompanied by a trained counselor, confront the drug user. They state specific facts about his or her behavior in an effort to help the user recognize the possibility of dependency.**

In any case, before those who are chemically dependent can change their behavior, they must first overcome their denial of abuse. Nearly all people with drug-related problems deny that they have a problem. Because their initial drug use had positive effects, they continue to seek that experience even when drug use can no longer provide it. This may explain why the relapse rate is high for addicts initially entering treatment. According to Herbert D. Kleber of the Office of National Drug Control Policy, addicts don't enter treatment the first time to get rid of their habit. Rather, they want "to get back to that honeymoon when the drug felt great and [they] could control it."[28]

Nevertheless, the acknowledgment of addiction to a drug is the first step. Giving up the drug is next.

Getting Help for Mild or Moderate Drug Problems Some drugs produce only mild or moderate withdrawal symptoms, and users are able to overcome their habits without great difficulties. If you think this might apply to you, there is much that you can do yourself. You should consider where you stand in your life and how extensive your drug use is. Think about what the drug does *for* you, and what your reasons are for giving up drugs. *(See ● Figure 4.)* In addition, you might try the following:

- ***Get treatment:*** Brief treatment includes such things as short-term counseling, discussions with family or friends, or simply reading self-help materials.

- ***Identify goals and methods:*** Set your goals for drug use, such as the extent to which you will limit your use, and the methods for controlling it. For example, you might make a contract with a friend listing goals, deadlines, rewards, and punishments.

- ***Identify how you will strengthen yourself and your life:*** Decide how you will change your environment and otherwise strengthen your life to help you break the habit. For example, you might identify drug-related social situations you will avoid, self-help groups you will join, exercise programs you will take up. Find other pleasures to replace drugs. Some healthy activities that people take up as alternatives to drugs are athletics, music, art, the outdoors.

Getting Help for Significant Drug Problems
People who suffer from chemical dependency often require specialized treatment, as follows:

- ***Detoxification: Detoxification—ridding the body of the drug—may require hospitalization or a stay in some other health-care facility.*** There withdrawal symptoms can be monitored and treated.

- ***Milieu treatment:*** **Inpatient residence programs, known as** *milieu treatment,* **are located in a hospital or drug rehabilitation facility.** They provide 2–6 weeks of treatment, including various kinds of counseling and psychotherapies, drug-withdrawal therapy, and drug education. Some famous treatment centers for chemical dependency are Hazelden in Center City, Minnesota, and the Betty Ford Center in Rancho Mirage, California.

SELF DISCOVERY 1

Are You Chemically Dependent?

The following questions were written by recovering addicts in Narcotics Anonymous.

	Yes	No
1. Do you ever use alone?	☐	☐
2. Have you ever substituted one drug for another, thinking that one particular drug was the problem?	☐	☐
3. Have you ever manipulated or lied to a doctor to obtain prescription drugs?		
4. Have you ever stolen drugs or stolen to obtain drugs?	☐	☐
5. Do you regularly use a drug when you wake up or when you go to bed?	☐	☐
6. Have you ever taken one drug to overcome the effects of another?	☐	☐
7. Do you avoid people or places that do not approve of you using drugs?	☐	☐
8. Have you ever used a drug without knowing what it was or what it would do to you?	☐	☐
9. Has your job or school performance ever suffered from the effects of your drug use?	☐	☐
10. Have you ever been arrested as a result of using drugs?	☐	☐
11. Have you ever lied about what or how much you use?	☐	☐
12. Do you put the purchase of drugs ahead of your financial responsibilities?	☐	☐
13. Have you ever tried to stop or control your using?	☐	☐
14. Have you ever been in a jail, hospital, or drug rehabilitation center because of your using?	☐	☐
15. Does using interfere with your sleeping or eating?	☐	☐
16. Does the thought of running out of drugs terrify you?	☐	☐
17. Do you feel it is impossible for you to live without drugs?	☐	☐
18. Do you ever question your own sanity?	☐	☐
19. Is your drug use making life at home unhappy?	☐	☐
20. Have you ever thought you couldn't fit in or have a good time without using drugs?	☐	☐
21. Have you ever felt defensive, guilty, or ashamed about your using?	☐	☐
22. Do you think a lot about drugs?	☐	☐
23. Have you had irrational or indefinable fears?	☐	☐
24. Has using affected your sexual relationships?	☐	☐
25. Have you ever taken drugs you didn't prefer?	☐	☐
26. Have you ever used drugs because of emotional pain or stress?	☐	☐
27. Have you ever overdosed on any drugs?	☐	☐
28. Do you continue to use despite negative consequences?	☐	☐
29. Do you think you might have a drug problem?	☐	☐

Are you an addict? This is a question only you can answer. Members of Narcotics Anonymous found that they all answered different numbers of these questions "yes." The actual number of yes responses isn't as important as how you feel inside and how addiction has affected your life. If you are an addict, you must first admit that you have a problem with drugs before any progress can be made toward recovery.

274

Chapter 8
Drug and Other
Dependencies:
Lifestyles and
Gratifications

● **Figure 4   Peace of mind.** Some benefits of quitting illegal drugs.

" *People who give up illegal drugs cut a lot of unnecessary risk and tension out of their lives. They no longer have to fear getting busted for possession or losing a job because of a positive drug test. They don't have to worry about getting the money for their next fix, rock, or pill, and they don't have to waste energy trying to look clean when they're using. They can stop associating with unsavory characters and quit aligning themselves with a system of greed and violence. Through abstinence they can resign from the rat race and rejoin the human race. Recovery brings them many gifts, not the least of which are the simple peace of sobriety and the welcome renewal of self-respect.* "

—Barbara Yoder (1990). *The recovery resource book.* New York: Fireside, p. 186.

- ***Outpatient treatment:*** Following inpatient treatment, recovering addicts are directed toward various kinds of outpatient treatment programs. Many drug-dependent people may skip the inpatient phase and go directly to an outpatient program. Treatment sometimes includes drug therapies, such as methadone maintenance for recovering heroin addicts.

  Newly abstinent addicts are urged to join Twelve Step programs, which follow the model pioneered by Alcoholics Anonymous. Examples are Narcotics Anonymous, Pills Anonymous, Marijuana Anonymous, Marijuana Addicts Anonymous, Cocaine Anonymous, and Cokenders.

Family Rehabilitation Programs Like alcoholism, drug addiction affects not only the individual but also the people with whom he or she has close relationships. Drug dependency of any kind, therefore, is considered a "family disease." Family therapy helps recovering addicts and their families to learn new ways of communicating with each other. In addition to counseling by trained family therapists, there are self-help organizations dedicated to helping family members of addicts with their problems. These include Families Anonymous, Al-Anon, Nar-Anon, and ToughLove.

Nondrug Forms of Dependence

▶ Define the term *dependence,* and explain when dependency poses a problem.

▶ Present both sides of the debate over whether a process addiction is a true addiction.

▶ Distinguish between substance and process addictions.

▶ Discuss the following dependencies: gambling, spending and debt, work, and codependency in terms of incidence, characteristics, and treatment.

The words "dependence" and "addiction" have become broadly applied to behavior other than drug use in recent years. Indeed, the word "addictive" has been used to characterize our society itself. For instance, psychotherapist Anne Wilson Schaef writes, in *When Society Becomes an Addict,* "the society in which we live is an addictive system. It has all the characteristics and exhibits all the processes of the individual alcoholic or addict."[29] Addictive systems are built on self-centeredness and dishonesty, she says. We live in a society "in which we are expected to cheat on our taxes and get away with as much as we can."[30] The notion that our society is an addictive system can stir up a good deal of debate. Let us consider some of the range of problems that now come under the heading of "addictions."

Can the Definition of "Addiction" Be Expanded?

Some propose that the meaning of *addiction* be expanded to cover two categories: (1) substances, including drugs and food, and (2) processes, including "mood-altering events," such as gambling, spending money, and workaholism. Many health experts disagree that addiction should be broadened beyond drug dependence.

276

*Chapter 8
Drug and Other
Dependencies:
Lifestyles and
Gratifications*

Figure 5 The broader meaning of addiction. In recent years, the meaning of the word "addiction" has been expanded to include far more than alcohol and drugs. However, many professionals do not agree with this widened definition.

"It's possible to become addicted to almost any ingestible substance or mood-altering event: Work. Money. Booze. Pills. Computers. Exercise. Sex. Religion. Sports. Television. Crossword puzzles. Cocaine. Tobacco. Food.

Any repeated use of a substance or event to numb pain or enhance pleasure, to take us out of our senses, away from ourselves, has the potential to become an addiction."

—Barbara Yoder (1990). *The recovery resource book.* New York: Fireside, pp. 2–3.

Dependence **means reliance on or need for something that is physical, psychological, or both.** It may be for food, for another person, for exercise, for cigarettes, or for drugs such as cocaine. However, in recent years the term "addiction" has been given wider meaning. *(See ● Figure 5.)* For instance, Schaef says that an *addiction* **"is any process over which we are powerless.** It takes control of us, causing us to do and think things that are inconsistent with our personal values and leading us to become progressively more compulsive and obsessive."[31] Schaef divides addictions into two major categories—*substance addictions* and *process addictions*:

- *Substance addictions: Substance addictions* **are addictions to mood-altering substances that are usually artificially refined or produced.** According to Schaef, these substances include *drugs*—caffeine, nicotine, alcohol, and more powerful mood-altering chemicals, such as tranquilizers, marijuana, cocaine, and heroin. They also include *food.* (We describe food-related disorders, such as overeating, anorexia, and bulimia, in another chapter.)

- *Process addictions: Process addictions* **consist of any specific series of actions or interactions, or "mood-altering events," on which one becomes extraordinarily dependent.** Some prominent examples include "addictions" to gambling, spending money, and work, which we describe below. Exercise can become an "addiction" (as we discuss in the chapter on physical activity). Sex and love can also become an addiction (as we discuss in the chapter on intimacy and sexuality). Even excessive television watching has been called "addictive." Finally, there is codependency, described as "an addiction to another person's addiction."[32]

Are "process addictions" true addictions? One study found that gambling, for instance, produced a euphoria that was similar to the euphoria produced by psychoactive drugs.[33] Another study found gamblers scored similarly to heroin addicts on an addiction scale.[34] However, other studies report different results. One found that gambling does not seem to involve dependence, as illegal drugs often do.[35] A second concluded that addiction involves physiological processes that do not appear to be present in cases of excessive gambling.[36]

Whatever one may think about these new additions to the category of addiction, they represent dependencies that ultimately limit personal freedom. "Dependencies become problems," write Andrew Weil and Winifred Rosen, "when they take up vast amounts of time, money, and energy; create guilt and anxiety; and control one's life."[37]

In the following sections, we examine four activities that can become "process addictions" or dependencies:

- Gambling
- Spending and debt
- Work
- Codependency

Gambling

Gambling's popularity has surged and is greater among high school and college students than among the general population. Pathological gamblers are unable to resist impulses to gamble, despite the dismal chances of winning, and the disruption that occurs in their lives.

Gambling is a major industry in the United States. Thirty-two states and the District of Columbia have lotteries.[38] Forty-eight of the 50 states allow some form of legal gambling (Hawaii and Utah are the exceptions). Then there is the $20-billion-a-year *illegal* sports-betting market. An estimated $253 billion is legally and illegally wagered in the United States each year ($2.5 billion on the Super Bowl alone).[39]

Compulsive Gamblers Compulsive gambling is a significant problem. Perhaps 3–4% of those who gamble are unable to control their betting and seem especially vulnerable to the hype that surrounds gambling. An additional 10–15% gamble more money than they can afford. However, according to one authority on compulsive gambling, these two groups may account for nearly *half* of all money wagered.[40] In states where gambling is legal 24 hours a day, such as Nevada

and New Jersey, the number of compulsive gamblers jumps to about 2½ times the national rate.[41]

Gambling by high school and college students has surged—and the rates seem to be higher than among the adult population. A study by sociology professor Henry R. Lesieur of New Jersey high school students found that 86% had gambled in the past year. Also, 32% had gambled at least once a week.[42] About 5% of the teenage population had lost control of their gambling activity and had become "pathological" or "compulsive" gamblers. This compares with 2–3% of the adult population. A survey by William C. Phillips of 2000 college students in six states found 87% had gambled, and 25% had gambled weekly. Eleven percent had gambled more than $100 in one day, with amounts ranging to $50,000 in one week.[43] About 5.7% were described as having pathological gambling behavior. That includes repeatedly betting in hopes of a big win to cover losses and continuing to gamble despite inability to pay debts. The study found that several students frequently gambled money set aside for college tuition.[44]

Compulsive gambling has been officially recognized as a psychiatric illness by the American Psychiatric Association since 1980. **Pathological gambling** has been defined, in the *Diagnostic and Statistical Manual of Mental Disorders,* Fourth Edition (DSM-IV), as a chronic and progressive failure to resist impulses to gamble. Gambling continues even though it disrupts or damages family, personal, and vocational pursuits.[45, 46] Originally, gambling was categorized as a disorder of impulse control, like the need to steal or to start fires. Indeed, some experts regard it as purely psychological. As one compulsive gambler put it, "People don't smell dice on your breath or see card marks on your arm."[47] However, researchers led by Alec Roy found pathological gambling to be linked to low levels of certain brain chemicals (byproducts of norepinephrine). These chemicals regulate arousal, thrills, and excitement. It is speculated that the deficit can lead to a need to engage in risky, exciting activities, such as gambling. These activities stimulate the brain to secrete more of these chemical substances.[48, 49]

Compulsive gambling has the hallmarks of an addiction, says psychologist Valerie Lorenz, who directs the National Center for Pathological

278

*Chapter 8
Drug and Other
Dependencies:
Lifestyles and
Gratifications*

Gambling in Baltimore. "It follows the classic course for an addiction: It becomes chronic and progressive, tolerance levels increase, and you lose all regard for the consequences of the habit."[50]

Pathological gamblers generally share certain characteristics:[51]

- ***They are intelligent:*** They often have above-average or superior intelligence.

- ***They are competitive and energetic:*** They are strongly competitive, are industrious workers, have a high energy level, often have outstanding athletic ability, and generally perform well academically.

- ***They seek challenge:*** They thrive on challenges, don't tolerate boredom well, and don't finish tasks they find dull.

- ***They prefer skill games:*** They prefer games of skill, such as those found in casinos (craps, blackjack, sportsbook), rather than games of chance, such as lotteries.

- ***They have had a "big win":*** Compulsive gamblers usually have had a history of a big win that equals or exceeds several months of salary. This establishes in their minds that it could happen again.

- ***They "chase" to recoup losses:*** As losing becomes intolerable, they "chase," or bet more money, to recoup losses. They borrow heavily to cover losses.

- ***They go into debt:*** They borrow until their own resources are exhausted, then turn to bookies and loan sharks for more. Eventually they may turn to writing bad checks, forgery, or embezzlement.

Strategy for Living Are any gamblers, even the non-compulsive ones, getting rich? Not very many. Among the 97 million Americans who wager on state lotteries, for instance, those who win $1 million are only .000008% of those who participate.[52] It is said that the odds of your winning a lottery grand prize are 1 in 5.2 million. You are much more likely to appear on the "Tonight Show" (1 in 490,000) or to be struck by lightning (1 in 600,000).[53] Casino gambling has better odds for gamblers, but the odds are always best for the house.

Yet few players seem to pay attention to the dismal chances of winning. The reason, accord-

ing to Dutch psychologist Willem Wagenaar, is faulty thinking. A trick of memory helps gamblers recall their wins more than their losses, preserving the illusion that their chances are far better than they really are.[54]

Compulsive gamblers may find help through organizations such as Gamblers Anonymous.

Spending and Debt

Compulsive spenders repeatedly engage in impulse buying to find self-assurance, escape anxiety, and achieve excitement. Compulsive spenders often become compulsive debtors who continually borrow money.

Over the last decade, many people have been spending beyond their means. As a result some 30 million Americans have financial troubles, according to the National Foundation for Consumer Credit. Personal bankruptcy increased 10% between 1988 and 1990.[55] Some of this was caused by job loss, illness, divorce, career setbacks, or family problems. However, many financial problems are caused by out-of-control spending.

Compulsive Spenders All of us occasionally make impulsive purchases for reasons that have nothing to do with the specific objects purchased, such as to cheer us up. But ***compulsive spenders,* or compulsive shoppers, repeatedly engage in impulse buying to provide self-assurance and self-worth and to escape anxiety and despair.** One particular hallmark of compulsive spending is making unnecessary purchases, sometimes of luxury items, that end up unused or even hidden away. In this case the *process* of buying is more important than the purchase itself. A shopping expedition that begins with feelings of euphoria and reckless excitement, however, often ends with feelings of self-recrimination and depression.

Not surprisingly, compulsive spenders often become ***compulsive debtors,* who continually borrow money from institutions, family, and friends to pay their bills.** Both compulsive spenders and compulsive debtors follow an "addiction cycle" similar to that of substance abusers. They resort repeatedly to their activity to obtain relief from depression and anxiety. But they develop a craving for the activity, and eventually lose control.

Compulsive spenders are 6% of the population and are at all income levels, according to a 1989 study by Thomas O'Guinn and Ronald Faber. They estimate that about 60% of compulsive spenders are women.[56] Because shopping is used to bolster low feelings of self-worth, the relationship with salespeople who make shopaholics feel good about themselves becomes important.

Some characteristics of compulsive spenders are as follows.[57]

- ***They are very anxious and depressed:*** Many compulsive spenders use shopping to alleviate their depressed feelings. Thus, they may go on shopping binges when their feelings are hurt.

- ***They often buy for other people:*** Because many compulsive shoppers have a desperate need for approval, they often buy things not for themselves but for other people.

- ***They may be "binge buyers," "daily shoppers," or "multiple buyers":*** Compulsive shoppers do not all act the same way, according to O'Guinn and Faber. People who are "binge buyers" may go off on a shopping binge only occasionally, perhaps triggered by an upsetting event. "Daily shoppers" go shopping every day and become upset if they do not. "Multiple buyers," a less common type, repeatedly buy several of the same item (perhaps because they like the sales clerk).

Strategy for Living People who are deeply in debt feel "helpless, angry, and confused," says former debtor Jerrold Mundis. "They become fearful, depressed, even suicidal. They live with a daily sense of impending disaster."[58]

How does one avoid or back away from this state of affairs? The obvious action is to rein in expenses, stay within a budget, and otherwise inject rationality into the shopping process. For example, one can draw up plans for shopping, ask others to do the shopping, or shop only when feeling calm. One can also destroy all credit cards, even those (such as American Express or department-store cards) that are supposed to be paid off in full every month.

For people having difficulty with their finances, there are several resources available, such as Debtors Anonymous.

Work

Workaholism is work addiction. Workaholics would rather work than play, are driven and perfectionistic, and let work interfere with their lives. Ultimately they may suffer from "burnout."

What is considered more socially productive than work? This thought is precisely the reason that so many people have difficulty understanding that work can be a compulsion, another "process addiction." Indeed, many people who work long hours are *not* compulsive workers. They like what they do and they take time out to relax and to be with their families.

Workaholics **Work addicts, or *workaholics*, are people who are self-destructively obsessed with their career and making a living.** How do you tell a work addict from someone who finds fulfillment in his or her work?

Here are some characteristics associated with workaholics:[59, 60]

- ***They would rather work than play:*** Workaholics often work anywhere and anytime. They don't take much time off to play and don't have much of a personal or love life. A great deal of their socializing and interpersonal relationships involves coworkers.

- ***They are driven and perfectionistic:*** Work-addicted people labor extremely hard in part because they have such great self-doubts. They often strive for perfection. As one writer describes it, "Nothing you produce at the office seems good enough, so you compulsively revise and polish each memo, letter, and presentation."[61] Even in their marriages they tend to be perfectionists and regard their spouse and children as extensions of their own egos.[62]

280

Chapter 8
Drug and Other
Dependencies:
Lifestyles and
Gratifications

- ***Their work interferes with their lives:*** Their long hours at the job cause workaholics problems with others. "Your family resents the amount of time you devote to your job and lets you know it. In addition, your coworkers are fed up with your unreasonable demands and expectations."[63] In the end, workaholism leads to such signs of stress as general exhaustion, fitful sleep, and headaches.

Strategy for Living At some point—perhaps after many years—work stops providing the workaholic the rewards it did: avoidance of intimacy, heightened self-esteem, perfection, total control. This is often known as "burnout." When this "hitting bottom" occurs, the work addict is in a position to begin to recover. Recovery is not giving up work completely (since most people need to support themselves) but learning to work less, and for fulfillment.

If you suspect you might be a workaholic, the first thing to do is to determine where your time goes. If you sleep 8 hours a day, that leaves 16 hours a day (112 hours a week) for everything else. Keep a diary of the time you spend preparing for work, commuting, working, unwinding from work, housework, and play or leisure activities. Then ask yourself if you are comfortable with the balance of time between work and play. How much more time would you like to spend with family and friends? What leisure activities would you like to schedule into your week? The principal self-help recovery program is Workaholics Anonymous. Its slogans are "Work smarter, not harder" and "If everything else fails, lower your standards."

Codependency

Codependents are family members or others close to a substance-dependent or process-addicted person who accommodate their lives to the addict.

Codependents were originally considered to be spouses of alcoholics, but the term now applies to others close to an alcoholic family member. **The chief characteristic of *codependents* is that they accommodate themselves to the alcoholic.**

In the last few years, however, the term "codependents" has been extended to people in families troubled by other addictions or compulsions. For example, people close to someone hooked on gambling or workaholism may be called codependent. Some critics complain that codependency is less a psychological disorder than "a business, generating millions of book sales [and] countless support groups. . . ."[64] Some self-proclaimed experts (many of whose credentials are simply those of self-described "recovering codependents") say that 96% of all Americans suffer from codependency. If so, the category may be so broad as to be meaningless. Nevertheless, the idea is useful because it helps us consider how our selves are formed within the fabric of family life and relationships.

People in Families of Addicts Codependency assumes that the *family or relationship* is more important than the *individual* within that family. Alcoholism and other addictions are considered family illnesses because of the tremendous impact that addicts have on those around them. In general, it may be said that codependent family members become concerned with others and neglect themselves; they also learn to not take responsibility for their own lives.

Some of the characteristics associated with codependents are as follows.

- ***They become addicted to the addict:*** People living with a person who is dependent on a mood-altering substance or activity take on a certain way of behaving. They base their self-esteem on what others think of them and organize their lives according to others' expectations of them. They become supporting actors to the major player, the addict. Their urge to help others turns into an obsession with other people, so that they lose their own identity and self-worth.

- ***They become enmeshed in a cycle of pain:*** Codependents assume responsibility for family well-being and attempt to manage the addict's life. Failing to control the addiction, they become obsessed with protecting the family and the addict from intervention or knowledge by outsiders. By "enabling" the addict and sparing him or her the consequences of addiction, they actually allow the cycle of pain to persist.

- **They remain stuck in codependent behavior:** Even after they or the addict leaves the family or relationship, codependents remain locked in a pattern of living their lives through other people. Thus, they may continue to look for other dependent or addicted people to take care of. They continue to deny their feelings of pain.

Strategy for Living Despite criticisms of the codependency notion, it helps many people discover they don't have to live their lives through someone else. They learn that they need to be whole themselves. The goal of any relationship should be *inter*dependency, or mutual dependency. That means a constantly changing task of trying to maintain independence within the confines of the relationship.

It's likely that nothing can change in an addict's family system until the codependent realizes that rescuing the addict isn't helping anyone. Once the codependent stops making excuses and taking on the responsibilities of the addict, the addict will have to face his or her own problem. Some codependents may be able to establish their independence by themselves, but many will need to reach out and get help. The principal self-help Twelve Step group is Co-Dependents Anonymous (CoDA). Other groups, such as Al-Anon, Nar-Anon, and Gam-Anon, are designed for codependents involved with specific types of addicts and addictions.

800-HELP

Alcoholism and Drug Addiction Treatment Center. 800-477-3447. Available 24 hours. Provides phone counseling and local referrals.

National Council on Alcoholism and Drug Dependence Hotline. 800-475-HOPE. Available 24 hours.

The National Council on Self-Help and Public Health. 800-922-9234. Formed under auspices of U.S. Surgeon General's office to foster public awareness of self-help's worth.

National Institute for Drug Abuse. 800-662-HELP. (In Spanish: 800-66-AYUDA.) Available M–F 9 A.M.–3 P.M., Sat.–Sun. noon–3 A.M. Gives counseling over the phone. Refers callers to local support groups and treatment programs.

800/Cocaine Hotline. 800-COCAINE. Available 24 hours.

Suggested Readings

Erich Goode (1989). *Drugs in American society.* New York: McGraw-Hill.

Stanton Peele (1985). *The meaning of addiction.* Lexington, MA: Lexington Books.

Andrew Weil (1973). *The natural mind.* Boston: Houghton Mifflin. Discusses how altered states of consciousness can be achieved without drugs.

Barbara Yoder. (1990). *The recovery resource book.* New York: Fireside/Simon & Schuster. Comprehensive guide to recovery resources for alcohol, drugs, food, compulsive debting, workaholism, gambling, etc.

People Confronting the Drug Sickness

Drugs—and the resistance to drugs, whether legal or illegal—affect people of all social classes, races, and genders. Some examples:

"As Sick as Your Secrets"

Her famous grandfather, novelist Ernest Hemingway, an alcoholic, committed suicide in 1961 by putting a rifle to his head. After two failed marriages and a ski accident that left her in constant pain, model and actress Margaux Hemingway herself became an alcoholic—a secret one who rarely drank at all in public. Eating problems ballooned her up to 200 pounds, and she began to hide and contemplate suicide.

At 35 she left despair for a chance at rebirth—quitting drinking and losing weight. "The thing about getting sober is that you have to live your life with rigorous honesty," she said. "Someone told me you're only as sick as your secrets."[65]

"We're Not Going Away"

Endesha Juakali, 34, went from his New Orleans housing project to college and then to law school. Concerned as drugs claimed a generation and a half of project dwellers, Juakali used a grant from the Housing Authority to create a "drug-free zone" in the project, with fenced off alleys and new sports fields.

While on patrol, Juakali was shot in the leg, but he continued to fight back. "The pushers have decided we're not going away," he said, "so maybe they'd better."[66]

"Daylight Always Comes Back"

At age 15 Rosendo Ruiz tried heroin for the first time. Four years later he was the youngest convict in the federal penitentiary in Fort Worth, Texas. Finally, after nearly three decades of committing burglaries and robberies by the thousands to support his drug habit—and most of that time spent behind bars—he decided he wanted to have choices about things as simple as when to turn out the lights and where to eat dinner. Now in his fifties, Ruiz speaks to prison inmates. He carries a business card that says "drug educator and consultant. Practical experience."

Drugs, he said, were the only reason he ever stole. "You're taking them because there is something lacking in your life," he said. "I needed to learn to deal with pain, with feelings. . . . I told myself, . . . 'I better start dealing with reality, because it always comes back—daylight always comes back.' "[67]

"The Best Part of Life Is the Struggle"

Every day Mimi Silbert, director of Delancey Street, receives letters: "I have watched helplessly as my brother's life slowly drains from his very being . . ." "When not high on drugs, my husband is a caring, loving father . . ."[68]

Silbert is a criminologist who since 1972 has dedicated herself to San Francisco–based Delancey Street, an organization that has received worldwide acclaim for its history of mending even the most broken of lives. Delancey has helped thousands of drug abusers, ex-convicts, and prostitutes to become healthy, productive citizens.

". . . [T]here's tremendous good in being able to get excited that rebuilding is possible," says Silbert. "Once you know it's possible, you can take the risk of starting again. Then the best part of life is the struggle."[69]

Infectious and Noninfectious Illnesses

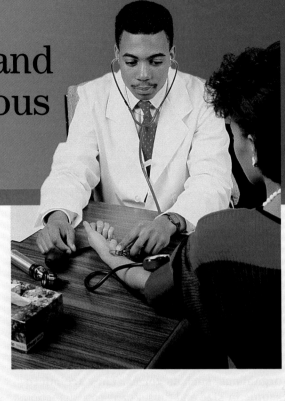

Where do those new diseases come from?

A mere two decades ago, we might have thought medical science was well on its way to controlling the world's dread diseases. Bubonic plague, which had swept medieval Europe, was no longer considered a problem. Syphilis, which had afflicted the Spanish colonizers of the New World, seemed to be behind us. Yellow fever, once a killer in American port cities, had disappeared. Tuberculosis, which had affected many Eskimos, and smallpox, which had wiped out many Native Americans, seemed to have been overcome.

Then *new* diseases began to appear: Lyme disease (first recognized in 1975), AIDS (1982), chronic fatigue syndrome (1984). There has also been a comeback among old diseases: tuberculosis, measles, influenza, syphillis, gonorrhea, and others.

Still, we in North America are fortunate to live in a time and place in which *taking care of and taking responsibility for oneself* will help avoid many infectious diseases. This chapter provides important information about diseases, boosting your body's defenses, and seeking treatment if you need it.

The Immune System and Infectious Diseases

▶ Explain the causes of infection, the pathogens, and discuss each of the six types of pathogens.

▶ Describe the process of infection—the transmission and four stages of infection.

▶ Discuss the defenses against infection—physical, chemical, and cellular, including the immune system and response.

▶ Compare and contrast the following types of infections: the common cold, flu, mononucleosis, chronic fatigue syndrome, hepatitis, staph infections, strep infections, pneumonia, tuberculosis, and Lyme disease.

▶ Explain the principal types of immunizations for children and for adults.

Many factors contribute to disease and associated illness. Some of them you can do nothing about, such as heredity, aging, or certain environmental pollutants outside your control. Some of them you probably can do something about, such as drug use and lifestyle. Some factors you have limited control over; these are *microorganisms* or *microbes—* **organisms, such as germs. They are microscopic in size** and thus escape easy detection. Avoiding some of the diseases transmitted by microorganisms may take a bit of luck. On the other hand, good luck is frequently brought about by design—by thoughtful planning.

The forms of illness transmitted by microbes may be thought of as a battle between invaders and defenders of your body. There are three important factors that influence one's vulnerability and ability to cope with communicable diseases:

- *The causes of infection:* The invaders are called *pathogens,* **microorganisms that have gained entry to the body and that cause disease.** The ability of particular pathogens to cause disease depends on their type, number, and *virulence—***the pathogen's power to overcome the body's defenses.**

- *The process of infection:* **Disease caused by a pathogen is called an** *infection.* **The infection proceeds through four steps,** as we will describe.

- *The protection against infection:* The body protects itself against infection, using physical, chemical, and cellular forms of defenses. One important protector is the *immune system,* **a system of cellular elements that protect the body from invading pathogens and foreign materials.**

Causes of Infection: Pathogens

Six kinds of harmful microorganisms, or pathogens, are viruses, bacteria, rickettsia, fungi, protozoa, and parasitic worms. Viruses are the smallest yet toughest, are commonplace (including the common cold), and vary in seriousness, means of transmission, and incubation periods. Drug treatment for viruses is limited. Bacteria are single-celled organisms that cause a variety of diseases such as pneumonia and tuberculosis and may be treated with antibiotics. Rickettsia grow inside living cells. Fungi consist of yeasts and molds. Protozoa are responsible for many tropical diseases, such as malaria. Parasitic worms cause problems by residing in the intestines.

Many of the microorganisms that surround us are beneficial, such as the bacteria in our intestines, which help in digestion. Here, however, we consider the types of microorganisms that are harmful—namely, pathogens. There are six kinds of pathogens, ranging in size from smallest to largest: *viruses, bacteria, rickettsia, fungi, protozoa, parasitic worms. (See* ● *Figure 1.)*

Viruses: The Smallest and Toughest
Viruses **may be the smallest of the pathogens, being visible only under an electron microscope. However, they are also the toughest to fight** because most drugs that will kill a virus also kill the diseased cell. In addition, viruses withstand heat, formaldehyde, and radiation.

A virus is such a primitive form of life that it cannot exist on its own. A virus is simply a protein structure containing the nucleic acids DNA

Viruses: Smallest pathogens
Typical diseases: Colds, influenza, herpes, rubella, mononucleosis, hepatitis, mumps, chicken pox, HIV

Bacteria: One-celled pathogens
Typical diseases: Strep throat, tetanus, bacterial pneumonia, Lyme disease, tuberculosis, scarlet fever, gonorrhea

Fungi: Plant-like pathogens
Typical diseases: Athlete's foot, candidiasis, ringworm

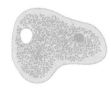

Protozoa: Simplest animal form
Typical diseases: amebic dysentery, giardia, malaria

Rickettsia: Virus-like microbes
Typical diseases: Typhus fever, Rocky Mountain spotted fever

Parasitic worms: Many-celled
Typical diseases: Pinworm, elephantiasis

● **Figure 1   Pathogens.** Examples of each of the six types of pathogens are shown.

or RNA. To survive and reproduce, it must attach itself to a cell and inject its own DNA or RNA. This tricks the cell's reproductive functions into producing new viruses. These new viruses expand the cell until it bursts, setting the viruses free to seek other cells to take over.

Common characteristics of viruses that are important to know are the following:

- *Viruses are common:* There are many viruses—200 for the common cold alone—making them the most common form of contagious disease. ***Contagious* means a disease is "catching"—it is easily transmitted from one person (carrier) to another**.

- *Viruses can vary in seriousness:* The differences in seriousness depend on which cells the viruses attack. For example, cold viruses attack respiratory cells, which can be replaced. However, the polio virus attacks nerve cells, which cannot be replaced, resulting in paralysis.

- *Viruses are transmitted in different ways:* Some highly contagious viruses, such as colds, are transmitted in the air, as when cold sufferers sneeze or cough. Hepatitis A is transmitted by water contaminated by sewage or other fecal-oral routes, as when infected food handlers don't wash their hands. HIV is transmitted through anal, vaginal, or oral sex with an infected partner or through sharing drug needles. HIV can also be passed by an infected pregnant woman to her fetus.

- *Viruses have varying incubation periods:* An *incubation period* is the time lapse between exposure to an organism and the development of symptoms. Cold viruses have short incubation periods, taking perhaps only 24 hours and lasting only 4–5 days. The flu, on the other hand, may develop after 4 days and last about 2 weeks. AIDS may not appear for 10–11 years after infection by HIV and may last 2 or more years.

- ***Drug treatment for viruses is limited:*** Viruses are hard to reproduce in laboratories, which makes antiviral drug development difficult. Drugs may block the reproduction of some viruses. For other viruses, drugs may control symptoms but not cure the problem.

  A natural protection against some viruses is *interferon*, a protein substance produced by our bodies. It helps protect healthy cells in their battle with invaders.

Bacteria: The Most Plentiful Next larger in size to viruses are bacteria. ***Bacteria* are single-celled organisms, visible through a standard microscope, and are the most plentiful of the pathogens. Unlike viruses, many bacteria do not enter cells but thrive on and around the cells.** Some bacteria are actually helpful, such as those in the digestive tract (*Escherichia coli*). About 100 of the several thousand species of bacteria actually cause disease in people.

The characteristics of bacteria include the following:

- ***Bacteria can cause a variety of diseases:*** Three types of bacteria are spirilla, cocci, and bacilli. Among the bacterial infections they cause are streptococcal (strep) infections (including strep throat), staphylococcal infections, pneumonia, tuberculosis, scarlet fever, and gonorrhea.

- ***Bacteria can be transmitted in a variety of ways:*** Some bacteria are transmitted through consumption of contaminated water or food. A type of bacteria called *chlamydia* (discussed later in this chapter) is largely transmitted by sexual intercourse.

- ***Bacteria can harm the body in several ways:*** Many bacteria release ***toxins*, poisonous substances,** that cause diseases such as tetanus, diphtheria, or even the traveler's diarrhea sometimes called "Montezuma's revenge."

  Within the body, some bacteria work locally, killing cells near the source of infection. The infection then spreads to other tissue, producing boils, abscesses, and soreness. Other bacteria spread via the bloodstream, causing fever or attacking organs.

Some bacteria simply grow until they obstruct vital organs, as in pneumonia.

- ***Antibiotics fight specific bacteria: Antibiotics* are bacteria-killing drugs.** One of the most well known antibiotics is ***penicillin*, a substance produced from a fungus.** (Other antibiotics you may recognize are such drugs as erythromycin, tetracycline, streptomycin, gentamicin, and the cephalosporins.)

  Specific antibiotics work on specific bacteria. A certain antibiotic, therefore, cannot be used to treat all bacterial infections. Moreover, an antibiotic is never appropriate for treating viral infections. In addition, antibiotics have to be taken properly in order to be effective. *(See ● Figure 2.)*

- ***Some bacteria may be drug-resistant:*** Because of inappropriate use and overuse of antibiotics, some antibiotic-resistant strains of bacteria have developed. Worse, some strains of bacteria—for instance, some forms of tuberculosis—have transformed into "superbugs" highly resistant or even invulnerable to antibiotics.[1–3]

Rickettsia Resembling bacteria but more complex than viruses, ***rickettsia* are disease-causing microorganisms that grow inside living cells. These organisms are generally transmitted by insects such as mites, ticks, and fleas.** Rickettsia may cause rashes and fever, such as ***typhus fever*, a disease characterized by high, disabling fever.** Infected ticks transmit ***Rocky Mountain spotted fever*, a disease marked by chills, fever, prostration, and pain in muscles and joints.**

Fungi: Yeasts, Molds, and the Like ***Fungi* are single-celled organisms (like yeasts) or multicelled organisms (like molds). Some fungi cause diseases on the skin, mucous membranes, and in the lungs. Two such diseases are *athlete's foot* and *jock itch*, with itching, burning, and scaling of the feet and of the scrotal skin. Both are caused by a fungus** that thrives in moist environments, such as locker-room shower floors. Another kind of fungal disorder is ***candidiasis*, a yeast infection of the vagina.** Treatment is with antifungal medications.

Protozoa: The Smallest Animals The smallest animals in existence are ***protozoa,*** **single-celled organisms responsible for many tropical diseases.** One example is among the most serious and widely spread tropical diseases, killing up to 2 million people a year. That is ***malaria,*** **the severe, recurrent disease borne by mosquitos.**[4,5] Another is ***African sleeping sickness,*** **a recurring disease whose chief characteristic is weariness and listlessness.** ***Amoebic dysentery*** **is a protozoan infection of the intestines.** If you hike or camp in North America, be aware that drinking unpurified water—even from mountain streams—may produce the protozoan called ***giardiasis.*** **Symptoms are diarrhea, abdominal cramps, and fatigue.**

Parasitic Worms ***Parasitic worms*** **may be microscopic in size or may range up to 10 feet long.** Intestinal parasites, such as the tapeworm, may be contracted by eating undercooked beef or pork. Some of these parasites are more of a problem in developing countries than in North America. However, pinworm is the most common worm infection in the United States.

The Process of Infection

Infectious diseases are transmitted in three ways: via people, via food and water (salmonella, botulism, trichinosis, cholera), or via animals and insects (encephalitis). Infection occurs in four phases: incubation, prodromal, peak, and recovery.

We move among trillions of exotic viruses, bacteria, fungal spores, and other unseen microorganisms. How shall we avoid the harmful microbes and ignore the others?

Transmission Infectious diseases are transmitted in three ways—by people, by food or water, and by animals and insects.

- ***People to people:*** Most of us need human contact, but we can also try to avoid disease from that contact. Disease organisms are transmitted by coughing, sneezing, touching, kissing, and sexual contact. You can't always avoid people coughing or sneezing in

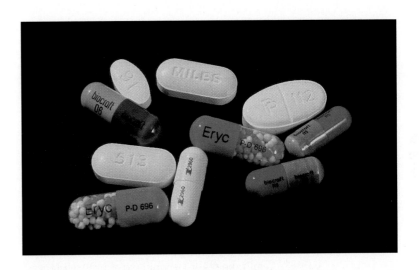

● **Figure 2   Using antibiotics right.** The safest way to use antibiotics is to take them only when you need them and to use them properly.

Some advice on using antibiotics:

1. **Take the drug *exactly* as prescribed.** Many antibiotics are prescribed for 7 days or more, and you should not stop taking them sooner even if you feel better sooner. Bacteria may be launching another attack, and if you're not taking the antibiotic, you may have a relapse. This not only means that you'll have to start over again but that you're increasing the chances the bacteria will become drug-resistant.
2. **Watch for a decline in symptoms.** You will probably know an antibiotic is working within a day or two by experiencing fewer symptoms. If they aren't disappearing, you may need to contact your health professional about changing medication. You could be fighting a resistant strain of bacteria.
3. **Never use someone else's prescription.** That person's antibiotic may not be the appropriate treatment for your problem. Moreover, some people have strong allergic reactions to some antibiotics.
4. **Throw out year-old prescriptions.** Old antibiotics have probably lost strength and are no longer effective.

your presence and it's considered unfriendly if you don't shake hands. Still, you can wash your hands after going to the bathroom and before handling food. Also, avoid sharing toothbrushes, and make sure eating utensils are clean.

Use judgment about kissing someone who seems to have cold symptoms or cold sores. Ask a prospective sexual partner about any problems they may have in the genital area—any blister or lesion, for example. Try to get a sense of his or her sexual history. Take precautions, including using condoms, with all sexual partners. Finally, as we describe in the discussion of HIV, you can take steps to avoid exposure to infected blood.

- *Food- and water-borne organisms:* Spoiled or incorrectly prepared or processed food can transmit diseases, especially bacteria. Three in particular are worth mentioning—*salmonella* infections, botulism, and trichinosis. Two examples of water-borne diseases are cholera and typhoid fever.

    (1) *Salmonella* **is a leading agent in bacterial food-borne diseases and is found throughout the environment.** Salmonella bacteria are found in about a third of the poultry in the United States and appear in some eggs as well. If food is not properly handled, cooked, or refrigerated, the *Salmonella* can produce *gastroenteritis (food poisoning).* **The results are nausea, vomiting, diarrhea, fever, and abdominal cramps lasting 1–3 days.** Gastroenteritis may occur, for example, if eggs are consumed raw or undercooked.

    (2) *Botulism* **is a food-related disease produced by a bacterium (Clostridium) that grows in improperly canned foods.** Home-canned vegetables and fruits sometimes cause botulism. Without treatment, botulism can produce paralysis and even death.

    (3) *Trichinosis,* **a disease caused by an intestinal worm, is transmitted as a result of eating raw or under-cooked meat,** especially pork. However, trichinosis is unusual in commercially processed meats. It produces diarrhea, nausea, fever, and later stiffness, pain, sweating, and insomnia.

    (4) *Cholera* **is an example of a water-borne disease transmitted by contaminated drinking water or in food washed with such water.** The disease causes severe diarrhea and vomiting, draining the body of vital fluids and often causing rapid death if treatment is not available.

- *Animal- and insect-borne diseases:* You can catch some diseases from animals. Dogs and cats, for example, may carry rabies. Houseflies may spread dysentery, which is why food should be kept covered. Some types of mosquitos may carry *encephalitis,* **such as** *eastern equine encephalitis (EEE).* **This is a relatively rare but usually fatal virus that attacks the brain, causing it to swell.**[6]

The Four Periods of Infection After a disease is transmitted, whether by people, water, food, animals, or insects, it then goes through four periods of infection. These are incubation, prodromal, peak, and recovery:

- *Incubation period—the beginning of the battle:* The period between the time a pathogen is transmitted to you and the time you actually notice its symptoms is the *incubation period.* For some diseases (the common cold, for example) this may be mere hours, for others (HIV) it may be years. For most illnesses, this is not a particularly contagious stage, although infection of others is possible.

- *Prodromal period—the invaders build their strength:* In the short second stage, or *prodromal period,* you begin to show vague, nonspecific signs and symptoms of a problem. With a cold, for instance, you may experience coughing, sneezing, and watery eyes. During this time, you are apt to be most contagious, capable of infecting other people.

- *Peak period—the battle is at its height:*
Also called the *acute period,* the *peak period* is when the illness is full-blown, reaching its highest point of development—and unpleasantness. All the symptoms and signs of the disease are now present in full force. You may continue to be infectious, likely to transmit the illness to others. At this point, your body is using all its available defense mechanisms.

- *Recovery period—the invaders are beaten back:* In the *recovery,* or *convalescent, period* your body (and any disease-fighting drugs) has triumphed over the invader. The pathogen is killed or reduced in power, and the signs and symptoms of the disease disappear. Until the time when all signs and symptoms have vanished, you are still somewhat contagious, but transmission is not as likely. With some infections (such as syphilis), the symptoms may disappear by themselves, but that doesn't mean the pathogen has gone away.

Defenses Against Infection

The body's three lines of defense against disease are physical, chemical, and cellular. The cellular defenses constitute the immune system that protects against pathogens and foreign materials. Two systems of immunity are cell-mediated (T-cells) and humoral (B-cells). Humoral immunity provides antibodies against specific invaders. Immunity is acquired naturally, artificially (vaccinations), and passively. Repelling the invasion of disease is known as the immune response. It is carried out by phagocytes, helper T-cells and killer T-cells, B-cells and antibodies, memory cells and suppressor T-cells. When the body overreacts to disease, the result is an allergy. When the body attacks itself, it produces autoimmune disorders, such as rheumatoid arthritis.

Consider hair in the nose: Is it just some relic of our furry ancestors or is it truly useful?

Actually, it is quite useful, it turns out. Nose hairs trap inhaled dust and other debris, preventing some of it from moving on into the nasal passages. Inside the nose and respiratory passages, tiny hairlike *cilia* sweep the foreign matter you breathe in, trapping it in *mucus* (thick secretions). When the debris is moved to the back of the throat, it is coughed out or swallowed and eliminated.

The Body's Defenses The body has three lines of defenses—physical, chemical, and cellular (the immune system)—against disease. *(See ● Figure 3.)*

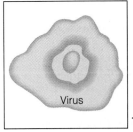

	First line of defense: physical barriers	**Second line of defense: chemical barriers**	**Third line of defense: cellular barriers**
Virus	Skin	Stomach acids and enzymes	Cell-mediated immunity
	Hair and cilia	GI tract acids and enzymes	Humoral immunity
Invading pathogen	Sweat, tears, and saliva	Sweat, tears, and saliva	
	Mucous membranes	Mucous membranes	
	Ear wax	Vaginal enzymes	
	Spleen and liver		
	Lymph nodes		

● **Figure 3**   **The body's three lines of defense against disease.**

- ***The first line—physical barriers:*** The first line of deterrence consists of *physical defenses,* which are primarily physical rather than chemical or cellular. These physical barriers are *external* and *internal.*

    Examples of external physical defenses are nasal hairs and cilia that filter the air. Another is the skin, which (when not broken) keeps out pathogens. Sweat, tears, and saliva wash away bacteria. The mucous membranes of the respiratory and gastrointestinal tracts trap invaders, as does the wax in the ears.

    Internal defenses include the spleen and the liver, organs that filter and purify the blood and eliminate dangerous substances. **The *lymph nodes* are small pea-sized glands in the neck, underarms, and groin that filter out and destroy harmful debris.** *(See ● Figure 4.)*

- ***The second line—chemical barriers:*** The second line of defense consists of *chemical barriers.* These include digestive enzymes and acids in the stomach and upper gastrointestinal tract. Sweat, tears, and saliva contain substances that repel or destroy bacteria. Vaginal enzymes also make life inhospitable for some microorganisms.

- ***The third line—cellular barriers, the immune system:*** The third line of defense consists of *cellular barriers.* This is called the ***immune system,*** **the internal system of cellular elements that protect the body from pathogens and foreign materials.**

Two Systems of Immunity: Cell-Mediated and Humoral When invaders slip by the physical and chemical barriers, the immune system—the cellular defense system—goes to work. The immune system actually consists of two groups of cells (called *lymphocytes*), which work in cooperation with each other to provide two kinds of immunity against invaders:

- ***T-cells—cell-mediated immunity:*** One group of cells are called *T-cells* because they originate in the thymus gland. *(Refer back to Figure 4.)* These cells provide T-cell–mediated immunity, or simply ***cell-mediated immunity.*** **The thousands of**

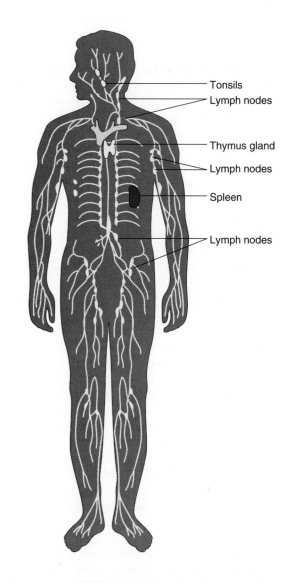

● **Figure 4   The defense effort.** Location of lymph nodes, the thymus gland, tonsils, and spleen, which are important in resisting disease organisms.

T-cells in cell-mediated immunity mainly protect the body against cancer cells, fungi, parasites, and foreign cells.

- ***B-cells—humoral immunity:*** The other group of cells are called *B-cells* because they originate in the bone marrow. They provide **humoral immunity, which is mainly effective in protecting against infections caused by viruses and by bacteria.**

Humoral immunity provides ***antibodies,*** **specific chemical compounds made by the B-cells that destroy specific kinds of invaders.** These invaders—toxins, foreign substances, and microorganisms—are called antigens. **An *antigen* is any foreign matter that enters the body and causes it to form antibodies.** Moreover, *once your body produces antibodies, you're protected against that particular antigen for life.* This is important to understand because it is the principle on which vaccines (for example, against polio) operate.

An example of how antigens and antibodies work is seen in the case of German measles, or rubella. Many colleges require students to show proof that they have had rubella or been inoculated against it before they can enroll. What they want to know is whether students have built up or acquired *antibodies* against the *antigen* of rubella, to protect them from infection.

Let us see how the body acquires an immunity to an infectious disease such as rubella.

Three Ways of Obtaining Acquired Immunity The two cellular systems of immunity—cell-mediated and humoral—are in place when we are born. However, they will not actually work against specific disease threats until they encounter antigens representing that disease. Once this encounter has happened, the immune system is "armed and ready," able to fight if that antigen appears again. That is, the body now has **acquired immunity; it has formed antibodies and specialized blood cells that can destroy the specific pathogen.**

This protection of acquired immunity can come about in three ways:

- **By exposure to the disease: *Naturally acquired immunity* means that you were exposed to the disease naturally.** For example, a family member had rubella and transmitted the rubella virus to you. Your body fought the infection, thereby developing antibodies that will protect you against being infected ever again.

- **By receiving a vaccination: *Artificially acquired immunity* means that you developed antibodies as a result of having pathogens introduced artificially into your body—by being vaccinated. In a** *vaccination*—also known as an *immunization* or inoculation—one receives (by injection or sometimes orally) **organisms that were prepared in a laboratory. The purpose is to build antibodies against a particular disease.** The organisms may be dead or alive. Either way, they constitute only a mild case of the disease against which they are supposed to build antibodies.

- **By receiving antibodies from outside the body: *Passively acquired immunity* means that you acquired antibodies from outside your body**—for example, microorganisms gamma globulin from animal sources or other people. In other words, you didn't develop the antibodies within your own body; you got them from somewhere else. Gamma globulin is administered as a preventative for hepatitis (although it is not completely effective).

Note that antibodies are specific: each antibody can deactivate only one type of antigen. A polio antibody, for example, won't work against a measles antigen.

The Immune Response: Repelling the Invasion Assuming your immune system is armed and ready, what happens when the invaders invade? First the antigens—whether microorganisms, foreign substances, or abnormal cells—have to penetrate physical and chemical defenses. Once they are inside the body, the cellular defense goes into operation, as follows.[7]

- ***"Eating cells" first:*** Front-line defenders consist of specialized white blood cells called phagocytes, from the Greek for "eating cells." ***Phagocyctes* are specialized white blood cells that confront the enemy and attempt to engulf and digest them.** These eating cells are of two types: ***granulocytes* roam the bloodstream, and *macrophages,* large white blood cells, line the blood vessels.**

- ***Helper T-cells and killer T-cells:*** On encountering the foreign organism, the macrophages summon helper T-cells to the scene. ***Helper T-cells*—part of cell-mediated immunity—identify the intruders.** The helper T-cells then call in ***killer T-cells*—also a part of cell-mediated immunity—to destroy the antigen.**

- ***B-cells and antibodies:*** In addition, the helper T-cells notify the *B-cells* (a component of humoral immunity). The B-cells are transformed into producers of *antibodies* capable of destroying the specific intruder.

- ***Memory cells and suppressor T-cells:*** Finally, two other cells also become activated. **Memory cells "remember" the specific attacking microbes and enable the body to respond more quickly against the antigen in subsequent infections.** In other words, they give your body acquired immunity. **Suppressor T-cells reduce or suppress the B-cells' production of antibodies once it is apparent that the battle against infection is being won.**

How can you tell these great struggles are going on inside you? Sometimes you may develop signs and symptoms such as a slight fever. Sometimes you develop inflammation in a specific place. **An *inflammation* is a buildup of cells and fluid, causing blood vessels to expand and making a site red and swollen.** Sometimes, as the body struggles with the invader in a specific location, it will form an ***abscess,* a cavity filled with pus. Pus is made up of white blood cells, fluid, and dead white blood cells.**

Sometimes our body's defense systems don't work the way they should to combat invading substances. When the immune system underreacts, it leads to *infection:* the invaders win, as when cancer overwhelms the body. At other times, **in *immune disorders,* the immune system overreacts or the body even attacks itself.** We consider these next.

Allergies: When the Body Overreacts Lots of people have allergies—41 million Americans get hay fever alone.[8] **An *allergy* is a hypersensitivity to a particular substance or environmental condition.** What happens is that the immune system overreacts to the stimulus, producing antibodies that attack it. The results are runny nose, watery eyes, itching, swelling, redness, rashes, and wheezing—or even worse.

The **sources of allergies, called *allergens,*** can be almost anything: dust, molds, plants, animals, insects, foods, medicines, chemicals, perfumes, and cigarette smoke. ***Pollen, a***

natural, powdery substance produced by trees and grass, is a common allergen. Some people are allergic to things most of us would not suspect, such as tap water or paper money.

Common allergic reactions take several forms, ranging from mild to life-threatening:

- ***Hay fever: Hay fever* is an allergic reaction not just to hay but to pollens and other allergens. It produces runny nose and eyes,** itching, sneezing, and loss of appetite.

- ***Hives: Hives,* a reaction to insect bites, drugs, chemicals, and certain foods, is characterized by raised, itchy red blotches** on the skin.

- ***Asthma: Asthma* is a chronic affliction of the airways in the lungs marked by chest constriction, labored breathing, wheezing, gasping, and coughing.** It affects 15 million Americans.[9]

- ***Anaphylaxis:*** In the worst cases, people get near-fatal and even fatal allergic reactions called ***anaphylaxis,* or *anaphylactic shock.* The air passages become constricted, causing difficulty breathing; the blood vessels expand, causing the blood pressure to drop; and the victim faints**. Without medical treatment, anaphylaxis can be fatal.[10]

Autoimmune Disorders: When the Body Attacks Itself Some of the most difficult disorders are ***autoimmune disorders.* These come about because the immune system fails to recognize its own tissue and attacks itself, causing progressive degeneration.** Three examples are:

- ***Rheumatoid arthritis: Rheumatoid arthritis* is a chronic, crippling form of arthritis (of which there are more than 100 varieties) that inflames small joints.** It often affects the joints of the fingers and wrists but can also attack the organs and connective tissues.[11]

- ***Multiple sclerosis: Multiple sclerosis* is a condition in which it is suspected that cells in the immune system turn against the body and attack the brain and spinal cord.** It leads to progressive, irreversible paralysis and death.[12]

- *Myasthenia gravis: Myasthenia gravis,* **an autoimmune disorder common in women ages 20–40, consists of a weakening of the muscles.** Vision and respiratory problems may occur, and even combing one's hair becomes difficult.[13]

These diseases, although they may progressively worsen, may be treated with drugs that suppress the immune system.

Let us now turn to some of the most common infectious diseases.

The Common Cold

The common cold, an infection of the lining of the upper respiratory tract, is caused by any of 200 viruses. It is transmitted by people contact. Treatment is with time, decongestants, expectorants, and cough suppressants, depending on the symptoms.

The common cold may be "common," but that does not mean that it is simple. A cold can be caused by not just one but any of 200 or so different viruses.

Prevention **The *common cold* is an infection of the membrane lining the upper respiratory tract: nose, sinuses, and throat.** The symptoms, as all of us know, are runny nose, watery eyes, general aches and pains, and sometimes a slight fever. Later symptoms might include a stuffy nose, sore throat, and coughing.

Whatever you hear about staying out of drafts or avoiding getting your hair wet, these are not ways you catch a cold. Frequent temperature changes also make no difference.[14] If college students are particularly apt to get colds, it is because they share classrooms and living spaces with many other people.

Colds are rarely spread through the air; most are hand-delivered. You could avoid shaking hands with people, but can you avoid touching doorknobs and telephones, some of which may be virus-contaminated? Washing your hands often and keeping your unwashed fingers away from your eyes and nose may help. So will using tissues rather than handkerchiefs, since cold viruses don't survive as long on tissues.[15]

High levels of stress may double your chances of getting a cold.[16] Stress impairs some of the body's defenses, such as the production of interferon, a natural antiviral agent, in the nasal passages.

Treatment Actually, you don't "treat" a cold so much as manage it, since there is no cure. Recommended cold management includes staying home, resting, and eating moderately (your sense of taste will be diminished). Drink plenty of fluids such as water and juices. Steam inhalation seems to have no beneficial effects.[17]

Since there are more than 800 over-the-counter cold remedies, which should you use? Here are some thoughts:

- *Avoid aspirin and acetaminophen:* The common painkillers aspirin and acetaminophen (Tylenol) may help any headache and muscle pain you might have. But they may also suppress the body's immune system, slowing down the production of antibodies against infection.[18] These drugs are just pain medications, but colds aren't usually painful, just uncomfortable. (Some cold medications include these painkillers.) Children and teenagers especially should avoid aspirin because of a possible link with a rare but potentially fatal illness called *Reye's syndrome.* This disorder is characterized by fever, vomiting, and swelling of the kidneys and brain.

- *Use decongestants with care:* **Decongestants are drugs that suppress mucus production by constricting the blood vessels in the nose.** Spray decongestants are considered the most effective, but they should be used sparingly. Overuse sometimes leads to *rebound congestion—excessive congestion that can worsen the problem.* (Oral decongestants can restrict blood vessels throughout the body, causing mouth dryness and other side effects in some people.)

- *Expectorants: Expectorants* **are supposed to stimulate coughing so that mucus in the chest will be loosened and can be coughed up.**

- *Use cough suppressants for dry coughs: Cough suppressants* act on the

brain's cough reflex to suppress the cough. Coughing is important for clearing phlegm from the throat and chest, so cough suppressants should be used only for a dry cough. A *dry cough* is marked by the absence or scantiness of secretions.

In recent years, many of these products have been combined into multipurpose or "shotgun" cough remedies. These remedies often contain antihistamines—useful for hay fever and similar allergies but not for the common cold—and decongestants. Some also have pain relievers, such as aspirin or acetaminophen. Cold experts consider these combinations irrational because people differ greatly in their cold symptoms. Most effective are single-ingredient drugs because you can target just the symptoms you have. Why take more medication than is really needed? Whatever course you take—even if you do nothing—the symptoms will subside after a few days.

In 1970, Nobel Prize-winning chemist Linus Pauling suggested that high doses of vitamin C would help prevent colds or diminish cold symptoms.[19] Studies have failed to support this, but the enormous sales of vitamin C supplements show that many people believe the idea anyway.[20]

The Flu: More Serious Than It Seems

Influenza, or the flu, is caused by three contagious viruses. Influenza is quite serious and has caused worldwide epidemics (pandemics) killing millions of people. Flu viruses are airborne, transmitted by sneezing and coughing. Inoculation with flu shots may help prevent infections.

The "flu" is the name most people give to influenza. Influenza is different from a cold, although distinguishing the two isn't always easy. Like the common cold, **influenza is caused by contagious viruses. There are only three principal strains (strains A, B, and C, within which are several subtypes).** However, people don't die directly from a cold as they do from flu. Flu and resulting complications kill an average of 10,000 Americans in a mild year, up to 70,000 in a severe one.[21] Indeed, the most common misconception about the flu is that it is not serious.[22] Yet it has caused some of the worst *pandemics*—**the word experts use for an epidemic that rages across national boundaries.** Flu pandemics occur every 10–12 years and minor regional epidemics every 2–3 years.[23]

Distinguishing Flu from Colds Unlike cold viruses that are not thought to be airborne, flu viruses can be airborne for up to 2 hours. They are transmitted by sneezing and coughing, can be airborne for up to 2 hours. This ability to be transmitted by air droplets makes them extraordinarily contagious. In general, influenza is much more uncomfortable than a cold. Most colds produce only slight aches and pains and do not often cause fevers or headaches. The flu, on the other hand, produces all these symptoms (with fevers up to 104°F). In addition, chest discomfort can be severe. If the condition advances to become bronchitis or pneumonia, it can be life-threatening.

Prevention Most health officials recommend annual influenza immunization for older adults and anyone with a chronic medical problem. The vaccines used consist of viruses that have been grown in laboratories and then killed. When injected into the body, the vaccine stimulates the production of antibodies that will fight an invading flu virus. The antibodies reduce the likelihood of infection and the severity of disease if an infection occurs. The vaccine is effective in 70–90% of people under the age of 65 and about half the people over age 65.[24,25]

Winter is usually flu season. People are advised to get their flu shots in the fall because the body needs a couple weeks to develop the virus-fighting antibodies.[26] Mid-October through mid-November are best for shots.[27] However, even an inoculation in February may lessen the severity of the virus, although it may not prevent infection.

Treatment If you already have the flu, a physician might prescribe the antiviral drug *amantadine*. This drug can be 70–90% effective in reducing flu symptoms—provided it is started within 48 hours after symptoms begin. Otherwise, treatment is similar to that used for a cold: bed rest and fluids. As with colds, children and teenagers should *not* take aspirin, which may cause Reye's syndrome.

Mononucleosis: The "Kissing Disease"

Mononucleosis is a common infectious disease that afflicts people ages 15–24 and can bring long periods of low energy. Treatment involves rest.

Sometimes called the "kissing disease" and frequently called just "mono," **mononucleosis is a common infectious viral disease among college students and other young people 15–24 years old. Initially, mononucleosis is experienced as a fever, headache, sore throat, chills, nausea, and prolonged tiredness or weakness. Later the lymph nodes may become enlarged, body rashes and joint aches develop, and there may be kidney, liver, and spleen complications.**

Mono is usually caused by the *Epstein-Barr virus (EBV)*, which is present in over 90% of American adults, though usually in latent form. Mono is diagnosed by means of a blood test. Although known as "the kissing disease," mononucleosis is not thought to be highly contagious, although kissing is always a possible transmission mode.

Treatment is much the same as for colds and the flu but principally involves extended rest. Alcohol should be avoided because it may increase the risk of liver complications.[28] A physician's advice should be sought. Returning to normal activity prematurely can bring about relapse.

Chronic Fatigue Syndrome: The Mysterious Disease of Exhaustion

Chronic fatigue syndrome is a disease of mysterious origins, perhaps a virus. Its principal effect is profound exhaustion, sometimes lasting for years. Various kinds of treatments are still being developed.

***Chronic fatigue syndrome (CFS)* starts out resembling mononucleosis, with patients reporting the same flulike symptoms. These include sore throat, tender lymph nodes, fever, chills, headaches, joint pain, and prolonged, debilitating fatigue and depression. However, the symptoms linger from 6 months to several years.**[29,30]

The cause of CFS has still not been identified. However, research suggests the debilitating disease could be linked to an immune system disorder that causes inflammation of the central nervous system.[31] Researchers also have found evidence of a virus among CFS sufferers, but it is not clear whether it causes the syndrome. It is possible that each case may arise from a mix of causes—viruses, immune abnormalities, genetic predisposition, and psychological makeup.

In general, doctors prescribe stress reduction, getting plenty of sleep, eating a balanced diet, and light exercise while avoiding overexertion. Antidepressants have been tried.

Hepatitis: Five Diseases of the Liver

Hepatitis is a name given to five virally caused inflammations of the liver, all of which have similar symptoms. Hepatitis A is spread by fecal contamination of food and water and sometimes oral-anal sex. Hepatitis B is a highly contagious virus that is transmitted by infected blood or body fluid, as in sexual contact or sharing drug needles. Vaccination against it is recommended. Hepatitis C is blood-borne, spread by shared needles and other blood contacts.

The Centers for Disease Control and Prevention recorded about 57,000 cases of viral hepatitis cases in 1988 in the United States. However, the number may actually be as high as 300,000.[32] *Hepatitis* **is generally defined as a virally caused inflammation of the liver. Its symptoms include fever, chills, headache, nausea, diarrhea, loss of appetite, skin rashes, and sometimes *jaundice,* the yellowing of skin and eyes.**

Actually, the term "hepatitis" covers at least five inflammatory diseases of the liver, accounting for 95% of viral hepatitis cases. The five forms are hepatitis A, B, C, D, and E. These diseases have similar symptoms but otherwise are different. We describe the first three, considered the principal health threats.

Hepatitis A—Transmitted by Hygiene Lapses Hepatitis A generally enters the body through the mouth. The virus is found in the feces of infected people and is spread by fecal contamination of food and water. Thus, it may be spread by restaurant workers or people working in day-care centers or homes with children in diapers. Another source of contamination is raw shellfish. However, the virus may also be transmitted by oral-anal contact during sex.[33]

The period of illness is usually 2–6 weeks. There is no treatment, although doctors can ease the symptoms of fever, lethargy, and pain. A vaccine called *immune globulin (IG),* recommended for travelers in developing countries, is available to boost immunity.[34,35]

Hepatitis B (HBV)—Transmitted by Infected Body Fluids This different hepatitis virus is transmitted through infected blood (or saliva, mucus, and semen). Transmission is typically by sexual contact, sharing of drug needles, needle-stick accidents, or even sharing of razors and toothbrushes. *(See ● Figure 5.)* It can also be transmitted by an infected mother to her baby at birth.

Although you might not think of it as a sexually transmitted disease (STD), today hepatitis B is one of the most common STDs in America.[36]

The most common reported risk factor for hepatitis B is sexual activity, particularly for people with multiple partners or whose partners have multiple partners.[37] Adolescents are particularly at risk because they tend to have sex more often with more partners and many do not use condoms.

Symptoms of hepatitis B include dark urine, muscle and joint aches, and fatigue. The disease lasts 2–6 months. People usually recover on their own, although in a small percentage of cases (1–3%) there are fatalities from liver failure. A drug called alpha interferon has shown promise of being effective in treatment.[38,39] A vaccine has been available for about a decade that has been found to be 80–95% effective. But health officials are concerned that many children and at-risk individuals have not been immunized.[40]

Hepatitis C—"Classic" Hepatitis, Also Blood-Borne It is not clear whether hepatitis C is spread by sexual contact, but as another blood-borne virus it has been found to be transmitted by IV drug use, needle-stick accidents, blood transfusion, and contact between infected women and their fetuses. Often the virus produces no symptoms, so victims may infect other people without knowing it. The disease is fatal in 2% of cases. No vaccine is available, but alpha interferon can manage the illness in some patients.

Protecting Against Hepatitis The hepatitis viruses, particularly hepatitis B, continue to spread principally because of ignorance. Hepatitis B is 100 times as contagious as HIV, the AIDS virus. It may be spread not only through sexual contact but also through sharing toothbrushes or razors. Even kissing in which there is an exchange of saliva can spread this highly contagious disease.[41] All sexually active people should use condoms. All babies should now get the vaccine for hepatitis B as part of their standard immunization program, according to the CDC. Indeed, *anyone*—every person in America—would be wise to be vaccinated against this widespread disease.

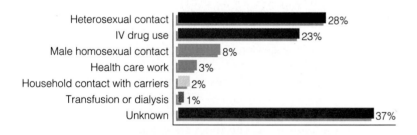

● **Figure 5   Hepatitis B.** Risk of infection by source, 1989. Heterosexual sex is the most common means of transmitting the disease, followed by IV (intravenous—by needles) drug use.

Staph Infections: From Acne to Toxic Shock Syndrome

Staph infections are caused by staphylococci bacteria. Commonplace staph infections are acne, boils, and styes. A potentially fatal disease is toxic shock syndrome.

Staph (or staphylococcal) infections are caused by bacteria called *staphylococci.* These bacteria are usually present on the skin and don't create problems unless they enter through a wound or cut.

Acne, Boils, and Styes Three commonplace staph infections are the following:

- *Acne: Acne* **is, of course, the disorder of the skin caused by inflammation of the oil glands in the skin and hair follicles. It produces pimples, cysts, and even scarring** on the face and elsewhere. The fluctuation in hormones brought about by puberty causes the oil glands in the skin to become overactive. They produce excess oil and plug up the glands, leading staph bacteria to attack. In defense, the body's white blood cells move to the area, forming pus that creates a "white head." Later, pigment-producing cells cause the formation of a "black head."

- *Boils and styes:* That famous affliction of the biblical Job, *boils* **are skin swellings and inflammations resulting from staphylococcal infection in a skin gland.** The swellings have a central hard core and form pus. *Styes* **are inflamed swellings of the oil glands at the margin of an eyelid**.

Acne is quite often solved by simply getting older, when the adolescent hormones subside. However, pharmacies also carry many over-the-counter preparations containing so-called *peeling agents* (salicylic acid, benzoyl peroxide). Physicians may also prescribe *antibiotics* (tetracycline, erythromycin, minocycline), although they may cause some side effects. A derivative of vitamin A called *Accutane*, which reduces acne by halting the oil glands' production, may be helpful for severe cases.

Toxic Shock Syndrome Acne and boils may be unsightly and bring about emotional pain, but at least they aren't fatal. Toxic shock syndrome can be. *Toxic shock syndrome (TSS)* **is a rare but potentially fatal infection in which bacteria release poisonous (toxic) wastes into the bloodstream.** The "shock" in toxic shock syndrome is associated with symptoms such as faintness, rapid pulse, and low blood pressure. Other symptoms are fever, headache, vomiting, sore throat, diarrhea, muscle aches, rash, peeling skin on palms and soles of feet, reduced urination, and disorientation. Without prompt treatment, TSS can cause permanent damage and is potentially fatal.

TSS sometimes occurs in people recovering from wounds or surgery and women within 6–8 weeks of giving birth. But it has been most dramatically discovered in women using high-absorbency tampons. In the last 10 years, TSS has declined because manufacturers have changed the absorbency and composition of tampons.[42] Even so, besides avoiding superabsorbent tampons, women are advised to change tampons every 3–4 hours and to allow themselves some tampon-free time every day.

Strep Infections: More Than "Strep Throat"

Strep infections are most familiar as strep throat. But they include the very serious disorders of rheumatic fever, which can lead to heart damage, and group A strep, linked to a fatal pneumonia.

"Strep throat" is familiar to most people. *Strep throat* **is a severe sore throat caused by *streptococci* bacteria. Symptoms are white or yellow pustules at the back of the throat and fever.** Indeed, strep throat is quite common, with perhaps up to 20 million Americans developing it every year.[43]

Most strep infections are not serious, especially those for children. But some forms found in adults, if not treated, can lead to potentially fatal diseases, including rheumatic fever and group A strep.

- *Rheumatic fever: Rheumatic fever is a streptococcal infection that occurs principally in children ages 5–15 and young adults such as military recruits. The disorder is characterized by fever, inflammation and pain around the joints, jerky and involuntary movement, and skin rashes. Half the victims develop a condition called rheumatic heart disease, which damages heart valves.*

    Rheumatic fever, like scarlet fever (an acute fever, sore throat, and rash), was supposed to have virtually disappeared since the mid-1900s. But in recent years it had made a return in parts of the United States. Because it is difficult to predict who will get rheumatic fever, everyone who might have strep should see a doctor.[44]

- *Group A strep: Group A strep is a bacteria that was linked to the return of rheumatic fever in the United States and to a rare and fatal form of pneumonia.* The new disease, also known as *streptococcal toxic-shock-like syndrome,* progresses quickly. It causes a high fever, cough, chills, skin rash, dizziness, sudden drop in blood pressure, and an interruption in circulation.

    Penicillin and other antibiotics are still effective in treating both infections, if they are caught early. Still, it is important to be aware of the dangers. Many people carry strep bacteria in their throats, which are transmitted by airborne droplets—a danger to susceptible people. No one knows why some people become ill and others don't. To guard against the toxic-shock-like syndrome, if you get a cut or burn you should wash the wound and keep it covered. See a doctor if the site becomes red and swollen or if flu-like symptoms develop.

Pneumonia: Inflammation of the Lungs

Pneumonia is an infection with different causes in which fluid fills the lung's tiny air chambers. Pneumonia, the most frequently fatal infection in the United States, is distinguished from a cold by its length and severity.

Pneumonia is an infection in the lungs, in which fluid fills the tiny air chambers. It can be caused by bacteria (such as group A strep), virus (such as influenza), or chemicals or other substances in the lungs (such as smoke). It can be a complication of childhood diseases such as measles, mumps, and rubella. Seventy-five years ago, pneumonia and influenza were the leading killers in the United States; today they are fifth. Every year, of the 2 million Americans who catch pneumonia, at least 40,000 die.[45]

Pneumonia caused by a bacterial infection can be controlled with antibiotics. Antibiotics are not effective for those strains caused by viruses or environmental exposure. A vaccine is available. It is recommended for everyone over age 65, those with weakened immune systems, and people with heart, lung, or kidney disease.[46]

Tuberculosis: A 19th-Century Killer Returns

Tuberculosis is a contagious bacterial disease that lodges in the lungs and then spreads to the rest of the body. TB is transmitted in airborne droplets via breathing, coughing, and sneezing. But the risk of acquiring TB rises only with prolonged contact with a carrier. People may be infected with TB, but it may not become active. The early form can nearly always be cured. People who drop out of treatment may develop drug-resistant TB strains.

Tuberculosis frequently causes disability and death in many parts of the world. In the United States, the scourge once called "consumption" killed more people in the 19th century than any other infectious disease. In this century, tuberculosis was thought to be largely controlled in North America; however, in a stunning development, it has come back.

    Caused by a germ called *Mycobacterium,* **tuberculosis (TB) is a contagious bacterial disease that mainly lodges in the lungs. There it slowly and painfully multiplies there. It can spread to and damage the brain, bone, eyes, liver and kidneys, spine, and skin. The common symptoms include coughing, chest pain, night sweats, and**

spitting up of blood.[47] Serious outcomes of initial TB infections most frequently occur in infants, adolescents, and adults.[48]

Who Gets TB and How TB is an airborne disease: it travels from person to person in airborne droplets when someone with active TB exhales, coughs, sings, or sneezes. Since it is airborne, it is far easier to transmit than blood-borne illnesses like hepatitis or HIV. "Catching tuberculosis requires no consensual act: only breathing," says one physician specializing in communicable diseases.[49] *(See ● Figure 6.)*

Even so, it is not as contagious as influenza, measles, or chicken pox. People with those diseases can infect nearly anyone who has not already had the disease.[50] TB occurs only after close and prolonged contact with an infected person. On average, healthy people who are heavily exposed to TB have a 50% chance of becoming infected. Such exposure might mean spending 8 hours a day for 6 months working or living with someone who is sick with TB. Exposure all day for 2 months has about the same odds, according to an administrator with the American Lung Association.[51]

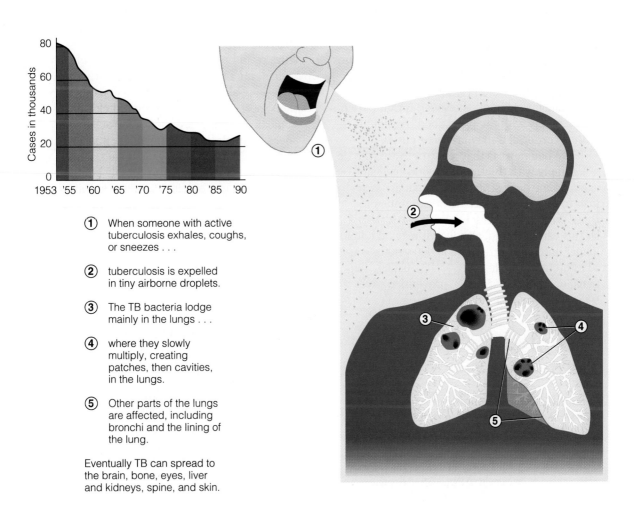

① When someone with active tuberculosis exhales, coughs, or sneezes . . .

② tuberculosis is expelled in tiny airborne droplets.

③ The TB bacteria lodge mainly in the lungs . . .

④ where they slowly multiply, creating patches, then cavities, in the lungs.

⑤ Other parts of the lungs are affected, including bronchi and the lining of the lung.

Eventually TB can spread to the brain, bone, eyes, liver and kidneys, spine, and skin.

● **Figure 6   The spread of tuberculosis.**

Treatment Tuberculosis may exist in two forms. In *latent TB,* no outward symptoms and signs are present. In *active TB,* a person becomes ill with coughs, fevers, and night sweats. To determine whether a person has latent TB, doctors use skin tests, chest X-rays, and cultures of sputum. Active TB is diagnosed with a chest X-ray.

Millions of people in North America are infected with the latent form but have no sign of the disease. Their immune systems control the latent infection, so that they have only a 1 in 10 lifetime chance of developing active TB.[52] Physicians don't know what makes TB progress from the latent to active stage. The trigger may be changes in the immune system that come with age, existing diseases, or infections such as HIV.

The good news is that the common, latent form of tuberculosis, if detected early, can be cured. Exceptions include drug-resistant strains of the disease. Drug therapy must continue for at least 6 months and may mean taking several drugs daily. A difficulty, however, is that patients must comply with the prescribed treatment *exactly* as ordered if they are to be cured.[53,54]

The bad news is that many of those who do not comply with treatment may become sick again. Some have strains of TB that are *resistant* to most drugs—and they can transmit those strains to others. Some drug-resistant strains can be cured, although it may take much longer and cost perhaps $250,000 versus $11,000 for a simple case.[55–57] As usually happens, every dollar spent on prevention saves several dollars later in treatment.

Lyme Disease: The Summer Pest

Lyme disease is spread by tick bites and can lead to difficulties such as heart problems. The most prominent symptom is a ringed rash at the site of the bite and flulike symptoms. Prevention means taking precautions when walking outdoors.

Lyme disease was identified only a few years ago, after a 1975 outbreak in Old Lyme, Connecticut. However, the bacteria that causes it (the bacterium *Borrelia burgdorferi*) seems to

have been around since 1940 in the United States.[58] ***Lyme disease is spread by the bite of deer ticks. It causes some extremely serious complications, including joint inflammation, heart problems, severe headaches, and nervous system disorders.***[59,60] Two-thirds of those who have been bitten develop a ringlike rash at the site of the bite about 2 days to a few weeks later. Within 48 hours after infection, most people also experience flulike symptoms, including fatigue, fever, headache, chills, a stiff neck, and muscle aches. Without treatment, the disease can spread to other organs, eventually leading to memory loss, poor coordination, and an irregular heartbeat. Weeks or even years after the bite, half of untreated patients develop arthritis.

Prevention Especially during May through July, avoid tick-infested areas, if possible, and be vigilant about walking in tall grass or woods. Wear long-sleeved shirts and long pants rather than shorts. Choose light-colored clothing, so you can see the ticks, and tuck trousers into socks or cinch them at the ankle. It is also helpful to spray your pant legs and shirt sleeves with tick or insect repellant (preferably containing DEET).[61] When outside during tick season, inspect your body every 3–4 hours. If you find a tick, remove it as soon as possible with tweezers, and save it if possible for professional identification. The greatest risk for infection is when a tick has been attached to the skin for more than 24 hours.[62] Children and furry pets should also be inspected for ticks.

Treatment If you suspect you have been bitten, you should see a healthcare professional at once. Treatment is with antibiotics, and it is safer and more cost-effective to begin treatment immediately rather than waiting for signs or symptoms.[63] When administered early, antibiotics can cure virtually all cases. Later, however, treatment is more difficult. Medical researchers have been working to come up with a vaccine that protects against Lyme disease.[64]

Strategy for Living: Immunizations for Staying Well

A vaccine is a preparation of organisms that helps increase one's immunity to a particular disease. All children ages 2 months to 16 years should have scheduled vaccinations: DPT combination, polio, MMR combination, meningitis, and hepatitis B. Adults, including college students, should also be immunized, depending on need: diphtheria-tetanus booster, MMR, hepatitis B, polio, and influenza and pneumococcal disease.

Immunizations or vaccinations are the injection of laboratory-prepared organisms into the body to increase one's immunity to a particular disease. The first *vaccine*—**the preparation of organisms**—was the virus of cowpox, used to produce immunity to smallpox. So successful has the immunization campaign been that *smallpox*, a once-dreaded disease that killed millions of people, was wiped out in 1977.

Both children and adults should receive immunizations. Vaccines needed during adulthood include "booster" shots or revaccinations for many common infectious diseases. There are also vaccines for diseases specific to countries to which a person may be traveling. Vaccines for chickenpox and Lyme disease are expected in the near future.

Immunizations for Children All children ages 2 months to 16 years should have vaccinations, on a scheduled basis, that include the following: *diphtheria-tetanus-pertussis (DPT) combination, polio, measles-mumps-rubella (MMR) combination, meningitis, and hepatitis B. (See ● Table 1.)* It's also wise to be immunized against tuberculosis—particularly preschool children in poor families.

The major kinds of vaccinations that should be given to children are as follows. The schedule of immunizations may vary slightly according to the recommendation of a child's pediatrician.

- *DPT—diphtheria-pertussis-tetanus:* This shot, which should be given six times in a child's life, protects against three diseases:

● **Table 1 Childhood immunization schedule.** DPT is combined vaccination for diphtheria-pertussis-tetanus; MMR is combined vaccination for measles-mumps-rubella.

Immunization	2 mos.	4 mos.	6 mos.	12 mos.	15 mos.	15–18 mos.	4–6 yrs.	11–12 yrs.	14–16 yrs.
DPT	●	●	●			●	●		●
Polio	●	●				●	●		
MMR				●			●[1]	●[1]	
Meningitis or HIB influenza	●	●	●	●		●			
Hepatitis B	●								
Cholera, typhoid fever, yellow fever	If possibility of being exposed								

[1]Advisory groups differ on whether a final MMR shot should be given at 4–6 years or 11–12 years; parents should consult their pediatrician.

Sources: Combined recommendations from the American Academy of Pediatrics and the Advisory Committee on Immunization Practices.

(1) *Diphtheria,* an infection involving the membranes of the mouth and throat, is a rare but dangerous disease. It can result in death from an obstructed windpipe or heart failure.

(2) *Pertussis* (whooping cough) is a bacterial infection that can develop into pneumonia, with possibly fatal results. Concern that the pertussis vaccination itself might lead to brain damage and death seems to have alleviated.[65-67]

(3) *Tetanus,* called "lock jaw" because one symptom is a painful stiffening of the jaw, can produce difficulty breathing and death. It is transmitted by puncture wounds, such as stepping on a nail, and by contamination with soil, dust, or feces containing the tetanus organism.

- *Polio:* Immunizations and booster shots for *polio* (short for *poliomyelitis*) should be given at four separate intervals for infants and young children. Often they coincide with the schedule for DPT vaccinations, depending on the pediatrician.

  After three decades of a program of vaccination, polio has almost disappeared in the United States. The only complication is that some adults who overcame the disease as children have found themselves weakened by a condition called *post-polio syndrome,* The syndrome has put them back on crutches.[68,69] Symptoms include problems with fatigue, weakness, joint and back pain, and intolerance to cold.[70,71]

- *MMR—measles-mumps-rubella:* This immunization, given once at 15 months and again later in childhood, is intended to prevent three diseases:

(1) *Measles* produces a rash on the face and body, eye inflammation, high fever, runny nose, cough, and fatigue. Serious cases may produce ear infections and pneumonia. One in 1000 cases produces *encephalitis,* an inflammation of the brain that can cause neurological disorders, mental retardation, or even death. As mentioned, the reduction in MMR vaccinations because of public health budget cuts produced an epidemic in the United States in 1990.

(2) *Mumps* is generally a mild though uncomfortable disease in childhood, that involves swelling of the salivary glands and fever. In rare cases it can produce deafness in one ear.[72]

(3) *Rubella* is also known as German measles, because it is a measles-like disease. Rubella can be devastating for the unborn.[73]

- **Meningitis or HIB:** The vaccine to immunize infants against bacterial *meningitis* is so effective that the sometimes lethal illness is nearly eliminated, one study shows.[74] Meningitis is an acute and sometimes deadly infection of the lining of the brain and spinal cord. Before the vaccine, it struck up to 15,000 young children in the United States and killed 5–10% of its victims.

  The bacterium that can cause meningitis in children (called *Haemophilus influenzae* type B) is abbreviated as HIB. *HIB* diseases include not only meningitis but also other childhood diseases such as pneumonia, arthritis, and inflammations of the bone marrow and the membrane around the heart. HIB infection of tissue in the throat can end in suffocation. The vaccine used to resist these diseases is known as the HIB vaccine.

We described the effects of, and vaccines for, hepatitis B, influenza, and tuberculosis above.

Immunizations for Adults, Including College Students Maybe you think you had all the vaccinations you needed as a child, or maybe you've simply "outgrown" those childhood diseases. Even adults, however, need to be immunized for some things, particularly since many of your childhood immunizations cannot confer lifetime immunity. *(See ● Table 2.)* Unfortunately, some of those so-called "childhood" diseases can be serious, even fatal, to adults. If, for instance, you are a parent and your child catches measles, you can catch the disease yourself. Indeed, measles is a serious health threat to college students.[75,76]

Even if you were vaccinated as a child, you may need to be *revaccinated.* This is particularly true if you plan to travel to less-developed countries or if you were born after 1956, one study suggests.[77] Here are some recommendations to consider:

- **Diphtheria-tetanus booster:** All college students and adults should have one of these every 10 years. Diphtheria can produce death from an obstructed windpipe or heart failure. Tetanus produces difficulty breathing and death.

- **MMR—measles-mumps-rubella:** All college students and adults born after 1956 should talk to a health care professional about having one of these immunizations. Health care workers and travelers to undeveloped countries should especially consider an MMR vaccination, which can be done anytime. Others needing vaccination include anyone born after 1956 who never had measles, mumps, or rubella (German measles) or a live measles vaccine. Measles and rubella are particularly dangerous to women of childbearing age.[78,79]

  (1) *Measles* in adults can cause severe pneumonia, ear infections, and encephalitis, and death occasionally occurs. Measles also can cause a pregnant woman to deliver a stillborn child.[80]

  (2) *Mumps* in adults can cause inflammation in the testicles and sometimes may cause sterility or mcningitis.[81]

  (3) *Rubella* (German measles) during pregnancy can cause miscarriage, stillbirth, or birth defects ranging from deafness to congenital heart disease.[82] All individuals, especially women of childbearing age, are urged to be vaccinated against rubella, which is increasing steadily in the United States.

- **Hepatitis B:** All health care workers, sexual partners of homosexual and bisexual men, hemophiliacs, and intravenous drug users need the three-shot series of vaccinations.

- **Polio:** Travelers to less-developed countries should get a polio booster shot.

- **Influenza and pneumococcal disease:** People 65 or older and anyone with chronic illness (especially heart or lung problems) should be vaccinated each fall for influenza.

● **Table 2   Adult vaccination schedule**

Immunization	How often to get it
Diphtheria-tetanus	If received no DPT shots as a child, should have series of 3 shots (second one 4–6 weeks after first, third one 6–12 months after second)
Diphtheria-tetanus booster	If did receive DPT shots as a child, should have booster shot once every 10 years
MMR—measles-mumps-rubella	Recommended for college students, health care workers, and travelers born after 1956 or anyone born after that year and not diagnosed with having had those diseases. (People born before 1957 are considered immune.)
Hepatitis B	Recommended for all health care workers, sexual partners of homosexual and bisexual men, heterosexuals who have multiple partners or whose sex partner does, hemophiliacs, and IV drug users; series of 3 shots anytime (second one 4 weeks after first, third one 5 months after second).
Polio	Booster shot recommended for travelers to less-developed countries before traveling.
Influenza and pneumococcal disease	Recommended for people 65 and older, anyone with chronic illness (heart or lung problems), or in contact with high-risk individuals. Influenza shot once a year before the flu season. Pneumococcal disease shot once or twice (second one at least 6 years after first).
Tuberculosis	Considered for those directly exposed to active tuberculosis

Sources: Adapted from: Anonymous. (1992). Immunization: Important for adults, too! *Patient Care, 26* (15), 124–129; Weinstock, C. (1992, January/February). Revaccinating adults. *American Health,* p. 15.

They should be vaccinated any time against bacterial pneumonia. The same is true of people in contact with such high-risk individuals.

- **Tuberculosis:** The homeless, poor, drug-addicted, or HIV-infected should be vaccinated, as should anyone coming into contact with such individuals.

Sexually Transmitted Diseases

▶ Discuss the causes, diagnosis, treatment, and prevention of HIV infection.

▶ Explain the two types of herpes simplex virus.

▶ Describe the human papilloma virus.

▶ Discuss chlamydia, gonorrhea, and syphilis.

▶ Explain parasite infections and infections of the urinary and reproductive systems.

▶ Describe how to avoid acquiring sexually transmitted diseases.

Formerly called *venereal diseases*, **sexually transmitted diseases (STDs) are infectious diseases that are transmitted as a result of (usually) sexual contact.** Although HIV infection is perhaps the most serious, the incidence of STDs is growing rapidly and may double by the end of the century.

HIV and AIDS: The Modern Scourge

HIV (human immunodeficiency virus) may progress over about 10 years through four stages into AIDS (acquired immune deficiency syndrome). HIV is diagnosed through an antibody test, but the test cannot predict if the person will actually develop AIDS. A few drugs are available to extend lives, but none kill the virus or cure the disease. HIV may infect both sexes and is principally transmitted by unprotected sex and by shared drug needles.

AIDS stands for *acquired immune deficiency syndrome*, **a sexually transmitted disease that is caused by a virus, HIV. AIDS is characterized by irreversible damage to the body's immune system.** *HIV, or human immunodeficiency virus*, **the virus causing AIDS, brings about a variety of ills, including the breakdown of the immune system. This breakdown allows the development of certain infections and cancers.** One variant of the virus is *HIV-1*, which causes most of the AIDS cases in the United States. Another is *HIV-2*, which is the dominant strain in Africa and is the cause of some cases in the United States. Because AIDS is relatively new, there are all kinds of fears and misunderstandings about it. Since it is a life-and-death matter, however, it's important to have *accurate knowledge* about it. The accompanying Self Discovery will help you determine what you know. *(See Self Discovery 1.)*

Since 1981, when a gay man walked into San Francisco General Hospital with a mysterious immune disorder, HIV has raged across the United States. It now affects about 1 million Americans, about a fifth of whom have developed AIDS.[83] *(See ● Figure 7.)* In the early years, the epidemic in the United States was primarily an affliction of homosexual men, intravenous drug users, and blood recipients. Infected products from blood banks went to people with hemophilia (a blood defect) and others (such as surgery patients).[84] Since then, the disease has spread in the United States along with epidemics of drug use and of sexually transmitted diseases such as syphilis. The number of cases of heterosexually acquired AIDS in this country is now doubling every 15 months.[85]

Throughout the world, HIV has infected more than 10 million adults—perhaps 40% of them women—and 1 million children.[86] About 2.5 million are already dead of AIDS. An estimated 40 million people will be infected by HIV by the end of the century.[87]

Who Has AIDS: The Politics of Definition
Who has AIDS? For a long time, people weren't considered to have AIDS until they showed symptoms of 23 indicator diseases. This disease list from the federal Centers for Disease Control and Prevention (CDC) included a rare pneumonia, specific cancers, and other infections. However, the definition has become a political as much as a medical issue. In the United States and Europe, for instance, the definition influences a person's ability to get care.

SELF DISCOVERY 1

What Do You Know About HIV and AIDS?

Answer true or false to each of the following statements:

	True	False
1. There is no known cure for AIDS.	___	___
2. AIDS is caused by inheriting faulty genes.	___	___
3. AIDS is caused by bacteria.	___	___
4. A person can "carry" and transmit the organism that causes AIDS without showing symptoms of the disease or appearing ill.	___	___
5. The organism that causes AIDS can be transmitted through semen.	___	___
6. Urinating after sexual intercourse makes infection with AIDS less likely.	___	___
7. Washing your genitals after sex makes infection with AIDS less likely.	___	___
8. Sharing drug needles increases the chance of transmitting the organism that causes AIDS.	___	___
9. The organism that causes AIDS can be transmitted through blood or blood products.	___	___
10. Donating blood makes it more likely you will be exposed to HIV.	___	___
11. You can catch AIDS like you catch a cold because whatever causes AIDS can be carried in the air.	___	___
12. You can get AIDS by being in the same classroom as someone who has AIDS.	___	___
13. You can get AIDS by shaking hands with someone who has AIDS.	___	___
14. A pregnant woman who has HIV can give AIDS to her baby.	___	___
15. Having a steady relationship with just one sex partner decreases the risk of getting AIDS.	___	___
16. Using condoms reduces the risk of getting AIDS.	___	___
17. A test to determine whether a person has been exposed to HIV is available.	___	___
18. A vaccine that protects people from getting AIDS is now available.	___	___

Correct Answers

1. True	4. True	7. False	10. False	13. False	16. True
2. False	5. True	8. True	11. False	14. True	17. True
3. False	6. False	9. True	12. False	15. True	18. False

Sources: Anderson, D. M., & Christenson, G. M. (1991). Ethnic breakdown of AIDS related knowledge and attitudes from the National Adolescent Student Health Survey. *Journal of Health Education, 22,* 30–34; Timoshok, L., Sweet, D. M., & Zich, J. (1987). A three-city comparison of the public's knowledge and attitudes about AIDS. *Psychology & Health, 1*(1), 43–60; Weiten, W., Lloyd, M. A., & Lashley, R. L. (1991). *Psychology applied to modern life: Adjustment in the 90s* (3rd ed.). Pacific Grove, CA: Brooks/Cole, p. 408.

In 1993 the CDC revised the definition. AIDS now includes HIV-infected people whose level of certain immune cells falls too low. These critical cells are **the body's master immune cells—called *T4 helper cells* or *CD4 cells*** (or CD4 positive lymphocytes). If T4-cell levels fall to 200 per cubic millimeter, or one-fifth of normal, an HIV-infected person is considered to have AIDS. A T4-cell count is an important measure of immune-system strength, with the normal level being around 1000.[88]

In addition, the CDC's new definition of AIDS includes diseases that are fatal to women infected with HIV. These include pulmonary tuberculosis, recurrent bacterial pneumonia, and invasive cervical cancer. Adding such disorders to the official definition of HIV cues physicians to test for AIDS in women with these symptoms. These diseases are also found in people without HIV.[89]

The Four-Stage Progression of HIV: From Infection to AIDS Although *official* definitions of HIV may change by the time you read this, the progression of the disease probably will not. What's important is that you be highly aware of four things:

1. AIDS itself comes only at the end of a long, slow collapse—averaging 8–10 years in adults—of the body's immune system.[90]

2. Often there are *no symptoms of illness* during the development of the disease, which means for perhaps 7–9 years.

3. So far *no one has ever recovered from AIDS.*

4. Yet *not everyone who is exposed to HIV gets AIDS,* just as not everyone exposed to polio virus develops paralysis.

There are four stages of development of HIV-related problems:

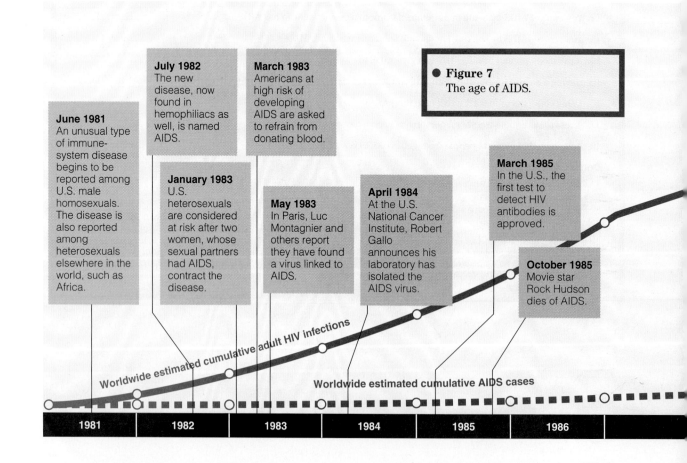

June 1981
An unusual type of immune-system disease begins to be reported among U.S. male homosexuals. The disease is also reported among heterosexuals elsewhere in the world, such as Africa.

July 1982
The new disease, now found in hemophiliacs as well, is named AIDS.

January 1983
U.S. heterosexuals are considered at risk after two women, whose sexual partners had AIDS, contract the disease.

March 1983
Americans at high risk of developing AIDS are asked to refrain from donating blood.

May 1983
In Paris, Luc Montagnier and others report they have found a virus linked to AIDS.

April 1984
At the U.S. National Cancer Institute, Robert Gallo announces his laboratory has isolated the AIDS virus.

March 1985
In the U.S., the first test to detect HIV antibodies is approved.

October 1985
Movie star Rock Hudson dies of AIDS.

● **Figure 7**
The age of AIDS.

Worldwide estimated cumulative adult HIV infections

Worldwide estimated cumulative AIDS cases

1981   1982   1983   1984   1985   1986

- ***Group I HIV infection, first 1–8 weeks—short-term illness may develop:*** The time between the virus entering the body and the occurrence of a short-term illness—beginning group I HIV infection—is 1–8 weeks. Many people show no symptoms, but some show signs similar to mononucleosis—fatigue, fever, swollen lymph nodes, and possibly a rash. Most people may simply ignore these. These initial symptoms disappear in a few weeks, and most people continue to feel normal. Some people may complain of chronically swollen lymph nodes.

- ***Group II HIV infection, 6 weeks to a year or more after transmission—no symptoms, diagnosis requires antibody test:*** The stage beginning when a person would first test positive in an HIV antibody test is group II HIV infection. It may occur within 6 weeks of transmission, but it can also be a year or more. During this period, people with HIV often show no

symptoms and feel fine. The HIV antibody test is a standard blood test that tests for HIV infection.

- ***Group III HIV infection, 1 week to 2 years or so after transmission—enlarged lymph nodes:*** The occurrence of new symptoms is known as group III HIV infection. This may occur between 1 week and 2 years or even longer after the virus enters the body.

    This is the cluster of symptoms that used to be known as *ARC*— short for *AIDS-related complex.*

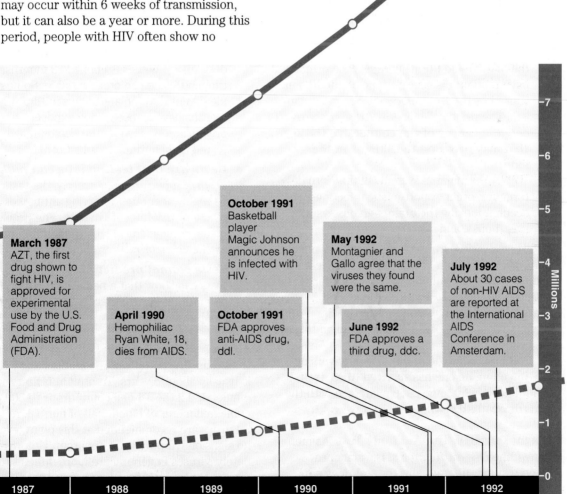

Year 2000 estimate: 30 million to 40 million worldwide

1992 12 million to 14 million worldwide

March 1987 AZT, the first drug shown to fight HIV, is approved for experimental use by the U.S. Food and Drug Administration (FDA).

April 1990 Hemophiliac Ryan White, 18, dies from AIDS.

October 1991 FDA approves anti-AIDS drug, ddI.

October 1991 Basketball player Magic Johnson announces he is infected with HIV.

May 1992 Montagnier and Gallo agree that the viruses they found were the same.

June 1992 FDA approves a third drug, ddc.

July 1992 About 30 cases of non-HIV AIDS are reported at the International AIDS Conference in Amsterdam.

Millions: 7, 6, 5, 4, 3, 2, 1, 0

1987 1988 1989 1990 1991 1992

The symptoms are less severe than those for AIDS itself. They consist of enlarged lymph nodes, loss of appetite, fever, lethargy, night sweats, diarrhea, and rashes. Later there may be slurred speech, memory loss, loss of feeling in hands and feet, and general mental deterioration.[91]

- *Group IV HIV infection, 6 months to 10 years after transmission—AIDS:* The AIDS disease is group IV HIV infection. It may come 6 months to 10 years after the virus enters the body. By this point, the T4-cell count has dropped from 1000 per cubic millimeter of blood (normal) to 200. The person with AIDS experiences rapid swelling of the lymph glands, weight loss, diarrhea, fatigue, headaches, fever, shortness of breath, and dry cough. There may be a white coating on the tongue and reddish-purplish bumps on the skin.

    As the HIV gradually weakens the body's immune system, other infections and cancer may invade the body. These are called "opportunistic infections," diseases the body would normally repel. The principal infectious disease is a type of pneumonia caused by the *Pneumocystis carinii* organism. The principal cancer is **Kaposi's sarcoma, a cancer of the connective tissues that may occur on the skin or in the mouth.**

    As the immune system continues to deteriorate, other opportunistic infections may occur, attacking the brain, nervous system, liver, bones, and skin.

The estimated average time from HIV infection to first symptom is approximately 5 years and to AIDS approximately 8–10 years. Very few patients are diagnosed with AIDS the first 2 years after infection, but after that the risk seems to be 5–10% per year. The use of anti-HIV medication might alter that.[92]

Although there do seem to be survivors of HIV infection, no one has survived AIDS itself. It is not known why some people infected with the virus develop AIDS while others stay healthy.

Diagnosing HIV: The Antibody Test As mentioned, the *HIV antibody test* is a standard blood test for HIV. Actually, the test does not detect the virus itself but rather the antibodies that the body forms in response to the appearance of the virus. **Antibodies are molecules that are secreted into the bloodstream, where they bind to the invading virus, incapacitating it.**

Two principal blood tests are used in sequence to detect HIV infection. The first one is the *EIA* or *ELISA*—short for the *enzyme immunoassay* and the *enzyme-linked immunosorbant assay*—which detect HIV antibodies. This first test may produce a false positive result—that is, the test suggests HIV is present, but it is in error. So a positive result is followed by the more expensive but more accurate *Western blot* test. *Negative* test results *can* mean positive news: the HIV may not be present. *Positive* test results *can* mean negative news: the HIV may be present. Still, anyone taking these tests needs to be aware of certain cautions:

- *Antibodies to the virus may not develop immediately:* If the test results are negative, it may mean the body has not been exposed to HIV. But it may also mean that antibody formation has not yet taken place. The time it takes for most people to develop antibodies is about 1–3 months, though this can be quite variable. Some people do not develop antibodies until 6–12 months have elapsed since exposure to the organism. (Meanwhile the person may be infected and continue to infect others.)

- *Be aware that testing labs can make errors:* If performed correctly, the tests can be highly accurate, detecting antibodies in 99.6% of HIV-infected people. The problem is that some medical labs have problems with high error rates in their testing.[93]

- *Tests cannot predict AIDS:* Currently, tests can show that a person has HIV. They cannot predict whether that HIV will develop into AIDS.

Treating HIV and AIDS In the absence of treatment, the path from HIV infection to AIDS is usually about 8 years. Treatment is first recommended if the T4-cell count drops to 500 per cubic millimeter of blood, half of normal. Antiviral drugs are recommended at this point, even if no signs or symptoms are apparent. Unfortunately, viruses in general are more difficult to treat with drugs than bacteria are, and HIV has turned out to be a very difficult virus to treat.

At present at least three major drugs are approved by the Food and Drug Administration (FDA) for treatment of AIDS—AZT, ddI, and ddC:

- ***AZT:*** First approved in 1987, AZT (azidothymidine or zidovudine) extends life an average of 18 months by postponing some of the symptoms of AIDS. Eventually, however, HIV mutates into a form that is less vulnerable to AZT. The drug's side effects of anemia and bone-marrow damage may also force patients to stop using it.[94]

- ***ddI:*** Approved by the FDA in October 1991, ddI (didanosine) works like AZT, but causes less viral resistance. The drug helps to protect uninfected cells, but does not destroy the virus in already-infected cells.[95]

- ***ddC:*** ddC (dideoxycytidine) is the same type of drug as AZT and ddI, but has less severe side effects. Before its FDA approval in 1992, ddC was smuggled into the United States by the AIDS underground.

AZT, ddI, and ddC are similar drugs and are likely to work best in combination. Although they do not rid the body of the virus and have limited effectiveness, they are thought to extend lives of some patients by 1–3 years. Another drug-treatment candidate is d4T, which may have fewer side effects than other AIDS drugs.

Drug researchers have developed a number of other compounds that were first thought to be promising. But all have been rejected as being ineffective or potentially toxic. Experimenters continue to push forward at top speed, but they say it may be years before any breakthrough is forthcoming. They warn that nations must prepare to care for millions of sick people who cannot be saved by drugs.[96]

Interestingly, one method that may lengthen the lives of people with HIV infection is something that requires no prescription: relaxation and aerobic exercise. One study found that such activities apparently enhanced the strength of the immune system and slowed the progress of HIV.[97,98]

Who Gets HIV/AIDS and How If there is one thing this disease has taught us it is that the past may not be a guide to the future. In 1993, the predominant number of reported U.S. AIDS cases were transmitted by male homosexual sex (47%). Next were those transmitted by intra-

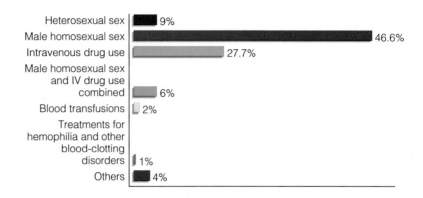

- ● **Figure 8   Where AIDS comes from.** Reported U.S. AIDS cases by type of transmission.

venous drug use (28%), with a small percentage of men (6%) falling into both categories. Heterosexual sex, as a means of transmission, was 9%. *(See ● Figure 8.)*

However, the sources of transmission of the disease have changed. Let's consider the categories of *heterosexual sex, male homosexual sex, intravenous drug use, blood transfusions and blood products, from mothers to infants,* and *accidental contacts:*

- ***Heterosexual sex—HIV risk is rising:*** There is some evidence that *men are more efficient at infecting women than women are at infecting men.*[99] Studies show that increasingly women are becoming HIV-infected through unprotected sex with bisexual men or male intravenous drug users.[100] Indeed, women are the fastest-growing category of people affected by the epidemic, particularly women of color.[101]

  Consistent with the current pattern of HIV infection emerging in North America, in Africa HIV and AIDS are spreading mainly through heterosexual intercourse. The virus strikes men and women alike, with the path eased by the presence of sexually transmitted diseases such as syphilis.[102] Indeed, heterosexual sex is thought to account for more than 80% of the adult cases of AIDS in Africa.[103]

- ***Male homosexual sex:*** During 1993, according to the Centers for Disease

Control and Prevention, there were 103,500 AIDS cases in the United States. Most cases (47%) occurred among homosexual or bisexual men.[104] HIV is no longer spreading explosively among gay men as it was in the late 1970s and 1980s, infecting them almost before they knew it. Still, AIDS is the second leading cause of death for men ages 25–44 in the United States.[105] As we shall discuss, one reason for the epidemic among men is that men are more apt to engage in risk-taking behavior.[106]

- *Intravenous drug use:* The incidence of AIDS has dropped in Canada, where clean needles have been distributed free to drug addicts in large Canadian cities.[107,108] In the United States, however, needle-swapping programs for intravenous drug addicts, such as heroin users, have been proposed. But the exchange of clean needles for used ones has been resisted for years on the grounds that free needles would increase drug use. The Canadian experience, however, found that there was no such increase in drug abuse: participants are almost always long-term abusers, not new.

- *Blood transfusions and blood products:* The Centers for Disease Control in 1991 reported that 2.2% of the AIDS cases in the United States came from blood transfusions. Another 0.8% of the cases were found in the nation's 25,000 hemophiliacs. **Hemophiliacs are people (nearly all males) with a blood defect that delays clotting of the blood. Poor clotting makes it difficult to control hemorrhage even after minor injuries.** Hemophiliacs require the use several times a week of a blood-clotting substance (Factor VIII) made from donated blood. HIV has infected almost every hemophiliac born before 1985, the year all blood donations and products were screened for HIV antibodies.[109]

Though not completely risk-free, the U.S. blood supply is now safer than ever, with HIV screening by the Red Cross and other blood banks. The odds of getting infected from a transfusion are said to be extremely low—perhaps 1 in 60,000 units.[110,111]

- *From mothers to infants:* Mothers who are HIV-infected may transmit the disease to their young in several ways: during pregnancy, labor and delivery, and during breastfeeding. Unfortunately, many women are unaware that they are infected with HIV until they give birth and their babies later develop AIDS.[112–114]

- *Accidental contacts:* HIV is not contracted by casual contact, as many people once believed.[115] You won't get it from being on a crowded bus or in a swimming pool, from a toilet seat, or from mosquitos. You are not likely to get it from sharing eating utensils, toothbrushes, or toilets with AIDS patients. Several studies confirm these findings. HIV survives poorly in saliva and is rarely recovered from the saliva of HIV-infected persons. Of 31 persons bitten by AIDS patients, none have turned out to be HIV-positive. The risk of infection from sticking oneself with a needle used on AIDS or HIV-infected persons is only 1% or less per stick.

At one time, people were worried about getting HIV from health care workers, but there seems to be no cause for alarm. The risk of being infected by a doctor, for instance, is considered "so remote that it may never be measured," as former Surgeon General C. Everett Koop put it.[116]

Although HIV is rarely transmitted in the workplace, the federal Occupational Safety and Health Administration has rules covering use of rubber gloves and protective clothing and housekeeping procedures. The rules are intended to prevent more than 200 deaths and 9200 blood-borne infections a year—most *not* related to AIDS.

Strategy for Living: The Relationship Between Gender Roles and HIV Most people become HIV-infected in two ways: (a) from unsafe sexual behavior or (b) from sharing drug needles.

Both men and women need to think about behaviors they consider masculine or feminine and how such behaviors increase risk of HIV.

- *Men's roles:* What, ask sociologists Michael Kimmel and Martin Levine, is the relationship between AIDS and masculinity? Per-

haps, they suggest, many men act in a "real man" kind of role of engaging in high-risk behaviors that ignore health risks.[117] *(See •
Figure 9.)* Indeed, they note, many gay men have acted more like "real men" than most straight men, wearing leather and short haircuts. They engage in quick and often anonymous sex with many partners. Similarly, IV drug users found drug use provided manly risk and adventure.

Recently, the patterns seem to have changed. Both gay and straight men are apparently having fewer sexual partners than in previous years and reporting more condom use.[118–120] Even so, many gay men apparently see themselves as less vulnerable to HIV infection. Their optimism is also found among sexually active adolescents.[121]

• ***Women's roles:*** Women are at risk for HIV, as we have shown, and many may not even know they are at risk. At the end of 1990, half the women with AIDS were found to have contracted it from IV drug use. Another 16% got it from blood transfusions and other categories. A third, however, contracted HIV through heterosexual contacts.[122] Presumably some HIV-positive women became infected from bisexual partners.

● **Figure 9   Is high-risk sex sexy?**

❝*How does one get AIDS? Not by being a homosexual or IV drug user, but by engaging in high-risk behaviors that ignore health risks. These behaviors also can confirm masculinity since masculinity typically is associated with risk-taking. Indeed, those whose masculinity is least secure are precisely those most likely to enact hypermasculine behavioral codes. . . .*

To men, . . . that which is safe is not sexy. Sex is about danger, risk, excitement; safety is about comfort, softness, security. Seen this way, it isn't surprising that one-fourth of gay men report they haven't changed unsafe sexual behaviors. What's astonishing is three-fourths are practicing safer sex.

What heterosexual men can learn from the gay community's response to AIDS is how to eroticize responsibility—something women have been trying to teach men for decades. ❞

—Michael Kimmel & Martin Levine. (1991, May 10). AIDS is a disease of men involved in risky behavior. *San Francisco Chronicle*, p. A25.

Other Sexually Transmitted Diseases

Besides HIV/AIDS, other serious STDs include hepatitis B, herpes, human papilloma virus, chlamydia, gonorrhea, syphilis, and parasite infections.

HIV/AIDS is perhaps the most dangerous and recent of the sexually transmitted diseases, but it is not the only one. As mentioned in the preceding section, *hepatitis B* is also a serious STD.

The STDs we will describe in the rest of this chapter include:

- Herpes simplex virus
- Human papilloma virus
- Chlamydia
- Gonorrhea
- Syphilis
- Parasite infections: pubic lice and scabies

Herpes: The Secret Virus

The STD known as the herpes simplex virus is of two types: Type 1 typically causes cold sores around the mouth. Type 2 is associated with sores around the genitals. Both types can be acquired in either area through oral-genital sex. The virus never completely disappears and may recur with or without symptoms, often triggered by stress.

A great number of people—30 million, or perhaps 16% of all Americans ages 15–74—have been infected with herpes. As many as 1 million more join their ranks every year.[123] This is unfortunate, for genital herpes can inflict a great deal of emotional as well as physical suffering.

Herpes is a viral infection that evades the body's immune defenses by hiding in the nervous system until reactivation of the virus occurs. There are six major types of herpes virus that affect humans (varicella-zoster virus, Epstein-Barr virus, cytomegalovirus, human herpes virus 6, and herpes simplex viruses types 1 and 2). The *herpes simplex virus, types 1 and 2* are the most common strains of the herpes virus family. They are sexually trans-

mitted strains (as is the cytomegalovirus) that produce cold-sore-like blisters in the areas of the genitals and mouth.

Two Types of Herpes Simplex Virus (HSV): 1 and 2 Herpes simplex virus (HSV) types 1 and 2, which are closely related to each other, are associated with STDs. *(See ● Figure 10.)*

- *Herpes simplex type 1: Herpes simplex virus type 1,* **which lies dormant in a nerve in the face, typically causes cold sores (fever blisters) around the mouth.** It can also cause genital herpes. It has been estimated that 90% of adults have been exposed to this virus.

- *Herpes simplex type 2: Herpes simplex virus type 2* **is commonly associated with genital herpes.** However, it too can be found in and around the mouth.[124] When located in the genital area, it lies dormant in a nerve track at the base of the spine. Generally, this strain recurs more frequently than the type 1—some people experience four or more attacks a year.

Oral-genital sex makes these distinctions less relevant, however. The type 2 genital virus can be acquired through oral sex with a partner who has a type 1 herpes virus outbreak in or on the mouth.

How It Feels, How It Spreads Many occurrences of genital and labial herpes are so mild they may not be noticed. For those who do have symptoms, two common patterns have been identified. Which pattern occurs depends on whether it is a primary (first) experience with the virus or a recurrence of the virus.

In both types, people may experience numbness, itching, or tingling where they have had contact with the virus. Next is an often painful eruption of water-filled blisters. Within 10 days of an initial exposure to the virus, people may feel flulike symptoms: fever, chills, nausea, headaches, fatigue, and muscle aches. The eruption crusts and scabs over, and then in about 2–3 weeks the skin appears normal.

After the first episode, the virus seems to disappear. Thereafter it emerges from time to time—sometimes as frequently as four or more times a year. Sometimes it will produce no symptoms. At other times it will produce outbreaks of blistering sores, although the flulike syptoms do not reappear. As time goes on, many find that the duration of symptoms becomes shorter and less severe.

The infection is active between the initial itch and tingle and the complete disappearance of symptoms. While it is active, the virus may be spread by skin-to-skin contact. However, in many women, perhaps half, the symptoms of infection are so slight that they easily escape notice.[125] Such women are said to have *asymptomatic viral shedding*. Thus, even highly motivated people who avoid sex during herpes flare-ups face the possibility of transmitting the disease to their partners.[126] Indeed, even doctors' standard methods of diagnosing genital herpes in women—routine physicals and patient histories—miss many cases.[127] If you think you should be screened for herpes, ask for a blood test, although no single test detects all cases.

The Effects of Herpes Among adults, apparently the principal effects of herpes are feelings of desperation and social inhibition. A great many herpes victims feel isolated and depressed and fear rejection in social situations. Although the negative effect of herpes on work and school performance and nonsexual socializing diminishes, it still causes distress in sexual relations.[128] One of the best coping mechanisms is to develop a social support system.

Much worse off is the baby born to a woman who has a herpes infection at the time of the birth. The baby is apt to contract the disease during the birth process.[129] Among the babies born with the virus, as many as 60% die. Half of the rest suffer blindness or brain damage.[130]

Prevention and Treatment People who know they have herpes are advised to abstain from sex until all symptoms have disappeared. At other times, they should use latex condoms along with a spermicidal jelly or cream containing nonoxynol-9. They should avoid touching infected areas and should wash their hands with soap and water if they do touch infected areas accidentally. Still, there are no guarantees. People who only have sex when they are free of symptoms and who use condoms may still have some potential to transmit the virus.[131]

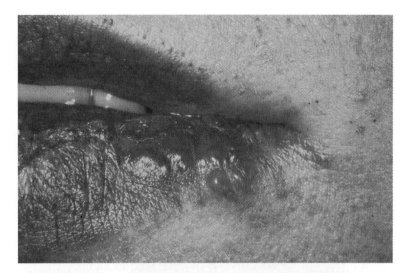

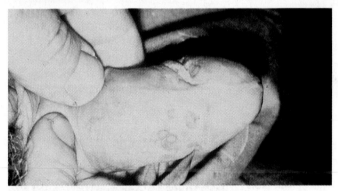

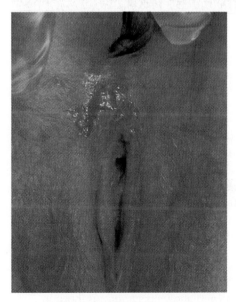

● **Figure 10 Herpes simplex.** *Top:* Fever blister—sore on lower lip. *Middle and bottom:* Blisters on male and female genitals.

There is no cure for herpes. Still, friction, sunlight, fever, stress, depression, and other psychological upsets seem to trigger recurrences.[132–134] Studies have found that infected people who have learned relaxation and other coping techniques suffer fewer herpes outbreaks.[135]

In addition, a prescription drug called *acyclovir*, if taken during the initial herpes outbreak, can ease the symptoms. The drug may also be given continuously (with a break every 6 months) for those suffering frequent outbreaks.

Human Papilloma Virus: The Fastest-Spreading STD

Human papilloma virus is associated principally with "genital warts," or fleshy growths in genital and other areas. Sometimes it has no symptoms at all. The disease is dangerous because it may increase the risk of cancer.

What is perhaps the *fastest-spreading* STD in the United States? It might be one you've never heard of: ***HPV*, short for *human papilloma virus*, which causes genital warts.** There are presently an estimated 12–24 million cases of HPV in the United States, with 750,000 new cases being added every year.[136] Indeed, nearly *half* of a sample of sexually active college women who had sexual relations with an average of four lifetime partners were HPV positive.[137]

HPV should not be taken lightly. At one time, it was thought that HPV caused only ***genital warts*—unpleasant but supposedly harmless fleshy growths. They occur on the penis, scrotum, anus, or urethra (the tube from the bladder to the outside) in men. They are found on the vulva, perineum, cervix, and anus in women, and in areas of the mouth** of both sexes.[138] However, some types of HPV have also been associated with cancer—for example, of the anus, penis, vulva, and cervix.[139, 140] Unfortunately, HPV also may be painless and show no symptoms, both in males and females. Many people with genital warts also have other STDs.

HPV is very contagious, being readily transmitted by sexual contact (including oral-genital sex). Newborns can acquire it from afflicted women during passage through the birth canal. On average the incubation period is 2–3 months after contact. Women who have had HPV should get an annual Pap test, the standard test for cervical cancer. However, the Pap test will not diagnose a *new, recent* HPV infection. Other tests (such as one called the Southern blot technique) are required for this.

Treatment is required not only for the patient but for his or her sexual partner, who may otherwise reinfect the patient.[141, 142] Genital warts are treated by freezing (cryotherapy), heat (diathermy), cauterization, laser therapy, chemicals, or surgical removal.

Chlamydia: The Most Common STD

Chlamydial infections, perhaps the most common of STDs, often show no symptoms. Serious complications in women are pelvic inflammatory disease, which can cause infections of the cervix, also possibly causing infertility. Infections of newborns can occur during childbirth. Two complications in men are epididymitis, which can lead to sterility, and nongonococcal urethritis.

If HPV is the fastest-growing sexually transmitted disease in the United States, chlamydia is perhaps the most common STD. It affects 3–4 million Americans every year, according to the Centers for Disease Control and Prevention.[143] ***Chlamydia*—or more accurately *chlamydial infections*—consists of a family of sexually transmitted diseases caused by a bacterium** (*Chlamydia trachomatis*). The disease is usually transmitted by sexual contact, including anal-genital and oral-genital sex.[144] A major problem with chlamydia is that it *often does not cause any symptoms*—especially early in the disease and in women. Yet if untreated it can cause lifelong damage. For example, one consequence is the eye infection ***trachoma*, a chronic conjunctivitis causing blindness.**

Infections in Women and Newborns About 50–70% of females show no early signs or symptoms. Those who do show symptoms may experience bleeding between menstrual periods, painful urination, abdominal pain, and vaginal discharge. Often women only become aware they have chlamydia when their sexual partners are diagnosed with it.

Untreated chlamydial infections in women can lead to some serious complications. Perhaps the three most important are *pelvic inflammatory disease, cervical infections,* and *infections of newborns*:

- **Pelvic inflammatory disease (PID): In pelvic inflammatory disease (PID) organisms ascend from the vagina or cervix to the uterus, fallopian tubes, and ovaries, finally infecting the pelvic area. The infection sometimes spreads to the liver and appendix. PID is characterized by lower abdominal pain, painful intercourse, irregular menstrual bleeding, abnormal vaginal discharge, painful urination, fever, and nausea and vomiting.** On the other hand, sometimes there are no symptoms at all.

  About half of all PID cases result from chlamydia—perhaps half a million American women a year, most among women under age 25 who are sexually active.[145] (PID also results from gonorrhea, discussed in a few pages.)

  At least a fourth of the women who develop PID suffer long-term consequences: One is chronic lower abdominal pain. Another is scarring of the fallopian tubes, which is held accountable for up to 30% of cases of infertility a year. PID is also associated with half of all cases of *ectopic pregnancy* (tubal pregnancy). **This occurs when a fertilized egg (ovum) implants itself outside the lining of the uterus in the fallopian tube or elsewhere.**[146]

  PID is treated with antibiotics. The earlier the treatment the better in terms of preventing scarring of the fallopian tubes and other complications. The risk of acquiring PID is reduced by avoiding high-risk sexual behaviors and by using condoms and diaphragms with spermicide containing nonoxynol-9.[147] Oral contraceptives may also protect some women against PID who are already infected with chlamydia.[148]

- **Cervical infections:** Chlamydial infections of the cervix usually cause no symptoms or only symptoms such as a slight vaginal discharge, which are sometimes missed. An untreated cervical infection, however, can lead to PID and result in infertility and even death. Treatment is with antibiotics (tetracycline).

- **Infections of newborns:** About two out of three infants born to women with chlamydial genital infections will become infected. It usually happens when they come into contact with an infected cervix during childbirth. Such infants, who may be born prematurely and with low birth weights, may develop eye infections (conjunctivitis) and pneumonia, if not treated at birth.[149,150]

Infections in Men As in women, early chlamydial infection in men often goes unrecognized. About 30% of infected men show no symptoms.[151] Those who do have symptoms may have a watery, puslike discharge from the penis and experience difficult, painful urination.

If untreated, two of the most common results of chlamydial infection in men are epididymitis and nongonococcal urethritis:[152]

- **Epididymitis: Epididymitis is an inflammation of the comma-shaped structure leading out of the testicle called the *epididymis*.** Most commonly found in sexually active males under age 35, epididymitis is characterized by tenderness in the testicles, fever, and swelling. If untreated, it can produce sterility.

- **Nongonococcal urethritis (NGU):** Chlamydia causes perhaps half the cases of **nongonococcal urethritis (NGU), an infection of the urethra in men.** (The other half of NGU cases are caused by gonorrhea.) The symptoms include mild burning during urination and discharge from the penis.

The symptoms of rectal infection are rectal pain, soreness, and anal discharge; oral-genital sex may produce an inflamed sore throat.[153] Diagnosis is by means of a lab test, often a culture of the affected area.

Treatment The standard treatment for chlamydia for both men and women is antibiotics, usually tetracycline. It is important to continue treatment as prescribed to prevent the continuation of the infection. Unfortunately, many people with the infection show no symptoms and thus aren't treated. A one-dose antibiotic (Zithromax) may help address this problem.[154]

Gonorrhea: An Old Enemy Comes Back

Gonorrhea is an easily transmitted STD presently on the increase after declining for some time. Infection is through sexual contact and during childbirth. Infected men may show inflammation called urethritis; infected women may show infections of the cervix and pelvic inflammatory disease. Both sexes may have rectal and throat infections and severe systemic blood-borne infection. Gonorrhea is treated with penicillin, although a penicillin-resistant strain has emerged.

Once upon a time, when the phrase "venereal disease" was in use, when people thought of sexually transmitted diseases they thought principally of gonorrhea ("clap" or "drip") and syphilis. For a time, in the 1970s and early 1980s, the incidence of these two diseases declined.[155] Recently, unfortunately, both the old enemies gonorrhea and syphilis have had a resurgence.

What It Is, How It Spreads *Gonorrhea* **is caused by the sexual transmission of a bacterium** (*Neisseria gonorrhoeae*). It is an organism that is easily transmitted. A man who has had sexual intercourse *once* with an infected woman has a 20–25% risk of getting the disease. A woman who has intercourse *once* with an infected man has a 50% chance of getting it.[156]

The disease may be spread from one person to another via genital, oral, or anal contact, both heterosexual and homosexual. It also spreads to babies during childbirth. Specifically:

- *Infection from sexual contact:* Because the gonorrhea bacterium needs warmth and humidity to thrive, it is harbored principally in warm, moist areas of the human body. Thus, one may contract gonorrhea from an infected person through genital, anal, and oral contact—including kissing.[157]

- *Infection of newborn babies:* Babies born to mothers who have gonorrhea may become infected as they pass through the birth canal. If not treated, they risk becoming blind. Thus, it is standard for newborns to have antiseptic or antibiotic placed in their eyes at birth to prevent blindness.

- *Probably not from toilet seats:* Toilet seats may harbor the gonococcus bacterium for a few seconds. However, despite the theoretical possibility of—and the folklore about—contracting the disease from toilet seats, the evidence does not show this occurs.[158]

Infections in Men Some men, perhaps 10–20%, show no signs of infection at all.[159] Otherwise, the main manifestation is urethritis. **Urethritis is a painful inflammation of the urethra, which discharges urine from the bladder.** Whether the form of urethritis is nongonococcal urethritis (NGU), as we discussed above under chlamydia, or gonococcal urethritis (GCU), the symptoms are unpleasant. There is burning pain during urination and discharge of pus—often watery or milkish at first, then greenish yellow—from the tip of the penis.

The burning sensation may subside in 2–3 weeks. But if the disease is not treated it spreads throughout the urinary and reproductive systems, causing scarring, obstructions, and sterility.

Infections in Women Early gonorrhea symptoms in women may be so slight that they are apt to be overlooked. Indeed, up to 80% of women show no symptoms at all. Women may only begin to suspect they have a problem when their partners are diagnosed.[160] When symptoms appear, they may take the following forms:

- *Infections of cervix:* Cervical infections can produce a yellowish or yellow-green puslike vaginal discharge, which can cause irritation of the vagina and painful and frequent urination. Someone who has an infected cervix may experience pain during sexual intercourse.

- ***Pelvic inflammatory disease:*** If untreated, gonorrhea, like chlamydia, can lead to pelvic inflammatory disease (PID) as the infection moves through the reproductive system. Scar tissue in the fallopian tubes, the long-term consequence of PID, may lead to sterility or ectopic pregnancies.

Infections in Either Sex In addition to the gender-specific symptoms above, gonorrhea may produce the following problems in either men or women:

- ***Rectal infections:*** Among men with a history of anal intercourse, there are almost as many rectal infections as there are instances of urethritis. Half of such men, however, show no symptoms.[161] Women who practice anal sex may also experience gonorrhea infection.
- ***Throat infections:*** Men or women who practice oral-genital contact may experience throat infections, which feel much like a sore throat.
- ***Severe systemic blood-borne infection:*** Gonorrhea can develop into a serious blood-borne systemic infection. This infection may lead to a form of arthritis in the joints and attack important organs in the body, from heart to brain to skin. This systemic infection can even be fatal.

Diagnosis and Treatment Gonorrhea is primarily diagnosed through laboratory tests, usually microscopic analysis of cultures taken from sites of infection. One test that is now available can detect the organism within 3 hours.

The principal treatment is use of antibiotics, especially penicillin. A very great problem recently, however, is the appearance of ***PPNG—*** **short for *penicillinase-producing Neisseria gonorrhoeae.* These are penicillin-resistant strains of gonorrhea.** The spread of PPNG is up 131% from 1988 to 1989.[162, 163] In place of penicillin, doctors are using other antibiotics (such as ceftriaxone).

Syphilis: The "Great Imitator" Returns

The symptoms of syphilis mimic many other disorders and diseases. Transmitted by sexual and oral contact and to newborns during childbirth, syphilis has four stages: primary, secondary, latent, and tertiary. The disease is detected by means of blood tests.

Syphilis, another old enemy like gonorrhea, is known as the "great imitator" because its sores and other symptoms mimic other disorders. For example, it may be mistaken for cancers, abscesses, hemorrhoids, and hernias.[164] Once thought to be under control in the United States, syphilis has returned with a vengeance. In 1990 it reached its highest level since 1949, zooming 75% in just 5 years. One reason for this epidemic, experts say, is the surge in crack cocaine use, which promotes high-risk sexual behavior. Some syphilitic patients have traded anonymous sex for money or drugs.[165, 166]

What It Is, How It Spreads *Syphilis* **is a sexually transmitted disease that is characterized by four stages.** Like gonorrhea, the disease is caused by a bacterium, in this case a **long, slender, spiral bacterium, or *spirochete,*** called *Treponema pallidum.* Syphilis is a serious STD because it can become a systemic infection, leading to possible brain damage, heart failure, and death.

The syphilis bacterium is a frail organism that requires warm, moist skin or mucous-membrane surfaces for survival. These spirochetes are present in **dime-sized or smaller sores, called *chancres,*** which may originate where the spirochete enters the body. Chancres may exist on the outside of the body—such as the lip, tongue, or finger—but also may be hidden within the vagina or rectum. *(See* ● *Figure 11.)* The disease can be transmitted to another person when these sores are present. Because the sores do not cause pain, they may not be noticed.

Specifically, syphilis is transmitted as follows:

- ***Infection by sexual and mouth contact:*** Syphilis is transmitted to a sexual partner through vaginal intercourse, anal intercourse, or oral-genital contact. It may be transmitted by kissing, if the sores are present in or around the mouth.

- ***Infection of fetus during pregnancy:*** A baby in the womb may acquire *congenital syphilis* because its mother is infected and the spirochetes cross the placental barrier. Syphilis can cause deafness, anemia, and damage to bones and teeth. In extreme cases, the infant may die before birth (stillbirth).

    Accordingly, pregnant women are advised to have blood tests for syphilis. Infection of the fetus apparently does not occur before the fourth month of pregnancy. Thus treatment of a woman with syphilis prior to the fifth month can prevent damage to the baby.[167]

The Four Stages of Syphilis Syphilis appears in four stages—primary, secondary, latent, and tertiary—as follows:

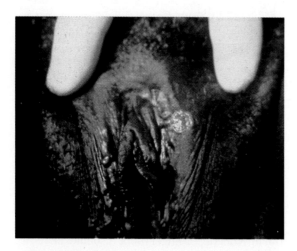

● **Figure 11 A chancre.** This dime-sized, painless sore may appear in the vulva (as shown), penis, anus, rectum, cervix, perineum, lips, tongue, fingers, and (rarely) other parts of the body. It contains the spirochetes that are the bearers of syphilis.

- ***Primary syphilis—painless sores that go away:*** In the first stage, one or more pink or red raised sores called *chancres* appear at the point of sexual contact. This may be the penis, vulva, vagina, cervix, anus, rectum, tongue, lips, breast, or wherever. The edges of the sore are hard, like cartilage. Because it is painless, it is often ignored or not noticed. The chancre appears within 10–90 days of infection.

    The chancre disappears by itself in 3–6 weeks. This may give the impression that the disease itself also has disappeared, but it has not.

- ***Secondary syphilis—rash and sores:*** About 6–12 weeks later, after the disappearance of the chancre, the spirochete spreads through the blood. This leads to symptoms of the second stage. These symptoms may be mistaken for the flu: swollen lymph nodes, sore throat, headache, and fever. There may also be loss of hair. The disease also produces a nonitchy rash on the hands or feet or all over the body. *(See ● Figure 12.)*

    In addition, large, moist sores may appear around the mouth or genitals. Because they are swarming with spirochetes, the sores make this second stage especially contagious to sexual partners. If untreated, the second-stage sores disappear in 2–6 weeks. This only means the disease has entered the next stage.

- ***Latent syphilis—unnoticed invasion of the body:*** In this stage, which may last from a few months to a lifetime, the disease goes underground. Only a blood test can show whether a person has the disease. The spirochetes burrow unnoticed into the blood vessels, bones, spinal cord, brain, and other organs. Some 50–70% of those with untreated syphilis remain in this latent stage the rest of their lives and experience no further problems. The rest develop late-stage syphilis.[168]

    During the first two years of the latent stage, the symptoms of secondary syphilis may reappear. On these occasions the person is highly contagious to sexual partners. After a year or two, the person is no longer contagious. An infected pregnant woman,

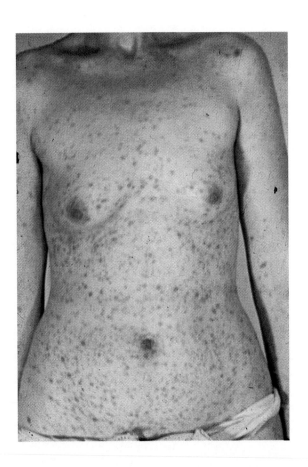

● **Figure 12   Rash of secondary syphilis.** A sign of the second stage of syphilis, this rash does not itch. It may appear all over the body or only part of it.

however, can always transmit the disease to her fetus.

● ***Tertiary syphilis—destruction of nervous system and organs:*** Years or even decades after the initial exposure to syphilis, untreated syphilis may result in major damage. It can affect the heart and major blood vessels, the central nervous system, or other organ systems. The results are impaired muscle control, paralysis, insanity, and death. This late-stage syphilis can also affect nearly all other organs: eyes (causing blindness), muscles, skin, lungs, liver, digestive organs, and endocrine glands.

Diagnosis and Treatment The re-emergence of syphilis has forced physicians to become highly suspicious about a disease that once had become relatively rare in North America.[169, 170] Health officials are also worried that the open sores of syphilis make it easier for HIV to enter the body.[171]

Syphilis is diagnosed by means of blood tests and the microscopic analysis of cultures of suspected spirochetes taken from sores. Blood tests are used as a standard screening device. Indeed, blood tests for possible syphilis are required to obtain marriage licenses in some states.

Syphilis is treated by antibiotics. Penicillin, for example, is the most common treatment for syphilis and can be highly effective if taken during the disease's primary stage.

Parasite Infections: Pubic Lice and Scabies

The parasite infections of pubic lice and scabies are transmitted by sexual means. They are far easier to control than other STDs.

The STDs we have described are transmitted by organisms that are microscopic in size. However, at least one of the parasitic insects transmitted by sexual contact, pubic lice, can be seen with just a magnifying glass. *(See ● Figure 13.)* Its eggs can be easily seen with the naked eye.

Pubic Lice: "Crabs" Called *crabs* because of their crablike appearance, ***pubic lice are wingless, gray insects, about 1/16th inch long. They live in human hair,*** particularly pubic hair, although they may move to underarm hair, eyebrows, eyelashes, and beards. Pubic lice feed on blood, causing itching and skin discoloration. Female lice lay eggs, or *nits,* that are attached to the hair.

Pubic lice are mainly transmitted during sexual intercourse but may also be picked up from bedding and infected clothing. Treatment is by washing with insecticide-containing shampoo available from health care professionals and as over-the-counter preparations available at pharmacies. In addition, the nits may be combed out with a fine-toothed comb. Contaminated clothing and linen should be washed.

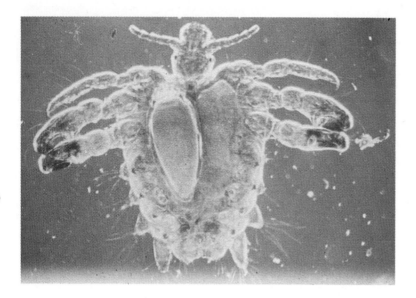

● **Figure 13   Pubic louse.** About ¹⁄₁₆ inch long, the pubic louse is often transmitted by sexual contact. Pubic lice live in body hair, feed on human blood, and cause itching.

Scabies: Skin Mites Scabies is a parasitic infection that spreads the same way as pubic lice—by sexual contact or contact with contaminated clothing or bedding. **Scabies are tiny mites that burrow under the skin and lay eggs, producing itching and discolored lines on the skin.** Treatment consists of washing oneself and other members of the household with insecticide-containing soap. Bedding and clothing should also be thoroughly washed.

Infections of the Reproductive and Urinary Systems

Troublesome disorders of the urinary and reproductive systems include bacterial vaginosis, trichomoniasis, yeast infections, and cystitis. These infections occur in both sexes.

Some infections of the urinary and reproductive systems are not transmitted exclusively by sexual contact, although it is one possible means of transmission. Still, that doesn't make them any less troublesome. We describe *bacterial vaginosis*, *trichomoniasis*, *yeast infections*, and *cystitis*.

Bacterial Vaginosis ***Bacterial vaginosis (BV), with slightly increased, malodorous vaginal discharge, is the most common cause of vaginal symptoms among women of childbearing age.***[172] BV may be a risk factor for pelvic inflammatory disease. The bacterial organism leading to bacterial vaginosis is probably transmitted by male partners during sexual intercourse. However, BV may also be present in the absence of sexual activity. Although some women show no symptoms, others reveal a white vaginal discharge. Diagnosis is made by performing laboratory tests, and treatment is with sulfa creams and antibiotics. Sexual partners should also be treated to prevent reinfection.

Trichomoniasis **The infection *trichomoniasis* ("trick") found in both sexes, is caused by a parasitic microorganism that is a protozoa** *(Trichomonas vaginalis)*. Some women show no symptoms at all, but 50–75% experience itching, burning, and vaginal discharge and find sexual intercourse painful. The infection generally remains in the genital and urethral area. Some women experience urinary symptoms. Many men show no symptoms. Those who do may experience a slight burning during urination. Trichomoniasis is highly contagious and is usually transmitted sexually. But it may also be transmitted in other ways, as from public toilet seats.[173] Treatment for both oneself and one's sexual partners is with oral or vaginal medications such as metronidazole (Flagyl).

Yeast Infections About 75% of women will at some point experience vaginal yeast infections.[174] **Yeast infections are caused by the fungus *Candida albicans* and other candida species. These organisms normally inhabit the intestinal tract, mouth, and vagina** but cause no problems or symptoms unless overgrowth of the organism occurs. In women, the symptoms of vaginal yeast infections can include severe itching, pain during intercourse, vaginal redness and soreness, and a white vaginal discharge. In men, the fungus may be present under the foreskin or scrotum, but most men have no symptoms.

Vaginal yeast infections can be precipitated by poor diet (excessive intake of sugar), use of antibiotics, diabetes, frequent douching, or pregnancy. Treatment of oneself and one's sexual partner is with antifungal vaginal suppositories or creams.

Urinary Tract Infections: Cystitis As with many other disorders of the urinary system, women appear more vulnerable than men to **cystitis, inflammation of the urinary bladder.** The reason for this inequality may be that the urethra in women is short (about 1½ inches long), compared to 6 inches in men. That gives bacteria a shorter distance to travel to reach the bladder in females. One in five women have a urinary tract infection sometime, and many are prone to recurrent infections. Sexual intercourse is a common way that bacteria gets introduced into the female urethra.

Cystitis can be caused by a variety of microorganisms, particularly those that normally inhabit the intestinal tract. Symptoms include burning during urination, urgency and frequency of urination, blood in the urine, fever, lower abdominal pain, and fatigue. Diagnosis is through a laboratory analysis of a urine culture. Early treatment, which usually consists of 7–10 days of antibiotics, is important to prevent the infection from migrating to the kidneys. There it could produce **pyelonephritis, inflammation of the kidneys.**

Noninfectious Illnesses

▶ Explain the mechanism of diabetes and differentiate between the two types.

▶ Describe three principal disorders of the nervous system: different types of headaches, multiple sclerosis, and two types of seizure disorders or epilepsy.

▶ Discuss the two important disorders of the bones and joints—low-back pain and arthritis.

▶ Describe the digestive-related disorders of inflammatory bowel disease and gallbladder disease.

▶ Discuss two principal disorders of the kidneys—kidney failure and kidney stones.

▶ Explain the two important respiratory disorders of asthma and chronic obstructive lung disease.

▶ Describe the two major dental diseases of cavities and gum disease and how they may be prevented.

Becoming ill because you caught some free-floating microorganism is easy to understand. All of us have been suddenly laid low by a cold virus or flu microbe—in other words, an infectious disease. Noninfectious illnesses also seem to come out of nowhere, although we can't say, "A germ did this to me." But these disorders, such as diabetes, headaches, low-back pain, asthma, and tooth decay, can be as troubling as any infection. This section explains some of the principal noninfectious conditions.

Diabetes: Failure to Use Glucose

Diabetes is a disease in which the body cannot properly metabolize food, especially carbohydrates. In people with diabetes, the pancreas cannot produce any insulin (Type 1 diabetes) or insufficient insulin (Type 2 diabetes).

SELF DISCOVERY 2

Are You at Risk for Diabetes?

Answer yes or no to each of the following statements:

	Yes	No
1. I have been experiencing one or more of the following symptoms regularly:		
a. Excessive thirst	____	____
b. Frequent urination	____	____
c. Extreme fatigue	____	____
d. Unexplained weight loss	____	____
e. Blurry vision from time to time	____	____
2. I am older than 30.	____	____
3. I am at least 20% over my ideal weight.	____	____
4. I am a woman who has had more than one baby weighing more than 9 pounds at birth.	____	____
5. I am of Native American descent.	____	____
6. I am of Hispanic or African American descent.	____	____
7. I have a parent with diabetes.	____	____
8. I have a brother or sister with diabetes.	____	____

Scoring

Score your yes answers as follows:

1a. 3	1c. 1	1e. 2	3. 2	5. 1	7. 1
1b. 3	1d. 3	2. 1	4. 2	6. 1	8. 2

Add your score: _____

Interpretation

3–5 points: You are at low risk for diabetes.

Over 5 points: You may be at high risk or even have diabetes. *See your doctor without delay.*

Preventive Steps

You can't change your heritage or your age, but you can change habits that may affect whether or not you get diabetes. Best are a low-calorie diet and a regular aerobic exercise program, which will keep your weight down.

Source: Adapted from The Diabetes Risk Test, American Diabetes Association, National Center, 1660 Duke Street, Alexandria, VA 22314.

As the seventh leading cause of death in the United States, diabetes is serious business.[175] Every year, 30,000 Americans die from it, and 300,000 more die from complications stemming from it. It doubles the risk of heart attack or stroke and is the leading cause of blindness in adults. It is associated with one-third of kidney failure cases.[176] Pregnant women with diabetes have higher risks of miscarriage or producing infants with developmental delays and birth defects.[177–179] Most disturbing, perhaps half of all Americans who have diabetes have not been diagnosed as having the disease. *(See Self Discovery 2.)*

Diabetes: What It Is, What It Does *Diabetes—more precisely known as diabetes mellitus—is a disease in which the body cannot properly metabolize food, especially carbohydrates.* A one-sentence definition only begins to cover it, however. The details are as follows:

1. To have energy and make replacement materials for itself, the body must metabolize—that is, chemically break down—food. Diabetes causes problems in metabolizing particular foods: carbohydrates and simple sugars.

2. Carbohydrates—fruits, milk, sugar, pasta, bread, vegetables, and other foods that include sugars and starches—act as the body's immediate fuel.

3. The body breaks down carbohydrates into *glucose*, or blood sugar. Glucose is the primary form of sugar that provides the body with energy. Both non-diabetics and diabetics are capable of producing glucose. The difference between them is what happens after that.

4. A critical organ is the pancreas. In healthy people, the level of glucose rises in the blood after a meal. This automatically causes the pancreas to release *insulin* into the blood. **The body needs *insulin*, a hormone, to move the sugar from the blood into the cells, which convert glucose into energy.**

5. In people with diabetes, unfortunately, the pancreas produces either no insulin or insufficient insulin or the person cannot use insulin effectively.

When *no* insulin is produced, the condition is called *Type 1 diabetes, insulin-dependent diabetes mellitus (IDDM), or juvenile onset diabetes.*

When *insufficient* insulin is produced, the condition is called *Type 2 diabetes, insulin-independent diabetes mellitus (IIDM), or adult onset diabetes.*

6. Without any insulin or not enough insulin, the glucose rising in the blood after a meal is unable to enter most body cells. This has two consequences: (a) The unused glucose has to go somewhere else, since it can't go into the cells. (b) The energy needs of the cells are not being met.

7. The unused glucose in the blood accumulates to such levels that the kidneys cannot process it. This excess glucose spills over into the urine, which is expelled.

8. When the energy needs of the cells are not met, the body begins to look within itself for another source of energy. Specifically, the body burns stored fats and proteins, in the course of which it produces dangerous acids called *ketones*. Ketones can lead to nausea, vomiting, abdominal pain, drowsiness, and even coma and death.[180]

Diabetics are at risk for heart and blood vessel disease, kidney disease, nerve damage, infection, slow healing for cuts and bruises, and blindness. This means that every diabetic should be under a doctor's care.

Diagnosis, Onset, and Risk Factors
Symptoms of diabetes include excessive thirst, frequent urination, fatigue and weakness, irritability, and a craving for sweets. Diagnosis is made on the basis of blood glucose tests.

The two types of diabetes have different patterns:

*   *Type 1 diabetes:* The onset of Type 1 diabetes, in which the body does not produce insulin at all, usually strikes in childhood or adolescence. However, it can develop at any time up to 35 years of age. Type 1 diabetes often comes about suddenly, the result of the body's own immune system destroying the insulin-producing cells of the pancreas.[181] Although the cause is unknown, in

some cases it may spring from virus-caused infection of the insulin-producing cells.[182]

*   *Type 2 diabetes:* Type 2 diabetes, in which insulin production is insufficient rather than totally lacking, is the less severe of the two types. It is far more common. Type 2 generally comes about gradually and occurs most often in adults who are over 35 and overweight. Here, too, the causes are unknown.

Fully 90% of all diabetics have Type 2 diabetes. It can occur in people with no family history of diabetes, but people with relatives who are diabetic are at high risk. Perhaps 75% of diabetics are overweight and don't exercise. Most are also over age 45.

Treatment   Diabetes cannot be cured, but it can be managed. The course of treatment is different for the two types:

*   *Type 1:* People with Type 1 diabetes cannot go much more than a day without insulin. It is usually self-administered either via injections (1–4 daily) or via an insulin pump.[183] *(See ● Figure 14.)* Too much or too little insulin can cause life-threatening complications. Signs of insulin overdose are weakness, impaired vision, tingling in hands, and drowsiness. If they occur, the person should take a fast source of sugar like sugar cubes or orange juice and seek medical help.

    Type 1 diabetics also need to take many of the same dietary and exercise measures as Type 2 diabetics do.

*   *Type 2:* People with Type 2 diabetes usually do not need daily insulin injections. They do need to take steps to maintain steady glucose and blood fat levels as much as possible. This means exercising, keeping their weight down, and watching their diet.

    The American Diabetes Association guidelines state that Type 2 diabetics may include up to 60% complex carbohydrates in their diet. (These are cereals, grains, breads, pasta, beans, fruits, and vegetables.) However, they should go easy on proteins (meat and milk) and fats and *very* easy on sugar and alcohol.

● **Figure 14   Insulin injection.** People with Type 1 diabetes require daily doses of insulin.

❝*Every moment of every day, the healthy human body performs an array of life-sustaining chores: The kidney filters toxins from the blood, the immune system battles foreign invaders, the lungs exchange carbon dioxide for precious oxygen. But for 14 million Americans stricken by diabetes mellitus—a chronic, incurable disease—one 'automatic' function, normally regulated by the pancreas, demands unrelenting attention: the conversion of sugar into fuel to power the body's cells.*

Diabetes robs its victims of the automatic pilot that regulates sugar processing. To compensate, diabetics must control their condition with an individually tailored regimen of diet, exercise and, when necessary, oral medication; many require daily insulin injections.❞

—Clare Collins. (1993, January/February). Diabolical diabetes. *American Health*, p. 68.

Neurological Disorders

Three neurological disorders, or disorders of the nervous system, are: (1) headaches, such as tension headaches induced by stress, migraine headaches, or cluster headaches; (2) multiple sclerosis (MS), possibly caused by a virus in which the immune system turns against the body; and (3) seizure disorders, or epilepsy, which includes convulsive seizures and nonconvulsive seizures.

There are a great many ***neurological disorders,*** **disorders of the nervous system.** Three that you may encounter are headaches, multiple sclerosis, and epilepsy.

Headaches Headaches—that mild to severe pounding pain in the head—can have all kinds of causes, some psychological, some organic. If they persist, they should be taken seriously.

Among the kinds of headaches are the following:

- ***Tension headaches:*** The most common kind of headache is ***tension headache,*** **discomfort caused by involuntary contractions of muscles in the neck, head, and scalp. They are usually brought about by stress.** They may be alleviated by stress-reduction techniques.

- ***Migraine headaches: Migraine headaches* have different causes. Blood vessels expand (dilate) in the brain, and chemicals leaked through the blood vessel walls inflame nearby tissues, sending pain signals.** Migraine attacks are often preceded by the sensation of glowing spots before the eyes, a condition known as an *aura.* Migraine headaches often run in families, are common, and can become increasingly severe over time. Migraines are treated with strong chemical painkillers and/or with relaxation.[184]

- ***Other headaches:*** One type of headache, most common in men, is the severely painful ***cluster headache.* It strikes on one side (and always the same side) of the head and occurs 1–14 times a day for many weeks.** Treatment is with prescription medications.

Some headaches are *secondary headaches* caused by some other condition. Causes include hunger (low blood sugar), colds, eyesight problems, badly fitting dentures, sexual activity, and so on. To treat the headache, one must first identify and treat the underlying cause.

Toxic headaches are types of secondary headaches caused by poisonous chemicals. Examples are toxins from bacterial infections, engine fumes, or alcohol (as with a hangover).

Multiple Sclerosis **Multiple sclerosis (MS) is a neurological disorder that, according to current theory, is caused by an unidentified virus. The virus causes cells in the immune system to turn against the body and attack the brain and spinal cord, slowing the nerve impulses.** In the beginning, symptoms include tremors, speech impediment, prickling and burning in the arms and legs, blurred vision, and changes in manner of walking. Often the disease goes into remission, in which one is free of symptoms for months or years. Ultimately, however, people suffer irreversible paralysis, and death occurs 20–25 years after onset.[185] The disease strikes as many as 350,000 Americans every year, primarily young adults around age 30.[186]

Treatment is with steroid, anti-inflammatory, and other drugs to relieve muscle spasms and physical therapy to reduce incapacitation. Psychotherapy and other forms of emotional support can help with depression.

Epilepsy and Seizure Disorders **Seizure disorders, also called *epilepsy* or *epilepsies*, are a collection of neurological disorders caused by abnormal electrical activity in the brain. They are characterized by sudden attacks, or seizures, of involuntary, sometimes violent muscle contractions and loss of consciousness.** About 1% of Americans suffer from some form of seizure-related disorder. The disorders are seldom fatal, although they can be dangerous if an attack occurs while one is driving or swimming.

The Epilepsy Foundation of America has simplified the classification of epilepsy into *convulsive* and *nonconvulsive*, as follows:[187]

- *Convulsive:* Often mistaken for a heart attack or a stroke, a ***convulsive seizure* is characterized by sudden rigidity and falls. These are most pronounced in a generalized major seizure (tonic-clonic or grand mal seizure).** This onset is followed by ***convulsions*—muscle jerks or involuntary muscle contractions.** Other symptoms are shallow or no breathing, perhaps loss of bladder or bowel control, frothy saliva on lips, and bluish skin. The attack usually lasts 2–5 minutes, followed by normal breathing, some confusion, and return to consciousness.

  If you see a person having such seizures, the main thing is to make sure he or she is not injured during the attack. Loosen clothing, protect the person's head, turn the person on his or her side to keep the airway clear, and check for medical identification. Take the person to an emergency room if the seizure lasts *longer* than 10 minutes. Do not try to restrain the person, put any implements in the mouth, or try to hold the tongue (which cannot be swallowed). Do not try to give liquids during or just after the seizure.

- *Nonconvulsive:* An attack of nonconvulsive seizures can be mistaken for daydreaming, intoxication, poor coordination, or mental illness. ***Nonconvulsive seizure* is a category covering a range of seizures. Types include brief muscle jerks, loss of contact with surroundings (psychomotor seizures), and loss of consciousness for several seconds (petit mal seizures).**

  If you are in the presence of a person having a nonconvulsive seizure, usually no first aid is required. You should expect the person to show momentary confusion and not understand you. The main thing is to provide reassurance and emotional support.

People with seizures are usually able to control their disorder with medications (such as carbamazepine and phenytoin). Most are able to drive, participate in athletics, go to school, and work.

Disorders of the Bones and Joints

Important disorders of bones and joints are low-back pain and arthritis, especially osteoarthritis and rheumatoid arthritis.

Disorders of the bones and joints are commonplace in part because we use them so frequently that injury is likely. Among the most common problems are *low-back pain* and *arthritis*.

Low-Back Pain Over a person's lifetime, 60–90% of people develop chronic back conditions.[188] Indeed, low-back pain is the second leading cause of missed work in the United States, right after the common cold.[189, 190] Even highly active people have bad backs. Chronic back conditions are the most frequent cause of activity limitation in people younger than age 45. They account for 23% of the activity limitation among people ages 18–44.[191]

Why is the back such a problem? One reason is that the disks, the gel-like pads separating each vertebra in the spine, wear out over time. Once they are too worn, a tiny stress—coughing, bending to pat the dog—can send a person into a paroxysm of pain. The sufferer may have a **herniated disk, the protrusion of the disk from its position between two vertebrae.** This condition may require surgery.

As you might expect, people whose jobs involve heavy lifting (garbage collectors, mechanics, nursing aides) are apt to suffer more low-back pain.[192] However, people who sit all week at their desks and then jump into weekend activity are also prime candidates for problems.

To avoid a back problem, note the following:

- **Don't demand too much of your back muscles:** The familiar advice for lifting something heavy is to keep the object close to your body and keep your back straight. *Bend your knees*, and *lift with your legs*. This advice is ignored with astonishing regularity, eventually to the sorrow of the lifter.[193]

  Any sport requiring lots of twisting, arching, and sudden starts and stops can put you at risk for back problems. Examples are racquet sports, golf, baseball, and basketball. Thus, you should do warm-ups,

stretches, and cool-downs before and after activity. Stretching helps lubricate the spinal joints.[194]

- **Build strong abdominal and back muscles:** Strong abdominal and back muscles help to support the spine and stabilize the lower back. Weak muscles allow your back to have an exaggerated curve that puts pressure on spinal nerves and discs.

  The best way to improve your abdominals is with exercise. The YMCA Healthy Back Program is devoted to strengthening the abdominal muscles. In one evaluation of the YMCA program, 82% of patients found their usual back pain stopped or decreased significantly.[195]

- **Move your body and don't smoke:** If you sit a lot, find ways to keep moving. Slump, fidget, cross and uncross your legs, stand up, sit down, and otherwise keep oxygenated blood circulating to the lower back muscles. Be aware that smoking restricts the flow of blood and oxygen to muscles.

If you suffer from periodic, mild low-back pain, you can try to alleviate it with rest, aspirin, heat, hot tubs, and massage. If it persists, however, you should consult a physician.

Arthritis **Arthritis is an umbrella term covering over 100 different types of inflammation of the joints.** The inflammation is frequently painful and often disabling and affects over 37 million Americans.[196] *(See ● Figure 15.)* Among the most common forms are *osteoarthritis* and *rheumatoid arthritis:*

- **Osteoarthritis:** Usually developing in people over age 40, **osteoarthritis is a progressive deterioration of the bones and joints. It is caused largely by weight bearing and deterioration of the joints.** Symptoms include swelling, pain, deformity, and restricted movement of joints.

- **Rheumatoid arthritis: Rheumatoid arthritis is a deterioration of the joints that results when the body's immune system attacks healthy cells in the joints.** Why the immune system attacks is not known. In about 2% of the population over age 15—more women than men—all the joints show symptoms of this disease. In the beginning, stiffness and joint pain are followed by swelling, deformity, and limitations in mobility.

If you have early morning stiffness, swelling or recurring pain in a joint, or inability to move a joint normally, see a physician. Treatment often includes drugs to reduce inflammation and relieve pain and physical therapy to maintain mobility. Sometimes artificial joints are implanted surgically.

Digestive-Related Disorders

Some serious digestive-related disorders are inflammatory bowel disease, which include Crohn's disease and ulcerative colitis, and gallbladder disease.

Is there anything more embarrassing than distress in the digestive system? Abdominal cramps and diarrhea are difficulties that are hard to bear in other people's company.

Some digestion-related disorders are merely uncomfortable. Others, however, are quite serious, such as inflammatory bowel disease and gallbladder disease.

Inflammatory Bowel Disease: Crohn's and Colitis *Inflammatory bowel disease* **encompasses two entities, Crohn's disease and ulcerative colitis. Both are disorders of unknown origin characterized by chronic inflammation of sections of the digestive tract.**

- *Crohn's disease:* **The most common symptoms of *Crohn's disease* are diarrhea, abdominal pain, cramps, and fever.** Diagnosis is made with an X-ray and examination of the inside of the intestine with a flexible, lighted tube (called a *colonoscopy*).

  Treatment is with drugs, including steroids and a drug called sulfasalazine. Surgery may be necessary to remove the diseased segment of the bowel.[197]

● **Figure 15 Arthritis.** Besides pain, arthritis often produces deformity of the joints.

66*Osteoarthritis is so common that nearly everyone over 40 shows some signs of it on X-rays—a gradual loss of the soft, smooth cartilage at joint surfaces, and frequently a compensatory overgrowth of bone at the joints. It's estimated that 20 million Americans have symptoms of this joint disease at any given time. . . .*

*Because of the pain and stiffness, the natural tendency is to minimize movement of arthritic joints. Unfortunately, this can simply lead to stiffer joints—and thus more pain—since inactivity weakens the muscles that stabilize joints.*99

—Editors of the University of California *Wellness Letter.* (1991). *The wellness encyclopedia.* Boston: Houghton Mifflin, p. 383.

- *Ulcerative colitis: Ulcerative colitis* **affects the colon and causes bouts of rectal bleeding and diarrhea.** After about 20 years of the disease, a patient has a significant chance of developing cancer of the colon.[198]

  Treatment is with antidiarrhea medications, drug therapy such as steroids and sulfasalazine, and change in diet.

Gallbladder Disease Imagine the sensation of having a hot poker thrust through your rib cage. That can be the feeling one has with a large gallstone. Roughly 20 million Americans have gallbladder disease, although only half seek treatment.[199] The disease typically affects middle-age women who are overweight.

The gallbladder is a small, pear-shaped sac attached to the underside of the liver. Its purpose is to store bile produced by the liver and release it into the small intestine to aid digestion. *Gallbladder disease* **occurs when the gallbladder has been irritated by infection or overuse, producing** *gallstones*—**formations of calcium, cholesterol, and minerals.** Often these are as small as grains of sand and produce no symptoms. However, when they become big, the size of walnuts, they become stuck in the bile duct. They then can cause several hours of intense pain, which may be mistaken for a heart attack. Diagnosis is made on the basis of X-rays as well as other imaging techniques.

Treatment may be through the removal of the gallbladder, an operation performed on an estimated 500,000 Americans every year.[200] Nowadays many people have this done in a 45-minute "keyhole surgery" that uses imaging equipment. Called a *laparoscopic cholecystectomy,* the operation leaves only a tiny scar and usually allows the patient to go home in less than a day.[201,202]

Kidney Disorders

When kidneys fail, a person must have a kidney transplant or have waste fluids cleared by using kidney dialysis. Kidney stones, which temporarily block the urinary system, are extremely painful.

Your two kidneys are part of the excretory system, organs for removing excess water, toxic waste products, and surplus chemicals from the body. For some whose kidneys fail, the damage is permanent. Kidney damage can be produced by infection, diabetes, poisoning by mercury or lead, high blood pressure, or other problems.

Kidney and Kidney Dialysis Once permanent damage has occurred, the only alternatives are kidney dialysis or kidney transplants. Kidney transplants are an involved surgical procedure requiring a tissue-matched organ from a living relative or from a cadaver. *Kidney dialysis* **consists of a mechanical process for doing what the kidneys can no longer do themselves—clear waste fluids from the body.** The patient is connected to a sophisticated filtering machine through which blood is circulated and impurities are removed.

Kidney Stones Having kidney stones, it is said, may be the closest men can come to knowing what women experience during the pain of childbirth.

The kidneys are located in the abdominal cavity, below the lowest rib. When difficulty with the kidneys occurs, it may at first be mistaken for a backache. However, the pain could indicate the presence of a *kidney "stone"* (technically called a *urinary calculus*). **The stone consists usually of crystallized salts and minerals that stick together.**[203] When it blocks the flow of urine from the kidney or bladder, the stone can cause excruciating agony. About 350,000 Americans every year have this frightening experience, accounting for more than 1% of the hospitalizations in the United States. Men, especially those aged 20–50, are more likely than women to have problems with kidney stones.[204]

Most of the time, the stones pass through on their own, bringing instant relief. However, if they do not, medical help must be sought to avoid kidney damage. The main nonsurgical procedure uses ultrasound to break up the stone. Recovery usually requires only a few days. Drugs may be used to reduce future kidney stones, but the main changes are dietary and beverage habits.

To avoid kidney stones and other kidney disorders, you should drink lots of fluids, perhaps 8 ounces every waking hour. This is especially necessary when you're very active or during the summer months when your body loses fluids through perspiration.

Respiratory Disorders

One important respiratory disorder is asthma, a chronic illness of the airways of the lungs. Another is chronic obstructive lung disease (COLD), which includes chronic bronchitis and pulmonary emphysema.

Among the worst of the respiratory afflictions are asthma and chronic obstructive lung disease (COLD).

Asthma *Asthma,* **a chronic illness of the airways in the lungs that leaves a person wheezing, coughing, and gasping for air, afflicts 15 million Americans.**[205] It is the most common chronic illness for children and adolescents. Repeated attacks can damage the lungs and heart. Death rates from asthma have increased significantly in recent years.[206,207]

Asthma attacks may be mild or severe. In an asthmatic person, the attacks may be triggered by an allergic reaction, as to dust, pollen, or cigarette smoke. Other triggers are bacterial infections, weather changes, exercise, and stress or fatigue. During the attack, there is swelling of the mucous membrane lining the small tubes in the lungs called bronchioles. This causes the bronchioles to constrict, obstructing airflow and producing blockage and spasms.

Asthma is diagnosed using lung-function tests and by exposing the patient to whatever agent is suspected of triggering the attacks. Treatment should be under the direction of a physician. It includes showing the patient what triggering factors to avoid, increasing exercise endurance, and alleviating any emotional distress. Medications are often in the form of bronchodilators that, when inhaled, widen the airways in the lungs. *(See ● Figure 16.)*

Chronic Obstructive Lung Disease
Chronic obstructive lung disease (COLD) **is characterized by the slow, progressive**

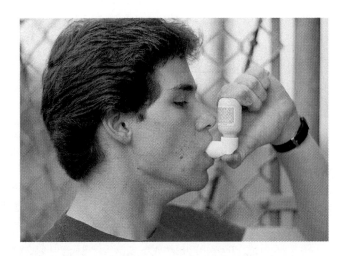

● **Figure 16** **Asthma treatment.** Some asthma patients need a bronchodilator to relieve their attacks.

❝*Once asthma begins, it establishes a powerful feedback loop that may not even need an allergen to trigger an attack. General irritants such as cigarette smoke and urban smog can cause the already inflamed airways to constrict. 'It is my opinion that parents and caregivers who smoke in the presence of a child are guilty of child abuse,' says Dr. Allan Luskin of the Rush Medical Center in Illinois. 'Smoke not only increases the risk of a child getting asthma in the first place, it makes asthma worse when it is there.'*❞

—Christine Gorman & Mary Cronin. (1992, June 22). Asthma: Deadly but treatable. *Time,* pp. 61–62.

interruption of air flow within the lungs. People who have COLD may have *chronic bronchitis, pulmonary emphysema,* or both:

- *Chronic bronchitis: Chronic bronchitis* **consists of inflamed airways to the lungs that lead to an increased production of mucus. The narrowed air passages and increased mucus produce shortness of breath,** labored breathing, and *sputum,* **the material coughed up from the throat.**

- *Pulmonary emphysema: Pulmonary emphysema is characterized by the loss of elasticity in the tiny air sacs (alveoli) of the lungs.* The air sacs become less elastic and thus less able to expand and contract. In time, these air sacs are stretched to the point that they rupture. The rib cage enlarges as it tries to accommodate the nonfunctional or overstretched air sacs, which makes the diaphragm work less efficiently.

    Ultimately, the impaired lung function interferes with the ability to exchange oxygen and carbon dioxide. This leads to continual shortness of breath and an overworked heart, which often leads to heart failure. Once the airways are destroyed, there is no way to reverse the process.

The biggest contributor to both chronic bronchitis and pulmonary emphysema is cigarette smoking.[208] Chronic bronchitis may also be brought about by inhaling sidestream (secondhand) smoke and environmental irritants such as chemicals. Both conditions are treated with drugs (such as antibiotics and epinephrine) and physical therapy.

Dental Disorders

Two major and very preventable dental diseases are cavities, caused mainly by the teeth-coating film called plaque, and gum disease. The principal defense is brushing and flossing.

Do you go to the dentist? Do you floss? According to one poll, 97% of Americans say regular dental checkups are important. Yet only 51% actually get a checkup at least twice a year. In addition, 80% say flossing is important, but only 36% floss at least once a day.[209] In short, dental care is an area where people don't practice what they preach.

Cavities and Gum Disease Most of us are concerned about having great smiles and avoiding bad breath. However, dental checkups and flossing are subjects a number of us don't want to think about. Half of Americans hate going to the dentist, surveys show. Perhaps 12 million

people show the sweaty-palms, heart-racing fear of dentists that constitutes a genuine phobia.[210] *(See ● Figure 17.)* Still, there are two major, and very preventable, dental diseases that can eventually affect your smile and your breath—cavities and gum disease:

- *Cavities:* About 95% of Americans have one or more **cavities, or *dental caries,* the demineralization of tooth enamel often called "tooth decay."**[211] Cavities are caused by ***plaque,* a sticky, colorless film containing bacteria that coats your teeth.** When mixed with sugar and starches or allowed to reproduce, plaque bacteria produce toxins that lead to tooth decay and gum disease. Sometimes you can recognize a cavity as a hole or discoloration in the tooth. More often it is discovered during a dental exam or because of a toothache.

- *Gum disease:* Cavities have actually been in decline, as a result of fluoridated water and toothpaste. Today only 4% of Americans under age 65 are toothless, compared to 40% a generation ago.[212] The culprit that dentists now worry about is **gum disease, or *periodontal disease*.**

    In its early and still reversible form, periodontal disease is manifested as gingivitis. **Signs of *gingivitis* include red and swollen gums that bleed easily,** especially during brushing. Gingivitis is caused by the migration of plaque bacteria beneath the gum line.

    If not treated, gingivitis is followed by more serious periodontal disease, ***periodontitis* (pyorrhea), characterized by permanent tooth, gum, and bone loss.**

If you're concerned about bad breath (halitosis), you should know that it can signal a form of periodontal disease. Gum disease now afflicts most children and adolescents, according to the American Academy of Periodontology.[213]

Strategy for Living: Brushing and Flossing
The weapons against bad breath and gum disease are well known: the toothbrush and dental floss:[214, 215]

- *Brushing:* Soft-bristle brushes are better than hard. Hard bristles can cause gum abrasions and wear down the tooth enamel.

They can even cause a groove in the soft roots of your teeth if your gums recede. Because plaque is soft, it can be removed with a soft brush moved in a small, circular, vibrating motion. As one dentist advised, "You should brush your teeth as if you were waxing an antique Porsche, not scrubbing the kitchen sink."[216] Electric toothbrushes are also effective, and, if your dentist advises it, an oral irrigator (such as Water Pik or Via-jet).[217]

- *Flossing:* "You don't have to floss all your teeth," says one writer, "only the ones you want to save."[218] People who say they don't have time to floss should consider keeping the floss next to the TV set. Or they could carry it in the car for use during traffic jams. Break off an 18-inch piece of floss (waxed or unwaxed, plain or flavored). Wind one end around the middle finger of one hand, the other around the middle finger of the other. Insert the floss between your teeth and move it back and forth in a gentle sawing motion.

Even conscientious brushing and flossing won't eliminate all the plaque. Thus, you need to visit the dentist twice a year to have the dentist or dental hygienist remove this for you. They will also check for signs of cavities and gum disease.

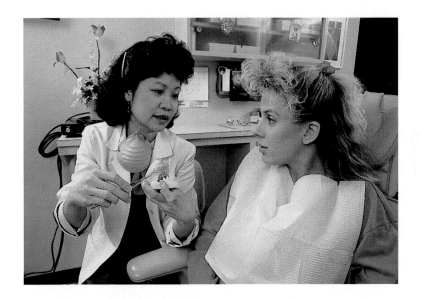

● **Figure 17   Fighting dental fear.**

"*If you're among the millions who avoid the dentist because of a fear of pain, remember that you are not without recourse, as these steps suggest:*

- *Ask dental schools to help you find phobia and pain clinics in your area.*
- *Ask for referrals to dentists who treat phobic or anxious patients.*
- *Ask the dentist how he or she deals with a patient's fear or pain. If your dentist seems unsympathetic, go to another.*
- *Make sure you take control. You need not be a victim.*
- *If one dentist hurts you, find another who doesn't. You'll keep smiling that way—with your own teeth.*"

—Carol Berczuk (1992, July 5). Are you afraid to go to the dentist? *Parade Magazine,* p. 13.

800-HELP

Acne Helpline. 800-222-SKIN. (In California, 800-221-SKIN.)

AIDS Hotline. 800-533-AIDS. (In Canada, 800-668-AIDS.)

AIDS Information Hotline. 800-342-AIDS. Public Health Service.

Allergy Information Hot Line. 800-727-5400. Sponsored by Allerest, this hotline offers a free allergy calendar.

Asthma and Allergy Foundation of America. 800-7-ASTHMA.

Crohn's and Colitis Foundation of America. 800-343-3637. Information on support groups for people coping with Crohn's disease and ulcerative colitis.

Juvenile Diabetes Foundation. 800-223-1138. (212-889-7575 in New York.)

Lungline. 800-222-LUNG. (In Colorado, 303-355-LUNG.) National Asthma Center.

National Asthma Center. 800-222-LUNG. (303-355-LUNG in Denver.)

National Headache Foundation. 800-843-2256. (800-523-8858 in Illinois.) Information on all types of headaches.

National Hemophilia Foundation. 800-424-2634. Answers questions about this blood-clotting disorder and provides local referrals for AIDS and HIV services, counseling, and treatment.

STD National Hotline. 800-634-3662. (In California, 800-982-5883.)

Suggestions for Further Reading

Ronald A. Baker, Jeffrey M. Moulton, & John Charles Tighe (1992). *Early care for HIV disease* (2nd ed.). San Francisco: San Francisco AIDS Foundation. Paperback book available at bookstores as well as from the foundation.

John G. Barlett & Ann K. Finkbeiner (1991). *The guide to living with HIV infection.* Baltimore: Johns Hopkins University Press. Developed at the Johns Hopkins University AIDS Clinic, this calm, clear, factual guide describes available treatments (both approved and unapproved), offers explicit advice for medical and legal decision-making, and tells how to find emotional support.

Jeffrey R. M. Kunz. (1987). *The American Medical Association family medical guide, revised and updated.* New York: Random House. Describes 650 illnesses, with flowcharts that lead the reader through self-diagnosis.

Mayo Clinic family health book. (1990). New York: William Morrow. In-depth descriptions of medical conditions, including symptoms and treatments.

Heart Disease, Cancer, and Personal Safety

Can there be a Silent Killer inside you without your knowing it?

In the United States, the No. 1 cause of death for the population as a whole is heart disease. The No. 2 cause of death is cancer. Because they have no immediate symptoms, people often don't know they are at risk for such health problems. High blood pressure, or hypertension, has been called the Silent Killer precisely because you can't tell you have it. Some health problems may not be avoidable: your predisposition toward getting heart disease or cancer may in part be hereditary. But family history is only one influence. People in other countries don't succumb to these diseases in the same way or at the same rate that Americans do. This means, then, that many of the risks have to do with *lifestyle*. And dedicating oneself to a healthy style of life is one of the fundamental arts of living.

The Way to a Healthy Heart

▶ Define *cardiovascular disease.*

▶ Describe the components of the cardiovascular system and describe how they work.

▶ Explain how blood pressure is measured and its significance.

▶ Identify and describe the five major groups of cardiovascular disease.

▶ Discuss the diagnostic procedures and treatment methods commonly used for cardiovascular disease.

▶ State what needs to be done in the event of a heart attack and how it may be treated.

▶ Discuss both predisposing and precipitating risk factors for cardiovascular disease.

▶ List the steps for preventing heart disease.

W hat would you say if you learned that a computer program suggests that adopting good heart-related health habits—stopping smoking, lowering cholesterol, and so on—would add only *3 years or so* to the average life span? You would probably say, "Why bother?"

A study by Dr. Joel Tsevat and others, based on a computer program developed by two Boston medical researchers, found exactly this. Eliminating all deaths from heart disease was estimated to extend the average life expectancy of a 35-year-old man by 3.1 years and a woman by 3.3 years.[1] The average life span in the United States today is 75.

There are, however, two important points about this. First, although the average increases might be small, the gains for *individuals* could be dramatic. For example, healthier habits could prevent some deaths from heart attacks at age 40 or 50. Second, adopting healthy habits that benefit the heart produce more healthy, fully active years.

Let us examine our deadliest enemy, **cardiovascular disease, defined as any disease or disorder of the heart and/or blood vessels.** But we need to keep in mind that it is just *one* potentially life-threatening disorder among many.

The Cardiovascular System: Blood, Circulation, and Heart

The cardiovascular system consists of blood, blood vessels, and heart. Blood carries nourishment to the body's cells. The circulatory system consists of the heart, blood vessels called arteries—which take blood out to the body from the heart—and veins, which bring it back. Blood pressure is a measure of the force of the blood in the blood vessels (systolic and diastolic).

Have a heart, the expression goes. What if you didn't have a heart, nor the circulatory system that goes with it? You would be like a city with no food-delivery and trash-removal trucks. Your body would have no means of delivering nutrients and oxygen to the cells or of removing the waste products of metabolism from the cells.

The closed system of heart, blood vessels, and blood is called the *cardiovascular system.* Blood does not flow through your body like a meandering stream. It is pushed through by the force of your heart's contractions and delivered by the blood vessels making up your circulatory system.

Let us see how it works, starting with the blood.

The Blood What, exactly, is that red liquid that seeps from your finger when you accidentally cut yourself? Blood is the substance that carries nourishment to the cells in your tissues and protects you against disease. Specifically, it consists of cells of several types and **a solution called *plasma, in which the cells are suspended.*** That is, it includes:

- *Red blood cells—45%:* About 45% of the blood consists of **red blood cells. Their purpose is to carry oxygen to the cells and carbon dioxide from the cells.**

- *White blood cells—1%:* About 1% of the blood is **white blood cells, an integral part of the immune system, whose purpose is to defend the body against a variety of organisms.**

- *Platelets—4%:* **Platelets are cell fragments in the blood that release substances necessary for clot formation.** Platelets clump together to help stop bleeding.

- *Plasma—50%:* About half the blood is made up of the watery substance plasma. It contains 90% water and various salts, sugar, cholesterol, proteins, minerals, and so on.

**The Circulatory System: Blood Routes in
the Body** The *circulatory system* **consists
of the heart and blood vessels.** The heart
pumps blood out through the arteries to the
body and then back to the heart through the
veins. *(See ● Figure 1.)*

    **The *arteries* are large-diameter blood
vessels that carry the blood from the heart
to smaller and smaller blood vessels. These
small blood vessels are called *arterioles*.**
The arterioles in turn branch into *capillaries*,
**tiny, thin-walled blood vessels that connect
the system of arteries with the system of
veins.** *(See ● Figure 2.)* **The *veins* return
the blood from the body to the heart.** The
blood in the capillaries delivers oxygen and nutrients to the cells in the tissues. The capillaries
also take up carbon dioxide and other waste
products of metabolism from the cells. These
wastes are sent to the heart through the veins.
Stretched end to end, all the vessels in the circulatory system would measure about 60,000
miles.[2]

    **The part of the circulatory system,
both arteries and veins, that has to do with
the lungs is called the *pulmonary circuit*.
The part that has to do with the rest of the
body is called the *systemic circuit*.** *(Refer
back to Figure 2.)*

The Heart The *heart* **is a hollow, muscular
pump with four chambers.** It is located between the two lungs in the middle of the chest.
(Two-thirds of the heart lies to the left of the
breastbone and one-third to the right.) This organ, which is about the size of two clenched fists
in an adult, pumps blood to the body's tissues
and cells. The pumping is relentless—about 70
times a minute, 100,000 times a day, 2.5 billion
times in a 70-year life span. It processes 75 gallons of blood every day of your life. Sometimes it
has to work harder than others. When you're
running hard, the heart can increase its output
to five times what it does when you're at rest.
Even when you're resting, the heart muscles
work twice as hard as the leg muscles of a person running at top speed.[3]

    The right side of the heart takes oxygen-
poor blood from the body. The blood enters the
heart through two *venae cavae* **(singular:**

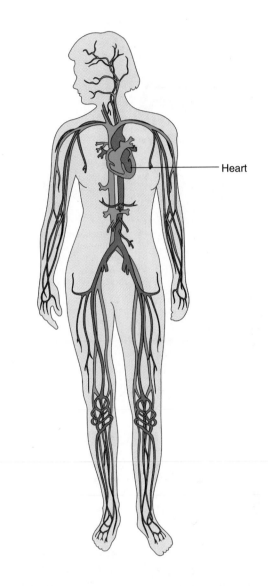

Heart

● **Figure 1   The circulatory system.** The
human circulatory system, including the
heart, arteries *(shown in red)*, and veins
(shown in blue).

vena cava), **the primary veins,** and is
pumped to the lungs. *(See ● Figure 3.)* The left
side takes oxygen-rich blood from the lungs and
pumps it out to the body by way of the **aorta,
the main artery of the body.** Blood does not
flow directly between the left and right sides
of the heart, which are divided by a thick wall.

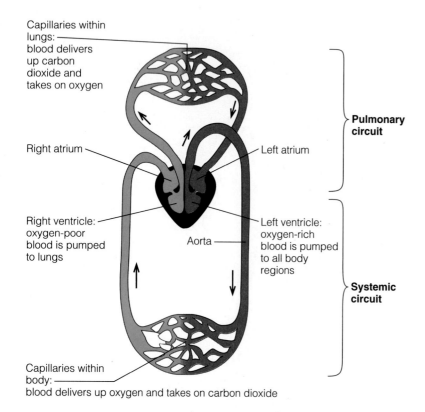

Capillaries within lungs: blood delivers up carbon dioxide and takes on oxygen

Right atrium

Left atrium

Pulmonary circuit

Right ventricle: oxygen-poor blood is pumped to lungs

Aorta

Left ventricle: oxygen-rich blood is pumped to all body regions

Systemic circuit

Capillaries within body: blood delivers up oxygen and takes on carbon dioxide

● **Figure 2   Diagram of general pattern of circulation.** Oxygen-rich (oxygenated) blood (*shown in red*) is taken from the lungs and pumped by the left side of the heart out to the blood vessels. They carry the blood to all body tissues. Oxygen-poor (deoxygenated) blood (*shown in blue*) is picked up from the capillaries. From here it is pumped back into the right side of the heart and back to the capillaries of the lungs. The blood returning to the heart carries carbon dioxide, which the lungs expel when you exhale.

However, the two sides contract at the same time.

Like any other part of the body, the heart muscle itself also needs nourishment. **The blood vessels that supply oxygen-rich blood to the heart muscle are the *coronary arteries.***

Each half of the heart (the right and left sides) has two holding chambers, an atrium and a ventricle. (*Refer back to Figure 3.*)

- *The atrium:* **The upper chamber on each side of the heart is called an *atrium* (plural: *atria*).** The right atrium receives oxygen-poor blood from the body. The left atrium receives oxygen-rich blood from the lungs. The blood from each atrium is then pumped through a valve into a corresponding lower chamber called a ventricle. The special *valves* between atria and ventricles prevent the blood from flowing in the wrong direction.

- *The ventricle:* **The *ventricle* is a holding chamber for blood.** Blood within each ventricle is pumped out of the heart through another valve to the arteries. Blood held within the right ventricle is pumped to the lung. Blood from the left ventricle is pumped to the body.

The contraction of the heart (your heartbeat) is actually a two-part process. First, muscles surrounding the top atria contract, forcing blood into the ventricles. Then, in quick succession, the heart muscle surrounding the ventricles contracts, forcing blood into the arteries.

When you feel your pulse, you are feeling the consequences of the contraction of the left ventricle. The resultant increased pressure of blood in the main arteries of the body causes these blood vessels to expand. You can feel the expansion with each heartbeat.

During the contraction phase, called *systole*, the heart forces blood into the arteries. During the relaxation phase, called *diastole*, the heart chambers fill with blood.

Blood Pressure   Your *blood pressure* is the measure of the pressure or force of circulating blood against the walls of your blood vessels. Since the pressure changes as the heart contracts and relaxes, blood pressure is expressed as:

- *Systolic pressure: Systolic blood pressure,* the highest pressure, occurs when the heart contracts and blood is forced into the arteries.

- *Diastolic pressure: Diastolic blood pressure,* the lowest pressure, occurs when the heart is relaxed.

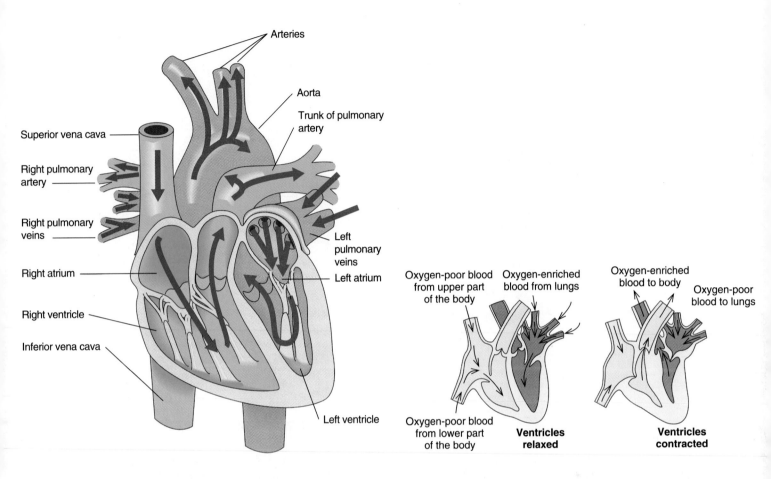

Arteries

Aorta

Trunk of pulmonary artery

Superior vena cava

Right pulmonary artery

Right pulmonary veins

Right atrium

Right ventricle

Inferior vena cava

Left pulmonary veins

Left atrium

Left ventricle

Oxygen-poor blood from upper part of the body

Oxygen-enriched blood from lungs

Oxygen-enriched blood to body

Oxygen-poor blood to lungs

Oxygen-poor blood from lower part of the body

Ventricles relaxed

Ventricles contracted

● **Figure 3   The heart.** *Left:* Partial view of the interior. *Right:* Blood flow through the heart during contraction and relaxation.

These pressures are expressed together as two figures—for example, 120/70, stated as "120 over 70." Here 120 is the systolic pressure, and 70 is the diastolic pressure. A blood pressure reading is taken with a device called a *sphygmomanometer* (pronounced "sfig-moe-man-*om*-e-ter"), or blood-pressure cuff, and a stethoscope. *(See ● Figure 4.)*

An average blood pressure reading for young adults is 120/80. Generally, any blood pressure under 140/90 is considered within the normal range. When blood pressure is low, people may feel faint or dizzy. It is not uncommon for children and young adults to have blood pressure readings of 100/60 or less. Many feel fine, but they may notice dizziness if they move from a lying to a standing position too quickly.

Cardiovascular Diseases: The Things That Can Go Wrong

The five major groups of cardiovascular disease are: (1) high blood pressure (hypertension); (2) coronary heart disease, which may lead to angina and heart attack; (3) stroke, impaired blood flow to the brain; (4) congenital heart disorders and rheumatic heart disease; and (5) other problems such as peripheral artery disease, congestive heart failure, and irregular heartbeat.

What mechanical or electrical machine has lasted a century or more of constant running

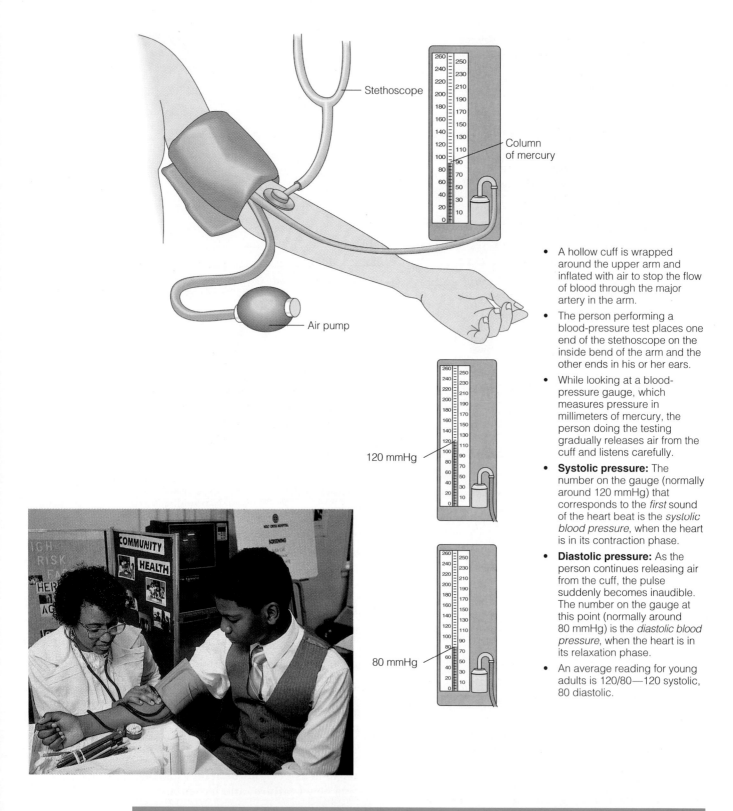

- A hollow cuff is wrapped around the upper arm and inflated with air to stop the flow of blood through the major artery in the arm.

- The person performing a blood-pressure test places one end of the stethoscope on the inside bend of the arm and the other ends in his or her ears.

- While looking at a blood-pressure gauge, which measures pressure in millimeters of mercury, the person doing the testing gradually releases air from the cuff and listens carefully.

- **Systolic pressure:** The number on the gauge (normally around 120 mmHg) that corresponds to the *first* sound of the heart beat is the *systolic blood pressure*, when the heart is in its contraction phase.

- **Diastolic pressure:** As the person continues releasing air from the cuff, the pulse suddenly becomes inaudible. The number on the gauge at this point (normally around 80 mmHg) is the *diastolic blood pressure*, when the heart is in its relaxation phase.

- An average reading for young adults is 120/80—120 systolic, 80 diastolic.

Stethoscope

Column of mercury

Air pump

120 mmHg

80 mmHg

● **Figure 4   Taking blood pressure.**

without failing? The answer is: none. Some human hearts, however, have functioned that long.

Still, like machines, hearts do break down. Heart and blood-vessel disease is the No. 1 cause of death in the United States. Coronary heart disease is the biggest killer of these; it alone kills more people in the United States than any other disease. **Stroke—a blockage of the blood supply to the brain**—is a major cause of death. *(See* ● *Figure 5.)* Strokes commonly represent a form of cardiovascular disease. The threat of cardiovascular disease and death, then, is enormously high for Americans. Unhealthy lifestyle habits are a major contributor to the problem. To understand the need for assessing and possibly changing your lifestyle for improved cardiovascular health, let us consider the common cardiovascular disorders.

In general, there are five major cardiovascular diseases, according to the American Heart Association:

- **High blood pressure:** High blood pressure results when there is marked resistance in blood vessels throughout the body that forces the heart to pump harder.

- **Coronary heart disease:** Coronary heart disease involves atherosclerosis, which severely narrows the vessels supplying blood to the muscle of the heart itself, and arteriosclerosis, which hardens the arteries and makes them less elastic. These problems may lead to angina and heart attack.

- **Stroke:** Stroke is the result of impaired blood flow to the brain.

- **Diseases of the young: congenital heart disorders and rheumatic heart disease:** A congenital defect is one that is present at birth. In this case, the defect is an abnormality of the heart. Rheumatic heart disease is heart damage resulting from a streptococcal infection that begins as strep throat.

- **Other problems:** Three other important problems are peripheral artery disease, congestive heart failure, and irregular heartbeat.

High Blood Pressure High blood pressure (along with coronary heart disease) is one of the two most common forms of cardiovascular dis-

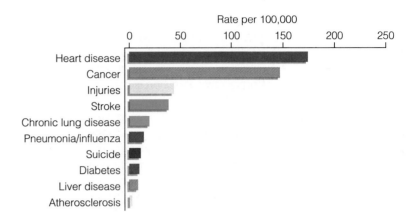

● **Figure 5   Leading causes of death.** Heart disease and stroke are among the major causes of death in the United States.

ease in the United States. How high is high? Today physicians agree that **blood pressure readings that are *consistently above 140/90* constitute *hypertension.*** This potentially life-threatening disease affects more than 60 million American adults and children.[4] The higher the blood pressure, the more serious the problem and the greater the need for treatment.

When having your blood pressure taken, it's recommended that a reading with abnormal results be repeated. Many people with normal blood pressure are so nervous in a doctor's office that their blood pressure rises, producing *whitecoat hypertension.*[5] Thus, most health professionals recommend that you repeat the reading over a few weeks' time to establish your true level.

Some key aspects of hypertension are:

- **Primary and secondary hypertension:** Hypertension is of two types, primary and secondary.

   In the form seen in 90% of cases, **primary (or essential) hypertension, the disease has no known cause.** It is probably related to uncontrollable and controllable factors. One uncontrollable factor is age (older people are more likely to have elevated blood pressure). Others are family history, diabetes, and race (African Americans are twice as likely as whites to develop hypertension).[6] The probable controllable factors include diet (salt and unsaturated fats), being overweight, alcohol and tobacco use, lack of exercise, and possibly stress. Primary hypertension is controllable but not curable.

***Secondary hypertension* is triggered by other primary diseases,** such as kidney disorders and disorders of the endocrine system like hypothyroidism. Blood-vessel diseases such as arteriosclerosis, or hardening of the arteries, can also produce hypertension.

- ***What having hypertension means:*** Is hypertension by itself a serious health problem or is it simply a symptom of other, graver disorders? The answer is: It may be both.

  You may not know you have hypertension—an estimated third of the 50 million Americans who have hypertension are unaware they have it.[7] Hypertension is called the "Silent Killer" because it is not associated with symptoms such as headaches, dizziness, or other adverse effects. Nevertheless, beneath the surface, and sometimes before it is detected, it takes its toll on vital organs. It speeds up the process of hardening of the arteries and forces the heart to work harder. It may narrow the blood vessels to the brain and even cause kidney damage.

- ***Treatment:*** Treatment for hypertension is of two types—lifestyle change and drugs.

  Taking a pill is easy. Making lifestyle changes may be more difficult. Most doctors will counsel their high-blood-pressure patients to lose weight, begin a program of regular exercise, and quit smoking. More advice: Don't consume more than two alcoholic drinks a day, stop salting food, eat a low-fat diet, and practice stress reduction. Lifestyle changes can significantly reduce blood pressure for some people. In one study, for example, men with mild hypertension took up moderate exercise for 10 weeks. (They did 20 minutes of aerobics and 30 minutes of weight training 3 times a week.) The exercise lowered their blood pressures as much as taking antihypertensive medication.[8]

Among the classes of drugs used to treat hypertension, two are particularly important. Many *antihypertensive drugs* open up (dilate) some of the smaller blood vessels, reducing the blood pressure. *Diuretic drugs* remove excess water from the bloodstream, lowering the volume of blood and thereby lowering the blood pressure. Many people who take medication for hypertension don't do so consistently. Reasons for noncompliance include misunderstandings about the disease, the lack of symptoms, and drug-related side effects. Drugs may have adverse side effects such as muscle weakness, impotence, depression, reduced sex drive, dizziness and fainting.

Hypertension cannot be cured, but it can be controlled. Continued efforts to have a healthy lifestyle along with collaboration with a health care practitioner on a regular basis assure optional control. Regardless of your medical history, take every available opportunity to have your blood pressure checked. If you receive a reading of 140/90 or higher, have it rechecked by a health care professional. High blood pressure can warn you to reduce hypertension risk. The same changes in habits can reduce your risk of other forms of heart disease.

Coronary Heart Disease: Atherosclerosis, Angina, and Heart Attack

Coronary heart disease (CHD) involves damage to the blood vessels to the heart. CHD is *the* leading cause of death of Americans today, killing 500,000 of us every year.[9] To explain how it happens, we first need to distinguish between *arteriosclerosis* and *atherosclerosis*, although you may hear the terms used interchangeably.

Arteriosclerosis is considered an *impairment* but not a disease. **Arteriosclerosis is "hardening of the arteries," a general condition often associated with aging in which the blood vessel walls thicken and harden.** In part this is because of buildups of fatty material from the diet. For some people, however, the rate of material building up is faster than others, and this is called atherosclerosis.

Atherosclerosis is considered a *disease*. **Atherosclerosis is a type of arteriosclerosis and is characterized by deposits of plaque on the inner lining of the arteries.**

***Plaque* consists of deposits of fat, cholesterol, calcium, cell parts, and a blood-clotting material (fibrin).** Over time, the channels in the artery become narrowed, reducing the supply of blood to the tissues fed by the affected arteries. A complete blockage may also occur. *(See ● Figure 6.)*

Atherosclerosis can occur in blood vessels throughout the body. It is particularly dangerous in a coronary artery, which supplies blood—and hence oxygen and nutrients—to the heart muscle itself. When the opening of the coronary artery is narrowed by 50–70% of its normal diameter, that is considered *coronary heart disease*. At this point, a person becomes vulnerable to angina or a heart attack:

- ***Angina: Angina*, or *angina pectoris*, is an intense pain in the chest behind the breastbone, owing to a diminished supply of oxygen to the heart.** The pain may also radiate to the arm, especially the left arm, and the neck or jaw. Angina can be triggered by emotional stress, exercise, a heavy meal, exposure to cold, or other factors.

  Angina is not itself fatal. Indeed, 2.5 million Americans presently live with angina, and some have had it for years and never suffered a heart attack. However, angina is a warning, particularly if it becomes longer in duration, more severe, or more frequent.

  Angina is treated with drugs. Nitroglycerin is frequently used because it is a *vasodilator—it widens blood vessels.* Other useful drugs lower blood pressure, slow the heart to reduce its need for oxygen, and reduce the chance of arterial spasms.

- ***Heart attack:* A heart attack is called a** *myocardial infarction (MI),* **which literally means "death of heart muscle."** Although often caused by impaired blood supply to part of the heart muscle, it may have other causes, such as electrical shock. The risk of fatality depends greatly on the extent and location of the damage.

  When a heart attack is underway, it is important to act quickly. This means not ignoring its principal signs: severe chest pain lasting more than 2 minutes, shortness of breath, sweating, nausea, dizziness, fainting,

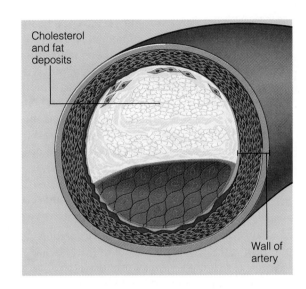

Cholesterol and fat deposits

Wall of artery

● **Figure 6   The effects of atherosclerosis.** An artery partially blocked by the plaque of atherosclerosis.

and poor skin color. The chest pain usually lasts 20 minutes or more and may radiate to the arms (especially the left arm), jaw, or neck.

A myocardial infarction may come about in three ways:

(1) It may be due to a ***coronary occlusion*—the slow buildup of atherosclerotic plaque within a coronary artery until the artery is blocked (occluded). Oxygen and nutrients cease to reach the heart.**

(2) It may be caused by a ***coronary thrombosis*—the sudden appearance of a wandering blood clot, called a *thrombus*, stuck to a blood vessel wall. The thrombus blocks the blood flow.**

(3) It may be a ***coronary embolism*—a blockage of the coronary artery by a clump of material—called an *embolus*—caused by a blood clot, bubble of air, gas, bacteria, or tissue.**

It is critical that someone having a heart attack get medical aid immediately. Sixty percent of deaths occur within an hour after first symptoms appear.[10] Don't transport the person yourself. Stay with the person and call for an ambulance. If the patient can be rushed to a hospital, he or she has a better chance of surviving. Clot-dissolving drugs can be used to get the blood flowing again.

Long-term treatment may involve the drugs used to treat angina, balloon angioplasty, coronary artery bypass graft, and other therapies we shall describe.

The atherosclerosis that produces angina and heart attacks can also occur in other blood vessels. For example, it may produce stroke or affect the supply of blood to the legs (peripheral artery disease).

Stroke Like a myocardial infarction, *a **stroke**, also known as a **cerebrovascular accident**, can be caused by a blockage in a blood vessel.* In this instance, however, the blockage is in an artery carrying blood to the brain.

The resulting loss of oxygen to the brain can produce dramatic changes: The face, arm, and leg on one side of the body suddenly becomes weak or numb. There may be a loss of the ability to speak, difficult or slurred speech, or inability to understand speech. There may be a complete or partial loss or dimming of vision, or memory loss. People experiencing a stroke may feel unsteady, dizzy, or suddenly fall. Because brain cells can perish very quickly after a stroke, it is crucial to take these warning signs seriously. Get the person to a hospital quickly. Again, call an ambulance—don't try to transport the person yourself.

As mentioned, strokes are a leading cause of death. About 500,000 Americans have strokes each year, and about 150,000 of them die.[11] Strokes are also a major cause of disability. Often the impairment is permanent, or recovery can take a long time. Nor are strokes a misfortune of the old; they are a leading cause of death among women in their late 30s.

The term *stroke* actually represents a group of diseases. There are two broad categories of stroke, *ischemic* and *hemorrhagic:*

- *Ischemic:* Accounting for about 70% of all strokes, *ischemic strokes are caused by lack of blood flow to the brain.*

One type of ischemic stroke is a **cerebral thrombosis, in which a clot blocks blood flow in a brain artery.** As with heart arteries, plaque builds up on the inner lining of an artery, eventually obstructing the flow of blood.

- *Hemorrhagic:* **Hemorrhagic strokes are those in which blood seeps from a hole in a blood vessel wall.** This type accounts for 20–25% of all strokes. The hemorrhage may be a *cerebral hemorrhage,* **a seepage of blood into the brain itself.** Or it may be sudden, through an *aneurysm,* **an outpouching or ballooning of a weakened area of the blood vessel, which ruptures.**

Some kinds of stroke, particularly the ischemic kinds, have warnings in the form of **"ministrokes" called *transient ischemic attacks (TIAs).* TIAs have the same symptoms as those for a stroke but last only a few minutes.** The symptoms are weakness or numbness on one side of the body, inability to speak, lack of coordination, and so on. Because they don't last long, people who have them tend to dismiss them as nothing. However, such an event should be taken seriously: about one third of those who experience TIA will go on to have a stroke.[12]

Anyone experiencing a stroke of any kind needs immediate medical help. Treatment depends on the underlying cause. Some patients undergo drug treatment, including use of anticoagulant (anti-clotting) drugs and aspirin. Others require surgery to repair blood vessels.

Heart Disease in the Young Two of the most common heart problems found in the young are congenital heart disease and rheumatic heart disease.

- *Congenital heart disorders:* The word *congenital* means "present at birth." *Congenital heart disorders* **are structural defects in the heart that develop while the baby is in the womb.** About 1% of newborn babies have some congenital heart malfunction, which means the condition is relatively rare. In only half the cases is the problem severe enough to require surgery or medical treatment.[13]

Congenital heart disorders include holes in the wall dividing the lower chambers of the heart (the ventricular septum), and damage to the heart valves. Or the arteries from the heart to the body and lungs may be switched. The term "blue babies" refers to babies who have *cyanosis.* Their blood is unable to carry enough oxygen and so produces a bluish skin color.

- *Rheumatic heart disease:* Developing mainly in children ages 5–15, *rheumatic heart disease is characterized by skin rashes and swollen joints. Damage to the heart valves results in about half the cases.* Rheumatic heart disease is the final stage of *rheumatic fever,* which develops in about 1% of acute streptococcal (strep) throat infections.[14] Treatment is use of antibiotics to prevent scarring of the heart valves.

Three Other Cardiovascular Problems
Other problems are peripheral artery disease, congestive heart failure, and irregular heartbeat.

- *Peripheral artery disease: Peripheral artery disease is damage from atherosclerosis that restricts the blood flow to the body's extremities.* The legs, feet, and sometimes hands may be affected. Symptoms are coldness, numbness, or tingling in areas deprived of blood flow, and cramps during exercise. Sometimes this can lead to tissue death, gangrene, and amputation.

  Treatment is with modified diet, exercise, drug therapy, weight loss, and elimination of smoking (because nicotine constricts the blood vessels). Sometimes surgery on the blood vessels is required.

- *Congestive heart failure: Congestive heart failure (CHF) occurs when the heart does not have the power to continue to pump blood normally. It is unable to pump out the blood that returns to it, so the blood flow starts to back up.* People with CHF experience difficulty breathing because **fluid collects in the lungs, a condition called** *pulmonary edema.* Swelling (edema) also occurs in the ankles and legs.

Congestive heart failure can result from lung disease, birth defects, rheumatic fever, heart attack, high blood pressure, or atherosclerosis. Treatment is with diet, rest, and drugs that will reduce the workload and improve the efficiency of the heart.

- *Irregular heartbeat:* Rheumatic fever, infections, drug use (including coffee, nicotine, and alcohol), and other problems can produce **irregular heartbeats called** *arrhythmias.* **The electrical activity associated with the heartbeats can be measured with an** *electrocardiogram (ECG).*

  The normal heart rate for adults at rest is 60–80 beats per minute. (It varies according to physical activity and other factors.) **An abnormally slow rate,** *bradycardia,* is below 60 beats per minute. **An abnormally high rate,** *tachycardia,* is more than 100 beats per minute. **In** *ventricular fibrillation,* **the ventricles are unable to pump blood because the cardiac muscle contracts haphazardly.** The ECG pattern for fibrillation is very uneven.

  Arrhythmias may be corrected by use of medication or, in some cases, by surgically implanting a mechanical *pacemaker.* **The pacemaker electrically stimulates the heart to beat at a normal rate.**

Help for the Sick Heart

Getting help for a heart attack means knowing how to recognize it and how to get emergency help. It helps to understand the tools for diagnosis, such as the electrocardiogram. Treatment may consist of bypass surgery, balloon angioplasty, or heart transplant, or a variety of lifestyle changes.

Every year, about half a million people die from heart attacks. What can you do to increase the survival chances for a friend, relative, or yourself if you observe the classic heart attack symptoms?

The Signs of Heart Attack Heart attacks sometimes happen without warning, but they often have characteristic signs and symptoms:

(1) steady, squeezing pressure or burning pain in the center of the chest lasting 2 minutes or more; (2) pain radiating from the center of the chest down the left or both arms or to the shoulders, neck, jaw, or back; (3) blue or grey skin color; (4) sweating or clamminess; (5) dizziness or fainting; (6) shortness of breath; (7) nausea or vomiting; and (8) a sense of anxiety or feeling of impending disaster.

Getting Emergency Help Individually, these signs may be symptoms of some disorder other than heart disease or heart attack. *However, people have died from heart attacks who might have been saved had treatment not been delayed because the signs were misinterpreted.* What if you become aware of any of these symptoms, in yourself or someone else? You should *immediately call the 911 emergency number or Emergency Medical Service and ask for an ambulance.*

Don't try to drive the person to a hospital emergency room yourself, unless you are in an extremely remote location. The Emergency Medical Service technicians will have the resources to administer to the victim en route to the emergency room. They may use oxygen, pain medication, and blood-clot-dissolving medication, for example.

While you are waiting for help to arrive, be reassuring and make sure the person is comfortable. If vomiting occurs, have the person sit up rather than lie down to prevent stomach contents from getting into the lungs. Don't give the person any drugs, foods, or liquids.

If the individual loses consciousness, you may need to start cardiopulmonary resuscitation (CPR). Once the victim arrives at the emergency room or coronary care unit of the hospital, health professionals may use a *defibrillator.* This delivers an electrical shock that will stimulate the heart back to a normal rhythm. They may also administer anticoagulants, pain medications, oxygen, and other treatment. The aim is to stabilize the person and prevent worsening of the problem.

Tools for Diagnosis If there is no medical emergency, doctors may still suspect a heart problem of some kind. They also routinely screen some individuals for the possibility of heart disease. They have a choice of several diagnostic tools:

- *The electrocardiogram:* As mentioned, the purpose of the electrocardiogram (ECG) is to provide information about heart rhythms and other clues to a heart problem. Electrodes, or leads, attached to the patient's chest or ankles. The electrical activity of the heart is recorded by an electrocardiograph.

- *Exercise stress testing:* The electrocardiogram just described is often called a "resting ECG," because it is administered while the patient is lying down. **In the exercise stress test, an electrocardiogram is taken while the individual walks on a treadmill or pedals a stationary bicycle.** The purpose of the test is to assess the action of the heart under conditions of increased oxygen demand. The idea is to elicit any symptoms, such as chest pain, that might occur under these conditions.

- *The echocardiogram:* **The echocardiogram is a one- or two-dimensional picture of the heart taken with sound waves.** It is used for diagnosing conditions, such as valve disorders, that require visualization of the heart's anatomy.

- *Nuclear cardiology:* In nuclear cardiology, a small amount of nonharmful radioactive material is injected into the bloodstream. A radiation-detecting device is then used to follow its progress through the circulatory system. The results are displayed by a computer as three-dimensional images of the heart.

- *Cardiac catheterization: Cardiac catheterization* **is the process of inserting a thin, hollow tube into a blood vessel in the leg or arm. From there it is passed into or around the heart.** Physicians may then take pressure readings or inject radiopaque dyes and see how the dyes show up on X-rays. (This type of X-ray is called an *angiogram.*)

Treatment Most people with cardiovascular problems can be treated with drugs. Various drugs lower blood pressure, control heart rhythms, relieve angina pain, or help the heart work better to overcome congestive failure. Other forms of treatment are coronary bypass surgery, balloon angioplasty, and heart transplants.

- ***Bypass surgery: Bypass surgery* is designed to alleviate the problem of blocking or narrowing of one or all of the arteries in the heart itself.** Because of their small diameter, the coronary arteries are particularly susceptible to blockage from plaque formation or a blood clot. In coronary bypass surgery, a section of a vein is first taken from the arm or leg. This vein is grafted on to the heart in a way that bypasses the blockage in the artery. *(See ● Figure 7.)* When the procedure must be done for all coronary arteries, it is called a "triple bypass."

  Unfortunately, bypass surgery does not always completely solve the problem. Many patients find that they must have a second bypass operation a few years later.

- ***Balloon angioplasty:*** Increasingly, bypass surgery is being replaced with a less risky procedure called balloon angioplasty. **In *balloon angioplasty,* using the process of cardiac catheterization, a miniature balloon is run inside a coronary artery. The balloon is then inflated, compressing the plaques and widening the artery to increase the flow of blood.**

  Balloon angioplasty is successful in about 85% of cases. One problem, occurring in 4–7% of cases, is that the arteries become narrow again within 6 months of the procedure.[15]

- ***Heart transplant:*** Heart transplants consist of the surgical removal of a defective heart and its replacement by a heart taken from a donor. (Usually the donor is a person of similar size, under age 35, who has suffered brain death, as from an auto accident.) Tissue matching, by blood type, is done through regional organ banks. The donor heart is flown to the hospital where the recipient is being prepared to receive it. Great care is taken to monitor possible rejection of the heart after the operation and to avoid infections.

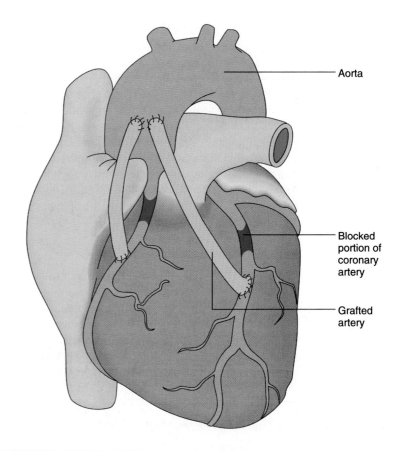

Aorta

Blocked portion of coronary artery

Grafted artery

● **Figure 7   Coronary bypass.** In this operation, two grafted arteries *(shown in green)* are used to bypass blocked portions of two coronary arteries.

Approximately 85% of patients are still alive after the first year and 65% after 5 years.[16] In recent years, there has also been excitement about the use of mechanical (artificial) hearts, such as the Jarvik heart. Some physicians wonder whether artificial hearts will ever be more than a temporary way to keep patients alive until donors are found. However, a 1991 study ordered by the Heart, Lung and Blood Institute suggests artificial hearts will improve. It predicts that self-contained mechanical pumps implanted in patients' bodies will be able to replace diseased human hearts within 20 years.[17]

Nonsurgical Treatment: Lifestyle Changes
In recent years, there has been some evidence that people with narrowed coronary arteries can reverse the problem without medication or surgery. In the Lifestyle Heart Trial study, San Francisco physician Dean Ornish and colleagues demonstrated that lifestyle changes alone could do the job. With a strict vegetarian (lowfat) diet, mild daily exercise, and stress-reduction techniques, patients actually reversed the progression of atherosclerotic plaques in coronary arteries.[18,19]

The Risk Factors for Heart Disease

Risk factors that increase the chances of getting heart disease consist of predisposing factors—heredity, gender, age, and race or ethnic group. They also consist of precipitating factors, such as cigarette smoking, high blood pressure, blood cholesterol levels, exercise, diabetes, weight, personality, and stress.

The term "risk factors" may not set alarm bells ringing in your head. But this dry, understated term means "danger signs." To physicians, **risk factors are those traits and behaviors that increase one's chances of getting—in this case—heart disease.** *(See Self Discovery 1.)*

Some risk factors are more controllable than others:

- **Not controllable—predisposing risk factors:** Those that cannot be controlled are called *predisposing risk factors* and they include your heredity, gender, age, and race or ethnic group.

- **Controllable—precipitating risk factors:** Those that can be controlled are called *precipitating risk factors.* They include cigarette smoking, high blood pressure, blood cholesterol levels, exercise, diabetes, weight, personality, and stress. The first three of these—smoking, hypertension, and cholesterol—are considered the Big Three controllable risk factors. All other risk factors mainly interact with these three to increase risk factors.

Predisposing Risk Factors: Age, Gender, Heredity, Race Nothing can be done to change predisposing risk factors. However, if you score high on any of these it might provide additional motivation for you to change precipitating risk factors:

- **Age:** The risk of cardiovascular disorders increases as you get older. Half of those who have heart attacks are 65 or older. Worse, 4 out of 5 people who die of heart attacks are over 65.

  Although nothing can be done to reduce age, paying attention to diet and fitness will delay the effects of aging.

- **Gender:** Men are more likely than women to develop cardiovascular disorders, particularly before age 40. Four times as many men as women develop atherosclerosis. Even so, coronary heart disease is the No. 1 cause of death among American women, though mainly in later life.

  It is speculated that male hormones (androgens) increase risk, whereas female hormones (estrogens) protect against atherosclerosis. This is supported by the fact that heart disease risk for women rises after menopause, when their bodies have stopped producing estrogen.

- **Heredity:** If you have close relatives who suffered heart attacks or strokes before age 50, it increases your chances of having the same. Some families have a history of very high levels of blood cholesterol, and this inherited tendency is passed on to younger generations.

  The good news is that there is nothing inevitable about this. After all, prior generations did not have the benefit of the sophisticated medical care we have now. Still, if you have a family history of heart attacks or strokes, you should be especially careful about controllable (precipitating) risk factors.

- **Race:** African Americans are twice as likely to have high blood pressure as whites.[20,21] *(See ● Figure 8.)* This may be because of societal factors, such as stress, poverty, and diet. The chances of having a heart attack are similar for blacks and whites. But in an African American the heart attack is more likely to be fatal.[22]

SELF DISCOVERY 1

Is Your Heart at Risk?

For each of the five following categories—weight, systolic blood pressure, blood cholesterol level, cigarette smoking, and (for women only) estrogen use—indicate the response that best describes you and your lifestyle.

1. Weight. Study the following chart and find your weight category. Indicate the points in the right-hand column.

Weight category	Points
A	−2
B	−1
C	+1
D	+2

Your points: _____

MEN
Weight category (lbs.)

Your height	A	B	C	D
5'1"	up to 123	124–148	149–173	174 +
5'2"	up to 128	127–152	153–178	179 +
5'3"	up to 129	130–156	157–182	183 +
5'4"	up to 132	133–160	161–186	187 +
5'5"	up to 135	136–163	164–190	191 +
5'6"	up to 139	140–168	169–196	197 +
5'7"	up to 144	145–174	175–203	204 +
5'8"	up to 148	149–179	180–209	210 +
5'9"	up to 152	153–184	185–214	215 +
5'10"	up to 157	158–190	191–221	222 +
5'11"	up to 161	162–194	195–227	228 +
6'0"	up to 165	166–199	200–232	233 +
6'1"	up to 170	171–205	208–239	240 +
6'2"	up to 175	176–211	212–246	247 +
6'3"	up to 180	181–217	218–253	254 +
6'4"	up to 185	186–223	224–260	261 +
6'5"	up to 190	191–229	230–267	268 +
6'6"	up to 195	196–235	236–274	275 +

WOMEN
Weight category (lbs.)

Your height	A	B	C	D
4'8"	up to 101	102–122	123–143	144 +
4'9"	up to 103	104–125	126–146	147 +
4'10"	up to 106	107–128	129–150	151 +
4'11"	up to 109	110–132	133–154	155 +
5'0"	up to 112	113–136	137–158	159 +
5'1"	up to 115	116–139	140–162	163 +
5'2"	up to 119	120–144	145–168	169 +
5'3"	up to 122	123–148	149–172	173 +
5'4"	up to 127	128–154	155–179	180 +
5'5"	up to 131	132–158	159–185	186 +
5'6"	up to 135	136–163	164–190	191 +
5'7"	up to 139	140–168	169–196	197 +
5'8"	up to 143	144–173	174–202	203 +
5'9"	up to 147	148–178	179–207	208 +
5'10"	up to 151	152–182	183–213	214 +
5'11"	up to 155	156–187	188–218	219 +
6'0"	up to 159	160–191	192–224	225 +
6'1"	up to 163	164–196	197–229	230 +

2. Systolic blood pressure. Use the first number from your most recent blood pressure test. If you do not know your blood pressure, estimate it by circling the number corresponding to your weight category (A = −2, B = −1, etc.).

Blood pressure/ weight category	Points if male	Points if female
A 119 or less	−1	−2
B 120–139	0	−1
C 140–159	0	0
D 160 or higher	+1	+1

3. Blood cholesterol level. Use the number from your most recent blood cholesterol test. If you do not know your blood cholesterol, estimate it by circling the number that corresponds to your weight category.

Blood cholesterol/ weight category	Points if male	Points if female
A 199 or less	−2	−1
B 200–224	−1	0
C 225–249	0	0
D 250 or higher	+1	+1

(continued)

SELF DISCOVERY 1
(continued)

4. Cigarette smoking

Amount smoked	Points
Do not smoke	−1
Smoke less than a pack a day or smoke a pipe	0
Smoke a pack a day	+1
Smoke more than a pack a day	+2

5. (For women only) estrogen use. Answer these two questions:
   a. Have you ever taken birth-control pills or other hormone drugs containing estrogen for 5 or more years in a row?
   b. Are you age 35 or older and now taking birth-control pills or other hormone drugs containing estrogen?

Usage	Points
"No" to both questions	0
"Yes" to one or both questions	+1

Scoring

Total the points circled. Be careful to *add* the plus numbers and *subtract* the minus numbers. Then add 10 points to your total.

Interpretation

Total points	Amount of heart risk
0–4	Very low
5–9	Low to moderate
10–14	Moderate to high
15–19	High
20+	Extremely high

Source: American Heart Association, 1985.

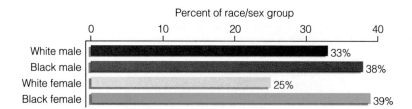

Percent of race/sex group

White male	33%
Black male	38%
White female	25%
Black female	39%

Hypertensives are defined as persons with a systolic level that is greater than or equal to 140 and/or a diastolic level that is greater than or equal to 90 or who report using antihypertensive medication.

● **Figure 8   High blood pressure and race.** Estimated percent of population with hypertension, by race and sex, U.S. adults ages 18–74.

Now let us turn to the controllable risk factors—the Big Three of smoking, hypertension, and blood cholesterol levels. We will also consider other risk factors that affect the Big Three—namely, exercise, diabetes, weight, personality, and stress.

Cigarette Smoking: The No. 1 Controllable Risk Factor By now people have gotten the message about the association between smoking and lung cancer. However, the bigger enemy strengthened by smoking is cardiovascular disease. Indeed, smoking is *the* No. 1 cause of heart disease in the United States. Moreover, of people who have heart attacks, smokers have less chance of surviving than nonsmokers do.[23]

Why is smoking so lethal? It seems that cigarette smoking accelerates atherosclerosis in three ways:[24]

- *Carbon monoxide damage:* The carbon monoxide in smoke is poisonous, and over time it damages the lining of the blood vessels. This makes it easier for fatty deposits to adhere to the walls.

- *Effect on cholesterol:* Smoking raises "bad" cholesterol and lowers "good" cholesterol, as we will describe, raising the risk and severity of atherosclerosis.

- *Blood clot increase:* Smoking increases the possibility of blood clots forming and blocking the arteries, raising the likelihood of heart attacks or stroke.

There is good news in this, however: The overall risk of having a heart attack starts to decline within the *first day* after one stops smoking. Within 1 year of quitting, the risk of heart disease is cut in half.[25]

High Blood Pressure: The No. 2 Controllable Risk Factor High blood pressure is a systolic level of 140 millimeters of mercury (mm Hg) or higher and/or a diastolic level of 90 mm Hg or higher. High blood pressure, or hypertension, results in the blood pressing against the artery walls. This increases the work the heart has to do, weakening it over time.

Controlling hypertension is imperative, since it can result in heart disease, stroke, and kidney failure. Nearly one third of people whose hypertension is not controlled die of heart disease. Another third die of stroke. Of the remaining, 10–15% die of kidney failure.[26] High blood pressure can be controlled with medication, exercise, and diet.

Blood Fats: The No. 3 Controllable Risk Factor **Blood fats, or serum lipids, include *cholesterol* and *triglycerides*.** These are the culprits that are believed to figure in the plaque buildup in the lining of the blood vessels. This build up produces atherosclerosis and heart disease.

Although it has a reputation almost like poison, **cholesterol is actually organic and is vital to the functioning of the body. It is found only in fats and oils produced by animals, never plants. The cholesterol in food is referred to as *dietary cholesterol*. The cholesterol in your body is *blood (serum) cholesterol*.**

Studies show that the level of blood cholesterol is a fairly reliable predictor of coronary heart disease and, to some extent, stroke.[27] Cholesterol levels are expressed as mg/dl, or milligrams of cholesterol per deciliter of blood. In general, experts consider cholesterol levels under 200 mg/dl to be normal, 200–239 to be borderline, and 240 and up to be dangerously high risk. About 1 out of 4 adults have cholesterol levels of 240 mg/dl or higher.

Cholesterol is carried within the circulatory system by *lipoproteins*, a word much in the news in the last few years. As the term suggests, **a *lipoprotein* can be thought of as "lipid plus protein." It is a compound of fat (lipid) and protein that carries cholesterol and other fats (such as triglycerides) through the bloodstream.** Several types of lipoprotein exist that have come to be known as the "good" and "bad" forms of blood cholesterol.

- ***"Bad" cholesterol—LDLs:*** *Low-density lipoproteins,* **abbreviated *LDLs,* transport blood cholesterol *to* the cells in the body.** This form is considered the "bad" lipoprotein because some gets deposited in fatty streaks in blood vessels, forming buildups of plaque.

- ***"Good" cholesterol—HDLs:*** **Abbreviated *HDLs, high-density lipoproteins* transport blood cholesterol *from* the cells in the body to the liver.** This form is considered the "good" lipoprotein because it removes excess cholesterol from blood vessels.

Now to get down to basics: The consensus about the effects of diet on heart and blood vessel disease seems to be as follows:[28]

- *High LDL and low HDL blood cholesterol levels mean high risk of heart disease:* The higher the blood levels of LDLs and the lower the levels of HDLs, the greater the severity of atherosclerosis. Eventually atherosclerosis can become coronary heart disease.

- *Eating saturated fats and dietary cholesterol increases blood cholesterol:* Avoid saturated fats—those found in meat and dairy products, palm and coconut oils, and cocoa butter. Saturated fats, and to some extent dietary cholesterol, promote the production of blood cholesterol in the body.

Weight Excess body fat appears to raise the risk of heart disease. The more the weight, the higher the risk. One study of 116,000 women found that the most obese group had three times the heart disease risk of the leanest group.[29]

Diabetes Mellitus People who develop a disorder of the endocrine system called *diabetes mellitus* have an increased risk of coronary heart disease and stroke. The risk is especially high for diabetes that begins later in life (Type II diabetes). Exercise and weight reduction can help to slow down the onset of diabetes.

Inactivity The evidence is convincing that regular exercise will reduce the likelihood of a heart attack. It may also improve the chances of survival if one does occur. Indeed, the authors of one study argued that inactivity should be considered as a primary rather than secondary risk factor for heart disease.[30] Exercise can certainly help control weight, and perhaps improve the body's ability to use insulin. It may also raise the HDL (the "good" cholesterol), and lower blood pressure, among other positive effects.

"Type A" Personality and Stress **People with *Type A personalities* are people who are hurried, deadline-ridden, and competitive, and who may also be hostile and antagonistic. *Type B personalities*, by contrast, are relaxed, unhurried, and carefree.** In the early 1970s, San Francisco physicians Meyer Friedman and Ray Rosenman suggested that Type A behavior was linked to stress-related heart disease, particularly if the person was hostile and aggressive. Type B personalities, they said, seemed less at risk.[31] Another study found that counseling could reduce both Type A behavior and the number of heart attacks.[32]

Not all experts agree that Type A behavior is a true cardiovascular risk factor. Still, job stress has been shown to raise blood pressure and lead to other detrimental physical changes that often precede heart disease.[33] Physician Dean Ornish has shown that stress-relieving techniques like yoga, visualization, and meditation along with changes in diet and exercise can actually reverse heart disease.[34–36]

Strategy for Living: Steps for Preventing Heart Disease

Nine steps for preventing heart disease are: (1) quit smoking, (2) reduce dietary fat and cholesterol, (3) reduce sodium, (4) add fiber, (5) moderate alcohol use, (6) keep weight down, (7) exercise, (8) consider taking aspirin, and (9) cope with stress.

A great part of the art of living well is learning that your habits really do matter. Nowhere is this more apparent than in the link between lifestyle habits and heart disease. In a way, having heart disease is a sign of *accelerated* aging. For many people, having heart disease means their bodies have run down sooner than nature intended—often because of certain choices they made about how they wanted to live.

Of course, when you're young you may not have any sense of urgency about quitting smoking, changing your diet, or taking up exercise. There seems to be no hurry to adopt these and other habits favorable to your heart's survival. What could induce you to make these changes? Perhaps it would be to ask cardiologists not what advice they give their patients but what lifestyle changes they have made *themselves*. After all, who better than a heart doctor would know the daily changes required to prevent heart disease?

In 1990 the *Wall Street Journal* surveyed 400 cardiologists. Based on their own example, the doctors rated the following as the most preventive steps for resisting heart disease: stopping smoking; altering diet to reduce cholesterol; limiting intake of salt; exercising; and taking aspirin.[37] Let us look at these and other steps.

Step 1: Quit Smoking Cardiologists are very strong on the subject of smoking. "I rarely see any patient with heart problems under the age of 65—unless they are smokers," said one.[38] Smokers have twice the risk of heart attack as nonsmokers do.

Step 2: Reduce Fat and Cholesterol in Your Diet You should get no more than 30% of your daily calories from fat in any form. No more than 10% should come from saturated fats.

To cut down fat, don't fry foods but broil or steam them instead. If you use cooking oils, use those that contain polyunsaturated fats—corn, safflower, soybean, sunflower, or cottonseed oils. Eat less butter and cheese, less red meat, such as beef and pork, and eat more fish and poultry.

Step 3: Reduce Sodium (Salt) in Your Diet Sodium can affect high blood pressure. Thus, reduce your consumption of processed foods (such as potato chips and canned vegetables), which are apt to be heavily salted. The same goes for condiments (such as mustard, catsup, and soy sauce). Don't add salt when cooking or eating food. Instead of salt, use herbs and spices as condiments.

Step 4: Add Fiber to Your Diet Fiber can reduce cholesterol levels, perhaps lower blood pressure, and make you feel "fuller" since it takes longer to digest. Fiber is found in whole grains, beans, legumes, fruits, and vegetables.

Step 5: Be Moderate in Your Alcohol Consumption Alcohol can raise the blood pressure. Drink only 2 alcoholic drinks or less a day.

Step 6: Keep Your Weight Down Being overweight can increase the chances of high blood pressure and other heart and blood-vessel diseases.

Step 7: Exercise Engaging in aerobic exercise three times a week about 30 minutes each time will lower blood pressure, maintain body weight, and reduce heart attack risk. Walking, jogging, bicycling, swimming, and dancing are all aerobic. *(See ● Figure 9.)*

Step 8: Consider Taking Aspirin Aspirin, the so-called "wonder drug," may be a potent protector against fatal heart attacks and strokes. Apparently it serves this purpose because aspirin makes the blood less susceptible to clotting and promotes the dilation of blood vessels. In the United States, aspirin is recommended to head off more serious attacks among patients who have already suffered a small stroke. It is also advised for those who have evidence of reduced blood flow to the brain. Their dose is baby

● **Figure 9   How much exercise?**

❝ *. . . To obtain a conditioning effect, a person must exercise three times a week for half an hour per session at a consistent intensity. One session is better than none, two is better than one, and three is still better than two. After three times a week, the gain in cardiovascular benefit, while still increasing, becomes progressively less. Additionally, when we start to exercise five, six, or seven times a week, orthopedic injuries become more of a problem. Therefore, there is a window of optimal frequency—three or four times each week, at which time the gain is near maximal while the injury risk is minor. More often becomes a threat to well-being—we wind ourselves too tightly.* ❞

—Walter M. Bortz II. (1991). *We live too short and die too long.* New York: Bantam Books, pp. 227–228.

aspirin (81 milligrams) daily or a regular, adult-sized aspirin tablet (325 milligrams) every second day.

Many Americans without a history of blood-vessel disease (including cardiologists) also take aspirin to prevent heart attacks and strokes. The dose is half an adult aspirin or one baby aspirin daily.[39,40] There is no advantage to taking more than one aspirin, which may lead to stomach distress, ulcers, and rectal bleeding. Nor should one take aspirin substitutes (such as Tylenol). Coated or buffered aspirin is less apt to cause internal distress. There is some concern about increased risk of stroke among aspirin users, but the evidence regarding stroke prevention remains inconclusive.

Step 9: Learn to Cope with Stress The stresses in our lives are ongoing and ever-changing. It is doubtful that we can ever get rid of all of them. However, we can learn to cope effectively with the stressors that confront us, using such relaxation techniques as progressive relaxation, meditation, visualization, and mental imagery.

Preventing and Conquering Cancer

▶ Define *cancer,* and discuss its causes and the process of metastasis.

▶ Name and describe the kinds of cancers that arise in major body systems.

▶ Describe the seven early warning signals and discuss several important cancers.

▶ Discuss how cancer is diagnosed and treated.

▶ Describe the predisposing risk factors and controllable risk factors for cancer.

▶ List the steps for preventing cancer.

Many diseases that were once practically synonymous with death—yellow fever, smallpox, scarlet fever—have been brought under control by medical progress. However, cancer—called "the Big C," by actor John Wayne, who died of lung cancer—still holds horror in the public mind.

However, when dealt with early, cancer no longer has the inevitable outcome once associated with it. True, cancer is the No. 2 cause of death in the United States, accounting for 1 out of 5 deaths. About 1 out of 3 Americans now living will eventually have cancer.[41] Even so, death rates have been steadily declining. Even better news, the potential for reducing cancer through prevention and early detection is quite large, as we shall show.

The first step in prevention is recognizing that cancer is not one disease but a constellation of more than 100 different diseases. What they have in common is the uncontrolled growth of abnormal cells.

Cancer: What It Is, What It Does

Cancer—abnormal cells spreading uncontrolled—is caused by initiators, promoters, and oncogenes. Cancer may spread in three ways—by direct extension, through the circulatory system, and through the lymphatic system. Tumors may be of four general types.

In only 9 months we grow from a single cell into a perfectly shaped human being. In the 18 or so years following our birth, we develop into a more or less fully formed adult. Along the way, as we suffer life's cuts, bruises, and diseases, our bodies produce new cells to repair the damage. These are the marvels of cellular growth.

Sometimes, however, cells don't follow this pattern. This is the beginning of the process called cancer.

What Is Cancer? *Cancer* **is a disease in which abnormal cells develop and often spread in an uncontrolled manner.** Picture a cell that doesn't follow the rules. Something happens to make it *mutate*—**change in a way that makes it lose its original ability to grow in orderly, regulated ways.** The single abnormal cell divides into two abnormal cells, then four, and so on. **Eventually these abnormal cells form clusters of cells called** *tumors*.

Tumors may be of two types:

- *Benign: Benign tumors* **are abnormal in some way, but, depending on where they occur, they are usually harmless,** such as freckles, moles, or fatty lumps in the skin. They may be left alone or removed, but they do not invade surrounding tissues.

- *Malignant: Malignant tumors* **have two characteristics: (1) they grow and** *infiltrate*, **or invade, surrounding tissues. (2) In time these malignant cells also** *metastasize*, **spreading like seeds to other parts of the body, where they start other growths.**

The only way to tell whether a tumor is benign or malignant is by examining the cells under a microscope. As you might expect, the sooner cancer is identified, the easier it is to treat and the better the prognosis (expected outcome).

The Causes of Cancer: Initiators, Promoters, and Oncogenes Normal growth—the doubling and copying of cells—is governed by genes within the cells. However, some normal genes may be transformed, for whatever reason, into *oncogenes*, **genes that promote the growth of cancer.** These genes alter the regulation of cells so that the cells become abnormal.

What kind of changes transform these genes? According to the "multiple hit theory," all cancers arise from at least two changes or "hits" to the genes in the cell.[42] The hits may be *initiators*, which initiate the cancer process, or they may be *promoters*, which accelerate the growth of abnormal cells:

- *Initiators:* Initiators may include tobacco and tobacco smoke, excessive radiation in the form of X-rays or exposure to sunlight, certain industrial agents or toxic substances, high-fat/low-fiber diet, and obesity. Other possible initiators are certain hormones and drugs, and certain sexual practices (as in unprotected sexual contact that increases one's vulnerability to STDs, including HIV).

- *Promoters:* Promoters may include alcohol use, which is a factor in 4% of cancers (especially of the head, neck, and liver). Another may be stress, which may weaken the immune system.

Heredity may also be a factor. As we shall explain, the risk of developing cancer comes down to three main factors: (1) your genetic makeup, (2) your environmental and occupational exposures to **cancer-causing, or** *carcinogenic*, **agents,** and (3) your personal lifestyle.

The Three Ways Cancer Spreads It is possible, but not usual, for tumors to grow in different parts of the body simultaneously. More commonly, a tumor begins in one place and then spreads to other areas. The spreading, called *metastasis*, may take place in three ways:[43]

- *Direct extension:* As the tumor grows in size, it invades tissues immediately next to it.

- *Through the circulatory system:* Tumor cells can grow through the walls of an artery or vein and enter the bloodstream. Then they circulate through the body until they invade other organs.

- *Through the lymphatic system:* Besides the circulatory system (of arteries, veins, and capillaries), the body has another vessel system, the lymphatic system. **The *lymphatic system* consists of a separate system of tiny vessels (lymphatics). They carry a liquid called *lymph*. The system drains infectious, toxic, and other waste materials from the body. These materials are trapped in bean-shaped vessels throughout the body called *lymph nodes*.** The lymph fluid is eventually returned to the heart.

Cancer cells can spread into the lymphatic system, perhaps eventually bypassing lymph nodes and getting directly into the body.

The Different Types of Tumors Physicians use an extensive classification system for types of malignancies. But to help us understand it we can say there are four general types of tumors, corresponding to four different kinds of tissues:

- *Carcinomas: Carcinomas* **are tumors that develop in an organ that secretes something.** These are tumors found in the skin, glands, or membranes and include lung, breast, rectal, oral, testicular, and pancreatic cancers. About 85% of malignant tumors are carcinomas.

- *Sarcomas: Sarcomas* **are tumors of the connective tissues of the body**—muscles, ligaments, bones, nerves, tendons, or blood vessels. Only 2% of malignant tumors are sarcomas.

- *Leukemias: Leukemias* **are tumors of the blood cells and blood-forming tissues,** including the cells in the bone marrow.

- *Lymphomas: Lymphomas* **are tumors that develop in the lymph glands.** Breast cancer, for instance, may initially spread from the breast to the lymph nodes in the armpit.

Most tumors fall in these four areas. However, many terms, from Hodgkin's disease to melanoma, have names that do not suggest which area the tumor is associated with.

Cancers and Warning Signs

Cancer may be noticed by any of seven early warning signals. Several important cancers are those of the lungs, breast, colon and rectum, prostate, blood and lymph systems, ovaries and uterus, oral cavity, skin, and testicles.

Some cancers have a higher risk of death than others. Every year the American Cancer Society reports the incidence and deaths associated with cancer in 12 different areas, covering about 40 organs and tissues. *(See ● Figure 10.)* Lung cancer and colon and rectum cancers are high on the list of deadly cancer for both men and women. Breast cancer is the second most likely to kill for women, and prostate cancer the third most likely to kill for men.

General Warning Signs of Cancer The American Cancer Society has published a list, called *Seven Early Warning Signals* for cancer. The first letters of the signals spell *C-A-U-T-I-O-N*. These are worth memorizing:

- *C:* Change in bowel or bladder habits.
- *A:* A sore that does not heal.
- *U:* Unusual bleeding or discharge.
- *T:* Thickening or lump in breast or elsewhere.
- *I:* Indigestion or difficulty in swallowing.
- *O:* Obvious change in wart or mole.
- *N:* Nagging cough or hoarseness.

Unfortunately, many people don't pay much attention to these warning signs. However, *the earlier cancer is diagnosed, the better the chances for treatment and survival.*

Often cancer symptoms are turned up during a routine physical examination, such as a yearly checkup. It is better still to take any sign seriously and have it checked out.

Lung Cancer Lung cancer, the leading cause of cancer death in the United States, would actually be somewhat rare except for cigarette smoking. Most cases are associated with exposure to tobacco smoke, both active smoking and passive (sidestream) smoking.

Identifying lung cancer early is difficult, because most signs don't appear until the disease

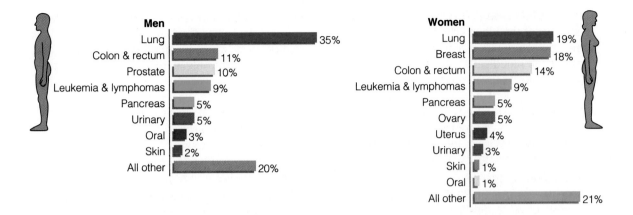

● **Figure 10   Risks of death, by cancer type.** The numbers express the percentage of fatalities for each type of cancer.

has spread. As with any disease, however, the earlier the detection, the better the chances of reversing its course. If you're a smoker or have spent many years in smoking environments, be alert for persistent cough. Watch for change in volume, odor, or color of sputum; shortness of breath; and frequent upper respiratory infections. Consult a health care professional for severe or continuing respiratory problems you experience.

Breast Cancer   For women, breast cancer is nearly as serious as lung cancer: nearly 1 out of 9 American women will develop this disease. Some women are more at risk than others: women who consume alcohol moderately to heavily; women with a family history of breast cancer; women who have had no children; women who have had children late in life; women whose diets are high in saturated fats; women whose menstrual periods began when they were young; and women whose menopause came later than usual.

In two-thirds of cases, the breast cancer is a painless mass in the upper outside quadrant (quarter) of the breast. In another few cases, the mass is experienced as painful. Sometimes there is nipple discharge.

Colon and Rectum Cancer   Lung cancer and breast cancer seem to grab all the headlines.

However, cancer of the colon and the rectum are nevertheless extremely common. **The *rectum* is the terminal part of the intestine, and the colon is the part of the large intestine joining the rectum.** Among cancers, colon and rectal cancer is the second cause of death of men, the third cause of death of women. A strong link is suspected between these cancers and a high-fat, low-fiber diet. Colon and rectal cancers may also tend to run in families. Symptoms include bleeding from the rectum, blood in the stool, or a change in bowel habits.

Prostate Cancer   **The *prostate gland*, which secretes a fluid that is part of the male ejaculatory fluid, is located just above the urethra.** Cancer of the prostate is the third most common form of cancer in males, and probably 1 out of 11 men will develop this disease. There has been an increase in prostate cancer during the last 20 years, perhaps partly related to the North American high-fat diet. Symptoms include difficulty urinating, blood in the urine, and persistent low-back pain.

Leukemia and Lymphomas   Leukemias are cancers of the blood system; lymphomas are cancers of the lymph system.

● ***Leukemia:*** There are several types of leukemia, but they all produce abnormal white blood cells that crowd out three substances of the blood. They crowd out healthy white blood cells, which fight infections; red blood cells, which prevent anemia; and platelets, which control bleeding.

Chronic leukemia often develops slowly and has few warning signs. Acute leukemia cause several symptoms: fatigue, weight loss, susceptibility to infections, paleness, susceptibility to bruising, or nosebleeds.

- *Lymphoma:* Lymphomas provide several warning signs, including swollen lymph nodes, fever, weight loss, or night sweats.

Cancers of the Ovaries and Uterus Known as *gynecological cancers,* cancers of the ovaries and uterus are responsible for about 9% of women's death by cancer every year.

- *Ovarian cancer:* **The ovaries are the female reproductive organs.** If the ovaries become cancerous, they often show no signs until later, although sometimes an enlarged ovary is felt during a pelvic exam.

- *Uterine cancer:* **The *uterus* is the pear-shaped muscle whose primary purpose is to contain the fetus until it is born.** About 70% of uterine cancers affect the **endometrium, the lining of the uterus.** Symptoms of endometrial cancer include abnormal bleeding between periods or other unusual vaginal discharge. The other 30% of uterine cancers affect the **cervix, the opening between the vagina and the uterus.** Warning signs include unusual vaginal discharge or bleeding between periods.

Oral Cancer Oral cancers occur anywhere between the lips and the throat—that is, anywhere in the oral cavity. Oral cancers may be associated with heavy smoking, excessive drinking, and use of chewing tobacco.

Symptoms include sores in the mouth that bleed easily or don't heal. Other symptoms are a lump or thickening in the mouth or on the lips, or whitish and hardened patches. Persistent sore throat and difficulty in chewing or swallowing may also signal oral cancer.

Skin Cancer Most skin cancers, called *basal and squamous cell carcinomas,* are not considered very hazardous. They are easily cured

by medicine applied to the skin or by outpatient surgery. However, the skin cancer known as *melanoma* (which means "black tumor") is an exception. "Not only is melanoma the most malignant of all skin cancers," write one team of experts, "it is among the most malignant of *all* cancers."[44] Although it is not a common cancer, it is increasing yearly, with 27,600 cases reported in a recent year.[45]

How do you tell the difference between less serious and harmful skin cancers?

- *Less serious skin cancer:* Basal and squamous cell carcinomas constitute about four-fifths of all skin cancers. The first symptom may be the appearance of a pale, waxlike, pearly nodule or a red, scaly patch.

- *Serious skin cancer:* **Malignant melanomas are most commonly found on the skin, but 10% arise in the eye. A melanoma often begins as a small, molelike growth. It gradually increases in size, changes color, becomes ulcerated, and bleeds easily** from the slightest injury.

Testicular Cancer Cancer of the **testicles, or sperm-producing organs,** is not a common form of cancer, but it *is* a common form for men between ages 20 and 34.[46] Fortunately, it is one of the most curable cancers if detected early.

One symptom of testicular cancer is the presence of a small, painless lump on the side of the testicle. Other signs are a change in shape of a testicle and a dull ache or heaviness in the groin or scrotum.

Help for Cancer

Cancer may be diagnosed by physical examination, laboratory tests, imaging techniques, endoscopy, and biopsy. Treatment may be by surgery, radiation therapy, chemotherapy, or immunotherapy, along with complementary treatments.

Suppose, as a result of some worrisome signs, you suspect you have cancer. Or suppose you learn in the course of a regular physical examination that your physician "has some suspicions" and "wants to run some tests."

At first, you may be engulfed by the terrifying feeling that you have received a death sentence. You may plunge abruptly through an emotional constellation of shock, confusion, despair, anger, and depression.

It's important to know, however, that *many cancers can be cured*—particularly if they are detected early. The challenge to a cancer patient is to decide to deal aggressively with the disease and to actively participate in fighting it.

Tools for Diagnosis A bit later in the chapter, we present strategies you can use to provide your own early-warning system against cancer. Here, however, let us look at the tools that physicians use to make a diagnosis.[47]

- *The physical examination:* A good physician will do an examination of the entire body, in particular touching and scrutinizing those parts that are most prone to develop cancers. These areas include:

  (1) The nose, throat, and larynx, to see if oral cancer is present.

  (2) The neck above the collarbone, under the arms, and in the groin—areas containing lymph nodes—to check for swellings. These might indicate lymphomas.

  (3) The abdomen, to check for enlargement of abdominal organs, such as the liver and spleen.

  (4) The rectum, using a rubber-gloved finger, to check for colon and rectal cancers. In men, the physician also checks for an enlarged prostate gland.

  (5) In women, the breasts and pelvic area to detect cancers of the ovaries, uterus, and cervix. A Pap test is used to detect evidence of abnormal cervical cells, indicating cervical cancer.

  The health care practitioner will also ask you about swallowing problems, hoarseness, bleeding, coughing up blood, and constipation. There will also be questions about cancer among close relatives.

- *Laboratory tests:* The health care practitioner may ask you to go to a lab and have blood drawn for several tests. Some of the blood tests may be nonspecific. But they may show results (such as a low blood count

from anemia) that suggest the presence of a problem. Other blood tests are fairly specific for particular kinds of cancer.

Besides blood tests, a physician may order tests of various body fluids, such as urine, or of the stools. These tests check whether a hidden cancer is possible.

The Pap test, mentioned above, is an example of a cytological test. Cytology is the study of cells. In the Pap test, the cervix is scraped. The cellular material removed is put on slides, stained with dyes, and examined under a microscope. The cytologist can then make a diagnosis as to whether the cells are abnormal or malignant.

- *Imaging techniques:* The original imaging technique was the X-ray, and this is still used extensively. For example, perhaps the best tool for early detection of breast cancer is **a diagnostic breast X-ray exam called mammography**. *(See ● Figure 11.)*

  In recent years, the arsenal of imaging techniques has been expanded. It now includes nuclear scans, computerized tomography (CT), magnetic-resonance imaging (MRI), and ultrasound.

- *Endoscopy:* Sometimes direct visualization is preferable to an imaging technique for diagnosis. Flexible fiber-optic "scopes" that can see around corners can be used to look directly at the tissue inside body cavities. They give physicians a direct view of possible tumor areas.

- *Biopsies:* **A *biopsy* is a procedure in which a specimen of tissue is removed from the body. The specimen is examined under a microscope by a specialist (pathologist) to see if the cells fit the characteristic profile for cancer.** Some biopsies can be performed with very thin needles and a local anesthetic. Other biopsies are performed during surgery that may be necessary to expose the potential tumor.

Treatment Suppose you are diagnosed as having cancer, perhaps by your primary physician, internist, or (if you're a woman) gynecologist. Next, a treatment team will be assembled. This team will include both internists—specialists in internal medicine—and **oncologists, internists with additional training in the**

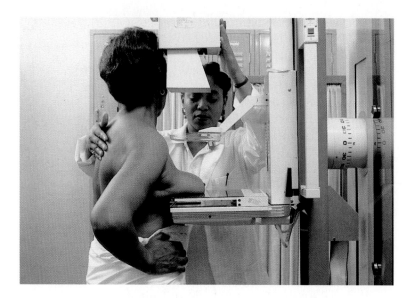

● **Figure 11 Mammography.** This diagnostic X-ray technique is one of the best tools for early detection of breast cancer.

treatment of cancer. They may be assisted by surgeons and radiation oncologists, who specialize in shrinking tumors with X-rays.

Cancer treatment includes *surgery, radiation therapy, chemotherapy,* and *immunotherapy* used alone or in some combination.

- *Surgery:* The oldest technique, surgery often works fine if (1) the tumor is in one location and the cancer has not spread, and (2) the tumor can be removed without damaging vital organs (such as the brain or the liver).

  Surgery is particularly recommended for cancers of the skin, gastrointestinal tract, breast, uterus, prostate, and testicles.

- *Radiation therapy: Radiation therapy is the use of X-rays, gamma rays, electrons, photons, or high-energy particles to treat cancer.* Radiation therapy attempts to shrink a tumor by damaging the tumor cells so they cannot reproduce themselves. The process is painless. Experiencing radiation is like having a chest X-ray, except the radiation is concentrated for several minutes instead of seconds.

It needs to be remembered that some healthy tissue may be destroyed along with the cancer cells. Radiation therapy is particularly suited to cancers of the skin, larynx, uterus, cervix, and lymphoid tissue. It can also be helpful in controlling the pain associated with some types of cancer.

- *Chemotherapy: Chemotherapy is actually a fairly broad term that means using drugs to fight any disease. However, people have come to associate the word with using drugs to fight cancer.* Often these anticancer drugs destroy the ability of the cancer cells to reproduce.

  Chemotherapy is generally used for cancers that have traveled through the blood and lymph systems and are in more than one place. The chemotherapy can also affect normal cells, resulting in such symptoms as fatigue, nausea, and hair loss (which is usually temporary). Although some people have moderate to severe side effects, most people tolerate them rather well. Moreover, side effects such as nausea can be alleviated with other drugs.

- *Immunotherapy: Immunotherapy tries to use the body's own immune system to fight disease. It bolsters natural immune mechanisms (lymphocytes such as T-cells) to destroy the cancer cells.* Immunotherapy consists mainly of using highly purified proteins (such as interferon and interleukin-2) to activate the immune system.

Several of these treatments may be applied simultaneously. For example, radiation and chemotherapy are combined to produce a more powerful anticancer effect than is possible with one therapy alone.

Additional Treatment—and Questionable Therapies Cancer specialists will recommend treatments in addition to the ones we've just described. These are called *complementary* or *adjunctive* treatments, because they are used along with standard therapies.[48] These include nutritional therapy, yoga, relaxation techniques, and the use of social-support systems. After all, fighting cancer can require a great deal of energy and overcoming a great many fears. These additional therapies can only assist in that struggle.

However, sometimes these therapies are promoted as having the power to cure cancer on their own, without traditional medical treatments. Thus, certain diets are advertised as cancer cures, guided imagery or relaxation programs are said to promote the right healing attitude, and so on. Some treatments are even more farfetched. In the 1970s, a substance prepared from apricot pits called Laetrile was offered as a cancer treatment. It has been shown to have no effect. Today clinics throughout the United States and in Mexico offer "oxygenation," or "natural therapy," or "cellular detoxification and restoration." Methods include cleansing of the colon or vitamin therapy.[49]

One can certainly sympathize with the plight of cancer patients desperate for the certainty of a cure. However, a treatment method should be studied scientifically and properly (reviewed and approved by other knowledgeable researchers). Promises and testimonials are not enough. Indeed, unproven methods can actually be harmful, diverting money and energy, causing patients to neglect legitimate treatments and raising false hopes.

Risk Factors for Cancer

Predisposing risk factors are age, gender, heredity, race, and viruses. Risk factors that can be controlled include tobacco, diet, sexual behavior, occupation, alcohol, environmental pollution, sunlight, and radiation.

As with heart disease, some risk factors for cancer are controllable. *(See ● Figure 12.)* Uncontrollable, or *predisposing,* risk factors include age, gender, heredity, race, and exposure to viruses, and infection. Controllable, or *precipitating,* risk factors include diet, smoking, sexual behavior, occupation, alcohol, environmental pollution, sunlight, radiation, and other matters. *(See Self Discovery 2.)*

Predisposing Risk Factors: Age, Gender, Heredity, Race, Viruses There is nothing you can do about these uncontrollable risk factors,

except to be alert to those factors that you *can* control.

- **Age:** Some forms of cancer seem to strike some age groups more than others: testicular cancer—ages 15–44; Hodgkin's disease—ages 20–40; endometrial cancer—ages 55–69. In general, however, the risk of cancer rises as one grows older.

- **Gender:** Some cancers are principally sex-specific, of course—testicular and prostate cancers in men, breast and gynecological cancers in women. Some men get breast cancer, too. Oral cancer and Hodgkin's disease show up more in males than in females.

- **Heredity:** Some cancers seem to be clustered in families: breast, ovarian, colon/rectum, prostate, stomach, and lung and leukemia. However, only about 2% of cancers are caused directly by heredity. That is, many family histories of cancer may be the result of environmental factors rather than genetic.[50] Children with Down syndrome are more apt to develop leukemia than most children.[51] Certain individuals may have genetic skin disorders (xeroderma pigmentosum and albinism) that predispose them to skin cancer.[52]

- **Race:** The role of race in cancer is seen quite specifically in skin cancers. Light-skinned people suffer a more adverse reaction to the sun's ultraviolet radiation.

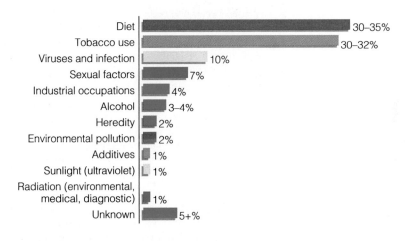

● **Figure 12   Cancer risk factors, with percentages.**

SELF DISCOVERY 2

What Is Your Risk of Cancer?

For each of the following questions, circle the answer that best describes you and your lifestyle.

Males: Answer questions for the first three sections only—the lung, colon/rectal, and skin cancer sections.

Females: Answer all questions, but if you have had a complete hysterectomy then skip the questions for cervical and endometrial cancers.

Lung Cancer

1. Sex
   a. Male (2)   b. Female (1)
2. Age
   a. 39 or less (1)   b. 40–49 (2)
   c. 50–59 (5)   d. 60+ (7)
3. Smoking behavior
   a. smoker (8)   b. nonsmoker (1)
4. Type of smoking
   a. cigarettes or little   b. pipe and/or cigar,
      cigars (1)   but not cigarettes (3)
   c. ex-cigarette   d. nonsmoker (1)
      smoker (2)
5. Amount of cigarettes smoked per day
   a. 0 (1)   b. less than ½ pack (5)
   c. ½–1 pack (9)   d. 1–2 packs (5)
   e. 2+ packs (20)
6. Type of cigarette by amount of tar/nicotine
   a. high tar/nicotine (20 mg tar/1.3 mg nicotine) (10)
   b. medium tar/nicotine (16–19 mg tar/1.15 mg
      nicotine) (9)
   c. low tar/nicotine (15 mg or less tar/1.0 mg or less
      nicotine) (7)
   d. nonsmoker (1)
7. Duration of smoking
   a. Never smoked (1)   b. ex-smoker (3)
   c. up to 15 years (5) d. 15–25 years (10)
   e. 25+ years (20)
8. Type of industrial work
   a. mining (3)   b. asbestos (7)
   c. uranium and radio- d. none of these (0)
      active products (5)

Colon/Rectum Cancer

1. Age
   a. 39 or less (10)   b. 40–59 (20)
   c. 60 and over (50)
2. Has anyone in your immediate family ever had:
   a. colon cancer (20)   b. one or more polyps
                             of the colon (10)
   c. neither (1)
3. Have you ever had:
   a. colon cancer (100) b. one or more polyps
                             of the colon (40)
   c. ulcerative colitis (20) d. cancer of the breast
                                  or uterus (10)
   e. none of the above (1)
4. Have you had bleeding from the rectum (other than
   obvious hemorrhoids or piles)?
   a. yes (75)   b. no (1)

Skin Cancer

1. Do you frequently work or play in the sun?
   a. yes (10)   b. no (1)
2. Do you work in mines, around coal tars, or around
   radioactivity?
   a. yes (10)   b. no (1)
3. Do you have fair and/or light skin?
   a. yes (10)   b. no (1)

Breast Cancer

1. Age
   a. 20–35 (10)   b. 35–49 (40)
   c. 50 and over (90)
2. Race
   a. black (20)   b. hispanic (10)
   c. oriental (5)   d. white (25)
3. Family history
   a. mother, sister, aunt, or grandmother with breast
      cancer (30)
   b. none (10)
4. Your history
   a. no breast disease (10)
   b. previous lumps or cysts (25)
   c. previous breast cancer (100)
5. Maternity
   a. first pregnancy before 25 (10)
   b. first pregnancy after 25 (15)
   c. no pregnancies (20)

Cervical Cancer

1. Age
   a. less than 25 (10)   b. 25–39 (20)
   c. 40–54 (30)   d. 55 and over (30)
2. Race
   a. black (20)   b. hispanic (10)
   c. oriental (20)   d. white (10)
3. Number of pregnancies
   a. 0 (10)   b. 1–3 (20)
   c. 4 and over (30)
4. Viral infections
   a. herpes and other viral infections or ulcer forma-
      tions on the vagina (10)
   b. never had such infections (1)
5. Age at first intercourse
   a. before 15 (40)   b. 15–19 (30)
   c. 20–24 (20)   d. 25 and over (10)
   e. never (5)
6. Bleeding between menstrual periods after
   intercourse
   a. yes (40)   b. no (1)

SELF DISCOVERY 2
(continued)

Endometrial Cancer

1. Age
   a. 39 or under (5)   b. 40–49 (20)
   c. 50 and over (60)
2. Race
   a. black (10)   b. hispanic (10)
   c. oriental (10)   d. white (20)
3. Births
   a. none (15)   b. 1–4 (7)
   c. 5 or more (5)
4. Weight
   a. 50 or more pounds overweight (50)
   b. 20–49 pounds overweight (15)
   c. underweight for height (10)
   d. normal (10)

5. Diabetes
   a. yes (3)   b. no (1)
6. Estrogen hormone intake
   a. yes, regularly (15) b. yes, occasionally (12)
   c. none (10)
7. Abnormal uterine bleeding
   a. yes (40)   b. no (1)
8. High blood pressure
   a. yes (3)   b. no (1)

Scoring

For each form of cancer, add up the numbers in parentheses following the answers you selected.

Interpretation

Numerical risks for skin cancer are difficult to state. A person with a dark complexion can work longer in the sun and be less likely to develop cancer than a light-complected person can. A person wearing a long-sleeved shirt and wide-brimmed hat may work in the sun and be less at risk than a person who wears a bathing suit for only a short time. The risk goes up greatly with age. Still, in general, the more questions to which you answered "yes," the greater your risks.

For other cancers, see the chart below.

Type of cancer	Very low risk	Low risk	Moderate risk	High risk	Very high risk
Lung/colon	6–24	25–49		50–74	75+
Rectum		13–29	30–69	70+	
Breast		45–100	100–199	200+	
Cervical		40–69	70–99	100+	
Endometrial		45–69	60–99	100+	

Source: American Cancer Society, 1981.

In general, cancer death rates are higher among blacks than among whites, and the average survival times are shorter.[53] However, this may be because of socioeconomic factors rather than race.

- *Viruses:* Viruses have been associated with certain cancers—of the blood, the liver, the cervix, the pharynx, and the lymph system. Human immunodeficiency virus (HIV) can so weaken the immune system that an otherwise rare cancer called *Kaposi's sarcoma* occurs in many who develop AIDS.

Although you cannot control your age, gender, heredity, race, or your exposure to certain viruses, you can control some other risk factors. These include tobacco, diet, sexual behavior, occupation, alcohol, environmental pollution, sunlight, and radiation.

Tobacco Despite the pronouncements of the cigarette-industry-sponsored Tobacco Institute to the contrary, over 50,000 studies have shown there is no question that smoking can cause cancer. In the early 1900s, lung cancer was a rare disease, with probably no more than 500 cases a year. In 1912, milder tobaccos came on the market that could be inhaled without causing excessive coughing, and smoking became much more commonplace. So did lung cancer. By 1950, when the first report was published linking smoking and lung cancer, there were 18,000 lung cancer deaths per year. By 1990 there were an estimated 160,000 deaths per year.[54] No effective treatment for lung cancer is available. Nearly 90% of lung cancer patients die within 5 years of diagnosis.[55]

Cigarette smoking is the major determinant of lung cancer risk, although exposure to asbestos, ionizing radiation, and radon decay products increases risk. Exposure to environmental (passive) tobacco smoke also increases the risk of lung cancer in people who have never smoked.

People who smoke pipes or cigars (and don't inhale) do not show high rates of lung cancer. Nor do those who use smokeless tobacco (chewing tobacco and dipping snuff). However, all these groups show high rates of oral cancer and cancer of the esophagus.

Diet Researchers seem to have found a number of links between diet and cancer. The riskiest diets include those that are high calorie, high fat, and low fiber. Other risks are foods that are pickled, salted, smoked, or grilled or that have additives such as nitrites and nitrates. High alcohol consumption is also linked to cancer.

- *High calories:* Obese people have a much higher risk of developing cancers of the uterus, breast, colon, stomach, gallbladder, and kidneys.

- *High fat/low fiber:* Diets that are high in fats—both saturated (hard, mostly animal) and unsaturated (liquid, mostly vegetable)—are risky. They are linked to cancers of the colon, rectum, prostate, testicles, breast, uterus, and gallbladder. Diets that are low in fiber are associated with the development of colon and rectum cancers.

- *Preserved and grilled foods:* Foods that are cured or smoked—such as smoked ham and sausage—may contribute to high rates of stomach cancer. Salted and pickled foods and nitrite- and nitrate-cured meats increase the risk of cancers of the stomach and esophagus. Foods grilled at high temperatures, as on barbecues, may have carcinogenic substances from the grease burning on the coals.

- *Low vitamins A and C:* People whose diets are low in vitamin A increase the risk of cancers of the larynx, esophagus, and lung. People with diets low in vitamin C

increase the risk of cancers of the stomach and esophagus.

Sexual Factors The more sex partners you have, the more likely you are to be exposed to sexually transmitted diseases. STDs include viruses that can cause cancers of the cervix, penis, and anus, as well as the head and neck. Women who have had their first sexual intercourse at an early age also have a higher risk of developing cervical cancer.

For women, childbearing reduces the risk of cancers of the breast, ovary, and uterus. Women who give birth before age 30 are less likely to have breast cancer in later life than those who never become pregnant or have their first child after age 30.

Occupation and Environment People who work around carcinogenic chemicals such as asbestos, coal products, cadmium, uranium, nickel, or nuclear wastes increase the risk of cancer. People living and working in areas with heavy air pollution may also be at greater risk.

Alcohol In about 4% of people (7% males, 3% females), alcohol can lead to cancers in the head, neck, larynx, liver, and pancreas.[56] Many people who drink also smoke, and the combination strongly raises the risk of oral cancers and cancer of the esophagus.

Sunlight *Ultraviolet radiation* **consists of the light rays emitted by the sun.** Even on cloudy days, these may affect your skin, and as the protective ozone layer becomes thinner, these rays are becoming even more intense.

The supposed beauty benefits of tanning, whether from the sun or from artificial tanning lights, are transitory at best and fatal at worst. After several years, tanning actually makes you look older, because of the leathery skin texture, wrinkles, and age spots. Worse, exposure to the sun may lead to basal-cell or squamous-cell cancers. It may even lead to the dangerous malignant melanoma, now the ninth most common cancer in the United States.

Strategy for Living: Steps for Preventing Cancer

Nine steps for preventing cancer are: (1) quit tobacco use; (2) eat a low-fat, high-fiber diet; (3) moderate alcohol use; (4) control weight through exercise; (5) protect yourself from STDs; (6) reduce exposure to sunlight; (7) reduce exposure to environmental carcinogens; (8) do regular self-exams; and (9) get regular professional evaluations.

Cancer can totally disrupt your life. It can inflict great emotional and physical pain and be enormously time-consuming and expensive to treat. It can completely undo all your life's routines and plans—maybe even permanently. People knowing what most cancer patients know should fully appreciate the chance to avoid undergoing this kind of agony. In a word, they have the chance to exercise *prevention.*

Prevention against cancer has two parts: (1) Take steps to increase the chances that cancer never happens to you. (2) Take steps to catch it in its earliest stage, when it is most curable.

Step 1: Avoid All Forms of Tobacco Use
Cure rates for cancer have increased steadily during the past half century—but not for lung cancer. Smoking is responsible for 85% of lung cancer cases, not to mention several other cancers. If you use smokeless tobacco, try to stop, to avoid oral cancer. If you find yourself continually breathing passive (sidestream) smoke, try to create a smoke-free environment for yourself. For example, put out signs that say THANK YOU FOR NOT SMOKING.

Step 2: Eat a Low-Fat, High-Fiber Diet
A cancer-fighting diet may mean changing a few old habits, but you'll be glad you did.

- ***Reduce your fat intake:*** Reduce the consumption of animal fats, especially red meats and dairy products. Trim excess fat from foods, cook with little or no fat, don't always butter your bread, and otherwise scale back fat consumption.

- ***Eat more fiber, cruciferous vegetables, and vitamins A and C:*** You can get fiber from whole grains, cereals, vegetables, and fruits. Cruciferous vegetables help reduce the risk of several cancers (such as colon cancer). Cruciferous vegetables are in the cabbage family (cabbage, brussels sprouts, turnips, and cauliflower). Vitamin A is found in dark-green and deep-yellow vegetables (such as cantaloupe, carrots, spinach, and sweet potatoes). Vitamin C is found in oranges, grapefruit, broccoli and cauliflower, among other foods.

- ***Avoid smoked or charcoal-broiled foods:*** You can still grill or broil foods, but try to keep them away from smoke and flames, which produce carcinogens. Wrap food in foil or place it in a pan before grilling. Stay away from meats that have been smoked, salted, or pickled.

Step 3: Use Alcohol in Moderation
Heavy alcohol users have increased oral cancers and cancer of the esophagus. If you drink, be sparing—say, 1–2 glasses a day.

Step 4: Control Your Body Weight Through Exercise
Being overweight produces excess hormones that may promote cancer growth. Indeed, women who are obese are more apt to develop cancer of the breast, uterus, and ovary. A good way to control your weight is through aerobic exercise, such as walking, swimming, or bicycling, about 30 minutes three times a week.

Step 5: Protect Yourself From STDs
Use condoms, when appropriate, to protect yourself from sexually transmitted diseases. There are increased incidences of cancer of the cervix and of the penis among people with multiple sexual partners.

Step 6: Reduce Your Exposure to Sunlight
Every spring college students head for the beaches to "catch a few rays," returning to show off their "healthy" tans. This is yet more proof, as if any were needed, that for many people appearance is more important than safety. Perhaps, however, with the thinning ozone layer and the rise in skin wrinkling and melanoma cases, this standard will change.

Some tips:

- ***Avoid sunlamps:*** Tanning parlors and sunlamps do the same thing as the sun itself, despite some manufacturers' claims. They all increase your risk of skin cancer.

- ***Know when UV rays are strongest:*** Between 10 A.M. and 3 P.M. is the time of day when ultraviolet (UV) rays are strongest. This is a good time to stay out of the sun or wear wide-brimmed hats and long sleeves. Be aware that UV rays are strongest at high altitudes, and that snow and water are powerful reflectors of the sun's rays.

- ***Understand the value of sunblock and use it:*** Even overcast skies do not filter the sun's rays. Thus, you should wear sunblock or sunscreen anytime you plan to be outside for more than a few minutes during the day. You can be surprised at how much sun you get after only a half hour of walking or gardening.

  In using sunblock, follow these guidelines:

  (1) Use sunscreen lotion containing PABA (para-aminobenzoic acid).

  (2) Make sure it has a sun protection factor (SPF) of 15 or more, especially if you are blond, red-headed, freckled, or light-skinned. Sunblocks are labeled with SPF ratings ranging from a low of 8 to a high of 30.

  (3) Apply it an hour *before* going into the sun.

  (4) Sunblock wears off when you're swimming or sweating and thus needs to be reapplied from time to time.

Step 7: Reduce Your Exposure to Work and Environmental Carcinogens If you work in industrial surroundings, where you might be exposed to cancer-causing chemicals such as benzene and industrial asbestos, make an effort to use protective equipment, such as masks, gloves, and overalls. If possible, avoid contact with such carcinogens altogether.

Step 8: Do Regular Self-Exams for Early Detection The foregoing steps are to try to prevent cancer from developing. These should be backed up with measures to ensure early detection should tumors develop. The first line of detection is self-examination, as follows:

- ***Men—checking for testicular cancer:*** Once a month, after a warm bath or shower (when the scrotum is relaxed), take about 3 minutes for this exam. Roll first one testicle, then the other, between thumbs and forefingers of both hands. Look or probe for lumps, tenderness, swelling, heaviness, or anything else unusual. *(See ● Figure 13.)*

  Testicular cancer is the most common malignancy among males ages 15–34. However, you cannot make the diagnosis yourself; it usually requires professional help. Thus, any irregularity you find should be examined promptly by a physician.

- ***Women—checking for breast cancer:*** A breast self-exam should be done once a month. Do it at the same time every month if you are not menstruating (during pregnancy, or after menopause or a hysterectomy). Do it or 2–3 days after your period, if you are menstruating. The self-exam should be done in three phases: (1) while in the shower or bath; (2) before a mirror; and (3) while lying down. *(See ● Figure 14.)*

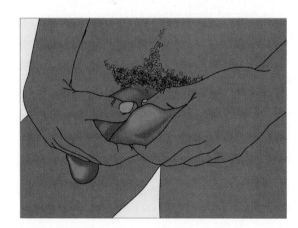

1. Roll each testicle between thumbs and forefingers of both hands.
2. Look or feel for pea-sized, painless lump. Also look for swelling, tenderness, or other irregularities.
3. If you find anything unusual, don't disregard it. Contact a physician immediately. Only a doctor can make an accurate diagnosis.

● Figure 13   Testicular self-exam.

● **Figure 14   Breast self-exam.**

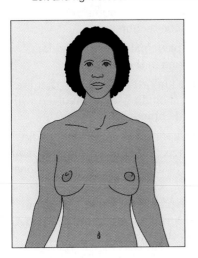

1. In the shower: Examine your breasts during bath or shower; hands glide more easily over wet skin. With fingers flat, move your hands gently over every part of each breast. Use your right hand to examine your left breast, left hand for your right breast. Check for any lump, hard knot, or thickening.

2. Before a mirror: While standing before a mirror, examine your breasts from three positions:
- Inspect your breasts with arms at your side.
- Next, raise your arms high overhead. Look for any changes in the contour of each breast: a swelling, dimpling of the skin, or change in the nipple.
- Then, rest your palms on your hips and press down firmly to flex your chest muscles.

   Left and right breast will not match exactly—few women's breasts do.

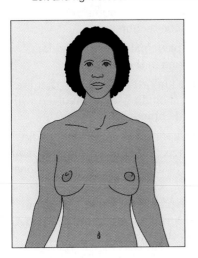
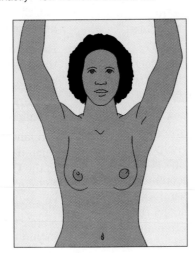
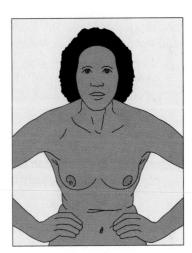

3. Lying down: To examine your right breast, put a pillow or folded towel under your right shoulder. Then do the following:
- Place your right hand behind your head—this distributes breast tissues more evenly on the chest.
- With your left hand, fingers flat, press gently in small circular movements around an imaginary clock face. Begin at the outermost top of your right breast for 12 o'clock, then move to 1 o'clock, and so on around the circle back to 12. A ridge of firm tissue in the lower curve of each breast is normal.

   Then move in an inch, toward the nipple, and keep circling to examine **every part of your breast,** including the nipple. This requires at least three more circles. Now slowly repeat this procedure on your left breast.
- Finally, squeeze the nipple of each breast gently between thumb and index finger. Any discharge, clear or bloody, should be reported to your doctor immediately.

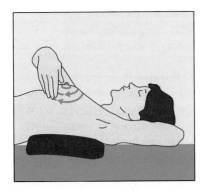
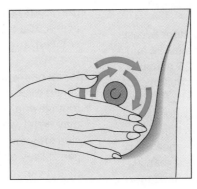
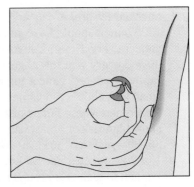

Many women's breasts normally feel lumpy. However, once you become familiar with these normal lumps, you will be able to notice any changes—lumps, hard knots, or thickenings. If you notice a change, you should see a physician immediately.

- ***Both males and females—monthly overall self-check:*** Once a month, use a full-length mirror and a hand mirror to check yourself all over. Look for suspicious lumps or patches on the skin, in the mouth, in and around the genitals, and around the rectal area.

Step 9: Get Regular Professional Evaluations During yearly physical examinations, the physician should use the following procedures and tests to check for cancer:

- ***For lung cancer:*** After age 40, an elective yearly chest X-ray and a blood chemistry profile should be done to check for lung cancer, especially for smokers.

- ***For colon cancer:*** A simple test for colon cancer, which can be done in the physician's office, detects blood in the person's stool. Another standard yearly test, recommended after age 40, is a digital rectal exam. After age 50, a sigmoidoscopy/colonoscopy (using a hollow, lighted tube) of the rectum and lower colon is recommended every 2–3 years.

- ***For gynecological cancers:*** Women should have a yearly pelvic examination, including a Pap test, to check for cervical, uterine, ovarian, and endometrial cancers.

- ***For breast and testicular cancers:*** A physician should in the course of a normal physical examination inspect a man's genitals for testicular and penile cancers. A woman's breast, chest, and armpits are checked for breast cancers.

  Women should be examined for breast cancer every 3 years between ages 20 and 40 and every year after age 40. A mammography can detect cancer lumps that are too small to feel. It is recommended as follows for women whose family history does not show high risk of breast cancer: ages 35–39—one time; ages 40–49—once every 1 or 2 years; over age 50—once a year. Women in high-risk groups may need more frequent mammograms.

Personal Safety: Preventing Accidents and Violence

▶ Explain people's different reactions to involuntary and voluntary risks and what matters affect risk.

▶ Describe traffic safety techniques for avoiding hurting others and hurting yourself with a motor vehicle, including motorcycle and bicycle safety techniques.

▶ List the various types of home accidents and some rescue techniques.

▶ Describe the principal types of accidents that may happen in the outdoors.

▶ Discuss some important disorders that are work-related, including those involved with chemicals and computers.

▶ Explain the importance of murder, gunfire-related violence, and other forms of assault in the United States. List some precautions to take.

▶ Discuss the dynamics of abusive relationships, and describe the abuse of children, including incest.

▶ Describe sexual harassment and rape, including date rape.

Chances Are: Risks and Accidents

Attitudes that affect personal safety include those relating to thrill seeking, drug taking, stress, aggression, inattention, denial, and failure to anticipate. Principal types of accidents are traffic, home-related, outdoor, and work-related.

If you're a white-knuckled flyer, you may be inclined to obsess about all that television news footage you've seen of crashed jetliners. Yet you may never worry about driving in a car. Television and newspapers can have that effect. Because they often emphasize the sensational, the media can make us worry unduly about airplane crashes, shark attacks, lightning, tornados, or earthquakes. In fact, however, your risk of death is far, far greater from being in an auto accident.

The Importance of Attitude in Reducing Risks You cannot control the risks inherent in some situations: when you're in a car, for example, you're at risk from other drivers' errors. However, there are ways you can improve your odds. This is where your attitude comes in. Do you or do you not drive fast, drive drunk, drive half asleep, drive with mechanical defects, drive without using seatbelts? All these are risks *you* can control.

Attitudes that affect your safety include thrill seeking, drug taking, stress, aggression, inattention, denial, and failure to anticipate:

- *Avoiding boredom and seeking thrills:* A lot of things we have to do in life are boring, but some people have trouble with that fact. Indeed, some people don't think they're alive unless they're living on the edge. Such sensation seekers clearly increase the risks of accidents to themselves. Are you one of them?

- *Alcohol and other drugs:* Excessive drinking is so widespread that you probably know someone who was arrested for drunken driving or had other problems when drunk. You may know someone who has been injured (or injured someone else) as a result of alcohol-related behavior. Is there a lesson in this?

  The same observations apply with other drugs, such as cocaine. While you're on them, drugs *may* make you feel almost larger than life, impervious to mistakes. But the statistics on accidents, as well as suicides and homicides, run the other way.

- *Stress:* Stress can distort your thinking. If you're late for a job interview, for example, you may tend to take chances on crossing the street or race the light at intersections. Stress can also distract you, as when you're worrying about an important exam or breaking up with your lover. Stress, in a word, makes you *careless.* Thus, when you're feeling tense, you should do what you can to lower your stress level.

- *Aggression:* Nothing can cloud your judgment like getting mad at somebody. You see this happen with drivers all the time. Otherwise civilized people become enraged when another driver cuts them off or beats them out of a parking place. They try to exact revenge ("That turkey needs a lesson!"). People become walking accidents because they allow matters of supposed "honor" or "respect" or "payback" to overwhelm rational ideas about personal safety.

- *Inattention:* Daydreaming or letting your mind wander can do you in. Many a driver has looked down to adjust the car radio and rear-ended the car ahead. Farmers, who work around dangerous equipment, have become injured when they looked away at a crucial moment. Boaters have gotten in trouble because they didn't look at tide tables and skiers because they didn't attend to weather reports. Pedestrians in crime-prone areas must learn how to keep their wits about them to avoid trouble.

- *Denial:* Some of the biggest risks aren't flashy and so they are easy to ignore or explain away. For instance, terrorism fears caused thousands of Americans to cancel overseas travel plans during the 1991 Gulf War. However, their chances of dying by a terrorist's hand has been pegged at only 1 in 650,000.[57] Yet you can be sure that many of these same Americans refuse to reconsider their smoking, drinking, and driving habits. Denial ("That will never happen to me") enables many people to disregard the threat of low-profile calamities such as car crashes and home accidents.

- *Failure to anticipate or prepare:* Although some accidents cannot be anticipated or prevented, many can. For example, some truck drivers with excellent safety records mentally practice "what-if" possibilities so they can react appropriately to avoid accidents. ("What if I rounded the bend and found a car stopped dead in the middle of the highway?" "What if a car pulled out of that side road?")

  Besides mental preparation, there are also other kinds of preparation. If you're driving for a weekend of skiing, for example, you need to listen to weather reports. Carry tire chains, flares, and food and water (in case you get stuck), and wear appropriate clothing. Once you get to the ski slopes, take lessons or otherwise become properly trained. The way to avoid bad luck, in other words, is to *anticipate the possibility* of bad luck.

Types of Accidents **Accidents are defined as unexpected events that produce injury or death.** In the United States, accidents are the fourth leading cause of death, after heart disease, cancer, and stroke.[58] For people ages 1–37—which includes many readers of this book—accidents are *the* leading cause of death.

As for types of accidents, they may be classified as follows:[59]

- *Traffic accidents:* Motor vehicle crashes (including motorcycle accidents) cause the greatest number of deaths, about 50,000 a year in the United States. In addition, 2 million people are seriously injured. We include bicycle accidents in this category.

- *Home-related accidents:* Because people spend so much time at home, that is where most accidents happen: falls, burns, poisonings, suffocations, electrical shock, and others.

- *Work-related accidents:* Deaths from work-related accidents are apt to be associated with farm machinery, construction, and heavy industry. However, severe injuries can happen in jobs you might not suspect, such as office work involving heavy use of a computer.

- *Outdoor accidents:* Outdoor accidents are often associated with recreation. The most common include drowning and near drowning, diving, falls, overexposure to heat and cold, and athletic injuries.

Let us consider some of these.

A Crash Course in Traffic Safety: Strategy for Living

Part of traffic safety is driving to avoid hurting others. Surround yourself with a defensive "bubble" of space. Don't speed, run red lights, drink and drive, drive while fatigued, or drive with distractions. The other part is driving to avoid hurting yourself. Use seat belts, learn crash-avoidance techniques, be patient, be in a safe car. Being on motorcycles and bicycles requires particular vigilance.

Not everyone drives, but most readers of this book, including bicyclists and pedestrians, are exposed to the dangers of driving. As the driver of a car, motorcycle, or bicycle, you have two concerns: to avoid injuring others and to avoid injuring yourself. Often both concerns overlap.

Driving to Avoid Hurting Others The young driver looked down to change a music tape in her dashboard tape deck. When she looked up again, she had drifted sideways, and it was too late to avoid hitting four bicyclists riding single file. All the bicyclists were killed. This college student was not only convicted of manslaughter but has to bear the pain of her experience the rest of her life.

About 95% of automobile deaths and injuries are due to careless or reckless driving such as this. (The rest are caused by mechanical failure of the vehicle.)[60] To avoid having a similar tragic episode in your life, here are some tips:

- *Surround yourself with a "bubble" of space:* Don't tailgate cars in front, avoid traveling next to cars in other lanes, and let cars crowding you from behind go around. This "bubble" or "defensive space" keeps you away from other cars and gives you some room to maneuver. When you enter situations such as interchanges or heavy traffic, slow down to allow for a smaller bubble.[61]

- *Don't speed:* Speed is a leading cause of accidents in general. The reasons are simple: the faster you go, the longer it takes to stop and the heavier the impact of hitting something. Speeding on rain-slicked or icy roads means you have no control over the vehicle. Speed-limit signs indicate the *maximum* speed allowed under *ideal* conditions. This means if you're driving at night or during bad weather, you should drive more slowly.

  So many people speed that it can feel uncomfortable to drive under the speed limit because people may crowd you from behind. But that's *their* problem. *Your* problem is to not let yourself feel harassed just because you're holding up someone who wants to go faster.

- ***Don't be a red light bandit:*** Then there are the rules-don't-apply-to-me drivers who try to beat the yellow light at an intersection. Not surprisingly, they find themselves going through on the red, which is extremely dangerous. In San Francisco, for instance, up to 29% of the injury accidents are caused by drivers who run red lights.[62]

- ***Don't drink and drive:*** Alcohol is responsible for about *half* of all automobile accidents and is the leading cause of automobile fatalities. No stronger message can be sent about the reasons not to drink and drive.

- ***Don't become fatigued:*** After alcohol, the second cause of serious accidents is fatigue (which is worst from 3 P.M. to 2 A.M.). Drowsiness can be caused not only by lack of sleep but also by certain medications. Avoid driving when taking tranquilizers, muscle relaxants, antidepressants, antihistamines, and some cold and flu remedies.[63]

- ***Don't smoke and drive:*** People who smoke while driving are 50% more likely to be involved in a mishap than those who don't smoke.[64] Fumbling with cigarettes, eye irritation, filmy windshields, and the interference of carbon monoxide with night vision are all reasons.

- ***Don't try to do two things at once:*** A nonscientific study of 500 traffic-school students in south Florida found that three-quarters of them drink, eat, or do both while driving. About half admitted applying makeup or writing notes. More than 40% said they sometimes kiss and drive at the same time.[65] You can't do these things and keep your mind on your driving.

Incidentally, many people are convinced they can hold a cellular phone to one ear while maneuvering 1½ tons of metal through traffic. There are no statistics on accidents related to wireless phones, but clearly mobile callers don't have their full attention on the road.[66]

Driving to Avoid Hurting Yourself Young drivers, ages 15–24, have the highest death rates, owing to lack of experience and judgment. The second highest death rate is among drivers over the age of 75 (almost tied with those in the 25–44 age group). Elderly drivers may have slower reaction times and deterioration of the senses. *(See ● Figure 15.)* Regardless of your age, you can reduce the chances of injuring or killing yourself by adopting the habits described above. Also do the following.

- ***Use seat belts:*** Some people think there's no need to buckle up when on short trips or when not driving fast. However, three-quarters of all crashes are within 25 miles of home and 80% of deaths and injuries occur under 40 mph.[67] Some people also think that in a crash they would be better off being "thrown clear." Not true: actually they would be 25 times more likely to be killed. Finally, although you may be a good driver yourself, you can't always prevent someone else—a drunk driver, say—from hitting you.

The single most effective thing you can do in a car to protect your life is to use a seat belt.

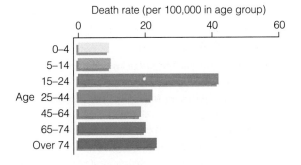

● **Figure 15 Deaths from motor vehicle accidents, by age.** Those ages 15–24 have the highest rate of deaths in motor vehicle (car and motorcycle) accidents. Those over age 74 have the second highest rate.

● **Figure 16   Crash-avoidance techniques.**

1. **ALWAYS try to avoid a head-on crash.** Your chances of surviving almost any other crash are better than those of surviving a head-on collision.

2. **Go off-road, if necessary.** Get rid of the idea that your car *always* belongs on the pavement. If you are close to having an on-road collision, and pedestrians, bicyclists, or motorcyclists are not in your way, *drive off the road.* Driving onto a sidewalk or lawn or into a field may save your life.

3. **Steer your way clear and brake gently off-road.** As you drive off the pavement, try to steer to avoid skidding. Also, don't brake too hard when you're off road, which may trip up the vehicle and cause it to roll over.

4. **Hit a car going your way.** If you are about to crash into a car stopped in front of you or approaching you, and have to hit another vehicle, *hit one going in the same direction you are.* Hitting one traveling beside you in the next lane will have less impact than hitting one in front.

5. **Hit objects that will yield somewhat, and hit with a glancing blow.** If you have to have a collision, don't hit a massive immovable object, such as a concrete abutment or a brick building. Try to pick something that has some "give," such as small trees, parked cars, or wood-frame buildings. Whatever object you run in to, try to give it a glancing blow, which will lessen the impact.

- ***Know crash-avoidance driving techniques:*** Many people don't know how to handle themselves when driving in bad weather. They drive as fast on rain-slicked pavements as on dry roads, and wonder why they go into a skid when they hit the brakes. In fog they pull close to the car or truck in front and follow its lights, eliminating room to stop.[68] When someone veers into their lane, they have a head-on accident rather than risk a less lethal crash by going sideways. It helps to learn some crash survival techniques that don't square with most people's driving habits. *(See ● Figure 16.)*

- ***Learn patience to avoid stress:*** It has been found that the longer people commute, the higher their blood pressure afterward and the worse the stress they feel. They also carry that stress into the office or home afterward.[69] How does one deal with this? Practice patience, or what psychotherapist Todd Berger, coauthor of *Zen Driving,* calls "moving meditation"— driving with full awareness and relaxed concentration.[70]

- ***Drive or ride in a safe car:*** Making sure the car you are in is mechanically sound or fully equipped can make a big difference. For instance, nearly half of all taxicabs nationwide have no seat belts or broken or inaccessible belts in the rear seat. This leads to serious head and neck injuries of passengers in the estimated 100,000 crashes cabs are involved in each year.[71]

Motorcycle Safety   Mile for mile, motorcycles are more dangerous than cars. The chief reasons are that motorcycles are hard to see and other motorists often forget that motorcycles are there. Some motorcyclists add to their chances of injury by "lane splitting," riding between traffic lanes when cars are slowing or stopped. Despite the argument (not true) that a helmet decreases vision, helmet laws have been shown to reduce head injuries.[72–76]

Bicycle Safety   Bicyclists also benefit from having helmets.[77] Of the 1300 bicyclists killed each year, most die from head injuries. The odds of injury are six times greater for the unhelmeted compared to the helmeted.[78] In addition,

● **Figure 17 Bicycle safety.**

Bicycling is . . .

- *. . . Like driving a car in some respects:* Many of the same traffic laws apply, including those of stop signs and traffic signals. Signal (using hand signals) your intention to change directions. Go in a straight line and don't weave. Slow down on rainy days.
- *. . . But you're much less visible than a car:* Drivers don't see bicycles as readily as they do other cars. Thus, at night you should have a rear red reflector, a light emitting a bright beam forward and to the sides, and reflectors on the frame or wheels, or reflecting tape on your clothes. In the daytime, wear bright clothes.
- *. . . And much more vulnerable than a motorist:* You need to be especially alert to the hazards of the road. Check for cars before you make a turn. Watch for sewer grates, pot holes, gravel, and low-hanging branches. Keep at least one hand on the handlebars. Avoid clothing that might get caught in the chain or spokes (long scarves and coats or baggy trousers or dresses). Wear a helmet.

bicyclists need to be sure they are visible to motorists, using bright-colored clothing, reflectors, and headlights and taillights at night. Ride as though your life depended on it, because it does. Stop at stop signs, signal for turns, and use bike lanes when available. When riding with others proceed single-file rather than side by side. *(See ● Figure 17.)*

Home Safe: Strategy for Living

Common home accidents are from falls, burns and fires, poisonings, electrical shocks, choking, and eye and limb injuries. A good rescue technique to know for choking is the Heimlich maneuver.

People tend to feel safest in their own homes, so it's ironic that is the place where most accidents and injuries occur. Most home accidents involve falls, fires and burns, poisonings, and suffocations. *(See ● Figure 18.)*

Falls Falls are the leading cause of nonfatal injuries in the United States and the second leading cause of death from injury (after motor vehicle accidents).[79] In one survey of 70,000 Americans by Rand Corporation, it was found that almost 2 out of 5 nonfatal injuries were due to slips and falls.[80] Falls on stairs and falls on the floor are the two leading causes of emergency-room visits for injuries.

Falls are a particular affliction of older people. In older bones, falls often produce hip fractures—about 172,000 every year in the United States. Roughly half the survivors never recover normal function.[81,82]

Burns and Fires Fires are the third leading cause of unintentional injury death in the United States (following falls and drownings). Each year, residential fires—in which most injuries from fire occur—are responsible for about 5000 deaths.[83]

Adults, not children, cause most fires. It is adults who leave pans on the stove, overload house wiring, and buy unsafe heaters. Adults also drink, and experts say alcohol plays nearly

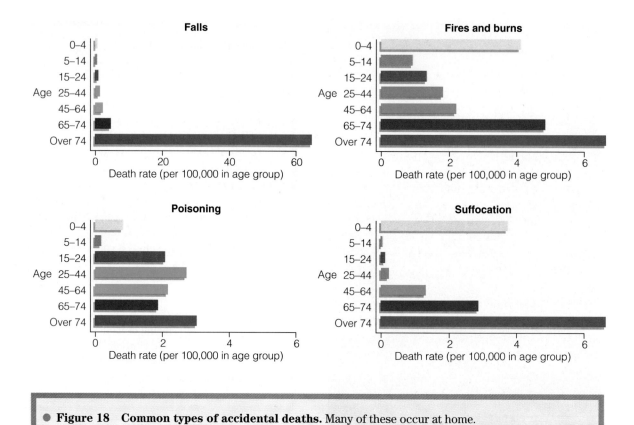

Figure 18   Common types of accidental deaths. Many of these occur at home.

as important a role in fires as it does in auto accidents. Alcohol is involved in 40% of all fatal fires and burns.[84] In addition, adults smoke, and cigarettes cause about 25% of residential fires, usually by setting fire to bedding or upholstery.[85] Smoking is responsible for 29% of deaths in home fires, and cooking causes 22% of injuries.[86]

Perhaps three factors can be significant in preventing fire injuries and fatalities: (1) Installing smoke detectors, and making sure they stay in working order, can make a real difference. (2) Unlike in Japan or the countries of Western Europe, in the United States the attitude is that "fires are not really anyone's fault."[87] A more realistic attitude is to decide that the view that no one is to blame for careless fires is simply incorrect. (3) Safety experts urge people to draw their home's floor plans and mark not just one but *two* escape routes from each room. Then practice the plan.

Poisoning   Unintentional poisonings account for 3300 deaths per year in the United States.[88] The largest affected group is of children under age 5, who think household chemicals and medications are food or candy. The next largest group is people older than age 65, who may take medications without checking the labels. *(See ● Figure 19.)* Reduction in childhood poisoning has been associated with federal legislation requiring child-resistant containers for aspirin, prescription drugs, household chemicals, and similar substances.

The biggest cause of gas poisoning is carbon monoxide, which is colorless and odorless. The way you know you've been affected is first when you feel headache, blurred vision, and shortness of breath, followed by dizziness and vomiting. Make sure wood stoves, furnaces, and gas and kerosene heaters are not leaking. Work on car engines, power mowers, and other gasoline-powered equipment outside rather than in closed garages.

Electrical Shock, Choking, Eye and Limb Injuries There is a whole grab-bag of other injuries that can happen around the house, some of which are particularly worth mentioning:

- *Electrical shocks:* Any electrical equipment that causes a tingling sensation when you touch it can mean bad news—especially if you have wet hands or are standing in water. People tend to shrug off electrical shocks, but the jolt can damage your heart or other organs more than it first seems. Avoid using frayed extension cords. Buy irons that turn themselves off when not in use and space heaters that shut down when tipped over. Above all, don't use electrical appliances when you're wet or touching water.

- *Choking:* Most choking is the result of haste. Food, such as a big piece of meat, that has not been chewed properly can block the windpipe. Often this happens with someone who has been drinking alcohol or using other drugs, but not necessarily. To avoid choking, it's best to eat in a relaxed fashion. Cut your food into small pieces, chew thoroughly, and don't try to talk when swallowing.

  If you see someone choking, or if you are choking yourself, you should *quickly* act to dislodge the food in the windpipe. The procedure used is the **Heimlich maneuver, manually applying sudden upward pressure on the abdomen to force the object from the windpipe.** (See ● *Figure 20.)*

- *Eye and limb injuries:* Power tools and lawn mowers, as well as games such as racquetball and squash, can be hazardous to the unprotected eye. As one emergency-room physician writes, "Virtually all eye injuries can be avoided by remembering three words: goggles, goggles, goggles."[89] If you wear eye glasses, an eye doctor can prescribe prescription goggles.

  When working around power tools, such as lawn mowers, chain saws, and snow blowers, you need to exercise extra care. To avoid accidentally cutting off fingers and toes, wear special gloves and steel-toed boots. Make sure long hair is tied back out of the way. Be certain to shut off the engine before unjamming equipment.

● **Figure 19   Sheer poison.**

To prevent poisoning in children:

- Keep pills, drugs, vitamins, and cosmetics out of children's reach. Buy products in child-resistant packaging or containers.
- Store cleaning supplies, rat and ant poisons, mothballs, and aerosol cans in a locked place. Never store them under the sink.
- Be sure hazardous materials in the garage or intended for outdoor use— paint, gasoline, lighter fluid, antifreeze, certain toxic plants—are secure.
- Don't leave a child alone with a toxic product even for a minute; take it with you to answer the phone or doorbell.

To prevent poisoning in older adults:

- If you are over 65, read the label before taking a pill. (Don't take it at night with the light off or without glasses.)
- Post a sheet and regularly check it off every time you take medication so you'll never be uncertain whether you took a pill or not.
- Check the expiration date and get rid of (in the toilet) those that are outdated.

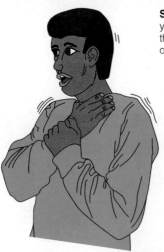

Step 1: Establish if the person is choking: Ask, "Are you choking?" or "Can you speak?" If the person nods and cannot speak, something is obstructing the windpipe. If the person can make some sounds, it may be better to let him or her clear the airway by coughing.

Step 2: Perform the Heimlich maneuver: If the person cannot speak, perform the following:
• Stand behind the person.
• Make a fist and put it slightly above the navel (higher on the chest in an obese or pregnant person). The thumb should be toward the choking person. Grasp the fist with your other hand (drawing).

• Thrust **forcefully and quickly** inward and upward against the person's abdomen to dislodge the obstruction. Repeat if necessary.

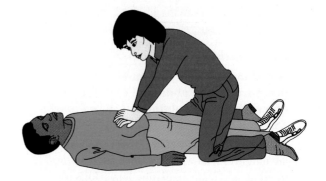

• If the person is unconscious, roll him or her on his back, straddle the person, place one hand above the navel with the second on top, and thrust both hands quickly upward into the abdomen.

● **Figure 20   The Heimlich maneuver.**

"*If you're choking, you don't have to rely on someone else to come to your rescue. Stand up and make a fist with one hand and place the thumb side on the abdomen just above your navel. Now grab your fist and press inward and upward with a quick, sharp thrust. If that doesn't dislodge the stuck food, try again, this time throwing your weight forward over the back of a chair, so your fist is driven up hard into your abdomen.*"

—Emergency-room physician Arnold G. Robinson, M. D. (1991, April). Painful mistakes. *Men's Health*, p. 33.

Survival in the Outdoors

Accidents in the outdoors result from lack of preparation for changes in weather, drowning, and animal bites.

You can get into trouble in the outdoors almost as much as you can indoors. Elsewhere in this book we described the difficulties of not adjusting your clothing and physical activity for weather. If you don't, in hot weather you risk heat exhaustion and heat stroke, and in cold weather frostnip, frostbite, and hypothermia. Even when weather is not a problem, however, there are at least two other hazards that require attention—drowning and animal bites.

Drowning About 7700 Americans die each year by drowning, including about 1200 in boating accidents.[90,91] The people at greatest risk are small children ages 1–3. Small children most often drown in backyard swimming pools because adults are unaware they have wandered near the water. These accidents are preventable with fences and latchgates.

The group at next greatest risk is males ages 15–24. *(See ● Figure 21.)* Adolescents and adults most often drown in lakes, rivers, and ponds while swimming, wading, diving, boating, rafting, and fishing. In other words, drownings most often happen in places that are not organized facilities with lifeguards.[92] Often the drownings occur when people (even strong swimmers) are exhausted or are swept into deep water.

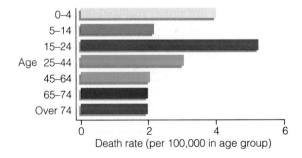

● **Figure 21   Drowning.**

It's important to know that alcohol and other drugs figure prominently in drowning and boating mishaps. About half of drowning victims are found to have a high blood alcohol level, and about 10% show evidence of having taken other drugs.[93]

First aid for drowning victims consists of administering CPR for as long as possible. Some people have recovered who have been submerged for more than an hour in cold water.

Animal Bites So you think meter readers, mail carriers, and dogcatchers are most apt to be bitten by animals? Actually, people in such lines of work are usually cautious and therefore rarely bitten. More likely victims are children. The great majority of the 2 million bite wounds reported annually in the United States, 80–85%, are inflicted by domestic dogs. Cats account for about 10%. About 20 Americans die every year from dog attacks, half of them by pit bull terriers.[94] Treatment must first be for traumatic damage and then for bacterial infection. A health professional should always examine the wound. As a preventative, make sure that tetanus and hepatitis B immunizations are up to date and pets have rabies vaccines.

Caution: Work May Be Hazardous to Your Health

Overexertion, being struck, and falls produce the most common work-related disabling injuries. Other injuries are caused by breathing tobacco smoke and exposure to industrial chemicals. Computer-related jobs may lead to serious repetitive strain injury (RSI), as well as eye strain, headache, and back and neck pains.

Work, says one writer, "kills more people each year than die from AIDS, drugs, or drunken driving and all other motor vehicle accidents."[95] The Occupational Safety and Health Act of 1970, legislation designed to enhance worker safety, was passed in 1970. Figures kept since then show that some 200,000 workers have been killed on the job in the United States. Two million more have died from diseases caused by the conditions in which they worked. Another 1.4

million have been disabled in workplace accidents.[96]

Restaurants and bars account for the largest number of occupational injuries. But meat packing and motor-vehicle manufacturing are by far the most dangerous industries.[97] The most disabling work injuries are overexertion, followed by being struck by or against an object and falls.[98] However, some other kinds of workplace hazards deserve mention—chemicals and computers.

The Hazards of Smoke and Other Ordinary Chemicals Waiters and waitresses, although they might not smoke themselves, have as much as five times more exposure to cigarette smoke than people in other workplaces and have a significantly higher risk of lung cancer—perhaps 50–90% more, according to one study.[99] Indeed the study found that waitresses die of lung cancer nearly four times more often than other women. Twice as many die of heart disease.

Tobacco smoke is not the only harmful chemical found in the workplace. Toxic solvents, dyes, lead dusts, plastics, metals, or other chemicals are part of the work environments of artists, art teachers, chemistry and biology teachers, operating room personnel, laboratory workers, machine operators, electrical or circuit board workers, launderers, dry cleaners, book binders, furniture refinishers, cosmetologists, health aides, telephone operators, automobile mechanics, and many other workers. If you are in such a job, you should follow safety guidelines and use protective clothing and equipment. Women who are pregnant should try to ask for a temporary job transfer.[100]

The Hazards of Computers For some people—clerical workers, word processors, postal clerks, journalists—the computer has turned out to be quite uncomfortable. For some it is even a job-killer. The reasons are repetitive strain injury, eyestrain and headache, and back and neck pains.[101]

- **Avoiding repetitive strain injury: Repetitive strain injury (RSI) is the name for a number of wrist, hand, arm, and neck pains resulting from fast, repetitive work. RSI is also called *repetitive motion injury* and *cumula-**

tive trauma disorders. RSI victims were once mainly slaughterhouse, textile, automobile workers, and musicians (because of long hours of practice). But the increase in computer users during the last decade has made RSI the fastest-growing work injury in recent years.[102–107]

One kind of RSI, called **carpal tunnel syndrome (CTS), consists of damage and pain to nerves and tendons in the hands.** It is virulent among heavy computer users, some of whom may make as many as 23,000 keystrokes a day. *(See ● Figure 22.)* Some CTS sufferers cannot type or even open a door. One result has been more interest in a field known as **ergonomics, defined as the study of human factors related to computers.** Ergonomics is concerned with fitting the job to the worker rather than the reverse.

- **Avoiding eyestrain and headache:** Human eyes were made to see most efficiently at a distance. However, computer screens require that you use your eyes at reasonably close range for a long time. This can lead to eyestrain, headache, and double vision.

  To avoid these difficulties, you should take a 15-minute break every hour or so. Position the screen so it's not in direct sunlight or reflected glare from lights. Keep the brightness of the screen and the surrounding area about the same, so your eyes won't have to keep adjusting. Consider installing an anti-glare filter.

- **Avoiding back and neck pains:** Many people work at computers in work situations that produce back and neck pain. Often the computers are simply installed on desks intended for typewriters, but the two kinds of equipment are not alike. To avoid problems, you should have a chair that is adjustable for height and back. The height of the keyboard, the computer screen, and the document holder should also all be adjustable.

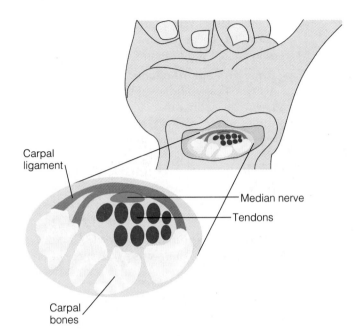

Carpal Tunnel Syndrome

The carpal ligament creates a tunnel across the bones of the wrist. When tendons passing through the carpal tunnel become swollen, they press against the median nerve, which runs to the thumb and first three fingers.

Carpal ligament

Median nerve

Tendons

Carpal bones

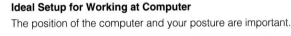

Ideal Setup for Working at Computer

The position of the computer and your posture are important.

Screen: At eye level or slightly lower. Your head should be about an arm's length from the screen. Avoid having light throw glare on the screen.

Keyboard: At or below elbow level. Elbows should be at about right angle. Hands and wrists should be straight and relaxed. Fingers should be gently curved. A wrist rest helps.

Chair: Chair should keep back upright or inclined slightly forward from the hips. Knees should be slightly lower than hips. Backrest should maintain the slight natural curve of the lower back.

Footrest: Feet should be planted firmly on floor; otherwise, use a footrest.

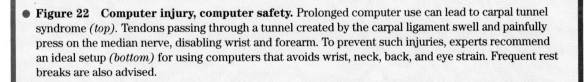

● **Figure 22   Computer injury, computer safety.** Prolonged computer use can lead to carpal tunnel syndrome *(top)*. Tendons passing through a tunnel created by the carpal ligament swell and painfully press on the median nerve, disabling wrist and forearm. To prevent such injuries, experts recommend an ideal setup *(bottom)* for using computers that avoids wrist, neck, back, and eye strain. Frequent rest breaks are also advised.

The Culture of Violence: From Murder to Sexual Harrassment

Murder is the 11th leading cause of death in the United States and is highest among young males. Next to traffic accidents, gunfire is the most common cause of death for young Americans. Avoiding assault and other violence means taking precautions. Consider when and where to walk and drive, protect your residence, and know what to do if attacked.

A critical part of the art of living is learning how to avoid violence in your life. We will discuss the issue of violence along a continuum, ranging from loss of life to sexual harrassment.

Murder Homicide is the 11th leading cause of death in the United States.[108] In 1991, murders in the United States were more than *twice* the *combined* figures for Canada, France, Germany, Britain, and Japan for 1988. (1988 was the latest year figures for those countries were available.) Canada's reputation as a safe country has been tarnished by a rapidly rising murder rate (762 cases in 1991, up 14% from the previous year). Still, that is a very long way from the 24,000 homicides in the United States that year, especially among young males.[109] *(See ● Figure 23.)* Among young African Americans ages 15–24, the homicide rate was more than 7 times that for white American males of similar age. (It was 87 per 100,000 people versus 11 per 100,000.)[110] The majority of murders were perpetrated by members of the same race: 90% of black male victims were murdered by blacks, and 87% of white males were murdered by whites. Moreover, in the majority of cases victims were murdered by someone who was known to them.[111]

The chances of being murdered or otherwise a victim of violence vary according to who and where you are:

- **Gender and age:** Three quarters of all homicide victims are males, perhaps because of gender differences in weapon-carrying behavior and social expectations for males and females.[112,113] Violent behavior is committed disproportionately by young males in their late teens through early 30s. Those are also the very people who are apt to be victims of violent acts.

- **Race and social class:** "Although there is an overrepresentation of blacks (44% of all homicide victims are black) and other non-whites in U.S. violence statistics," points out one group of scholars, "it is increasingly clear that socioeconomic status is a greater predictor of violence than racial status."[114] Both perpetrators and victims of violence are apt to be in the lowest levels of socio-economic status.[115]

- **Urban and suburban areas:** Between 1980 and 1988, there was a 50% increase in mortality of children and adolescents living in cities as opposed to suburbs. Firearm-related homicides accounted for the majority of homicide deaths.[116]

- **Friends and murderers:** Most murders occur between people who have some sort of prior relationship with each other. In only 15% of murders are assailant and victim strangers to each other.[117]

- **Arguments, alcohol, and weapons:** Half of homicides are precipitated by an argument. Alcohol and other drugs seem to lead to violence by stimulating aggression and reducing inhibitions and impairing judgment. Indeed, nearly half of all convicted criminals, whatever the crime, were intoxicated at the time of their offense.[118] Having immediate access to a weapon or carrying a weapon also increases the possibility for violence.[119]

- **Homicide on the job:** Murder is the No. 3 cause of death on the job and is the leading cause of death of women at work.[120]

Guns and Harm There are about 200 million guns in the hands of American civilians. Four million more guns, including 2 million handguns, are being added each year.[121] Next to traffic accidents, gunfire is the most common cause of death for Americans ages 15–19.[122]

Every day, 10 Americans who are 19 years of age or under are killed by guns, in homicides, suicides, or accidents. Only 5% of all firearms fatalities are unintentional.[123] The largest number of deaths from guns happen from nonaccidents.

Thus, there are two concerns—the safe handling of guns to prevent accidents, and their safe handling to prevent deliberate use.

- *Firearms safety:* Most inadvertent firearm injuries occur in or around the house. Too often the victims are children. To prevent such accidents, the Center to Prevent Handgun Violence recommends that guns should be stored in a locked container. Guns should be unloaded and uncocked, and stored separately from their ammunition.

  A revolver may be child-proofed with a special padlock that goes around the cylinder and behind the trigger. A semiautomatic pistol may be child-proofed by locking the trigger with a special lock or by disconnecting the slide encasing the barrel. Or at the least the magazine or clip of bullets should be pulled out from the handle.[124]

- *The question of gun control:* The Justice Department estimates that over one-half million Americans are confronted each year by criminals carrying pistols, including 9200 people who are killed.[125] Should this trend be allowed to continue?

  In the United States, national debate over crime control, declared one writer, "a gun, depending on one's view, is either an agent of evil that ought to be banned or restricted, or a constitutionally enshrined defense against evil."[126] Even a small decrease in firearms deaths would mean some progress, however. In 1989, there were 35,000 firearms-connected deaths, including 15,000 homicides, 18,000 suicides, 1500 accidents, and other unspecified deaths.

  There is a dilemma: With so many guns in circulation, should new laws try to do a better job of keeping firearms away from criminals? Or should they also restrict legal gun ownership in order to reduce the number of guns in public hands?[127] By contrast, consider Canada's 1991 gun-control law. It banned the import of military assault weapons and made it harder to obtain gun permits. It also raised the minimum age for gun ownership from 16 to 18.[128] Few of these controls exist in the United States.

Dealing with Crime and Violence: Strategy for Living Just as crime has risen in American

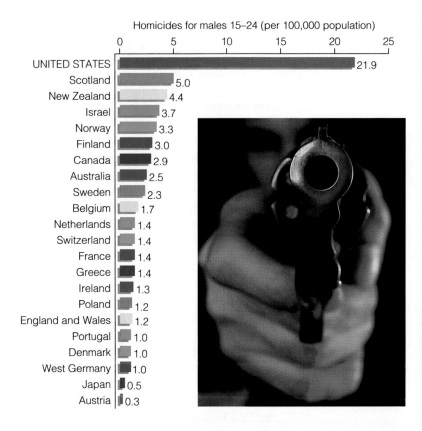

Homicides for males 15–24 (per 100,000 population)

UNITED STATES	21.9
Scotland	5.0
New Zealand	4.4
Israel	3.7
Norway	3.3
Finland	3.0
Canada	2.9
Australia	2.5
Sweden	2.3
Belgium	1.7
Netherlands	1.4
Switzerland	1.4
France	1.4
Greece	1.4
Ireland	1.3
Poland	1.2
England and Wales	1.2
Portugal	1.0
Denmark	1.0
West Germany	1.0
Japan	0.5
Austria	0.3

● **Figure 23   World murder rates, males 15–24.** The homicide rates for males ages 15–24 in 1986 or 1987 was 4 times higher in the United States than in Scotland, the next highest country.

society at large, so it has also come to the college campus. Safety is a major issue on many campuses. At your college, you may see posters, brochures, and newspaper articles that address dormitory security, date rape, and nighttime escorts to parked cars. The federal Campus Security Act requires that students and prospective students and their parents receive campus crime statistics for the previous 3 years. They must also receive a description of security procedures.[129]

Whether you are on campus or off, there are a number of precautions you can take to decrease your risks of becoming a victim of crime:

- *When walking or out in public:* At night or early morning, don't walk alone or jog alone. Stay with groups. Take advantage of campus escort services. Stick to well-populated, well-lighted areas.

Don't show money or valuables in public. Discreetly tuck away your cash after using an automatic teller machine.

When on foot, walk rapidly and look as though you're going somewhere. If someone makes signs of wanting to talk to you, just keep on going. It's less important that you be polite than that you be safe.

- *When in a car:* When in a car, make sure all doors are locked. Don't open them for anyone you don't know. Keep windows rolled up so someone can't reach in and snatch your purse, wallet, or keys. Remain alert when stopped at intersections, day or night. If you stop for gas or to use a pay phone, choose well-lighted, busy facilities. Park in well-lighted areas, and get an escort to your car whenever possible.

  If your car is bumped from behind and you don't feel comfortable getting out, signal to the other person to follow you. Then drive to the nearest police station, service station, hospital, or fire station.[130,131]

  If you are the victim of a *carjacking*—**someone approaches with a weapon, demanding your car or money**—turn it over to them.

- *When in your residence or campus buildings:* Lock your dorm-room or residence doors, even when you go to the shower. Theft is a big problem in some residence halls. Don't let strangers into your residence hall. Ask any stranger whom he or she wants to see. Don't leave backpacks, purses, or briefcases unattended, even in your residence lounge.

- *If you sense you might be attacked:* If you are facing an armed criminal, the risk of injury may be minimized by cooperating with his or her demands. Avoid any sudden movements and give the criminal what he or she wants.

  If you sense your life is in immediate danger, *use any defense you can think of: screaming, kicking, running.* Your objective is to get away. In a violent crime, it is generally ineffective for the victim to cry or plead with the attacker. Such actions tend to reinforce the attacker's feeling of power over the victim.[132]

Intimate Violence: Abusive Relationships, Child Abuse, and Incest

Both men and women are involved in abusive relationships. It's important to understand why people abuse others and why people stay in abusive relationships. Many children are also physically, mentally, and sexually abused, by their parents and others. Incest can be a difficult matter to detect and to deal with.

"American women have far more to fear from the men they know and once loved than from any stranger on the street," writes health reporter Jane Brody. "Domestic violence is the leading cause of injury and death to American women, causing more harm than vehicular accidents, rapes, and muggings combined."[133]

Abusive Relationships and Domestic Violence Domestic violence is found in all types of families, among all races, religions, economic groups, and educational levels.[134] Some men are abused by women, siblings are abused by siblings, and some gays and lesbians by their partners. But most abuse is experienced by women in what has been called "domestic captivity."[135] Sometimes the effects have been compared to the terror men feel in war, inflicting posttraumatic stress disorder.[136] Perhaps 6 million women—wives and girlfriends—every year are beaten by the men they live with. An estimated 30% of murdered women are killed by men with whom they have a "family" relationship.[137] Perhaps 30–40% of teenage girls, including women in college, have been hit in the course of dating.[138] *(See Self Discovery 3.)*

Some critical questions need to be answered: What kind of men are abusers, and why? Why do women stay in abusive relationships?

- *Men who are abusers and why:* Michigan psychologist Donald Saunders finds there are three types of men who abuse their partners:[139]

  (1) Men who are violent only in the home, who overcontrol their hostility. They act like doormats until they drink too much

and then erupt. Half the time their violence is linked to alcohol.

(2) Men who are violent inside and outside the home, whose violence is severe and tied to alcohol. They have rigid attitudes about sex roles and often have arrest records.

(3) Less violent men who are psychologically abusive, who have rigid attitudes about sex roles and fear losing their partners.

Why do men do it? The speculation is that many abusive men were abused themselves as children or observed their fathers physically or verbally abusing their mothers.[140] Perhaps also men in general have been socialized by cultural stereotypes about masculinity—reinforced by violence in the media and toy manufacturing. They learn the varied arts of violence and destructiveness.[141] Finally, if men are domineering and aggressive it may be because of raging hormones—specifically, the male sex hormone testosterone.[142]

- ***Why women stay in abusive relationships:*** If you had been assaulted, even seriously injured, why would you stay in the relationship? Often women first try to accommodate their abusers. Some may even believe their batterer's rationalization that the beating "is for your own good."[143] Indeed, some researchers think the behavior of battered women falls in the category of the so-called ***Stockholm syndrome. This condition was named for a 1973 bank holdup in Sweden. The victims held hostage came to "bond" themselves to their captors out of fear that it was the only way to survive.***[144]

Economics presents one major reason why women stay with those who batter them. Many do not have enough money to live by themselves (particularly if they have children requiring day-care). Many also have trouble finding places to live. There are not enough shelters for battered women and the majority of shelters do not accept children.[145]

Perhaps fear is the biggest part. Women who leave are afraid their spouses will gain custody of their children. They are also

afraid the law will not protect their safety and that their abusers will track them down. Indeed, there is some basis for this belief. Justice Department statistics show that 75% of assaults against lovers or wives occur *after* separation.[146]

Child Abuse In 1991, an estimated 2.7 million youngsters were physically, mentally, and sexually assaulted by their parents, according to the National Center for Child Abuse and Neglect.[147] According to the center, parents who are more likely to maltreat their children are emotionally

---

SELF DISCOVERY 3

Are You Abused?

Answer the following yes or no:

Does your partner . . .   **Yes   No**

1. Constantly criticize you and your abilities? ___ ___
2. Become overprotective or extremely jealous? ___ ___
3. Threaten to hurt you, children, pets, family, or friends? ___ ___
4. Prevent you from seeing family or friends? ___ ___
5. Have sudden bursts of anger? ___ ___
6. Destroy personal property? ___ ___
7. Deny you access to family assets or control all finances and force you to account for what you spend? ___ ___
8. Use intimidation or manipulation to control you or your children? ___ ___
9. Hit, punch, slap, kick, shove, or hit you? ___ ___
10. Prevent you from going where you want when you want? ___ ___
11. Force you to have sex when you don't want to? ___ ___
12. Humiliate or embarrass you in front of others? ___ ___

Interpretation

If you answer yes to *any* of these questions, you may be in an abusive relationship.

Source: Victim Services, New York City. (212-577-7777). Questionnaire appeared in: Brody, J. E. (1992, March 18). Each year, six million American women become victims of abuse without ever leaving home. *New York Times*, p. B6.

immature or needy. They may be isolated, with no family or friends to depend on. As children, abusive parents have often experienced abuse, deprivation, and neglect. As a result, they feel worthless and feel they have never been cared about. In addition, such parents are frequently alcohol or drug abusers.[148] Child abuse is more likely to occur in lower-income families (under $15,000 a year) than higher-income families. However, abuse is found at all economic and educational levels.

Child sexual abuse is a crime—and a social taboo—that all involved, adult and child, frequently want to keep hidden. Yet the phenomenon may be widespread: perhaps as many as 500,000 children are sexually assaulted in the United States each year.[149] In one study in Los Angeles, 15% of 6th–12th graders, both boys and girls, reported having had at least one unwanted sexual experience. In a number of cases, the incident occurred with an adult authority figure, usually male family members and friends.[150] The sexual assault may include sexual contact, but it may also mean coercion to watch or perform sexual acts.

The most common form of child sexual abuse is incest. *Incest* **is defined as sexual contact between a child or adolescent and a person who is closely related or perceived to be related to the child.**[151] The abusive person may be a parent, stepparent, sibling, uncle, or cousin. If the child is repeatedly abused by trusted nonfamily members, such as neighbors or childcare workers, the emotional impact may be like incest. The abuse may range from fondling of genitals or breasts to vaginal, oral, or anal sex. Incest often involves some form of coercion and psychological manipulation.[152]

Unwanted Sex: From Sexual Harrassment to Rape

Members of either sex may be victims of forced or unwanted sexual attention or actions. Unwanted sex ranges from sexual harrassment to sexual assault, including statutory, acquaintance, and date rape. It's important to learn techniques for preventing, resisting, or coping with acquaintance or stranger rape.

A grave problem for both sexes, but particularly for women, is that of dealing with unwanted sexual attention or demands. This may range from listening to sexual remarks to rape.

Sexual Harassment *Sexual harassment* **is unwelcome sexual attention, physical or verbal, that creates an intimidating, hostile, or offensive work or learning environment.** Such harassment may include sexual remarks, suggestive looks, pressure for dates, letters and calls, deliberate touching, or pressure for sexual favors. Legally, the U.S. Supreme Court has ruled that sexual harassment is a form of employment discrimination just as serious and as illegal as racial or religious discrimination.[153]

So what do you do if you are confronted with sexual harassment by someone who has power over your college or work career? Proving harassment in court is difficult, and other institutional arrangements are predisposed to protect the harasser.[154,155] Thus, one needs to proceed deliberately. First keep a log, recording dates, times, nature of incidents, and any witnesses. According to one survey, just asking or telling the person to stop worked for 61% of the women. Telling coworkers, or threatening to, worked 55% of the time. Pretending to ignore the offensive behavior usually didn't work at all.[156] If the harassment persists, stronger measures may be required. (See ● *Figure 24.*)

Rape: Date Rape and Other Sexual Assaults Sex may be pleasurable, but forced sex is in the same category as any other attack. Assault is assault, whether it is with a gun, a club, a fist—or a penis. *Rape* **is defined as sexual penetration of a male or female by intimidation, fraud, or force.** Most rape victims are women, but one study of 3000 randomly chosen Los Angeles residents found that one third of victims of attempted sexual assault were men.[157] In a 1988 survey done of Stanford University Students, 1 in 3 women and 1 in 8 men reported having unwanted sexual activity.[158]

Rape victims can be of all ages. But the shocking fact is that 61% of rape victims were younger than 18 when attacked, according to the National Victim Center.[159] In almost 80% of cases, the victim knew the rapist. (See ● *Figure 25.*)

Three kinds of rape are particularly worth mentioning:

- ***Statutory rape: Statutory rape* is unlawful sexual intercourse between a male over age 16 and a female under age 12 or 21,** depending on the state. As the National Victim Center report showed, 3 out of 10 rape victims had not reached their 11th birthdays.

- ***Acquaintance rape: Acquaintance rape* is rape by a person known by the victim, whether related or unrelated.** The National Victim Center report found that 78% of rapists were known to their victims.

- ***Date rape: Date rape* is a particular kind of acquaintance rape in which the rapist is someone with whom the victim has had a date,** as on a college campus. Once nonconsensual sex on dates might have been thought to be a form of female error or lack of resistance. But today sexual activity that is abhorrent to females is considered assault.[160]

Strategy for Living: Avoiding and Coping with Rape Men and women interpret sexual cues differently. For instance, in one study, men and women were asked whether certain behaviors indicated a willingness to have sex. The behaviors included going back to a date's room, kissing, French kissing, and taking off one's shirt. Men interpreted all these behaviors as more indicative of consent than women did.[161] These are the kinds of misunderstandings, resulting from misinterpretations of nonverbal cues, that can hurt someone.

To cope with rape, here are some suggestions:

- ***To avoid acquaintance or date rape:*** Be aware of your surroundings and intentions. Stay out of ambiguous situations (such as bedrooms) and be clear in communicating what you want and don't want. Learn to listen carefully to your partner's messages about what he or she wants and doesn't want. Use a neutral tone and speak in "I" statements: "I want to be taken home." *Trust your instincts.* If you're uncomfortable with a situation, follow your intuition. Don't be afraid of hurting somebody's feelings.

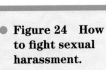 **Figure 24 How to fight sexual harassment.**

If sexual harassment persists, here are some steps to take:

- *Document:* Keep a detailed written record of the incidents, with dates, times, places, names, and quotes. Keep any notes you receive.

- *Confide in co-workers or friends:* You may tell trusted co-workers, friends, family members, a minister, or others, saying you may have to file a grievance and that you want them to know what is happening.

- *Find witnesses or supporting evidence:* If there are witnesses, ask them to write a statement for you. If you are receiving harassing phone calls, have someone be an "ear witness" by listening in and taking notes. Look for other people in your same situation who may have been harassed by the same person.

- *Confront the harasser:* Say the behavior must stop immediately, and let him or her know you will file a complaint if it does not. If necessary, write a letter—or follow up your conversation with a memo summarizing your talk—and hand it to the harasser in the presence of a witness. Keep a copy.

- *Talk to the harasser's supervisor:* Talk to an appropriate third party such as the harasser's supervisor or someone in the human resources department or equal opportunity officer.

- *File a complaint:* If your company or institution does not take steps to stop the harassment, file a legal complaint based on state or federal antidiscrimination laws. Your state may have a department of fair employment or you may take your case to the U.S. Equal Employment Opportunity Commission (call 800-USA-EEOC).

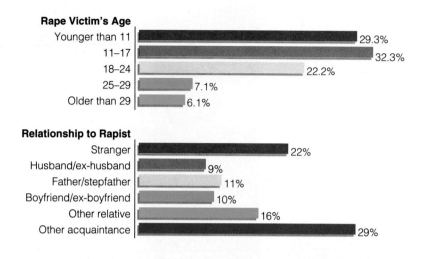

Rape Victim's Age

Age	
Younger than 11	29.3%
11–17	32.3%
18–24	22.2%
25–29	7.1%
Older than 29	6.1%

Relationship to Rapist

Stranger	22%
Husband/ex-husband	9%
Father/stepfather	11%
Boyfriend/ex-boyfriend	10%
Other relative	16%
Other acquaintance	29%

● **Figure 25   Age of rape victim and relationship to rapist.**

- ***To avoid stranger rape:*** When on the street, be aware of your surroundings, anticipate how you would respond to an attack. Look behind you, stay in the middle of the sidewalk, and walk with a confident stride. Use extra caution in parking garages. If you're alone on an elevator, get out if a stranger gets on and pushes the button for the basement. Have your keys in hand when you approach your car so you won't have to stand there fumbling.

- ***To resist rape of any kind:*** Don't be too polite to fight. Be loud, be rude, cause a scene. Attackers count on the fear of embarrassment. Research shows that women who fight back, especially against acquaintances, have a better chance of escaping than those who plead or cry.[162]

- ***To cope with rape:*** Call the police and a rape crisis center or rape treatment center. Don't bathe or wash yourself or your clothes or touch anything in the location of the rape. If a condom was used, try to remember where it was discarded. Try to remember everything about the rapist, his car, clothing, scars, haircut, and things he said and did. Report any weapons or restraints used, and if bruises show up later, have photographs taken by the police. Go to a hospi-

tal and be tested and/or treated for sexually transmitted diseases.

Afterward, expect emotional aftershocks, even if you weren't hurt physically. Tell your physician and try to institute a health strategy that includes psychological as well as physical factors. Confide your feelings in a friend.[163] Many women tend to blame themselves when attacked, especially by men they trust. Only later—perhaps years later—do they decide that they have been sexually assaulted.[164]

800-HELP

Suggestions for
Further Readings

Malin Dollinger, Ernest H. Rosenbaum, & Greg Cable (1991). *Everyone's guide to cancer therapy: How cancer is diagnosed, treated, and managed day to day.* Kansas City, MO: Andrews and McMeel (Somerville House). Explanations of types of cancers and options for therapy.

Patricia Evans (1992). *The verbally abusive relationship: How to recognize it and how to respond.* Holbrook, MA: Bob Adams. A valuable book in the literature of domestic violence.

Ann Jones & Susan Schechter (1992). *When love goes wrong: What to do when you can't do anything right.* New York: HarperCollins. Strategies for women with controlling partners.

Paul Kivel (1992). *Men's work: How to stop the violence that tears our lives apart.* New York: Ballantine. One of the founding members of the Oakland Men's Project in California shares an approach to stopping male violence.

Lee Nisbet (Ed.) (1990). *The gun control debate: You decide.* Buffalo, NY: Prometheus. Essays of pros and cons on public access versus prohibition of handguns in the U.S. by historians, criminologists, jurists, and public health officials.

Dean Ornish (1990). *Dr. Dean Ornish's program for reversing heart disease: The only system scientifically proven to reverse heart disease without drugs or surgery.* New York: Ballantine. Presents evidence of the reversal of heart disease without drugs or surgery. The program explores the psychological, emotional, and spiritual as well as physical sides of recovery.

Jane Schoenberg & JoAnn Stichman (1990). *Heart family handbook.* Philadelphia: Hanley & Belfus. Geared mainly to heart disease patients and their families.

Barry L. Zaret, Marvin Moser, Lawrence S. Cohen, & Genell J. Subak-Sharpe (Eds.) (1992). *Yale University School of Medicine heart book.* New York: Hearst Books. Comprehensive, practical lay reference guide from one of the country's finest medical schools.

Men Making the Most of Their Lives

I live for today because nobody has promised me tomorrow," says 24-year-old Sean Murray of Ardmore, Pennsylvania. Words of wisdom for anyone, Murray is especially able to appreciate them: at age 7 he was diagnosed with leukemia.[165] Murray is a survivor, one of those able to carry away a positive message from one of life's nightmares. Here are others.

The Teacher

Junior high school history teacher Hugh McCabe of Gaithersburg, Maryland, succumbed at age 47 to lung cancer—but not before putting the remainder of his life on a documentary film to capture his physical decline. His message: to force children to listen to his plea—Don't smoke. McCabe had smoked since age 13.

Scare tactics normally don't work, because kids think they're immortal, explained a spokesperson for the American Lung Association, which sponsored the film. "We thought that by showing a particular man, that could have a little more impact."

McCabe continued to carry a full teaching load during his final semester. By doing so he hoped to set an example in both a positive and negative way. "Positive—to keep striving for your goal," he said. "Don't let death or some of these things be deterrents. And negative—to show that you should not be smoking."[166]

The Employer of Gang Members

Jamaican-born Baxter Sinclair, who had come to the U.S. and become owner of a pipeline construction business, worried that gangs would steal equipment off his job in a South Los Angeles housing project. He had an idea: he hired 10 gang members to provide security, and as a result didn't even lose a shovel.

Then he began hiring other gang members, extending opportunities to young men with criminal records who couldn't find work. Sinclair plays a tough guy who does not tolerate tardiness, sloppiness, or drug use. "The streets are full of kids who, if somebody gave them a chance to do something, could turn around," he said.[167]

The Cholesterol Warrior

MCDONALD'S, YOUR HAMBURGERS STILL HAVE TOO MUCH FAT! said the newspaper ad, which ran in 1990, AND YOUR FRENCH FRIES STILL ARE COOKED WITH BEEF TALLOW. The relatively unknown industrialist who sponsored it, Phil Sokoloff, 67, a "little guy out here in Omaha," as he called himself, probably had an impact. Today most fast-food restaurants, including McDonald's, use vegetable oils instead of beef fat, which can raise cholesterol levels, a heart disease risk factor.

A slender nonsmoker who exercised regularly, Sokoloff suffered a heart attack at age 43 and discovered his cholesterol was dangerously high. In 1985 he began to finance ads against food companies using saturated fats. Sokoloff said he planned to keep on trying to improve the American diet. "How can I stop," he said, "as long as there are people out there I can help?"[168,169]

The Cameraman

Diagnosed at age 17 with the form of cancer known as Hodgkin's lymphoma, Randy Kerry, 30, of Texarkana, Arkansas, during treatment "got a 35mm camera and started taking pictures." Later he parlayed his interest into a job as a television news cameraman.

Kerry also found that the experience with cancer made him better able to face everyday problems. "I realize life is valuable now," he said. "If I see a car with three flat tires, I'll look at the one that's still up."[170]

CHAPTER

11 Environmental Health

"We should all be concerned about the future because we will have to spend the rest of our lives there."

Is there a better reason than this, stated by scientist Charles F. Kettering, why we should care about the environment? The world around us presents us with two environmental challenges to our health—personal and global.

- ***Personal environmental challenges to your health:*** How do you defend yourself against such personal irritants as high-decibel noise, indoor chemicals that make your eyes water, or strange-tasting water? Fortunately, there *are* things you can do to control these threats, and the first half of this chapter shows you how.

- ***Global environmental challenges to your health:*** Billions of people crowd the planet, poverty and famine are widespread, toxic and nuclear wastes are handled carelessly. Add to these acid rain, global warming, holes in the ozone, war. All these threats may look very much like a case of the environment controlling you. Fortunately, there are things you—in concerted action with others—can do to minimize these threats, too.

Personal Environmental Challenges

▶ Discuss the primary environmental challenges to health.

▶ Explain the effects of noise and how the decibel scale works.

▶ Describe the controversy about possible hazards from electromagnetic fields.

▶ Discuss ionizing radiation and radioactivity.

▶ Explain the factors behind sick building syndrome and environmental illness.

▶ Explain the effects of air pollution on health.

▶ Discuss the problems of solid waste disposal, especially of toxic and nuclear wastes.

Concerns about environmental health may begin with large concepts. An orange sun sinking through a brown haze at sunset, supertanker oil spills, or old tires in vacant lots arouse concern. However, environmental health concerns are also apt to begin as extremely personal matters. Consider, for instance, the impact of noise.

Noise Pollution

The intensity of sound is measured in decibels, where each 10-point increase on the decibel scale is 10 times as loud. Exposure to excessive noise produces hearing loss and stress. Premature hearing loss is being found more among young Americans, often because of amplified music.

Mike Negron, 20, who lives near Fordham University in the Bronx, New York, didn't get it. So what if his car stereo had four 300-watt Super-Pro speakers, a 280-watt Sherwood amplifier, and a pair of powerful tweeters. "I don't play it loud," he said. Nevertheless, Bronx police seized Negron's car for noise violation. They measured sound coming from it exceeding the legal threshold of 80 decibels measured at 50 feet.[1] **A decibel is a unit for measuring the intensity of sound.** (See ● Figure 1.)

How much is 80 decibels? Actually, it's only as loud as a ringing alarm clock 2 feet away, or a vacuum cleaner, or a car alarm, or a minibike. Yet it's the beginning of the danger zone for loss of hearing. Truly loud music, as heard in the front row at a rock concert, might be 120 decibels (like a jackhammer at 3 feet). A blaring stereo might be 130 decibels (equal to a jet engine at 100 feet). Nevertheless, if Negron's "boombox car" registered 80 decibels at 50 feet away, imagine what it was like inside the car. Amplified car stereos can hit 140 decibels at full volume—like the sound of a jet taking off.

What's important to note is that, on the decibel scale, 20 is not twice as loud as 10 but rather *10 times as loud.* That is, each 10-decibel increase represents a tenfold increase in the intensity of sound. Thus, *50 decibels is 1000 times louder than 20 decibels.*

The Effects of Noise One in three Americans over 65 has a hearing loss great enough to make communication difficult. Now hearing loss is being found among people much younger. One study examined first-year students at the University of Tennessee at Knoxville. Six of ten students were found to have hearing loss of the kind formerly found mainly among elderly people.[2] In a survey in Fountain Valley, California, researchers testing hearing found failure rates of 13% among high school seniors. That was a significant increase from 10 years earlier.[3] Once destroyed, the sensory cells in the ear can never be restored. To see if you might have a problem with your hearing, try the accompanying Self Discovery. (See Self Discovery 1.)

Exposure to excessive noise has two principal effects:

- ***Hearing loss:*** The U.S. Public Health Service says almost half of the 81 million Americans with hearing loss owe their impairment to noise exposure.[4]

- ***Stress:*** Noise increases tension. As the "fight-or-flight" mechanisms are triggered, adrenaline rises, increasing heart rate and blood pressure. Various studies have examined effects of noise of 85 decibels (a crowded school bus) up to 115 decibels (Sony Walkman). These studies associated prolonged exposure to these noise levels with an "assortment of physical, mental and social problems ranging from hypertension to helplessness, from learning disabilities to birth defects," says one report.[5]

Strategy for Living: Shutting Out Noise
Workers exposed to factory noise may not experience hearing loss for as long as 10 years.[6] Musicians playing amplified music may run the risk a lot sooner. In 1984, punk-rock musician Kathy Peck woke up after a concert with a ringing in her ears that wouldn't go away. Today Peck, who

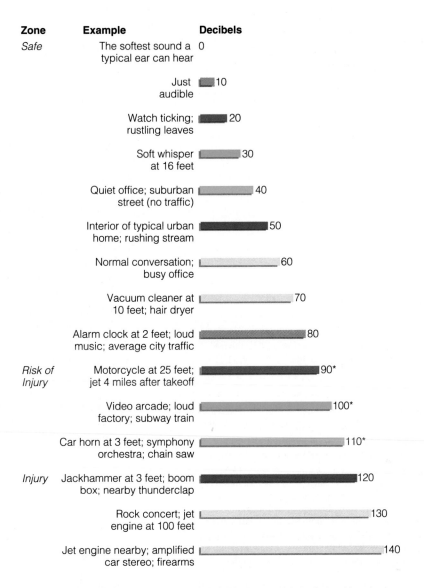

Zone	Example	Decibels
Safe	The softest sound a typical ear can hear	0
	Just audible	10
	Watch ticking; rustling leaves	20
	Soft whisper at 16 feet	30
	Quiet office; suburban street (no traffic)	40
	Interior of typical urban home; rushing stream	50
	Normal conversation; busy office	60
	Vacuum cleaner at 10 feet; hair dryer	70
	Alarm clock at 2 feet; loud music; average city traffic	80
Risk of Injury	Motorcycle at 25 feet; jet 4 miles after takeoff	90*
	Video arcade; loud factory; subway train	100*
	Car horn at 3 feet; symphony orchestra; chain saw	110*
Injury	Jackhammer at 3 feet; boom box; nearby thunderclap	120
	Rock concert; jet engine at 100 feet	130
	Jet engine nearby; amplified car stereo; firearms	140

*Note: The maximum exposure allowed on the job by federal law, in hours per day, is as follows: 90 decibels—8 hours; 100 decibels—2 hours; 110 decibels—1/2 hour.

● **Figure 1   How loud is loud?** An increase of 10 decibels represents a tenfold increase in acoustic energy or intensity of sound. The human ear perceives these 10 decibels as a doubling of loudness. Thus, the 100 decibels of a subway train sounds much more than twice as loud as the 50 decibels of a rushing stream.

SELF DISCOVERY 1

How's Your Hearing?

Answer each of the following statements "true" or "false."

	True	False
1. Sounds are loud enough, but not clear.	____	____
2. Soft sounds, such as my watch ticking, birds singing, and voices from another room, are very difficult to hear or simply cannot be heard anymore.	____	____
3. People often seem to be mumbling or talking too fast.	____	____
4. Understanding what is being said is very difficult when there is any background noise.	____	____
5. Group conversations are difficult to follow.	____	____
6. Loud sounds may seem more annoying than before.	____	____
7. My hearing is good when I'm fresh and rested, but seems to deteriorate quickly.	____	____
8. My family tells me that the television or stereo is uncomfortably loud for them.	____	____

If you answered true to one or more of these questions, it's possible you may have a hearing loss, even one that you're not conscious of. To take it to the next step, call 800-322-EARS (in Pennsylvania, 800-345-EARS) to be referred to a number in your area that offers a simple hearing test by phone. The 800 number operates Monday through Friday 9 A.M. to 5 P.M., Eastern Standard Time. The local numbers operate 24 hours a day.

When you call the local number, a recording will play four tones for each ear and a message. You should hear all the tones. If not, you may need to have your hearing checked by a professional. This service is provided by Occupational Hearing Service, which can also make referrals to audiologists and ear, nose, and throat doctors. You can also call the American Speech-Language-Hearing Association at 800-638-8255.

Source: Deborah Huning, certified audiologist. Cited in: Anonymous. (1992, June). Danger signs of hearing problems. *Men's Health*, p. 10.

---

has lost 40% of her hearing and wears a hearing aid, is warning others. She is active in the organization called HEAR (Hearing Education and Awareness for Rockers), which urges rock musicians and concertgoers to wear earplugs.[7] Even personal stereos, headset radios and tape players, and car stereo systems can be dangerous when played at the levels that many people prefer.

Here are some tips for preventing premature hearing impairment:

- **Turn it down!** "People with more than moderate hearing loss can probably no longer appreciate the nuances of the very music that brought about their disability," points out one writer.[8] People wearing headphones often turn up the volume to block out the sounds of noisy surroundings. However, the experts' rule of thumb warns about headphone music loud enough to be heard by a person next to you. At that level it can cause damage if used more than 2 hours a day, or even less for some individuals.[9]

- **Watch out for loud environments—and deal with them:** You know you're in a too-loud place when you have trouble hearing someone a few feet away. It is too loud when you have to raise your voice to be heard. When afterward your ears are ringing or you have a temporary hearing loss, it was definitely too loud.

  If you find yourself in a loud place (bowling alley, disco), get out after a couple hours, even for a short walk. If you engage in a noisy activity in which you can't protect your ears, such as motorcycling or snowmobiling, take breaks. That gives your ears a rest.[10]

- **Use earplugs—even at concerts:** Record producer Jeff Baxter was formerly a guitarist in the 1970s with the rock groups Steely Dan and the Doobie Brothers. He was noted for blocking out the booming sound of on-stage amplifiers with an earmuff-style headset. That is why, he says, he still has his hearing today so he is able to produce records.[11]

  Baxter says that people can enjoy the experience of being surrounded by sound at a loud concert but still protect their hearing. Foam earplugs will let sound pass through but cut down on the volume.

- **Minimize the sound of the environment:** If you live in a noisy place, you can dampen sound by using fabric, rugs, curtains, and acoustic tile. Noisy appliances, such as blenders or computer printers, can be put on rubber pads or covered with sound-proofing material. If street noise or loud neighbors bother you, you can try turning on the fan in your air conditioner. Or buy "white noise" machines, which give off a sound similar to what you hear on a TV channel that's not receiving. Static-like white noise acts as a masking device, drowning out unwanted sounds.

It's important to note that susceptibility to noise varies. Some people can tolerate sound that would damage the hearing of someone else. The sound level you find acceptable on a radio may drive other people on the beach or in the neighborhood to distraction.

Electromagnetic Fields

Electromagnetic fields are fields of electrical and magnetic energy, which travel in waves. Low-frequency waves are at one of the electromagnetic spectrum, and high-frequency waves are at the other. Prolonged exposure to high-frequency waves, such as X-rays, may be dangerous to health. There is speculation that exposure to low-frequency waves, such as those of power lines, computers, and cellular phones, may also be hazardous.

Are our household appliances our enemy? Are the corner power pole, the computer, and the cellular phone exposing us to magnetic fields that may cause childhood leukemia, brain cancer, and other diseases?

The Effects of Electromagnetic Fields
Electromagnetic fields **are invisible fields of electrical energy and magnetic energy, which travel in waves.** These waves cover an *electromagnetic spectrum,* with low-frequency waves at one end and high-frequency waves at the other. If we were to represent this spectrum with appliances and machines, video-display terminals and hair dryers would be at the low-frequency end. It would range up through electric heaters, walkie-talkies, cellular phones, radar, and microwave ovens. At the high-frequency end would be infrared "nightscope" binoculars, ultraviolet-light tanning machines, X-ray machines, and gamma-ray machines for food irradiation.

The higher the wave frequency, the greater the energy. X-rays, which are very high frequency, have so much energy that they can ion-

ize atoms (release electrons from atoms). They can also cause cancer, which is why physicians and dentists recommend limiting your exposure to X-rays. This has been known for years. What is a relatively recent concern, however, is whether *low*-frequency waves may be harmful. Does exposure to high-voltage power lines, video-display terminals, microwave ovens, and cellular phones lead ultimately to ill health? The answer is: so far no one is sure.

In the United States, a 1991 study by John M. Peters and Stephanie J. London seemed to show a problem. Their study suggested that childhood leukemia is approximately doubled in homes with higher concentrations of nearby electric power lines. It also appeared to be somewhat higher in homes reporting frequent use of appliances such as electric hair dryers and black-and-white television sets.[12] Two 1992 long-term epidemiological studies in Sweden showed clear associations between exposure to extra-low frequency fields and brain cancer and leukemia.[13] A 1992 study in Finland found a correlation between extra-low frequency fields and miscarriages in women who use video-display terminals at work.[14]

The foregoing studies investigated the effects of extra-low frequency (ELF) fields and health. Even less is known about radio frequency (R) fields and microwave fields, which are higher on the electromagnetic spectrum. Two 1990 studies by biophysicist Stephen Cleary used normal human blood cells and one type of cancer cell. The cells grew abnormally after 2-hour exposures to the frequency at which microwave ovens operate or a lower frequency.[15]

The risk to health from electromagnetic radiation seems far less than that from smoking or a high-fat diet. Still, it may be that, in the term used by the Environmental Protection Agency, we should all exercise *prudent avoidance.* That is, we can make easy changes without changing our whole lives or spending a fortune to minimize exposure to electromagnetic fields.[16,17]

Strategy for Living: Reducing Electromagnetic Radiation Most people move in and out of extra-low frequency (ELF) fields throughout the day, and brief exposures probably don't cause risk. However, in the interests of "prudent avoidance," it might be wise to avoid prolonged exposure within a field. Thus, you might want to analyze where you and any children for whom you are responsible spend most of your time. Following are some tips for reducing ELF.[18–20]

- *Reduce children's exposure:* For example, keep them 5 feet away from color TVs.
- *Distance yourself from appliances:* For example, move clocks and fans 3 feet away from your bed.
- *Avoid ELF-producing devices at work:* Stay an arm's length from video-display terminals.

If you're particularly concerned about ELF fields, have your home measured with a gauss-meter (available for about $100). Some utilities will do this for you.

Hazardous Radiation

High-intensity radiation, called ionizing radiation, can form ions, or electrical charges, that can damage living tissue. Overexposure to radioactive particles can produce radiation sickness. Sources of radiation, which is measured in rads and rems, include X-rays and radioactive elements used in medicine and dentistry. Other sources are radon, nuclear reactors, and nuclear weapons plants.

The word *radiation* is a scare word to many people, evoking memories of the nuclear age's worst consequences (the World War II atom-bombing of Hiroshima). It may remind them of terrible accidents (the 1979 near-meltdown of the nuclear power plant at Pennsylvania's Three Mile Island). In fact, however, we are surrounded by radiation all the time—from the sun, mineral deposits, industrial wastes, and other things. Most of this exposure produces negligible health risks. What we are concerned about in this section, however, is the kind that *does* produce health risks.

Radiation **is simply energy sent or emitted in the form of waves or particles.** Thus, it includes *nonionizing electromagnetic radiation,* **the low-intensity electromagnetic radiation of radio waves, microwaves, infrared light, and ordinary light.** These we just described. However, radia-

tion also includes **high-intensity *ionizing radiation.* This is fast-moving particles or high-energy radiation (such as gamma rays) capable of dislodging electrons from atoms they hit.** The significance of ionizing radiation is that it can form charged *ions*—atoms with positive (+) or negative (−) electrical charges. Ions can react with and damage living tissue.

Radiation: How Much Is Too Much? In small doses, ionizing radiation such as X-rays can benefit your health. High doses, however, whether from radiation for cancer therapy or from a nuclear accident, are harmful, perhaps even fatal. Of particular concern are radioactivity, which emanates from substances such as uranium, and radiation sickness, which can be fatal.

- *Radioactivity:* **Radioactivity refers to the emission of harmful rays or particles from the nucleus of an atom.** Radioactive materials emit three kinds of particles or rays:

   (1) *Alpha particles* cannot pass through skin and are not considered hazardous unless the substance is eaten or breathed.

   (2) *Beta particles* penetrate the body slightly; if the radioactive substance is eaten, it can affect bones and the thyroid gland.

   (3) *Gamma rays,* which can pass through the human body, are the most hazardous.

- *Radiation sickness:* **The result of overexposure to radioactive materials is *radiation sickness.* This illness is characterized by low white-blood counts, nausea, weight loss, immune deficiencies, hair loss, bleeding from mouth and gums, and ultimately death.**

   It's difficult to know how much radiation you are being exposed to because, as we mentioned, so much of it is natural radiation. There is also radiation from human activities. Radiation exposure is measured in rads and rems.

- *Rads:* **A *rad* is a measure of the amount of radiation absorbed by an organism.** A rad is used to measure dosages of radiation in treating cancer. A normal chest X-ray is about 1/10 of a rad. Between 50 and 150 rads will produce radiation sickness; 650 rads will kill one outright.

- **Rems: A *rem* is a measure of the relative danger of exposure to ionizing radiation.** Smaller doses are millirems (mrems), which are thousandths of a rem. The average annual exposure per person in the United States to ionizing radiation is 230 millirems. Of that, 130 mrems come from natural radiation and the rest from human activities. You should not receive more than 100 millirems from human-made sources in a year. *(See Self Discovery 2.)*

Sources of Radiation   Let us now consider some important sources of human-made radiation. We must hasten to mention, however, that at the moment radioactive hazards do *not* include *irradiated food*. **This is food that has been exposed to low doses of ionizing radiation,** such as gamma rays. Irradiation, in use since the mid-1980s, is designed to rid foods of harmful bacteria, and make them stay fresh longer. At least 20 nations already irradiate produce and spices. The World Health Organization encourages the practice, which can help eradicate salmonella and trichinosis and prevent spoiling.[21]

Some more legitimate sources of worry about radiation are the following:

- **Medical and dental X-rays—do the minimum:** You might wonder why the dental assistant makes such a production about putting a lead apron on you and then vanishing from the room while the X-ray machine clicks. You might especially wonder why, considering the dose you get from a full set of dental X-rays. It is equivalent to the amount of natural "background" radiation you might just pick up being outside over 11 days' time.[22] However, your dentist is just being cautious: although the risk is small, it's always a good idea to minimize the dose. Radiation exposure during pregnancy is especially risky.

  Guarding against too much exposure is even more important for chest and other medical X-rays. Every time someone suggests an X-ray might be a good idea, you should ask, "Why is this necessary?" It may only be because physicians are trying to

---

SELF DISCOVERY 2

How Much Annual Radiation Are You Exposed To?

Follow the directions to fill in the column at right to find out your estimated annual dose of radiation, in millirems (mrems):

	Millirems
Natural Radiation	
1. Cosmic rays from space:	
At sea level (U.S. average)	40
Add 1 mrem for every 100 feet you live above sea level	___
2. Radiation in rocks and soil (U.S. average)	55
3. Radiation from air, water, and food (U.S. average)	25
Radiation from Human Activities	
4. Medical and dental X rays and treatments (U.S. average)	80
5. Add 40 if you live in a stone or brick building	___
6. Add 40 if you work in a stone or brick building	___
7. Add 40 if you smoke one pack of cigarettes per day	___
8. Nuclear weapons fallout (U.S. average)	4
9. Add 2 for each 1500 miles of air travel per year	___
10. Add 4 for each 2 hours of exposure to television per day	___
11. Add 4 for each 2 hours of exposure to computer screen per day	___
12. Occupational exposure (U.S. average)	0.8
13. Add 76 if you live next to nuclear power plant with boiling water reactor	___
14. Add 4 if you live next to nuclear power plant with pressurized water reactor	___
15. Add 0.6 if you live within 5 miles of nuclear power plant	___
16. Exposure to normal operation of nuclear power plants, fuel processing, and research facilities (U.S. average)	0.1
17. Miscellaneous radiation exposure—industrial wastes, some watch dials, smoke detectors (U.S. average)	2
Your total points:	___

Interpretation

The average annual exposure for people in the United States is 230 mrems—130 from natural radiation and 100 from human activities. Your exposure could be higher, depending on occupation, location of residence, health behavior, medical tests, and the like.

The International Commission on Radiation Protection recommends a person receive no more than 100 mrems from human-made sources in a year. Do you see ways you might reduce your risk?

Source: Adapted from G. Tyler Miller, Jr. (1990). *Living in the environment: An introduction to environmental science* (6th ed.). Belmont, CA: Wadsworth, p. 296.

protect themselves in the event of a malpractice suit. The reason for concern is that X-ray exposure is *cumulative* and no exposure is by itself absolutely safe.

- **Radioactive elements used for medical treatment:** A number of radioactive elements are useful for medical diagnosis and treatment. For example, radioactive iodine (iodine-131) is used in tests of thyroid disorders. Cobalt-60, iodine-125, cesium-137, and radium-226 are used to treat cancer.[23] If you are being treated for cancer, the effects of the radioactive elements might seem of secondary concern. Nevertheless, they are potentially harmful to health.

- **Radon—radioactive gas beneath the house: Radon is an odorless, colorless, radioactive gas given off by underground uranium deposits.** At one time, there was a good deal of worry about radon seeping up into homes along water and sewage pipes or through foundation cracks. Radon could be inhaled, releasing radioactive particles that could damage lung tissue and lead to cancer.[24–26] More recently, some scientists have argued that the risks have been overblown. They say the EPA's original estimates for lung cancer caused by radon were too high.[27,28]

  Radon self-tests ($10–$50) are available through hardware stores and supermarkets, although some are better than others. There are also companies that test for radon, but few are licensed by the states. The gas can be reduced by sealing cracks in basement floors and ventilating crawl spaces, although repairs may be expensive.

- **Nuclear reactors—should you move if you live near one?** In 1991, nine countries generated a third or more of their electricity from nuclear reactors.[29] In the United States, the 110 reactors now in operation generate about 20% of the nation's electricity.[30]

  Are such plants safe? In 1979, operator mistakes, design flaws, and mechanical failures allowed overheating at the nuclear power plant at Three Mile Island, Pennsylvania. The plant was destroyed when it overheated to 2500° Fahrenheit, and cleanup took 14 years.[31] However, no in-

crease in cancer rates near the plant associated with the accident has been found.[32] In 1986, the Chernobyl nuclear plant in Ukraine (then in the Soviet Union) erupted in a volcano of deadly radioactivity. Evacuation from the 18-mile zone around the plant involved 116,000 people, and 600,000 people worked on the cleanup. In the aftermath, there have been reports of a soaring increase in thyroid cancer rates.[33–35]

Less serious accidents have been reported since at other American nuclear power plants. The nonprofit advocacy group Public Citizen said that in 1990 U.S. commercial nuclear reactors reported 1,921 safety-related incidents to the Nuclear Regulatory Commission (NRC). However, the NRC said the numbers were lower than in previous years, showing steady safety improvements.[36,37] In 1990, the National Cancer Institute found no increased risk of death from cancer for people living near nuclear power plants. The same was true of other nuclear installations.[38]

One major problem is that over the next 25 years, more than half of the nation's nuclear plants will turn 40. Their operating licenses will expire when they do.[39,40] At that point, many of the plants will need to be torn down and their radioactivity-permeated remains somehow disposed of safely. This is a social problem of awesome proportions.

- **Nuclear weapons plants:** Knowledge about radioactivity and radiation safety standards has changed through the nuclear age. Increased cancer cases have occurred among the 600,000 employees who since 1942 have worked in federal nuclear research centers and weapons plants. Work site studies include Tennessee's Oak Ridge National Laboratory.[41,42] Some Nevada, Utah, and Arizona "down-winders" of openair nuclear testing have also established relationships between cancer and exposure to radioactive materials. Colorado uranium miners of the 1950s have done the same.[43–45] Even in the 1990s, serious safety problems were turned up at nuclear weapons plants in Colorado and Oklahoma. The Occupational Safety and Health Administration in 1991 found more than 600 safety violations and basic defects at these and other government weapons facilities.[46-48]

Strategy for Living: Reducing Sources of Radioactivity Some radiation matters you have some control over, such as the amount of X-rays and other radioactive medical treatments you receive. You can have the basement of your house checked for radon levels. If living close to a nuclear power plant bothers you, conceivably you could move. Dealing with other radioactive hazards—nuclear waste dumps, stockpiled nuclear weapons, decaying nuclear power plants in Eastern Europe—is not so simple. It requires political efforts. We describe these in the second half of this chapter.

Indoor Pollution and Environmental Illness

Indoor air pollution may cause headaches, dizziness, and other symptoms of so-called sick building syndrome (SBS). Pollution in buildings may derive from carbon monoxide, formaldehyde, asbestos, and lead. Household chemicals may also turn houses into unhealthy toxic-waste sites. Some people experience an extreme sensitivity to chemicals called environmental illness (EI).

Sick buildings, toxic houses, and *environmental illness* are terms that were hardly known a few years ago. Let us consider these.

Sick Buildings and Chemicals A malaise recognized by the World Health Organization, ***sick building syndrome (SBS)* is illness that comes from indoor air pollution.** Symptoms may consist of some or all of the following: stinging eyes, hoarseness, headaches, nausea, runny nose, dizziness, and lethargy.[49,50] As in other work-related illness, however, people's feelings about their jobs and working conditions could play a role. A tipoff that the building is the cause might be if the symptoms worsen during the workday but improve at other times.

SBS health problems may occur in older buildings with deficient ventilation and ancient air-conditioning systems or in new, tightly

sealed, energy-efficient buildings. Sometimes the condition may be traced to a single contaminant, such as a fungus or tobacco smoke.[51] However, chemical engineer Richard Shaughnessy, who directs an indoor-air research program, says that everything contributes: "Copiers, ventilation systems, the air brought in from outdoors, the number of people in a work space."[52]

Houses, too, may also cause SBS, because they often have been weatherized to save energy, thereby sealing in air pollutants. The culprits may be natural, as in radon gas. Or they may be in such building materials as particle board, wood adhesives and carpet fibers, paint and wood finishes, and insulation. *(See ● Figure 2.)*

Among some of the principal polluters of buildings are the following.

- ***Carbon monoxide: Carbon monoxide* is a colorless, odorless gas.** It can be produced by furnaces, water heaters, space heaters, and gas stoves as a result of incomplete combustion. At high doses, the gas can be fatal, but at low doses it can produce headache, nausea, dizziness, and fatigue. However, at low doses most people are quickly restored by breathing pure oxygen.

- ***Formaldehyde:*** This was once used widely as an adhesive in particle board and plywood. ***Formaldehyde* is a chemical that in low levels can cause breathing problems, dizziness, and eye and skin irritations.** In high concentrations, formaldehyde can cause cancer in laboratory animals. Although most manufacturers of wooden building materials no longer use formaldehyde, it is present in older homes. The best advice is to avoid pressed-wood products, and keep humidity and temperature levels moderate to discourage release of the formaldehyde gas. Also, have adequate ventilation.

- ***Asbestos: Asbestos* is a fibrous, heat-resistant mineral. It can produce chest and abdominal cancers, lung diseases, and other illnesses in people exposed to it over 20–30 years on the job.** Those exposed include pipefitters and shipyard workers.[53] Used for many years for insulation and other building materials, asbestos is now banned. However, it is still found

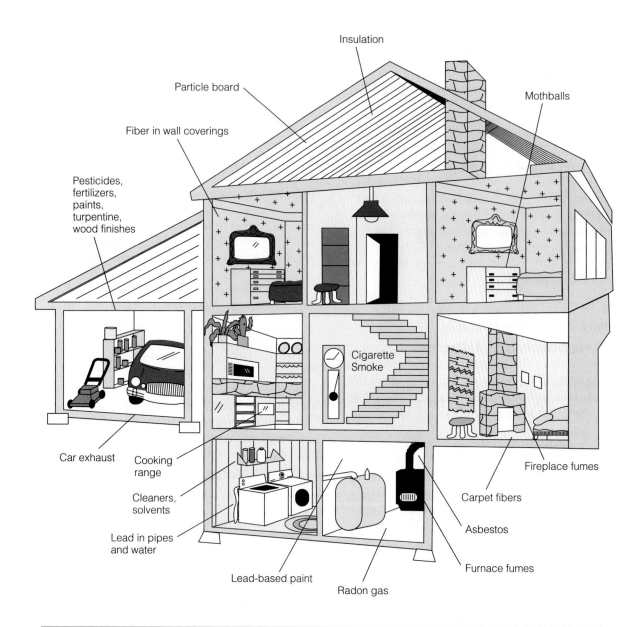

Insulation

Particle board

Fiber in wall coverings

Mothballs

Pesticides,
fertilizers,
paints,
turpentine,
wood finishes

Cigarette
Smoke

Car exhaust

Cooking
range

Cleaners,
solvents

Lead in pipes
and water

Lead-based paint

Radon gas

Fireplace fumes

Carpet fibers

Asbestos

Furnace fumes

● **Figure 2   The sick building.** Scientists have given the name "sick building syndrome" to illness that comes from indoor air pollution. Here are some of the sources.

around household pipes and some older furnaces. There, janitors, maintenance workers, and others may be exposed to fibers from disturbed asbestos. Still, most people who work in well-maintained buildings have little to worry about.[54,55]

In recent years, researchers thought that old asbestos should be removed from schools and public buildings. Today, however, the advice seems to be: Leave it alone. Or, if it is damaged or crumbling, have certified experts remove it.[56,57]

- *Lead: Lead* **is a soft, gray-blue metal.
  When consumed in sufficient amounts,
  it can lead to mental retardation, liver
  damage, paralysis of the extremities,
  and sometimes convulsions and collapse.** Its effects cannot be reversed.
  Impaired intellectual development from
  prenatal and early childhood exposure to
  lead occurs in children of all socioeconomic
  backgrounds.[58]

Lead used to be in most cans of paint
and all gasoline. Although by and large eliminated from those products, it is still found
in the paint of old houses. Indeed, perhaps
three-quarters of all occupied housing units
built before 1980 contain lead paint.[59]
Young children live in 3.8 million homes that
have peeling deteriorated lead-based paint
or lead in dust.[60] Lead is also found in old
water pipes and in new plumbing fixtures
where lead leaches from solder linking copper and brass.[61–63] Finally, lead is found in
materials that have nothing to do with buildings, including car batteries and soldered
cans of imported products. It may be in food
(lead occurs naturally in soil), some imported table wines, and ceramic tableware
and old china.[64–68]

Houses as Toxic-Waste Sites Besides being
sick buildings themselves, houses may also be
their own toxic-waste dumps. Indeed, the average American household generates 15 pounds of
hazardous waste a year.[69] These are ordinary
consumer goods ranging from shoe polish to
oven cleaner, house paint to turpentine, weed
killer to motor oil. Car owners who do their own
oil changes produce as much as 400 million gallons of waste oil every year. That equals 36 of
the Alaskan *Exxon Valdez* oil-tanker spills. But
only 12% of that is disposed of properly, as
through a service station or recycler. The rest is
poured into the ground, streams, or sewers—
and 1 gallon of oil can make a million gallons of
water undrinkable.[70]

According to the Environmental Protection
Agency, products designated as hazardous must
use "signal words" on labels: DANGER, POISON,
WARNING, CAUTION. Typically they fall into
five categories: (1) paints and solvents; (2) vehicle fluids; (3) pesticides; (4) household cleaners
and polishes; and (5) miscellaneous—including

batteries, art supplies, pharmaceuticals, and
some cosmetics.

Household toxic waste leads to two problems. (1) If left around the house, it may be a
respiratory hazard or a fire hazard. To children,
it could be a poison and pose skin and eye danger. (2) If thrown in the garbage or poured in
the ground or down a storm drain, it could end
up in the groundwater or nearby lakes.

Environmental Illness If you smell fumes
from some paints, automobile exhaust, or am-
monia, do you get blurred vision and headaches?
Does your speech begin to slur? Does a magazine "scent strip"—the perfume advertising insert—make you ill? The National Academy of
Sciences has suggested that about 15% of the
population has a heightened sensitivity to chemicals.[71]

With some people, chemical sensitivity is so
extreme that they are suspected of having the
syndrome known as *environmental illness
(EI)*. **Also called *multiple-chemical sensitivity*, this involves violent reactions to the
numerous chemicals and toxins that are a
part of everyday life.** (From 1945 to 1988,
production of synthetic organic chemicals went
from under 1 billion pounds to 273 billion
pounds.[72])

Although many health professionals don't
accept the existence of EI as such, they agree
that many patients have multiple chemical sensitivities.[73] Symptoms range from fatigue, hives,
and forgetfulness to severe headaches, joint
pain, and a paralyzing disorientation that makes
people unable to speak.

What causes EI? Clinical ecologists (physicians specializing in EI) say patients' vulnerability "may be caused by initial overdose or acute
exposure to chemicals, by biochemical differences in the individual, by overall stress load, by
viral or bacteriologic accompaniment, or by
complex biological processes in the body which
we don't yet fully understand."[74] It's also likely
that pollutants often interact with each other so
in effect two pollutants make you sicker than
one (the additive effect).

Strategy for Living: Dealing with Indoor Chemicals If we spend 90% of the time *indoors,* as has been discovered, what can we do to make our indoor environment safer?[75] Here are a few tips:

- **Deal with your sick building:** If you suspect you suffer from sick building syndrome, the first thing to do is the obvious: get as much ventilation and fresh air as possible. See whether the air is actually moving around existing ventilation systems. See if office machines are near functioning vents. Open vents that have been sealed to conserve energy. Ask the building maintenance supervisor if filters and drain pans have been cleaned or replaced. Also ask if pesticides or renovation work are near the air supply. Use a desk ionizer.

  Suspect tobacco smoke, toxins in old building materials, and fungus if there is water in the ductwork. Suspect fumes from carpeting and upholstery. Suspect old paint, which may be lead-based. Suspect heavy chemicals used by janitorial services.

  Get a plant: as NASA scientists found out, certain houseplants absorb formaldehyde and other health-threatening pollutants. (Efficient plants include the peace lily, gerbera daisy, English ivy, chrysanthemum, bamboo palm, mother-in-law's tongue, Janet Craig dracaena, moss cane, and marginata dracaena.[76,77])

- **Dispose of household toxins—properly:** What are you supposed to do with hazardous wastes? If possible reuse them yourself. Give such things as paints, pesticides, and cleaners to a garden club, local theater troupe, school, or homeless project. At the least, dispose of them properly. If your house connects with a wastewater plant (not a septic tank), you can dump *some* materials down a laundry sink or bathroom toilet. Do it slowly and don't mix materials—but first call the local water authority to be sure.[78]

  The following should be taken to a household hazardous-waste event (some communities have an annual toxic roundup or collection drive): paints, strippers, stains/finishes, wood preservatives, metal primers, pesticides, furniture polish, batteries, motor oil, prescription drugs.[79]

A word about lead in dishes: There is no way to tell by looking whether a piece of ceramicware is safe. But you can be sparing in your use of old or handcrafted china or china with a corroded glaze or dusty chalky glaze.

Water Pollution: Fear at the Faucet?

Unsafe drinking water can produce intestinal distress such as gastroenteritis. Water pollutants include infectious microorganisms, pesticides, lead, and chemicals such as PCBs and heavy metals. Chlorine and fluoride have been found to be beneficial.

Water symbolizes purity. But is the water we drink, in fact, pure? The Safe Drinking Water Act has been law since 1974. But in 1990 the General Accounting Office of Congress found inadequate tracking and enforcement by the states and the Environmental Protection Agency.[80] In 1992, a National Water Education Council study said the nation's water-supply systems might require $500 billion over the next 20 years. Crumbling water-supply and sewer systems must be repaired or improved to meet federal requirements for clean water.[81]

The Effects of Unsafe Drinking Water A good indicator of the infection potential of a particular tap water is whether people who drink it get *gastroenteritis.* **This inflammation of the lining membranes of the stomach and intestines has such symptoms as vomiting, diarrhea, nausea, and cramps.** People have come to accept the symptoms as the "one-day flu" and as "normal." However, this condition may represent the activity of a class of viruses called *enteroviruses.* Some enteroviruses (poliovirus, Hepatitis A, Coxsackie virus) are linked to long-term, serious illness. One Canadian experiment found that Montreal residents were 30–35% more likely to get gastroenteritis from regular tap water than highly filtered tap water.[82]

Types of Pollutants Viruses, bacteria, protozoa, and parasitic worms enter the water supply through human sewage and human wastes.

mobile exhaust and nitrogen oxides from industrial processes combine under sunlight. Even in healthy individuals, ozone can cause chest tightness, shortness of breath, decreased lung capacity, coughing, and nose and throat irritation. It aggravates emphysema and other respiratory illnesses.[99]

- *Smog and cancer:* Loma Linda University researchers who studied 6000 Californians found that smog increases cancer risks, particularly among women. Women in the Los Angeles Basin were found to have a 37% greater chance of getting all cancers because of particle pollution.[100]

- *Smog and lung abnormalities:* Pathologist Russell Sherwin found that 30 of 107 young Los Angeles residents who died from accidents or violence had severe lung abnormalities caused by air pollution.[101]

- *Carbon monoxide and heart risks:* Carbon monoxide—a pollutant from auto exhaust and industrial smokestacks—may provoke dangerous heartbeat irregularities in people with coronary artery disease.[102]

Strategy for Living: Can You Survive Smog? The good news is that there *are* some improvements. For instance, because of tough motor-vehicle emission controls, air pollution has dropped by 50% in much of southern California since 1982. Danger peak levels have dropped by more than 25%. These improvements were reported in 1992 by the California Air Resources Board.[103] The goal is blue skies over Los Angeles by the year 2007. Here and in other smoggy cities, individual actions will count, as we will describe.

If you live in a smoggy area and are concerned about guarding your health, what do you do? For people who have asthma, bronchitis, emphysema, or other respiratory problems, it is a particularly serious matter. Children, too, suffer more because their lungs are smaller and they take in more air than adults do. In general, the best advice is as follows:

- *Minimize efforts on smoggy days:* On days when there are air-pollution alerts, you should avoid exercise and stay indoors as much as possible. When exercising on

non-alert days, stay away from heavy traffic areas.

- *Don't smoke:* Cigarette smoke and smog have a worse effect on your lungs together than either do by themselves.

Other aspects of air pollution that may not affect you now have the most serious long-term consequences for our planet. Acid rain, global warming, the greenhouse effect, and destruction of the ozone layer won't be solved by staying indoors. As we describe in the second half of the chapter, they require political action.

Land Pollution

Solid waste in landfills tends not to be biodegradable or to turn to compost. Despite misconceptions, most solid waste is paper. Dumps are now being more closely regulated, especially toxic-waste dumps. The disposal of nuclear waste is a particularly difficult problem, because this dangerous material can endure for thousands of years.

"One of the critical problems of our time is *stuff*," writes columnist Molly Ivins. "Nobody seems to understand how they come to have so much stuff."[104] College students may have less accumulated than other people do. However, a look around may surprise you. One person turned up "old magazines, out-of-fashion or threadbare clothing, half-dead running shoes, extra kitchenware, broken furniture, old notebooks," and so on.[105] What do you do with this?

Who Is Harmed by Land Pollution? Unused possessions and junk—much of which can be given away or recycled—are not difficult to deal with, given a little time. What's harder are the nastier aspects of garbage. Let us see what the problems are.

Garbage and Landfills For more than two decades, archaeologist William L. Rathje has sorted through numerous garbage cans and landfills—what scholars call the *solid-waste stream.* **Solid waste is any unwanted or discarded material that is not a liquid or a gas.** One important discovery Rathje has made is that a great deal of garbage dumped in landfills tends *not* to be **biodegradable. That means it cannot be broken down by bacteria into basic elements and compounds.** Nor does much turn to **compost, in which organic matter becomes a humuslike product that can be used as a soil conditioner.** Biodegradation occurs, but it takes place over centuries rather than decades. The problem with landfills, say Rathje and his coauthor, is that they "are not vast composters; rather, they are vast mummifiers."[106]

In recent years, a number of other interesting facts have come to light regarding Americans and their garbage:

- **Garbage doesn't lie, people do:** Rathje's field of **garbology—the study of trash, refuse, rubbish, and litter**—has produced some interesting insights. For example, surveys about food consumption don't match the contents of the same respondents' trash containers. People consistently understate the amount of junk food they eat and underreport their alcohol consumption by 40–60%. They overstate the quantities of fruit and diet soda they consume and embellish on the amount of recycling they do. Heads of households, conscious of their roles as "good providers," exaggerate the amount of food their families consume.[107]

- **Misconceptions about what fills the landfills:** Most people, says Rathje, believe that landfills are 20–30% fast-food packaging and 30–40% polystyrene foam (used for coffee cups and packing "peanuts"). They think another 25–45% is disposable diapers—all in all making up perhaps 75% of landfills.[108]

  In fact, fast-food packaging made up one-quarter of 1%. Polystyrene products accounted for 0.9%.[109] The 16 billion disposable diapers thrown away every year made up only 0.8%. Incidentally, research shows that the energy to manufacture and launder cloth diapers and to fuel diaper-service delivery trucks exceeds that for disposables.[110–112]

  The largest component of landfills is, appropriately for the information age, paper. (*See ● Figure 4.*) From 35% of the volume of refuse in 1970, paper has become 50%.[113]

The most common kind of paper is newspaper, which occupies 10–15% of landfill volume. Yard waste, consisting of grass clippings and leaves, and construction debris make up two other major categories.

- **Complex choices about waste disposal:** Federal regulations now require town dumps to close unless they meet new regulations by 1993. These rules, designed to prevent dumps from polluting air and groundwater, require that new landfills be built with plastic and clay liners. They must have liquid and treatment systems and other expensive environmental equipment. As a result, 6500 old community dumps will be closed in the next few years. Solid waste will be concentrated in 1000 or so modern—and much larger—landfills.[114]

  Landfills are only one option of disposal, but they are the largest. Burning is attractive because it can reduce the volume of waste by 90% and the heat can be used to generate electricity. However, burning raises problems of safety and environmental nuisance.[115] Despite incineration, composting, and recycling, the amount of garbage going into landfills amounts to 130 million tons a year. By century's end, however, the Environmental Protection Agency projects less landfill use and more recycling and converting of solid waste to energy.[116]

Toxic Waste People don't like having dumps nearby. They especially hate being near **toxic-waste dumps—containing everything from chemicals to motor oils to, in special cases, radioactive materials.** Any time officials contemplate opening a new dump, particularly one for toxic waste, they are confronted with the phenomenon of NIMBYism. **NIMBY stands for Not In My Back Yard.** The term NIMBY, says one writer, "is usually applied broadly to people who don't want to bear social burdens or risks of any kind. Yet technological fears are a separate category deserving special attention."[117] In other words, although NIMBYism can be selfish and irresponsible, it also need not be, as we shall explain.

There are two problems with nonnuclear toxic waste:

- ***Cleaning up of old toxic-waste dumps:***
In 1980, Congress passed what came to be
known as the Superfund program. The superfund is to be used by the Environmental
Protection Agency to clean up abandoned
or inactive hazardous-waste dump sites. In
the past decade, the EPA spent $11 billion
on emergency measures at 400 abandoned
sites and full-scale cleanups at 60 others.
Yet the cleanup has only begun.[118] The Con-
gressional Office of Technology estimates
that the final list might include 10,000 sites
and take 50 years to clean up.[119]

  People living near old toxic-waste sites
naturally worry that the chemicals will find
their way into air and water. Problem sites
include leaking underground storage tanks,
inactive uranium dumps, and abandoned
mine lands. However, analysts believe the
risks are overestimated. The EPA estimates
that roughly 1000 cancer cases a year can
be linked to public exposure to hazardous
waste. This is not a negligible problem, but
it is far behind other cancer risks. More cancer cases are linked to exposure to chemicals in the workplace or to radon gas leaking
underneath houses.[120]

- ***Relocating hazardous wastes to new
dumps:*** In time, contaminated dumps and
buildings, as at old chemical factories, will
be cleaned up or at least isolated. But what
should be done with the toxic waste being
generated now? Trucks and trains carry
toxic waste from one state to another and
even one country to another.

  Industrialized nations in North America
and Europe, finding disposal of such waste
more restricted and more costly at home,
are exporting it. Not so long ago a favored
location was Africa. There a ton of toxic
waste could be disposed of for as little as
$2.50 compared to $2000 in the United
States. More recently, more and more has
gone to Latin America. Despite millions of
tons of dangerous cargo moving around the
world, no global monitoring system exists to
police hazardous waste exports.[121,122]

Paper: Includes packaging, newspaper, telephone books, glossy magazines, & mail-order catalogs — 50%

Organic: Includes wood, yard waste, & food scraps — 13%

Plastic: Includes milk jugs, soda bottles, food packaging, garbage bags, & polystyrene foam — 10%

Metal: Includes iron as well as aluminum & steel cans for food & beverages — 6%

Glass: Includes beverage bottles, food containers, & cosmetics jars — 1%

Miscellaneous: Includes construction and demolition debris, tires, textiles, rubber, & disposable diapers — 20%

● **Figure 4   What's in the garbage?** When trash ends up in a
landfill, it's not polystyrene and disposable diapers that take up
most of the volume. Half of it is paper.

Nuclear Waste Radioactive waste is in a class by itself. A 1992 Environmental Protection Agency study said 45,361 sites across the United States are *potentially*—the qualifier is important—contaminated by radioactivity.[123] Many of the locations, which include factories and hospitals, are not likely to be dangerous. But some have highly radioactive liquids and solids from nuclear reactors and nuclear-weapons plants.

Until 1993, only three repositories (in Nevada, South Carolina, and Washington) existed for permanent disposal of low-level radioactive waste. Low-level waste comes from medical facilities and research laboratories. However, the three states objected to being dumping grounds for the nation's low-level waste. So federal law decreed that states now have to dispose of wastes themselves or enter into regional compacts with other states. Every year enough low-level waste is produced in the United States to fill a dozen Olympic-size swimming pools.[124]

The government classifies radioactive-waste materials into five groups, of which low-level is the least problematic. Above that are uranium mill-tailings, spent fuel, transuranic (elements heavier than uranium), and high-level. Most troublesome are these higher-level nuclear wastes, probably the most difficult garbage problem we face. Some of it comes from the nation's 110 nuclear reactors. Most reactors store radioactive wastes in indoor water pools originally designed to hold small quantities for only a few years.[125–127] This means that when the plants themselves reach the end of their 40-year operating licenses, they cannot really shut down; the control rooms, miles of plumbing, and deep pools of water holding the spent fuel must be monitored 24 hours a day. Tearing down and disposing of decommissioned plants themselves, whose walls and equipment are permeated with radioactivity, is another problem. Again, there seems to be no present solution. Eventually, however, all these reactors will probably have to come down.[128]

The same difficulty exists at the government's 17 nuclear weapons-production reservations. Nuclear wastes are stored in pools of water or above ground in sealed casks. Government experts have said that catastrophic explosions are possible at million-gallon waste tanks at the Hanford bomb plant in Washington State. There has been deep concern about Hanford and other nuclear weapons plants.[129] In addition, the end of the Cold War means the United States and Russia have to start retiring their nuclear arsenals. Together, there are nearly 40,000 nuclear warheads and hundreds of tons of bomb materials like plutonium 239 and uranium 235.[130,131]

What we have not mentioned so far is *how long* these radioactive materials remain dangerous. **The amount of time over which the radioactive potency of any substance diminishes to half its original value is called the *half-life*.** Radioactive phosphorus-32, used in hospitals, has a half-life of 14 days. Tritium has a half-life of 12.26 years. Carbon 14 has a half-life of 5780 years. Even after achieving its half-life, a material can still be dangerous. Weapons-grade uranium will continue to emit radiation for *billions* of years.[132]

Are there no solutions for choosing sites for solid-waste dumps, particularly for radioactive materials? Advocates of nuclear technology say that high-level wastes can be safely disposed of permanently deep in the Earth in rock or salt formations. Sites have been identified that have not moved or had moisture in them for millions of years.[133]

This may be so, but the U.S. Energy Department has already postponed use of one such site. Officials concluded they cannot withdraw radioactive material from civilian power plants to store underground permanently by 1998, as the law requires it to.[134,135] An enormous reactor-waste burial site had been built in Yucca Mountain, Nevada, 100 miles from Las Vegas. Yucca Mountain was chosen because apparently there had not been a major earthquake in the area in perhaps 10,000 years. However, a 1992 earthquake caused $1 million worth of damage to a building just 6 miles from the site. Since then, Nevada residents have succeeded in getting officials to postpone taking fuel until 2010.[136] Opponents also have delayed movement of nuclear waste into sites in Idaho and New Mexico.[137–139]

In the meantime, a growing number of people support "intermediate storage" for 50–100 years or until a good disposal method is found. Decommissioned nuclear plants, for instance, could be simply mothballed rather than dismantled and transported to a burial site. The British government has announced it will mothball reactors for at least 130 years.[140]

Other possibilities include nuclear burial at
sea or reprocessing and recycling of nuclear
waste. Or the answer might be a process (trans-
mutation) that accelerates the radioactive decay
(half-life) and reduces the radioactive danger.
Other experiments attempt to use jimsonweed
to digest plutonium. A bacterium called GS-15
may transform uranium waste water into a solid
form that can be easily filtered out.[141–144]

**Strategy for Living: Dealing with Land Pol-
lution** At least one writer believes that NIMBY-
ism against solid-waste dumps, toxic-waste
dumps, and nuclear weapons plants occur
because opponents have reason for skepticism.
Given the past 40 years' experience, people no
longer believe that science and government offer progress or protection from unwanted hazards.[145] When NIMBYists have the facts, they
may become a political power that can force
industries and government to take better precautions.

From the standpoint of safeguarding your
personal health from garbage and toxic waste,
we might offer the following suggestions:

- *Cleaning up public litter:* When picking
  up public or roadside litter, as around your
  house, wear heavy clothing and durable
  gloves that fit tightly at the wrist. A mask
  may be desirable if odors are a problem.
  Wash your hands frequently and clean them
  with alcohol-saturated towelettes. The same
  sorts of advice apply if you are disposing of
  household chemicals.

- *Dealing with nearby waste facility:* Is
  your neighbor an industry or even an individual (such as someone who works on
  cars) that you suspect of pollution? If they
  pollute the ground or the water supply in a
  way that might endanger you, you may find
  you have a choice: You can move. Or you
  can take up some form of political action.

At this point, you may see why we started
with forms of environmental pollution you could
individually do something about. With land-
pollution problems, it is possible to see that the
environmental problems that affect you are not
always amenable to individual solutions. You
need to join forces with others.

Global Environmental Challenges

▶ Describe the principal concerns behind
  four overriding world environmental problems: population growth, poverty, pollution,
  and war.
▶ Discuss the personal health benefits of
  voluntarism.

Toxic wastes, dwindling rain forests, holes
in the ozone, and global warming may
seem to be environmental problems that
are far from your personal concerns. They may
also seem to be insurmountable. Yet in recent
years people acting together have made a
tremendous difference. They have halted nuclear power development, reduced air and water
pollution, and saved millions of acres of wilder-
ness. Some of our problems seem so overwhelming as to warrant cynicism. Yet the examples of
environmental achievement should inspire us to
realize that individuals—in the company of
others—*do* make a difference.

The Four Horsemen of Our Time: Population, Poverty, Pollution, and War

There are perhaps four overriding world
environmental problems affecting our
health. The first is excessive population
growth, which needs to be reduced so the
fertility rate equals the replacement rate.
The second is poverty, along with hunger
and disease, which must be remedied with
sustainable development. The third is pollution brought about by acid rain, rainforest deforestation, the greenhouse effect
and global warming, and the disappearing
ozone layer. These pollution problems require international action. The fourth is
war, which requires regulation on proliferation of nuclear weapons.

In the Bible, Revelation 6.1–8, the allegorical figures of the Four Horsemen of the Apocalypse are war, famine, pestilence, and death. Although these scourges remain with us today, let us suggest the Four Horsemen for our time: *population, poverty, pollution,* and *war.*

Population Every year there are nearly 100 million more people on the planet. This means the world *annually* gains slightly more people than live in Great Britain, Ireland, Iceland, Belgium, Denmark, Norway, Sweden, and Finland *combined.*[146] Where is all this leading us?

- *World population growth:* The number of people born every year is getting larger. The famed biologist Paul Ehrlich wrote his book *The Population Bomb* in 1968, warning of the dangers of overpopulation. Since then, the world has gone from 3.5 billion people to 5.5 billion. By 2025—within the lifetime of many people reading this—it will be 8.5 billion, says a United Nations Population Fund report.[147] By 2036, Ehrlich and population groups predict, it will be more than *twice* what it is today—11 billion.[148,149] *(See ● Figure 5.)* China and India have two-fifths of the world's population and account for one in three of the new people added each year.[150]

- *U.S. population growth:* What about the United States, which has a slower growth rate than other countries? Between 1950 and 1992, we grew from 150 million to 255 million. The U.S. Census Bureau now estimates there will be 275 million by the end of this century and *383 million* by 2050.[151] This is a stunning 50% increase in only six decades. (This increase assumes fertility rates averaging 2.1 births per woman. It adds in legal and illegal immigration of between 880,000 and 1.4 million a year for the next six decades.) Next time you can't find a parking place or a roomy beach, think how a 50% increase will affect quality of life.

- *The rise of megacities and edge cities:* Where will these people go? Probably where most of them go now: to the cities. For instance, in 1950, only 42% of Latin Americans were city dwellers. Today almost 73% are, creating shantytowns and slums everywhere, according to the United Nations.[152,153] By century's end, there are expected to be 23 **so-called** *megacities*—**metropolitan areas of the world with 10 million people or more.**[154] Two U.S. megacities already exist—the New York area, with 18 million people, and the Los Angeles area, with 14.5 million. Regardless of what country they're in, megacities have much in common. *(See ● Figure 6.)*

  In the United States, decades of movement from small towns and farms have put 50% of the population in cities and suburbs. That is up from 30% in 1950, according to the Census Bureau.[155] There are now 39 metropolitan areas with 1 million people or more. Indeed, demographers now speak of these metropolises as "metropolitan systems" that spread well beyond the central cities. Some have what one writer calls "edge cities," with their own city centers. The United States has nearly 125 edge cities, each bigger than Memphis.[156]

- *What Americans think:* Most Americans find such rapid population growth, both at home and in the world, extremely troubling. A 1992 poll commissioned by the World Population Crisis Committee, a population-stabilization organization, found Americans expressed the following concerns regarding overpopulation:[157]

(1) Concern for environmental degradation and poverty. More than 85% of all Americans believe that rapid population growth is ruining the world's environment. It will continue to contribute to environmental degradation and poverty if nothing is done, they say.

600 650 700 750 800 850 900 950 1000 1050 1100 1150 1200 1250

(2) Worries about immigration and jobs. More than three-quarters of those surveyed felt rising world population would cause more illegal immigrants to come to the United States. The same number said they thought American jobs would move to countries where people would work for less.

(3) Belief in family-planning assistance. The survey found that most Americans want the government actively involved in international family planning. Fifty-five percent said the United States should pay directly for overseas abortion services.

No challenge is more urgent, says Werner Fornos, president of the nonprofit Population Institute, than stabilizing world population. The knowledge and technology exist to reach the objective. Only the will is missing.[158]

The highest priority is *population stabilization.* As Fornos and many others point out, population control and family-planning assistance must be accelerated from all sources. The goal is to stabilize populations. That means the ***fertility rate*—the average number of children a woman will bear**—equals the replacement rate. The ***replacement rate* is having the number of persons born in a generation equal, rather than exceed, the number dying.** The goal should be a fertility rate of 2.4 children per woman, according to Fornos, to stabilize population at present death rates. The world can achieve that goal by the year 2000, the World Bank reports, if 72% of couples in developing countries use contraception. The proportion now is 40%.[159]

Poverty, Hunger, and Disease If the world were a village of only 1000 people, North Americans would make up only 60 of them.* Moreover, of those 1000 people, 60 would control half the total income. In addition, 500 would be hungry, 600 would live in shantytowns, and 700 would be illiterate.[160]

These kinds of figures make it plain how shockingly unequal the distribution of the world's wealth, food, housing, and education is. The poorest fifth of the world's population dispose of only 4% of the world's wealth, while the richest fifth dispose of 58%.[161] Incredibly, the world is actually producing enough food to feed all of the human race, according to the United Nations Food and Agricultural Organization.[162] The difficulty is one of distribution, so that starvation and malnutrition affect as many as half a billion people today.[163] The problem of poverty and hunger, which in turn exposes people to disease, is aggravated by more children born to families in underdeveloped nations.

Some observers have pointed out a certain arrogance exists among the West's more affluent nations. For poor people to stop having so many children, for example, they must know that the children they do have will survive. This means making available health, education, and employment opportunities that we North Americans take for granted. However, if people in developing countries tried to live as we do, the result

*The rest: 80 South Americans, 86 Africans, 210 Europeans, and 564 Asians. The 1000 villagers would also include 300 Christians (183 Catholics, 84 Protestants, 33 Orthodox), 175 Moslems, 128 Hindus, 55 Buddhists, 47 Animists, and 210 without any religion or who are atheist.

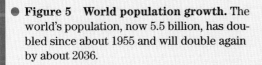

● **Figure 5   World population growth.** The world's population, now 5.5 billion, has doubled since about 1955 and will double again by about 2036.

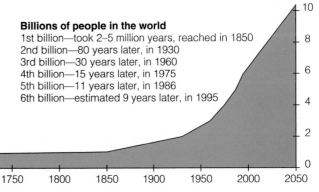

Billions of people in the world
1st billion—took 2–5 million years, reached in 1850
2nd billion—80 years later, in 1930
3rd billion—30 years later, in 1960
4th billion—15 years later, in 1975
5th billion—11 years later, in 1986
6th billion—estimated 9 years later, in 1995

● **Figure 6   Megacities.** By the year 2000, there are expected to be 23 cities in the world with 10 million people or more. Janice Perlman, founder of The Mega-Cities Project at New York University, points out that developed (first-world) and underdeveloped (third-world) cities have much in common.

>*Moving people around, moving garbage around, housing low-income people and matching people with jobs are universal problems. Every third-world city has a first-world city in it; every first-world city has a third-world city in it.*
>
>—Janice E. Perlman. Quoted in: Roberts, S. (1990, June 25). 'Mega-cities' join to fight problems. *New York Times,* p. A13.

would be ecological disaster. ***Sustainable development—striking a balance between ecological and economic concerns***—is supposed to be the answer. But many people in North America and Europe regard sustainable development as something poorer nations need to practice but they themselves don't.[164]

In fact, says Paul Ehrlich, one American does 20–100 times more damage to the planet than one person in a developing country. One rich American causes 1000 times more destruction.[165] People who drive cars, air condition

homes, and eat food produced through high-intensity agriculture do far more damage than subsistence farmers, he says. Yet this criticism doesn't mean Americans need adopt a peasant lifestyle. In Sweden, for instance, the average person consumes about 60% as much energy as the average American.

Pollution: Acid Rain, Global Warming, and the Ozone Layer Is Ehrlich right? Are we in North America (and others in the richest part of the world) responsible for most of Earth's pollution problems? In 1992, the World Watch Institute in Washington, D.C. issued a study that echoed Ehrlich's views. The study states that the consumption by the richest fifth of the world is responsible for releasing virtually all ozone-depleting chemicals. It also produces two-thirds of greenhouse gases and pollutants that cause acid rain, and a large share of pesticides and radioactive waste.[166] Worse, the study said, the actions of the "consumer class" inspire poor countries to want to adopt the consumer lifestyle. Witness, for example, the global spread of shopping malls.

The people of the developing world also contribute to global pollution, although much of it represents the desperation of poverty. For example, the United Nations says that half the world's population depends on wood to heat homes and to cook, pulling down trees and even shrubs. Many other impoverished people clear land for marginal farming. As a result, natural forests have all but disappeared in Haiti, Greece, and El Salvador.[167–169] The resulting deforestation contributes to increased levels of carbon dioxide, a principal greenhouse gas responsible for global warming, as we discuss.

What are the major pollution problems that need to be confronted to make Earth livable? The following are key:

- ***Industrial pollution in Eastern Europe:*** We have described the problems of disposing of toxic chemicals and nuclear waste in North America. The former USSR and its satellites, including Russia, East Germany, and Poland, are mired in pollution and backward industries. They are an environmental menace to the rest of the world.[170–174] They have poisoned air, water, and land; dying forests; aging nuclear reactors; and radioactive waste dumps. The poisoning of one-sixth of the Earth's land mass must somehow be dealt with. One statistic shows the seriousness of the problem: although the United States contributed 17.6% of greenhouse emissions in 1989, the former USSR contributed 13.6%.[175]

- *Acid rain and destruction of forests:* **Acid rain is rain (or snow, fog, or clouds) containing sulfuric acid and nitric acid.** The acid rain comes about because water droplets in the air mix with smoke from sulfur-content fuels (such as coal) and nitric oxide. Nitric acid comes from auto emissions and some industrial processes. The clouds or precipitation may be carried several miles, doing severe damage well outside the country of origin.

  Acid rain is a serious problem in the northeastern United States and southeastern Canada. The emissions come from coal- and oil-burning plants in industrial parts of the United States. Acid rain also plagues northern and central Europe and other areas. Besides damaging car finishes, buildings, statues, lakes, rivers, fish, and crops, acid rain has been destructive of forests. In turn, deforestation and the burning of fossil fuels have a consequence unanticipated a generation ago: the *greenhouse effect,* as we shortly describe.

- *Destruction of tropical forests:* There are 10 billion acres of forests left in the world, including 5 million acres of tropical rain forest. More than half the tropical rain forest is in Latin America.[176] Today tropical forests are half the size they were a century ago, and the destruction has proceeded especially rapidly in recent years. Forest over 324,000 square miles in size—equal to two Californias—was destroyed in Latin America alone in the years 1981–1990.[177] (Canada's once-vast rain forest has also been logged off at such a rate that experts say it will disappear within a generation.[178]) Most Latin American tropical rain forest destruction (often through burning) has come about because of the "three Cs," says anthropology and biology professor William Durham. The Cs are coca (for cocaine), cattle, and colonization.[179] However, impoverished people

hunting fuel, loggers, gold miners, and American oil companies are also responsible.[180]

Destruction of the rain forest has three possible consequences that should concern us:

(1) Fewer forests mean fewer plants to absorb carbon dioxide. This is the most important of the gases accumulating in the atmosphere that seem to be causing the greenhouse effect.[181]

(2) There are perhaps 10 million species on Earth today, from one-celled microbes to redwood trees to whales. Normally extinction is slow, 1–10 species a year. With the loss of tropical forests, perhaps 50,000 species disappear every year. As one writer put it, "One of the great mass extinctions in history appears to be underway."[182]

(3) For thousands of years plants have been the primary source of medicine. In the United States one in four prescriptions still comes from plants. Of 121 prescription drugs used widely around the world, nearly three-quarters came from following up folklore claims.[183] Currently Western companies are trying to tap the knowledge of people in rainforest cultures to develop leads for new medicines.[184] This search is part of increasing interest in harvesting the rain forest. Recent studies have suggested systematic harvesting of products— fruits, pigments, oils—from the Amazon rain forest. The studies show that steady harvests can be more profitable than cutting down the trees for lumber and running cattle on the land.[185]

- *The greenhouse effect and global warming:* The burning of rain forests and fossil fuels and the rapid deforestation of the planet are causing a great climatic change. The change is a global warming from the greenhouse effect.

  "Greenhouse gas"—carbon dioxide and certain other gases—is building up because of deforestation and the burning of fossil fuels and wood. The buildup is making the atmosphere act more than ever like the window pane in a gardener's greenhouse. "Greenhouse gas" is made up of four gases:

(1) *Carbon dioxide* (56%), mostly from fossil fuels

(2) *CFCs* or chlorofluorocarbons (23%), the gas that was used in refrigeration, air conditioning, and spray cans (now being phased out under a 1987 international agreement in Montreal)

(3) *Methane* (14%), released largely by cattle and rice farming and by leaks from natural-gas pipelines

(4) *Nitrous oxides* (7%), produced by cattle and engines

The *greenhouse effect* occurs when the "greenhouse gas" of carbon dioxide, CFCs, methane, and nitrous oxides makes the atmosphere act like glass in a greenhouse. The gas increases the warming effects of sunlight: it lets in the sun's light but retains heat. That causes the world's climate to warm up. *(See ● Figure 7.)*

So why worry about a little global warming? The problem is flooding from melting glaciers and Antarctic ice sheets. If the world were to increase in temperature by only 7°F (4°C), as it might 100 years from now, sea levels could rise by 2 feet. Floods would threaten coastal cities and agricultural lowlands everywhere.[186]

• **The thinning ozone layer: Ozone is a form of oxygen that reacts readily with other substances and, on close exposure, can be harmful to living things.** However, **the *ozone layer* high up in the atmosphere gives us a shield against excessive ultraviolet radiation from the sun.** Ultraviolet radiation has been found to cause skin cancer, cataracts, and suppression of the immune system in human beings. It also harms wildlife and crops.

Since 1967, however, there has been a 10% reduction in ozone over the middle latitudes of Europe and North America. Worse, there has been a loss of ozone at the poles, particularly over Antarctica. A loss of 50% has been reported there—a so-called "ozone hole."[187] Satellite measurements in late 1992 showed the ozone hole over Antarctica to be the largest on record. It is almost

three times larger in area than the United States.[188] People living in the southernmost part of South America, not far from the ozone hole, have reported ultraviolet radiation damage. They say cattle and sheep have been blinded by temporary cataracts and ranch hands' eyes and skin have been damaged.[189]

In 1992, environmental officials from 93 countries agreed to eliminate the use of ozone-depleting chemicals *4–9 years earlier* than previously agreed. The speedup is an effort to save Earth's protective layer.[190] Earlier, in 1987, signatories to the Montreal Protocol had agreed to reduce CFCs and carbon tetrachloride by half by 1998.[191] In the November 1992 meeting, they agreed to phase out *all* these chemicals by January 1, 1996. (CFCs are used in refrigeration, air conditioners, and aerosol spray cans. Carbon tetrachloride is used in dry cleaning and fumigation.) They also moved up the elimination of halons (in firefighting foam) and methyl chloroform (used in dry cleaning) from 2000 to 1994. They also agreed to an accelerated phaseout of HCFCs (hydrochlorofluorocarbons), used as a substitute for CFCs but also found to be dangerous.

Will the kinds of measures being taken against acid rain, global warming, and the vanishing ozone work? Or will the climate continue to be thrown out of kilter? In 1957, the late Roger Revelle of the University of California wrote of the changing atmosphere that humankind "is inadvertently conducting a great geochemical experiment."[192] The experiment is continuing.

War We have been fortunate, despite some close calls, to have endured more than 40 years of Cold War without nuclear war. Yet there has been appalling loss of life from other kinds of wars. Lentz Peace Research laboratory researchers in St. Louis have been keeping a computerized database on war deaths. They found that in 1987 there were more wars—26—than in any year in recorded history. The wars were responsible for 2.2 million deaths—84% of which were civilian casualties.[193]

Wars are of two principal kinds—nuclear and nonnuclear:

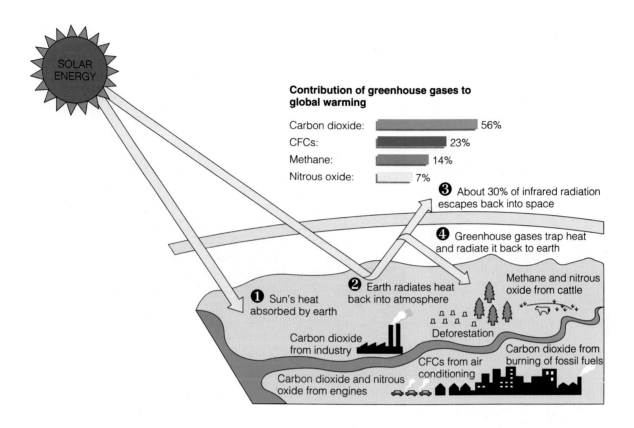

Contribution of greenhouse gases to global warming

Carbon dioxide: 56%
CFCs: 23%
Methane: 14%
Nitrous oxide: 7%

❸ About 30% of infrared radiation escapes back into space

❹ Greenhouse gases trap heat and radiate it back to earth

❶ Sun's heat absorbed by earth

❷ Earth radiates heat back into atmosphere

Methane and nitrous oxide from cattle

Carbon dioxide from industry

Deforestation

Carbon dioxide from burning of fossil fuels

CFCs from air conditioning

Carbon dioxide and nitrous oxide from engines

● **Figure 7   The greenhouse effect.** Like a window pane in a gardener's greenhouse, the collection of gases collectively called "greenhouse gas" lets in light but retains heat. Earth's climate thus warms up. (The gases are carbon dioxide, CFCs, methane, nitrous oxide.)

- **Nuclear war:** There has been only one hostile use of nuclear weapons since the birth of the atomic age. This was by the United States against Japan, when two atom bombs were dropped on Hiroshima and Nagasaki in August 1945. *(See ● Figure 8.)*

  The bomb that destroyed Hiroshima was equivalent to 13 kilotons, or the explosive power of 13,000 tons of TNT. The first hydrogen bomb, tested by the United States in 1952, was 700 times as powerful as the Hiroshima bomb. A single nuclear submarine can carry firepower equivalent to eight times *all* the firepower of World War II.

  Since the end of the Cold War, the greatest worries have become the following:

  (1) Who will get control of the remaining nuclear warheads in the former Soviet Union's far-flung arsenal? The United

States and Russia have agreed to arms cuts. But three independent neighboring states of Russia (Ukraine, Belarus, and Kazakhstan) hold nuclear weapons in their territories.[194,195]

  (2) What can be done to curtail the proliferation of nuclear weapons—including so-called "basement-built atom bombs"—to other countries or terrorist groups?[196,197]

  It seems clear that vigilance will be required throughout our lifetimes.

- **Nonnuclear war:** So-called "conventional wars" are ongoing. In 1986, Ruth Leger Sivard published a table listing all wars in the 20th century with deaths of 100,000 or more.[198] The table listed 43 wars or conflicts throughout the world, with a total loss of life of 83,642,000 people.

● **Figure 8   Nuclear weapons.** *Top left:* A mushroom cloud from an atomic-bomb test. *Top right:* Nagasaki after the A-bomb attack.

Yet this table listed only *major* conflicts between 1900 and 1986. Including so-called minor wars—those with deaths *under* 100,000—the total number of fatalities would probably have been over 100 million. And the 20th century still had another 14 years to run.

There may well be, say, 15 wars going on right now throughout the world. Most of the casualties will probably be civilian and from less developed nations. Civilians in advanced nations are generally not affected (except tourists or journalists in the war zones). However, judging by the past, the governments of the rich countries—led by the United States—sell armaments to the poor countries. The arms are then used against these countries' own populations, their minorities, and their neighbors.[199–201]

The Art of Living: Make Your Life Larger Than Yourself

To avoid catastrophic events in the future, immediate cooperative action is required. This can be done by adopting personal styles of living that are environmentally sound, such as avoiding overconsumption. People who do volunteer work not only benefit others but may also increase their life expectancy and gain vitality and purpose.

Is it too late to save the Earth? If a special "World3" computer model can predict the future, the answer may be: yes, it is too late.[202] This model plotted future scenarios, based on population growth trends, use of energy and resources, food production, pollution, and so on. It found that—without any major intentional changes—the future presents an extremely unhappy picture. In that future are famine, deforestation, species extinction, polluted water, global warming, depletion of the ozone layer, and social and political instability.

However, the authors believe, change is possible and collapse can be averted, provided action is immediate. The changes will require, however, that we and the rest of the world learn to live with limits on our consumption. Population growth, poverty, and pollution cannot be ended by indefinite material growth.

What can you do? Part of the art of living is to *make your life mean something more than just living for yourself.*

Personal Action Many people have begun a quiet revolution in their own lives.[203] They take a stand on the population issue by having few or no children themselves or by adopting children. They support the decisions of friends and relatives who have two, one, or no children. They don't overconsume, following the adage "Use it up, wear it out. Make it do, or do without." They are avid recyclers. They use their votes and their influence to support reproductive planning, abortion, and land-use planning that preserves agricultural land and open space. They also come to terms with their feelings about money.

In *Your Money or Your Life,* Joe Dominguez and Vicki Robin point out that money is something we choose to trade our "life energy" for. They write:

> *Our life energy is our allotment of time here on earth, the hours of precious life available to us. When we go to our jobs we are trading our life energy for money. . . .*
>
> *This definition of money gives us significant information. Our life energy is* more *real in our actual experience than money. You could even say money* equals *our life energy. So, while money has no intrinsic value, our life energy does—at least to us. It's tangible, and it's finite. Life energy is all we have. It is precious because it is limited and irretrievable and because our choices about how we use it express the meaning and purpose of our time here on earth.*[204]

It thus becomes important, they point out, to decide whether you receive satisfaction and value in proportion to the life energy expended. Consider also whether an expenditure of life energy is in alignment with your values and purpose.

Many people have learned to live on less and enjoy it more.[205] It has been called an ecological lifestyle, a creative lifestyle, conspicuous conservation, or voluntary simplicity. These are not people on the fringes, but mainstream, often well-educated men and women. Many are choosing to clean out the clutter in their homes, buy fewer gadgets, consume fewer disposable goods, and avoid expensive car and house payments. They may ride bicycles to work, use solar power, share child care with neighbors, or grow their own vegetables.

The rewards can be less consumer debt, less stress in work, and less worry about living costs. There is less concern about *buying things* as a means of satisfying the soul. In return, there is more time to be with friends and do volunteer work or otherwise do things you think are important.

Voluntarism and Its Rewards for Health
Many people are cynical about the state of our society. As one writer put it, they "feel too jaded to lift a finger, other than to change channels with the remote control."[206] It may be that the focus on the self has led people into "cocooning," withdrawing into comfortable private worlds. Yet sociologist Todd Gitlin points out, "The more people withdraw energy from their public lives, the more unsatisfying it becomes to participate."[207]

Actually, getting out and helping others can benefit the helper as much as the person being helped. In 1988, when Allan Luks was director of New York City's Institute for the Advancement of Help, he surveyed 3300 volunteers. He found that 95% experienced significant reductions in stress after helping acts.[208] James House and his colleagues at the University of Michigan's Survey Research Center studied how social relationships affected health. Their work included 2700 people studied for more than a decade. They found that doing regular volunteer work, more than any other activity, dramatically increased life expectancy and probably vitality.[209]

"To make ourselves healthier and to make the world a better place," says Luks, "we need to stop trying to protect ourselves and start opening up more. It's not easy, though. People need a push sometimes."[210]

Sometimes people become helpers because of a personal tragedy. Wayne Bates became the "Ralph Nader of the Railways," championing railroad safety, after his brother was seriously injured in a train accident.[211] Richard Eustice, 30, who experienced the first symptoms of rheumatoid arthritis at age 19, volunteers during his vacation at a summer camp for children with arthritis.[212]

Anger, points out David Walls in *The Activist's Almanac,* can also make a difference. Many activists begin with a sense of anger—at social injustice, at discrimination, or at the needless destruction of nature.[213] Anger may make one finally take the steps to join an organization and to effect social change. These steps, says Walls, can include "checkbook activism," for those with a little money but not much time. There are letter writing, telephoning, fundraising, and other activities for those who have some time and want to work with others. Computer networking with other activists and devoting full time to activism as a career are yet other steps.

Helping others helps your own health. Yet health is not a goal in itself but a means to serving a purpose in life.

Thus, we come full circle.

800-HELP

American Speech-Language-Hearing Association. 800-638-8255. (In Maryland, 301-897-8682.) Offers advice on hearing protection, hearing aids, and audiologists.

Dial A Hearing Screening Test. 800-222-EARS. (In Pennsylvania, 800-345-EARS.) Refers you to a number in your area that offers a simple screening test by phone.

Environmental Protection Agency Resource Conservation and Recovery Act Hotline. 800-424-9346. (In Washington, DC, 202-382-3000.) Referrals to local government agencies for disposal of hazardous waste.

National Institute of Occupational Safety and Health (NIOSH). 800-35NIOSH. Will provide information on where to go for a health hazard evaluation of your office or workplace.

National Pesticides Telecommunications Network. 800-858-7378. Makes disposal recommendations for pesticides, herbicides, and paint.

National Volunteer Hotline. 800-HELP-664.

Radon Information Hot Line. 800-767-7236. Advice on measuring and dealing with this radioactive gas beneath houses.

Safe Drinking Water Hot Line. 800-426-4791. Call for testing information about drinking water.

Suggestions for Further Reading

Debra Lynn Dadd (1986). *The nontoxic home.* Los Angeles: Jeremy P. Tarcher.

Duane Elgin (1993). *Voluntary simplicity: Toward a way of life that is outwardly simple, inwardly rich.* New York: Morrow.

Allan Luks (1992). *The healing power of doing good.* New York: Ballantine. Shows that volunteer work benefits the helper as much as the person being helped.

David Walls (1993). *The activist's almanac: The concerned citizen's guide to the leading advocacy organizations in America.* New York: Simon & Schuster. Information on 105 nonprofit, public-supported activist organizations and issues, from environmental to human rights, from animal welfare to foreign policy.

Richard Wolfson (1991). *Nuclear choices: A citizen's guide to nuclear technology.* Cambridge, MA: MIT Press. Stresses connections between nuclear technologies, so you can make your own choice about nuclear policy.

CHAPTER 12

Aging Well and Coping with Death

"Life isn't a mountain that has a summit. Nor is it a game that has a final score."

So says John W. Gardner, founder of the public-interest group Common Cause. Rather, he says, "Life is an endless unfolding, and if we wish it to be, an endless process of self-discovery, an endless and unpredictable dialogue between our own potentialities and the life situations in which we find ourselves."[1]

You can take the steps now to live both longer and well. A healthy lifestyle begun at age 30 can extend the average person's life expectancy of 70-plus years by another 15 years. Not just any old 15 years, as one writer points out, but "15 *healthy* years. The same smart behaviors that help you live long can also help you live well."[2]

Aging and drawing closer to death present an opportunity. As historian Page Smith says, when we get older, our reflections on our youth "becomes a crucial element in an expanded consciousness of the infinite, incommensurable power and beauty and strange variety of life, so that we literally live in wonder all our latter days."[3]

Successful Aging

▶ Explain the difference between life span and life expectancy. Distinguish between the "time-bomb" and "spacecraft" models of aging.

▶ Describe three possible ways age and vitality may be extended.

▶ Discuss the various physical changes that are typical of growing older. Explain what disorders are often associated with aging but are not inevitable.

▶ Identify the psychosocial changes associated with aging.

▶ Discuss what can be done to avoid disability in later life.

The oldest living things are trees. Individual redwood trees can live over 3000 years, and bristlecone pines, on the eastern slope of the Sierra Nevada Mountains, even longer. People, of course, don't even come close. Although from time to time we hear of 130-year-old Chinese (who attribute their longevity to a diet rich in lizards) or similarly long-lived people, there is usually an absence of documentation.[4]

How Long Will You Live?

Life span is the maximum years a person can live; life expectancy is the average age people are expected to live to be. The "time-bomb" model of aging holds that the human organism is programmed to die upon reaching a specific age. The "space-ship" model holds that humans can do things to increase their life expectancy. Three possible ways to extend age may be to fight cell damage with antioxidants, eat less, or administer human growth hormone.

Most Americans would like to live to be 100.[5] Is that possible, if we're really serious about it? How long *can* a human live?

Both the number and percentage of **centenarians—people over 100**—is increasing throughout the world. The U.S. Census counted 35,808 people 100 years old and older in 1990—double the number 10 years previously.[6] Still, according to the *Guinness Book of Records*, only one person in 2 billion lives to be more than 115.[7] The present record holder is Jeanne Calment of France, the world's oldest citizen at 118.

Life Span Versus Life Expectancy Life span and life expectancy are two different things:

- *Life span: Life span refers to the maximum number of years that a human being can live.* The apparent *maximum* life span is 120 years, based on the evidence. The *average* biological limit to life is considered to be 85 years.[8]

- *Life expectancy: Life expectancy refers to the average age that people born at a certain time are expected to live to be.* For example, the average life expectancy for newborns in America has risen to 75 years today from 47 in 1900.[9]

Life expectancy increases with age: the older you already are, the better your chances of living longer. Thus, a 35-year-old woman is expected to live to age 80, but a 65-year-old woman to age 84.

Today **gerontologists, specialists in the study of aging,** are concerned not only with decline but also with *vitality* and *resilience*. What is it that enables some people to play tennis in their 80s, run marathons in their 90s, and take dance classes in their 100s?

The Time-Bomb Versus Spaceship Models of Aging There are several theories about aging, some of them rather technical, all of them fascinating. Here, however, let us consider some of those with practical applications for life extension.

In general, there are two basic models of aging:

- *Time bomb:* The *time-bomb model* assumes, as age researcher James R. Carey puts it, "when you attain a certain age, you self-destruct."[10, 11] Gerontologist James Fries agrees and says there is essentially a "death gene." Fries says the gene takes effect about age 85, give or take 7 years—excepting some people who hang on past 100. In this view, the body is programmed to run down and end at a certain time.[12–16] Some propose that a centralized clock controlling aging is located in the pineal gland in the brain.[17]

- *Spaceship:* The other model, says Carey, is the *spaceship model*: a spaceship engineered to reach a particular goal may be capable of going a little further. Carey and James W. Curtsinger and colleagues have grown fruit flies and found that, past a certain age, their life expectancy actually increases.[18,19] In other words, it was not true

• *Eyesight:* Although it doesn't happen to everyone, one of the more irritating signs that you're getting older is the need for eyeglasses. By their late 40s, most people become *farsighted,* **unable to see things as clearly close up.** The cause is that the ocular lens does not expand and contract as readily. This is when most people find they need reading glasses. On the other hand, some people who had been *nearsighted,* **unable to see things clearly at a distance,** find their sight is almost normal. The phenomenon of farsightedness may cancel some nearsightedness.

By age 60, only a third as much light reaches the retina as at age 20. That decreases the ability to distinguish detail and see in the dark. Also, as people get into their 60s, they may develop *cataracts,* **a clouding of the lens of the eye.** Some older people, especially those with a family history of the disease, develop *glaucoma,* **the buildup of fluid in the eye. Untreated glaucoma can damage the optic nerve and cause blindness.**

• *Hearing:* By the mid-30s, people's ability to hear high-pitched sounds declines. Louder sounds are required to hear the same thing at 35 that we could hear at 25. Nowadays, the hearing decline is being found at younger ages because of prolonged or repeated exposure to electronic amplification and urban noise.

Metabolism One of the reasons the body so easily gains weight as you age is that your metabolism slows down. The slowing process begins gradually after adolescence and increases dramatically in later life. Every 10 years, the rate at which food is converted into energy slows by about 3%.[41]

Heart and Blood Vessels Depending on your level of fitness, your resting heartbeat can remain about the same lifelong, although the amount of blood pumped with each beat lessens. With age, circulation also tends to slow, owing to the buildup of fat and cholesterol within the blood vessels. The blood pressure rises. Two of the major disorders of old age are heart disease and stroke.

Lungs and Respiration Age greatly reduces **the lungs' *vital capacity*—the amount of air that can be expelled after a big inhalation.** By age 75, a man's vital capacity is half that at 17. A woman's vital capacity is a third of that of her 20s. This is a consequence of reduced elasticity in the tissues surrounding the chest and the capillaries within the lungs. By 85, even though lung size has doubled, capacity is only half that of a 30-year-old. Still, the ability to *use* oxygen depends on your physical fitness. Athletic runners in their 60s are able to use their oxygen better than nonathletic people in their 20s.

Muscles, Bones, and Joints: Coping with Osteoporosis and Arthritis People who continue to exercise and stay physically active experience less loss of muscle strength and mass than those who don't. Still, by age 60, a man may have lost up to 20% of his muscle strength and women more than that. In addition, in losing 3–5% of our muscle mass each year, we become more susceptible to strains and cramps. Thus, warm-ups and cool-downs become more important before and after exercise.

In addition, as back muscles weaken and discs between **the small bones making up the spine, the *vertebrae,*** deteriorate, we lose height. Most people are an inch shorter in old age than they were in young adulthood.

In your 20s, after your bones have stopped growing, they begin to lose calcium and other minerals. That makes them more brittle and less able to heal quickly. Joints also weaken and become susceptible to cartilage damage, especially if you continue high-impact activities such as teeth-rattling forms of aerobic exercise.

Two particularly significant disorders of aging are osteoporosis and arthritis:

• *Osteoporosis: Osteoporosis* **is a condition, common in older people, in which the bones become soft and porous, increasing the risk of fracture.** Half of all women over 50 have had an osteoporosis-related fracture. By age 75 one-third of all men are affected by the disease. Women who have otherwise normal menstrual periods may lose bone rapidly if they do not ovulate during every monthly cycle, according to one study.[42] This means that women who do not ovulate regularly or at all may have to take progesterone supplements to preserve their bones. Another possibility why American women are unusually prone to osteoporosis is that losing weight also loses bone mass.[43]

Older women can strengthen bones by taking the recommended daily allowance (800 milligrams) of calcium accompanied by vitamin D.[44, 45] Combined estrogen and progesterone therapy can also reduce the risk of cervical spine and hip fractures, according to a Swedish study.[46, 47] Certain new drugs also seem to increase bone mass and prevent bone loss in the spine.[48, 49] Contrary to popular belief, moderate exercise alone will not prevent bone loss in older women. Exercise should be combined with hormonal replacement and calcium.[50]

The best advice for young women seems to be to take calcium supplements and get enough aerobic exercise activity and weight training. Make sure some exercise is of a *weight bearing* type; swimming, for example, won't build bone.

- **Osteoarthritis: Osteoarthritis is a disintegration of the cartilage between bones, which produces pain, stiffness, and lack of mobility.** It affects about 16 million Americans, most of them 60 and older.[51] Research links it to a genetic defect.[52] However, it may also be affected by sports injuries or similar accidents to the joints. Obesity also puts extra pounds on the joints, which may produce arthritis of the knees.[53]

The Brain: Intellectual Power, Memory, and Alzheimer's By age 30, less blood is traveling to the brain than at younger ages. The brain also shrinks as it ages, losing about 10% of its weight.[54] Although the shrinkage may cause some mental loss, neuropathologist Robert D. Terry says, "normal elderly people are largely intact intellectually."[55] Still, it has long been accepted that the aging brain declines, bringing a loss of intellectual powers. Is this true?

- **Normal memory decline—for one kind of memory:** Memory can be quite complex on a psychological level, regardless of age, for remembering is an act of *reconstruction*, not *reproduction*.[56] For instance, 13%

of people ages 18–44 have trouble sometimes or frequently remembering names, and this rises to 35% for ages 45–54.[57] If you're over 30, you're losing your memory. Psychologist and memory expert Thomas H. Crook says that loss of 6–8% memory for each decade is normal.[58–60] This kind of memory is called *episodic memory*— memory about specific events, such as what happened at yesterday's meeting.

The loss of episodic memory is called *age-associated memory impairment (AAMI)*. Because of AAMI, older people have more trouble than they used to remembering what happened a few minutes, hours, or days ago. AAMI varies tremendously from person to person. It also can be reversed. For example, young people may repeat a string of numbers or words until they learn them. But many older people— anxious that they are losing their memory— give up after only a few tries. Retention can be helped by practice and by analyzing surroundings, people's names, and so on, so that details can be remembered later.[61]

- **Kinds of memory that do not decline with age:** Episodic memory is only one kind of memory; there are other kinds, and older people (in good health) do not lose these. *Semantic memory*—factual knowledge—does not decline with age. Nor does *implicit memory*, remembering skills one mastered automatically, such as how to swim.[62] Indeed, psychologist David Mitchell, an expert on memory, says that "semantic memory is the seat of wisdom. When you make decisions and judgments, you draw on this store of knowledge." Moreover, he says, "Semantic memory does not decline with age."[63] This is good news indeed.

- **Memory impaired by illness:** Older people lose their memories for many reasons, many of them reversible. Examples range from clinical depression to head injury to poor circulation. These may be serious problems, but with the help of a health care professional something potentially can be done about them. Unfortunately, a form of brain disease called *dementia* corresponds to memory problems that are more likely irreversible.

may become dependent on the hormone—it improves mood and sense of well-being.[87]

Hormone replacement therapy is clearly not for every woman. Some alternatives include vitamin E and clonidine, a drug used to treat high blood pressure, either of which may reduce hot flashes.[88] Aerobic and weight-bearing exercise, like walking and cycling, also can strengthen bones and lower the risk of heart problems.

With the interest in menopause in recent years, there has also come an interest in the possibility of a *male menopause*. Is there such a thing? Actually, the jury is still out on this question. Nevertheless, some studies have suggested that levels of testosterone drop gradually with age, perhaps by 30–40% between ages 48 and 78.[89] Nobody knows, however, if boosting blood levels of testosterone would affect older men's sexuality.[90]

Does Greater Longevity Mean Being Sicker Longer? Some disabilities make it difficult for older people to have sex. Then again, points out one sex therapist, some older people are afraid to attempt sexual lovemaking because of their health problems.[91] Patients recovering from heart disease, for example, may be afraid they will collapse during sex. People suffering from the pain of arthritis are reluctant to attempt "the more athletic forms of sexual expression."

More than 10 million Americans, most over age 65, have to deal with **urinary incontinence—urinary seepage owing to lack of bladder control.**[92] As a result of this embarrassment, many older people stop having sex for fear they will urinate during the act. However, almost all of those troubled by urinary incontinence can be helped or cured. Methods include bladder control training, scheduled urination, pelvic muscle exercises, drugs to fight infection or treat underlying physical problems, and surgery.[93]

These and other health problems of the elderly got little public attention when most people died in their 40s, in 1900. However, because of the good news—namely, that Americans are living longer—we also have some bad news: people are sicker longer. Still, as psychology writer Daniel Goleman points out, "lengthened life means that, on average, people will have more years of being well before becoming ill."[94]

● **Figure 2   Sex after 60.** Men and women engaging in frequent sex after 60 report the happiest marriages. More than a third of married couples over 60 make love once a week or more.

As we will show, many kinds of illness associated with growing older can be forestalled. Before we describe these, however, let us look at some of the psychological and social changes associated with growing older.

Psychosocial Changes of Aging

The "midlife crisis" is only one of many psychosocial turning points associated with growing older. Ideas that older workers aren't adaptable or that retired people are either wealthy or poor are myths. Some older people's attitudes affect their mental health, leading to depression, medication and alcohol abuse, and suicide, but these are not inevitable. Growing older brings new relationships with one's parents and new challenges for dealing with change and loss.

When is the happiest time of life? Interestingly, when older people are asked that, their answer is often the *retirement* years. (See ● *Figure 3.*)

Age of respondent

"I think the best years are..."

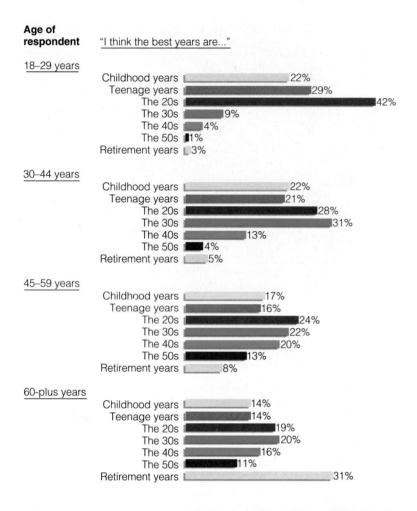

18–29 years

Childhood years 22%
Teenage years 29%
The 20s 42%
The 30s 9%
The 40s 4%
The 50s 1%
Retirement years 3%

30–44 years

Childhood years 22%
Teenage years 21%
The 20s 28%
The 30s 31%
The 40s 13%
The 50s 4%
Retirement years 5%

45–59 years

Childhood years 17%
Teenage years 16%
The 20s 24%
The 30s 22%
The 40s 20%
The 50s 13%
Retirement years 8%

60-plus years

Childhood years 14%
Teenage years 14%
The 20s 19%
The 30s 20%
The 40s 16%
The 50s 11%
Retirement years 31%

● **Figure 3   The best years of our lives.** "People feel differently about what years are the best time of a person's life. Which of these do you think are the best time of life?" People of different ages who were asked this question in a Roper Organization poll gave quite different answers. Interestingly, among older people, the best time was not the younger years but the retirement years.

Independent observers have also found older people feel psychologically better than young people, with fewer worries and higher self-esteem.[95]

Still, just as young people have some distinctive psychosocial problems—like choosing a career and a permanent companion—so do people in their middle and older years.

Middle Adulthood and Old Age "Adults hope that life begins at 40," Daniel Levinson writes, "but the great anxiety is that it ends there."[96] Levinson reported that 80% of all adults experience a midlife transition, a reassessment of their personal goals. At this important turning point, many people become depressed, despairing, and anxious, according to Levinson. They may begin to worry that they've wasted their lives and have been heading in the wrong direction.

There are indeed turning points, but sociologist John Clausen finds that many are childhood events and most come *before* the middle years.[97] Clausen surveyed people about their turning points. He asked people whether there was any time in their lives when they felt so disappointed with work or lacked satisfaction to such an extent that they thought they would "throw things over." More than 85% of the people who had passed through middle age identified one or more turning points. The most traumatic were divorce or death of a spouse, getting married, having children, and choice of first career job. "Turning points during college" were also cited as significant.

The main concerns of most middle-aged adults are earning a living, trying to make a valuable contribution, raising children. For many, another role is caring for their own elderly parents. However, many middle-aged adults view their lives positively. A 1989 survey of Americans asked several age groups whether they found life "exciting, pretty routine, or dull." Of those aged 36–41, 53% found life exciting, compared to 46% of young adults (aged 18–23) and 33% over 65.[98] People in another survey said that the middle years are years of positive growth. As many as 89% associated this period with compassion, caring, and purposeful contribution.[99]

When does middle age end and old age begin? In one national study, a majority of 1200 people survey said midlife was the period between 46 and 66.[100] Interestingly, 30% of those over 76 said they considered themselves middle-aged! Some older people speak of inner feelings of youthfulness despite physical infirmities and weaknesses that remind them of their actual age. "I feel so young inside," says one, "and yet my old body requires that I acquiesce in a role that life demands of us all."[101]

Aging, Work, and Money We have seen that episodic memory may begin to falter as one gets older and reaction times may be slower. However, judgment, accuracy, and general knowledge actually improve with age—qualities of experience that are celebrated in many cultures. Moreover, creative abilities may actually improve with age. Indeed, most artists, musicians, and writers really begin to hit their stride at midlife and continue on into their later years.

Despite these productive qualities, there are two stereotypes about older people that have to do with their work performance and financial abilities.

- *Myth—older workers aren't as adaptable:* A 1989 survey of 400 firms for the American Association of Retired Persons found that personnel managers appreciate older employees. They have work habits and a "work ethic" that include commitment to quality, company loyalty, coolness in crisis, and practical knowledge.[102] These managers did question the ability of people over 50 to adapt to new technology. But a 1991 study concluded that older workers could be retrained in new technologies. Indeed, older workers learned to use computers as quickly as younger people. They also stay on the job longer and take fewer sick days, and are often better salespeople than younger workers.[103, 104] Even so, some employers still continue to discriminate against older workers. Many older persons said they avoid searching for a job because they think nobody will hire them.

  The federal Age Discrimination in Employment Act is intended to combat this kind of *ageism—discrimination against older people.* But it is not always easy to prove that discriminatory practices have been going on.[105, 106]

- *Myths—retired people are poor/are wealthy:* Retired women workers receive less in the way of Social Security and pension benefits than men do. They get 76 cents for every dollar paid to retired male workers, according to a report by the Older Women's League. The principal reason is that women who take time off to have a child or care for an ill partner are penalized.[107]

Does this mean that retired men are not financially needy—or are they also? We keep getting two views: (1) Millions of older adults could be thrown into poverty by cuts in Social Security. (2) Older Americans are getting an outsize share of government funds, forcing the nation to shortchange others, particularly the young.[108, 109] The facts are that the poorest 20% of elderly households have an average net worth of about $3400. The top 20%—for whom the cruise ship ads are intended—are worth almost 90 times as much.[110] In other words, there is no single image of the financial standing of the aging.

From a health standpoint, it certainly makes a difference which income and education group one is in. Researchers comparing four income groups found the health of those with low education and income deteriorated most rapidly in later life. The health of those with high education and income declined comparatively slowly.[111–114]

As you might expect, the biggest difference between Americans over 65 and other adults is that they don't work. Retirement frees up 25 hours for men and 18 hours for women, on the average.[115]

Mental Health If you live to be older, you are more apt to have physical health problems. What is important for mental health, however, is people's *attitude* toward their disabilities. Some people do very well managing severe problems, while others feel overwhelmed by relatively minor ones.[116, 117]

Among some of the important mental-health indicators are depression, medication and alcohol abuse, and suicide:

- *Depression: Depression—persistent feelings of sorrow and apathy—*is considered a major health problem among older Americans. About 15% of elderly adults show signs of depression and nearly two-thirds go untreated.[118] The good news, however, is that 80% of depressed older people can be treated successfully. Therapies include counseling, antidepressant drugs, and electroshock therapy.

  The stacking of stressors in later years can be the most brutal of life, says Marvin

Rosenberg, a therapist specializing in geron-tology.[119] The transition of retirement, health deterioration, the death of friends, financial problems, and living alone may all occur quickly. Depression may be mani-fested in behavior thought to be typical of old age, such as irritability or withdrawal.

- *Medication and alcohol abuse:* Misuse of prescription and over-the-counter drugs has been called a major problem among the elderly.[120] One in five people over 60 has had an adverse reaction to a prescription drug, causing serious problems for 43% of them.[121] Some older people use long-lasting sleeping pills or tranquilizers. These med-ications can lead to drowsiness, amnesia, and dementia-like side effects that can land the user in a nursing home. They can also cause falls and hip fractures.[122–124]

  Alcohol abuse is another serious prob-lem with people in their 60s and beyond, as it is with other age groups. The prevalence of alcoholism among the elderly is estimated at 2–5%, and even higher in hospitals and health facilities. Because the elderly popula-tion is the fastest growing in the United States, there will probably be more elderly alcoholics in the next few decades.[125, 126]

- *Suicide:* A National Institutes of Mental Health study says the suicide rate among people 65 and older is 36% higher than among young adults. Another study, by the American Association of Retired Persons, says white males over 65 have a suicide rate four times the national average.[127]

  Some psychiatrists suggest that people tend to consider suicide after experiencing a series of personal losses—perhaps physi-cal health, job, spouse, or partner.

Life's Changes: Your Relationship to Your Parents Emerging from adolescence into adult-hood involves learning to interact with parents from your own vantage point, says psychoana-lyst John Oldham. Then, as you become middle-aged, you perceive your parents as being less "magically omnipotent." Finally, as parents grow old and die, children may idealize them once more. As people grow older themselves, they may see that their parents did their best and for-give their limitations and mistakes.[128]

In some families, there are adult children who never quite detach from their parents, either financially or emotionally. This may occur at the end of adolescence, when children are resisting the transition to adulthood. Or it may happen during middle age, when grown children are facing a crisis at home or at work.[129] It is best, however, if each generation can maintain a relationship of independence yet interdepen-dence with each other.

Strategy for Living: Build Yourself to Last

Most people would like to live a long time, if in good health. To avoid disabilities in later life, one should learn to manage stress, stay physically active, eat right, maintain normal weight, avoid tobacco, go easy on alcohol, and stay involved socially.

Many people would like to live to be old but are afraid of being crippled by disabilities. In a 1991 survey for the Alliance for Aging Research, two-thirds of Americans said they wanted to live to be 100. However, 75% stated they were worried about losing control of their lives in their older years. Nearly 80% said they feared ending up in a nursing home.[130]

The concern about disabilities in the later years is something you can begin to address now—by building yourself to last. The following paragraphs offer a crash course in how to pro-mote longevity and vitality and prevent many health problems to which we can become prone.

Manage Stress Think how much of people's lives is organized around trying to avoid or re-duce stress. For instance, people drink, smoke, and use drugs because they say life is too stress-ful, although these diversions actually aggravate the stresses.

As long as you live, there will never come a time when you are completely without stress. To be alive, to experience change, is to experience stress. The only real question is: Will you handle it, or will it handle you?

How do you handle stress? The answer is, with practice. Building *mental toughness,* or re-silience, comes with practice, as in learning and using the stress management techniques we describe elsewhere.

Stay Physically Active Among the truest words ever uttered are: "Use it or lose it." Being physically active seems to be the closest thing there is to an anti-aging pill. Even people who take up exercise in later life show benefits in increased strength and stamina.

It's best, however, if you've stayed active throughout your entire life. Physically the pay-offs are increased energy, stamina, flexibility, strength, and endurance. Mentally the rewards may be even better—a positive outlook and greater alertness. Older people who are physically active even score higher on intelligence tests than the less active do. The benefits of exercise also extend to what Americans say they fear most in old age—disabilities. Exercise reduces osteoporosis and heart and blood-vessel diseases, including stroke.

Eat Right Eating is indeed one of life's great pleasures. But food need not be greasy and sugary to be pleasurable. Some people have just a handful of personal eating rules to keep things simple. They won't eat red meat more than once a week. Or they stay away from any food that comes from a four-footed animal (which includes cheese and other dairy products). Or in restaurants they always ask for sauces and salad dressings to be served "on the side." Such dietary prescriptions still leave a lot of room for eating in a way that need not be boring or complicated. Salads, breads, chicken, fish, and raw fruits and vegetables will help you stay away from fat. They provide the fiber, vitamins, and minerals that help ward off heart disease, diabetes, obesity, and other afflictions of older people.

Maintain Normal Weight As you age, your metabolism slows, so if you eat and exercise the same way you always did you will *automatically* gain weight. While there's probably nothing wrong with gaining ½ pound a year after age 20, you should avoid putting on much more. Obesity not only hurts appearance and self-esteem, it also speeds premature aging and increases the risk for many health problems.

Avoid Tobacco If you smoke, you're essentially trading a minute of life for every minute you smoke. That may not sound like much to give up, but it means an average 12 years cut from life. Moreover, despite the image of virility and vitality in cigarette ads, smokers usually physically decline years before their deaths. They show everything from prematurely wrinkled skin to loss of sex drive to hacking coughs to more colds and chronic, disabling respiratory diseases.

Go Easy on the Alcohol You may be aware that heavy alcohol use impairs the liver and kidneys and is a factor in the majority of traffic deaths. What you may not know is that heavy drinking in effect pickles the brain. What if you drink 8 drinks a day for more than 20 years? According to University of Florida researchers, you may experience a 40% reduction in chemicals vital to learning and memory.[131] This will most certainly produce the diminished intellectual capacities that many people fear in conjunction with aging.

Stay Involved Socially Compared to the 1950s, adult Americans in the 1970s were less likely to be married and more likely to be living alone. They were less likely to belong to voluntary organizations and to visit informally with others. These trends, say three sociologists, will only be accelerated in the 21st century. Fewer older people will have spouses or children—the very people to whom most elders turn to for relatedness and support.[132] People with few or poor-quality relationships are less healthy, both psychologically and physically, and more likely to die sooner. It's important, therefore, that you not isolate yourself from social relationships.

Your First and Last Day of Life Today could be the last day of your life—a fact of which many older people are well aware. This knowledge also gives impetus to the corny but altogether true expression, "Today is the first day of the rest of your life."

"We love youth," says clinical psychologist Mark Gerzon and author of *Coming Into Our Own: Understanding Adult Metamorphosis.* "In America we're all in love with staying young.

That works until a certain point in life. But if you only love what's young, eventually you'll start to hate yourself."[133] The second half of your life does not mean there is no change or growth. On the contrary, it can be a time of reinvention, self-renewal, and altruism—giving something back to the community. As many have discovered, Act II of their lives may be the best part. *(See ● Figure 4.)*

● **Figure 4   Act II: Is the best yet to come?** The second half of life can be a time of reinvention, self-renewal, and altruism.

The End of Life

▶ Describe how people seem to handle feelings about death and the value of personal death awareness.

▶ Explain the different definitions of death, the definition of a coma and of a persistent vegetative state.

▶ Discuss the questions of right to die and euthanasia.

▶ Explain the different kinds of advance directives and their benefits.

▶ Discuss these death-related situations: near-death experiences, stages of adjustment to death, pain relief, hospices, feelings during impending death. Describe after-death practicalities, such as death certificates and funeral arrangements.

▶ List the four stages of mourning, describing different ways people react to grief. Discuss how you can help a person in bereavement.

I f you have a lot of unfinished business," said terminal cancer patient Howard Eckel, "maybe that's where the pain comes from dying."[134]

What is *your* unfinished business? What is it that you would devote your remaining life energy to? Your *life energy* is your allotment of time here on earth, the hours of precious life available to you.[135] Those hours could end at any time, as though you turned the next page and found the rest of the book blank. How you use your limited and irretrievable life energy expresses the meaning and purpose of your presence here on earth.

Thus, death is at the core of discovering the art of living. Despite the unpleasant associations, thinking about death forces you to consider what you want to do with your life. It also makes you come to terms with how to deal with those close to you, whose lives also will end.

In this section, we deal with the following important areas:

- Facing your feelings about death
- The definitions of death and decisions about ending life
- Making plans for your hospitalization and your death
- The process of dying
- Dealing with others' deaths
- Preparing for your own end

Your Feelings About Death

Feelings about death are often characterized by denial of the fact of death. Personal death awareness, however, represents an opportunity to put one's life in meaningful perspective.

We live in a society that conditions us to deny death. Most Americans no longer die at home. Seventy percent, in fact, die in hospitals, nursing homes, and extended-care facilities.[136] Often in such places death is considered the enemy, and people cling to their degenerating bodies hoping for some miraculous medical turnaround. Children and the rest of us are exposed to mock death thousands of times a day on television. Yet we are rarely at the bedside when a grandparent or relative dies. With more cremations and fewer open-casket funerals, it is possible to go one's whole life without seeing a dead person. If, at some point, death rudely inserts itself into our lives, it may register itself simply by a person's *absence.* Literally, they are here today, gone tomorrow, as when someone is killed in a car crash.

Death and Denial When we do have to think about death, it evokes "a murky swirl of emotions: terror, sadness, anxiety," as one writer says. "The more we try to counteract the natural deterioration of the body and the more attached we become to our accomplishments and our possessions, the more we dread our own demise."[137] And the more we are apt to deny that it can happen to us. A reasonable amount of denial is useful and helps us get through day-to-day difficulties. But excessive denial of death—as in smoking cigarettes or driving fast without seat belts—can actually hasten our own end. To

examine your own feelings about death, you may wish to take the accompanying Self Discovery. *(See Self Discovery 1.)*

Personal Death Awareness: An Opportunity Where does the recent interest in *danger sports*—mountain climbing, hang gliding, sky diving, and the like—come from? One writer suggests these "may all be ways we have of tricking ourselves into the present." Focusing on death is a way of becoming fully alive, for wherever attention and awareness are, that is what we experience. He goes on:

> *Many say they "feel so alive" when doing these sports because they demand attention. Perhaps that is why so many who are dying also say they have never felt so alive. When we take death within us we stop reinforcing our denial, our judging, our anger, or continuing our bargaining. We don't push our depression away.*[138]

***Personal death awareness*—accepting the fact that you are going to die**—is an opportunity to confront your life. You can try to put it into meaningful perspective. Some matters you might want to try to deal with:

- ***How would I like my epitaph to read?* Many gravestones or monuments have no *epitaphs*, or inscriptions,** just birth and death dates. However, some express the best memories the survivors have of the person. How would you like to be remembered on your monument? Your proposed death inscription could actually become your words to *live* by.

- ***What would I want an obituary or eulogy to say about me?*** Writing your own ***obituary notice*—a short account of your life,** like those published in the newspaper death notices—can be useful. It becomes a statement of your life purpose and how you would like to be remembered. Or write your own imaginary ***eulogy*, the kind of speech or praise given about the deceased at a memorial service.**

- ***Make a list to avoid aimlessness:*** All life journeys end at the same place. The difficulty lies in figuring out what events, depending on the choices available to you, you want your journey to include. If aimlessness suits you, that's fine, but realize that

SELF DISCOVERY 1

How Do You Feel About Death?

This questionnaire is not designed to test your knowledge. Instead, it should encourage you to think about your present attitudes toward death and how these attitudes may have developed.

Answer the questions to the best of your knowledge by circling the appropriate letter.

1. Who died in your first personal involvement with death?
   a. Grandparent, great-grandparent
   b. Parent
   c. Brother or sister
   d. Other family member
   e. Friend or acquaintance
   f. Stranger, or public figure
   g. Animal
2. To the best of your memory, at what age were you first aware of death?
   a. Under 3
   b. 3–5
   c. 6–10
   d. 11 or older
3. When you were a child, how was death talked about in your family?
   a. Openly
   b. With some sense of discomfort
   c. Only when necessary, with an attempt to exclude children
   d. As though it were a taboo subject
   e. Never recall any discussion
4. Which of the following best describes your childhood conceptions of death?
   a. Heaven-and-hell concept
   b. After-life
   c. Death as sleep
   d. No physical or mental activity
   e. Mysterious and unknowable
   f. Something other than the above
   g. No conception, or can't remember
5. To what extent do you believe in life after death?
   a. Strongly believe in it
   b. Tend to believe it
   c. Uncertain
   d. Tend to doubt it
   e. Convinced it does not exist
6. Regardless of your belief about life after death, what is your wish about it?
   a. I strongly wish there were a life after death.
   b. I am indifferent.
   c. I definitely prefer that there not be a life after death.
7. Has there been a time in your life when you wanted to die?
   a. Yes, mainly because of great physical pain
   b. Yes, mainly because of great emotional upset
   c. Yes, mainly to escape an intolerable social or interpersonal situation
   d. Yes, mainly because of great embarrassment
   e. Yes, for a reason other than above
   f. No
8. What does death mean to you?
   a. The end, the final process of life
   b. The beginning of a life after death; a transition, a new beginning
   c. A joining of the spirit with a universal cosmic consciousness

d. An endless sleep; rest and peace
   e. Termination of this life but with survival of the spirit
   f. Don't know
   g. Other (specify)
9. What aspect of your own death is the most distasteful to you?
   a. I could have no experiences.
   b. I am afraid of what might happen to my body after death.
   c. I am uncertain as to what might happen if there is life after death.
   d. I could no longer provide for my dependents.
   e. It would cause grief to my relatives and friends.
   f. All my plans and projects would come to an end.
   g. The dying process may be painful.
   h. Other (specify)
10. How is your present physical health?
    a. Excellent
    b. Very good
    c. Moderately good
    d. Moderately poor
    e. Extremely bad
11. How is your present mental health?
    a. Excellent
    b. Very good
    c. Moderately good
    d. Moderately poor
    e. Extremely bad
12. Based on your present feelings, what is the probability of your taking your own life in the near future?
    a. Extremely high (I feel very much like killing myself)
    b. Moderately high
    c. Between high and low
    d. Moderately low
    e. Extremely low (very improbable)
13. In your opinion, at what age are people most afraid of death?
    a. Up to 12 years
    b. 13–19 years
    c. 20–29 years
    d. 30–39 years
    e. 40–49 years
    f. 50–59 years
    g. 60–69 years
    h. 70 years and over
14. When you think of your own death (or mortality), how do you feel?
    a. Fearful
    b. Discouraged
    c. Depressed
    d. Purposeless
    e. Resolved, in relation to life
    f. Pleasure in being alive
    g. Other (specify)

15. What is your present orientation to your own
death?
    a. Death-seeker
    b. Death-hastener
    c. Death-accepter
    d. Death-welcomer
    e. Death-postponer
    f. Death-fearer
16. If you were told that you had a limited time to
live, how would you want to spend your time until
you died?
    a. I would change my lifestyle; satisfy hedonistic
needs (travel, sex, drugs, other experiences).
    b. I would become more withdrawn, reading, con-
templating, or praying.

c. I would shift from my own needs to a concern
for others (family, friends).
d. I would attempt to complete projects, tie up
loose ends.
e. I would make little or no change in my lifestyle.
f. I would try to do one very important thing.
g. I might consider suicide.
h. I would do none of these.

17. How do you feel about having an autopsy done on
your body?
    a. Approve
    b. Don't care one way or the other
    c. Disapprove
    d. Strongly disapprove

In one sentence, state what feelings you felt while filling out this questionnaire.

_____

_____

Now examine your attitudes toward death and discuss your feelings with classmates, friends, and family. Although we read about death in the newspapers every day, we rarely come in close contact with it. By completing this questionnaire, you are taking a step toward facing the reality of death.

Source: Edwin Schneidman. (1970, August). You and death questionnaire. *Psychology Today.*

aimlessness is a choice like any other. Perhaps making a list of all the things you'd like
to do and places you'd like to see will help
focus you. Or list the two or three important
things you'd like to do if you had only a year
to live. Don't forget to include people in
your plans—how you would like to treat and
be treated by people important to you. And
in focusing on the future, don't neglect the
present: enjoying sunsets, birds, music, a
meal with a friend—simple pleasures.

Some day the tomorrows will stop rolling in.
Within the limits of your mortality, you must determine the art of living for yourself.

What Are the Definitions of Death, and Who Decides Who Dies?

Death is defined in different ways: cessation of heart and lungs, cellular death,
brain death, and cortical death. In between
life and death is coma and a persistent
vegetative state. This state raises the
question of who should decide when a person should die and whether suicide should
be allowed. Euthanasia, or "mercy killing,"
may be either passive or active.

Technology has changed all our ways of dealing
with death—everything except our feelings
about it. Medical devices have become more
sophisticated, permitting critically ill persons,
even those in a coma, to be kept alive for years.
Thus "the definition of death edges closer to
life," as one writer points out.[139]

Definitions of Death Religions consider death
to be a spiritual event, the moment when the
soul leaves the body. However, death is also a
medical and legal event—and the definition of it
keeps changing. Consider:

- **Heart and lungs cease:** Not so long ago,
a physician had to let a person's heart stop,

completely on its own, before death could be declared.[140] At the same time, or shortly before, the lungs would also have ceased to function. The lack of heartbeat and breathing is determined by feeling for a pulse or listening through a stethoscope. It is one of the classical clinical signs of death.

- *Cellular death:* In earlier eras, some cultures considered putrefaction the only acceptable proof of death.[141] This, of course, takes time, for cells can live on for a little while. Indeed, they often do, if an organ is transplanted to another human's body. Still, the presence of *rigor mortis,* **when the body shows rigidity, indicates that the body has experienced cellular death.** That is, the cells in tissues and organs are no longer functioning.

- *Brain death:* The brain can continue to function for a short time (perhaps 10 minutes or less) after the heartbeat ceases. However, **a person who has irreversibly lost all brain function may be considered legally dead—declared** *brain dead*—despite a heart beat.

    Brain death is indicated by the absence (flat line) of brain-wave activity on a device called an electroencephalograph. An *electroencephalograph (EEG)* **is an instrument that records the electrical activity of the brain, using electrodes attached to the scalp.** To declare a person brain-dead, a physician must find brain-wave activity absent on the first measurement and then again 24 hours later.

- *Cortical death: Cortical death,* **also called** *cerebral* **or** *cognitive death,* **means that the person is brain dead, except the brain stem is still functioning. The** *brain stem,* **or** *medulla,* **is the part of the brain that controls breathing and heartbeat.** Cortical death is a new criterion of death that is being discussed but has not been legally accepted.

    If cortical death is accepted, a person could be declared dead whose breathing, heartbeat, blood pressure, temperature, and other signs were normal. The person would show no detectable brain waves—no evidence of cerebral cortex function. The *cerebral cortex* **is that part of the brain responsible for higher brain functions such as thought, memory, love, and voluntary muscle movement.**[142]

Persistent Vegetative State: Loss of Consciousness and Personhood Nancy Cruzan was 25 years old when her car overturned on a country road, and it was 15 or 20 minutes before paramedics could restart her heart. That was long enough to deprive her brain of oxygen. For almost 8 years, Cruzan was kept alive by a feeding tube implanted in her abdomen. Though she could breathe, her mind was obliterated. After several years of legal efforts by her parents, the U.S. Supreme Court ruled that the feeding tube could be disconnected. Cruzan died at the age of 33.[143–148] The court's ruling gives urgency to having a "living will" or other advance directive about what you want done should you become incapacitated.

Cruzan, doctors said, was in a persistent vegetative state, which is not the same as a coma:

- *Coma:* **A** *coma* **is a state of profound unconsciousness. People sometimes awaken from a coma.**

- *PVS:* **People in a** *persistent vegetative state (PVS)* **are completely paralyzed and show no signs of awareness or reflexes. Yet they have sleep-wake cycles, can often breathe on their own after having artificial respiration, and have all the normal vital signs.** They do not, however, show evidence of consciousness.[149] There are 15,000–25,000 PVS people, according to one report.[150]

Under the definition of cortical death, Nancy Cruzan and other PVS victims are not actually alive but already dead. "Once consciousness is irreversibly lost, the person is lost," says one psychiatrist, Stuart Youngner, who advocates the definition of cortical death. "What remains is a mindless organism."[151] The loss of personhood, he says, "leaves only a body that has outlived its owner."

Reporter Mark Dowie, who investigated the matter of PVS and cortical death, asked everyone he interviewed a troubling question: How do we know that PVS victims are not experiencing some form of consciousness, even bliss, that existing technology cannot describe? The unanimous answer is: We don't.

In that case, asks Dowie, do we have the right to declare them dead, simply to remove the emotional and economic burden of keeping them alive?[152] Once again, such questions urge us to guard our close relatives from years of emotional turmoil and economic catastrophe. It is imperative to communicate clear instructions now on what we want done should we be in a PVS or similar state.

The Right to Die: Who Should Decide?
Seemingly miraculous cures do happen. Patients in comas do sometimes come out of them. Resuscitation does bring back patients whose hearts have stopped. However, many doctors think that resuscitation is wasteful, painful, and brutal to patients who are chronically sick, very elderly, or terminally ill.[153]

From one viewpoint, marvelous medical technology prolongs living. From another, it prolongs dying. But who should decide who has the right to live or die—the patient's family, the physicians, the courts? Many doctors believe that consulting with the family is important. But they also believe that giving the family ultimate authority in do-not-resuscitate and similar life-support measures is a mistake. *(See ● Figure 5.)*

Medical ethicist Bruce Hilton states that a key word in whether or not to remove life-support equipment is *futile*. "If the treatment isn't working, and clearly isn't going to," he says, "doctors have no legal, moral, or professional obligation to keep it up."[154] If the medical treatment is futile, then the physician is under no obligation to continue it, even if the patient wants to go on. However, sometimes extending futile treatment may be justified for a short time.

According to the Patient Self-Determination Act, hospitals must advise all patients admitted of their right to sign "advance directives" for health-care decisions. The directives include whether one wants to be kept on life-support. We describe this in detail in another few pages. Of course, a patient who is brought to an emergency room unconscious is in no position to sign an advance directive.

Euthanasia: The Question of Mercy *Euthanasia,* **sometimes called "mercy killing," is any method of causing death to**

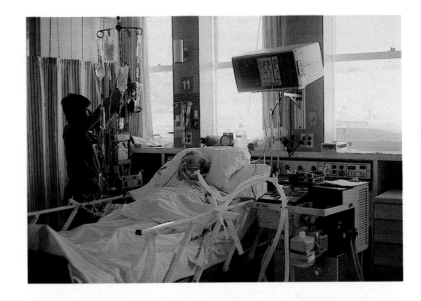

● **Figure 5   A patient on life support: Who decides the right to die?** Respirators, feeding tubes, intravenous fluids, and other technology can prolong living or prolong dying. Who should decide if and when such life-sustaining equipment should be removed—the family, the physicians, or the courts?

"*Typically, nobody knows what the patient would want because everyone was so good at denying their mortality. Family members are divided because they still don't want to face it. And you have heart-rending waiting-room scenes with hopeful loved ones rising and falling on the ebb and flow of the doomed patient's good days and bad days. What's a success or failure at the end of life? Everyone is distraught and afraid. And we're living in a horror movie that doesn't end after two weeks, let alone two hours.*"

—Poughkeepsie, New York, physician Donald E. Berman. Quoted in: Malcolm, A. H. (1991, November 29). Decisions about life and death. *New York Times*, p. A16.

a desperately ill patient. There are two types of euthanasia, passive and active:

- *Passive euthanasia—allowing someone to die: Passive euthanasia* **is withholding life-sustaining aid or life-saving techniques.** For example, physicians or nurses might disconnect respirators or tube feeders, or not use drugs that could continue life. Or they may not exercise life-saving techniques such as cardiopulmonary resuscitation (CPR).

- *Active euthanasia—intentionally inflicting death:* **Active euthanasia, sometimes called "assisted suicide," involves someone administering lethal drugs or poison or in some other way ending the patient's life.** The person assisting may be a physician or a relative, and the means used may be depressants, potassium chloride, or carbon monoxide. This is murder when it is not done by the patient's own hand.

     In recent years, physician Jack Kevorkian became famous for helping set up the equipment and chemicals for "suicide machines." With these, severely ill patients, such as Alzheimer's disease or multiple sclerosis victims, could press a button and take their own lives.[155–161] Most such incidents took place in Michigan, which for a time had no law specifically barring assistance in a suicide.

The American Hospital Association estimates that 70% of the 6000 daily deaths in the United States are already somehow timed or negotiated. Medical technology is withdrawn or not applied at all—what could be called forms of passive euthanasia.[162] Yet some physicians have admitted, nearly always anonymously, that they actually helped patients commit suicide.[163, 164] One who spoke for the record was Timothy Quill. Quill said that he had prescribed enough barbiturates to kill to a 45-year-old leukemia patient and had told her the size of a lethal dose.[165] A New York grand jury declined to indict the doctor for the crime of aiding in a suicide. The crime carries a prison sentence of up to 15 years.[166] In the Netherlands, where euthanasia is illegal but widely tolerated, a study showed that doctors deliberately caused about 1.8% of all deaths. The doctors acted on their patients' orders, typically cancer patients in their early 60s.[167, 168]

As might be expected, physicians in many circumstances are torn. Their Hippocratic oath demands they prolong life in all instances. That sometimes conflicts with alleviating pain and suffering and extending the quality of life if hope is nonexistent.[169–173]

Suicide Perhaps severe or terminal illness has always been a reason for suicide. Recently it has even taken the form of a self-help movement and made Derek Humphry's controversial suicide guide, *Final Exit,* a bestseller.[174] No one knows what proportion of suicides are motivated by illness. But the American Hospital Association gives one example: every year 12,000 of the 80,000 patients on artificial kidney machines voluntarily quit, bringing about a self-inflicted end within 2 weeks.[175]

Leaders of the country's largest Christian groups, the Roman Catholic Church and the Southern Baptist Convention, oppose all forms of euthanasia or suicide. However, religious advocates, mostly from liberal and mainline Protestant churches, express affirmation for individual choice in such matters.[176] The courts, at least in one Florida case, state that dying people have a right to refuse food. Thus they need not have a court's approval to stop forced feeding.[177]

Choosing Death: The Importance of Making Plans

To avoid becoming a not-quite-living burden to yourself or your family, it's advisable to write an advance directive giving instructions about resuscitation and use of life-support equipment. This can take the form of a living will, a health-care proxy, or a durable power of attorney. Organ-donor cards and wills should also be considered.

Modern medicine can extend our lives, but it can also make the end of our lives a living—or not-quite-living—hell. Both patients and families suffer. Thus everyone, even young people, should give clear instructions about what types of treatment they do and do not want. Give instructions in writing and in as much detail as possible to family, friends, and doctors. These instructions, known as **advance directives** or **medical directives, allow you to specify how much or how little treatment you want. They also allow you to designate a family member or friend to make decisions on your behalf** if you become too ill.

Under the Patient Self-Determination Act, all patients over age 18 must be informed of their right to fill out an advance directive. The law applies to virtually all hospitals, nursing homes, and health-maintenance organizations. (You are not required to have one, only to be advised of your *right* to have one.)

Advance directives may include living wills, health-care proxies, and durable power of attorney for health care. These documents vary from state to state, and it's important to comply with state law. *(See ● Figure 6.)* In some cases, patients who have said they did *not* want "heroic treatment" have nevertheless been kept on life-support systems.[178] This is because the living wills in many states become effective only when you are in a "terminal" condition. That could exclude people with PVS. Other state living wills allow the withdrawal of tube feeding only under very limited conditions, regardless of a patient's preference.

In this section we discuss:

- Living wills
- Health-care proxies
- Durable power of attorney for health care forms
- Organ donor card
- Wills

Living Will **A *living will* specifies what treatments you would or would not want if you become irreversibly incapacitated and dependent on life-sustaining equipment.** Some people may want to specify that they actually want *any* type of treatment available, and it's important to spell this out. The issue here is about choice, not about "pulling the plug."[179]

Some living-will forms allow you to state you do not want "heroic" treatment measures taken, but it's better to be specific. You can state whether you do or don't want cardiac resuscitation, mechanical respiration, tube feeding, kidney dialysis, or antibiotics. You can ask for painkilling drugs, or to be allowed to die at home.[180] Specifically, the measures you can decide about are the following.

- ***Cardiac resuscitation:*** Cardiac resuscitation includes measures to stimulate a stopped heart or to regulate aberrant heart rhythms. It includes the use of chest compressions, electrical shock, intravenous insertion of a pacemaker, and medications like epinephrine.

A Living Will

This living will applies to New York State. Forms for other states are available from Choice in Dying, 200 Varick St., 10th floor, New York, NY 10014-4810.

I, _____, being of sound mind, make this statement as a directive to be followed if I become permanently unable to participate in decisions regarding my medical care. These instructions reflect my firm and settled commitment to decline medical treatment under the circumstances indicated below:

I direct my attending physician to withhold or withdraw treatment that merely prolongs my dying, if I should be in an incurable or irreversible mental or physical condition with no reasonable expectation of recovery.

These instructions apply if I am (a) in a terminal condition; (b) permanently unconscious, or (c) if I am minimally conscious but have irreversible brain damage and will never regain the ability to make decisions and express my wishes.

I direct that treatment be limited to measures to keep me comfortable and to relieve pain, including any pain that might occur by withholding or withdrawing treatment.

While I understand that I am not legally required to be specific about future treatments, if I am in the condition(s) described above I feel especially strongly about the following forms of treatment:
I do not want cardiac resuscitation.
I do not want mechanical respiration.
I do not want artificial nutrition and hydration.
I do not want antibiotics.

However, I *do want* maximum pain relief, even if it may hasten my death.
Other directions (insert personal instructions):
These directions express my legal right to refuse treatment, under the law of New York. I intend my instructions to be carried out, unless I have rescinded them in a new writing or by clearly indicating that I have changed my mind.

Signed: _____ Date: _____
Witness: _____
Address: _____
Witness: _____
Address: _____

● **Figure 6** **Advance directives.** Example of a living will. This is for New York State.

Some doctors think that cardiac resuscitation is misapplied and overused. Only 5–15% of patients on whom resuscitation is attempted will survive to leave the hospital.[181] Nevertheless, under existing law physicians must make the effort even if they think it's useless, as on people with widespread cancer. The exception is for patients who have formally signed a "Do Not Resuscitate" (DNR) form or indicated this in a living will.

In some localities, paramedics will respect the wishes of people wearing leg or arm bands that say "Do Not Resuscitate." Usually the patient is in the last stages of life.

- *Mechanical respiration:* Mechanical respiration or artificial ventilation is used if a patient stops breathing or is unable to get enough oxygen to the organs. Generally, a respirator is used that forces oxygen into the lungs through a tube inserted through the nose or mouth.

- *Tube feeding:* For patients incapable of feeding themselves, nutrition is given intravenously or through a feeding tube into the stomach.

- *Antibiotics and painkillers:* Antibiotics and certain other medicines previously prescribed may be continued or withheld, according to your wishes. You can also state whether or not you want maximum pain relief.

Living wills vary from state to state. You can get the right one from a local hospital, financial planner, or stationery store. Or request one (no charge) from Concern for Dying/Society for the Right to Die (250 West 57th Street, New York, NY 10017). The document should be signed in the presence of two witnesses. Neither can be a potential heir or the attending doctor, nurse, or health-care facility employee. Some states require that the living will be notarized. Give copies to your immediate family, doctor, and anyone else involved. To keep the documents legally binding, they should be signed (and if necessary notarized) again every couple of years.[182] You can also send your living will to Concern for Dying to be recorded in their computerized Living Will Registry. You will get a wallet-size plastic mini-will with the registry number printed on it.

In some counties, people are permitted to wear "Do Not Resuscitate" arm or leg bands.

Health-Care Proxy A *health-care proxy* **form appoints an agent—friend or family member—to act for you in health-care matters if you become incapacitated.** It is often included within a living will. You should also indicate someone else as a backup, in case your first choice cannot be available. Laws regarding health-care proxies also vary from state to state and may give only limited powers. They may en-

able the agent to act for a person with terminal illness but not a person in a coma or with Alzheimer's disease, for example.

Durable Power of Attorney A more inclusive document than the health-care proxy is **the durable power of attorney for health care decisions. This document permits your representative to act for you in most health-care matters,** including those you might not have considered. Thus you can control your own affairs through your own agent—again, a friend or family member. The alternative is relying on a court to appoint a conservator. This form, which should be completed along with a living will, is also available from Concern for Dying.

Organ-Donor Forms There is currently a great need for organs, so great that in California half the patients waiting for transplants die before getting an organ. Many of these are children.[183]

Because of medical technology, many parts of the body can be transplanted: heart, lungs, kidneys, liver, pancreas, corneas, ligaments, tendons, bone, skin, heart valves, veins, and the tiny bones of the middle ear.[184] If you die as a result of an auto or motorcycle accident, murder, or other tragedy, you can still help someone else. It might comfort your survivors to know you helped a person with a bad heart to survive or a child to see. An organ-donor card is available at state motor-vehicle departments (or from The Living Bank, POB 6725, Houston, TX 77265). It should be filled out, signed with two witnesses, and attached to the back of your driver's license or identification card. *(See ● Figure 7.)*

Will Some people become quite involved with "taking care of their affairs" in the event of their death. But complicated estate planning, living trusts, and the like are not essential. However, you *should* have a will, particularly if there are family changes. Marriage, divorce, the birth of a child, or death of a prospective heir should be addressed in a will. If you die without a will—what is called *intestate*—the state's laws take over. The decisions that are made then about disposal of your property or other wishes might not be as you would have liked.

If you own property, are married, or have children, you should probably hire a lawyer to do the will. By telephoning different lawyers, you can find out what the rates are—often they are not expensive. Or, you can do a **holographic will, which is written entirely in ink in your own hand. It specifies who you wish to have your property and who should raise your children,** if any. You can also specify any funeral arrangements you want. Designate a family member or friend as the executor, who will carry out your wishes.

Surviving Others' Mortality: Dying and Death

Because you may be present when someone you know dies, you should be knowledgeable about a number of death-related situations: near-death experiences, Kübler-Ross's five stages of adjustment to death, telling dying people the truth, giving relief from pain, dying in a hospice or at home, and dealing with feelings during impending death. You may also be associated with certain practicalities after death: death certificate, autopsy, organ donation, and funeral arrangements.

It is possible you will not be a witness to your own passing, that you will be blessed with a sudden, virtually painless end. But before that day, you may well be caught up in the dying of family members or friends. That involves you in events that you can't control and that are tremendously saddening but that call upon you to give comfort and assist in making decisions. There are important lessons here.

In this section, we will describe the following:

- Near-death experiences
- The emotional stages of dying
- The final days—including pain relief, hospice care, and autopsies
- Grieving, including for children
- Death rituals, including funerals and wakes

Near-Death Experience What is it like, really like, to die? Since most people die only once, we

---

UNIFORM DONOR CARD

of_____
Print or type name of donor
In the hope that I may help others, I hereby make this anatomical gift, if medically acceptable, to take effect upon death. The words and marks below indicate my wishes:
I give: (a)_____any needed organs or parts
(b)_____only the following organs or parts
_____
Specify the organ(s), tissue(s), or part(s)
for the purposes of transplantation, therapy, medical research or education;
(c)_____my body for anatomical study if needed.

Limitations or special wishes, if any:_____

● **Figure 7 Organ-donor card.**

"*Dear Abby: Last May, our 22-year-old son, Michael, was involved in a motorcycle accident. He was pronounced brain dead three days later. Because of an article he had read in your column, he carried an organ donor card in his wallet.*

The lord took our precious son 10 days later, but we were comforted knowing that Michael gave two blind people the gift of sight, and a young father who had been on a kidney machine for three years is now living a normal life. . . ."

Michael's Father

—Letter to columnist "Dear Abby" (Abigail Van Buren). (1990, April 23). Gifts of life from son's death. *San Francisco Chronicle*, p. F10.

can't be sure. There is, however, a highly exclusive group of people who have had a **near-death experience (NDE). Most are people whose hearts had stopped but who were brought back, usually through the intervention of medical technology.**

A study by Kenneth Ring of over 100 NDEers found that all shared some core experiences: They had an out-of-body experience, during which one seems to float above one's body, viewing surrounding activities and hearing conversations. They had a feeling of well-being and peace. They reported a movement into darkness or a tunnel, discovering a bright light, and deciding to enter that light. They make a decision to either move toward death or to return to life to complete unfinished business. There was a feeling of sadness upon leaving this blissful dimension.[185] People also report meeting dead relatives, historical religious figures, or beings of light and undergoing a reevaluation of the events in their lives.[186]

According to Ring, "while the process of dying may be scary as we contemplate the end of everything, what we enter into at the moment of death is so magnificent, so beautiful, so full of love, that it's a very powerful source of hope and comfort."[187] Some believe that the near-death experience is a glimpse of the afterlife or of past lives.[188] Neurologists may consider NDEs hallucinations of a dying brain.[189] Researchers Justine Owens, Ian Stevenson, and Emily Cook reported the experiences of 30 people who merely thought they were going to die. They were remarkably similar to the experiences of 28 people who were in fact desperately ill. The similarity suggests both physiological and psychological causes of NDE.[190]

The Emotional Stages of Dying The final act may bring "intense feelings of joy, love, and peace," as Raymond Moody put it in his book *Life After Life.*[191] But getting there, particularly if it is a slow process as for someone with a terminal illness, can be agonizing. Based on observations of dying patients, psychiatrist Elisabeth Kübler-Ross described five stages of feelings or behavior that she says constitute adjustment to death.[192] *(See ● Figure 8.)*

- *Stage 1—Denial ("No, not me; it cannot be true"):* Told that he or she is going to die, a terminally ill patient will first show *denial*—disbelief. Patients will refuse to acknowledge their condition, and may visit several physicians and perhaps alternative healers (such as faith healers). Denial may actually be helpful because it allows patients to gather their resources for the challenging and sometimes grim days to come.

- *Stage 2—Anger ("Why me?"):* Patients now begin to feel resentment, that they've been cheated. In *anger* they vent their fears, frustration, and rage about their impending death against relatives, doctors, and nurses.

If you are trying to give comfort to a dying person, this is where you can offer solace and patience.

- *Stage 3—Bargaining ("Get me through this, God [or Doctor], and I'll give half my money to the church [or hospital]"):* In this stage, the patient may try to *bargain*—perhaps with God, a religious leader, or even their doctor. In return for the extension of life he or she will promise good behavior. Some people undergo religious conversions at this time.

- *Stage 4—Depression ("All I can do is wait for the bitter end"):* The stage of *depression* is one of grieving for one's anticipated death. The grief is also for the loss of friends and loved ones and of unfinished work. Sighing, crying, and prolonged periods of silence are to be expected.

If you are trying to offer comfort to someone dying you can simply listen, not trying to cheer him or her up. If the patient shows signs of wanting to be alone, you should respect it.

- *Stage 5—Acceptance ("This is the final rest before the long journey"):* In *acceptance,* the final stage, the person is psychologically ready to die, seeing the moment as inevitable. He or she does not wish news of the outside world, even news of a new treatment that might prolong life. Kübler-Ross says this stage "is almost void of feelings. It is as if the pain had gone, the struggle is over, and there comes a time for 'the final rest before the long journey' as one patient phrased it."[193]

The person may ask to see only a few friends or visitors as he or she begins separating from the present. If so, you can honor those wishes. If you are the principal companion, you may be the one the dying person wishes to have for support.

Just as life is not simple, neither is death. Not all people proceed through these stages in just this way. Some people skip some stages, some stages may occur at the same time, some may not occur in the order given here. And throughout the process, denial may return from time to time. The way people face death is very much the way they face life: the same skills, or lack of them, that they bring to bear on life problems will apply here.

Family and close friends may well go through many of the same kinds of emotions as the dying person. They may experience denial, anger, bargaining, depression, and finally acceptance. If someone close to you is in the process of dying, you should be alert to these feelings within yourself as well.

Leveling: Telling a Dying Person the News
At one time, in the 1950s, doctors were encouraged to withhold bad news from terminal patients and to tell a relative instead. The reasoning was that, if told directly, the patient might be shocked, agitated, or depressed. As a result, he or she might have a heart attack, stop eating, or commit suicide. Now doctors realize that withholding information impairs their communication with their patients. It also prevents people from making choices, puts nurses and family on the spot, and exposes doctors to malpractice suits. Worse, says ethicist Bruce Hilton, this silence leaves patients to perform their leave-taking, perhaps the most important moment of their life, all alone.[194]

Many patients are usually less worried about dying than they are about being abandoned or suffering intractable pain, says one physician. When reassured on these two counts, they deal well with approaching death.[195] The National Institute on Aging also found that patients are less afraid of death than of pain and chronic disability.[196]

Dying and Pain Perhaps the greatest fear associated with dying is the prospect of having to endure nearly endless, unrelieved pain. A great deal of the time, however, pain is not present. A study of older men and women found that 61% were free of pain on the day they died and over half died in their sleep without pain.[197] Moreover, the majority were in good health the year preceding their deaths.

Terminal patients often do experience a fair amount of physical pain, but nowadays physicians are more conscious of this. They used to give painkilling drugs only when the patient asked for them. Doctors now usually prescribe drugs that are delivered in ongoing, timed doses or by constant infusion.

Hospices and Homes **A *hospice* is a facility or program designed to provide medical**

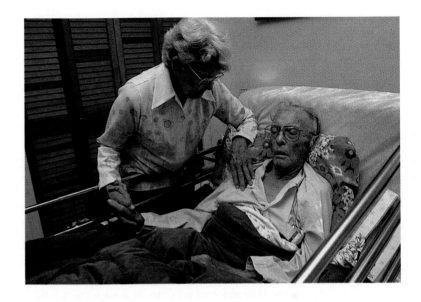

Figure 8   Kübler-Ross's five stages of adjustment to death.

and emotional care for terminally ill people. It may be part of a hospital but more often is a separate facility entirely or an at-home program. Most hospitals are designed to provide short-term treatment rather than long-term maintenance.

In recent years, specialized hospices for AIDS patients have been established.[198, 199] The staff consists of physicians and nurses, social workers, mental-health and spiritual counselors, and others as needed. Volunteers are widely used, and visiting hours flexible. The hospice tries to make the patient's last days as comfortable and pain-free as possible.

More people find dying at home a welcome alternative to clinical settings and to ending their lives around strangers. However, most families have not had the experience of our forebears of "sitting with the dying." They will have the physical and emotional strain of cleaning, changing, and comforting someone they love. Thus, it becomes important for care-givers to learn how to use formal support, such as hospice services, home health aides, and social workers. They need to find support systems to take care of their own needs so that they can effectively administer to their loved ones.[200]

Dealing with Feelings During Impending Death Care-givers are whipsawed by emotions, many of which correspond to those people in bereavement must handle. If, for instance, your parent is dying, you and other family members may reassess your relationships with the dying parent and each other. "It is a chance to resolve loose ends before it is too late," says one writer. "Knowing that they will soon die often makes parents more willing to discuss topics that had previously been avoided and to reconnect with estranged children."[201] Even close-knit families have many things they wish to settle. Public-health professor Robert Veninga says many people wish they had been able to thank their parents before they died.[202]

Parents who are seriously ill themselves may also have to deal with telling their young children about their disease. The temptation may be to avoid discussing serious illness or impending surgery—to protect children and not worry them. However, children prefer to know rather than be threatened by the unknown.[203]

After Death: The Practicalities After a person dies, there are a number of matters that close family members will have to deal with. Unfortunately, they come at a time of considerable emotional turmoil.

- *Death certificate:* A physician or medical examiner will need to fill out and sign a death certificate. The certificate showing the cause of death and disposition of the body must be filled out and filed with local authorities.

- *Autopsy:* If there is uncertainty about the cause of death, an autopsy will be performed. This is done to gather evidence, in case there is a criminal or legal proceeding.

An *autopsy* **is a medical examination of the body after death, which may include the removal of some organs for study.**

- *Arrange for donations of organs, if necessary:* If there is no autopsy and the deceased has filled out the Uniform Donor Card or its equivalent, make arrangements quickly. A medical school or organ bank can have the organs recovered for surgical transplantation to someone else.

- *Notify all who need to know:* If you are in charge of handling the death arrangements, you or someone you designate will need to telephone family members. Also call close friends, employer, and all others who should be notified personally. You should write an obituary, including time and place of any memorial service, and send it to the newspapers.

- *Make arrangements for disposition of the body:* The deceased may have made arrangements to donate his or her body to a medical school to advance medical science. Otherwise, most people opt to be disposed of in two principal ways:

(1) *Burial,* the method of disposition of perhaps 80% of bodies, usually requires the purchase of a cemetery plot. Or the body may be *entombed* in above-ground cemetery structures called mausoleums.[204] Most graves are lined with concrete, brick, metal, or other materials, which help protect groundwater.

(2) *Cremation* is now used in about 17% of deaths, up from 11% 10 years ago.[205] *Cremation* **consists of burning a body at very high temperature (up to 2200°F) until what's left are large bone fragments.** The bones are usually pulverized into sandlike grains (called the "cremains") for storage in an urn. Ashes may be scattered (state laws permitting), buried, or entombed in vaultlike areas called niches.

At $200–$500, cremation is considerably cheaper than burial, which averages about $5200 when embalming, funeral services, and burial plot and marker are included.[206] (With services and burial plot and marker, cremation averages $2400.)

Funeral Services and Memorial Societies
In 41 states, a family has the right to handle all the death arrangements of their deceased without a funeral director. Still, as one woman who handled the burial arrangements for her husband pointed out, "Not everyone is inclined—or even able—to build a casket, transport a body, or even, at a time of grief, assemble the information needed for a death certificate or an obituary."[207] Funeral directors (morticians) provide these services.

Besides helping to take care of the paperwork of death certificates and obituaries, funeral directors offer the following services.

- *Embalming:* **The process of injecting fluids containing formaldehyde into the circulatory system to replace blood is** *embalming.* **It was once promoted as a defense against the spread of disease (long since discredited).** Embalming came about because, at a time when refrigeration was not available, it preserved bodies for later viewing by family members and friends. This is still its principal purpose.

  The average cost of embalming, which is optional (except under certain circumstances), is $226. Other preparations for viewing, such as hairdressing and cosmetology, average about $90.

- *Rituals—visiting hours, funeral service, and burial ceremony:* The funeral home will make available a private room for visiting hours or calling hours. At those times family and friends may view the body (if the casket is open) or pay their respects to the dead person.

  A funeral service or religious service may take place a few days after death. It is usually in a church or in a chapel within the funeral home. After this, the body is usually transported by hearse to the cemetery. A processional of mourners follows for a graveside service.

It is easy to spend great sums of money on embalming, caskets, and burial—where the biggest profits are for the mortician. The family is ill-prepared emotionally to do competitive shopping. As a result, many thoughtful people

have joined together to form nonprofit ***memorial societies. These groups help members make simple, priceworthy burial or cremation arrangements in advance.***

Many people also specify in advance that they prefer to have a *memorial service* rather than (or even in addition to) a funeral. This enables the community of mourners to concentrate on the person's life rather than death.

Individualizing Ritual Some death rituals are quite formal, others are less so. In New Orleans, families in the black community sometimes hire a jazz band to lead mourners from the church service to the cemetery. *(See ● Figure 9.)* Elsewhere families charter a boat and invite friends of the departed to join them in scattering ashes

● **Figure 9   A New Orleans funeral.** A jazz band leads mourners from church to cemetery.

at sea. In urban ghettos, on the site where lives have ended violently, temporary memorials of flowers and candles spring up. In graveyards, personalized monuments—etched with guitars, flowers, teddy bears, or photographs of the departed—have become widespread. They are now referred to as "cemetery art."[208] Or friends plant a tree or donate money to save a redwood in memory of the deceased. Through such practices, the dead live on in the minds of the survivors.

Grief: Understanding Our Losses

Grief and loss may bring about four stages of mourning—shock, longing, depression and despair, and recovery. Different people respond to grief in different ways. You can help the bereaved to recover by listening and sympathizing and by being aware that bereavement takes lots of time.

For some survivors, black crepe and funerals may provide the solace they need to help them through their bereavement. For others, grief really only *begins* with the person's death—particularly if the survivor lost a child or a long-time companion. *(See ● Figure 10.)* Young adults are usually spared this agony, but for many the AIDS epidemic has decimated their neighborhood, profession, family, or circle of friends.[209]

Grief and Loss Even if we have never lost someone close to us, we have all felt grief because we have all felt *loss*. Some of the losses, says Lillian Chance, a psychiatric nurse specializing in grief counseling, are obvious: "a separation, the end of a romantic relationship, a job loss, a physical infirmity, aging, moving, a child leaving home." Other losses in life are more intimate: "the loss of a cherished dream, of a beloved pet, of innocence, or trust in a friend. . . ."[210]

Any change or turning point in your life—even positive ones—means leaving something behind. It may be marrying or committing to someone, or gaining a career opportunity. It may even be, as Chance says, the "loss of a self-destructive substance abuse." All these can bring on the process and feelings of grief.

The Stages of Mourning To be sensitive to a grieving person's needs or your own feelings of loss, consider these descriptions of four distinct stages of mourning. Note, however, that they do not follow an orderly schedule:[211, 212]

- *Stage 1—shock:* Some people in the *shock* phase seem dazed and distant, others calm and rational. A degree of numbness, disbelief, and detachment nearly always occurs at first. One may feel swept up by a sense of unreality, asking "What happened?" or "Did it really happen?" Becoming involved in the immediate problems—funeral arrangements, out-of-town guests, and the various documents—can postpone the feeling of letdown.

- *Stage 2—longing:* In this stage, the bereaved person has an intense *longing* to be with the departed person. His or her mind is filled with yearnings, memories, and dreams about the deceased. Some forms of denial or guilt may be present: it's normal to wish the loss had never happened.

- *Stage 3—depression and despair:* The third stage of *depression and despair* is expressed in despondency, sudden anger, and disordered thinking. Someone close to the bereaved may find their behavior irrational, as they suddenly change neighborhoods or buy things they cannot afford. The anger may be directed against the departed for "disappointing or deserting" them.

- *Stage 4—recovery:* The second and third stages can average 18–24 months, although everyone's grief period is different. In the last stage of mourning, *recovery*, the survivor finally puts the death into perspective and is able to move on. This means realizing there is no *returning* to normal but creating a *new* form of normality. It means recognizing also what was not lost, of the good that is left in one's life.

Helping the Bereaved to Recover What can you do to help a bereaved person? Here are some suggestions:

- *Listen and sympathize:* The first two tasks of grief are to accept the reality of the loss and experience the pain.[213] Be aware that powerful emotions are at work. If the feelings are bottled up and never dealt with,

● **Figure 10   The agony of grief.** The conventional trappings of mourning, such as funerals, may help some people with bereavement. But for others grief may last for months or years.

❝ *What is there to say about grief? Grief is a tidal wave that overtakes you, smashes down upon you with unimaginable force. . . .*

Grief means not being able to read more than two sentences at a time. It is walking into rooms with intentions that suddenly vanish. . . .

Grief makes what others think of you moot. It shears away the masks of normal life and forces brutal honesty before propriety can stop you. ❞

—Stephanie Ericsson. (1991, September/October). The agony of grief. *Utne Reader*, pp. 75–78.

the person could be in a continual state of depression and anxiety. Thus, you should be prepared to listen and sympathize. Indeed, you should try to detect if the bereaved person is hiding his or her feelings.

• *Be aware bereavement takes lots of time:* Months and even years may pass before the bereaved person can finally be said to have passed into the stage of recovery. Throughout he or she may demand sympathy and social support—and you should be prepared to offer it. Do not dis-

courage saving photographs, talking about shared experiences, or visiting the gravesite. Expect ***anniversary reactions*—expressions of grief and sorrow on birthdays or the anniversary of the death. These may start a new burst of mourning.**

Eventually, the bereaved person should be able to confront the loss and, just as important, recognize what was *not* lost. At that point, the bereaved may have developed a deeper appreciation of human relationships.[214]

Strategy for Living: The Will to Live and a "Good Death"

The will to live may postpone death.

One study shows that some people seem to actually tell death to wait, that the *will to live* matters. It is folk wisdom to say that people often stave off death for important occasions. Two studies found sharp drops in death rates among Chinese women before the Harvest Moon Festival and Jewish men before Passover.[215] The delayed deaths were most noticeable in stroke, heart disease, and cancer cases.

Most people want to die a "good death," a swift, pain-free, dignified death surrounded by people they love. Meanwhile, there are things to do, people to be close to, a world to see—these constitute our "will to live." Think about what is in your life that would make you want to postpone your mortality for a "good death."

800-HELP

Alzheimer's Disease and Related Disorders Association. 800-621-0379. (In Illinois, 800-572-6037.) Provides phone numbers of local support groups for families of patients with Alzheimer's disease or vascular dementia.

Arthritis Foundation Information Line. 800-283-7800. Provides information about osteoarthritis.

Choice In Dying. 800-989-WILL. Provides statutory advance directives for each state free of charge, as well as other materials relating to end-of-life medical care.

HOSPICELINK. 800-331-1620. (Except Connecticut.) Provides information on hospices and referrals to local hospices. Also offers supportive listening.

The Living Bank Organ Donor Registry and Referral Service. 800-528-2971. Sends information to anyone interested in becoming an organ donor.

National Council on the Aging. 800-424-9046. National information and consulting center for the aged.

National Funeral Director Association Funeral Service Consumer Arbitration Program. 800-662-7666. Acts as liaison or arbitrator between consumers and funeral services.

Simon Foundation for Continence. 800-23-SIMON. Provides help for problems of urinary incontinence.

The Sudden Infant Death Syndrome Alliance. 800-221-7437. Provides information on "crib death."

United Network for Organ Sharing. 800-24-DONOR. Provides information on becoming an organ donor.

Suggested Readings

Robert M. Baird & Stuart E. Rosenbaum (Eds.). (1989). *Euthanasia: The moral issues.* Buffalo, NY: Prometheus Books. Essays from advocates and opponents on this burning issue.

Derek Humphry. (1991). *Final exit: The practicalities of self-deliverance and assisted suicide for the dying.* Eugene, OR: Hemlock Society. Provides prescriptive information for those wanting to end their lives.

Danielle Lapp. (1987). *Don't forget: Easy exercises for a better memory at any age.* New York: McGraw-Hill. Helps train people to better memories.

Stephen Levine. (1982). *Who dies?* New York: Doubleday. The writer states that conscious dying begins with conscious living.

Rose Oliver & Frances A. Bock. (1989). *Coping with Alzheimer's: A caregiver's emotional survival guide.* New York: Dodd, Mead. A book offering training on how to cope with taking care of Alzheimer's disease and retaining one's own sanity.

David E. Outerbridge & Alan R. Hersh. (1991). *Easing the passage.* New York: Harper Perennial. Provides guidance for having a living will, personal medical directives, and other medical and legal resources.

Gail Sheehy. (1991). *The silent passage: Menopause.* New York: Random House. A well-written account of "the change of life."

David H. Solomon, Elyse Salend, Anna Nolen Rahman, Marie Bolduc Liston, & David B. Reuben. (1992). *A consumer's guide to aging.* Baltimore: Johns Hopkins University Press. Tips on physical and mental health, medical care, personal finances, relationships and other subjects for people over 50.

Notes

Explanation of abbreviations:

AH: American Health
AIM: Annals of Internal Medicine
AJPH: American Journal of Public Health
JAMA: Journal of the American Medical Association
LAT: Los Angeles Times
MMWR: Morbidity & Mortality Weekly Report
NEJM: New England Journal of Medicine
NYT: New York Times
PT: Psychology Today
SFC: San Francisco Chronicle
SFE: San Francisco Examiner
WSJ: Wall Street Journal

TO THE STUDENT

1. Longman, D. G., & Atkinson, R. H. (1992). *College learning and study skills* (2nd ed.). St. Paul, MN: West 4.
2. Douglass, M., & Douglass, D. (1980). *Manage your time, manage your work, manage yourself.* New York: American Management Association.
3. Beneke, W. M., & Harris, M. B. (1972). Teaching self-control of study behavior. *Behavior Research & Therapy, 10,* 35–41.
4. Zechmeister, E. B., & Nyberg, S. E. (1982). *Human memory: An introduction to research and theory.* Pacific Grove, CA: Brooks/Cole.
5. Bromage, B. K., & Mayer, R. E. (1986). Quantitative and qualitative effects of repetition on learning from technical text. *Journal of Educational Psychology, 78,* 271–78.
6. Longman & Atkinson, 1992, 148–53.
7. Lindgren, H. C. (1969). *The psychology of college success: A dynamic approach.* New York: Wiley.
8. Palkovitz, R. J., & Lore, R. K. (1980). Note taking and note review: Why students fail questions based on lecture material. *Teaching of Psychology, 7,* 159–61.
9. Palkovitz & Lore, 1980, 159–61.
10. Robinson, F. P. (1970). *Effective study* (4th ed.). New York: Harper & Row.
11. Langan, J., & Nadell, J. (1980). *Doing well in college: A concise guide to reading, writing, and study skills.* New York: McGraw-Hill, 93–110.
12. Langan & Nadell, 1980, 104.

CHAPTER 1: LEARNING HOW TO LIVE

1. Eberst, R. M. (1984). Defining health: A multidimensional model. *Journal of Social Health, 54,* 99–104.
2. Garfield, C. (1986). *Peak performers: The new heroes of American business.* New York: Morrow.
3. Ferguson, T. (1992, January–February). Patient, heal thyself: Health in the information age. *The Futurist,* 9–14.
4. Fiorello, J., & Siegel, B. Cited in: Ferguson, 1992.
5. Editors of the University of California, Berkeley, *Wellness Letter.* (1991). *The wellness encyclopedia: The comprehensive family resource for safeguarding health and preventing illness.* Boston: Houghton Mifflin.
6. Angier, N. (1992, June 21). Bedside manners improve as more women enter medicine. *NYT,* sec. 4, 18.
7. Council on Scientific Affairs. (1990, March 2). Home care in the 1990s. *JAMA, 263,* 1241–44.
8. American Medical Association. Cited in: Colburn, D. (1991, October 24). Are physicals worth it? *SFC,* B5.
9. American Society of Internal Medicine. Cited in: Editors of the University of California, Berkeley, *Wellness Letter.* (1991).

10. Willensky, D. (1992, March). Vital signs. *AH,* 100–103.
11. Brody, J. E. (1992, September 16). Ignoring the doctor's orders has become a costly and deadly epidemic. *NYT,* B6.
12. National Council on Patient Information and Education. Cited in: Brody, 1992.
13. Anonymous. (1990, May). Generic drugs: Still safe? *Consumer Reports,* 310–13.
14. Anonymous. (1991). Are drugs approved by the FDA safe and risk free? *National Medical-Legal Journal, 2,* 8.
15. Hilts, P. J. (1990, May 27). Dangers of some new drugs go undetected, study says. *NYT,* 10.
16. Chastain, S. (1992, February–March). The accidental addict: Are you hooked on your prescriptions? *Modern Maturity,* 39.
17. Katzenstein, L. (1991, April). Rx to OTC: Who pays and who profits when prescription drugs go over the counter. *AH,* 49–53.
18. Edeson, E. (1991, November). What a relief: A guide to nonprescription pain medication. *AH,* 63–65.
19. Cowley, G., & Hager, M. (1990, March 12). Some counter intelligence. *Newsweek,* 82, 84.
20. Roine, R., Gentry, R. T., Hernandez-Munoz, R. et al. (1990). Aspirin increases blood-alcohol concentrations in humans after ingestion of ethanol. *JAMA, 264,* 2406–08.
21. Krieger, L. M. (1990, April 8). Beware what's over the counter. *SFE,* D-16, D-15.
22. Edeson, 1991.
23. Wootton, F. T., & Lee, W. M. (1990). Acetaminophen hepatotoxicity in the alcoholic. *Southern Medical Journal, 83,* 1047–49.
24. Foust, R. T., Reddy, K. R., Jeffers, L. J. et al. (1989). Nyquil-associated liver injury. *American Journal of Gastroenterology, 84,* 422–25.
25. Gengo, F. M. Cited in: Zoler, M. L. (1990). Antihistamines can bomb drivers. *Medical World News, 31,* 19.
26. Horowitz, J. M., & Lafferty, E. (1991, November 4). Why new age medicine is catching on. *Time,* 68–76.
27. Begley, S. (1992, April). Alternative medicine: A cure for what ails us? *AH,* 39–40, 44, 46.
28. Shekelle, P. G., & Brook, R. H. (1991). A community-based study of the use of chiropractic services. *AJPH, 81,* 439–42.
29. Vickery, D. M. (1990). *Life plan.* Evergreen, CO: Health Decisions, 23.
30. U.S. Department of Health and Human Services, Public Health Service (1990). *Healthy people 2000: National health promotion and disease prevention objectives.* DHHS Pub. No. (PHS)91-50213.
31. Brody, J. E. (1991, January 31). In pursuit of the best possible odds of preventing or minimizing the perils of major disease. *NYT,* B6.
32. Moog, C. (1990). *"Are they selling her lips?": Advertising and identity.* New York: Morrow.
33. Klaidman, S. (1991). *Health in the headlines: The stories behind the stories.* New York: Oxford University Press.
34. Glick, D. (1992, July 13). New age meets Hippocrates. *Newsweek,* 58.
35. Barrett, S. (1991, March). Quack, quack: 30 ways to duck medicine's con artists. *AH,* 59–63.
36. Kahane, H. (1988). *Logic and contemporary rhetoric: The use of reason in everyday life* (5th ed.). Belmont, CA: Wadsworth.
37. Winslow, R. (1989, October 5). Sometimes, talk is the best medicine. *WSJ,* B1.
38. Fishman, S. (1993, April). The powerful patient. *Health,* 74–78.

39. Bilich, M., quoted in: Ray, M., & Myers, R. (1986). *Creativity in business.* Garden City, NY: Doubleday, 68.
40. Ellis, D. (1991) *Becoming a master student* (6th ed.). Rapid City, SD: College Survival, Inc., 18.
41. Ray & Myers, 1986, 51.
42. Ellis, 1991, 16.
43. Anonymous. (1988, July 4). A holiday for heroes. *Newsweek,* 41.
44. Baer, S. (1990, April 22). And justice for all. *SFC, Sunday Punch,* 6; reprinted from *Baltimore Sun.*
45. Stewart, P. (1988, July 2). Woman gives 27 kids an early break. *SFC,* A2.
46. Shavelson, L. (1990, October 14). New lives on wheels: A Berkeley wheelchair designer mobilizes the Third World's disabled. *This World, SFC,* 12–14.
47. Anonymous, 1988, 55.
48. Taylor, S. C. (1990, June-July). Everyday heroes: Meet ten people who make a difference day in, day out. *Modern Maturity,* 45.

CHAPTER 2: PSYCHOLOGICAL HEALTH

1. Leonard, G. (1983, December). Abraham Maslow and the new self. *Esquire,* 331–32.
2. Maslow, A. H. (1968). *Toward a psychology of being* (2nd ed.). Princeton, NJ: Van Nostrand Reinhold.
3. Maslow, A. H. (1970). *Motivation and personality* (2nd ed.). New York: Harper & Row.
4. Harre, R., & Lamb, R. (Eds.). (1983). *The encyclopedia dictionary of psychology.* Cambridge, MA: MIT Press.
5. Schneiderman, L. Cited in: Sylvester, D. A. (1990, April 10). Schools join self-esteem movement. *SFC,* A1, A4.
6. McGinnis, A. L. (1990). *The power of optimism.* San Francisco: Harper & Row.
7. Ornstein, R., & Sobel, D. (1989). *Healthy pleasures.* Reading, MA: Addison-Wesley.
8. Ornstein, R. E., & Sobel, D. S. (1989, May). Healthy pleasures. *AH,* 53–62.
9. Szent-Györgyi, A. Quoted in: von Oech, R. (1983). *A whack on the side of the head.* Menlo Park, CA: Creative Think, 7.
10. Hyatt, C., & Gottlieb, L. (1987). *When smart people fail.* New York: Simon & Schuster, 20.
11. Garfield, C. Quoted in: Rozak, M. (1989, August). The mid-life fitness peak. *PT,* 32–33.
12. Harre & Lamb, 1983, 359.
13. Curtis, R. C., & Miller, K. (1986). Believing another likes or dislikes you: Behaviors making the beliefs come true. *Journal of Personality & Social Psychology, 51,* 284–90.
14. Lazarus, R. S. (1981, July). Little hassles can be hazardous to health. *PT,* 61.
15. Charney, D. Cited in: Goleman, D. (1990, August 22). Flashback terror: It's biological. *SFC,* "Briefing" section, 7; reprinted from *NYT.*
16. Selye, H. (1974). *Stress without distress.* New York: Lippincott, 27.
17. Selye, 1974, 28–29.
18. Lazarus, R. S., & Folkman, S. (1982). Coping and adaptation. In W. D. Gentry (Ed.), *Handbook of behavioral medicine.* New York: Guilford.
19. Selye, 1974.
20. Wittmeyer, I. W. Cited in: Doheny, K. Health & Fitness News Service. (1990, October 3). Illness 'all in your head'? Maybe not. *SFC,* B3.
21. Krueger, E., & Krueger, G. R. (1991). How does the subjective experience of stress relate to the breakdown of the human immune system. *In Vivo, 5,* 207–15.
22. Shavit, Y., Terman, G. W., Martin, F. C., Lewis, J. W.,

Liebeskind, J. C., & Gale, R. P. (1985). Stress, opioid peptides, the immune system, and cancer. *Journal of Immunology, 135,* 834S–37S.

23. Kiecolt-Glaser, J., & Glaser, R. Major life changes, chronic stress, and immunity. (1988). *Advances in Biochemical Psychopharmacology, 44,* 217–24.

24. Kiecolt-Glazer, J. et al. (1987) Stress, health, and immunity: Tracking the mind/body connection. Presentation at American Psychological Association meeting, New York, August 1987.

25. Kannel, W. B. (1990). CHD risk factors: A Framingham study update. *Hospital Practice, 25,* 119.

26. Eliot, R., & Breo, D. (1984). *Is it worth dying for?* New York: Bantam.

27. Holmes, T. H., & Rahe, R. H. (1967). The social readjustment rating scale. *Journal of Psychosomatic Research, 11,* 213–18.

28. Friedman, M., & Rosenman, R. H. (1974). *Type A behavior and your heart.* Greenwich, CT: Knopf.

29. Friedman, M., Thoreson, C. E., Gill, J. J. et al. (1986). Alteration of Type A behavior and its effect on cardiac recurrences in post myocardial infarction patients: Summary results of the recurrent coronary prevention project. *American Heart Journal, 112,* 653–65.

30. Dembroski, T. M., & Costa, P. T. (1988). Assessment of coronary-prone behavior: A current overview. *Annals of Behavioral Medicine, 10,* 60–63.

31. Dembroski, T. M., MacDougall, J. M., Costa, P. T. Jr. et al. (1989). Components of hostility as predictors of sudden death and myocardial infarction in the Multiple Risk Factor Intervention Trial. *Psychosomatic Medicine, 51,* 514–22.

32. Colby, B. N. (1987). Well-being: A theoretical program. *American Anthropologist, 89,* 879–95.

33. McCulloch, A., & O'Brien, L. (1986). The organizational determinants of worker burnout. *Children & Youth Services Review, 8,* 175–90.

34. Jaffe, P., Wolfe, D., Wilson, S. et al. (1986). Similarities in behavioral and social maladjustment among child victims and witnesses to family violence. *American Journal of Orthopsychiatry, 56,* 142–46.

35. Jaffe, P., Wolfe, D. A., Wilson, S. et al. (1986). Emotional and physical health problems of battered women. *Canadian Journal of Psychiatry, 31,* 625–29.

36. Kilpatrick. Cited in: Goleman, D. (1990, May 3). Second assault on crime victims: Long-term mental troubles. *NYT,* B7.

37. American Psychiatric Association. (1994). *Diagnostic and statistical manual of mental disorders* (4th ed). Washington, DC: American Psychiatric Association.

38. Burge, S. K. (1988). Post-traumatic stress disorder in victims of rape. Special Issue: Progress in traumatic stress research. *Journal of Traumatic Stress, 1,* 193–210.

39. Gersons, B. P. (1989). Patterns of PTSD among police officers following shooting incidents: A two-dimensional model and treatment implications. *Journal of Traumatic Stress, 2,* 247–57.

40. Goodwin, J. (1988). Post-traumatic symptoms in abused children. *Journal of Traumatic Stress, 1,* 475–88.

55. Kleinman, 1990. Cited in Goleman, 1990, B7.

41. Rinear, E. E. (1988). Psychosocial aspects of parental response patterns to the death of a child by homicide. *Journal of Traumatic Stress, 1,* 305–22.

42. Trice, A. D. (1988). Posttraumatic stress syndrome-like symptoms among AIDS caregivers. *Psychological Reports, 63,* 656–58.

43. Benson, H. (1975). *The relaxation response.* New York: Avon.

44. Benson, H., & Proctor, W. (1984). *Beyond the relaxation response.* New York: Times.

45. Miller, L. (1989, November). What biofeedback does (and doesn't). *PT,* 23.

46. Page, R. M. (1990). Loneliness and adolescent health behavior. *Health Education, 21,* 14–18.

47. Beck, A. T., & Young, J. E. (1978, September). College blues. *PT,* 80–92.

48. Spitzberg, B. H., & Hurt, H. T. (1987). The relationship of interpersonal competence and skills to reported loneliness across time. *Journal of Social Behavior & Personality, 2,* 157–72.

49. Zimbardo, P. (1977). *Shyness: What it is; what to do about it.* Reading, MA: Addison-Wesley, 12.

50. National Foundation for Depressive Illness. Cited in: Gertz, K. R. (1990, November). Mood probe. *Self,* 165–68, 204–206.

51. Ray, M., & Myers, R. (1986). *Creativity in business.* Garden City, NY: Doubleday.

52. Averill, J. R. (1983). Studies on anger and aggression: Implications for theories of emotion. *American Psychologist, 38,* 1145–60.

53. Tavris, C. (1982). *Anger: The misunderstood emotion.* New York: Touchstone, 189.

54. Tavris, 1982, 223.

55. American Psychiatric Association. (1994). *Diagnostic and statistical manual of mental disorders* (4th ed.).

56. Kalat, J. W. (1990). *Introduction to psychology* (2nd ed.). Belmont, CA: Wadsworth.

57. Jacobsen, F. M., Sack, D. A., Wehr, T. A. et al. (1987). Neuroendocrine 5-hydroxytryptophan in seasonal affective disorder. *Archives of General Psychiatry, 44,* 1086–91.

58. Wenzlaff, R. M. Quoted in: Adler, V. (1989, January/February). Accentuate the positive. *AH,* 50.

59. Low, B. P., & Andrews, S. F. (1990). Adolescent suicide. *Medical Clinics of North America, 74,* 1251–64.

60. Low & Andrews, 1990.

61. Blumenthal, S. J., & Kupfer, D. J. (1986). Generalizable treatment strategies for suicidal behavior. *Annals of the New York Academy of Sciences, 487,* 327–40.

62. Peterson, L. G., Peterson, M., O'Shanick, G. J. et al. (1985). Self-inflicted gunshot wounds: Lethality of method versus intent. *American Journal of Psychiatry, 142,* 228–31.

63. Kalat, 1990, 515.

64. Wolpe, J., & Rowan, V. C. (1988). Panic disorder: A product of classical conditioning. *Behaviour Research & Therapy, 26,* 441–50.

65. Myers, J. K., Weissman, M. M., Tischler, G. L. et al. (1984). Six-month prevalence of psychiatric disorders in three communities. *Archives of General Psychiatry, 41,* 959–67.

66. Wolpe, J. (1961). The systematic desensitization treatment of neuroses. *Journal of Nervous & Mental Disease, 132,* 189–203.

67. Hughes, H. Quoted in: Fowler, R. D. (1986, May). Howard Hughes: A psychological autopsy. *PT,* 22–33.

68. Smith, M. L., Glass, G. V., & Miller, R. L. (1980). *The benefits of psychotherapy.* Baltimore: Johns Hopkins Press, 183.

69. Elkin, I. (1986). Outcome findings and therapist performance. Paper presented at the American Psychological Association convention.

70. Singer, J. L. (1981). Clinical intervention: New developments in methods and evaluation. In L. T. Benjamin, Jr. (Ed.), *The G. Stanley Hall Lecture Series,* (Vol. 1). Washington, DC: American Psychological Association.

71. Smith, D. (1982). Trends in counseling and psychotherapy. *American Psychologist, 37,* 802–809.

72. Kihlstrom, J. F. (1979). Hypnosis and psychopathology: Retrospect and prospect. *Journal of Abnormal Psychology, 88,* 459–73.

73. Udolf, R. (1981). *Handbook of hypnosis for professionals.* New York: Van Nostrand Reinhold.

74. Flach, F. F. (1988). *Resilience: Discovering new strength at times of stress.* New York: Ballantine.

75. Flannery, R. (1990). *Becoming stress-resistant.* New York: Crossroads/Continuum.

76. Flannery, R. Cited in: Springer, I. (1991, March). The tough get going. *AH,* 12.

77. McKee, S. (1991, March). Just do it. *AH,* 12.

78. Haskall, A. (1992, November). Stop worrying. *Self,* 134–37.

CHAPTER 3: EATING RIGHT: NUTRITION AND WEIGHT MANAGEMENT

1. American Dietetic Association survey, October 9, 1991. Reported in: Associated Press. (1991, October 10). People know they could improve diet. *SFC,* D4.

2. Anonymous. (1993, April). 14 dietary habits you can stop feeling guilty about. *Tufts University Diet & Nutrition Letter,* 3–6.

3. Featherstone, J. D. B. (1987). The mechanism of dental decay. *Nutrition Today, 22,* 10–16.

4. Dews, P. B. (1987). Summary report of an international aspartame workshop. *Food Chemistry Toxicology, 25,* 549–52.

5. Klurfeld, D. M. (1987). The role of dietary fiber in gastrointestinal disease. *Journal of the American Dietetic Association, 87,* 1172–77.

6. Centers for Disease Control and Prevention. (1994). Daily dietary fat and total food-energy intakes—NHANES III, phase 1, 1988–91. *JAMA, 271,* 1309.

7. U.S. Public Health Service (1990). *Healthy people 2000: National health promotion and disease prevention objectives.* DHHS Pub. No. (PHS)91-50212. Washington, DC: U.S. Government Printing Office, 112. 1

8. Cohen, L. A. (1987). Diet and cancer. *Scientific American, 257,* 42–48.

9. Cohen, 1987.

10. U.S. Public Health Service (1988). *The Surgeon General's report on nutrition and health.* DHHS Pub. No. (PHS) 88-50210. Washington, DC: U.S Government Printing Office.

11. Glomset, J. (1985). Fish, fatty acids, and human health. *NEJM, 312,* 1253–54.

12. Phillipson, B. E., Rothrock, D. W., Connor, W. E. et al. (1985). Reduction of plasma lipids, lipoproteins, and apoproteins by dietary fish oils in patients with hypertriglyceridemia. *NEJM, 312,* 1210–16.

13. Kromhout, D., Bosschieter, E. B., & Coulander, C. D. (1985). The inverse relation between fish consumption and 20-year mortality from coronary heart disease. *NEJM, 312,* 1205–09.

14. U.S. Public Health Service, 1988.

15. Saltman, P., Gurin, J., Mothner, I. et al. (1987). *The California nutrition book.* Boston: Little, Brown, 216–17.

16. Pauling, L. C. (1970). *Vitamin C and the common cold.* San Francisco: Freeman.

17. Chalmers, T. C. (1975). Effects of ascorbic acid on the common cold. *American Journal of Medicine, 58,* 532–36.

18. Cameron, E., & Pauling, L. (1976). Supplemental ascrobate in the supportive treatment of cancer: Prolongation of survival times in terminal human cancer. *Proceedings of the National Academy of Science USA, 73,* 3685–89.

19. Creagan, E. T., Moertel, C. G., O'Fallon, J. R. et al. (1979). Failure of high-dose vitamin C (ascorbic acid) therapy to benefit patients with advanced cancer. *NEJM, 301,* 687–90.

20. Bruce, W. R., Eyssen, G. M., Ciampi, A. et al. (1981). Strategies for dietary intervention studies in colon cancer. *Cancer, 47,* 1121–25.

21. Jacob, R. A. (1994). The case for vitamin supplementation. *Journal of the American*

College of Nutrition, 13, 111–12.

22. Reynolds, R. D. (1994). Vitamin supplements: Current controversies. *Journal of the American College of Nutrition, 13*, 118-26.

23. Shangraw, R. F. (1990, July-August). Standards for vitamins and nutritional supplements: Who and when. *Pharmacopeial Forum*, 751–58.

24. Beauchamp, G. K. (1987). The human preference for excess salt. *American Scientist, 75*, 27–33.

25. U.S. Public Health Service, 1988.

26. Holmes, J. H. (1964). Thirst and fluid intake problems in clinical medicine. In M. J. Wayner (Ed.), *Thirst*. New York: Macmillan.

27. Houts, S. S. (1988). Lactose intolerance. *Food Technology, 3*, 110–13.

28. Kreutler, P. A., & Czjka-Narins, D. M. (1987). *Nutrition in perspective* (2nd ed.). Englewood Cliffs, NJ: Prentice Hall.

29. Costill, D., & Miller, J. (1980). Nutrition for endurance sports: carbohydrate and fluid balance. *International Journal of Sports Medicine, 1*, 2–14.

30. Costill & Miller, 1980.

31. McQuillan, S. (1994, May). The new food labels. *American Health*, p. 101.

32. Whitney, E. N., & Hamilton, E. M. N. (1987). *Understanding nutrition*. St. Paul: West, 47–49.

33. U.S. Senate Select Committee on Nutrition and Human Needs. (1977). *Dietary goals for the United States* (2nd ed.). Washington, DC: U.S. Government Printing Office.

34. U.S. Department of Agriculture and the Department of Health and Human Services. (1985). *Nutrition and your health: Dietary guidelines for Americans* (2nd ed.). Home and Garden Bulletin No. 232. Washington, DC: U.S. Government Printing Office.

35. U.S. Department of Health and Human Services. (1980). *Promoting health/preventing disease: Objectives for the nation*. Washington, DC: U.S. Government Printing Office.

36. U.S. Public Health Service, 1988.

37. National Research Council. (1989). *Diet and health: Implications for reducing chronic disease risk*. Washington, DC: National Academy Press.

38. National Research Council, 1989.

39. National Research Council, 1989.

40. Wolf, N. (1991). *The beauty myth: How images of beauty are used against women*. New York: Morrow, 184.

41. Anonymous. (1991). Great bodies come in many shapes. *University of California, Berkeley, Wellness Letter, 7*, 2.

42. Gallup Organization, December 1990 survey. Cited in: Sietsema, T. (1991, January 2). Fat's back. *SFC*, Food section, 1, 5.

43. Wolf, 1991, 17.

44. Stallones, R. A. (1980). The rise and fall of ischemic heart disease. *Scientific American, 243*, 53–59.

45. Bray, G. A. (1980). Definition, measurement, and classification of the syndromes of obesity. In G. A. Bray (Ed.), *Obesity: Comparative methods of weight control*. Westport, CT: Techomic.

46. Bray, G. A. (1979). *Obesity in America*. Washington, DC: U.S. Department of Health, Education, and Welfare.

47. Consensus Development Conference Statement. (1985). *Health implications of obesity*. Bethesda, MD: National Institutes of Health.

48. U.S. Public Health Service, 1990, 403.

49. Knittle, J. L., & Hirsch, J. (1968). Effect of early nutrition on the development of rat epididymal fat pads: Cellularity and metabolism. *Journal of Clinical Investigation, 47*, 209.

50. Grinker, J. A. (1982). Physiological and behavioral basis for human obesity. In D. W. Pfaff (Ed.), *The physiological mechanisms of motivation*. New York: Springer-Verlag.

51. Nisbett, R. E. (1972). Hunger, obesity, and the ventromedial hypothalamus. *Psychological Review, 79*, 433–55.

52. U.S. Public Health Service, 1990.

53. Herzog, D. B., & Copeland, P. M. (1985). Eating disorders. *NEJM, 313*, 295–303.

54. Comerci, G. D. (1990). Medical complications of anorexia nervosa and bulimia nervosa. *Medical Clinics of North America, 74*, 1293–1310.

55. Moore, D.-J. (1989, November/December). I invented bulimia. *Medical Self Care, 32*.

56. Siegel, M., Brisman, J., & Weinshel, M. (1988). *Surviving an eating disorder*. New York: Harper & Row.

57. Saltman et al., 1987, 148.

58. Brody, J. E. (1991, June 27). Study links yo-yo dieting to an increased death rate. *NYT*, A9.

59. Gallup poll. Cited in: Brownell, K. (1988, March). The yo-yo trap. *AH*, 78–84.

60. Lissner, L., Odell, P. M., D'Agostino, R. B. et al. (1991). Variability of body weight and health outcomes in the Framingham population. *NEJM, 324*, 1839–44.

61. Brownell, 1988.

62. Meade, J. (1991, February). Drop a fast 10 pounds. *Men's Health*, 55–56, 92.

63. Kayman, S., Bruvold, W., & Stern, J. S. (1990). Maintenance and relapse after weight loss in women: Behavioral aspects. *American Journal of Clinical Nutrition, 52*, 800–07.

64. Anonymous. (1991). The four keys to losing weight and keeping it off. *Johns Hopkins Medical Letter, Health After 50, 3*, 7.

65. Brownell, K. D. Cited in: Brody, J. D. (1991, July 3). Personal health: Regardless of the weight-loss program you follow, successful dieting is really in the mind. *NYT*, B6.

66. Brownell, K. D. (1989, June). When and how to diet. *PT*, 40–46.

CHAPTER 4: PHYSICAL FITNESS

1. Nagler, W. Quoted in: Sims, S. M. (1990, April). Dr. Nagler says 'keep moving.' *Self*, 165–68, 211.

2. Ornstein, R., & Sobel, D. (1989). *Healthy pleasures*. Reading, MA: Addison-Wesley, 106.

3. Ornstein & Sobel, 1989, 103.

4. Taylor, H. (1991, October). Has the fitness movement peaked? *American Demographics*, 10–11.

5. Centers for Disease Control (1990). Coronary heart disease attributable to sedentary lifestyle—selected states, 1988. *JAMA, 264*, 1390, 1392.

6. Dietz, W. H. Jr., & Gormaker, S. L. (1985). Do we fatten our children at the television set? Obesity and television viewing in children and adolescents. *Pediatrics, 75*, 807–12.

7. Singer, D. G. (1983, July). A time to reexamine the role of television in our lives. *American Psychologist*, 815–16.

8. Fahey, V. (1992, December/January). TV by the numbers. *In Health*, 35.

9. Cooke, P. (1992, December/January). TV or not TV. *In Health*, 33–43.

10. Anonymous. (1991, November). Better health with a twist of the wrist. *Prevention*, 116.

11. Flippin, R. (1989, October). Beyond endorphins: The latest research on runner's high. *AH*, 78–83.

12. Greist, J. H., Eischens, R. R. et al. (1978). Running out of depression. *The Physician & Sportsmedicine, 6*(12), 49–56.

13. Monahan, T. (1986). Exercise and depression: Swapping sweat for serenity? *The Physician & Sportsmedicine, 14*(9), 192–97.

14. Morgan, W. P., & O'Connor, P. J. (1987). Exercise and mental health. In R. K. Dishman (Ed.), *Exercise adherence*. Champaign, IL: Human Kinetics.

15. Farmer, M. E., Locke, B. Z., Moscicki, E. K. et al. (1988). Physical activity and depressive symptoms: The NHANES I epidemiologic follow-up study. *American Journal of Epidemiology, 128*, 1340–51.

16. Tucker, L. A., Cole, G. E., & Friedman, G. M. (1986). Physical fitness: A buffer against stress. *Perceptual & Motor Skills, 63*, 955–61.

17. Sime, W. E. (1984). Psychological benefits of exercise. *Advances, 1*, 15–29.

18. Roth, D. L., & Holmes, D. S. (1987). Influence of aerobic exercise training and relaxation training on physical and psychological health following stressful life events. *Psychosomatic Medicine, 49*, 355–65.

19. Mott, P. (1990, October 7). Mental gymnastics. *LAT*, E1, E18–E19.

20. Gondola, J. C. Cited in: Cardozo, C. (1990, September). The new feel-great prescription: Even a few minutes of exercise can enhance creativity, self-esteem, and chase away the blues. *Self, 122*, 124–25.

21. Thayer, R. E. (1988, October). Energy walks. *PT*, 12–13.

22. Thayer, R. E. (1987). Energy, tiredness, and tension effects of a sugar snack versus moderate exercise. *Journal of Personality & Social Psychology, 52*(1), 119–25.

23. McCleary, K. (1991, December/January). The no-gimmick weight-loss plan. *In Health*, 83.

24. Paffenbarger, R. S., Hyde, R. T., Wing, W. L. et al. (1986). Physical activity, all-cause mortality, and longevity among college alumni. *NEJM, 314*, 605–13.

25. Leon, A. S., Connett, J., Jacobs, D. R. et al. (1987). Leisure-time physical activity levels and risk of coronary heart disease and death. *JAMA, 258*, 2388–95.

26. Frisch, R. E., Wyshak, G., Albright N. L. et al. (1985). Lower prevalence of breast cancer and cancers of the reproductive system among former college athletes compared to non-athletes. *British Journal of Cancer, 52*, 885–91.

27. Lee, I.-M., Paffenbarger, J. Jr., & Hsieh, C. (1991). Physical activity and risk of developing colorectal cancer among college alumni. *Journal of the National Cancer Institute, 83*, 1324–29.

28. Horton, E. Quoted in: Chang, K. (1991, July 18). Exercise can prevent adult diabetes, study says. *SFC*, A4.

29. Helmrich, S. P., Ragland, D. R., Leung, R. W. et al. (1991). Physical activity and reduced occurrence of non-insulin-dependent diabetes mellitus. *NEMJ, 325*, 147–52.

30. Kirkpatrick, M. K., Edwards, R. N., & Finch, N. (1991). Assessment and prevention of osteoporosis through use of a client self-reporting tool. *Nurse Practitioner, 16*(7), 16–26.

31. Whitten, P., & Whiteside, E. J. (1989, April). Can exercise make you sexier? *PT*, 42–44.

32. Bortz, W. Quoted in: Chinnici, M. (1991, April). How to protect your body from time. *Self*, 128–29.

33. Nieman, D. Citedc in: Drexler, M. (1991, July 14). Tuning up immunity. *SFC, This World*, 14–15; reprinted from *Boston Globe Magazine*.

34. Biddle, S., & Smith, R. A. (1991, September). Motivating adults for physical activity: Towards a healthier present. *Journal of Physical Education, Recreation & Dance*, 39–48.

35. American College of Sports Medicine (1990). *Achieving and maintaining physical fitness*. Indianapolis, IN: American College of Sports Medicine.

36. Raskin, D. (1991, January 28). Updated guidelines to improve fitness. *NYT*, B7.

37. American College of Sports Medicine (1990). The recommended quantity and quality of exercise for developing and maintaining cardiorespiratory and muscular fitness in healthy

adults. *Medicine & Science in Sports & Exercise, 22,* 265–74.

38. Borg, G. (1973). Perceived exertion: A note on history and methods. *Medicine and Science in Sports, 5,* 90–93.

39. Borg, G. (1982). Psychophysical bases of perceived exertion. *Medicine & Science in Sports & Exercise, 14,* 380.

40. Flippin, R. (1991, July/August). Mix-and-match aerobics. *AH,* 88.

41. Kaufmann, E. (1989, December). The new rhythms of fitness. *AH,* 45–49.

42. Brody, J. E. (1991, May 2). Roller blading: A new sport that can be fun as well as an aerobic activity to enhance fitness. *NYT,* B8.

43. Fisher, L. (1991, September). Step right. *AH,* 66–70.

44. McKee, S. (1991, April). The balance of power. *AH,* 62–67

45. DeWitt, J., & Roberts, T. (1991, September). Pumping up an adult fitness program. *Journal of Physical Education, Recreation, & Dance,* 67–71.

46. McKee, 1991, 62–67.

47. Bensimhon, D. (1991, October). Exercise for dumbbells: How to use hand weights for a total-body workout. *Men's Health,* 28–29.

48. Thaxton, N. A. (1988). *Pathways to fitness: Foundations, motivation, applications.* New York: Harper & Row, 244.

49. Morrow, J., & Harvey, P. (1990, November). Exermania! *AH,* 31–32.

50. Morrow, J., & Harvey, P. (1990, November). How do you compare to the marathoners? *AH,* 31.

51. Cobb, K. (1989, October). When is too much of a good thing bad? *AH,* 79–84.

52. Morgan & O'Connor, 1987.

53. Thaxton, 1988, 343–44.

54. Halim, A. (1980). Fluid and electrolyte balance and physical training in hot climates. *Journal of Sports Medicine, 20,* 350.

55. Thaxton, 1988.

56. American National Red Cross. (1973). *Standard first aid and personal safety.* New York: Doubleday, 160–65.

57. Thaxton, 1988, 345–46.

58. Home, J. A. Quoted in: Israeloff, R. (1990, November 15). Feeling a bit drowsy? Join the club. *SFC,* B3–B4; reprinted from *Working Woman.*

59. Lamberg, L. (1990, November). The boy who ate his bed...and other mysteries of sleep. *AH,* 56–60.

60. Dement, W. (1992, March). The sleep-watchers. *Stanford,* 56.

61. Aldrich, M. S. (1990). Narcolepsy. *NEJM, 323,* 389–94.

62. Dement, W. C., Carskadon, M., & Ley, R. (1973). The prevalence of narcolepsy. *Sleep Research, 2,* 147.

63. Roth, B. (1980). *Narcolepsy and hypersomnia.* Basel: Springer-Verlag, 94–95.

64. Krueger, J. M., & Dinarello, C. A. Reported in: Moffat, A. S. (1988, July/August). "Get a good night's rest." *AH,* 54.

65. Nordheimer, J. (1991, September 8). It's Sunday afternoon, and in counterpoint to Friday highs, blues settle in. *NYT,* 15.

66. Kolata, G. (1990, May 3). Light resets body rhythms for the night worker. *NYT,* A10.

67. Dinges, D. F., & Broughton, R. J. (Eds.) (1989). *Sleep and alertness: Chronobiological, behavioral, and medical aspects of napping.* New York: Raven Press.

68. Kates, W. (1990, March 30). America is not getting enough sleep. *SFC,* B3.

69. Maas, J. Cited in: Kates, 1990, B3.

70. Williams, T. F. (1990, July 1). Scientists looking at sleep disorders have made some eye-opening discoveries. *LAT,* A9.

71. Jacobs, G. D. (1992, January). The zzzzzz plan. *Prevention,* 44–47, 114–20.

72. Lipman, D. S. (1990, November). Snore no more! *Prevention,* 39–46.

73. Associated Press. (1993, July 1). Big feat for one-leg skater. *SFC,* C1.

74. Schylman, A. (1990, October 22). Role model urges taking the plunge. *NYT,* B8.

75. Associated Press. (1992, August 23). Black man busts broncos, and rodeo's racial barriers. *SFE,* B-9.

76. Rubien, D. (1990, November 19). Sporting seniors. *SFC,* E1.

CHAPTER 5: INTIMACY, SEXUALITY, AND SAFER SEX

1. Burns, D. D. (1985). *Intimate connections.* New York: Signet, 29.

2. Ishii-Kuntz, M. (1990). Social interaction and psychological well-being: Comparison across stages of adulthood. *International Journal of Aging & Human Development, 30*(1), 15–36.

3. Claes, M. E. (1992). Friendship and personal adjustment during adolescence. *Journal of Adolescence, 15*(1), 39–55.

4. Stein, J. (Ed.) (1973). *The Random House dictionary of the English language.* New York: Random House.

5. Schaefer, M. T., & Olson, D. H. (1981). Assessing intimacy: The pair inventory. *Journal of Marital & Family Therapy, 7,* 47–60.

6. Jorgensen, S. R., & Gaudy, J. C. (1980). Self-disclosure and satisfaction in marriage: The relationship examined. *Family Relations, 29,* 281–87.

7. Rice, F. P. (1989). *Human sexuality.* Dubuque, IA: Wm. C. Brown.

8. Shea, J. A., & Adams, G. R. (1984). Correlates of male and female romantic attachments: A path analysis study. *Journal of Youth & Adolescence, 13,* 27–44.

9. Rubin, L. (1973). *Liking and loving.* New York: Holt, Rinehart & Winston.

10. Hatfield, E., & Sprecher, S. (1986). *Mirror, mirror...The importance of looks in everyday life.* Albany: State University of New York Press.

11. Dutton, D., & Aron, A. (1974). Some evidence for heightened sexual attraction under conditions of high anxiety. *Journal of Personality & Social Psychology, 30,* 510–17.

12. Hatfield, E., & Walster, G. W. (1978). *A new look at love.* Reading, MA: Addison-Wesley.

13. Viorst, J. (1979). Just because I'm married, does it mean I'm going steady? In B. J. Wishart & L. C. Reichman (Eds.), *Modern sociological issues.* New York: Macmillan, 283–89.

14. Saxton, L. (1977). *The individual, marriage, and the family* (3rd ed.). Belmont, CA: Wadsworth.

15. Phillips, D. (1980). *How to fall out of love.* New York: Fawcett.

16. Wholley, D. (1988). *Becoming your own parent.* New York: Doubleday.

17. Saluter, A. F. (1990). Singleness in America. Studies in marriage and the family. *Current Population Reports,* Series P-23, No. 162. Washington, DC: U.S. Department of Commerce, Bureau of the Census.

18. United Press International (1990, August 13). Many single women aren't desperate to wed. *SFC,* B5. [Report of F. Kaslow, The thirty-something women: Companionship, children, and career choices. Presented at August 1990 American Psychological Association meeting, Boston, MA.]

19. Curran, J. P. (1982, October). Dating anxiety. *Medical Aspects of Human Sexuality, 16,* 160–75.

20. Curran, 1982, 165.

21. Whyte, M. Quoted in: United Press International. (1990, May 4). Dating a lot won't net good marriage. *SFC,* B7.

22. Rindfuss, R. Cited in: Larson, J. (1991,

November). Cohabitation is a premarital step. *American Demographics,* 20–21.

23. Rindfuss, 1991, 20.

24. Associated Press. (1992, September 3). Why live-ins get divorced. *SFC,* B3. [Report of study by W. Axinn & A. Thornton in August 1992 *Demography*]

25. Bennett, N. Cited in: Hall, H. (1988, July/August). Marriage: Practice makes perfect? *PT,* 15.

26. Hall, 1988.

27. Baker, J. N., & Lewis, S. D. (1990, March 12). Lesbians: Portrait of a community. *Newsweek,* 24.

28. Blumstein, P., & Schwartz, P. (1983). *American couples.* New York: Morrow.

29. Patterson, C. Cited in: Tuller, D. (1992, November 23). Lesbian families—study shows healthy kids. *SFC,* A13.

30. Gross, J. (1991, February 11). New challenge of youth: Growing up in gay home. *NYT,* A1, A12.

31. National Center for Health Statistics. (1989, April 28). Births, marriages, divorces, and deaths for 1988. *Monthly Vital Statistics Report,* U.S. Department of Health and Human Services, vol. 37, no. 12, suppl. DHHS Pub. No. (PHS)89-1120.

32. Umberson, D. (1989, May). Marital benefits for men vs. women. *Medical Aspects of Human Sexuality,* 56.

33. Hu, Y. R., & Goldman, N. (1990). Mortality differentials by marital status: An international comparison. *Demography, 27*(2), 233–50.

34. Wilson, B. F. (1991, October). The marry-go-round. *American Demographics,* 52–54.

35. Umberson, 1989.

36. Bozzi, V. (1988, March). Brains and beauty merge. *AH,* 116.

37. Olson, D. H. Quoted in: Kochakian, M. J. (1992, October 27). Study finds many marriages unhappy. *SFC,* D3; reprinted from *Hartford Courant.*

38. Cleek, M., & Pearson, A. (1985). Perceived causes of divorce: An analysis of interrelationships. *Journal of Marriage & the Family, 47,* 179–83.

39. U.S. Census Bureau. Cited in: Anonymous. (1991, October 4–6). Liz leads at the altar. *USA Today,* 1A.

40. U.S. Census Bureau. Cited in: Staff, *American Demographics.* (1990, August 3). Romance in America, and how it pans out. *WSJ,* B1.

41. Arbetter, S. R. (1989). The way it is: The remarried family. *Current Health 2, 17,* 17–19.

42. National Center for Health Statistics. Reported in: Associated Press. (1990, April 4). Marriage can be habit-forming. *SFC,* A7.

43. Crooks, R., & Baur, K. (1990). *Our sexuality* (4th ed.). Redwood City, CA: Benjamin/Cummings, 522.

44. Weiten, W., Lloyd, M. A., & Lashley, R. L. (1991). *Psychology applied to modern life: Adjustment in the 90s* (3rd ed.). Pacific Grove: CA: Brooks/Cole.

45. Eisler, R. M., Skidmore, J. R., & Ward, C. H. (1988). Masculine gender-role stress: Predictor of anger, anxiety, and health-risk behaviors. *Journal of Personality Assessment, 52*(1), 133–41.

46. Gillespie, B. L., & Eisler, R. M. (1992). Development of the feminine gender role stress scale: A cognitive-behavioral measure of stress, appraisal, and coping for women. *Behavior Modification, 16*(3), 426–38.

47. American Academy of Pediatrics. (1989). Report of the Task Force on Circumcision. *Pediatrics, 84,* 383–91.

48. Arrighi, H. M., Guess, H. A., Metter, E. J. et al. (1990). Symptoms and signs of prostatism as risk factors for prostatectomy. *Prostate, 16,* 253–61.

49. Fowler, F., Wennberg, J., Timothy, R. et al. (1988). Symptom status and quality of life following prostatectomy. *JAMA, 259,* 3018–22.

50. Barry, M. J. (1990). Epidemiology and natural history of benign prostatic hyperplasia. *Urologic Clinics of North America, 17*, 495–507.
51. Avant, R. F. (1988). Dysmenorrhea. *Primary Care; Clinics in Office Practice, 15*, 549–59.
52. Izzo, A., & Labriola, D. (1991). Dysmenorrhea and sports activities in adolescents. *Clinical & Experimental Obstetrics & Gynecology, 18*, 109–16.
53. Osofsky, H. J. (1990). Efficacious treatments of PMS: A need for further research. *JAMA, 264*, 387.
54. Sedney, M. (1987) Development of androgyny: Parental influences. *Psychology of Women Quarterly, 11*, 311–26.
55. Crooks & Baur, 1990.
56. Crooks & Baur, 1990.
57. Centers for Disease Control. Cited in: Associated Press. (1992, November 23). Risky sex declining among teens. *SFC*, C4.
58. Crooks & Baur, 1990.
59. Crooks & Baur, 1990.
60. Crooks & Baur, 1990.
61. Pauly, I., & Edgerton, M. (1986). The gender identity movement: A growing surgical-psychiatric liaison. *Archives of Sexual Behavior, 15*, 315–30.
62. Green, R. (1974). *Sexual identity conflict in children and adults*. New York: Basic.
63. Pauly, I. (1974). Female transsexualism: Part II. *Archives of Sexual Behavior, 3*, 509–26.
64. Tollison, C. D., & Adams, H. E. (1979). *Sexual disorders: Treatment, theory, and research*. New York: Gardner Press.
65. Lundstrom, B., Pauly, I., & Walinder, J. (1984). Outcome of sex reassignment surgery. *Acta Psychiatrica Scandinavica, 70*, 289–94.
66. Kinsey, A., Pomeroy, W., & Martin, C. (1948). *Sexual behavior in the human male*. Philadelphia: Saunders.
67. Bloch, H., Donley, M., & Lafferty, E. (1992, August 17). Bisexuality: What is it? *Time*, 49–51.
68. Barinaga, M. (1991). Is homosexuality biological? *Science, 253*, 956–57.
69. Bailey, J. M., & Pillard, R. C. Cited in: Bishop, J. E. (1991, December 17). Study of brothers of gay men suggest genetic tendency for homosexuality. *WSJ*, B4.
70. LeVay, S. (1991). A difference in hypothalamic structure between heterosexual and homosexual men. *Science, 253*, 1034–37.
71. Allen, L. S., & Gorski, R. A. (1992). Sexual orientation and the size of the anterior commissure in the human brain. *Proceedings of the National Academy of Sciences of the United States of America, 89*, 7199–7202.
72. Gallup Organization. (1992, June 12). Poll finds most disapprove of gay lifestyle. *SFC*, A27.
73. Masters, W., & Johnson, V. (1966). *Human sexual response*. Boston: Little, Brown.
74. Masters & Johnson, 1966.
75. Masters & Johnson, 1966.
76. World Health Organization. (1992). *Reproductive health: A key to a brighter future*. Cited in: Associated Press. (1992, June 25). U.N. agency on sex: Pitfalls and promise. *NYT*, A4.
77. Klein, M. (1992, June). The answer guy. *Men's Health*, 84–85.
78. Friday, N. (1991). *Women on top: How real life has changed women's sexual fantasies*. New York: Simon & Schuster, 191.
79. Zilbergeld, B. (1992). *The new male sexuality*. New York: Bantam.
80. Sue, D. (1979). Erotic fantasies of college students during coitus. *Journal of Sex Research, 15*, 299–305.
81. Crooks & Baur, 1990.
82. Kinsey, Pomeroy, & Martin, 1948.
83. Kinsey, A., Pomeroy, W., Martin, C. et al. (1953). *Sexual behavior in the human female*. Philadelphia: Saunders.
84. Follingstad, D., & Kimbrell, D. (1986). Sexual fantasies revisited: An expansion and further

clarification of variables affecting sex fantasy production. *Archives of Sexual Behavior, 15*, 475–86.
85. Hunt, M. (1974). *Sexual behavior in the 1970s*. Chicago: Playboy Press.
86. Crooks & Baur, 1990.
87. Huey, C., Kline-Graber, G., & Graber, B. (1981). Time factors and orgasmic response. *Archives of Sexual Behavior, 21*, 111–18.
88. Hass, A. (1979). *Teenage sexuality*. New York: Macmillan.
89. Kinsey, Pomeroy, Martin, & Gebhard, 1953.
90. Hunt, 1974.
91. Harold, E., & Way, L. (1983). Oral-genital sexual behavior in a sample of university females. *Journal of Sex Research, 19*, 327–29.
92. Consumers Union. (1989, March). Can you rely on condoms? *Consumer Reports*, 135–41.
93. Hunt, 1974.
94. Westoff, C. (1974). Coital frequency and contraception. *Family Planning Perspectives, 6*, 136–41.
95. Trussell, J., & Westoff, C. F. (1980). Contraceptive practice and trends in coital frequency. *Family Planning Perspectives, 12*, 246–49.
96. Greenblatt, C. S. (1983). The salience of sexuality in the early years of marriage. *Journal of Marriage & the Family, 45*, 289–99.
97. National Opinion Research Center, University of Chicago. (1990, February). Report on sexual behavior. Presented to February 1990 American Association for the Advancement of Science Meeting, New Orleans. Cited in: Petit, C. (1990, February 19). Sex survey says Americans are faithful—once a week. *SFC*, A1.
98. National Opinion Research Center, 1990.
99. Marin, P. (1983, July). A revolution's broken promises. *PT*, 50–57.
100. Byer, C. O., & Shainberg, L. W. (1991). *Dimensions of human sexuality* (3rd ed.). Dubuque, IA: Wm. C. Brown.
101. Kaminer, W. (1992, November 29). Exposing the new authoritarians: Censorship under the guise of protecting women. *SFE*, D-1, D-4, D-5; exerpted from *The Atlantic* (1992, November).
102. Martin, G. (1991, August 11). The body trade. *SFC, This World*, 7–10.
103. Goldberg, L. (1991, November 10). Walking away from the wild side. *SFE*, C-5.
104. Hoigard, C., & Finstad, L. (1992). K. Hanson, N. Sipe, & B. Wilson (trans.), *Backstreets: Prostitution, money, and love*. University Park, PA: Pennsylvania State University Press.
105. Anonymous. (1992, April 23). Sex for sale (editorial). *The Times* (London), 13.
106. Knopf, J., & Seiler, M. (1990). *Inhibited sexual desire*. New York: Morrow.
107. Josselson, R. (1992). *The space between us*. San Francisco: Jossey-Bass.
108. Bechtel, S. (1991, August). Burning down the house. *Men's Health*, 78–80.
109. Carnes, P. (1983). *Out of the shadows: Understanding sexual addiction*. Minneapolis: CompCare.
110. Levin, R., & Levin, A. (1975, September). Sexual pleasure: The surprising preferences of 100,000 women. *Redbook*, 51–68.
111. Fisher, J. D. Cited in: Adler, J., Wright, L., McCormick, J. et al. (1991, December 9). Safer sex. *Newsweek*, 52–56.
112. Montefiore, S. S. (1992, October). Love, lies and fear in the plague years... *PT*, 30–35.
113. Merson, M. H., World Health Organization. Cited in: Altman, L. K. (1992, July 21). Women worldwide nearing higher rate for AIDS than men. *NYT*, B8.
114. Alan Guttmacher Institute. Cited in: Barringer, F. (1993, April 1). 1 in 5 in U.S. have sexually caused viral disease. *NYT*, A1, B9.

115. Alan Guttmacher Institute. Cited in: Barringer, 1993.
116. Adler et al., 1991.
117. Cochran, S. D., & Mays, V. M. (1993). Sex, lies, and HIV (letter). *NEJM, 322*, 774–75.
118. Cochran, S. Quoted in: Roberts, M. (1988, December). Dating, dishonesty and AIDS. *PT*, 60.
119. Centers for Disease Control. (1988). Leads from the MMWR. Condoms for prevention of sexually transmitted diseases. *JAMA, 259*, 1925–27.

CHAPTER 6: BIRTH CONTROL, PREGNANCY, AND CHILDBIRTH

1. Anonymous. Quoted in: Adler, J., Wright, L., McCormick, J. et al. (1991, December 9). Safer sex. *Newsweek*, 52–56.
2. D.B. (1989, April). Conception misconceptions. *PT*, 10–11.
3. Forrest, J. D. (1987). Has she or hasn't she? U.S. women's experience with contraception. *Family Planning Perspectives, 19*, 133.
4. Kost, K., Forrest, J. D., & Harlap, S. (1991). Comparing the health risks and benefits of contraceptive choices. *Family Planning Perspectives, 23*, 54–61.
5. Starr, C., & Taggart, R. (1989). *Biology: The unity and diversity of life* (5th ed.). Belmont, CA: Wadsworth.
6. Hatcher, R., Guest, F., Stewart, F. et al. (1990). *Contraceptive technology: 1990–1992* (15th ed.). New York: Irvington.
7. Hatcher et al., 1990.
8. Hatcher et al., 1990.
9. Kost, Forrest, & Harlap, 1991.
10. Hatcher et al., 1990.
11. Jarow, J., Budin, R. E., Dym, M. et al. (1985). Quantitative pathologic changes in the human testis after vasectomy. *NEJM, 20*, 1252–56.
12. Hilts, P. J. (1990, December 16). Birth-control backlash. *New York Times Magazine*, 41, 55, 70–74.
13. Kaeser, L. (1990). Contraceptive development: Why the snail's pace? *Family Planning Perspectives, 22*, 131–33.
14. Leary, W. E. (1992, February 1). U.S. Panel backs approval of first condom for women. *NYT*, 7.
15. Turner, R. (1990). Vaginal ring is comparable in safety and efficacy to other low-dose, progestogen-only methods. *Family Planning Perspectives, 22*, 236–37.
16. Silvestre, L., Dubois, C., Renault, M. et al. (1990). Voluntary interruption of pregnancy with mifepristone (RU 486) and a prostaglandin analogue. *NEJM, 322*, 645–48.
17. National Center for Health Statistics. (1989, September 26). Advanced report of final mortality statistics, 1987. *Monthly Vital Statistics Report*, vol. 38, no. 5, sppl. DHHS Pub. No. (PHS)89-1120. Washington, DC: U.S. Department of Health and Human Services.
18. Kolata, G. (1992, January 5). In late abortions, decisions are painful and options few. *NYT*, sec. 1, 1, 12.
19. Lasker, J., & Borg, S. (1990). *When pregnancy fails: Families coping with miscarriage, ectopic pregnancy, stillbirth, and infant death* (2nd ed.). New York: Bantam.
20. Adler, N. E., David, H. P., Major, B. N. et al. (1990). Psychological responses after abortion. *Science, 248*, 41–44.
21. Lunneborg, P. (1992). *Abortion: A positive decision*. South Hadley, MA: Bergin & Garvey.
22. Dagg, P. K. (1991). The psychological sequelae of therapeutic abortion—denied and completed. *American Journal of Psychiatry, 148*(5), 578–85.
23. Rosenblatt, R. (1992). *Life itself: Abortion in the American mind*. New York: Random House.

24. Rivers, R., & Williamson, N. (1990). Sickle cell anemia: Complex disease, nursing challenge. *RN, 53*, 24–27.

25. Barrett, J. M., Abramoff, P., Kumaran, A. K. et al. (1986). *Biology.* Englewood Cliffs, NJ: Prentice Hall.

26. Schmeck, H. M. Jr. (1990, April 29). Battling the legacy of illness. *New York Times Magazine, The Good Health Magazine*, 36-37, 46-50.

27. National Center for Health Statistics. Cited in: Anonymous. (1990, December). Older mothers: chromosome defects. *AH*, 11.

28. Ahlborg, G. Jr., & Bodin, L. (1991). Tobacco smoke exposure and pregnancy outcome among working women: A prospective study at prenatal care centers in Orebro County, Sweden. *American Journal of Epidemiology, 133*, 338–47.

29. Williams, M. A., Lieberman, E., Mittendorf, R. et al. (1991). Risk factors for abruptio placentae. *American Journal of Epidemiology, 134*, 965–72.

30. Savitz, D. A., Whelan, E. A., & Kleckner, R. C. (1989). Self-reported exposure to pesticides and radiation related to pregnancy outcome—results from National Natality and Fetal Mortality Surveys. *Public Health Reports, 104*, 473–77.

31. Kulhanjian, J. A., Soroush, V., Au, D. S. et al. (1992). Identification of women at unsuspected risk of primary infection with herpes simplex virus type 2 during pregnancy. *NEJM, 326*, 916–20.

32. Althaus, F. (1990). Folic acid supplementation during early pregnancy appears to lessen risk of neural tube defects. *Family Planning Perspectives, 22*, 140–41.

33. Tamura, R., Goldenberg, R. L., Freeberg, L. E. et al. (1992). Maternal serum folate and zinc concentrations and their relationships to pregnancy outcome. *American Journal of Clinical Nutrition, 56*, 365–70.

34. Carlsen, E., Giwercman, A., Keiding, N. et al. (1992). Evidence for decreasing quality of semen during past 50 years. *British Medical Journal, 305*, 609–13.

35. Fraga, C. G., Motchnik, P. A., Shigenaga, M. K. et al. (1991). Ascorbic acid protects against endogenous oxidative DNA damage in human sperm. *Proceedings of the National Academy of Sciences of the United States of America, 88*, 11003–6.

36. Emanuele, M. A., Tentler, J., Emanuele, N. V. et al. (1991). In vivo effects of acute EtOH on rat alpha and beta luteinizing hormone gene expression. *Alcohol, 8*, 345–48.

37. Brody, J. E. (1991, December 25). Possible links are being explored between babies' health and fathers' habits and working conditions. *NYT*, 15.

38. Zhang, J., Cai, W. W., & Lee, D. J. (1992). Occupational hazards and pregnancy outcomes. *American Journal of Industrial Medicine, 21*, 397–408.

39. Waldrop, J. (1991, September). The birthday boost. *American Demographics*, 4.

40. Leifer, M. (1980). *Psychological effects of motherhood: A study of first pregnancy*. New York: Praeger.

41. Carpenter, M. (1979). Physicians ponder popularity of pregnancy self-test kits. *Medical News, 14*, 18.

42. Rice, F. P. (1989). *Human sexuality.* Dubuque, IA: Wm. C. Brown.

43. Guttmacher, A. F. (1983). *Pregnancy, birth, and family planning* (rev. ed.). New York: New American Library.

44. Antle, K. (1978). Active involvement of expectant fathers in pregnancy: Some further considerations. *Journal of Obstetric, Gynecologic, & Neonatal Nursing, 7*, 7–12.

45. Lipkin, M. J., & Lamb, G. S. (1982). The couvade syndrome: An epidemiologic study. *AIM, 96*, 509–11.

46. Conner, G. K., & Denson, V. (1990). Expectant fathers' response to pregnancy: Review of literature and implications for research in high-risk pregnancy. *Journal of Perinatal & Neonatal Nursing, 4*, 33–42.

47. Longobucco, D. C., & Freston, M. S. (1989). Relation of somatic symptoms to degree of paternal-role preparation of first-time expectant fathers. *Journal of Obstetric, Gynecologic, & Neonatal Nursing, 18*, 482–88.

48. Jackson, B. (1984). *Fatherhood.* London: George Allen and Unwin.

49. Gelles, R. J. (1975). Violence and pregnancy: A note on the extent of the problem and needed services. *Family Coordinator, 24*, 81–86.

50. Kitzinger, S. (1983). *The complete book of pregnancy and childbirth.* New York: Knopf.

51. National Center for Health Statistics. (1990). *Health, United States, 1989, and prevention profile.* DHHS Pub. No. (PHS)90-1232. Hyattsville, MD: U.S. Department of Health and Human Services.

52. U.S. Public Health Service. (1990). *Healthy people 2000: National health promotion and disease prevention objectives.* DHHS Pub. No. (PHS)91-50212. Washington, DC: U.S. Government Printing Office.

53. Scott, J. (1990, December 31). Low birth weight's high cost. *LAT*, A1, A20.

54. King, J. C. (1991). New National Academy of Sciences guidelines for nutrition during pregnancy. *Diabetes, 40*(suppl. 2), 151.

55. Scholl, T. O., Hediger, M. L., Khoo, C. S. et al. (1991). Maternal weight gain, diet and infant birth weight: Correlations during adolescent pregnancy. *Journal of Clinical Epidemiology, 44*, 423–28.

56. Hall, D. Quoted in: Longstreet, D. (1992, June). Expecting the best. *AH*, 89.

57. Caan, B. J., & Goldhaber, M. K. (1989). Caffeinated beverages and low birthweight: A case-control study. *AJPH, 79*(9), 1299–1300.

58. Fenster, L., Eskenazi, R., Windham, G. C. et al. (1991). Caffein consumption during pregnancy and fetal growth. *AJPH, 81*(4), 458–61.

59. Moore, K. (1989). *Before we are born* (3rd ed.). Philadelphia: Saunders.

60. McLaren, N., & Nieburg, P. (1988, August). Fetal tobacco syndrome and other problems caused by smoking during pregnancy. *Medical Aspects of Human Sexuality*, 69–75.

61. Niebyl, J. (1988, September). Smoking presents many risks to mother and fetus. *Medical Aspects of Human Sexuality*, 10–24.

62. Coleman, S., Piotrow, P. T., & Rinehart, W. (1979, March). Tobacco: Hazard to health and human reproduction. *Population Reports,* Series L (1).

63. Mason, J. O., Tolsma, D. D., Peterson, H. B. et al. (1988). Health promotion for women: Reduction of smoking in primary care settings. *Clinical Obstetrics & Gynecology, 31*, 989–1002.

64. Carroll, C. R. (1989). *Drugs in modern society.* Dubuque, IA: Wm. C. Brown.

65. Carroll, 1989.

66. Ostrea, E. M. Jr., & Chavez, C. J. (1979). Perinatal problems (excluding neonatal withdrawal) in maternal drug addiction: A study of 830 cases. *Journal of Pediatrics, 94*, 292–95.

67. Scher, J., & Dix, C. (1983). *Will my baby be normal? Everything you need to know about pregnancy.* New York: Dial Press.

68. Fried, P. A., Watkinson, B., Grant, A. et al. (1980). Changing patterns of soft drug use prior to and during pregnancy: A prospective study. *Drug & Alcohol Dependency, 6*, 323.

69. Hingson, R., Alpert, J., Day, N. et al. (1982). Effects of maternal drinking and marijuana use on fetal growth and development. *Pediatrics, 70*, 539–46.

70. Coles, C. D., Platzman, K. A., Smith, I. et al. (1992). Effects of cocaine and alcohol use in pregnancy on neonatal growth and neurobehavioral status. *Neurotoxicology & Teratology, 14*, 22–33.

71. Janke, J. R. (1990). Prenatal cocaine use: Effects on perinatal outcome. *Journal of Nurse-Midwifery, 35*, 74–77.

72. Mayes, L. C., Granger, R. H., Bornstein, M. H., & Zuckerman, B. (1992). The problem of prenatal cocaine exposure. *JAMA, 267*, 406–408.

73. Gupta, C., Yaffe, S. J., & Shaprio, B. H. (1982). Prenatal exposure to phenobarbital permanently decreases testosterone and causes reproductive dysfunction. *Science, 216*, 640–42.

74. O'Brien, T. E., & McManus, C. E. (1978). Drugs and the fetus: A consumer's guide by generic and brand name. *Birth & the Family Journal, 5*, 58–86.

75. Brent, R. L. (1986). The complexities of solving the problem of human malformations. In J. L. Sever & R. L. Brent (Eds.), *Teratogen update: Environmentally induced birth defect risks.* New York: Liss.

76. Stewart, A., & Kneale, G. W. (1970). Radiation dose effects in relation to obstetric X-rays and childhood cancers. *Lancet, 1*, 1495.

77. Raloff, J. (1986). Even low levels in mom affect baby. *Science News, 130*, 164.

78. U.S. Public Health Service. (1990). *Healthy people 2000: National health promotion and disease prevention objectives.* DHHS Pub. No. (PHS)91-50212. Washington, DC: U.S. Government Printing Office.

79. Public Health Service, 1990.

80. Beck, M. (1988, August 15). Miscarriages. *Newsweek*, 46–52.

81. Guttmacher, 1983.

82. Moore, K. (1989). *Before we are born* (3rd ed.). Philadelphia: Saunders.

83. Larsen, J. W. (1986). Congenital toxoplasmosis. In J. L. Sever & R. L. Brent (Eds.), *Teratogen update: Environmentally induced birth defect risks.* New York: Liss.

84. Berger, K. S. 1988). *The developing person through the life span* (2nd ed.). New York: Worth.

85. Greenwood, S. (1989, March/April). Prenatal testing update. *Medical Selfcare*, 19–20.

86. Haddow, J. E., Palomaki, G. E., Knight, G. J. et al. Prenatal screening for Down's syndrome with use of maternal serum markers. *NEJM, 327*, 588–93.

87. Anonymous. (1992, August 19). A simpler screening for Down risks. *NYT*, B6. [Report of study led by N. J. Wald.]

88. Bean, C. (1974). *Methods of childbirth.* New York: Dolphin.

89. Crooks, R., & Baur, K. (1990). *Our sexuality* (4th ed.). Redwood City, CA: Benjamin/Cummings.

90. Declercq, E. R. (1992). The transformation of American midwifery: 1975 to 1988. *AJPH, 82*, 680–84.

91. Kay, B. J., Butter, I. H., Chang, D. et al. (1988). Women's health and social change: The case of lay midwives. *International Journal of Health Services, 18*, 223–36.

92. Otis, C.H. (1990, November/December). Midwives still hassled by medical establishment. *Utne Reader, 32*, 34.

93. Health Insurance Association of America. Cited in: Weinhouse, B., & Burgower, B. (1990, August 30). Answers to questions about birth styles. *SFC*, B3, B5.

94. Duran, A. M. (1992). The safety of home birth: The farm study. *AJPH, 82*, 450–53.

95. Albers, L. L., & Katz, V. L. (1991). Birth setting for low-risk pregnancies: An analysis of the current literature. *Journal of Nurse-Midwifery, 36*, 215–20.

96. Tyson, H. (1991). Outcomes of 1001 midwife-attended home births in Toronto, 1983–1988. *Birth, 18*, 14–19.

97. Thorp, J. M. Jr., & Bowes, W. A. Jr. (1989). Episiotomy: Can its routine use be defended? *American Journal of Obstetrics & Gynecology, 160,* 1027–30.

98. Bromberg, M. H. (1986). Presumptive maternal benefits of routine episiotomy: A literature review. *Journal of Nurse-Midwifery, 31,* 121–27.

99. Wilson, R. J., Bacham, C. T., & Carrington, E. R. (1975). *Obstetrics and Gynecology.* St. Louis: Mosby.

100. Whipple, B., Josimovich, J. B., & Komisaruk, B. R. (1990). Sensory thresholds during the antepartum, intrapartum, and postpartum periods. *International Journal of Nursing Studies, 27,* 213–21.

101. Leventhal, E. A., Leventhal, H., Shacham, S. et al. (1989). Active coping reduces reports of pain from childbirth. *Journal of Consulting & Clinical Psychology, 57,* 365–71.

102. Felton, G., & Segelman, F. (1978). Lamaze childbirth training and changes in belief about personal control. *Birth and Family Journal, 5,* 141–50.

103. Lamaze, F. (1970). *Painless childbirth.* Chicago: Regency.

104. Leboyer, F. (1975). *Birth without violence.* New York: Alfred Knopf.

105. Miller, B. C., & Bowen, S. L. (1982). Father-to-newborn attachment behavior in relation to prenatal classes and presence at delivery. *Family Relations, 31,* 71–78.

106. Nortzon, F. C., Placek, P. J., & Taffel, S. M. (1987). Comparisons of national cesarean-section rates. *NEJM, 316,* 386–89.

107. Winslow, R. (1990, January 2). C-sections tied to economic factors in study. *WSJ,* B4.

108. Anonymous. (1992, May 13). Caesareans decline, but rate is called too high. *NYT,* C12.

109. Stichler, J. P., & Alfonso, D. D. (1980). Cesarean birth. *American Journal of Nursing, 80,* 466–68.

110. Anonymous. (1991, February). The effects on mother and child. *Consumer Reports,* 122.

111. Klaus, M., & Kennel, J. (1982). *Parent-infant bonding* (2nd ed.). St. Louis: Mosby.

112. Salk, L. (1974). *Preparing for parenthood.* New York: Bantam.

113. Harlow, H. F., & Suomi, S. J. (1970). Nature of love—simplified. *American Psychologist, 25,* 161–68.

114. Anonymous. (1992). Sudden infant death syndrome—United States, 1980–1988. *MMWR, 41,* 515–17.

115. Ryan, A. S., Rush, D., Krieger, F. W. et al. (1991). Recent declines in breast-feeding in the United States, 1984 through 1989. *Pediatrics, 88,* 719.

116. Macfarlane, A. (1977). *The psychology of childbirth.* Cambridge, MA: Harvard University Press.

117. Medical Tribune News Service. (1991, September 9). Breast-milk benefits extend to adulthood. *SFC,* D3.

118. Sears, C. (1991, December). Baby bottle blues. *AH,* 17.

119. Lucas, A., Morley, R., Cole, T. J. et al. (1992). Breast milk and subsequent intelligence quotient in children born preterm. *Lancet, 339,* 261–64.

120. Karjalainen, J., Martin, J. M., Knip, M. et al. (1992). A bovine albumin peptide as a possible trigger of insulin-dependent diabetes mellitus. *NEJM, 327,* 302–307.

121. McCary, S. P., & McCary, J. L. (1984). *Human sexuality* (3rd ed.). Belmont, CA: Wadsworth.

122. Crooks & Baur, 1990.

123. Marchbanks, P. A., Peterson, H. B., Rubin, G. L. et al. (1989). Research on infertility: Definition makes a difference. The Cancer and Steroid Hormone Study Group. *American Journal of Epidemiology, 130,* 259–67.

124. Rice, 1989.

125. Rice, 1989.

126. Rice, 1989.

127. Bates, G. W., & Boone, W. R. (1991). The female reproductive cycle: New variations on an old theme. *Current Opinion in Obstetrics & Gynecology, 3,* 838–43.

128. Luke, B., Witter, F. R., Abbey, H. et al. (1991). Gestational age-specific birthweights of twins versus singletons. *Acta Geneticae Medicae Et Gemellologiae, 40,* 69–76.

129. Luke, B., & Keith, L. G. (1992). The contribution of singletons, twins and triplets to low birth weight, infant mortality and handicap in the United States. *Journal of Reproductive Medicine, 37,* 661–62.

130. Quigley, M. M. (1992). The new frontier of the reproductive age (editorial). *JAMA, 268,* 1320–21.

131. Bachrach, C. A., Stolley, K. S., & London, K. A. (1992). Relinquishment of premarital births: Evidence from national survey data. *Family Planning Perspectives, 24,* 27–32.

132. Gubernick, L. (1991, October 14). How much is that baby in the window? *Forbes,* 90–98.

133. Carroll, J. (1990, November 8). Why Feinstein believes in fate. *SFC,* B3, B6.

134. Seawell, M. A. (1989, October). Unwanted celebrity status. *Stanford Observer,* 5.

135. Leary, W. E. (1992, September 13). A determined breaker of boundaries. *NYT,* sec. 1, 18.

136. Manegold, C. S. (1994, September 11). The Citadel's lone wolf: Shannon Faulkner. *NYT Magazine,* 56–59.

CHAPTER 7: CAFFEINE, TOBACCO, AND ALCOHOL

1. Levenson, H. S., & Bick, E. C. (1977). Psychopharmacology of caffeine. In M. E. Jarvik (Ed.), *Psychopharmacology in the practice of medicine.* New York: Appleton-Century-Crofts, 451–63.

2. Lecos, C. W. (1988). Caffeine jitters: Some safety questions remain. *FDA Consumer.* HHS Pub. No. (FDA)88-2221. Rockville, MD: U.S. Government Printing Office.

3. Bashin, B. J. (1988, February 28). The jolt in java. *SFC, This World,* 12–13.

4. Weidner, G., & Itvan, J. (1985). Dietary sources of caffeine (letter). *NEJM, 313,* 1421.

5. Gilbert, R. M. (1984). Caffeine consumption. *Progress in Clinical Biological Research, 158,* 185–213.

6. Ray, O., & Ksir, C. (1990). *Drugs, society, and human behavior* (5th ed.). St. Louis: Times Mirror/Mosby.

7. Leonard, T. K., Watson, R. R., & Mohs, M. E. (1987). The effects of caffeine on various body systems: A review. *Journal of the American Dietetic Association, 87,* 1048–53.

8. Ashton, C. H. (1987). Caffeine and health. *British Medical Journal, 295,* 1293–94.

9. Leonard, Watson, & Mohs, 1987.

10. Ray & Ksir, 1990.

11. Gilliland, K., & Andress, D. (1981). Ad lib caffeine consumption, symptoms of caffeinism, and academic performance. *American Journal of Psychiatry, 138,* 512–14.

12. Kenny, M., & Darragh, A. (1985). Central effects of caffeine in man. In S. D. Iversen (Ed.), *Psychopharmacology: Recent advances and future prospects.* Oxford: Oxford University Press, 278–88.

13. Gilliland & Andress, 1981.

14. Ray & Ksir, 1990.

15. van Dusseldorp, M., & Katan, M. B. (1990). Headache caused by caffeine withdrawal among moderate coffee drinkers switched from ordinary to decaffeinated coffee: A 12 week double blind trial. *British Medical Journal, 300,* 1558–59.

16. Klag, M. Cited in: Friend, T. (1991, March

15–17). Coffee tied to increase in heart risk. *USA Today,* 1A. [Study reported at 1991 American Heart Association meeting, Florida.]

17. LaCroix, A. Z., Mead, L. A., Liang, K. et al. (1986). Coffee consumption and the incidence of coronary heart disease.

18. Rosenberg, L., Palmer, J. R., Kelly, J. P. et al. (1988). Coffee drinking and nonfatal myocardial infarction in men under 55 years of age. *American Journal of Epidemiology, 128,* 570–78.

19. Tverdal, A., Stensvold, I. Solvoll, K. et al. (1990). Coffee consumption and death from coronary heart disease in middle-aged Norwegian men and women. *British Medical Journal, 300,* 566–69.

20. Grobee, D. E., Rimm, E. B., Giovannucci, E. (1990). Coffee, caffeine, and cardiovascular disease in men. *NEJM, 323,* 1026–32.

21. Willet, W. Study reported in: Kolata, T. (1990, October 11). Study disputes coffee's tie to heart disease risk. *NYT,* B7.

22. National Institutes of Health. (1989). Caffeine may be associated with reduced fertility. *JAMA, 261,* 1864.

23. Joesoef, M. F., Beral, V., Rolfs, R. T. et al. (1990). Are caffeinated beverages risk factors for delayed conception? *Lancet, 335,* 136–37.

24. Aaronson, L. S., & Macnee, C. L. (1989). Tobacco, alcohol, and caffeine use during pregnancy. *Journal of Obstetric, Gynecologic, & Neonatal Nursing, 18,* 279–87.

25. Caan, B. J., & Goldhaber, M. K. (1989). Caffeinated beverages and low birthweight: A case-control study. *AJPH, 79,* 1299–300.

26. Fenster, L., Eskenazi, R., Windham, G. C. et al. (1991). Caffeine consumption during pregnancy and fetal growth. *AJPH, 81*(4), 458–61.

27. Brooke, O. G., Anderson, H. R., Bland, J. M. et al. (1989). Effects on birth weight of smoking, alcohol, caffeine, socioeconomic factors, and psychosocial stress. *British Medical Journal, 298,* 795–801.

28. Rossignol, A. M., & Bonnlander, H. (1990). Caffeine-containing beverages, total fluid consumption, and premenstrual syndrome. *AJPH, 80,* 1106–10.

29. Lubin, F., & Ron, E. (1990). Consumption of methylxanthine-containing beverages and the risk of breast cancer. *Cancer Letters, 53*(2–3), 81–90.

30. Phelps, H. M., & Phelps, C. E. (1988). Caffeine ingestion and breast cancer: A negative correlation. *Cancer, 61*(5), 1051–54.

31. Ray & Ksir, 1990.

32. Joesoef et al., 1990.

33. LaVecchia, C., Gentile, A., Negri, E. et al. (1989). Coffee consumption and myocardial infarction in women. *American Journal of Epidemiology, 130,* 481–85.

34. Grobbee et al., 1990.

35. DiFranza, J. R., & Tye, J. B. (1990). Who profits from tobacco sales to children *JAMA, 263,* 2784–87.

36. U.S. Bureau of the Census, U.S. Department of Commerce. (1990). *Statistical abstract of the United States 1990.* Washington, DC: U.S. Department of Commerce, 123.

37. Fielding, J. E. (1987). Smoking and women: Tragedy of the majority. *NEJM, 317,* 1343–45.

38. Fried, J. L. (1994). Women and young girls...High risk populations for tobacco use. *Health Values, 18,* 33–40

39. Johnston, L. D., O'Malley, P. M., & Bachman, J. G. (1990). *Illicit drug use, smoking, and drinking by America's high school students, college students, and young adults: 1975–1989.* Rockville, MD: National Institute on Drug Abuse.

40. Pierce, J. P., Fiore, M. C., Novotny, T. E. et al. (1989). Trends in cigarette smoking in the United States: Educational differences are increasing. *JAMA, 261,* 56–60.

41. U.S. Department of Health and Human Services. (1990). *Smoking and health: A national status report*. Rockville, MD: U.S. Department of Health and Human Services.

42. Istvan, J., & Matarazzo, J. D. (1984). Tobacco, alcohol, and caffeine use: A review of their interrelationships. *Psychological Bulletin, 95*, 301–26.

43. Bradstock, M. K., Marks, J. S., Forman, M. R. et al. (1987). Drinking-driving and health lifestyle in the United States: Behavioral risk factors surveys. *Journal of Studies on Alcohol, 48*, 147–52.

44. Peele, S., Brodsky, A., & Arnold, M. (1991). *The truth about addiction and recovery: The life process program for outgrowing destructive habits*. New York: Simon & Schuster, 101.

45. Kilbourne, J. (1988). Cigarette ads target women, young people. *Alcoholism & Addiction, 9*, 22–23.

46. Carroll, C. R. (1989). *Drugs in modern society*. Dubuque, IA: Wm. C. Brown.

47. Nesbitt, P. D. (1972). Chronic smoking and emotionality. *Journal of Applied Social Psychology, 2*, 187–96.

48. U.S. Surgeon General. (1988). *Nicotine addiction: The health consequences of smoking*. Rockville, MD: U.S. Department of Health and Human Services, Office on Smoking and Health.

49. Peele, Brodsky, & Arnold, 1991.

50. Marsh, A. (1984). Smoking: habit or choice? *Population Trends, 37*, 19–20. Quoted in: Peele, Brodsky, & Arnold, 1991, 102.

51. Kilbourne, 1988, 22–23.

52. Kilbourne, 1988, 23.

53. U.S. Surgeon General, 1988.

54. Blum, K. (1984). *Handbook of abusable drugs*. New York: Gardner Press.

55. Hughes, J. R., Grist, S. W., & Pechacek, T. F. (1987). Prevalence of tobacco dependence and withdrawal. *American Journal of Psychiatry, 144*, 205–208. Cited in: Maisto, S. A., Galizio, M., & Connors, G. J. (1991). *Drug use and misuse*. Fort Worth, TX: Holt, Rinehart and Winston, 147.

56. Gallagher, J. E. (1990, March 5). Under fire from all sides. *Time*, 41. [Describes report of U.S. Senator Edward Kennedy during Senate hearings in which a new regulatory group was proposed to curb tobacco use.]

57. Russell, M. A. (1990). The nicotine addiction trap: A 40-year sentence for four cigarettes. *British Journal of Addiction, 85*, 293–300.

58. Centers for Disease Control. (1991). Smoking-attributable mortality and years of potential life lost—United States, 1988. *MMWR, 40*(4), 62.

59. Gilliam, H. (1991, June 2). Taking the risk: A sensible guide to environmental dangers. *SFC, This World*, 11.

60. Dinman, B. D. (1980). The reality and acceptance of risk. *JAMA, 244*, 1226–28.

61. Gilliam, 1991.

62. Ockene, J. K., Kuller, L. H., Svendsen, K. H. et al. (1990). The relationship of smoking cessations to coronary heart disease and lung cancer in the Multiple Risk Factor Intervention Trial (MRFIT). *AJPH, 80*, 954–58.

63. 1990 U.S. Surgeon General's report on smoking. Reported in: Perlman, D. (1990, September 26). Big benefits for smokers who can kick the habit. *SFC*, A2.

64. Office on Smoking and Health. (1989). *Reducing the health consequences of smoking: 25 years of progress. A report of the Surgeon General*. DHHS Pub. No. (CDC)89-8411. Washington, DC: U.S. Department of Health and Human Services.

65. Benfield, J. R. Cited in: Anonymous. (1991, May–June). Lung cancer and women. *The Futurist*, 6.

66. McLemore, T. L., Adelberg, S., Lieu, M. C. et al. (1990). Expression of cypial gene in patient

with lung cancer: Evidence for cigarette smoke–induced altered gene regulation in primary pulmonary carcinomas. *Journal of the National Cancer Institute, 82*, 1333–39.

67. Willett, W. C., Green, A., Stampfer, M. J. et al. (1987). Relative and absolute excess risks of coronary heart disease among women who smoke cigarettes. *NEJM, 317*, 1303–09.

68. La Vecchia, C., Franceschi, S., Decarli, A. et al. (1987). Risk factors for myocardial infarction in young women. *American Journal of Epidemiology, 125*, 832–43.

69. Abbott, R. D., Yin, Y., Reed, D. M. et al. (1986). Risk of stroke in male cigarette smokers. *NEJM, 315*, 717–20.

70. Tosteson, A. N. A., Weinstein, M. C., Williams, L. W. et al (1990). Long-term impact of smoking cessation on the incidence of coronary heart disease. *AJPH, 80*, 1481–86.

71. Kaduance, D. P., Burr, R., Gress, R. et al. (1991). Cigarette smoking: Risk factor for premature facial wrinkling. *AIM, 114*, 840–44.

72. Glina, S., Reichelt, C., Leao, P., & Reis, J. (1988). Impact of cigarette smoking on papaverine-induced erection. *Journal of Urology, 140*, 523–24.

73. Berg, A. T., Shapiro, E. D., & Capobianco, L. A. (1991). Group day care and the risk of serious infection disease. *American Journal of Epidemiology, 133*, 154–63.

74. Midgette, A. S., & Baron, J. A. (1990). Cigarette smoking and the risk of natural menopause. *Epidemiology, 1*, 474–80.

75. Stevenson, J. C., Lees, B., Devenport, M. et al. (1989). Determinants of bone density in normal women: Risk factors for future osteoporosis? *British Medical Journal, 298*, 924–28.

76. Hellberg, D., Nilsson, S., Haley, N. J. et al. (1988). Smoking and cervical intraepithelial neoplasia: Nicotine and cotinine in serum and cervical mucus in smokers and nonsmokers. *American Journal of Obstetrics & Gynecology, 158*, 910–13.

77. Layde, P. N., & Broste, S. K. (1989). Carcinoma of the cervix and smoking. *Biomedicine & Pharmacotherapy, 43*, 161–65.

78. Licciardone, J. C., Brownson, R. C., Chang, J. C. et al. (1990). Uterine cervical cancer risk in cigarette smokers: A meta-analytic study. *American Journal of Preventive Medicine, 6*, 274–81.

79. Goldbaum, G. M., Kendrick, J. S., Hogelin, G. C. et al. (1987). The relative impact of smoking and oral contraceptive use on women in the United States. *JAMA, 258*, 1339–42.

80. Coste, J., Job-Spira, N., & Fernandez, H. (1991). Increased risk of ectopic pregnancy with maternal cigarette smoking. *AJPH, 81*, 199–201.

81. Ray & Ksir, 1990.

82. Mason, J. O., Tolsma, D. D., Peterson, H. B. et al. (1988). Health promotion for women: Reduction of smoking in primary care settings. *Clinical Obstetrics & Gynecology, 31*, 989–1002.

83. Ray & Ksir, 1990.

84. Miller, L. G. (1990). Cigarettes and drug therapy: Pharmacokinetic and pharmacodynamic considerations. *Clinical Pharmacy, 9*(2), 125–35.

85. Handlin, D. Reported in: Goldfarb, B. (1990, October 22). Smokers need more time in recovery room. *USA Today*, 1D. [Describes report at October 1990 meeting of American Society of Anesthesiologists.]

86. Sears, C. (1990, January/February). Oral cancer: Room for improvement. *AH*, 26.

87. Logan, R. F., & Kay, C. R. (1989). Oral contraception, smoking, and inflammatory bowel disease: Findings in the Royal College of General Practitioners Oral Contraception Study. *International Journal of Epidemiology, 18*(1), 105–107.

88. Royce, R. A., & Winkelstein, W. Jr. (1990). HIV infection, cigarette smoking and CD4+

T-lymphocyte counts: Preliminary results from the San Francisco Men's Health Study. *AIDS, 4*, 327–33.

89. Botkin, J. R. (1988). The fire-safe cigarette. *JAMA, 260*, 226–29.

90. Patetta, M. J., & Cole, T. B. (1990). A population-based descriptive study of housefire deaths in North Carolina. *AJPH, 80*, 1116–17.

91. Christen, A. G., McDonald, J. L., Olson, B. L. et al. (1989). Smokeless tobacco addiction: A threat to the oral and systemic health of the child and adolescent. *Pediatrician, 16*(3–4), 170–77.

92. Glover, E. D., Laflin, M., Flannery, D. et al. (1989). Smokeless tobacco use among American college students. *Journal of American College Health, 38*, 81–85.

93. Winn, D. M. (1988). Smokeless tobacco and cancer: The epidemiologic evidence. *Ca: A Cancer Journal for Clinicians, 38*, 236–43.

94. Benowitz, N. L., Porchet, H., Sheiner, L. et al. (1988). Nicotine absorption and cardiovascular effects with smokeless tobacco use: Comparison with cigarettes and nicotine gum. *Clinical Pharmacology & Therapeutics, 44*(1), 23–28.

95. Brownson, R. C., diLorenzo, T. M., Van Tuinen, M. et al. (1990). Patterns of cigarette and smokeless tobacco use among children and adolescents. *Preventive Medicine, 19*(2), 170–80.

96. Grady, D., Ernster, V. L., Stillman, L. et al. (1991). Short term changes a surprise with smokeless tobacco. *Journal of the American Dental Association, 122*(1), 62–64.

97. Creath, C. J., Sheldon, W. O., Wright, J. T. et al. (1988). The prevalence of smokeless tobacco use among adolescent male athletes. *Journal of the American Dental Association, 116*(1), 43–48.

98. Christen et al., 1989.

99. Ray & Ksir, 1990.

100. Hoffman, D., Djordjevic, M. V., & Brunnemann, K. D. (1991). New brands of oral snuff. *Food & Chemical Toxicology, 29*, 65–68.

101. National Institutes of Health. (1988). NIH consensus statement: Health implications of smokeless tobacco use. *Biomedicine & Pharmacotherapy, 42*(2), 93–98.

102. Christen et al., 1989.

103. Winn, 1988.

104. Christen et al., 1989.

105. Grady et al., 1991.

106. Clark, G. C. (1990). Comparison of the inhalation toxicity of kretek (clove cigarette) smoke with that of American cigarette smoke. *Archives of Toxicology, 64*(7), 515–21.

107. Council on Scientific Affairs. (1988). Evaluation of the health hazard of clove cigarettes. *JAMA, 260*, 3641–44.

108. Ray & Ksir, 1990.

109. Bruno, K. (1990, January/February). The perils of passive smoke. *AH*, 15–17.

110. Ray & Ksir, 1990.

111. U.S. Public Health Service. (1986). *The health consequences of involuntary smoking: A report of the Surgeon General*. DHHS Pub. No. (CDC)87-8398. Washington, DC: U.S. Government Printing Office.

112. U.S. Environmental Protection Agency. Reported in: Associated Press. (1991, May 30). Secondhand smoke blamed for 53,000 deaths each year. *NYT*, A14.

113. Associated Press. (1990, December 6). Criticized panel backs the condemnation of second-hand smoke. *NYT*, A14.

114. Wells, A. J. (1991). Breast cancer, cigarette smoking, and passive smoking (letter). *American Journal of Epidemiology, 133*, 208–10.

115. Cowley, G. (1990, June 11). Secondhand smoke: Some grim news. *Newsweek*, 59.

116. Greenberg, R. A., Bauman, K. E., Strecher, V. J. et al. (1991). Passive smoking during the first year of life. *AJPH, 81*, 850–52.

117. U.S. Public Health Service, 1986.
118. Associated Press, 1990.
119. U.S. Public Health Service, 1986.
120. Ray & Ksir, 1990.
121. Novello, A. Quoted in: Perlman, 1990, A2.
122. LaCroix, A. Quoted in: Associated Press. (1991, June 6). Study says old smokers live longer by quitting. *SFC*, A5.
123. LaCroix, A. Z., Lang, J., Scherr, P. et al. (1991). Smoking and mortality among older men and women in three communities. *NEJM, 324*, 1619–25.
124. Carmody, T. P. (1990). Preventing relapse in the treatment of nicotine addiction: Current issues and future directions. *Journal of Psychoactive Drugs, 22*(2), 211–38.
125. Goodkind, M. (1989, Spring). The cigarette habit. *Stanford Medicine*, 13.
126. Okene, J. K. (1989). Promoting cessation. *Journal of the American Medical Women's Association, 44*(2), 60–63.
127. Fortman, S. Cited in: Goodkind, 1989, 14.
128. Fiore, M. C., Novotny, T. E., Pierce, J. P. et al. (1990). Methods used to quit smoking in the United States: Do cessation programs help? *JAMA, 263*, 2760–65.
129. Fiore et al., 1990.
130. Glynn, T. J. (1990). Methods of smoking cessation—finally, some answers (editorial). *JAMA, 263*, 2795–96.
131. Ray & Ksir, 1990.
132. Gourley, S. G., & McNeil, J. J. (1990). Antismoking products. *Medical Journal of Australia, 153*(11–12), 699–707.
133. Hughes, J. R., Gust, S. W., Keenan, R. M., Fenwick, J. W., & Healey, M. L. (1989). Nicotine vs placebo gum in general medical practice. *JAMA, 2*, 1300–1305.
134. Higgins, L. C. (1990). Arm patch may help kick the butt. *Medical World News, 31*, 29.
135. Spiegel, D. Cited in: Goodkind, 1989.
136. Williamson, D. F., Madans, J., Anda, R. F. et al. T. (1991). Smoking cessation and severity of weight gain in a national cohort. *NEJM, 324*, 739–45.
137. Skoog, K. Quoted in: Associated Press. (1991, January 30). Weight gain by ex-smokers points to success. *SFC*, B3.
138. Kozlowski, L. T., Wilkinson, D. A., Skinner, W. et al. Pope, M. (1989). Comparing tobacco cigarette dependence with other drug dependencies: Greater or equal 'difficulty quitting' and 'urges to use,' but less 'pleasure' from cigarettes. *JAMA, 261*, 898–901.
139. Roine, R., Gentry, R. T., Hernandez-Munoz, R. et al. (1990). Aspirin increases blood alcohol concentrations in humans after ingestion of ethanol. *JAMA, 264*, 2406–08.
140. Maisto, S. A., Galizio, M., & Connors, G. J. (1991). *Drug use and misuse*. Fort Worth, TX: Holt, Rinehart and Winston, 207–208.
141. Kinney, J., & Leaton, G. (1987). *Loosening the grip: A handbook of alcohol information* (3rd ed.). St. Louis: Times Mirror/Mosby, 21.
142. Addiction Research Foundation, Toronto, in pamphlet, "Know the Score." Cited in: Maisto, Galizio, & Connors, 1991, 208.
143. Kinney & Leaton, 1987, 41–42.
144. Herd, D. (1989). The epidemiology of drinking patterns and alcohol-related problems among U.S. blacks. In *Alcohol use among U.S. ethnic minorities*. Rockville, MD: National Institute on Alcohol Abuse and Alcoholism, 3–50.
145. Caetano, R. (1989). Drinking patterns and alcohol problems in a national sample of U.S. Hispanics. In *Alcohol use among U.S. ethnic minorities*. Rockville, MD: National Institute on Alcohol Abuse and Alcoholism, 147–62.
146. Vaillant, G. E. (1983). *The natural history of alcoholism: Causes, patterns, and paths to recovery*. Cambridge, MA: Harvard University Press, 61.
147. Vaillant, 1983.

148. Peele, Brodsky, & Arnold, 1991, 55.
149. Kinney & Leaton, 1987, 71.
150. Bedell, T. (1991, February). Saintly suds. *Men's Health*, 58–61.
151. Miller, A., & Springen, K. (1990, March 5). This safe suds is for you. *Newsweek*, 42.
152. Stampfer, M. J., Colditz, G. A., Willett, W. C. et al. (1988). A prospective study of moderate alcohol consumption and the risk of coronary disease and stroke in women. *NEJM, 319*, 267–73.
153. Centers for Disease Control. (1990). Alcohol-related mortality and years of potential life lost—United States, 1987. *MMWR, 39*(11), 173–77.
154. Centers for Disease Control, 1990.
155. Vegega, M. E., & Klein, T. M. (1991). Alcohol-related traffic fatalities among youth and young adults—United States, 1982–1989. *JAMA, 265*, 1930.
156. Caudill, B. Reported in: King, P. (1989, December). Heavy drinkers often take the wheel. *PT*, 12.
157. Kinney & Leaton, 1987, 25.
158. Centers for Disease Control, 1990.
159. Kinney & Leaton, 1987, 25.
160. Centers for Disease Control, 1990.
161. Mello, N. K. (1987). Alcohol abuse and alcoholism: 1978–1987. In H. Y. Meltzer (Ed.), *Psychopharmacology: The third generation of progress*. New York: Raven Press, 1515–20.
162. Wilsnack, S. C., Klassen, A. D., & Wilsnack, R. W. (1984). Drinking and reproductive dysfunction among women in a 1981 national survey. *Alcoholism: Clinical and Experimental Research, 8*, 451–58.
163. Plant, M. A. (1990). Alcohol, sex and AIDS. *Alcohol & Alcoholism, 25*, 293–301.
164. Parsons, O. A. (1986). Alcoholics' neuropsychological impairment: Current findings and conclusions. *Annals of Behavioral Medicine, 8*, 13–19.
165. U.S. Department of Health and Human Services (1987). *Alcohol and health*. Rockville, MD: U.S. Department of Health and Human Services.
166. Maisto, Galizio, & Connors, 1991, 209, table.
167. Willett, W. C., Stampfer, M. J., Colditz, G. A. et al. E. (1987). Moderate alcohol consumption and the risk of breast cancer. *NEJM, 316*, 1174–80.
168. Graham, S. (1987). Alcohol and breast cancer. *NEJM, 316*, 1211–12.
169. Carroll, 1989, 127.
170. Carroll, 1989, 128.
171. Schoenborn, C. A. (1991). Exposure to alcoholism in the family: United States, 1988. *Advance Data from Vital and Health Statistics of the National Center for Health Statistics*. Washington, DC: U.S. Department of Health and Human Services.
172. Anonymous child. Quoted in: Woodside, M. (1986). Children of alcoholics: Breaking the cycle. *Journal of School Health, 56*, 448.
173. Mull, S. S. (1990). Help for the children of alcoholics. *Health Education, 21*, 42–45.
174. Starling, B. P., & Martin, A. C. (1990). Adult survivors of parental alcoholism: Implications for primary care. *Nurse Practitioner, 15*(7), 16–24.
175. Harwood, H. J., Napolitana, D. M., Kristiansen, P. L., & Collins, J. J. (1984). *Economic costs to society of alcohol and drug abuse and mental illness: 1980*. Research Triangle Park, NC: Research Triangle Institute.
176. Stark, L. (1987, Spring). A century of alcohol and homelessness: Demographics and stereotypes. *Alcohol Health & Research World*, 8–13.
177. Pinkney, D. S. (1990, May 11). Specialists give new definition of alcoholism. *American Medical News*, 28.
178. Blum, K., Nobele, E. P., Sheridan, P. J. et al. (1990). Allelic association of human dopamine

D₂ receptor gene in alcoholism. *JAMA, 263*, 2055–60.
179. Gordis, E., Tabakoff, B., Goldman, D. et al. (1990). Finding the gene(s) for alcoholism (editorial). *JAMA, 263*, 2094–95.
180. Waldholz, M. (1991, July 15). New studies lend support to 'alcoholism gene' finding. *WSJ*, B1, B4.
181. Schuckit, M. A. (1987). Biology of risk of alcoholism. In H. Y. Meltzer (Ed.), *Psychopharmacology: The third generation of progress*. New York: Raven Press, 1527–33.
182. Donovan, J. M. (1986). An etiologic model of alcoholism. *The American Journal of Psychiatry, 143*, 1–11.
183. Johnson, V. E. (1980). *I'll quit tomorrow: A practical guide to alcoholism treatment*. New York: Harper & Row. Described in: Kinney & Leaton (1987), 153–58.
184. Johnson, V. E. (1986). *Intervention: How to help someone who doesn't want help*. Minneapolis: Johnson Institute.
185. Institute of Medicine (1989). *Prevention and treatment of alcohol problems: Research opportunities*. Washington, DC: National Academy Press.
186. Institute of Medicine (1990). *Broadening the base of treatment for alcohol problems*. Washington, DC: National Academy Press. 252.
187. Stipp, D. (1991, July 8). Heroin medication may help alcoholics avoid relapses. *WSJ*, B1–B2.
188. Anonymous. (1987). Aversion therapy: Council on Scientific Affairs. *JAMA, 258*, 2562–66.
189. Wegscheider-Cruse, S. (1989). *Another chance: Hope and health for the alcoholic family*. Palo Alto, CA: Science & Behavior.
190. Robertson, N. (1988). *Getting better: Inside Alcoholics Anonymous*. New York: Morrow, 88.

CHAPTER 8: DRUG AND OTHER DEPENDENCIES

1. Weil, A., & Rosen, W. (1983). *Chocolate to morphine: Understanding mind-active drugs*. Boston: Houghton Mifflin, 1.
2. Schuster, C. Cited in: Medical Tribune News Service (1991, January 25). High school seniors report less drug use. *SFC*, A12.
3. Shedler, J., & Block, J. (1990, May). Adolescent drug use and psychological health. *American Psychologist*, 612–24.
4. Perlman, D. (1990, May 14). Furor over report on teenage drug use. *SFC*, A10.
5. World Health Organization (1981). Nomenclature and classification of drug- and alcohol-related problems: A WHO memorandum. *Bulletin of the World Health Organization, 59*, 227.
6. Carroll, C. R. (1989). *Drugs in modern society*. Dubuque, IA: Wm. C. Brown.
7. Girdano, D. A., & Dusek, D. E. (1988). *Drug education: Content and methods* (4th ed.). New York: Random House.
8. Weil & Rosen, 1983.
9. Maisto, S. A., Galizio, M., & Connors, G. J. (1991). *Drug use and misuse*. Fort Worth, TX: Holt, Rinehart and Winston.
10. McCarty, D. (1985). Environmental factors in substance abuse: The microsetting. In M. Galizio & S. A. Maisto (Eds.), *Determinants of substance abuse: Biological, psychological, and environmental factors*. New York: Plenum Press, 247–82.
11. Flynn, J. C. (1991). *Cocaine: An in-depth look at the facts, science, history and future of the world's most addictive drug*. New York: Carol, 50.
12. Gillin, J. C. (1991). The long and short of sleeping pills (editorial). *NEJM, 324*, 1735–36.
13. National Institute on Drug Abuse (1986). *Highlights of the 1985 National Household*

Survey on Drug Abuse. Rockville, MD: National Institute on Drug Abuse.

14. Johnson, B. A. (1990). Psychopharmacological effects of cannabis. *British Journal of Hospital Medicine, 43*, 114–16.

15. Jones, R. T. (1980). Human effects: An overview. In R. C. Peterson (Ed.), *Marijuana research findings: 1980*. Rockville, MD: National Institute on Drug Abuse, 54–80.

16. Maisto, Galizio, & Connors, 1991.

17. Johnson, 1990.

18. Abraham, H. D. (1983). Visual phenomenology of the LSD flashback. *Archives of General Psychiatry, 40*, 884–89.

19. Carroll, 1989.

20. Young, T., Lawson, G. W., & Gacono, C. B. (1987). Clinical aspects of phencyclidine (PCP). *The International Journal of Addictions, 22*, 1–15.

21. Maisto, Galizio, & Connors, 1991, 341.

22. Smith, D. E., & Gay, G. R. (Eds.). (1972). *It's so good don't even try it once: Heroin in perspective*. Englewood Cliffs, NJ: Prentice Hall.

23. Jaffe, J. H., & Martin, W. R. (1985). Opioid analgesics and antagonists. In A. G. Gilman, L. S. Goodman, & A. Gilman (Eds.), *Goodman and Gilman's The pharmacological basis of therapeautics* (7th ed.) New York: Macmillan, 491–531.

24. Treaster, J. B. (1991, April 28). A more potent heroin makes a comeback in a new, needleless form. *NYT*, Sec. 4, 4.

25. Treaster, J. B. (1991, February 4). Search for better heroin high is fatal allure of synthetics. *NYT*, C11.

26. Rangel, C. B. (1990, August 14). The killer drug we ignore. *NYT*, A19.

27. Beck, J., & Morgan, P. A. (1986). Designer drug confusion: A focus on MDMA. *Journal of Drug Education, 16*, 287–99.

28. Kleber, H. D. Quoted in: Smith, L. (1991, May 6). Getting junkies to clean up. *Fortune*, 108.

29. Schaef, A. W. (1987). *When society becomes an addict*. San Francisco: Harper & Row, 4.

30. Schaef, 1987, 57.

31. Schaef, 1987, 18.

32. Sullivan, B. (1990, August 12). Becoming the 'thoroughly diseased society.' *SFE*, D-1; reprinted from *Chicago Tribune*.

33. Hickey, J. E., Haertzen, C. A., & Henningfield, J. E. (1986). Simulation of gambling responses on the Addiction Research Center Inventory. *Addictive Behaviors, 11*(3), 345–49.

34. Blaszczynski, A. P., Buhrich, N., & McConaghy, N. (1985). Pathological gamblers, heroin addicts and controls compared on the E.P.Q. "Addiction scale." *British Journal of Addiction, 80*(3), 315–19.

35. Shaffer, H. J., & Gambino, B. (1989). The epistemology of "addictive disease": Gambling as predicament. *Journal of Gambling Behavior, 5*(3), 211–29.

36. Walker, M. B. (1989). Some problems with the concept of "gambling addiction": Should theories of addiction be generalized to include excessive gambling? *Journal of Gambling Behavior, 5*(3), 179–200.

37. Weil & Rosen, 1983, 168.

38. Farmer, J. J. (1989, October 15). Legal gambling: America's biggest growth industry. *SFE*, A-2.

39. Welles, C. (1989, April 24). America's gambling fever. *Business Week*, 112–20.

40. Custer, R. L. Cited in: Welles, 1989.

41. Powers, L. (1989, July 16). Nevada has over twice as many compulsive gamblers. *Reno Gazette-Journal*, 1E.

42. Welles, 1989.

43. Walters, L. S. (1990, June 18). Teen gambling is the latest addiction of choice. *SFC*, B5; reprinted from *Christian Science Monitor*.

44. Associated Press. (1989, June 23). 1 in 20 college students are compulsive gamblers—survey. *Reno Gazette-Journal*, 6D.

45. American Psychiatric Association. (1994). *Diagnostic and statistical manual of mental disorders* (4th ed.). Washington, DC: American Psychiatric Association.

46. Volberg, R. A., & Steadman, H. J. (1988). Refining prevalence estimates of pathological gambling. *American Journal of Psychiatry, 145*, 502–05.

47. O'Connor, J. J. (1990, June 29). The urge to gamble, and how to fight addiction. *NYT*, B10.

48. Roy, A., Adinoff, B., Roehrich, L. et al. (1988). Pathological gambling: A psychobiological study. *Archives of General Psychiatry, 45*(4), 369–73.

49. Roy, A., De Jong, J., & Linnoila, M. (1989). Extraversion in pathological gamblers: Correlates with indexes of noadrenergic function. *Archives of General Psychiatry, 46*(8), 679–81.

50. Lorenz, V. Quoted in: Goleman, D. (1989, October 15). Gambling—the odds are it's biological. *SFC, Sunday Punch*, 5; reprinted from *NYT*.

51. Peck, C. P. (1986). A public mental health issue: Risk-taking behavior and compulsive gambling. *American Psychologist, 41*, 461–65.

52. Will, G. F. (1989, May 8). In the grip of gambling. *Newsweek*, 61.

53. Siskin, B., Staller, J., & Rorvik, D. (1989). *What are the chances? Risks, odds, and likelihood in everyday life*. New York: Plume.

54. Wagenaar, W. Cited in: Goleman, 1989.

55. de la Pena, N., & Miller, A. (1990, April 1). Going for broke. *Newsweek*, 40–41.

56. O'Guinn, T., & Faber, R. Cited in: Goleman, D. (1991, July 17). Reining in a compulsion to spend. *NYT*, B1, B8.

57. Goleman, 1991, B8.

58. Mundis, J. (1986, January 5). A way back from deep debt. *New York Times Magazine*, 23.

59. Machlowitz, M. (1980). *Workaholics*. Reading, MA: Addison-Wesley.

60. Topolnicki, D. (1989, July/August). Workaholics: Are you one? *PT*, 25.

61. Topolnicki, 1989, 25.

62. Pietropinto, A. (1986, May). The workaholic spouse. *Medical Aspects of Human Sexuality*, 89–96.

63. Topolnicki, 1989, 25.

64. Kaminer, W. (1990, February 11). Chances are you're codependent too. *New York Times Book Review*, 1, 26–27.

65. Robins, C. (1990, April 15). Sun also rises on Margaux Hemingway. *SFC*, E-4.

66. Anonymous. (1989, July 10). A salute to everyday heroes. *Newsweek*, 47.

67. Minton, T. (1990, June 13). Three stories of 'hopeless' lives turned around. *SFC*, B3–B4.

68. Pogash, C. (1988, July 31). Would you please welcome Mimi Silbert. *Image, SFE*, 14–23.

69. Whittemore, H. (1992, March 15). Hitting bottom can be the beginning. *Parade Magazine*, 4–6.

CHAPTER 9: INFECTIOUS AND NONINFECTIOUS ILLNESSES

1. Wright, K. (1990). Bad news bacteria. *Science, 249*, 22–24.

2. Nash, J. M. (1992, August 31). Attack of the superbugs. *Time*, 62–63.

3. Skolnick, A. (1991, January 2). New insights into how bacteria develop antibiotic resistance. *JAMA, 265*, 14–16.

4. Rasche, R. E. (1991). Mapping malaria. *Today, 16*, 26–28.

5. Rosenthal, E. (1991, February 12). Outwitted by malaria, desperate doctors seek new remedies. *NYT*, B5, B8.

6. Mitchell, C. J., Niebylski, M. L., Smith, G. C. et al. (1992). Isolation of eastern equine encephalitis virus from *Aedes albopictus* in Florida. *Science, 257*, 526–27.

7. Jaret, P. (1986, June). The wars within. *National Geographic*, 702–34.

8. American College of Allergy and Immunology. Cited in: Brody, J. E. (1991, April 11). Old advice as well as new hope for millions who are allergic to the pollens of springtime. *NYT*, B8.

9. Gorman, C. (1992, June 22). Asthma: Deadly...but treatable. *Time*, 61–62.

10. Sampson, H. A., Mendelson, L., & Rosen, J. P. (1992). Fatal and near-fatal anaphylactic reactions to food in children and adolescents. *NEJM, 327*, 380–84.

11. Firestein, G. S. (1992). Mechanisms of tissue destruction and cellular activation in rheumatoid arthritis. *Current Opinion in Rheumatology, 4*, 348–54.

12. Perlman, D. (1990, May 24). MS clue found—Cells that attack brain. *SFC*, A2. [Report in 5/23/92 *Nature* of Stanford and Australian researchers.]

13. Anonymous. (1991, January). Myasthenia gravis: The 'weakening' disorder. *Mayo Clinic Health Letter*, 6.

14. Brody, J. E. (1992, January 1). Setting the record straight on how to live with the minor discomforts of winter. *NYT*, 13.

15. Anonymous. (1989, January). Cold remedies: Which ones work best? *Consumer Reports*, 8–11.

16. Cohen, S., Tyrrell, D. A., & Smith, A. P. (1991). Psychological stress and susceptibility to the common cold. *NEJM, 325*, 606–12.

17. Macknin, M. L., Mathew, S., Medendorp, S. V. (1990). Effect of inhaling heated vapor on symptoms of the common cold. *JAMA, 264*, 989–91.

18. Graham, N. M., Burrell, C. J., Doublas, R. M., Debelle, P., & Davies, L. (1990). Adverse effects of aspirin, acetaminophen, and ibuprofen on immune function, viral shedding, and clinical status in rhinovirus-infected volunteers. *Journal of Infectious Diseases, 162*, 1277–82.

19. Pauling, L. C. (1970). *Vitamin C and the common cold*. San Francisco: Freeman.

20. Chalmers, T. C. (1975). Effects of ascorbic acid on the common cold. *American Journal of Medicine, 58*, 532–36.

21. Advisory Committee on Immunization Practices. (1987). Prevention and control of influenza. *MMWR, 36*, 373–87.

22. Gunn, W. Quoted in: Associated Press. (1990, November 10). Doctors, warning of flu danger, say ignoring risk could be fatal. *NYT*, 9.

23. Le, C., & Chang, R. S. (1988). In T. W. Hudson, M. A. Reinhart, S. D. Rose et al. (Eds.), *Clinical preventive medicine: Health promotion and disease prevention*. Boston: Little, Brown, 615–17.

24. Gunn. Quoted in: Associated Press, 1990.

25. Ruben, F. L. (1987). Prevention and control of influenza: Role of vaccine. *American Journal of Medicine, 82*, 31–34.

26. Altman, L. K. (1991, December 3). Gaps shown in flu fight. *NYT*, A1, B6.

27. Levine, D. (1992, November). Prevent the flu. *AH*, 11–12.

28. Anonymous. (1991). Infectious mononucleosis. *Postgraduate Medicine, 89*, 54.

29. Shafran, S. D. (1991). The chronic fatigue syndrome. *American Journal of Medicine, 90*, 730–39.

30. Katzenstein, L. (1992, May). Sick & tired. *AH*, 51–56.

31. Schlueederberg, A., Straus, S. E., Peterson, P. et al. (1992). NIH conference. Chronic fatigue syndrome research: Definition and medical outcome assessment. *AIM, 117*, 325–31.

32. Felts, W. M., & Knight, S. M. (1992). The nature and prevention of viral hepatitis: What health educators should know. *Journal of Health Education, 23*, 267–74.

33. Navarro, M. (1992, March 6). Health officials see increase in hepatitis among gay men. *NYT*, A9.

34. Centers for Disease Control. (1990). Recommendations for IG prophylaxis for hepatitis A. *MMWR, 39*, 3–5.

35. Anonymous. (1992). Hepatitis A: A vaccine at last. *Lancet, 339*, 1198–99.

36. Kingsley, L. A., Rinaldo, C. R., Lyter, D. W. et al. (1990). Sexual transmission efficiency of hepatitis B virus and human immunodeficiency virus among homosexual men. *JAMA, 264*, 230.

37. Brody, J. E. (1991, September 11). U.S. seeks vaccination of babies to avert the growing danger of hepatitis B. *NYT*, B8.

38. Carey, W. D. (1990). Interferon for chronic hepatitis. *Cleveland Clinic Journal of Medicine, 57*, 218–19.

39. Perrillo, R. P., Schiff, E. R., Davis, G. L. et al. (1990). A randomized, controlled trial of interferon alpha-2b alone and after prednisone withdrawal for the treatment of chronic hepatitis B. *NEJM, 323*, 295–301.

40. Felts & Knight, 1992.

41. Brody, 1991 (September 11).

42. Schucat, A., & Broome, C. V. (1991). Toxic shock syndrome and tampons. *Epidemiologic Reviews, 13*, 99–112.

43. Beck, M., Crandall, R., & Hager, M. (1990, July 23). A mean strain of strep. *Newsweek*, 57.

44. Brody, J. E. (1990, November 15). Resurgence of rheumatic fever puts focus on treatment of strep throat. *NYT*, B8.

45. Gable, C., Holzer, S. S., Engelhart, L. et al. (1990) Pneumococcal vaccine: Efficacy and associated cost savings. *JAMA, 264*, 2910–15.

46. Shapiro, E. D., Berg, A. T., Austrian, R. et al. (1991). The protective efficacy of polyvalent pneumococcal polysaccharide vaccine. *NEJM, 325*, 1453–60.

47. Flynn, N. Tuberculosis. In Hudson et al. (Eds.), 1988, 620–27.

48. Benenson, A. S. (Ed.). (1990). *Control of communicable disease in man*. Washington, DC: American Public Health Association.

49. Benjamin, R. Quoted in: Craffey, B. (1992, June 14). A killer returns. *SFE, Image*, 6–13.

50. Altman, L. K. (1992, January 25). For most, risk of contracting tuberculosis is seen as small. *NYT*, 1, 9.

51. Reichman, L. B. Cited in: Altman, 1992, 9.

52. Altman, 1992 (January 25).

53. Cowley, G., Leonard, E. A., & Hager, M. (1992, March 16). Tuberculosis: A deadly return. *Newsweek*, 53–57.

54. Specter, 1992 (October 11).

55. Specter, 1992 (October 11).

56. Rosenthal, E. (1992, August 1). Drug-resistant TB is seen spreading within hospitals. *NYT*, 1, 9.

57. Rosenthal, E. (1992, August 13). Scientists identify what is making TB resistant to drugs. *NYT*, A1, A9.

58. Pershing, D. H., Telford, S. R. 3d, Rys, P. N. et al. (1990). Detection of *Borrelia burgdorferi* DNA in museum specimens of *Ixodes dammini* ticks. *Science, 249*, 1420–23.

59. Cunha, B. A. (1990). Lyme disease: Strategies for this summer. *Emergency Medicine, 22*, 75–97.

60. Harbit, M. D., & Willis, D. (1990). Lyme disease: Implications for health educators. *Health Education, 21*, 41–43.

61. Fultz, O. (1991, June). The tick that ate summer. *AH*, 52–57.

62. Travis, J. (1992). Biting back at Lyme disease. *Science, 256*, 1623.

63. Magid, D., Schwartz, B., Craft, J., & Schwartz, J. S. (1992). Prevention of Lyme disease after tick bites: A cost-effective analysis. *NEJM, 327*, 534–41.

64. Edelman, R. (1991). Perspective on the development of vaccines against Lyme disease. *Vaccine, 9*, 531–32.

65. Maniace, L. (1991, June). The perils of pertussis. *AH*, 8.

66. Gershon, A. A. (1990). Immunization practices in children. *Hospital Practice, 25*, 91–107.

67. Camfield, P. (1992). Brain damage from pertussis immunization: A Canadian neurologist's perspective. *American Journal of Diseases of Children, 146*, 327–31.

68. Farizo, K. M., Cochi, S. L., & Patriarca, P. A. (1990). Poliomyelitis in the United States: A historical perspective and current vaccination policy. *Journal of American College Health, 39*, 137–43.

69. Anonymous. (1991, May 27). New worries about old diseases. *Newsweek*, 68.

70. Smith, D. W. (1989). Polio and postpolio sequelae: The lived experience. *Orthopaedic Nursing, 8*(5), 24–28.

71. Agre, J. C., Rodriquez, A. A., & Sperling, K. B. (1989). Symptoms and clinical impressions of patients seen in a postpolio clinic. *Archives of Physical Medicine & Rehabilitation, 70*, 367–70.

72. Smith, H. (1990). Mumps. *The Practitioner, 234*, 903–904.

73. Hudson, W. T. (1988). Rubella and pregnancy. In Hudson et al. (Eds.), 124–29.

74. Black, S. B., & Shinefield, H. R. (1992). Immunization with ogligosaccharide conjugate Haemophilus influenzae type b (HbOC) vaccine on a large health maintenance organization population: Extended follow-up and impact on Haemophilus influenzae disease epidemiology. The Kaiser Permanente Pediatric Vaccine Study Group. *Pediatric Infectious Disease Journal, 11*(8), 610–13.

75. Kennedy, D. H. (1990). Measles. *The Practitioner, 234*, 895–900.

76. Centers for Disease Control. (1990). Public health burden of vaccine-preventable diseases among adults: Standards for adult immunization practice. *MMWR, 39*, 725–29.

77. Hilton, E., Singer, C., Kozarsky, P. et al. (1991). Status of immunity to tetanus, measles, mumps, rubella, and polio among U.S. travelers. *AIM, 115*, 32–33.

78. Centers for Disease Control, 1990, *MMWR, 39*, 725–29.

79. Anonymous. (1990). Immunization: Important for adults, too! *Patient Care, 26*, 124–25.

80. Kennedy, 1990.

81. Smith, 1990.

82. Ellis, M. (1990). Rubella. *The Practitioner, 234*, 906–10.

83. Centers for Disease Control. (1992). The second 100,000 cases of acquired immunodeficiency syndrome—United States, June 1981–December 1991. *MMWR, 41*, 28–29.

84. Brundage, J. F. (1991). Epidemiology of HIV infection and AIDS in the United States. *Dermatologic Clinics, 9*, 443–52.

85. Peaceman, A. M., & Gonik, B. (1991). Sexually transmitted viral disease in women. *Postgraduate Medicine, 89*, 133–40.

86. Mann, J. M. (1992). AIDS—the second decade: A global perspective. *Journal of Infectious Diseases, 165*, 245–50.

87. Centers for Disease Control. (1991). The HIV/AIDS epidemic: The first 10 years. *MMWR, 40*, 357.

88. Anonymous. (1991, November 17). The long road from HIV to AIDS. *NYT*, sec. 4, 1.

89. Associated Press. (1992, September 3). Women seek to expand list of illnesses in defining AIDS. *NYT*, A6.

90. Blattner, W. A. (1991). HIV epidemiology: past, present, and future. *Faseb Journal, 5*, 2340–48.

91. Byer, C. O., & Shainberg, L. W. (1991). *Dimensions of human sexuality* (3rd ed.). Dubuque, IA: Wm. C. Brown.

92. Giesecke, J., Scalia-Tomba, G., Hakansson, C. et al. (1990). Incubation time of AIDS: Progression of disease in a cohort of HIV-infected homo- and bisexual men with known dates of infection. *Scandinavian Journal of Infectious Diseases, 22*, 407–11.

93. Snell, J. J., Supran, E. M., Esparza, J. et al. (1990). World Health Organization quality assessment programme on HIV testing. *Aids, 4*, 803–806.

94. Moore, R. D., Hidalgo, J., Sugland, B. W. et al. (1991). Zidovudine and the natural history of the acquired immunodeficiency syndrome. *NEJM, 324*, 1412–16.

95. Kolata, G. (1991, November 4). Patients turning to illegal pharmacies. *NYT*, A1, A10.

96. Garrison, J. (1992, February 2). Experts glum as new drugs for AIDS flop. *SFE*, A-1, A-10.

97. Antoni, M. H., Schneiderman, N., Fletcher, M. A. et al. (1990). Psychoneuroimmunology and HIV-1. *Journal of Consulting & Clinical Psychology, 58*, 38–39.

98. LaPerriere, A. R., Antoni, M. H., Schneiderman, N. et al. (1990). Exercise intervention attenuates emotional distress and natural killer cell decrements following notification of positive serologic status for HIV-1. *Biofeedback & Self Regulation, 15*, 229–42.

99. Padian, N. S., Shiboski, S. C., & Jewell, N. P. (1991). Female-to-male transmission of human immunodeficiency virus. *JAMA, 266*, 1664–67.

100. Staver, S. (1990, June 1). Women found contracting HIV via unprotected sex. *American Medical News*, 4–5.

101. Kerr, D. L. (1991). Women with AIDS and HIV infection. *Journal of School Health, 61*, 139–40.

102. Eckholm, E., & Tierney, J. (1990, September 16). AIDS in Africa: A killer rages on. *NYT*, sec. 1, 1, 10.

103. Eckholm, E. (1990, September 16). What makes the 2 sexes so vulnerable to epidemic. *NYT*, sec. 1, 11.

104. Centers for Disease Control and Prevention, 1994, *MMWR, 43*, 155–60.

105. Centers for Disease Control, 1991, *MMWR, 40*, 357.

106. Kimmel, M., & Levine, M. (1991, May 10). AIDS is a disease of men involved in risky behavior. *SFC*, A25.

107. Addiction Research Foundations. Reported in: Reuters. (1991, July 10). Needle swap credited for Canada's drop in AIDS. *SFC*, A9.

108. Coates, R. A., Rankin, J. G., Lamothe, F. et al. (1992). Needle sharing behaviour among injection users (IDUs) in treatment in Montreal and Toronto, 1988–1989. *Canadian Journal of Public Health, 83*, 38–41.

109. Kolata, G. (1991, December 25). Hemophiliacs, hard hit by H.I.V., are angrily looking for answers. *NYT*, 1, 7.

110. Sandler, S. G., & Popovsky, M. A. (1990, July). New technologies for a safer blood supply. *Technology Review*, 23–31.

111. Nelson, K. E., Donahue, J. G., Munoz, A. et al. (1992). Transmission of retroviruses from seronegative donors by transfusion during cardiac surgery. *AIM, 117*, 554–59.

112. Kerr, 1991.

113. Blanche, S., Rouzious, C., Moscato, M. L. et al. (1989). A prospective study of infants born to women seropositive for human immunodeficiency virus type 1. HIV Infection in Newborns French Collaborative Study Group. *NEJM, 320*, 1643–48.

114. Van de Perre, P., Simonon, A., Msellati, P. et al. (1991). Postnatal transmission of human immunodeficiency virus type 1 from mother to infant: A prospective cohort study in Kigali, Rwanda. *NEJM, 325*, 593–98.

115. Holmberg, S. D., & Curran, J. W. (1990). The epidemiology of HIV infection in industrialized countries. In K. K. Holmes, P. Maroh, P. F. Sparling et al. (Eds.), *Sexually transmitted diseases* (2nd ed.). New York: McGraw-Hill, 1990, 343–53.

116. Koop, C. E. Quoted in: Hilts, P. J. (1991, September 20). Experts oppose AIDS tests for doctors. *NYT*, A11.

117. Kimmel, M., & Levine, M. (1991, May 10). AIDS is a disease of men involved in risky behavior. *SFC*, A25.

118. Winkelstein, W. Jr., Samuel, M., Padian, N. S. et al. (1987). Selected sexual practices of San Francisco heterosexual men and risk of infection by the human immunodeficiency virus. *JAMA*, *257*, 1470.

119. Joseph, J. G., Montgomery, S. B., Emmons, C.-A. et al. (1987). Perceived risk of AIDS: Assessing the behavioral and psychosocial consequences in a cohort of gay men. *Journal of Applied Social Psychology*, *17*, 231–50.

120. Fineberg, H. V. (1988). Education to prevent AIDS: Prospects and obstacles. *Science*, *239*, 592–96.

121. Bauman, L. J., & Siegel, K. (1987). Misperception among gay men of the risk for AIDS associated with their sexual behavior. *Journal of Applied Social Psychology*, *17*, 329–50.

122. Centers for Disease Control. (1991, January). *HIV/AIDS Surveillance Report*, 1–22.

123. Davies, K. (1990). Genital herpes: An overview. *Journal of Obstetric, Gynecologic & Neonatal Nursing*, *19*, 401–406.

124. Corey, L., & Holmes, K. K. (1983). Genital herpes simplex virus infections: Current concepts in diagnosis, therapy, and prevention. *AIM*, *98*, 973–83.

125. Brock, B. V., Selke, S., Benedetti, J. et al. (1990). Frequency of asymptomatic shedding of herpes simplex virus in women with genital herpes. *JAMA*, *263*, 418–20.

126. Mertz, G. J., Benedetti, J., Ashley, R. et al. (1992). Risk factors for the sexual transmission of genital herpes. *AIM*, *116*, 197–202.

127. Koutsy, L. A., Stevens, C. E., Holmes, K. K. et al. (1992). Underdiagnosis of genital herpes by current clinical and viral-isolation procedures. *NEJM*, *326*, 1533–39.

128. Lynch, P. J. (1988). Psychiatric, legal, and moral issues of herpes simplex infections. *Journal of the American Academy of Dermatology*, *18*, 173–75.

129. Brown, Z. A., Benedetti, J., Ashley, R. et al. (1991). Neonatal herpes simplex virus infection in relation to asymptomatic maternal infection at the time of labor. *NEJM*, *324*, 1247–52.

130. Subak-Sharpe, G. J. (Ed.). (1984). Genital herpes. In *The physician's manual for patients*. New York: Times, 370–72.

131. Mertz et al., 1992.

132. Longo, D. J., & Clum, G. A. (1989). Psychosocial factors affecting genital herpes recurrences: Linear versus mediating models. *Journal of Psychosomatic Research*, *33*, 161–66.

133. Futterman, A. D., Kemeny, M. E., Shapiro, D. et al. (1992). Immunological variability associated with experimentally-induced positive and negative affective states. *Psychological Medicine*, *22*, 231–38.

134. Rand, K. H., Hoon, E. F., Massey, J. K. et al. (1990). Daily stress and recurrence of genital herpes simplex. *Archives of Internal Medicine*, *150*, 1889–93.

135. Longo, D. J., Clum, G. A., & Yaeger, N. J. (1988). Psychosocial treatment for recurrent genital herpes. *Journal of Consulting & Clinical Psychology*, *56*, 61–66.

136. Goldsmith, M. F. (1989). 'Silent epidemic' of 'social disease' makes STD experts raise their voices. *JAMA*, *261*, 3509–10.

137. Bauer, H. M., Ting, Y., Greer, C. E. et al. (1991). Genital human papillomavirus infection in female university students as determined by a PCR-based method. *JAMA*, *265*, 472–77.

138. Gordon, A. N. (1990, February). New STD menace: HPV infection. *Medical Aspects of Human Sexuality*, 20–24.

139. Daling, J. R., Weiss, N. S., Hislop, T. G. et al. (1987). Sexual practices, sexually transmitted diseases, and the incidence of anal cancer. *NEJM*, *317*, 973–77.

140. Nuovo, G., & Pedemonte, B. (1990). Human papillomavirus types and recurrent cervical warts. *JAMA*, *263*, 1223–26.

141. Bergman, A. (1991, December). HPV infection in men: Severing the link to cervical cancer. *Medical Aspects of Human Sexuality*, 20–30.

142. Carlson, J. W., Hill, P. S., & Robertson, A. W. (1990, August). Evaluation and treatment of human papillomavirus infection in men. *Medical Aspects of Human Sexuality*, 58–62.

143. Waldholz, M. (1992, September 24). Cost may limit use of Pfizer drug against chlamydia. *WSJ*, B4.

144. Jones, R. B., Rabinovitch, R. A., Katz, B. P. et al. (1985). Chlamydia trachomatis in the pharynx and rectum of homosexual patients at risk for genital infection. *AIM*, *102*, 757–62.

145. Washington, A., Arno, P., & Brooks, M. (1986). The economic cost of pelvic inflammatory disease. *JAMA*, *255*, 1735–38.

146. Chow, J. M., Yonekura, L., Richwald, G. A. et al. (1990). The association between *Chlamydia trachomatis* and ectopic pregnancy: A matched-pair, case-control study. *JAMA*, *263*, 3164–67.

147. McCormack, W., Rosner, B., McComb, D. et al. (1985). Infection with *Chlamydia trachomatis* in female college students. *American Journal of Epidemiology*, *121*, 107–15.

148. Wolner-Hanssen, P., Eschenbach, D. A., Paavonen, J. et al. (1990). Decreased risk of symptomatic chlamydial pelvic inflammatory disease associated wtih oral contraceptive use. *JAMA*, *263*, 54–59.

149. Holmes, K. K. (1981). The *Chlamydia* epidemic. *JAMA*, *245*, 1718–23.

150. Martin, D., Kotitsky, L., Eschenbach, D. et al. (1982). Prematurity and perinatal mortality in pregnancies complicated by maternal *Chlamydia trachomatic* infections. *JAMA*, *247*, 1585–1615.

151. White, D. M., & Felts, W. M. (1989b, Spring). Chlamydial infection: The quiet epidemic. *Our Sexuality Update*, 1, 4–5.

152. Holmes, K., & Stamm, W. (1981, October). Chlamydial genital infections: A growing problem. *Hospital Practice*, 105–17.

153. Rice, F. P. (1989). *Human sexuality*. Dubuque, IA: Wm. C. Brown.

154. Waldholz, 1992.

155. Schwebke, J. R. (1991, March). Gonorrhea in the '90s. *Medical Aspects of Human Sexuality*, 42–46.

156. Platt, R., Rice, P., & McCormack, W. (1983). Risk of acquiring gonorrhea and prevalence of abnormal adnexal findings among women recently exposed to gonorrhea. *JAMA*, *250*, 3205–09.

157. Zenilman, J. M. (1990). Update on gonorrhea. *Hospital Medicine*, *26*, 21–37.

158. Gilbaugh, J. H. Jr., & Guchs, P. C. (1979). The gonococcus and the toilet seat. *NEJM*, *301*, 91–93.

159. Rein, M. F. (1982, February). Asymptomatic gonorrhea in men. *Medical Aspects of Human Sexuality*, 103–107.

160. Starcher, E., Kramer, M., Carlota-Orduna, B. et al. (1983). Establishing efficient interview periods for gonorrhea patients. *AJPH*, *73*, 1381–84.

161. Zenilman, 1990.

162. Anonymous. (1990, August). Resistant gonorrhea on the rise. *Medical Aspects of Human Sexuality*, 37.

163. Schwarcz, S. K., Zenilman, J. M., Schnell, D. et al. (1990). National surveillance of antimicrobial resistance in *Neisseria gonorrhoeae*. *JAMA*, *264*, 1413–17.

164. Altman, L. K. (1990, November 13). Syphilis fools a new generation. *NYT*, B7.

165. Anonymous. (1991). Primary and secondary syphilis—United States, 1981–1990. *MMWR*, *40*, 314–23.

166. Goldsmith, M. F. (1988). Sex tied to drugs equals STD spread. *JAMA*, *260*, 2008.

167. Byer & Shainberg, 1991.

168. Rice, 1989.

169. Handsfield, H. H. (1990). Old enemies: Combating syphilis and gonorrhea in the 1990s (editorial). *JAMA*, *264*, 1451–52.

170. Rosen, T. (1990, January). The reemergence of syphilis. *Medical Aspects of Human Sexuality*, 20–22.

171. Stamm, W. E., Handsfield, H. H., Rompalo, A. M. et al. (1988). The association between genital ulcer disease and acquisition of HIV infection in homosexual men. *JAMA*, *260*, 1429.

172. Hillier, S., & Holmes, K. K. (1990). Bacterial vaginosis. In Holmes et al., 457–59.

173. Chapel, T. A. (1982, August). Dissemination of trichomoniasis. *Medical Aspects of Human Sexuality*, 145–49.

174. Tortora, G., Funke, B. R., & Case, C. L. (1989). *Microbiology* (3rd ed.). Menlo Park, CA: Benjamin/Cummings.

175. U.S. Public Health Service. (1990). *Healthy people 2000: National health promotion and disease prevention objectives*. DHHS Pub. No. (PHS)91-50212. Washington, DC: U.S. Government Printing Office.

176. Haffner, S. M., Stern, M. P., Hazuda, H. P. et al. (1990). Cardiovascular risk factors in confirmed prediabetic individuals: Does the clock for coronary heart disease start ticking before the onset of clinical diabetes? *JAMA*, *263*, 2893–98.

177. Centers for Disease Control. (1990). Perinatal mortality and congenital malformations in infants born to women with insulin-dependent diabetes mellitus—United States, Canada, and Europe, 1940–1988. *MMWR*, *39*, 363–65.

178. Mulder, E. J., & Visser, G. H. (1991). Growth and motor development in fetuses of women with type-1 diabetes. I. Early growth patterns. *Early Human Development*, *25*(2), 91–106.

179. Ramos-Arroyo, M. A., Rodriguez-Pinilla, E., & Cordero, J. F. (1992). Maternal diabetes: The risk for specific birth defects. *European Journal of Epidemiology*, *8*, 503–508.

180. Porth, C. (1986). *Pathophysiology* (2nd ed.). Philadelphia: Lippincott.

181. Stein, J. (Ed.). (1989). *Internal medicine: Diagnosis and therapy, 1988–1989*. Boston: Little, Brown.

182. Coleman, R., Lombard, M., Sicard, R. et al. (1989) *Fundamental immunology*. Dubuque, IA: Wm. C. Brown.

183. Carey, B. (1991, January/February). Dodging diabetes. *In Health*, 18.

184. Pryse-Phillips, W., Findlay, H., Tugwell, P. et al. (1992). A Canadian population survey on the clinical, epidemiologic and societal impact of migraine and tension-type headache. *Canadian Journal of Neurological Sciences*, *19*, 333–39.

185. Perlman, D. (1990, May 24). MS clue found—Cells that attack brain. *SFC*, A2.

186. Anderson, D. W., Ellenberg, J. H., Leventhal, C. M. et al. (1992). Revised estimate of the prevalence of multiple sclerosis in the United States. *Annals of Neurology*, *32*, 333–36.

187. Wolf, P. (1991). The phenotype: Seizures and epilepsy syndromes. *Epilepsy Research—Supplement*, 4, 19–29.

188. Farnham, A. (1992, December 14). Backache. *Fortune*, 132–41.

189. Public Health Service, 1990.

190. Garg, A., & Moore, J. S. (1992). Epidemiology of low-back pain in industry. *State of the Art Reviews: Occupational Medicine*, 7, 593–608.

191. Public Health Service, 1990.
192. Stipp, D. (1989, September 26). Low-back pain gives up some secrets. *WSJ*, B1.
193. Anonymous. (1990). Proper lifting. *Mayo Clinic Health Letter, 8*(11), 4.
194. Gutfield, G. (1991, October). Building a defensive back. *Men's Health*, 70–75.
195. Gutfield, 1991.
196. Abyad, A., & Boyer, J. T. (1992). Arthritis and aging. *Current Opinion in Rheumatology, 4*, 153–59.
197. Anonymous. (1990). Crohn's disease. *Mayo Clinic Health Letter, 8*(11), 4–5.
198. Gumaste, V. V., & Zimmerman, M. J. (1990). Diagnosis: Ulcerative colitis. *Hospital Medicine, 26*, 31–48.
199. Bronson, G. (1990, November/December). Mitigated gall. *Assets*, 92–93.
200. Anonymous. (1990). Gallbladder removal. *Mayo Clinic Health Letter, 8*(11), 1–2.
201. Bankhead, C. D. (1990). One-day cholecystectomy popular. *Medical World News, 31*(13), 48–49.
202. The Southern Surgeons Club. (1991). A prospective analysis of 1518 laparoscopic cholecystectomies. *NEJM, 324*, 1073–78.
203. Pak, C. Y. (1991). Etiology and treatment of urolithiasis. *American Journal of Kidney Diseases, 18*, 624–37.
204. Brody, J. E. (1992, July 8). Treating kidney stones becomes faster and safer. *NYT*, B8.
205. Gorman, C. (1992, June 22). Asthma: Deadly...but treatable. *Time*, 61–62.
206. Buist, A. S., & Vollmer, W. (1990, October 3). Reflections on the rise in asthma morbidity and mortality. *JAMA, 264*, 1719–20.
207. Weiss, K., & Wagener, D. (1990, October 3). Changing patterns of asthma mortality: Identifying target populations at high risk. *JAMA, 264*, 1683–87.
208. Ogushi, F., Hubbard, R. C., Vogelmeier, C. et al. (1991). Risk factors for emphysema: Cigarette smoking is associated with a reduction in the association rate of lung alpha 1-antitrypsin for neutrophil elastase. *Journal of Clinical Investigation, 87*, 1060–209. Harris poll for Teledyne Water Pik. Cited in: Anonymous. (1991, November). Preach yes, practice no. *AH*, 22.
210. Berczuk, C. (1992, July 5). Are you afraid to go to the dentist? *Parade*, 12–13.
211. Wyngaarden, J. P. (1989). *Cecil-textbook of medicine* (29th ed.). Philadelphia: Saunders.
212. United Press International. (1990, June 9). Americans keeping their teeth longer, dental study finds. *SFC*, A8.
213. Brody, J. E. (1990, October 18). With cavities on decline, flossing is key weapon in battle for dental health. *NYT*, B8.
214. Addy, M., Dummer, P. M., Hunter, M. L. et al. (1990). The effect of toothbrushing frequency, toothbrushing hand, sex and social class on the incidence of plaque, gingivitis and pocketing in adolescents: A longitudinal cohort study. *Community Dental Health, 7*, 237–47.
215. Sicilia, A., Noguerol, B., Hernandez, R. et al. (1990). Relationship of dental treatment and oral hygiene to caries prevalence and need for periodontal treatment [Spanish]. *Avances En Odontoestomatologia, 6*, 343–49.
216. Papas, A. Quoted in: Bensimhon, D. (Ed.). (1991, October). Ask Men's Health. *Men's Health*, 16.
217. Hughes, R. (1993, January/February). Breaking the gum disease cycle. *AH*, 17.
218. Bedell, T. (1991, December). Floss, anyone? *Men's Health*, 20–21.

CHAPTER 10: HEART DISEASE, CANCER, AND PERSONAL SAFETY

1. Tsevat, J., Weinstein, M. C., Williams, L. W. et al. (1991). Expected gains in life expectancy from various coronary heart disease risk factor modifications. *Circulation, 83*, 1194–1201.
2. Zaret, B. L., Moser, M., Cohen, L. S. et al. (Eds.) (1992). *Yale University School of Medicine heart book*. New York: Hearst.
3. Zaret et al., 1992.
4. American Heart Association. (1991). *1991 Heart and stroke facts*. Dallas: American Heart Association.
5. McGrady, A., & Higgins, J. Jr. (1990, February). Effect of repeated measurements of blood pressure on blood pressure in essential hypertension: Role of anxiety. *Journal of Behavioral Medicine, 93*, 93–101.
6. American Heart Association, 1991.
7. Cohen, L. S. (1992). What can go wrong. In Zaret et al. (Eds.), 11–20.
8. Kelemen, M. H., Effront, M. B., Valenti, S. A. et al. (1990). Exercise training combined with antihypertensive drug therapy: Effects on lipids, blood pressure, and left ventricular mass. *JAMA, 263*, 2766–71.
9. Cohen, 1992.
10. Cohen, 1992.
11. Brass, L. M. (1992). Stroke. In Zaret et al. (Eds.), 215–33.
12. Brass, 1992.
13. Kleinman, C. S. (1992). Heart disease in the young. In Zaret et al. (Eds.), 247–62.
14. Kleinman, 1992.
15. Kuntz, R. E., Piana, R., Pomerantz, R. M. et al. (1992). Changing incidence and management of abrupt closure following coronary intervention in the new device era. *Catheterization & Cardiovascular Diagnosis, 27*, 183–90.
16. Baldwin, J. C., Elefteriades, J. A., & Kopf, G. S. (1992). Heart surgery. In Zaret et al. (Eds.), 313–29.
17. Associated Press. (1991, July 24). Total mechanical heart expected in 20 years. *SFC*, A3.
18. Ornish, D. M., Brown, S. E., Scherwitz, L. W. et al. (1990). Can lifestyle changes reverse coronary heart disease? The Lifestyle Heart Trial. *Lancet, 336*, 129–33.
19. Ornish, D. (1990). *Dr. Dean Ornish's program for reversing heart disease: The only system scientifically proven to reverse heart disease without drugs or surgery*. New York: Ballantine.
20. Kittner, S. J., White, L. R., Losonczy, K. G. et al. (1990). Black-white differences in stroke incidence in a national sample. *JAMA, 264*, 1267–70.
21. Murray, R. F. (1991). Skin color and blood pressure. *JAMA, 265*, 639–40.
22. Ostfeld, A. (1992). Racial and ethnic differences in heart disease. In Zaret et al. (Eds.), 273–80.
23. Black, H. R. (1992). Cardiovascular risk factors. In Zaret et al. (Eds.), 23–26.
24. Zahler, R., & Piselli, C. (1992). Smoking, alcohol, and drugs. In Zaret et al. (Eds.), 71–84.
25. Zahler & Piselli, 1992.
26. Luckmann, J., & Sorenson, K. (1987). *Medical-surgical nursing: A psychophysiologic approach* (3rd ed.). Philadelphia: Saunders.
27. U.S. Public Health Service. (1989). *Report of the expert panel on dection, evaluation, and treatment of high blood cholesterol in adults*. DHHS Pub. No. (NIH)89-2925. Washington, DC: U.S. Department of Health and Human Services.
28. U.S. Public Health Service (1988). *The Surgeon General's report on nutrition and health*. DHHS Pub. No. (PHS)88-50210. Washington, DC: U.S Department of Health and Human Services.
29. Manson, J. E., Tosteson, H., Ridker, P. M. et al. (1990). A prospective study of obesity and risk of coronary heart disease in women. *NEJM, 326*, 1406–16.
30. Ekelund, L G., Haskell, W. L., Johnson, J. L. et al. (1988). Physical fitness as a predictor of cardiovasular mortality in asymptomatic North American men. The Lipid Research Clinics Mortality Follow-up Study. *NEJM, 319*, 1379–84.
31. Friedman, M., & Rosenman, R. H. (1974). *Type A behavior and your heart*. Greenwich, CT: Knopf.
32. Friedman, M., Thoreson, C. E., Gill, J. J. et al. (1986). Alteration of Type A behavior and its effect on cardiac recurrences in post myocardial infarction patients: Summary results of the recurrent coronary prevention project. *American Heart Journal, 112*, 653–65.
33. Schnall, P. L., Pieper, C., Schwartz, J. E. et al. (1990). The relationship between 'job strain,' workplace diastolic blood pressure, and left ventricular mass index. *JAMA, 263*, 1929–35.
34. Ornish, D. M., Scherwitz, L. W., Doody, R. S. et al. (1983). Effects of stress management training and dietary changes in treating ischemic heart disease. *JAMA, 249*, 54–59.
35. Ornish, D. M. (1983). *Stress, diet, & your heart*. New York: New American Library (Signet).
36. Ornish et al., 1990.
37. Koten, J., & McWethy, V. L. (1990, May 11). Do as we do. *WSJ*, R26.
38. Koten & McWethy, 1990.
39. Willard, J. E., Lange, R. A., & Hillis, L. D. (1992). The use of aspirin in ischemic heart disease. *NEJM, 327*, 175–200.
40. Brody, J. E. (1991, October 31). Lower dose of aspirin is safe and effective, new study finds. *NYT*, A17.
41. U.S. Public Health Service. (1990). *Healthy people 2000: National health promotion and disease prevention objectives*. DHHS Pub. No. (PHS)91-50212. Washington, DC: U.S. Department of Health and Human Services.
42. Dollinger, M., Rosenbaum, E. H., & Cable, G. (1991). *Everyone's guide to cancer therapy: How cancer is diagnosed, treated, and managed day to day*. Kansas City, MO: Andrews & McMeel (Somerville House).
43. Dollinger, Rosenbaum, & Cable, 1991.
44. Mitchell, M. S. (1991). Melanoma. In Dollinger, Rosenbaum, & Cable (Eds.), 428.
45. American Cancer Society (1990). *Cancer facts and figures*. Atlanta: American Cancer Society.
46. U.S. Public Health Service. (1987). *Testicular cancer: Research report*. Pub. No. (NIH)87-654. Washington, DC: U.S. Department of Health and Human Services.
47. Dollinger, M., & Rosenbaum, E. H. (1991). How cancer is diagnosed. In Dollinger, Rosenbaum, & Cable (Eds.), 11–20.
48. Cassileth, B. R. Questionable and unproven cancer therapies. (1991). In Dollinger, Rosenbaum, & Cable (Eds.), 91–96.
49. Cassileth, 1991.
50. Rosenbaum, E. H., Dollinger, M., & Newell, G. R. (1991). Risk assessment, cancer screening and prevention. In Dollinger, Rosenbaum, & Cable (Eds.), 186–92.
51. Finklestein, J. Z. Childhood cancers. (1991). In Dollinger, Rosenbaum, & Cable (Eds.), 285–93.
52. Slater-Freedberg, J. R., & Arndt, K. A. Skin. (1991). In Dollinger, Rosenbaum, & Cable (Eds.), 503–509.
53. U.S. Public Health Service, 1990.
54. Rosenbaum, Dollinger, & Newell, 1991.
55. U.S. Public Health Service, 1990.
56. Rosenbaum, Dollinger, & Newell, 1991.
57. Farley, C. J. (1991, March 28). Guarding against day-to-day, often deadly, risks. *USA Today*, 6D.
58. National Safety Council. (1988). *Accident facts*. Chicago: National Safety Council.
59. National Safety Council, 1988.
60. National Safety Council, 1988.
61. Blyskal, J. (1993, January/February). Crash course: How to steer clear of your next auto accident. *AH*, 74–79.

62. Zane, M. (1992, January 28). More drivers running the signals. *SFC*, A1.

63. Brody, J. E. (1990, July 5). Why drivers fall asleep, and how to avoid becoming a statistic. *NYT*, B8.

64. Deutsch, G. (1990, October). Cruise control. *Men's Health*, 47, 82.

65. Associated Press. (1992, July 23). Drivers keep themselves busy. *SFC*, D3.

66. Ramirez, A. (1992, May 14). The life you save may be on the phone. *NYT*, D5.

67. Traffic Safety Now. (1987). *Buckle up.* Detroit: Traffic Safety Now, Inc.

68. Cushman, J. H. Jr. (1991, April 27). Officials say little is done to cut crashes in fog. *NYT*, 8.

69. Public Policy Research Institute, University of California, Irvine. (1987). *Orange County annual survey: 1987 final report.* Irvine, CA: University of California.

70. Berger, T. Cited in: Greenwald, J. (1992, April). Driving yourself sane. *Health*, 86–89.

71. Anonymous. (1991, September.) A tip for the taxi. *University of California, Berkeley, Wellness Letter*, 6.

72. Anonymous. (1992, December). Nonfatal vision. *Men's Health*, 27.

73. Sosin, D. M., Sacks, J. J., & Holmgreen, P. (1990). Head injury-associated deaths from motorcycle crashes: Relationship to helmet-use laws. *JAMA*, 264, 2395–99.

74. Miller, T. C. (1992, July 28). Motorcycle fatalities decline. *SFC*, A15–A16.

75. Braddock, M., Schwartz, R., Lapidus, G. et al. (1992). A population-based study of motorcycle injury and costs. *Annals of Emergency Medicine*, 21, 273–78.

76. Muelleman, R. L., Mlinek, E. J., & Collicott, P. E. (1992). Motorcycle crash injuries and costs: Effect of a reenacted comprehensive helmet use law. *Annals of Emergency Medicine*, 21, 266–72.

77. Williams, M. (1991). The protective performance of bicyclists' helmets in accidents. *Accident Analysis & Prevention*, 23, 119–31.

78. Thompson, R., Rivara, F., & Thompson, D. (1989, May 25). A case-control study of the effectiveness of bicycle safety helmets. *NEJM*, 320, 1361–67.

79. Centers for Disease Control. (1988). Public health surveillance of 1990 injury control objectives for the nation. *MMWR Surveillance Summary*, 37, 1–68.

80. Rand Corporation. Cited in: Otten, A. L. (1991, May 17). Accidents take big toll on health, earnings. *WSJ*, B1.

81. Baker, S. P., & Harvey, A. H. (1985). Fall injuries in the elderly. *Clinical Geriatric Medicine*, 1, 501–12.

82. Cummings, S. R., Kelsey, J. L., Nevitt, M. C. et al. (1985). Epidemiology of osteoporosis and osteoporotic fractures. *Epidemiologic Reviews*, 7, 178–208.

83. Centers for Disease Control, 1988.

84. Brodzka, W., Thornhill, H. L., & Howard, S. (1985). Burns: Causes and risk factors. *Archives of Physical Medicine & Rehabilitation*, 66, 746–52.

85. U.S. Preventive Services Task Force. (1990). Counseling to prevent household and environmental injuries. *American Family Physician*, 42, 135–42.

86. National Fire Protection Association. Cited in: McNeil, D. G. Jr. (1991, December 22). Why so many more Americans die in fires. *NYT*, sec. 4, 3.

87. McNeil, 1991.

88. National Safety Council. (1985). *Accident facts.* Chicago: National Safety Council.

89. Robinson, A. G. (1991, April). Painful mistakes. *Men's Health*, 32.

90. Centers for Disease Control, 1988.

91. Spyker, D. A. (1985). Submersion injury: Epidemiology, prevention, and management. *Pediatric Clinics of North America*, 32, 113–25.

92. Wintemute, G. J., Kraus, J. F., Teret, S. P. et al. (1988). The epidemiology of drowning in adulthood: Implications for prevention. *American Journal of Preventive Medicine*, 4, 343–48.

93. Wintemute et al., 1988.

94. Powers, R. D. (1990). Taking care of bite wounds. *Emergency Medicine*, 22, 131–39.

95. Serrin, W. (1991, January 28). The wages of work. *Nation*, 80.

96. Serrin, 1991.

97. Monthly Labor Review. (June 1991). Cited in: Anonymous. (1991, October). Careful with that knife. *American Demographics*, 18.

98. National Safety Council. Cited in: Milbank, D. (1991, March 29). Companies turn to peer pressure to cut injuries as psychologists join the battle. *WSJ*, B1, B3.

99. Siegel, M. Cited in: Fernandez, E. (1992, October 23). Study says smoky air endangers waitresses. *SFE*, A-1, A-22.

100. Greenwood, S. (1989, November/December). Workplace hazards. *Medical SelfCare*, 19–20.

101. Hopkins, A. (1990). The social recognition of repetition strain injuries: An Australian/American comparison. *Social Science & Medicine*, 30, 365–72.

102. Mandel, S. (1990). Overuse syndrome in musicians: When playing an instrument hurts. *Postgraduate Medicine*, 88, 111–14.

103. Thompson, J. S., & Phelps, T. H. (1990). Repetitive strain injuries: How to deal with 'the epidemic of the 1990s.' *Postgraduate Medicine*, 88, 143–49.

104. Hembree, D., & Sandoval, R. (1991, August). RSI has become the nation's leading work-related illness. How are editors and reporters coping with it? *Columbia Journalism Review*, 41–46.

105. Kilborn, P. T. (1990, June 24). Automation: Pain replaces the old drudgery. *NYT*, sec. 1, 1, 11.

106. Horowitz, J. M. (1992, October 12). Crippled by computers. *Time*, 70–72.

107. Roel, R. E. (1991, July/August). Wrist watch. *AH*, 72–75.

108. Mercy, J. A., & O'Carroll, P. W. (1988). New directions in violence prediction: The public health arena. *Violence & Victims*, 3, 285–301.

109. Reuters. (1992, March 27). Canada worries about climbing murder rate. *SFC*, A10.

110. Fingerhut, L. A., & Kleinman, J. C. (1990). International and interstate comparisons of homicide among young males. *JAMA*, 263, 3292–95.

111. Fingerhut & Kleinman, 1990.

112. Spivak, H., Hausman, A. J., & Prothrow-Stith, D. (1989). Practitioners' forum: Public health and the primary prevention of adolescent violence: The violence prevention project. *Violence & Victims*, 4, 203–12.

113. Page, R. M., Kitchin-Becker, S., Solovan, D. et al. (1991). Interpersonal violence: A priority issue for health education. *Journal of Health Education*, 23, 286–91.

114. Page et al., 1991, 287.

115. Messner, S. F. (1988). Research on cultural and socioeconomic factors in criminal violence. *Psychiatric Clinics of North America*, 11, 511–25.

116. Ropp, L., Visintainer, P., Uman, J. et al. (1992). Death in the city: An American childhood tragedy. *JAMA*, 267, 2905–10.

117. Page et al., 1991.

118. U.S. Department of Health and Human Services. (1987). *Alcohol and health.* DHHS Pub. No. (ADM)87-1519. Washington, DC: Department of Health and Human Services.

119. Page et al., 1991.

120. Bell, C. A. (1991). Female homicides in United States workplaces, 1980–1985. *AJPH*, 81, 729–32.

121. Eckholm, E. (1992, March 8). Ailing gun industry confronts outrage over glut of violence. *NYT*, sec. 1, 1.

122. Hilts, P. J. (1992, June 10). Gunshot wounds become second-leading cause of death for teen-agers. *NYT*, A14.

123. National Safety Council, 1985.

124. Blumenthal, D. (1991, March 30). How to keep guns safely. *NYT*, 4.

125. Associated Press. (1990, July 9). Justice Dept. says pistols used in 44 percent of murders. *SFC*, A4.

126. Kilborn, P. T. (1992, March 9). The gun culture: Fun as well as life and death. *NYT*, A1.

127. Eckholm, E. (1992, April 3). Thorny issue in gun control: Curbing responsible owners. *NYT*, A1, A15.

128. Reuters. (1991, November 8). Canada's Parliament votes for gun control legislation. *NYT*, A6.

129. Marcus, J. (1992, September 13). Crime reports reveal dangers on campuses. *SFE*, A-4.

130. Trost, C. (1992, September 30). Carjacking spreads to nation's suburbs, raising fear there are no safe havens. *WSJ*, B1, B10.

131. McDowell, E. (1992, October 28). Threat of crime rises on the main highways. *NYT*, A7.

132. San Jose State University Police Department. (1989). *Safety and security at San Jose State.* San Jose, CA: San Jose State University, Police Department, Investigations/Crime Prevention Unit.

133. Brody, J. E. (1992, March 18). Each year, six million American women become victims of abuse without ever leaving home. *NYT*, B6.

134. Todd, J. S. (1992, December). A terrible national secret. *Living Well*, 108.

135. Herman, J. L. (1992). *Trauma and recovery.* New York: Basic.

136. Sonnenberg, S. M. (1988). Victims of violence and post-traumatic stress disorder. *Psychiatric Clinics of North America*, 11, 581–90.

137. Brody, 1992 (March 18).

138. Kutner, L. (1991, November 14). A large number of teen-age girls have become caught up in abusive relationships. *NYT*, B4.

139. Saunders, D. B. Cited in: Anonymous. (1992, September/October). Men of mean. *PT*, 18.

140. Brody, 1992 (March 18).

141. Miedzian, M. (1991). *Boys will be boys: Breaking the link between masculinity and violence.* New York: Doubleday.

142. Gray, A., Jackson, D. N., & McKinlay, J. B. (1991). The relation between dominance, anger, and hormones in normally aging men: Results from the Massachusetts Male Aging Study. *Psychosomatic Medicine*, 53, 375–85.

143. Brody, 1992 (March 18).

144. Irving, C. (1991, August 18). Why battered women stay with abusers. *SFE*, A-5. [Graham, D., & Rawlings, E. Paper presented to American Psychological Association convention, San Francisco, August 17, 1991.]

145. Brody, 1992.

146. U.S. Department of Justice. Cited in: French, M. (1992). *The war against women.* New York: Summit.

147. National Center for Prevention of Child Abuse. Cited in: Toufexis, A. (1992, November 23). When kids kill abusive parents. *Time*, 60–61.

148. U.S. Department of Health and Human Services. (1989). *Child abuse and neglect: A shared community concern.* DHHS Pub. No. (HDS)89-30531. Washington, DC: Clearinghouse on Child Abuse and Neglect Information.

149. Thomas, J. N., Rogers, C. M., Lloyd, D. et al. (1985). *Child sexual abuse: Implications for public health practice.* Rockville, MD: Division of Maternal and Child Health, U.S. Department of Health and Human Services.

150. Turner, R. (1991). One in seven 6th–12th graders had an unwanted sexual encounter, including one in five females. *Family Planning Perspectives, 23*, 286–87.

151. Maltz, W. (1990, December). Adult survivors of incest: How to help them overcome the trauma. *Medical Aspects of Human Sexuality*, 42–47.

152. Maltz, 1990.

153. U.S. Supreme Court, *Meritor Savings Bank v. Vinson.* Cited in: Goldstein, L. (1991, November). Hands off at work. *Self*, 110–13.

154. Anonymous. (1991, October 12). Proving harassment is tough in court, lawyers say. *SFC*, C10; reprinted from *NYT*.

155. Karl, T. Cited in: O'Toole, K. (1991, November–December). How to handle harassment. *Stanford Observer*, 8.

156. U.S. Merit Systems Protection Board. Cited in: Deutschman, A. (1991, November 4). Dealing with sexual harassment. *Fortune*, 145–48.

157. Anonymous. (1989, April). Offering resistance: How most people respond to rape. *PT*, 13.

158. Stanford Rape Education Project. Cited in: Anonymous. (1991, January–February). Men, women interpret sexual cues differently. *Stanford Observer*, 15.

159. National Victim Center. Cited in: Anonymous. (1992, May 4). Unsettling report on an epidemic of rape. *Time*, 15.

160. Celis, W. 3d. (1991, January 2). Growing talk of date rape separates sex from assault. *NYT*, A1, B7.

161. Stanford Rape Education Project, 1991.

162. Coffe, J. (1993, January/February). To escape rape. *AH*, 18.

163. Schroepfer, L. (1992, November). When the victim is a woman. *AH*, 20.

164. Gross, J. (1991, May 28). Even the victim can be slow to recognize rape. *NYT*, A6.

165. Peterson, K. S. (1991, January 30). Adults bound back from early illness. *USA Today*, 1D–2D.

166. Henderson, G., United Press International. (1986, December 24). Teacher turns his cancer death into final lesson. *SFC*, 11.

167. Baker, B. (1988, April 24). The man who put L.A.'s toughs to work. *SFC, Sunday Punch*, 7; reprinted from *LAT*.

168. Robbins, W. (1990, July 22). One man with purpose takes on heart disease. *NYT*, 12.

169. Katz, M. (1990, September). Heart attack: One man's crusade to unclog the American food chain. *AARP Bulletin*, 20.

170. Peterson, 1991.

CHAPTER 11: ENVIRONMENTAL HEALTH

1. Ravo, N. (1991, October 6). Noise police crackdown takes boom out of Bronx. *NYT*, sec. 1, 20.

2. Anonymous. (1990). Noise and haring loss: National Institutes of Health Consensus Development Conference on Noise and Hearing Loss. *JAMA, 263*, 3185.

3. Flodin, K. C. (1992, January/February). Now hear this. *AH*, 58–62.

4. U.S. Public Health Service. Cited in: Wing, E. (1992, February). Now hear this. *Self*, 116–17, 149.

5. Barron, J. (1990, August 14). Above the clamor of New York City, more clamor. *NYT*, A16.

6. U.S. Public Health Service. (1990). *Healthy people 2000: National health promotion and disease prevention objectives.* DHHS Pub. No. (PHS)91-50212. Washington, DC: U.S. Government Printing Office.

7. Flodin, 1992.

8. Anonymous. (1991, October). Play it softly, Sam: Decibel overload. *Consumer Reports*, 660.

9. Monroe, L. R. (1990, December 13). Personal stereos called a threat to kids' hearing. *SFC*, A14; reprinted from *LAT*.

10. Flodin, 1992.

11. Monroe, 1990.

12. Peters, J. M., & London, S. J. Cited in: Petit, C. (1991, January 20). Electrical links to leukemia studied. *SFC*, A3.

13. Kirkpatrick, D. (1993, March 8). Do cellular phones cause cancer? *Fortune*, 82–89.

14. Kirkpatrick, 1993.

15. Kirkpatrick, 1993.

16. Petit, C. (1991, June 11). Fear of man-made magnetism. *SFC*, A1, A4.

17. Kirkpatrick, D. (1990, December 31). Can power lines give you cancer? *Fortune*, 80–85.

18. Hacinli, C. (1992, January/February). A gauss in the house. *Garbage*, 40–43.

19. Kirkpatrick, 1990.

20. Kirkpatrick, 1993.

21. Gibson, R. (1992, March 9). Despite vocal critics, wary consumers, food makers move toward irradiation. *WSJ*, B1, B4.

22. Delaney, L. (1993, January/February). X-ray vision. *Men's Health*, 32–34.

23. Dollinger, M., Rosenbaum, E. H., & Cable, G. (1991). *Everyone's guide to cancer therapy.* Kansas City, MO: Somerville House.

24. Elias, M. (1989, March). The radon that came in from the cold. *AH*, 15.

25. Office of Health and Environmental Research. (1990). *Indoor radon and decay products: Concentration, causes, and control strategies.* Washington, DC: U.S. Department of Energy.

26. Office of Health and Environmental Research. (1991). *Radon research program— annual report, FY 1990.* Washington, DC: U.S. Department of Energy.

27. Leary, W. E. (1991, February 2). U.S. study finds reduced danger from radon seeping into homes. *NYT*, A14.

28. Brody, J. E. (1991, January 8). Some scientists say concern over radon is overblown by EPA. *NYT*, B7.

29. Broad, W. J., & Wald, M. L. (1992, December 1). Milestones of the nuclear era. *NYT*, B8.

30. Wald, M. L. (1991, June 24). Due up for license renewal: The future of nuclear power. *NYT*, A1, B1.

31. Anonymous. (1992, November 25). Cleanup resumes at 3 Mile Island. *SFC*, A8.

32. Hatch, M. C., Wallenstein, S., Beyea, J., Nieves, J. W., & Susser, M. (1991). Cancer rates after the Three Mile Island nuclear accident and proximity of residence to the plant. *AJPH, 81*, 719–24.

33. Brooke, J. (1991, November 3). Chernobyl said to affect health of thousands in a Soviet region. *NYT*, sec. 1, 1, 6.

34. Kolata, G. (1992, September 3). A cancer legacy from Chernobyl. *NYT*, A4.

35. Medvedev, Z. A. (1990). *The legacy of Chernobyl.* New York: W. W. Norton.

36. Associated Press. (1991, April 26). Safety of U.S. A-plants questioned. *SFC*, A10.

37. Schneider, K. (1991, May 12). Is nuclear winter giving way to nuclear spring? *NYT*, sec. 4, 4.

38. Shabecoff, P. (1990, September 20). No added cancer risk is found near A-plants. *NYT*, A15.

39. Wald, 1991.

40. Wald, M. L. (1992, August 16). Nuclear power plants take early retirement. *NYT*, sec. 4, 7.

41. Burns, R. (1990, July 14). U.S. knew in 1948 of A-plant's risks. *SFC*, A2.

42. Wing, S., Shy, C. M., Wood, J. L. (1991). Mortality among workers at Oak Ridge National Laboratory: Evidence of radiation effects in follow-up through 1984. *JAMA, 265*, 1397–1402.

43. Atchison, S. D. (1990, October 15). 'These people were used as guinea pigs.' *Business Week*, 98.

44. Schneider, K. (1990, July 13). Report warns of impact of Hanford's radiation. *NYT*, A8.

45. Abramson, R. (1990, July 13). Thousands found exposed to Hanford plant radiation. *LAT*, A1, A32.

46. Schneider, K. (1992, November 25). Troubled nuclear factory is to be shut in Oklahoma. *NYT*, A7.

47. Wald, M. L. (1991, July 25). As U.S. struggles to restart Colorado bomb plant, critics question its need. *NYT*, A12.

48. Anonymous. (1991, March 22). Workers in jeopardy at A-plants. *SFC*, A15.

49. Kreiss, K. (1990). The sick building syndrome: Where is the epidemiologic basis. *AJPH, 80*, 1172–73.

50. Anonymous. (1991, July). Can a building really make you sick? *University of California, Berkeley, Wellness Letter*, 1–2.

51. Rice, F. (1990, July 2). Do you work in a sick building? *Fortune*, 86–87.

52. Shaughnessy, R. Quoted in: Griffin, K. (1993, February 14). When your office calls in sick. *SFC, This World*, 8–10; reprinted from *Health*.

53. Associated Press. (1992, August 11). Asbestos settlements may reach $1 billion. *SFC*, A6.

54. Stevens, W. K. (1991, September 26). Study asserts intact asbestos poses little risk for most inside buildings. *NYT*, C19.

55. Stevens, W. K. (1991, August 7). Doctors reassess risk of asbestos. *NYT*, A15.

56. Harris, T. (1993, December/January). The asbestos mess. *Garbage*, 44–49.

57. Norris, R. (1992, March). Safe houses. *AH*, 88–90.

58. Brody, J. E. (1992, October 29). Study documents lead-exposure damage in middle-class children. *NYT*, A14.

59. Yulsman, T. (1991, April 28). Lead hazards at home. *New York Times Magazine, The Good Health Magazine*, 28, 46–51.

60. Needleman, H. L. (1991). Childhood lead poisoning: a disease for the history texts. *AJPH, 81*, 685–87.

61. Rosewicz, B. (1991, May 8). EPA issues rules to reduce lead levels in drinking water of American homes. *WSJ*, B4.

62. Specter, M. (1992, October 21). E.P.A. tests find high lead levels. *NYT*, A15.

63. Anonymous. (1992, December 16). California lawsuit says faucets leach dangerous levels of lead. *NYT*, p. C18.

64. Brody, J. E. (1992, November 18). Lead is public enemy no. 1 for American children. *NYT*, p. B8.

65. McCoy, C. (1991, November 13). Ceramic-tableware lead levels spur California lawsuits; firms deny peril. *WSJ*, B7.

66. Reinhold, R. (1991, November 13). California moves to limit leaching of lead from tableware. *NYT*, A11.

67. Burros, M. (1992, February 26). With concerns being raised about lead in ceramics, you are what you eat on. *NYT*, B5.

68. Leary, W. E. (1991, September 11). F.D.A. seeks a limit on lead content in wine and a ban on foil capsules. *NYT*, B8.

69. Bellafante, G. (1990, March/April). Minimizing household hazardous waste. *Garbage*, 44–48.

70. *Consumer Reports.* Cited in: Anonymous. (1991, July). Fascinating facts. *University of California, Berkeley, Wellness Letter*, 1.

71. National Academy of Sciences. Cited in: Krattenmaker, T. (1990, October 14). Environmentally ill cry for medical recognition. *LAT*, B3.

72. Krattenmaker, 1990.

73. Poore, P. (1990, March/April). Clinical ecology: Medicine for the chemical-sensitive? *Garbage*, 30–35.

74. Poore, 1990, 30.

75. Marinelli, J. (1990, March/April). Plants for healthier homes. *Garbage*, 36–43.

76. Marinelli, 1990.

77. Anonymous. (1991, October–November). Plants help cut indoor pollution. *Modern Maturity*, 12.

78. Sharp, D. (1992, December/January). What a dump! *In Health*, 56–60.

79. Bellafante, G. (1990, March/April). Minimizing household hazardous waste. *Garbage*, 44–48.

80. Anonymous. (1990, October 8). U.S. is faulted for role in water quality. *NYT*, A7.

81. Associated Press. (1992, December 8). $500 billion may be needed to fix urban water systems. *SFC*, A4.

82. Bashin, B. J. (1992, August 23). Fear of faucets. *SFC, This World*, 7, 12–14; reprinted from *Eating Well*.

83. Miller, G. T. Jr. (1990). *Resource conservation and management*. Belmont, CA: Wadsworth.

84. Miller, 1990.

85. National Academy of Sciences. Cited in: Miller, 1990.

86. Gutfeld, R. (1992, October 21). Lead in water of many cities is found excessive. *WSJ*, B6.

87. Altman, L. K. (1992, July 1). Tiny cancer risk in chlorinated water. *NYT*, A12.

88. Sears, C. (1989, October). Fluoridation: Friends and foes. *AH*, 36–38.

89. Brody, J. E. (1991, March 21). Water fluoridation: A much-hailed measure still hampered by lingering doubts. *NYT*, B7.

90. Miller, 1990.

91. Bashin, 1992.

92. Bashin, 1992.

93. Simons, A. (1989, March/April). Diarrhea: On the runs. *Medical SelfCare*, 60–61.

94. Secter, B., & Abramson, R. (1990, May 3). U.S. poised to clean up the air in Grand Canyon. *SFC*, A12; reprinted from *LAT*.

95. Anonymous. (1990, November 24). Smog is hurting trees in Yosemite. *SFC*, A6.

96. Ayres, B. D. Jr. (1991, May 2). Pollution shrouds Shenandoah Park. *NYT*, A10.

97. Stevens, W. K. (1990, July 17). If it's east of the Mississippi, it's blanketed in pollution's haze. *NYT*, B10.

98. Associated Press. (1990, July 27). Council ranks states as world polluters. *SFC*, A12.

99. Reinhold, R. (1990, September 14). Citing medical evidence on smog, California lowers threshold for its health alerts. *NYT*, A10.

100. Anonymous, 1991. Evidence piling up that smog is L.A. health hazard to all.

101. Sherwin, R. Cited in: Boly, W. (1992, April). Smog City wants to make this perfectly clear. *Health*, 54–64.

102. Winslow, R. (1990, September 4). Air polluted with carbon monoxide poses risk to heart patients, study shows. *WSJ*, B4.

103. California Air Resources Board. Cited in: Dolan, M. (1992, July 22). 50% cut in smog in L.A. since '82. *SFC*, A13; reprinted from *LAT*.

104. Ivins, M. (1989, July/August). Too much stuff! Our accumulating crisis. *Utne Reader*, 77–79; reprinted from *Ms.*

105. Kotzsch, R. E. (1989, July/August). Just say no to junk. *Utne Reader*, 79; reprinted from *East West*.

106. Rathje, W., & Murphy, C. (1992). *Rubbish! The archaeology of garbage*. New York: HarperCollins.

107. Rathje & Murphy, 1992.

108. Rathje, W. L. (1991, May). Once and future landfills. *National Geographic*, 116–34.

109. Rathje & Murphy, 1992.

110. Rathje & Murphy, 1992.

111. Anonymous. (1991, August). Which are best for the environment? *Consumer Reports*, 555–56.

112. Specter, M. (1992, October 23). Among the earth baby set, disposable diapers are back. *NYT*, A1, A20.

113. Rathje, 1991.

114. Schneider, K. (1992, January 6). Rules force towns to pick big new dumps or big costs. *NYT*, A1, A10.

115. Passell, P. (1992, February 26). The garbage problem: It may be politics, not nature. *NYT*, C1, C6.

116. Schneider, 1992.

117. Brown, P. (1992, July). Addressing public distrust. *Technology Review*, 68.

118. Passell, P. (1991, September 1). Experts question staggering costs of toxic cleanups. *NYT*, sec. 1, 1, 12.

119. Miller, 1990.

120. Passell, 1991.

121. Kay, J. (1990, September 23). Global dumping of U.S. toxics is big business. *SFE*, A-2.

122. Nash, N. C. (1991, December 16). Latin nations getting others' waste. *NYT*, A6.

123. Environmental Protection Agency. Cited in: Anonymous. (1992, April 10). U.S. says 45,000 sites may be nuclear hazards. *International Herald Tribune*, 3.

124. Grossman, D., & Shulman, S. (1993, December/January). Doing their low-level best. *Garbage*, 32–37.

125. Wald, M. L. (1992, September 20). As nuclear plants close, costs don't shut down. *NYT*, sec. 4, 18.

126. Wald, M. L. (1992, October 3). Nuclear plants held hostage to old fuel. *NYT*, 6.

127. Bauerlein, M. (1992, July/August). Plutonium is forever. *Utne Reader*, 34–37.

128. Breen, B. (1992, March/April). Dismantling nuclear power plants. *Garbage*, 40–47.

129. Wald, M. L. (1992, December 24). Nuclear hazard festers after alarm. *NYT*, A1, A10.

130. Schneider, K. (1992, February 26). Nuclear disarmament raises fear on storage of 'triggers.' *NYT*, A1, A8.

131. Broad, W. J. (1992, July 6). Nuclear accords bring new fears on arms disposal. *NYT*, A1, A4.

132. Grossman & Shulman, 1993.

133. Long, R. L. (1991, November 11). NIMBYism stalls action on nuclear waste sites. *SFC*, A21.

134. Lippman, T. W. (1992, December 19). Energy Dept. can't store nuclear fuel by deadline. *SFC*, A3; reprinted from *Washington Post*.

135. Wald, M. L. (1992, October 20). States' pressure over nuclear waste. *NYT*, C5.

136. Coates, J. (1992, July 12). Damage forces officials to rethink nuclear dump site. *SFE*, A-2; reprinted from *Chicago Tribune*.

137. Kenyon, Q. (1991, October 6). Nuclear waste starts rolling into Idaho. *Albuquerque Journal*, A3.

138. Schneider, K. (1991, October 10). U.S. delays opening of a waste site. *NYT*, A19.

139. Schneider, K. (1992, August 30). Wasting away. *New York Times Magazine*, 42–45, 56–58.

140. Bauerlein, 1992.

141. Skerrett, P. J. (1992, February/March). Nuclear burial at sea. *Technology Review*, 22–23.

142. Browne, M. C. (1991, October 29). Modern alchemists transmute nuclear waste. *NYT*, B5, B7.

143. Fialka, J. J. (1991, June 18). Salute the jimson! The noxious weed may save our planet. *WSJ*, A1, A7.

144. Anonymous. (1991, April 9). Bacterium may combat nuclear waste. *SFC*, A9; reprinted from *NYT*.

145. Piller, C. (1992). *The fail-safe society: Defiance and the end of American technological optimism*. New York: Basic.

146. Ehrlich, P. R., & Ehrlich, A. H. (1990, April 11). People a lethal disease for earth. *SFC*, Briefing section, 8; reprinted from *LAT*.

147. Anonymous. (1991, May 14). New prediction on world's population. *SFC*, A7.

148. Ehrlich, P. Cited in: Reuters. (1992, June 19). Author still predicting a world 'population bomb.' *SFC*, A6.

149. Allen, F. E. (1991, September 13). Overpopulation takes center stage in 1990s. *WSJ*, B1.

150. Crossette, B. (1992, September 16). Population policy in Asia is faulted. *NYT*, A7.

151. U.S. Census Bureau. Cited in: Pear, R. (1992, December 4). New look at the U.S. in 2050: Bigger, older and less white. *NYT*, A1, A10.

152. United Nations. Cited in: Nash, N. C. (1992, October 11). Squalid slums grow as people flood Latin America's cities. *NYT*, sec. 1, 1, 10.

153. Lowe, M. D. (1992, July–August). Alternatives to shaping tomorrow's cities. *The Futurist*, 28–34.

154. Roberts, S. (1990, June 25). 'Mega-cities' join to fight problems. *NYT*, A13.

155. U.S. Census Bureau. Cited in: Vobejda, B. (1991, February 21). Half of population lives in urban areas. *Washington Post*, A1, A12.

156. Garreau, J. (1991). *Edge city: Life on the new frontier*. New York: Doubleday.

157. Gordon S. Black Corp. survey for Population Crisis Committee. Cited in: McLeod, R. G. (1992, March 2). Poll finds U.S. concern about world population. *SFC*, A3.

158. Fornos, W. (1991, February/March). Population politics. *Technology Review*, 45–51.

159. World Bank. Cited in: Fornos, 1991.

160. *IRED Forum* [a publication of the Geneva-based Innovations et Reseaux pour le Developpement], cited in: Anonymous. (1990, July/August). The global village. *Utne Reader*, 144; excerpted from *World Development Forum* (1990, April 15).

161. Sadik, N. (1991, March–April). World population continues to rise. *The Futurist*, 9–14.

162. United Nations Food and Agricultural Organization. Cited in: Associated Press. (1992, September 21). World producing enough food, U.N. study says. *SFC*, A10.

163. Sadik, 1991.

164. Anonymous. (1992, June 29). Notes and comment. *New Yorker*, 25–26.

165. Ehrlich, P. Cited in: Associated Press. (1990, April 6). Americans accused of ruining the planet. *SFC*, A11.

166. Durning, A. (1992). *How much is enough?* Washington, DC: The Worldwatch Institute.

167. Sadik, 1991.

168. United Nations. Cited in: Allen, 1991.

169. Jungerman, E. (1992, May 29). Confronting a threatened planet. *SFC*, A7.

170. Hofheinz, P. (1992, July 27). The new Soviet threat: Pollution. *Fortune*, 110–14.

171. Fesbach, M., & Friendly, A. Jr. (1992). *Ecocide in the U.S.S.R.: Health and nature under seige*. New York: Basic.

172. Bogert, C. (1992, November 2). Get out the geiger counters. *Newsweek*, 64–65.

173. Lewis, P. (1992, May 21). U.S. and six plan nuclear cleanup in Eastern Europe. *NYT*, A1, A7.

174. Kinzer, S. (1992, July 8). 7 leaders fail to agree on pact for A-plant safety. *NYT*, A6.

175. Intergovernmental Panel on Climate Change, 1990. Cited in: Jungerman, 1992.

176. Reuters. (1991, June 14). Expert says deforestation is suicidal. *SFC*, A16.

177. United Nations Food and Agriculture Organization. *Forest resources assessment, 1990 project*. Cited in: Jungerman, 1992.

178. Egan, T. (1990, April 20). Canada rain forest falling like Brazil's. *SFC*, A26; reprinted from *NYT*.

179. Durham, W. Cited in: Seawell, M. A. (1990, April–May). *Stanford Observer*, 5.

180. Larmer, B. (1991, August 12). The rain forest at risk. *Newsweek*, 42.

181. Shabecoff, P. (1990, June 8). Loss of tropical forests is found much worse than was thought. *NYT*, A1, A9.
182. Jungerman, 1992.
183. Sears, C. (1992, October). Jungle potions. *AH*, 70–75.
184. Barnum, A. (1992, December 22). Taking stock in the rain forest. *SFC*, C1.
185. Anonymous. (1990, April 30). The rain forest goes commercial. *SFC*, C2; reprinted from *NYT*.
186. Starr, C., & Taggart, R. (1992). *Biology: The unity and diversity of life* (6th ed.). Belmont, CA: Wadsworth.
187. Shabecoff, P. (1990, June 24). Scientists report more deterioration in earth's ozone layer. *NYT*, sec. 1, 16.
188. Anonymous. (1992, September 30). Dramatic increase in ozone hole. *SFC*, A5.
189. Larmer, B. (1991, December 9). Life under the ozone hole. *Newsweek*, 43.
190. Associated Press. (1992, November 26). New timetable for ban on ozone-depleting chemicals. *SFC*, A13.
191. Makhijani, A., Bickel, A., & Makhijani, A. (1990, May/June). Still working on the ozone hole. *Technology Review*, 53–56.
192. Revelle, R. Quoted in: Jungerman, 1992.
193. Lentz Peace Research. Cited in: Farhat, L. (1990, October 23). Computer analysis tells a grim tale of war. *SFC*, A21.
194. Perlman, D. (1992, December 3). World still lives in nuclear fear. *SFC*, A1, A4.
195. Deutch, J. M. (1992, February/March). Nuclear weapons in the new world order. *Technology Review*, 68.
196. Rathjens, G. W., & Miller, M. M. (1991, August/September). *Technology Review*, 25–32.
197. Church, G. J. (1991, December 16). Who else will have the bomb? *Time*, 42–48.
198. Sivard, R. L. (1986). *World military and social expenditures, 1986.* Washington, DC: World Priorities, 26.
199. Farhat, 1990.
200. Pear, R. (1991, August 11). U.S. ranked no. 1 in weapons sales. *NYT*, 8.
201. Klare, M. T. (1990, May/June). Who's arming who? The arms trade in the 1990s. *Technology Review*, 42–50.
202. Meadows, D. H., Meadows, D. L, & Randers, J. (1992). *Beyond the limits: Confronting global collapse, envisioning a sustainable future.* Post Mills, VT: Chelsea Green.
203. Paulsen, M. (1991, May/June). How to undermine overpopulation. *Garbage*, 49, 51.
204. Dominguez, J., & Robin, V. (1992). *Your money or your life.* Bergenfield, NJ: Penguin.
205. Nix, S. (1991, January 22). Living on less, enjoying it more. *SFC*, B3, B5.
206. Schlender, B. R. (1992, January 27). The values we will need. *Fortune*, 75.
207. Gitlin, T. Quoted in: Schlender, 1992, 76.
208. Luks, A. Cited in: Flippin, R. (1992, November). Good Luks: A champion of volunteerism insists helping is healthy. *AH*, 27–29.
209. House, J. Cited in: Growald, E. R., & Luks, A. (1988, March). Beyond self. *AH*, 51–53.
210. Luks, A. Quoted in: Flippin, 1992, 27–28.
211. Theiler, (1990, November/December). The power of one. *Common Cause Magazine*, 36–40.
212. Wade, J. (1992, November/December). Volunteering on vacation. *Arthritis Today*, 60–62.
213. Walls, D. (1993). *The activist's almanac: The concerned citizen's guide to the leading advocacy organizations in America.* New York: Simon & Schuster.

CHAPTER 12: AGING WELL AND COPING WITH DEATH

1. Gardner, J. W. (1991, June 16). Commencement address, Stanford University,
Stanford, CA. Quoted in: Anonymous. (1991, June 17). Life is an endless unfolding Stanford graduates are told. *NYT*, 91.
2. Lafavore, M. (1990, October). Living long *and* well is a better revenge. *Men's Health*, 6.
3. Smith, P. (1991, January 13). The two great ages. *SFC, This World*, 5–6.
4. Ignatius, A. (1990, March 9). Secrets of Bama: In a corner of China, they live to be 100. *WSJ*, A1, A14.
5. Belden & Russonello survey, October 9–17, 1991, conducted for Alliance for Aging Research. Cited in: Associated Press. (1991, November 18). Two-thirds in U.S. survey want to be 100. *SFC*, A2.
6. U.S. Census Bureau. Cited in: Beck, M., Chideya, F., & Craffey, B. (1992, May 4). Attention, Willard Scott. *Newsweek*, 75.
7. Hocking-Vigie, P. (1992, May 17). 117-year-old woman's secret? Attitude. *LAT*, A6.
8. Olshansky, S. J., Carnes, B. A., & Cassel, C. (1990). In search of Methuselah: Estimating the upper limits to human longevity. *Science*, 250, 634–40.
9. Otten, A. L. (1991, November 15). Charting future course of longevity gains. *WSJ*, B1.
10. Carey, J. R. Quoted in: Kolata, G. (1992, October 16). Fruit fly study challenges accepted longevity theory. *NYT*, A13.
11. Carey, J. R., Liedo, P., Orozco, D. et al. (1992). Slowing of mortality rates at older ages in large medfly cohorts. *Science*, 258, 457–61.
12. Fries, J. Cited in: Waldholz, M. (1992, October 16). Fountain of youth may not be a fairy tale, study finds. *WSJ*, B1.
13. Fries, J. Cited in: Opatrny, D. J. (1991, November 24). Simple question: Why do we die? *SFE*, A-1, A-6.
14. Fries, J. F. (1992). Strategies for reduction of morbidity. *American Journal of Clinical Medicine*, 55, 1257S–62S.
15. Fries, J. F., Williams, C. A., & Morfeld, D. (1992). Improvement in intergenerational health. *AJPH*, 82, 109–12.
16. Fries, J. F. (1989). The compression of morbidity: Near or far? *Milbank Quarterly*, 67(2), 208–32.
17. Kloeden, P. E., Rossler, R., & Rossler, O. E. (1990). Does a centralized clock for ageing exist? *Gerontology*, 36, 314–22.
18. Carey, J. R., Liedo, P., Orozco, D. et al. (1992). Slowing of mortality rates at older ages in large medfly cohorts. *Science*, 258, 457–61.
19. Curtsinger, J. W., Fukui, H. H., Townsend, D. R. et al. (1992). Demography of genotypes: Failure of the limited life-span paradigm in *Drosophila melanogaster*. *Science*, 258, 461–63.
20. Ahlburg, D. A., & Vaupel, J. W. (1990). Alternative projections of the U.S. population. *Demography*, 27, 639–52.
21. Vaupel, J., Gerontological Society of America meeting, San Francisco, October 1991. Quoted in: *Opatrny*, 1991, A-6.
22. Gaziano, J. M., Manson, J. E., Buring, J. E. et al. (1992). Dietary antioxidants and cardiovascular disease. *Annals of the New York Academy of Sciences*, 669, 249–58.
23. Angier, N. (1990, April 17). Radical diet gives animals long lives. *SFC*, A1, A8.
24. Effros, R. B., Svoboda, K., & Walford, R. L. (1991). Influence of age and calorie restriction on macrophage IL-6 and TNF production. *Lymphokine & Cytokine Research*, 10, 347–51.
25. Spindler, S. R., Grizzle, J. M., Walford, R. L. et al. (1991). Aging and restriction of dietary calories increases insulin receptor mRNA, and aging increases glucocorticoid receptor mRNA in the liver of female C3B10RF1 mice. *Journal of Gerontology*, 46(6), B233–37.
26. Walford, R. L. (1990). The clinical promise of diet restriction. *Geriatrics*, 45, 81–83, 86–87.
27. Walford, R. L., & Crew, M. (1989). How dietary restriction retards aging: An integrative
hypothesis (editorial). *Growth, Development, & Aging*, 53, 139–40.
28. Walford, R. (1988). *The 120-year diet.* New York: Pocket.
29. Sobel, D. (1991, September). The 120-year man. *AH*, 18–21.
30. Roth, G. Cited in: Angier, 1990.
31. Roth, G. S., Ingram, D. K., & Cutler, R. G. (1991). Caloric restriction in non-human primates: A progress report. *Aging*, 3, 391–92.
32. Cutler, R. G., Davis, B. J., Ingram, D. K. et al. (1992). Plasma concentrations of glucose, insulin, and percent glycosylated hemoglobin are unaltered by food restriction in rhesus and squirrel monkeys. *Journal of Gerontology*, 47(1), B9–12.
33. Rudman, D., Fellder, A. G., Nagraj, H. S. et al. (1990). Effects of human growth hormone in men over 60 years. *NEJM*, 323, 1. 34. Stephens, R. (1990, September). Turning back the clock? *AARP Bulletin*, 10–12.
35. Anonymous. (1990, December). Human growth hormone: Fountain of youth? *Medical Aspects of Human Sexuality*, 10.
36. Schneider, E. Quoted in: Opatrny, 1991, A-6.
37. Emerit, I. (1992). Free radicals and aging of the skin. *EXS*, 62, 328–41.
38. Anonymous. (1993, January–February). Baldness: The many stages of loss. *Men's Health*, 93.
39. Hilchey, T. (1992, November 25). Scientists pursue new ways to fight baldness. *NYT*, B6.
40. Brody, J. E. (1992, May 13). Perplexing syndrome of sudden baldness. *NYT*, C12.
41. Whitney, E. N., & Hamilton, E. M. N. (1987). *Understanding nutrition* (4th ed.). St. Paul: West.
42. Tanouye, E. (1992, July 1). Estrogen use cuts fracture rate for female osteoporosis sufferers. *WSJ*, B4.
43. Brody, J. (1992, October 14). Loss of weight is tied to the risk of osteoporosis. *NYT*, B7.
44. Dawson-Hughes, B., Dallal, G. E., Krall, E. A. et al. (1990). A controlled trial of the effect of calcium supplementation on bone density in postmenopausal women. *NEJM*, 323, 878–83.
45. Krall, E. A., Sahyoun, N., Tannenbaum, S. et al. (1989). Effect of vitamin D intake on seasonal variations in parathyroid hormone secretion in postmenopausal women. *NEJM*, 321, 1777–83.
46. Naessen, T., Persson, I., Adami, H. O. et al. (1990). Hormone replacement therapy and the risk for first hip fracture: A prospective, population-based cohort study. *AIM*, 113, 95–103.
47. Naessen, T., Persson, I., Ljunghall, S. et al. (1992). Women with climacteric symptoms: A target group for prevention of rapid bone loss and osteoporosis. *osteoporosis international*, 2, 225–31.
48. Riggs, B. L., Watts, N. B., Harris, S. T. et al. (1990). Intermittent cyclical etidronate treatment of postmenopausal osteoporosis. *NEJM*, 323, 73–79.
49. Love, R. R., Mazess, R. B., Barden, H. S. et al. (1992). Effects of tamoxifen on bone mineral density in postmenopausal women with breast cancer. *NEJM*, 326, 852–56.
50. Prince, R. L., Smith, M., Dick, I. M. et al. (1991). Prevention of postmenopausal osteoporosis: A comparative study of exercise, calcium supplementation, and hormone-replacement therapy. *NEJM*, 325, 1189–95.
51. Anonymous. (1990, November). Osteoarthritis. *Mayo Clinic Health Letter*, 6.
52. Ala-Kokko, L., Baldwin, C. T., Moskowitz, R. W. et al. (1990). Single base mutation in the type II procollagen gene (COL2A1) as a cause of primary osteoarthritis associated with a mild chondrodysplasia. *Proceedings of the National Academy of Sciences of the United States of America*, 87, 6565–68.
53. Turk, M. (1992, October). Warding off arthritis. *AH*, 7.

54. Kolata, G. (1991, April 16). The aging brain: The mind is resilient, it's the body that fails. *NYT*, B5, B8.

55. Terry, R. D. Quoted in: Chollar, S. (1988, December). Older brains don't fade away. *PT*, 22.

56. Toufexis, A., Blackman, A., Dolan, B. et al. (1991, October 28). When can memories be trusted? *Newsweek*, 86–88.

57. Associated Press. (1993, February 27). Forget something? You're not alone. *SFC*, C1.

58. Crook, T. H. Cited in: Trotter, B. (1991, April). Better memory through chemistry. *AH*, 12.

59. West, R. L., Crook, T. H., & Barron, K. L. (1992). Everyday memory performance across the life span: Effects of age and noncognitive individual differences. *Psychology & Aging, 7*, 72–82.

60. Crook, T. H., Larrabee, G. J., & Youngjohn, J. R. (1990). Diagnosis and assessment of age-associated memory impairment. *Clinical Neuropharmacology, 13*, Suppl. 3, S81–91.

61. Randal, J. (1990, November 16). It's true: Older people do forget more easily. *SFC*, B3, B5.

62. Salthouse, T. A., Legg, S., Palmon, R. et al. (1990). Memory factors in age-related differences in simple reasoning. *Psychology & Aging, 5*(1), 9–15.

63. Mitchell, D. Quoted in: Goleman, D. (1990, March 27). Not all memory fades with age, studies show. *SFC*, A2; reprinted from *NYT*.

64. National Institute on Aging. (1992). *Bound for good health: A collection of Age Pages*. Gaithersburg, MD: National Institute on Aging.

65. Alzheimer's Disease and Related Disorders Association. Cited in: Anonymous. (1992, December). Down with APP. *Living Well*, 21–22.

66. Kolata, G. (1991, February 28). Alzheimer's disease: Dangers and trials of denial. *NYT*, B15.

67. Wolf-Klein, G. P. (1990). Symptoms, diagnosis, and management of Alzheimer's disease. *Comprehensive Therapy, 16*(9), 25–29.

68. Kolata, G. (1991, October 6). Mental gymnastics. *New York Times Magazine*, 15–17, 42.

69. Anonymous. (1990, June 1). Older women gain freedom by driving. *SFC*, A4; reprinted from *NYT*.

70. Fost, D. (1991, September). Who's too old to drive? *American Demographics*, 8–10.

71. National Institute on Aging. Cited in: Otten, A. L. (1992, June 1). Older drivers appear safer but more frail. *WSJ*, B1.

72. Opatrny, D. J. (1990, November 18). New tests planned for state's drivers. *SFE*, B-1, B-5.

73. Rauch, K. D. (1992, July 12). Sex for life. *SFC, This World*, 7.

74. Greeley, A. M. (1992). *Sex after sixty: A report*. Cited in: Woodward, K. L., & Springen, K. (1992, August 24). Better than a gold watch. *Newsweek*, p. 71.

75. Butler, R. N. Quoted in: Rovner, S. (1989, January 15). Older love. *SFC, This World*, 22; reprinted from *Washington Post*.

76. Weg, R. B. Cited in: Rovner, 1989.

77. Byer, C. O., & Shainberg, L. W. (1991). *Dimensions of human sexuality* (3rd ed.). Dubuque, IA: Wm. C. Brown.

78. Hamilton, J. A., Parry, B. L., & Blumenthal, S. J. (1988). The menstrual cycle in context, I: Affective syndromes associated with reproductive hormonal changes. *Journal of Clinical Psychiatry, 49*, 474–80.

79. Sutherland, F. N. (1990). Psychological aspects of menopause. *Maternal and Child Health, 15*(1), 13–14.

80. Matthews, K. A. (1992). Myths and realities of the menopause. *Psychosomatic Medicine, 54*, 1–9.

81. Kolata, G. (1991, September 17). Women face dilemma over estrogen therapy. *NYT*, B8.

82. Anonymous. (1991, September). The estrogen question: Is it a natural supplement or a dangerous drug? *Consumer Reports*, 587–91.

83. Ziegler, J. (1992, April). The dilemma of estrogen replacement. *AH*, 68–71.

84. Wright, K. (1992, December). Menopause: Change and choice. *Living Well*, 66–71.

85. Stampfer, M. J., Colditz, G. A., Willett, W. C. et al. (1991). Postmenopausal estrogen therapy and cardiovascular disease: Ten-year follow-up from the nurses' health study. *NEJM, 325*, 756–62.

86. Colditz, G. A., Stampfer, M. J., Willett, W. C. (1990). Prospective study of estrogen replacement therapy and risk of breast cancer in postmenopausal women. *JAMA, 264*, 2648–53.

87. Bewley, S., & Bewley, T. H. (1992). Drug dependence with oestrogen replacement therapy. *Lancet, 339*, 290–91.

88. Brody, J. E. (1992, May 20). For menopausal women, there are effective and painless alternatives to hormone replacement. *NYT*, B7.

89. Angier, N. (1992, May 20). Is there a male menopause? Jury is still out. *NYT*, A1, B7.

90. Miles, W. Cited in: Rauch, 1992.

91. Hamilton, E. (1992, November 5). Ailing oldsters can have sex. *Point Reyes Light* (Calif.), 6.

92. Barasch, D. (1992, December). Urinary incontinence. *Living Well*, 94.

93. Leary, W. E. (1992, March 24). U.S. issues guidelines on bladder problems. *NYT*, B6.

94. Goleman, D. (1991, May 16). A modern tradeoff: Longevity for health. *NYT*, B8.

95. Rubinstein, C., & Shaver, P. (1982). *In search of intimacy: A report on loneliness and what to do about it*. New York: Delacorte.

96. Levinson, D. (1978). *The seasons of a man's life*. New York: Alfred A. Knopf.

97. Clausen, J. (1990, October 9). Study fails to find 'midlife crisis.' *SFE*, A2.

98. National Opinion Research Center General Social Survey. Cited in: Riche, M. F. (1991, January 4). Zestful outlook starts to get on in years. *WSJ*, B1.

99. New World Decisions, Inc. 1990 survey for American Board of Family Practice. Cited in: Anonymous. (1990, August–September). Mapping out middle age...crisis or conquest? *Modern Maturity*, 88.

100. New World Decisions, Inc. survey, 1990.

101. Anonymous. Quoted in: Smith, P. (1991, September 15). Voices of experience. *SFC, This World*, 5–6.

102. Daniel Yankelovich Group survey, 1989, for American Association for Retired People. Cited in: Stephens, R. (1989, December). *AARP Bulletin*, 1, 4.

103. IFC study for Commonwealth Fund, 1991. Cited in: Teltsch, K. (1991, May 21). New study of older workers find they can become good investments. *NYT*, A10.

104. Bennet, J. (1992, January 21). Older job applicants find fewer opportunities. *NYT*, 21.

105. Lewis, R. (1991, December). Advantage: bosses. *AARP Bulletin*, 1, 12.

106. Older Women's League. Cited in: Lewin, T. (1991, May 9). *SFC*, B3; reprinted from *NYT*.

107. Older Women's League. Cited in: Cox News Service. (1990, May 10). Pension report says women lagging. *SFC*, A16.

108. Longino, C. F. Jr., & Crown, W. H. (1991, August). Older Americans: Rich or poor? *American Demographics*, 48–54.

109. Smith, L. (1992, January 13). The tyranny of America's old. *Fortune*, 68–72.

110. Longino & Crown, 1991.

111. Otten, A. I. (1990, December 24). Healthy aging hinges on income, education. *WSJ*, 9.

112. Kessler, R. C., Foster, C., Webster, P. S. et al. (1992). The relationship between age and depressive symptoms in two national surveys. *Psychology & Aging, 7*, 119–26.

113. Herzog, A. R., House, J. S., & Morgan, J. N. (1991). Relation of work and retirement to health and well-being in older age. *Psychology & Aging, 6*, 202–11.

114. House, J. S., Kessler, R. C., & Herzog, A. R. (1990). Age, socioeconomic status, and health. *Milbank Quarterly, 63*, 383–411.

115. Robinson, J. P. (1991, May). Quitting time. *American Demographics*, 34–36.

116. Wingard, D. Cited in: Goleman, 1991.

117. Kaplan, R. M., Anderson, J. P., & Wingard, D. L. (1991). Gender differences in health-related quality of life. *Health Psychology, 10*, 86–93.

118. Friedhoff, A. Cited in: Medical Tribune News Service. (1991, November 7). Depressed elderly ignored. *SFC*, B5.

119. Rosenberg, M. Cited in: Rauch, K. D. (1992, July 12). Red flags of depression. *SFC, This World*, 10.

120. National Academy of Sciences. Cited in: Altman, L. K. (1990, November 6). More preventive care sought for older people. *NYT*, B8.

121. Elias, M. (1991, February 19). Reactions to medicine affect 20% of seniors. *USA Today*, 1A.

122. Kolata, G. (1992, February 2). Elderly become addicts to drug-induced sleep. *NYT*, sec. 4, 4.

123. Associated Press. (1989, December 15). Tranquilizers linked to hip fractures. *SFC*, A7.

124. Ray, W. A., Griffin, M. R., & Downey, W. (1989) Benzodiazepines of long and short elimination half-life and the risk of hip fracture. *JAMA, 262*, 3303–7.

125. Beresford, T. P., Blow, F. C., & Brower, K. J. (1990). Alcoholism in the elderly. *Comprehensive Therapy, 16*(9), 38–43.

126. National Institute on Alcohol Abuse and Alcoholism. (1988, October). Alcohol and aging. *Alcohol Alert*, 1–3.

127. Freedman, M. (1992, May 16). Suicide rates high among the elderly. *SFC*, A8.

128. Oldham, J. Cited in: Anonymous. (1991, August). The middle of life: A good place to be. *University of California, Berkeley, Wellness Letter*, 4–5.

129. Kutner, L. (1991, May 23). Some adult children still look to their parents for much of their emotional and financial support. *NYT*, B5.

130. Belden & Russonello survey, October 1991, for Alliance for Aging Research. Cited in: Associated Press, November 18, 1991.

131. Anonymous. (1989, January–February). Pickled brains. *PT*, 23.

132. House, J. R., Landis, K. R., & Umberson, D. (1988). Social relationships and health. *Science, 241*, 540–45.

133. Gerzon, M. Quoted in: Lipstein, O., Mauro, J., & Scanlon, M. (1992, October). Act II: Why it's not such a drag getting old. *PT*, 54–60, 94.

134. Eckel, H. Quoted in: Bill Moyers' "Healing and the mind," television documentary, February 24, 1993, Public Broadcasting System.

135. Dominguez, J., & Robin, V. (1992). *Your money or your life*. Bergenfield, NJ: Penguin.

136. Leming, M. R., & Dickinson, G. E. (1990). *Understanding dying, death, and bereavement* (2nd ed.). Fort Worth, TX: Holt, Rinehart & Winston.

137. Cordes, H. (1991, September/October). Facing death. *Utne Reader*, 65.

138. Levine, S. (1982). *Who dies?* New York: Doubleday.

139. Dowie, M. (1990, October). The biomort factor. *AH*, 18–19.

140. Dowie, 1990.

141. Dowie, 1990.

142. Dowie, 1990.

143. Greenhouse, L. (1990, June 27). Right to reject life. *NYT*, A13.

144. U.S. Supreme Court. Quoted in: Anonymous. (1990, June 26). Excerpts from

court opinions on Missouri right-to-die case. *NYT*, A12.

145. Associated Press. (1990, December 15). Missouri judge says comatose woman can die. *SFC*, 1.

146. Malcolm, A. H. (1990, December 7). Right-to-die case nearing a finale. *NYT*, A14.

147. Lewin, T. (1990, December 27). Nancy Cruzan dies, outlived by debate over right to die. *NYT*, A1, A13.

148. Anonymous. (1990, December 27). Nancy Cruzan's accomplishment (editorial). *NYT*, A18.

149. Dowie, 1990.

150. *JAMA*. Reported in: Hilton, B. (1990, February 4). Making the toughest decisions. *SFE*, D-19.

151. Youngner, S. Quoted in: Dowie, 1990, 18.

152. Dowie, 1990.

153. Rosenthal, E. (1990, October 4). Rules on reviving the dying bring undue suffering, doctors contend. *NYT*, A1, B6.

154. Hilton, B. (1991, January 13). In the news: Right to die turned around. *SFE*, D-14.

155. Belkin, L. (1990, June 6). Doctor tells of first death using his suicide device. *NYT*, A1, A13.

156. Wilkerson, I. (1990, June 7). Physician fulfills a goal: Aiding a person in a suicide. *NYT*, A13.

157. Schmidt, W. E. (1990, December 15). Prosecutors drop criminal case against doctor in suicide case. *NYT*, 9.

158. Wilkerson, I. (1991, October 25). Rage and support for doctor's role in suicide. *NYT*, A1, A8.

159. Gibbs, N., & Gregory, S. S. (1991, November 4). Dr. Death strikes again. *Time*, 78.

160. Associated Press. (1992, July 22). Murder charges against Kevorkian are dismissed. *NYT*, A6.

161. Associated Press. (1992, November 24). 'Dr. Death' assists in his 6th suicide. *SFC*, A3.

162. American Hospital Association. Cited in: Malcolm, A. H. (1990, December 27). What medical science can't seem to learn: When to call it quits. *NYT*, sec. 4, 6.

163. Vorenberg, J. (1991, November 5). Going gently, with dignity. *NYT*, A15.

164. Altman, L. K. (1991, March 12). More physicians broach forbidden subject of euthanasia. *NYT*, B6.

165. Quill, T.E. (1991). Death and dignity—a case of individualized decision making. *NEJM*, *324*, 691–94.

166. Altman, L. K. (1991, July 27). Jury declines to indict a doctor who said he aided in a suicide. *NYT*, 1, 7.

167. Simons, M. (1991, September 11). Dutch survey casts new light on patients who choose to die. *NYT*, B8.

168. Steinfels, P. (1991, November 2). Dutch

study is euthanasia vote issue. *NYT*, 10.

169. Conwell, Y., & Caine, E. D. (1991). Rational suicide and the right to die. *NEJM*, *325*, 1100–2.

170. Carton, R. W. (1990). The road to euthanasia (editorial). *JAMA*, *263*, 2221.

171. Sprung, C. L. (1990). Changing attitudes and practices in forgoing life-sustaining treatments. *JAMA*, *263*, 2211–15.

172. Singer, P. A., & Siegler, M. (1990). Euthanasia—a critique. *NEJM*, *322*, 1881–83.

173. Cassel, C. K., & Meier, D. E. (1990). Morals and moralism in the debate over euthanasia and assisted suicide. *NEJM*, *323*, 750–52.

174. Humphry, D. (1991). *Final exit: The practicalities of self-deliverance and assisted suicide for the dying*. Eugene, OR: The Hemlock Society.

175. American Hospital Association. Cited in: Malcolm, 1990, December 23.

176. Steinfels, P. (1991, October 28). At crossroads, U.S. ponders ethics of helping others die. *NYT*, A1, A15.

177. Associated Press. (1990, September 14). Dying have right to refuse food, Florida high court rules. *NYT*, A14.

178. Angell, M. (1990, July 23). The right to die in dignity. *Newsweek*, 9.

179. Rowland, M. (1992, March 22). Planning for the end of life. *NYT*, sec. 3, 17.

180. Anonymous. (1990, March). Why you need a living will. *University of California, Berkeley, Wellness Letter*, 1–2.

181. Rosenthal, E. (1990, October 4). Rules on reviving the dying bring undue suffering, doctors contend. *NYT*, A1, B6.

182. Ames, K., Wilson, L., Sawhill, R. et al. (1991, August 26). Last rights. *Newsweek*, 40–41.

183. Decarlo, T. (1990, November 12). Looking for families willing to make a final gift of life. *SFC*, B3, B5.

184. Thomas, S. (1991). The gift of life. *Nursing Times*, *87*(37), 28–31.

185. Ring, K. (1980). *Life at death: A scientific investigation of near-death experience*. New York: Coward, McCann & Geohegan.

186. Perry, P. (1988, September). Brushes with death. *PT*, 14–17.

187. Ring, K. Quoted in: Peay, P. (1991, September/October). Back from the grave. *Utne Reader*, 72–73; reprinted from *Common Boundary*.

188. Moody, R. A. Jr. (1991). *Coming back*. New York: Bantam.

189. Krier, B. A. (1990, September 21). New reports from the great beyond. *SFC*, B3, B5; reprinted from *LAT*.

190. Owens, J., Stevenson, I., & Cook, E. Cited in: Farrell, J. (1991, May). Near-death trips may start when stress blows a brain circuit. *AH*, 14.

191. Moody, R. A. Jr. (1975). *Life after life*. Cited in: Ferris, T. (1991, December 15). A cosmological event. *New York Times Magazine*, 44. 52–53.

192. Kubler-Ross, E. (1969). *On death and dying*. New York: Macmillan.

193. Kubler-Ross, 1969.

194. Hilton, B. (1991, January 27). All about lying at death's door. *SFE*, D-14.

195. Anonymous. Cited in: Hilton, 1991, January 27.

196. National Institute on Aging. (1981). *Aging and the circumstances of death*. Bethesda, MD: National Institute on Aging.

197. Somerville, J. (1991, January 7). The final days. *American Medical News*, 7.

198. Malcolm, A. H. (1991, July 5). Giving a dose of empathy to the dying. *NYT*, A12.

199. Egan, T. (1991, January 8). Creating a pleasant stop on the journey to death. *NYT*, A10.

200. Belkin, L. (1992, March 2). Choosing death at home: Dignity with its own toll. *NYT*, A1, B12.

201. Kutner, L. (1992, January 9). A parent's impending death can lead family members to reassess relationships with the parent. *NYT*, B3.

202. Veninga, R. Cited in: Kutner, 1992.

203. Frankel, M. R., & Canepa, L. (1988, September/October). Telling your kids you have cancer or any serious illness. *Medical SelfCare*, 37–41, 69–71.

204. Leming & Dickinson, 1990.

205. Leary, W. E. (1991, August 27). Not even death ends anti-pollution crusade. *NYT*, B8.

206. Horn, P. (1992, May 31). Death: The bottom line. *Reno Gazette-Journal*, 11A.

207. Carlson, L. (1991, September/October). Caring for our own dead. *Utne Reader*, 79–81; excerpted from *Woman of Power*.

208. Schwartz, N. (1992, September 3). Trend in gravestones is highly personal; it's 'cemetery art.' *WSJ*, A1, A4.

209. Rosenthal, E. (1992, December 6). Struggling to handle bereavement as AIDS rips relationships apart. *NYT*, sec. 1, 1, 21.

210. Chance, L. Quoted in: Malcolm, A. H. (1991, October 11). *NYT*, B16.

211. Kalish, R. A. (1985). The social context of death and dying. In Binstock, R. H., & Shanas, E. (Eds.). *Handbook of aging and the social sciences*. New York: Van Nostrand Reinhold.

212. Kastenbaum, R. (1986). *Death, society, and the human experience*. Columbus, OH: Merrill.

213. Trunnell, E. P., Caserta, M. S., & White, G. L. (1992, July/August). Bereavement: Current issues in intervention and prevention. *Journal of Health Education*, *23*, 275–79.

214. Berger, K. S. (1988). *The developing person through the life span* (2nd ed.). New York: Worth.

215. Goleman, D. (1991, March 25). People good at predicting own deaths. *SFC*, D3; reprinted from *NYT*.

Glossary

*Terms printed in **boldface type** within the definition are defined elsewhere in the glossary.*

abscess Localized collection of pus (product of inflammation partly made up of cells) in a cavity formed by the disintegration of tissues.

absorption The passage of substances into or across membranes or tissues.

acquired immune deficiency syndrome (AIDS) An illness, often sexually transmitted, caused by the **human immunodeficiency virus (HIV)**; irreversibly damages the body's immune system.

acquired immunity State in which body encounters **antigens** representing a particular disease, which help the body form **antibodies** that combat greater threats of the disease later.

acupressure Ancient Chinese treatment in which gentle finger pressure is used to treat pain.

acupuncture Ancient Chinese treatment in which a needle or a staple is inserted in a specific part of the body, often the outer ear, to alter the body's electroenergy fields to cure disease.

acute Of short and usually severe duration; opposite of **chronic.**

adaptation Method of dealing with **stress** that does not change the **stressor** or one's reaction to it.

addiction Pattern of being dependent on a drug or a sensation; characterized by continued repetition of the activity despite negative consequences.

additive Chemical that may be added during food production to change color, enhance flavor, or extend storage life.

additive interaction State in which the effect of two drugs is the same as the sum of the effects of the drugs used.

aerobic Physical activity in which oxygen taken in is equal to or slightly more than the oxygen used by the body; compare with **anaerobic** and **nonaerobic.**

aerobic endurance Indicator of efficiency with which one's body uses oxygen, which is needed for cardiovascular fitness.

alcoholism Chronic, progressive, and potentially fatal disease characterized by a growing compulsion to drink.

allergy Overreaction by the **immune system,** producing hypersensitivity to a substance or environmental condition.

Alzheimer's disease Form of dementia characterized by loss of numbers of brain cells; over several years, memory and reasoning ability are progressively lost, and eventually death results.

amino acids Essential building blocks of proteins; synthesized by the body or obtained from dietary sources.

amniocentesis Test used to detect fetal abnormalities, through withdrawal of portion of **amniotic fluid** and analysis of fetal cells for genetic defects.

amniotic fluid In pregnancy, the fluid enveloping and protecting the **fetus.**

amoebic dysentery A protozoa-caused intestinal infection.

amphetamine Laboratory-made drug that stimulates the central nervous system and produces exaggerated feelings of well-being and less fatigue but also impaired judgment.

anaerobic Physical activity in which the body develops an oxygen deficit, producing energy when the oxygen taken in is not enough to meet the oxygen required; compare with **aerobic.**

analgesic Painkilling drug that acts on the **central nervous system** to block pain messages sent to the brain.

anaphylaxis (anaphylactic shock) Life-threatening constriction of air passages resulting from allergic reaction.

androgynous Having the characteristics of both male and female.

anemia Decreased ability of the blood to carry oxygen because levels of **red blood cells** or **hemoglobin** are low.

aneurysm Ballooning of a weakened area of an artery.

angina (angina pectoris) Intense chest pain resulting from impaired blood flow to heart muscles.

anorexia nervosa Psychological disorder in which appetite and hunger are suppressed, leading to severe weight loss and even death.

anorgasmic Unable to have an orgasm during intercourse.

antagonistic interaction Action in which one drug neutralizes the effects of another.

antibiotic Bacteria-killing drug.

antibodies Chemical compounds produced by the **immune system** that destroy disease-producing **antigens.**

antigens Disease-producing microorganisms that, when introduced into the body, cause the formation of **antibodies.**

antihistamine Drug used to block the release of histamine, which plays a role in allergic reactions.

antioxidants Special vitamins that protect other compounds from the harmful effects of oxygen.

anxiety disorders Irrational fears and worries that constitute some common psychological disorders; these include: **generalized anxiety disorder; panic disorder; phobias; obsessive-compulsive disorders**.

aorta Primary artery of the body arising from the left ventricle of the heart.

arrhythmia Irregular heartbeat rhythm.

arteries Any large tubular blood vessels that carry oxygen-rich blood from the heart through the body.

arterioles Any of the small terminal twigs of an **artery** that ends in **capillaries.**

arteriosclerosis Disease characterized by hardening, thickening, and loss of elasticity in blood vessel walls.

arthritis Inflammation of the joints.

artificial insemination Process of collecting **sperm** from male partner or anonymous donor and depositing it into the female reproductive tract to enable **conception.**

artificially acquired immunity The development of **antibodies** after specially prepared **pathogens** are injected into the body; such injection is called *vaccination,* **immunization,** or *inoculation.*

asthma Chronic affliction of lung airways, producing wheezing, coughing, and gasping; repeated attacks can damage the heart and lungs.

atherosclerosis Serious form of **arteriosclerosis** in which **plaque** builds up in blood vessels, causing narrowing that results in less blood, and thus less oxygen and nutrients, passing through.

atrium Part of the heart that takes in and pumps blood to the chamber below, the **ventricle,** which then contracts to send the blood to the **aorta** and lungs.

autoimmune disorder Disorder in which the **immune system** attacks the body's own tissues; examples include **rheumatoid arthritis, multiple sclerosis,** and **myasthenia gravis.**

aversion therapy Therapy intended to change habits by inducing dislike for them through association with a negative stimulus; also called *aversive conditioning.*

bacteria One-celled microscopic organisms (singular: *bacterium*).

bacterial vaginosis (BV) Slightly increased, malodorous vaginal discharge; the most common cause of vaginal symptoms among women of childbearing age.

balloon angioplasty Use of **cardiac catheterization** to insert and then inflate a tiny balloon inside a blocked **coronary artery** to open areas of narrowing.

barbiturates Chemical compounds that are dispensed by prescription in pill or liquid form to be used as sleeping aids and tension relievers and to control epileptic seizures.

basal-body-temperature (BBT) method Method that aids in conception; uses a special thermometer to check body temperature to detect the slight drop and then sharp rise that signals **ovulation.**

basal metabolic rate Refers to energy spent to sustain a person's life when in a resting position.

behavior modification Method of psychological treatment in which rewards are given for desirable behaviors and withheld for undesirable behaviors.

behavior therapies Types of psychotherapy in which therapists try to relieve psychological distress not by searching out underlying problems but by using learning principles to change underlying behavior.

benign tumor Abnormal cells that are usually harmless; unlike cancer cells, they do not grow uncontrollably or invade surrounding tissues; opposite of **malignant tumor.**

benzodiazepines Group of chemicals used as **tranquilizers.**

bilirubin Yellow pigment in skin, which causes the yellow color of **jaundice** if not removed by the liver.

biofeedback Method of stress reduction in which one is attached to a machine that monitors internal changes in the body and communicates, or feeds, this information back.

biopsy Surgical removal of sample of tissue in order to give it a microscopic examination for signs of cancer.

bipolar disorder Emotional disorder characterized by mood swings between the two extremes, or poles (hence, "bipolar") of **depression** and **mania;** also known as *manic-depressive disorder.*

blackout Short-term amnesia resulting from alcohol-induced interference in ability to transfer information from short-term to long-term memory.

blood alcohol concentration (BA) Amount of alcohol in the blood, expressed as a ratio of milligrams (mg) of alcohol per 100 milliliters (ml) of blood.

blood cholesterol Fatty material that is necessary for production of **hormones,** cell metabolism, and other vital processes but that in high levels is a contributing factor to coronary heart disease; also known as *serum cholesterol.*

blood pressure Force exerted by the blood pushing against the walls of the blood vessels. *See also* **systolic blood pressure** and **diastolic blood pressure.**

boils Localized swellings and inflammations of the skin caused by infection in a skin gland.

borderline personality disorder Emotional disorder characterized by lack of stable sense of self, feelings of inadequacy, and difficulty making decisions about values, careers, and relationships.

botulism Possibly fatal food poisoning resulting from a bacterium growing in improperly canned foods.

bradycardia Abnormally slow heart rate, below 60 beats per minute.

brain death Irreversible loss of all brain functions.

brain stem Part of the brain that controls breathing and heartbeat.

breech birth Kind of childbirth in which the infant is being born buttocks- or feet-first, instead of head-first.

brief therapy Type of psychotherapy in which patient and therapist agree on meeting for treatment for a short period (generally 2–6 months) and to concentrate on specific problems identified in advance; two examples are **cognitive therapy** and **transactional analysis.**

bulimia nervosa Psychological disorder of binge eating often followed by forced vomiting of food.

bypass surgery Operation during which veins from elsewhere in the body are grafted to the heart in order to bypass blocked **coronary arteries** and allow the heart to receive more blood.

caffeine A mild stimulant found in coffee, tea, cocoa, and many cola drinks.

calendar method Method of natural family planning in which the beginning and duration of a woman's fertile period each month is calculated based on her menstrual cycle.

Calories Units of heat (energy); 1 Calorie (kilocalorie) is the heat required to raise 1 kilogram of water 1 degree Celsius.

cancer Disease in which malignant cellular tumor develops that is capable of spreading to other parts of the body.

candidiasis Yeast infection of the vagina.

cannabis (*Cannabis sativa*) Plant from which the psychoactive drugs **marijuana** and **hashish** are derived.

capillaries Small blood vessels that deliver deoxygenated blood into **veins,** which return to the heart.

carbohydrate Chemical compound such as starch, sugar, or glycogen, which is composed of carbon, hydrogen, and oxygen; carbohydrates are the body's primary source of energy.

carcinogen Substance that stimulates the development of cancer.

carcinoma Cancer that develops in organs that secrete, such as skin and some glands.

cardiac catheterization Insertion of a thin tube through a blood vessel and into the heart to take readings or inject dyes for X-ray diagnosis.

cardiovascular disease Any disease or disorder of the heart and/or blood vessels.

carpal tunnel syndrome (CTS) Damage and pain in nerves and tendons of the hands; a form of **repetitive strain injury.**

cataracts Clouding of the lens of the eye.

catatonia Type of **schizophrenia** characterized by being motionless or constantly in motion, neither condition being related to outside stimuli.

cell-mediated immunity Form of **acquired immunity;** specialized **white blood cells** are used to destroy specific **antigens.**

central nervous system Part of the nervous system made up of the brain and the spinal cord.

cerebral cortex Part of the brain responsible for thought, memory, emotion, and voluntary movement.

cerebral embolism Wandering blood clot that wedges in an artery leading to the brain.

cerebral hemorrhage Form of **hemorrhagic stroke** caused by blood seepage into the brain, resulting in severe headaches and decreased or lost consciousness.

cerebral thrombosis Blood clot in the brain that develops when **plaque** builds on an artery wall and partly obstructs blood flow.

cervical cap Small, thimble-shaped rubber or plastic cap that fits directly onto the cervix for purposes of contraception.

cervical mucus method Method of birth control in which females check for clear, thin mucus discharge from the cervix, an indication of fertility.

cervix Opening between **uterus** and **vagina.**

cesarean section Surgical delivery of an infant through an incision in the mother's abdominal wall.

chancre A sore or ulcer at the entry point of a pathogen; a sign of **syphilis.**

chemotherapy Treatment of cancer with drugs that hinder the ability of cancer cells to reproduce.

chlamydia Bacterial **sexually transmitted disease;** may have no early symptoms, especially in women, but if untreated may lead to trachoma.

cholera Any of several diseases marked by severe gastrointestinal symptoms, such as diarrhea and vomiting, and possibly fatal dehydration; may be contracted from drinking or washing food in contaminated water.

cholesterol Organic substance found in animal fats and oil.

chorionic villi Fingerlike extensions of the fetal part of the placenta, which carry blood vessels from fetus close to the blood vessels of the mother.

chorionic villus sampling (CVS) Test for identifying genetic defects during pregnancy, consisting of insertion of a tube through the **cervix** or a needle through the abdominal wall to obtain a sample of the developing placenta for analysis; may be performed earlier in pregnancy than **amniocentesis.**

chromosomes Structures in the cell nucleus that carry **genes,** or hereditary units; each chromosome is made of **deoxyribonucleic acid (DNA).**

chronic Marked by long duration or frequent recurrence; opposite of **acute.**

chronic bronchitis Persistent inflammation and infection of smaller airways in the lungs; caused by pollutants and tobacco smoke.

chronic fatigue syndrome (CFS) Illness of unknown origin characterized by debilitating fatigue, aches, and depression, which lasts from 6 months to several years.

chronic obstructive lung disease (COLD) Respiratory disorder characterized by the slow, progressive interruption of air flow within the lungs; the two main types are **chronic bronchitis** and **pulmonary emphysema.**

circadian rhythm Body's built-in clock of daily physiological cycles.

circuit training Indoor version of **cross training.**

circulatory system The system of heart, blood vessels, blood, and lymphatics concerned with the circulation of the blood and lymph.

circumcision Surgical removal of the foreskin for health or religious reasons.

cirrhosis Disease characterized by irreversible scarring of the liver, which is then unable to metabolize various toxins and drugs; results from heavy alcohol consumption.

climacteric The 3–5 years before the final menstrual period and the onset of **menopause;** periods become less regular and often either lighter or heavier.

clitoris In females the most sexually sensitive organ; it is protected by a hood formed by the joining of the inner lips above the vaginal opening.

cocaine hydrochloride White crystalline powder, the drug most people call simply "cocaine"; it is highly addictive.

codeine Painkiller found in opium; principally derived from **morphine;** found in cough medicines and combined forms of aspirin.

cognitive therapy School of psychotherapy that assumes that our thinking influences our feelings and our reactions to events.

coitus interruptus Removal of the penis from the vagina before ejaculation.

colon Part of the large intestine that connects with the rectum.

colostrum Yellowish milk produced in the breasts of new mothers a few days after childbirth.

colpotomy Type of female sterilization, consisting of surgical incision made through the back of the vagina, which leaves no outside scar.

combination pill Birth control pill that contains two hormones, **estrogen** and **progesterone,** which prevent **ovulation.**

common cold **Virus**-caused infection of membranes lining the nose, sinuses, and throat; usually spread by direct contact with infected people or the things they recently touched.

complex carbohydrates **Carbohydrates**—primarily starches and fibers—that provide the body with sustained rather than short-term energy; compare with **simple carbohydrates.**

compulsion Repetitive, almost irresistible action, as in constant biting of fingernails.

conception The moment when a male reproductive cell, the **sperm,** enters its counterpart female cell, the **ovum** or egg, and fuses with it; also called *fertilization.*

condom A thin sheath, often made of latex; when unrolled over the penis, it prevents semen from being transmitted during sexual acts.

congener In alcoholic beverages, a byproduct of fermentation and preparation.

congenital heart disorder Abnormalities of the heart existing at birth.

congestive heart failure Inability of the heart to pump sufficient blood, resulting in an accumulation of fluids in the lungs, abdomen, and legs.

contagious Communicable by contact.

contraception Prevention of **conception;** birth control.

convulsion Abnormal, involuntary muscle jerk or contraction.

convulsive seizure Condition lasting 2–5 minutes in which person becomes rigid, falls, and has **convulsions.**

coping State of changing a **stressor** or one's reaction to it.

coronary arteries Blood vessels that supply oxygenated blood to heart muscle tissues.

coronary embolism A blockage of coronary artery by a clump of material, **embolus,** caused by a blood clot, bubble of air, gas, bacteria, or tissue.

coronary heart disease Disease of the heart caused by narrowing of the **coronary arteries,** resulting in reduced blood flow to the heart.

coronary occlusion Blockage of a **coronary artery,** preventing the heart from functioning properly.

coronary thrombosis Sudden appearance of a blood clot, **thrombus,** stuck to a blood vessel wall, which blocks the blood flow.

cortical death Type of death in which the **cerebral cortex** no longer functions; also called *cerebral death* or *cognitive death.*

Cowper's glands Two small glands discharging into the male **urethra;** in the first stage of sexual arousal they secrete a fluid that makes the urethra more alkaline.

crack Drug consisting of **cocaine hydrochloride** dissolved with baking soda or other alkaline solution, producing hard lumps, or "rocks," which may be smoked in a pipe.

Crohn's disease Type of bowel disorder producing diarrhea, abdominal pain, cramps, and fever.

cross tolerance Transfer of **tolerance** from one drug to another; also called *cross-addiction.*

cross-training Use of more than one **aerobic** activity to achieve physical fitness.

circuit training Indoor version of **cross-training.**

cumulative Characterized by an accumulation of a drug (e.g., alcohol) in the body because it is taken in faster than the body can process and excrete it.

cunnilingus Oral stimulation of the **clitoris** or vulva.

curette Small plastic tube inserted through woman's **cervix** into the **uterus** during type of **abortion** known as **suction curettage.**

cystic fibrosis Genetic condition of the respiratory system in which excess production of mucus impairs lung function.

cystitis Inflammation of the urinary bladder.

cytomegaloviral (CMV) infection Infection passed from mother to infant in cervical secretions at birth or during breast-feeding; may produce brain or liver damage, blindness, deafness, mental retardation, cerebral palsy, or seizures.

Daily Values (DVs) Government recommendations for total fat, saturated fat, cholesterol, sodium, total carbohydrate, dietary fiber, protein, and some vitamins and minerals.

decibel (dB) Unit for measuring the intensity of noise.

dehydration Abnormal depletion of fluids from the body.

delirium tremens (DTs) Violent delirium, with trembling, fevers, hallucinations, and delusions, resulting from prolonged, excessive consumption of alcohol.

delta-9-tetrahydrocannabinol (THC) Principal psychoactive agent in **cannabis.**

delusions of grandeur A person's false belief that he or she is supremely important.

delusions of persecution A person's false belief that people are trying to harm him or her.

delusions of reference A person's false beliefs that many messages personally refer to himself or herself.

denial Defense mechanism in which one refuses to admit to or to face unpleasant realities.

dental dams Latex sheets, which may be used to prevent saliva and vaginal fluids from being exchanged when a woman receives oral sex.

deoxyribonucleic acid (DNA) Complex molecule found in all living cells and the carrier of hereditary information; DNA is made up of thousands of **genes.**

dependence Physical and/or psychological reliance on or need for a chemical substance.

dependent personality disorder Poorly adaptive type of **personality disorder** characterized by lack of self-confidence and preference for letting other people make decisions.

depersonalization Distortion in how people see their bodies and themselves, as happens in some kinds of drug use.

depressant Drug that slows down or sedates the central nervous system.

depression Persistent feelings of sorrow, apathy, and despair; as a mental illness, inability to function normally.

designer drugs Types of **psychoactive drugs** closely related in chemical structure to regulated or banned drugs; also called *analog drugs.*

detoxification Process of supervised removal of alcohol or other drug from the body, usually in a hospital or similar setting.

diabetes (diabetes mellitus) Disease in which the body in unable to break down **carbohydrates** at a normal rate because of the inadequate production of **insulin.** *See also* **type 1 diabetes, type 2 diabetes.**

Diagnostic and Statistical Manual of Mental Disorders (Fourth Edition) Classification of psychological disorders published by American Psychiatric Association; commonly known as *DSM-IV.*

diaphragm   Contraceptive consisting of a latex cup used with **spermicide** and placed over the **cervix** for birth-control purposes.

diastole   Relaxation phase in the cardiac cycle when the heart chambers fill with blood; compare with **systole.**

diastolic blood pressure   Force exerted by the blood on walls of blood vessels during the relaxation phase when the heart is between contractions; compare with **systolic blood pressure.**

dietary cholesterol   Type of **cholesterol** in food that comes only from animal sources.

dilation   Expansion.

dilation and curettage (D and C)   Method of **induced abortion** in which the cervix is dilated (expanded) and a spoonlike instrument (curette) is used to scrape the uterine wall and remove the contents.

dilation and evacuation (D and E)   Method of **induced abortion** in which the cervix is dilated (expanded) and suction and forceps (an instrument for grasping) are used to extract the uterine contents.

dispositional tolerance   Type of **tolerance** to drugs in which the user's metabolism rate increases the body's ability to break down and get rid of the drug.

distress   Type of **stress** in which the source is a negative event; opposite of **eustress.**

distressor   Type of **stressor** that is negative, such as being fired; opposite of **eustressor.**

diuretic   Drug that increases the elimination of body fluid via urination.

diverticulosis   A condition in which the intestinal wall develops outpouchings called diverticula.

dominant gene   A **gene** that has the major influence in determining a particular inherited characteristic, such as eye color; opposite of **recessive gene.**

dosage   Amount of a drug.

douching   Attempted method of birth control consisting of rinsing out the vagina with a chemical immediately after sexual intercourse.

Down (or Down's) syndrome   Genetic disorder consisting of physical and mental retardation caused by extra number-21 **chromosome.**

drug   Chemical that changes a person's mental or physical state or function.

drug abuse   Excessive use of a drug that has dangerous side effects or use of a drug for nonmedical reasons; also called *illicit drug use.*

drug effect   Action of drug on the body.

drug expectancy   User's expectation of what use of a drug will produce.

drug misuse   Use of a drug for purposes other than those for which it was originally intended or prescribed.

drug use   Use of a legal drug for purposes and in amounts for which it was intended or prescribed.

durable power of attorney for health care decisions   Legal document empowering a patient's representative, such as a friend or relative, to act on the patient's behalf in health care matters.

dysfunctional family   Family in which one or both parents act negatively or destructively toward each other or toward their children.

dysmenorrhea   Painful menstruation.

dyspareunia   Painful or difficult sexual intercourse.

eating disorder   Abnormal, possibly dangerous pattern of food consumption; includes **anorexia nervosa, bulimia nervosa,** and bulimarexia.

echocardiogram   Diagnostic technique for heart disease in which sound waves are used to create a picture of the heart.

eclectic   In psychotherapy, the use by a therapist of a combination of methods and approaches.

ectopic pregnancy   A pregnancy in which a fertilized egg becomes implanted at a site other than the lining of the **uterus;** typically it is in the **fallopian tube.**

ejaculatory duct   Tube connecting the **seminal vesicles** and **vas deferens.**

electrocardiogram (ECG, EKG)   Recording of electric currents associated with heartbeats.

electroconvulsive therapy   Treatment for depression in which brief electrical shock is applied to a patient's brain to induce a convulsion; also called *electroshock treatment.*

electroencephalograph (EEG)   Record of electrical activity in the brain.

electromagnetic field   Invisible field of electrical energy and magnetic energy generated by an electrically charged conductor.

embolus   Blood clot.

embryo   Developing human from the end of the second week to about the eighth week of pregnancy.

emotional health   The ability to be aware of and express one's feelings in an appropriate way.

emphysema   Disease in which the lungs lose their normal elasticity, causing extreme difficulty breathing.

enabler   Family member who protects an alcoholic from the negative consequences of addiction and thereby unintentionally promotes the alcoholic's drinking.

encephalitis   Relatively rare but usually fatal virus, such as eastern equine encephalitis, that attacks the brain, causing it to swell.

endometriosis   Condition in which cells of the uterine lining grow in pelvic or abdominal cavities

endometrium   Mucus membrane lining the **uterus,** broken down and discharged during **menstruation.**

endorphin (enkephalin)   Natural mood-elevating, painkilling chemical released by the brain, as during some types of exercise.

energy   The capacity to do work.

energy balance   State in which Calories expended are the same as those consumed.

energy-yielding nutrients   Types of **nutrients—carbohydrates, proteins,** and **fats**—that produce energy when they are used (oxidized or burned) by the body for movement, heat, or growth.

environmental illness (EI)   Condition of violent reactions or heightened sensitivity to certain common chemicals; also called *multiple-chemical sensitivities.*

enzymes   Chemical substances that regulate physiological processes.

epididymis   Coiled tubes in the **scrotum** in which **sperm** mature.

epididymitis   Inflammation of tissue leading out of the **testicles,** which may result in sterility; symptoms are testicular tenderness, fever, and swelling.

episiotomy   During birth process, a small surgical incision sometimes made in the **perineum** to prevent possible tearing of vaginal tissue.

ergonomics   Study of human factors to consider in designing tools for safe and effective use.

essential   In nutrition, describes a substance that the body requires for energy growth, and maintenance but cannot make in sufficient amounts.

essential amino acids   Types of **amino acids** that are indispensable to life and growth and that must come from the diet; compare with **nonessential amino acids.**

essential nutrients   Chemicals that the body needs for growth, maintenance, and repair and that must be obtained from food.

estrogen   A **hormone,** secreted by the **ovaries,** that spurs **endometrium** buildup and generally controls the **menstrual cycle.**

estrogen replacement therapy   Estrogen administered medically to replace **estrogen** lost as a result of **menopause.**

ethanol (ethyl alcohol)   Intoxicating agent in alcoholic beverages.

eustress   Type of **stress** in which the source is positive; opposite of **distress.**

eustressor   Type of **stressor** that is positive, such as falling in love; opposite of **distressor.**

euthanasia   Assisted method of causing a terminally ill person to die painlessly.

exercise dependency   Compulsion to overexercise; also called *exercise addiction.*

exercise stress test   Test for heart reaction to increased work, consisting of **electrocardiogram** taken as the patient walks on a treadmill or pedals a stationary bicycle.

external cue theory   Theory of obesity holding that the body eats in response to external cues, such as time of day.

fallopian tubes Two canals through which **ova** pass from the **ovaries** to the **uterus.**

false labor Contractions of the uterus that resemble those of true labor.

family therapy Type of psychotherapy that treats an individual's family as well as the individual, on the assumption that a person's problems may stem from problems of interaction within the family.

farsighted Unable to see things clearly at close range without glasses; differs from **nearsighted.**

fats Nutrients composed of fatty acid and glycerol; the body's most concentrated source of energy.

fat-cell theory Theory of obesity suggesting that overfeeding in early childhood increases the number of fat cells.

fatfold test Test using a pincer-like instrument called skin calipers to measure the percentage of body fat.

fat-soluble vitamins Vitamins A, D, E, and K, which are **soluble** in **fat;** compare with **water-soluble vitamins.**

fatty acids Basic chemical units of **fat;** they are of two types—**saturated fats** and **unsaturated fats.**

fellatio Oral stimulation of the penis.

female condom Disposable contraceptive device consisting of soft polyurethane sheath that lines the **vagina;** also called *vaginal pouch.*

fentanyl **Opiate** used to produce anesthesia in surgery and sometimes sold as an illegal street drug; it is 80 times as potent as **morphine.**

fetal alcohol effects (FAE) Developmental disability in a child resulting from mother's use of alcohol while pregnant.

fetal alcohol syndrome (FAS) Birth disorder characterized by a common pattern of birth defects and mental retardation resulting from mother's use of alcohol while pregnant.

fetus Human organism developing in the **uterus** from ninth week until birth.

fiber Indigestible part of plants; found in cereal, fruits, and vegetables.

fibrocystic breast disease Noncancerous (benign) breast lumps.

flashbacks Unexpected re-experienced parts of a hallucinogenic episode or perceptual distortions, which can occur weeks or even years after a **hallucinogen** was used.

flexibility Ability to move through the full range of motions allowed by the joints.

flooding Type of therapy for diminishing a **phobia** by exposing the patient to the object of the phobia suddenly instead of gradually.

follicle-stimulating hormone (FSH) A **hormone** produced by the **pituitary gland** that stimulates the growth of **ova** in females and **sperm** in males.

foreskin Extension of the skin that covers the penis shaft.

freebase cocaine Form of cocaine mixed with ether or another solvent that can be smoked.

frost nip Painless condition resulting from overexposure to cold weather and characterized by lightening of the skin; it may develop into **frostbite.**

frostbite Condition resulting from overexposure to cold weather and characterized by frozen tissue with discolored skin and pain and then pale skin and numbness, until the area is thawed and bluish skin and blisters develop.

functional tolerance Condition in which user's brain and central nervous system become less sensitive to a drug's effect.

fungus (fungi) Organism that reproduces by means of spores, such as yeasts or molds.

gallbladder disease Disease in which the gallbladder has been irritated by infection or overuse, producing gallstones—formations of calcium, cholesterol, and minerals—which become stuck in the bile duct and can cause intense pain.

gamete intrafallopian transfer (GIFT) Technique for treating **infertility** in which **ovum** and **sperm** are positioned in the **fallopian tube** for **conception,** then moved into the **uterus** for **implantation.**

gastritis An inflammation of the membrane of the stomach.

gastroenteritis Food poisoning or bacterial infection caused by eating contaminated food, producing inflammation of the stomach and intestinal linings, and characterized by nausea, vomiting, diarrhea, fever, and abdominal cramps.

gastrointestinal (GI) tract The stomach and large and small intestines.

gender identity Perception of oneself as male or female.

gender role Set of attitudes and behaviors considered appropriate for a given sex within a particular culture.

general (systemic) Affecting the body in general; said of the action of a drug.

general adaptation syndrome Standard physical response to sudden stress, consisting of three phases—alarm, resistance, and exhaustion.

general anesthesia Type of drug used to render a person unconscious before surgery.

generalized anxiety disorder Emotional disorder characterized by excessive or unrealistic worries, especially over a period of 6 months or more.

genes The biological units of heredity; elements on the **chromosomes** that determine the characteristics of a species and of an individual.

genital warts A type of **sexually transmitted disease** characterized by fleshy growths on the penis, **scrotum,** anus, or **urethra** in men or, in women, on the **vulva, perineum, cervix,** or anus.

Gestalt therapy School of psychotherapy that tries to help patients to become aware of and express their feelings and to take responsibility for their feelings and actions; it combines the emphasis of

psychoanalysis on making one aware of unconscious feelings with the emphasis of humanistic therapy on immediate experience and current behavior.

giardia Common disorder resulting from water impurity that causes diarrhea, abdominal cramps, and fatigue.

gingivitis Early form of **periodontal disease** characterized by swollen red gums that bleed easily.

glans The most sensitive part of the **penis,** located just below its head.

glaucoma Disorder consisting of high pressure in the eye, which if left untreated can lead to blindness.

glucose Blood sugar, the body's principal source of energy.

gonad The principal reproductive organs—**testes** in a male and **ovaries** in a female.

gonorrhea A bacterial **sexually transmitted disease;** if not treated, it can lead to an inflammation of the **urethra** in males and to **pelvic inflammatory disease** in females.

granulocyte A form of **phagocyte** that circulates in the bloodstream.

greenhouse effect Environmental problem in which various gases—carbon dioxide, chlorofluorocarbons (CFCs), methane, and nitrous oxide—exceed their normal amounts in the atmosphere and act like panes of glass in a greenhouse, trapping heat.

group A strep Type of streptococcal toxic-shock-like syndrome, which causes flu-like symptoms, then skin rash, dizziness, sudden drop in blood pressure, and interrupted circulation; if not treated quickly, it can be fatal.

group therapy Type of psychotherapy in which a trained therapist directs a group of 8–10 patients, with the goal of developing self-understanding and behavior change.

half-life Measure of the time necessary for radioactive material to degrade until it emits half its present radiation.

hallucinations Sensory visual and aural experiences that are distortions of reality.

hallucinogens Drugs such as **mescaline, psilocybin, LSD,** and **phencyclidine (PCP)** that can alter consciousness in profound ways and produce **hallucinations;** also known as *psychedelics.*

hash oil A **psychoactive drug** that is a concentrated liquid extract of the hemp plant; more potent than **marijuana** or **hashish.**

hashish A **psychoactive drug** that is made by drying and compressing gum-like secretions (resin) produced by the hemp plant.

hay fever Allergic reaction caused by pollen; characterized by runny nose and eyes, itching, sneezing, and loss of appetite.

health The achievement of physical, mental, social, emotional, and spiritual well-being.

health-care proxy Legal document that appoints a friend or family member to make health care decisions on one's behalf in case of incapacitation.

heart Four-chambered muscular pump that moves blood through the vascular system to every living cell in the body.

heat cramps Painful arm, leg, and abdominal spasms resulting from exposure to excessive heat.

heat exhaustion Prostration caused by excessive fluid loss in hot weather; characterized by increased sweating, raised body temperature, cool wet skin, and lack of coordination.

heat stress Disorder resulting from exposure to excessive heat; characterized by lowered blood pressure, dizziness, and blurred vision.

heat stroke Potentially fatal disorder brought on by exposure to excessive heat; characterized by lack of sweating, hot and dry skin, fast breathing, seizures, and coma.

Heimlich maneuver Rescue procedure used to dislodge object stuck in a person's throat; consists of applying sudden upward pressure on the abdomen to force out the object.

helper T-cells Cells in the body's immune system that identify **antigens,** or foreign organisms, in the body.

hemoglobin The oxygen-carrying part of the blood.

hemorrhagic stroke Damage to the brain caused by blood seeping from an opening in the wall of a blood vessel in the head.

hemorrhoids Swollen blood vessels in the anus.

hepatitis A **virus**-caused infection and inflammation of the liver; characterized by fever, chills, headache, nausea, diarrhea, loss of appetite, skin rashes, and sometimes the yellowing of skin and eyes called **jaundice.** There are five principal strains, designated A, B, C, D, and E.

herniated disk Protrusion of a disk from between two **vertebrae,** requiring surgery.

heterozygous Having different genes for a given inherited trait; opposite of **homozygous.**

high-density lipoproteins (HDLs) Beneficial molecules that help remove excess **cholesterol** from the body.

histrionic personality disorder Type of emotional disorder characterized by excessive emotionality and attention-seeking and a constant demand for praise.

hives Allergic reaction characterized by raised, itchy skin blotches.

holistic health Concept of the nature of health that views an individual as a whole person with five interacting dimensions of health: physical, emotional, social, intellectual, and spiritual.

homeostasis The human body's natural balance or stability of physiological and psychological systems.

homozygous Having identical genes for a given inherited trait; opposite of **heterozygous.**

hormone replacement therapy Taking **estrogen** and **progesterone** to ease problems associated with **menopause.**

hormones Specialized chemicals released in the blood that regulate specific body functions.

human growth hormone (HGH) A **hormone** produced by the **pituitary gland** which spurs bone growth in children and keeps tissues healthy in adults; when it declines after about age 30, signs of aging begin.

human immunodeficiency virus (HIV) A **virus** transmitted by blood, semen, and vaginal fluids that gradually destroys cells of the immune system, weakening its defense against other diseases; HIV is the cause of **acquired immune deficiency syndrome (AIDS).**

human papilloma virus (HPV) A **sexually transmitted disease** that causes **genital warts** and risk of cervical cancer.

humoral immunity Form of **acquired immunity** in which **antibodies** are used to counter specific **antigens.**

hydromorphone An **opiate** painkiller more potent than morphine; also called *dilaudid.*

hymen Thin fold of mucous membrane that may cover the vaginal opening.

hypertension Consistently high blood pressure, which increases the risk of heart attack **(myocardial infarction), stroke,** and kidney failure because it adds to the workload of the heart; hypertension may also damage the walls of the **arteries.**

hypertrophy To increase in size.

hyperventilating Excessive rate of respiration, leading to loss of carbon dioxide from the blood.

hypnotic Sleep- or relaxation-inducing drug.

hypochondria Imaginary physical ailment.

hypothermia Abnormally low body temperature.

hysterectomy Surgical removal of the **uterus**.

immune disorder Malfunction in which the **immune system** overreacts or even attacks the body.

immune system The organs, tissues, cells, and mechanisms providing defense against disease by producing **antibodies** to fight invading **pathogens.**

immunization Administration of a **vaccine** to prevent development of a disease; also called *inoculation* or *vaccination.*

immunotherapy Use of the body's **immune system** to treat disease, as in bolstering the body's natural cancer-fighting mechanisms.

implantation Embedding of the fertilized **ovum** in the lining of the **uterus.**

in vitro fertilization (IVF) Technique for treating **infertility** in which an egg is removed from a woman at the time of **ovulation** and is fertilized in a glass dish, and then the developing **embryo** is implanted into the mother's **uterus**.

incubation period The time between a person's exposure to an infectious agent and the development of symptoms.

induced abortion Purposeful termination of pregnancy; also called *elective abortion.*

infection Process in which the body's **immune system** is unable to resist invading organisms.

infertility Inability to conceive a child.

inflammation Localized response to injury; buildup of cells and fluids, causing blood vessels to expand, making a site on the body red and swollen.

inflammatory bowel disease Chronic inflammation of the digestive tract.

influenza (flu) Any of a number of contagious **virus**-caused diseases that are characterized by chills, malaise, cough, muscle aches, nausea, vomiting, and diarrhea.

ingestion Taking a drug by swallowing.

inhalants Drugs such as certain aerosols and anesthetics that when inhaled have **psychoactive** effects.

inhalation Taking a substance into the lungs.

injection Using a hypodermic needle to insert a drug; the method may be under the skin (subcutaneously), into a muscle (intramuscularly), or into a blood vessel (intravenously).

insomnia Inability to achieve adequate or restful sleep.

insulin A **hormone** secreted by the pancreas that converts **glucose** and other compounds into energy.

interferon Protein substance produced by the body to help protect cells.

interval training Method of exercise that alternates intense exertion with low-intensity periods in a single session.

intervention Process in which trained counselors, family members, and friends confront an alcohol-dependent person with evidence of his or her behavior, with the goal of compelling that person to seek treatment.

intrauterine device (IUD) Birth-control device consisting of plastic or copper device placed in the **uterus,** inhibiting **implantation** of a fertilized egg.

ion Atom with positive or negative electrical charge.

ionizing radiation High-energy radiation that dislodges electrons from the atoms it hits; the energy produced can react with and damage living tissue.

irradiation Process of exposing food to low doses of ionizing radiation, ultraviolet light, gamma rays, or high-energy electrons to prevent insect growth or sterilize foods.

irritable bowel syndrome (IBS) A disorder, often stress-related, that is characterized by chronic diarrhea or constipation accompanied by abdominal pain.

ischemic stroke Damage to the brain brought on by lack of blood flow to part of the brain.

isokinetic exercise Muscle-developing exercise performed on weight machines that allow full range of movement and provide resistance equal to the force applied by the user.

isometric exercise Strengthening exercise in which a muscle group is contracted without moving the joint to which the muscles are attached, as in pushing against an immovable object.

isotonic exercise Strength training that requires the application of force while moving, as in using weights or calisthenics to strengthen muscles.

jaundice Disease characterized by yellowing of the skin, caused by the liver's inability to remove bile pigments from the blood.

Kaposi's sarcoma Cancer of connective tissues; often associated with **acquired immune deficiency syndrome (AIDS).**

kidney dialysis Mechanical filtering of impurities from the blood following kidney failure.

kidney stone (urinary calculus) A concentration of crystallized salts and minerals that causes blockage of urine flow from the kidney or bladder.

killer T-cells Components of the **immune system** that destroy **antigens.**

kilocalorie The amount of heat required to raise the temperature of a liter of water 1° Celsius; also known as the **Calorie.**

Korsakoff's syndrome Disorder characterized by memory and learning dysfunction, mental confusion, and hallucinations; caused by alcohol abuse, although it may also have a nutritional basis.

labia majora Fleshy outer lips of the vulva that surround and protect the **clitoris** and opening to the **vagina.**

labia minora Fleshy inner lips of the **vulva** that surround and protect the **clitoris** and opening to the **vagina.**

Lamaze method Method of childbirth preparation in which an expectant woman, in cooperation with her partner (the prospective father or a friend), is taught breathing, massage, and pushing techniques to help her cope with the discomfort of labor.

laparoscopy Type of female sterilization in which a tubelike instrument, the laparoscope, is inserted through a half-inch surgical incision in the area of the woman's navel and the **fallopian tubes** are then blocked or cut.

laparotomy Type of female sterilization in which a 2-inch-long surgical incision is made in the woman's abdomen and the **fallopian tubes** are blocked or cut.

Leboyer method Method of childbirth intended to reduce discomfort for the newborn through the use of dim lights, quiet, caressing, and delay in cutting the umbilical cord.

leukemia A cancer that develops in the blood cells and in blood-forming tissues such as the bone marrow.

leukoplakia A precancerous condition characterized by appearance of thick, hardened, wrinkled, white patches on the mucous membrane lining the mouth; is often brought about by the use of smokeless tobacco.

life expectancy The average age to which a given group of people born at a given time will live.

life span The maximum number of years a human being can live; the biological limit for a species.

lipids **Fats** and fatty compounds.

lipoprotein Molecules composed of **lipids** and **proteins** that carry fatty materials through the bloodstream; associated with heart and blood vessel disease.

living will A legal document that states a person's wishes regarding the withholding of life-sustaining medical procedures in the event of severe and irreversible illness or injury.

local Describes drug action that affects one part of the body but not others, as when dentists use novocaine as a local anesthetic; opposite of **general.**

low-density lipoproteins (LDLs) Molecules that deposit excess **cholesterol** on the walls of the blood vessels.

LSD A hallucinogenic drug, lysergic acid diethylamide, that produces perceptual distortions.

luteinizing hormone (LH) A **hormone** produced by the **pituitary gland** that stimulates **ovulation** in females and production of **testosterone** in males.

Lyme disease Bacterial infection contracted through the bite of deer ticks, characterized first by a ring-like rash at the site of the bite, then flu-like symptoms; without treatment, memory loss, poor coordination, irregular heartbeat, and arthritis may follow.

lymph nodes Pea-sized glands in the neck, underarms, and groin that trap cellular debris and filter out harmful foreign materials.

lymphatic system Complex network of vessels that helps filter foreign materials and bacteria and contributes to the body's immunity.

lymphoma Cancer that develops in the **lymphatic system.**

macrominerals Seven elements that should be consumed in amounts greater than 100 milligrams per day: calcium, phosphorus, sulfur, potassium, sodium, chloride, and magnesium.

macronutrients Category of **nutrients** present in foods in large quantities—**carbohydrates, proteins,** and **fats.**

macrophages Specialized white blood cells, types of **phagocytes,** that line the

blood vessels and as part of the body's **immune system,** attempt to destroy invading **antigens.**

major depression A severe **depression** that lasts 2 weeks or longer.

major stimulant A **stimulant** that is either closely regulated by the government or illegal; compare with **minor stimulant.**

malaria Disease borne by mosquitos and characterized by periodic bouts of chills and fever.

malignant tumors Abnormal cells that are harmful and invade other tissues; opposite of **benign tumor.**

mammogram X-ray photograph of the breasts.

mammography X-ray examination of the breast for early detection of cancer.

mania Emotional disorder characterized by constant, driven activity and lack of inhibitions; part of the cycle of **bipolar disorder.**

marijuana A **psychoactive** drug consisting of the leafy top portion and flowers of the hemp plant; the active ingredient is the drug **delta-9-tetrahydrocannabinol (THC).**

maximum heart rate Maximum number of times the heart can beat per minute; estimated by subtracting one's age from 220.

medication (medicine) Drug used for the purpose of diagnosing, preventing, or treating disease; may also help in the care of an individual during illness.

meditation Stress-reduction techniques using quiet setting and breathing or chanting to eliminate mental distractions and relax the body.

medulla The brain stem.

megadose A quantity of a **vitamin** or **mineral** that far exceeds the Recommended Daily Allowance (RDA); in some cases may be toxic.

melanoma Skin cancer in the form of a small molelike growth that gradually increases in size, changes color, becomes ulcerated, and bleeds easily.

memory cells In the immune system, cells that store the characteristics of an invading **antigen** so that immunity is acquired and the antigen can be combatted quickly if it is encountered again.

menarche Onset of **menstruation** at puberty.

menopause Permanent end of the cycle of **ovulation** and **menstruation;** normally occurs between ages 45 and 55.

menstrual cycle Nearly monthly cycle in which a woman's body matures an **ovum** to be available for fertilization by a sperm and also prepares the lining of the **uterus** for **implantation** of the fertilized egg; also called the *fertility cycle*. The menstrual cycle has three phases: **menstrual phase, proliferative phase,** and **secretory phase.**

menstrual phase The phase of the **menstrual cycle** characterized by menstrual bleeding.

menstruation The monthly shedding of blood and the **endometrium** in a woman who is not pregnant and is of premenopausal age.

mental health State of psychological wellness, ability to think reasonably clearly and to perceive reality as it is; also called *intellectual health.*

mental imagery Stress-reduction technique in which one essentially daydreams an image or desired change, anticipating that the body will respond as if the image were real; also called *guided imagery* or *visualization.*

meperidine An **opiate** used as a painkiller and sedative which has proven to be addictive; also called *demerol.*

mescaline A **hallucinogen** derived from the peyote cactus, causing hallucinations and euphoria.

methadone An **opiate** used as a painkiller and as a substitute narcotic in the relief of **heroin** addiction; also called *Dolophine.*

microbes Microscopic organisms.

microminerals The **minerals** present in small amounts in the body; also known as *trace minerals.*

micronutrients The **nutrients** present in foods in small amounts, such as **vitamins** and **minerals.**

microorganism Microscopic organisms, germs.

migraine headache Severe, recurrent head pains, in which blood vessels in the brain expand and leak chemicals that inflame nearby tissues.

minerals Inorganic substances, small amounts of which are essential to life; among the functions they perform in the body are digestion, bone formation, synthesis of **enzymes,** and regulation of the heart rhythm.

minilaparotomy Type of female sterilization consisting of 1-inch-long surgical incision in the woman's abdomen and cutting of the **fallopian tubes.**

minipill Birth control pill that contains **progesterone** only and thus has fewer side effects than the **combination pill** or the **multiphasic pill,** though it is also less effective in preventing pregnancy.

minor stimulant A **stimulant** that is legally and readily available; compare with **major stimulant.**

mononucleosis Infectious viral disease characterized by fever, headache, sore throat, chills, nausea, and prolonged tiredness or weakness.

monounsaturated fat Form of fat found in both plant and animal foods, such as peanut and olive oils.

mons pubis Mound of fatty tissue over the pubic bone; it is covered with hair after puberty.

mood disorders Mental disorders characterized by prolonged or severe **depression** or **mania** (elation) or swings between these extremes; also called *affective disorders.*

morning glory seeds A **psychoactive** drug consisting of pulverized seeds of the morning glory plant.

morphine A painkiller and narcotic derived from the principal component of **opium.**

multiphasic pill Birth control pill that provides a changing dosage of **estrogen** and **progesterone,** which mimics the body's natural cycle of hormones; compare with the **combination pill,** which offers a steady dosage.

multiple sclerosis (MS) An **autoimmune disorder** in which the **immune system** attacks the brain and causes slowing nerve impulses, paralysis, and eventual death.

muscle endurance The ability of the body to use muscles to function over time; a measure of muscle fitness.

muscle strength The amount of force one's muscles can exert against resistance; a measure of muscle fitness.

myasthenia gravis An **autoimmune disorder** that causes progressive weakening of the muscles.

myocardial infarction (MI) The death of some part of the heart muscle; better known as a *heart attack.*

Naegele's formula Method of calculating expected date of birth of a **fetus;** 3 months are subtracted from the first day of the last menstrual period and 7 days are added.

narcissistic personality disorder Mental disorder characterized by an exaggerated self-centeredness that can interfere with one's ability to form attachments to others; people with this disorder actually have a deep sense of worthlessness, so that they need attention and admiration to bolster their self-esteem.

narcolepsy Irresistible urge to fall asleep, an ongoing condition that can't be fully relieved by any amount of sleep; opposite of **insomnia.**

natural childbirth Form of childbirth in which no medications are used and there is no intervention in the birth process.

naturally acquired immunity Aspect of the **immune system** in which chemicals produced by the body are used to develop **antibodies** against a particular disease.

near-death experience (NDE) Experience by people who have almost died, as in those whose hearts have stopped but have been resuscitated; common attributes are feelings of peace, movement through darkness toward a bright light, sadness at returning, and sometimes appearance of dead relatives or religious figures.

nearsighted Unable to see things far away without glasses; differs from **farsighted.**

neurological disorder Disorder of the nervous system.

neurons Active cells of the nervous system that transmit and receive messages.

neurotransmitters Chemicals enabling **neurons** to transmit impulses.

nonaerobic Physical activity in which oxygen taken in is always sufficient to meet the oxygen needed, so that heart and lungs do not need to put out much effort; opposite of **aerobic.**

nonconvulsive seizures State covering symptoms ranging from brief muscle jerks to brief loss of consciousness or of contact with surroundings; no first aid is required, but the person may be momentarily confused.

nonessential amino acids Types of **amino acids** that the body can manufacture for itself; compare with **essential amino acids.**

nongonococcal urethritis (NGU) Infection of the urethra by organisms other than **gonorrhea;** characterized by mild burning during urination.

noninsulin-dependent diabetes Chronic disease in which the body does not effectively process **insulin,** the **hormone** regulating blood sugar levels, resulting in too much sugar in the blood and urine.

nonionizing electromagnetic radiation Low-intensity **radiation;** includes visible light, radio waves, and microwaves.

nonnutrient Food substance that is not required by the body for its growth, maintenance, and repair but may serve another healthful purpose.

nonoxynol-9 Spermicide used in many contraceptive foams and jellies.

non-REM Type of quiet, mainly nondreaming sleep.

nutrients Components found in food necessary for the body's growth, energy, and repair.

obesity Condition in which a person's weight exceeds desirable weight by more than 20%.

obsession A repetitive, unwanted idea, image, or stream of thought.

obsessive-compulsive disorder (OCD) Mental health disorder characterized by **obsessions** or **compulsions** that interfere with the ability to function.

oils Fats in liquid form.

omega-3 fatty acids Types of beneficial **polyunsaturated fats** that may decrease the risk of heart and blood-vessel disease and cancer; they are found in fish oils, Chinook salmon, and albacore.

omega-6 fatty acids Types of beneficial **polyunsaturated fats** that are important for growth; they are found in plant oils (e.g., corn and peanut oil).

oncogene A gene that may cause a normal cell to become cancerous when activated by a virus or radiation.

opiates Narcotics that act as pain relievers, such as **morphine.**

opium A narcotic consisting of dark brown chunks or powder that is derived from the Asian poppy plant (*Papaver somniferum*).

osteoarthritis   A disintegration of the cartilage between bones, causing pain, stiffness, and lack of mobility.

osteoporosis   A disease primarily affecting women after **menopause** in which the bones become porous and brittle and thus more easily fractured.

ova   The female egg cells (singular: *ovum*).

ovarian follicles   Sacs in the **ovaries** in which individual **ova** develop.

ovaries   Female organs that produce **ova;** they also produce **estrogen** and **progesterone.**

overweight   Condition in which a person's body weight exceeds desirable weight by 1–19%.

ovulation   The release of mature **ova** from the **ovaries** into the **fallopian tubes** approximately 14 days prior to the onset of **menstruation.**

oxycodone   An **opiate** pain reliever.

ozone   Type of oxygen that exists in the upper atmosphere and is sometimes formed in the lower atmosphere when certain automobile and industrial emissions combine chemically under sunlight; it can cause breathing problems.

ozone layer   An upper layer of the atmosphere that shields the earth against ultraviolet light and radiation from the sun.

pancreatitis   Inflammation of the pancreas; characterized by nausea, vomiting, diarrhea, and upper abdominal pain.

panic attack   Sudden, emotionally intense experiences of fear, characterized by pounding heart, racing pulse, shortness of breath, sweating, faintness, and fears about going crazy or dying.

panic disorder   Constant, moderate level of anxiety that is interspersed by **panic attacks.**

Pap smear   Laboratory test in which cells removed from the **cervix** are examined under a microscope for signs of cancer; also called *Pap test.*

parasitic worm   Worm such as tapeworm or pinworm that invades the intestine as a result of a person's eating undercooked pork or beef.

partitioned foods   Food composed of only parts of the plant and animal tissues needed for nutrients.

passively acquired immunity   Temporary immunity brought about by injecting **antibodies** from another person or animal.

pathogen   A disease-causing microorganism.

pelvic inflammatory disease (PID)   Inflammation that may spread from the **vagina** or **cervix** to the **uterus, fallopian tubes, ovaries,** and pelvis; characterized by lower abdominal pain, abnormal vaginal discharge, painful urination, and fever.

penicillin   A type of **antibiotic.**

penicillinase-producing *Neisseria gonorrhoeae* **(PPNG)**   A form of **gonorrhea** that is resistant to **penicillin.**

Percent Daily Value (%DV)   Percentage of a day's worth of a nutrient a food item contains, based on a recommended diet.

percutaneous umbilical blood sampling (PUBS)   Testing method in which a needle is inserted into the umbilical cord of a fetus to obtain a blood sample that can be analyzed to detect some diseases and disorders.

perineum   The area between the anus and the **vagina** in the female and the anus and the **scrotum** in the male.

periodontal disease   Gum disease caused by bacterial migration under the gumline; the early and reversible form is manifested as **gingivitis,** the serious form as **periodontitis.**

periodontitis   Stage of periodontal disease characterized by permanent teeth, gum, and bone loss; also called *pyorrhea.*

peripheral artery disease   Damage resulting from restricted blood flow to the legs and feet, and sometimes hands, which may make the affected body parts tingle or numb; also called *peripheral vascular disease.*

persistent vegetative state (PVS)   State of **cortical death,** though bodily vital signs may be normal; a person in such a state is permanently and completely paralyzed and has no reflexes or awareness.

person-centered therapy   Type of psychotherapy in which the therapist focuses on the patient's own conscious self-insights rather than on the therapist's interpretations.

personality disorder   Maladaptive, inflexible way of dealing with the environment and other people.

phagocytes   Specialized white blood cells that engulf and destroy invading organisms.

phencyclidine (PCP)   A chemical classed as a hallucinogen that causes users to experience perceptual changes or distortions in body image.

phenylketonuria (PKU)   An inherited metabolic disease in which one is unable to oxidize a specific metabolic product of phenylalanine; characterized by severe mental deficiency.

phobia   Exaggerated and persistent fear of a specific situation, person, group, or idea.

physical dependence   Need to continue use of a drug in order to avoid **withdrawal** and to maintain normal body function.

physical health   The dimension of health that means not only the absence of disease or risk behaviors that might lead to disease, but also physical fitness, functioning body systems, and minimal exposure to such abuses as drugs, stress, and environmental hazards.

pituitary gland   The master gland of the endocrine system; it produces a variety of **hormones,** which are sent throughout the body.

placenta   An organ that allows blood, oxygen, and nutrients to pass from mother to **fetus** and waste to be removed; it is expelled shortly after birth of the child.

placenta praevia   Premature separation of the **placenta** from the wall of the **uterus.**

plaque   (1) Accumulation of fat, **cholesterol,** calcium, cell parts, and blood-clotting material that builds up along blood vessel walls. (2) Bacteria-laden film on the teeth, which can lead to tooth decay.

plasma   Watery solution that holds the blood components that supply energy to the cells; components include: **red blood cells, platelets,** and **white blood cells.**

platelets   Components of blood that help in clotting.

pneumonia   Any of a group of infections characterized by fluid filling tiny air chambers of the lungs; may be caused by any of several **microorganisms.**

polyunsaturated fat   Form of fat found principally in fish and plant products; it is mainly found in the form of oils.

positive signs   Signs by which a physician determines that a woman is definitely pregnant, such as detecting movement of the fetus; compare with **presumptive signs** and **probable signs.**

post-traumatic stress disorder   Repeated re-experiencing of a trauma through recollection, as in nightmares.

potentiating interaction   Phenomenon in which one drug intensifies the effect of a second drug.

precursor   Compound that is not a **nutrient** but from which a nutrient can be formed; the body has to convert some **vitamins** from precursors.

premature labor   Labor that occurs before a fetus is 36 weeks old.

premenstrual syndrome (PMS)   Physical and mental distress occurring in some women 7 or more days before **menstruation** and lasting as long as 2 weeks; symptoms may include mood swings, irritability or hostility, muscle aches, pelvic cramps, breast tenderness, dizziness, bloating, and diarrhea.

prepared childbirth   Childbirth that follows a series of classes intended to prepare the expectant mother to actively participate in the delivery of her baby and to avoid or minimize the use of pain-relieving drugs; also called *participatory childbirth.*

presumptive signs   Subjective signs, such as **morning sickness,** by which a woman guesses she may be pregnant; compare with **probable signs** and **positive signs.**

primary hypertension   Type of **hypertension** in which there is no known cause; it is also known as *essential hypertension;* compare with **secondary hypertension.**

principle of complementation Nutritional principle in which two or more of the right plant foods are eaten together to provide the **essential amino acids** needed by the body.

probable signs Signs by which a physician determines that a woman is probably pregnant, including positive pregnancy tests; compare with **presumptive signs** and **positive signs.**

process addiction Type of **addiction** in which one becomes extraordinarily dependent on or attached to an activity rather than a substance, such as gambling, work, spending, or sex; compare with **substance addiction.**

progesterone Sex **hormone** found in greater quantities in females than in males; it stimulates the **uterus,** preparing it to accept a fertilized egg.

progressive muscular relaxation A stress-reduction method in which the tension in the muscles is reduced by contracting and then relaxing certain areas of the body.

proliferative phase A phase of the **menstrual cycle** in which a new thick, spongy **endometrium** of blood and mucus develops so that a fertilized egg may be implanted in it.

propoxyphene (Darvon) Legal synthetic **opiate** once widely prescribed for all kinds of pain, from menstrual cramps to cancer.

prostaglandins Chemical substances that stimulate smooth muscle contractions.

prostate enlargement Enlargement of the **prostate gland,** a condition that happens to most men at some point after age 40 and causes pressure on the **urethra,** restricting urine flow; also called *benign prostatic hypertrophy.*

prostate gland An organ located beneath the bladder and surrounding the **urethra,** which produces a substance that makes the semen more alkaline and thus more suitable for **sperm.**

proteins Compounds essential for life that are present in the body and in foods and are composed of hydrogen, oxygen, and nitrogen.

protozoa Single-celled microorganisms that can cause many diseases, such as **malaria, amoebic dysentery,** and **giardia.**

provitamin The name given to vitamin **precursors.**

psilocybin A type of **psychoactive drug** found in several kinds of "magic mushrooms" and known for the strong visual distortions it produces.

psychoactive drugs Drugs capable of altering people's moods, thinking, perceptions, and behavior.

psychoanalysis (1) A theory of psychology developed by Sigmund Freud that suggests that personality develops according to how well children resolve five stages of **psychosexual development.** (2) A form of **psychotherapy,** the first

of the **talking therapies,** that is intended to help people uncover and confront their suppressed fears and innermost feelings through such techniques as dream analysis, free association, and transference.

psychological dependence Emotional or mental attachment to a drug.

psychological disorder Pattern of behavior associated with distress (pain), disability (impaired functioning), or risk of pain, death, or loss of freedom.

psychological health Dimension of health that refers to the state of both mental and emotional well-being; consists of having good **mental health** (intellectual health) and good **emotional health.**

psychosis Severe psychological disturbance that grossly impairs contact with reality.

psychosomatic illness Physical disorder caused at least in part by emotional problems.

psychosurgery Attempt to change behavior through surgical removal or destruction of brain tissue.

psychotherapy Treatment designed to make changes by psychological rather than physical means, using persuasion, reassurance, and support.

pubic lice Wingless insects that live in human hair and cause itching and skin discoloration; they may be transferred from another person during sex or other close body contact or from bedding or clothing.

pulmonary circuit The system of **arteries** and **veins** leading to and from the lungs; compare with **systemic circuit.**

pulmonary edema Fluid in the lungs.

pulmonary emphysema Loss of elasticity and subsequent rupture of the tiny air sacs in the lungs.

pyelonephritis Inflammation of the kidney.

quackery Medical fakery or other pretensions to cure illness.

rad A measure of the amount of **ionizing radiation** absorbed by an organism.

radiation sickness Illness caused by overexposure to radiation; symptoms include low white-blood-cell count, nausea, weight loss, immune deficiencies, hair loss, bleeding from mouth and gums, and ultimately death.

radiation therapy Use of high-energy radiation to damage or destroy cancer cells.

radioactivity The emission of radiation from the nucleus of an atom in three forms: alpha particles, which cannot pass through human skin; beta particles, which can penetrate the body slightly and may affect bones or the thyroid gland; and gamma rays, which can pass through the body and may cause considerable harm.

rapid-eye movement (REM) sleep A phase of sleep during which the most

active dreaming takes place and the sleeper's eyes move quickly.

rational-emotive therapy A type of **psychotherapy** created by Albert Ellis that assumes that thoughts, or rationality, lead to emotions and that irrational thoughts and beliefs can be replaced with rational ones to relieve emotional illnesses.

recessive gene A type of **gene** that has a minor influence in determining a particular inherited characteristic, such as hair color; opposite of **dominant gene.**

red blood cells Component of the blood that carries oxygen to, and carbon dioxide from, body cells.

relaxation response Predictable, beneficial physiological changes that occur in both body and mind when a person is truly relaxed.

rem Measure of the relative danger of exposure to different amounts and types of **radiation.**

repetitive strain injury (RSI) Inflammation or pain in the wrist, hand, arm, or neck caused by fast, repetitive motions; also called *repetitive motion injury.*

resilience People's ability to cope with disruptive, stressful, or challenging events so that they gain additional protective and coping skills.

resting heart rate The number of heartbeats per minute when the body is at rest.

Rh disease (erythroblastosis) Disorder in which **antibodies** in the mother's blood cause the **fetus** to be stillborn or suffer brain damage; the condition can occur in the second and subsequent children of couples in which the mother's blood is Rh-negative and the father's is Rh-positive.

rheumatic fever A disease occasionally found in children and young adults that is characterized by fever, inflammation and pain around the joints, jerky and involuntary movement, skin rashes, and sometimes **rheumatic heart disease.**

rheumatic heart disease Damage to the heart valves caused by **rheumatic fever.**

rheumatoid arthritis Deterioration of joints after an attack on them by the body's immune system; early symptoms are stiffness and joint pain, followed later by swelling, deformity, and limited mobility.

rhythm method Attempted method of contraception in which sexual intercourse is avoided during perceived fertile periods of the woman's **menstrual cycle.**

rickettsia Microorganisms that grow inside living cells and are usually transmitted to people by insects.

Rocky Mountain spotted fever A disease caused by **rickettsia** transmitted by a wood tick and characterized by chills, fever, prostration, pains in muscles and joints, and a purple eruption.

RU 486 pill Hormone compound that, if used within 5 weeks of conception, ends pregnancy by inducing bleeding and contractions of the **uterus.**

rubella Infectious disease that, if contracted by pregnant women, may cause birth defects in their offspring; also called *German measles.*

saline induction Method of abortion also known as *instillation,* in which a salt solution or **prostaglandins** are injected into the sac around the **fetus** to induce simulated labor that expels the fetus; used for **induced abortion** in weeks 16–20 of pregnancy.

salmonella Type of **bacteria** that cause food poisoning.

sarcoma Cancer that develops in muscles, ligaments, bones, nerves, tendons, or blood vessels.

saturated fats Unhealthful type of **fats** found mainly in animal products but also in some vegetable fats; compare with **unsaturated fats.**

scabies Tiny mites that burrow and lay eggs under the skin.

schizophrenia Several types of emotional disorders characterized by severe breaks with reality and symptoms such as **hallucinations** and delusions, thought disorders, and inappropriate emotions.

scrotum The external pouch that hangs behind and below the penis and holds the **testes.**

seasonal affective disorder (SAD) Condition in which people become seriously depressed in winter and normal or slightly manic in summer.

secondary hypertension Type of **hypertension** triggered by other primary diseases, such as kidney disorders; compare with **primary hypertension.**

secondary sex characteristics Physical changes associated with the development of maleness or femaleness that are brought about by sex **hormones.**

secretory phase Phase of the **menstrual cycle** in which the mature egg moves down the **fallopian tube,** where fertilization by sperm may take place.

sedative Drug that induces sleep or a trancelike state.

seizure disorders (epilepsy, epilepsies) Collection of neurological disorders caused by abnormal electrical activity in the brain; characterized by sudden attacks (seizures) of involuntary, violent muscle contractions and loss of consciousness.

selective Type of action in which a drug affects one organ or body system more than others.

self-defeating personality disorder Emotional disorder characterized by a fear of achieving success, as expressed in self-handicapping symptoms.

seminal vesicles Glands in the male reproductive system that secrete a nutrient for **sperm.**

seminiferous tubules Coiled tubes within the **scrotum,** held within the **epididymis,** in which **sperm** mature.

serotonin A chemical made from tryptophan that is one of the brain's main **neurotransmitters;** depending on the foods one eats, the level may be raised or lowered after a meal, with corresponding effects on mood.

setpoint theory A theory about obesity that holds that everyone has an unconscious control system for keeping the body fat at a certain set point, or predetermined level.

sexual addiction Intense sexual preoccupation that deters normal sexual relationships; also called *compulsive sexual behavior (CSB).*

sexually transmitted diseases (STDs) Diseases transmitted by sexual contact, including human **immunodeficiency virus (HIV), chlamydia, gonorrhea,** genital herpes, **human papilloma viruses,** and **syphilis.**

sickle-cell anemia Potentially fatal, genetically transmitted blood disorder characterized by sickle-shaped blood cells, primarily affecting African Americans.

side effects Reactions other than those a drug is intended to produce.

simple carbohydrates Sugars.

simple phobia Fear of a specific object, such as spiders, or situation, such as flying in a plane.

social health A person's well-being in interactions with others.

soluble Capable of being dissolved.

solvents Chemicals found in many cleaning products and adhesives that act as **depressants** and produce **delirium.**

sperm The male reproductive cell.

spiritual health Dimension of health that includes trust, integrity, principles and ethics, feelings of selflessness, and commitment to some higher process or being.

spirochete Bacteria that cause **syphilis.**

spontaneous abortion An abortion that happens without outside inducement; also called *miscarriage.*

sterilization Surgical procedure that causes **infertility.**

stimulant Drug such as **caffeine, cocaine,** or **amphetamines** that excites the nervous system, speeding up brain activity and body processes.

stimulant psychosis Psychological disorder caused by drugs such as **amphetamines** and characterized by paranoid delusions, **hallucinations,** and disorganized behavior.

Stockholm syndrome Condition in which hostages bond and identify with their captors because they fear it is the only way to survive.

strep throat Severe sore throat caused by streptococci **bacteria.**

stress Nonspecific, generalized reaction of our bodies to demands by **stressors** made on them; may take the form of **distress** or **eustress.**

stressor The specific source of **stress;** may be **distressor** or **eustressor.**

stroke Damage to part of the brain when its blood supply is interrupted; also called *cerebrovascular accident (CVA).*

substance addictions Addictions to mood-altering substances and drugs that are usually artificially produced, such as caffeine, nicotine, alcohol, **tranquilizers, marijuana, cocaine,** and **heroin;** it may also include addiction to food.

suction curettage A method of **induced abortion,** usually employed in weeks 6–12 of pregnancy, in which a suction device is used to extract the contents of the **uterus.**

sudden infant death syndrome (SIDS) The unexpected death of an apparently healthy baby, usually between the ages of 1 week and 1 year; also known as *crib death.*

suppressor T-cells In the **immune system,** cells that suppress the production of **antibodies** once the infection is under control.

surfactant Substance produced in the lungs of a **fetus** in the latter weeks of pregnancy that enables it to breathe on its own.

sympto-thermal method Method of birth control that combines the **calendar method,** the **basal-body-temperature method,** and the **cervical mucus method** to help determine a woman's fertile period.

synapse Space between any two **neurons** over which **neurotransmitters** must cross.

synergistic interaction Type of drug interaction in which the effect of two drugs together is greater than the sum of the effects of each drug used alone.

synesthesia Perception of a stimulus by a sense other than the one in which it was presented, as in "seeing music."

syphilis A **sexually transmitted disease** caused by **bacteria;** it advances through three stages, ending with death unless treated.

systematic desensitization Method of combating a **phobia** that works to reduce the fear by gradually exposing a person to the object that arouses that fear.

systemic circuit The system of **arteries** and **veins** leading to and from the parts of the body other than the lungs; compare with **pulmonary circuit.**

systole Contraction phase in the cardiac cycle when the heart chambers force blood into the arteries; compare with **diastole.**

systolic blood pressure Force exerted by the blood on walls of blood vessels when the heart is contracting; compare with **diastolic blood pressure.**

T-cells Components of the **immune system; helper T-cells** identify invading foreign organisms and **killer T-cells** destroy them.

T4 helper cells (CD4 cells) The body's master immune cells.

tachycardia Abnormally rapid heart-beat, over 100 beats per minute.

talking therapies Types of psychotherapy in which a patient interacts in a confiding way, for the purpose of achieving insight into the reasons for his or her behavior, either individually with a trained therapist or in a group led by a therapist; also called *insight-oriented therapies.*

target heart rate Number of times per minute that the heart must beat to produce a training effect; normally this is 60–80% of the maximum heart rate.

testicles (testes) The part of the male reproductive system that produces **sperm** and **testosterone.**

testosterone Sex **hormone** found in greater quantities in the male than in the female; it induces the changes that take place in males at puberty.

thrombus Blood clot that blocks an artery.

tolerance Increasing loss of sensitivity to the effects of a particular quantity of a certain drug.

toxemia Abnormal condition associated with the presence of toxic substances in the blood.

toxic shock syndrome Potentially fatal infection in which **bacteria** in the **vagina** create toxins that enter the bloodstream; characterized by fever, vomiting, diarrhea, and often shock.

toxicity The level at which a substance causes temporary or permanent damage to the body.

toxins Poisonous substances that are usually the metabolic products of living organisms, such as **bacteria.**

toxoplasmosis Infection caused by a parasite in uncooked or undercooked meat and in dust or water contaminated by cat feces.

tranquilizers Antianxiety drugs; minor tranquilizers include **benzodiazepines** and are used primarily to treat minor anxieties, to ease muscle tension, and to induce sleep, whereas major tranquilizers are used to treat people with serious mental disorders in institutional settings.

transactional analysis A form of psychotherapy that is concerned with how people communicate, or "transact," with each other.

transient ischemic attack (TIA) "Ministrokes" with the same symptoms as regular **strokes** but lasting only a few minutes.

trichinosis Illness caused by intestinal worms that may be in raw or undercooked pork; symptoms are diarrhea, nausea, fever, and later stiffness, pain, sweating, and insomnia.

trichomoniasis Infection caused by parasitic **protozoa** that is sometimes a **sexually transmitted disease;** women may experience itching, burning, vaginal discharge, and urinary complaints, and men experience slight burning during urination.

triglycerides Three **fatty acids** joined to a molecule of glycerol; high triglyceride levels in the blood may be a warning of heart and blood-vessel disease.

tubal ligation Method of female sterilization in which the **fallopian tubes** are surgically cut and tied.

tubal occlusion Method of female sterilization in which the **fallopian tubes** are surgically blocked by cauterizing (burning) them or with a clamp, clip, or band of silicone.

tubal sterilization Female sterilization; the surgical and usually permanent interruption of reproductive capacity by closing off the **fallopian tubes** by either **tubal ligation** or **tubal occlusion.** *See also* **laparotomy, mini-laparotomy, laparoscopy, colpotomy.**

tuberculosis (TB) A bacterial disease usually lodging in the lungs and characterized in its later stages by coughing, chest pain, night sweats, and spitting up of blood.

type 1 diabetes (insulin-dependent diabetes mellitus) Juvenile onset diabetes, the type of diabetes generally seen for the first time in childhood or adolescence.

type 2 diabetes (insulin-independent diabetes mellitus) Adult onset diabetes, the type of diabetes generally found for the first time in people 35 or older.

type A personality A hurried, deadline-ridden, and competitive person, whose traits appeared to be linked to stress-related heart disease.

type B personality A relaxed, unhurried, and carefree person, whose traits appear to be less prone to stress-related heart disease.

typhoid fever A bacterium-caused infectious disease that is characterized by fever, diarrhea, prostration, headache, and intestinal **inflammation.**

typhus fever Disease caused by **rickettsia** that is characterized by high, disabling fever.

ulcer An open sore of the mucous membrane, as in the stomach lining.

ulcerative colitis Disorder affecting the colon and causing bouts of rectal bleeding and diarrhea, often leading to colon cancer if untreated.

ultrasound (ultrasonography) A technology using high-frequency sound waves to view internal body structures, such as the **fetus** in a pregnant woman; also called *prenatal sonograph.*

ultraviolet radiation (UV) Form of radiation emitted by the sun which causes sunburn in humans; normally it is screened out by the **ozone layer** in the earth's upper atmosphere.

underweight State in which person is 10% below Metropolitan Life table values.

unsaturated fats Types of **fatty acids,** consisting of two kinds—**monounsaturated fats** and **polyunsaturated fats.**

urethra In both males and females, the tube that carries urine from the bladder for excretion; in males, the urethra also carries semen.

urinalysis Medical test consisting of an examination of a sample of a person's urine.

uterus The pear-shaped and pear-sized muscle in the female reproductive system in which the **embryo** is implanted and in which the **fetus** develops.

vaccine A weakened strain of a **virus** or **bacterium** that is produced in a laboratory and is used to bolster the **immune system** so as to fight off the actual disease.

vagina In the female reproductive system, the elastic muscular tube connecting the exterior opening with the **uterus;** it is the canal through which sperm must travel to fertilize an egg and through which a baby is born.

vaginal contraceptive film (VCF) A form of contraceptive that dissolves into a spermicide-containing gel over the opening to the **cervix.**

vaginal contraceptive sponge A form of contraceptive that blocks **sperm** from entering the **uterus.**

vaginal ring A form of contraceptive that is similar to a **diaphragm** but releases contraceptive hormones and may be worn for up to 3 months.

vaginal spermicide A form of contraceptive consisting of a chemical inserted into the vagina before intercourse to kill or neutralize **sperm** before they enter the **uterus.**

vaginismus A sexual disorder in which a female experiences involuntary muscle spasms in the vagina, so that the penis cannot enter.

valves In the heart, devices located between the two atria and two ventricles that prevent blood from flowing in the wrong direction.

vas deferens In the male, tubes carrying **sperm** from the **testes** to the **urethra.**

vascular dementia Death of brain tissue and memory loss caused by blood vessel changes in the brain due to a **stroke.**

vasectomy Surgical procedure for male sterilization, consisting of cutting and tying the **vas deferens** through incisions made in the **scrotum.**

vasodilator Medication such as nitroglycerin used to dilate, or expand, blood vessels so blood can flow more easily.

vein Any of the blood vessels that carry blood from the capillaries to the heart.

venae cavae The primary **veins** that return blood to the right atrium of the heart.

ventricle Either of the two lower chambers of the heart, which pump blood out of the heart and into the arteries.

ventricular fibrillation Disorder in which the heart cannot pump blood because it contracts haphazardly.

vernix caseosa Cheeselike coating found on the skin of the **fetus,** beginning at the end of the fifth month.

vertebrae Any of the small bones of the spine.

virulence The ability of a **pathogen** to overcome the body's defenses.

virus An infectious microorganism that can survive and reproduce only by attaching itself to a cell and tricking that cell into producing new viruses.

vital signs Indicators of physiological functioning, including body temperature, blood pressure, pulse rate, and breathing rate.

vitamins Organic substances that the body requires in small amounts to help regulate metabolic functions and nutrition.

water of metabolism Water produced during many chemical reactions in the body; one source of body fluids.

water-soluble vitamins Eight B-complex vitamins and vitamin C, which do not need fat or bile to be absorbed by the body; compare with **fat-soluble vitamins.**

Wernicke's syndrome Disorder caused by alcohol abuse; characterized by paralysis of eye nerves, mental confusion, loss of memory, and staggering gait.

white blood cells Components of the blood that help the **immune system** combat invading organisms.

withdrawal (1) Unpleasant negative symptoms that appear when a drug-dependent person stops using the drug. (2) Form of attempted birth control during sexual intercourse consisting of removal of the penis from the **vagina** before ejaculation.

workaholic Work addict; person self-destructively obsessed with his or her career and making a living.

X chromosome **Gene** associated with female characteristics.

Y chromosome **Gene** associated with male characteristics.

yeast infection **Fungus**-caused vaginal infection; in females, symptoms are severe itching, pain during intercourse, vaginal redness and soreness, and a white discharge.

yoyo syndrome Unhealthy, ineffective cycle of weight loss and weight gain.

zygote A fertilized **ovum.**

zygote intrafallopian transfer (ZIFT) Method of promoting fertility in infertile couples consisting of uniting **ovum** and **sperm** in the laboratory, then placing the resulting **zygote** in the **fallopian tube.**

Index

Boldface page numbers indicate definitions.